Russia,
Bolshevism,
and the
Versailles
Peace

STUDIES OF THE RUSSIAN INSTITUTE
COLUMBIA UNIVERSITY

Russia, Bolshevism, and the Versailles Peace

JOHN M. THOMPSON

PRINCETON, NEW JERSEY

PRINCETON UNIVERSITY PRESS

1966

The Russian Institute of Columbia University sponsors the *Studies of the Russian
Institute* in the belief that their publication
contributes to scholarly research and public
understanding. In this way the Institute,
while not necessarily endorsing their conclusions, is pleased to make available the
results of some of the research conducted
under its auspices. A list of the *Studies of
the Russian Institute* appears at the back
of the book.

Contents

[v]

MAPS

Russia, Bolshevism, and the Versailles Peace

Russia was probably among the worst problems before the Peace Conference. . . . It was the Banquo's ghost sitting at every Council table.

HERBERT HOOVER

The psychological and political effects of the tragedy of war have been very far-reaching. The spirits of nations have broken under this accumulated strain. The old institutions on which militarism and autocracy flourished lie crumbled in the dust; a great wave of advanced democracy is sweeping blindly over Europe. . . . For there is no doubt that mankind is once more on the move. The very foundations have been shaken and loosened, and things are again fluid. The tents have been struck and the great caravan of humanity is once more on the march.

GENERAL JAN CHRISTIAN SMUTS

Introduction

RUSSIA WAS NOT officially represented at the Paris Peace Conference of 1919; consequently her role there has seldom been treated in the extensive literature on the conference. Except for a few German studies and the pioneering articles of Fritz Epstein and George Kennan, Western scholars have ignored the Russian question at Paris or have dealt with it only in passing, while Soviet historians have interpreted it as a demonstration of the "worldwide" significance of the Bolshevik Revolution or as "proof" of the responsibility of Western leaders, especially Woodrow Wilson, for continued Allied intervention in Russia.[1] Even Temperley, one of the ablest historians of the conference, treats the Russian question cursorily, arguing that since the Bolsheviks denied the authority of the conference, their actions lie outside its history.[2]

The Russian specter at Paris cannot be exorcised so easily. To some extent the success of the whole peace settlement hinged upon a solution of the Russian problem. How could there be peace while civil war and revolution kept one sixth of the world in turmoil? How could the affairs of Europe be resolved without arranging for Russia's future role on that continent? How could the statesmen at Paris build a new order without settling accounts with Bolshevism, challenging, as it did, the very bases on which they hoped to construct that order? Wilson's biographer and press secretary at the conference, Ray Stannard Baker, has aptly summarized the significance of the Russian question for the peacemaking: "The effect of the Russian problem on the Paris Conference . . . was profound; Paris cannot be understood without Moscow. Without ever

[1] Erwin Hölzle, *Der Osten im Ersten Weltkrieg* (Leipzig, 1944) and, written from the Nazi point of view, Andreas Hohlfeld, *Die besiegten Sieger: Foch und Churchill im Kampf gegen der Bolschiwsmus* (Hamburg, 1943); Fritz T. Epstein, "Studien zur Geschichte der 'Russischen Frage' auf der Pariser Friedenskonferenz von 1919," *Jahrbücher für Geschichte Osteuropas*, N.F. 7, 3 (1959), 431–78; George F. Kennan, "Russia and the Versailles Conference," *The American Scholar*, Vol. 30, No. 1 (Winter 1960–1961), 13–42 (later reprinted as chs. 9 and 10 of his *Russia and the West under Lenin and Stalin* (Boston, 1961).

[2] H. W. V. Temperley, ed., *The History of the Peace Conference at Paris* (6 vols.; London, 1920–1924), VI, viii and 311.

[3]

being represented at Paris at all, the Bolsheviki and Bolshevism were powerful elements at every turn." [3]

The peacemakers themselves attached considerable importance to the Russian question. In preparing for the conference they placed Russian affairs high on its agenda. The Russian problem cropped up repeatedly during consultations among the Western statesmen before the opening of the conference. In the first two weeks of the conference the Allied rulers spent more time discussing Russia than any other subject, and they returned to it frequently during the remainder of the conference. Almost all the leaders of the conference stressed the necessity of effecting some sort of settlement in Russia, although often with different aims and from different motives. Marshal Foch and French Foreign Minister Pichon depicted the eradication of the Bolsheviks as essential to the security of the postwar world. Lloyd George, who favored an accommodation with the Bolsheviks and an effort to draw them into the European comity of nations, several times emphasized the importance of finding a peaceful solution to the Russian riddle. On January 16, 1919, only a few days after the conference opened, he argued for mediation in the Russian civil war on the ground that there could be no peace for the world if the conference left half of Europe and half of Asia still in flames.[4] In his famous "Memorandum of Fontainebleau" of March 25, 1919, the British prime minister reiterated this warning. Woodrow Wilson, speaking on behalf of his colleagues, declared in the preamble to the proposal for a Russian peace conference on the Prinkipo Islands: "The Associated Powers are now engaged in the solemn and responsible work of establishing the peace of Europe and of the world, and they are keenly alive to the fact that Europe and the world cannot be at peace if Russia is not." [5]

At the same time it is clear that the Allied leaders, while recognizing the significance of the Russian question for their work, had to be—and were—primarily preoccupied with the immediate and central task of making peace with Germany and with their other defeated enemies. This was their principal concern, and it naturally took up the greater part of their time, energy, and deliberations. During the relatively leisurely first weeks of the conference, and again after the draft treaty had been presented to Germany, the heads of government discussed Russia at some length. In the interval, however, the terms of peace with Germany were

---

[3] Ray Stannard Baker, *Woodrow Wilson and World Settlement* (3 vols.; New York, 1922), ii, 64. Hereafter cited as Baker, *Settlement*.

[4] Department of State, *Papers Relating to the Foreign Relations of the United States: Paris Peace Conference, 1919* (13 vols.; Washington, 1942–1947), iii, 583. Hereafter cited as *Peace Conference*.

[5] *Ibid.*, iii, 691.

[4]

the overriding issue, and the Russian problem was left to Colonel House, Herbert Hoover, Winston Churchill, and other subordinates. This meant that the Russian question received less high-level attention than its complexity required, with results, as we shall see in this study, that were often far from satisfactory. Some of the impracticality and inconsistency of the Russian policies developed at the conference can be traced to the haphazard and hurried way in which they were formulated. In the circumstances of the conference the careful consideration, concern for detail, and continued exertion that the Russian question needed were virtually impossible.

Thus, compared with the German question, that of Russia seemed of secondary importance to the peacemakers. This feeling was reinforced by their sense of helplessness and frustration before the Russian tangle. Moscow was far away, the situation in Russia appeared hopelessly confused and chaotic, and there seemed to be little the Allied statesmen could do to control and direct events there. Perhaps if they had seen a clear course to follow, and if they had believed they could act effectively in Russia, the men at Paris would not only have talked about the need to settle Russian affairs but would have done just that.

To be sure, the Russian problem that confronted them was a complex and far-reaching one, consisting of at least three distinct elements. First, there was the question of settling boundaries, diplomatic claims, and minority problems in which Russia had an interest. This proved to be a constantly worrisome but almost entirely unresolved aspect of the work of the conference. The peacemakers were much concerned over this matter since they were reluctant to leave unsettled issues which might later cause friction and trouble in Eastern Europe and which might endanger the security and stability of the newly formed or expanded states along Russia's western borders. At the same time the Allied leaders hesitated to act. Russia was not officially represented at the conference; in her absence did they have the right to settle matters directly affecting her interests? The current situation in Russia was fluctuating, confusing, and uncertain, but many Western statesmen believed—or at least hoped— that a democratic Russia would soon be reestablished. Would it not be better, therefore, to wait, to postpone settlement of issues involving Russia?

The United States, the most consistent champion of preserving Russia's territorial integrity, firmly maintained that no disposition of Russian land or of Russian rights could be made without her participation. It was the United States which most strongly—and successfully— opposed recognition by the conference of the Baltic states; it was the American delegation which almost singlehandedly blocked confirmation by the conference of the experts' recommendation that Bessarabia be given to Rumania; and it was the American government which protested the conference's late decision to accord *de facto* recognition to the states of the Caucasus. Appeals and arguments from the anti-Bolshevik Russian diplomats in Paris and Washington were designed to bolster and reinforce the United States attitude. France often sided with the United States and was quite sympathetic to the position of the unofficial Russian representatives in Paris. At the same time, as we shall see in chapter two, the French sometimes pursued a dual policy respecting Russia's borders with Poland and Rumania, nations which they considered within a French sphere of influence and which they hoped to include in an Eastern alliance system against both Germany and Bolshevik Russia, should a great undivided Russia not be reconstituted. Thus the French supported Poland's claim to Eastern Galicia but were reluctant to accede to the maximum Polish demands for territory in the west Russian borderlands.

With these uncertainties and reservations in mind, the Allied statesmen asserted in the first months of the conference that territorial and diplomatic issues affecting Russia could not be considered until a general policy toward Russia had been formulated.[6] After the conference had exchanged notes with the anti-Bolshevik government of Admiral Kolchak in late May and early June 1919, reference was usually made to the principles enunciated at that time. But since Kolchak merely promised to submit territorial issues to a future all-Russian constituent assembly, this simply meant further postponement of any decisions. Technical experts of the American delegation attempted in midsummer of 1919 to obtain action by the conference on Russian territorial issues by recommending that a special commission make provisional settlement of the status and boundaries of all areas of the former Russian empire, pending establishment of a recognized Russian government. This recommendation was supported in Washington by the State Department and by President Wilson, but the Supreme Council of the conference never considered the plan.[7] Finally, near the close of the conference the statesmen maintained that issues affecting Russia would have to be settled either by the League of Nations or by a special conclave of the Allied powers outside of the peace conference. Consequently, although various commissions of the peace conference prepared recommendations on almost all of the territorial and diplomatic questions in which

[6] See, as examples, discussions by the conference of the Aaland Islands on February 28 and of Bessarabia on May 16, *ibid.*, IV, 171–72, 719–20.

[7] Memorandum of August 6 by Prof. A. C. Coolidge on behalf of all the "area experts" involved. Records of the American Commission to Negotiate Peace, National Archives, File 861.014/1.

Russia had an interest, the Supreme Council of the conference took no action, except to approve a provisional delimitation of the Russo-Polish frontier.

At the time, however, the conference's failure to act seemed of little consequence. A number of the questions at issue were soon settled; some—without the participation of Soviet Russia—by multilateral agreement, as in the case of Spitzbergen, or with the assistance of the League of Nations, as in the cases of the Aaland Islands and of Memel; [8] and some by direct agreement between the Soviet government and its neighbors, as in regard to Finnish territorial claims, the boundaries of the Baltic states, and the Turkish boundary of Armenia. The interests of Russia in the questions of the Straits and of Constantinople were recognized in principle in the abortive Treaty of Sèvres, concluded by the Allies after the peace conference had closed; it provided for Russian membership on the proposed international authority to govern these areas, if and when Russia became a member of the League of Nations. Soviet Russia's interest in the Straits was acknowledged in the Lausanne Conference of 1923. However, Soviet Russia never recognized the granting of Bessarabia to Rumania by the post-conference Treaty of Paris of October 1920. The Russo-Polish frontier was determined only after a war between the two states in 1920, but the causes of the war transcended territorial issues and the tentative action of the conference respecting the Russo-Polish border was not a decisive factor in the outbreak of the war.

Later, on the eve of the Second World War, these arrangements between Russia and her neighbors became sources of conflict and instability in Eastern Europe. Some have argued that the failure of the Paris conference to determine these issues, and the later settlement of some of them without Soviet Russia's participation, contributed importantly to the upheavals in the area in the 1930's. But in 1919 the key issues between Russia and her neighbors and between Russia and the West were political; the territorial questions, rooted in history and ethnology, were of secondary importance. If it had been possible to achieve a political settlement in Russia, the other issues could probably have been worked out in a mutually satisfactory way. For example, if the Allies had been able to establish in Russia a government both democratic and friendly to the West, they might have been able to stabilize its relations with the border states, which some of the Allies also supported. But unable either

---

[8] The Soviet government protested strongly against settlement of both the Spitzbergen and Aaland Islands questions without its participation. See Jane Degras, ed., *Soviet Documents on Foreign Policy* (3 vols.; London, 1951–1953). Hereafter cited as Degras, *Soviet Documents*.

to destroy the Bolsheviks or to establish peaceful relations with them— for reasons which it is the purpose of this study to investigate—the Western powers were compelled to acknowledge an uneasy stalemate of power in Eastern Europe. This could hardly form the basis for lasting territorial settlements, once Russia had regained strength and Germany had come to dominate continental Europe.

Thus, for two reasons—because, in my view, the political aspect of the Russian question at Paris was paramount, and because the conference in any case had little effect on the eventual settlement, after its dissolution, of territorial problems affecting Russia—this work will not deal with the treatment of these problems by the conference.[9] Only when such issues had a significant bearing on consideration by the conference of the general political problem of Russia will they be dealt with here.

The second element of the Russian problem at Paris was the question of power in Russia itself. The military defeat and revolutionary disintegration of the Tsarist empire had created a vacuum in Russia. In the rush of forces into that vacuum the nascent Soviet state clashed bitterly with a medley of counterrevolutionary and separatist groups, many of them backed by Allied troops and aid. The Western nations had defended their intervention in Russian affairs as an effort to reestablish an Eastern Front against the Central Powers. After their victory in the war, the Allies had to redefine their relations with the Bolsheviks and other Russian groups and decide what course in Russia they should now pursue. Were they to intervene further, or attempt to make peace?

A third factor, which was of great significance and which influenced much of the peacemaking, was the problem of Bolshevism. The Soviet government was not simply one among many contestants for power in Russia; it stood as an intruder at the door of the Western world, denouncing the basic premises and institutions of the peacemakers and holding out to the war-weary and discontented peoples of Europe a promise of the millennium. This attack came at a difficult time for the West. The war had been a violent and dramatic symptom of the great changes taking place in Western society under the impact of nationalism and industrialization. Yet the war had tended to exacerbate rather than

[9] The record of the consideration of these problems is contained in the minutes of the commissions involved, especially the Commissions on Polish Affairs, on Rumanian and Yugoslav Affairs, and on Baltic Affairs, which are included in *Recueil des actes de la conférence* (8 parts; Paris, 1922–1934). Ample material on the position of the anti-Bolshevik Russians concerning these issues can be found in the Maklakov Papers at the Hoover Institution. Also at the Hoover Institution is a large collection of material prepared by the various non-Russian nationalities involved. For an important interpretation of some of the central territorial issues, see the article by Epstein cited in n. 1 above.

to resolve the fundamental problems generated by these changes. In 1919 Western society faced the exacting test of adjusting itself to dynamic forces of economic development, social equalization, and national self-consciousness. The war, by weakening and dislocating the traditional Western system, had made more difficult an already demanding task. The reordering of the world had to be attempted in the face of shattering material and moral damage, and in an atmosphere of bitterness, exhaustion, and insecurity.

Precisely at this moment of debilitation and flux in the West, the Bolsheviks challenged the peacemakers from their precarious foothold in Moscow, proclaiming the inevitable destruction of the capitalist system and a Utopian future for all under socialism. The Western statesmen not only had to attempt to set their own house in order but had also to thwart a determined effort to raze the whole structure. Bolshevik jeers greeted their peace proposals, and Bolshevik threats of imminent revolution clouded their deliberations. To the dispirited peoples of Europe the Bolsheviks offered a disarmingly simple peace program—"peace without annexations or indemnities"—and the promise of a new world of plenty and justice. In other times and better conditions the West might have shrugged off this challenge. But now the Bolshevik virus could penetrate and be nurtured in places where the West was exposed and weak. Disillusionment, resentment, immorality were easily exploited. At times it seemed as if Europe might succumb before peace could be made and stability recovered.

The two issues—the threat of Bolshevism and the struggle for power in Russia—were, of course, linked through the Soviet government in Moscow. The aim of this volume is to examine how, and from what motives, the peacemakers dealt with these related problems. How far did they succeed in countering the challenge of Bolshevism and in resolving the Russian conflict? To the extent that they failed, what were the reasons for their failure? What effects did this failure have on the Versailles peace settlement? In attempting to answer these questions primary emphasis will be given to the relationships between the peace conference and the Soviet and White Russian governments. Although basic tenets of Allied, Soviet, and White Russian policy will be discussed, the focus will remain on the peace conference itself. At the same time, since general Allied policy toward Russia was largely determined at the conference, at least until mid-1919, this study embraces much of the history of the West's relations with Russia in this first significant year of the interwar period. It was not a promising start.

CHAPTER ONE

An Uneasy World

IN CONFRONTING the problems of Russia and Bolshevism the peacemakers' efforts were circumscribed by the heritage of the past; the men at Paris could not write policy toward Russia on a clean slate. In many respects it was apparent, then as now, that the Bolshevik seizure of power in Russia in November 1917 had marked a major watershed in European history and in international relations. The Bolshevik Revolution had had a number of immediate and long-range effects which the Allied leaders at Paris could not ignore. Soviet Russia's withdrawal from the war and the Bolsheviks' renunciation of the secret treaties had endangered the Western war effort against the Central Powers and had forced a reexamination of Allied war aims. The American and Entente responses to these pressures, which will be discussed briefly later in this chapter and at the beginning of chapter two, inevitably conditioned the actions of the peacemakers respecting Russia.

But the long-run implications of the Bolshevik Revolution were of even greater import for the statesmen at Paris. Russia's defeat in the war and the consequent disorganization and weakness of that vast area radically upset the balance of power in Europe. The French could no longer count on Russian manpower and Russian strength as a counterpoise to Germany, while the British—relieved, from the standpoint of their imperial interests, at the diminution of Russian strength—could not but fear now either German or French domination of the European continent. The altered situation had to be taken into account and was bound to influence not only Allied policy toward Russia but the peace settlement as a whole.

A related problem was the deep concern of the Allied leaders that Germany might take advantage of Russia's prostration to establish German influence, perhaps even domination, over Russia. In the view of Western statesmen this ominous possibility would continue to exist, whether Germany were completely defeated or whether the war ended in a stalemate. This anxiety constantly troubled the Allies and affected their policies, both in the year between the Bolshevik Revolution and the Armistice, and throughout the succeeding months of peacemaking, as we shall see in this study.

At the same time the menace of Bolshevism greatly complicated and intensified these issues. It was not simply that Russia had collapsed but that she had been overcome by a virulent disease. Thus, even if it were possible to vanquish Germany, and in the process keep her from dominating Russia, the danger remained that Bolshevism might spread from Moscow into Central and Eastern Europe, infecting Germany and undercutting the Allied victory purchased at such enormous cost. Moreover, if this occurred the Western governments and systems themselves would be threatened.

Concern at the peace conference over the Russian-German-Bolshevism nexus was heightened by Western memories of German policy toward Russia in 1918. To be sure, the German government, like the Allied ministries, had wavered between two strands of policy: an accommodation and *modus vivendi* with the Soviet government, or a limited intervention designed to replace the Bolsheviks with a conservative, pro-German regime, as was accomplished in the Ukraine. But, in Western eyes, either of these raised the specter of the vast resources and potential power of Russia being controlled and exploited by the Germans. It was a nightmare the men at Paris could not easily forget.

Not only the past influenced and circumscribed actions of the peace conference in regard to Russia. Another major limitation was public opinion. It is, of course, true that this study, as an analysis of the efforts of the Western nations, to readjust their relations with Russia at the close of the war, is primarily concerned with matters of policy and diplomacy. Attention is focused on the discussions and decisions of statesmen and diplomats. Issues of power, national interest, and economic advantage are treated. Yet underlying and deeply affecting the pursuit of policy toward Russia in the postwar months was a key intangible factor —the mood and spirit of the times. The attempts of the peacemakers to settle the Russian question and to meet the challenge of Bolshevism can be understood only in the context of the existing climate of opinion, which enveloped and influenced their every thought and act. With respect to Russian policy, as we shall see, popular feelings and attitudes were often decisive.

The Temper of the Times

For many in the West the end of the war symbolized the beginning of the millennium, the dawning of that "brave new world" they had fought for and believed in. Hysterical rejoicing greeted the Armistice, but the "morning after" of peacemaking brought only disillusionment and re-

sentment. Neither personal nor world problems were miraculously resolved by the cessation of hostilities. In fact, in many respects conditions
seemed worse than before the war. Unemployment, hunger, and strife
plagued Europe; these and other postwar problems had to be faced by
peoples who were exhausted and dispirited. The supreme patriotic effort
of the war, demanding self-sacrifice, teamwork, and heroism, was suddenly over. The cement of a common purpose was dissolved, and individual, group, and national attitudes disintegrated into familiar competing patterns, marked by self-interest and jealousy. Hatreds previously
channeled against the enemy were suddenly released within each society.
After the years of strain and exaltation, the psychological letdown was
abrupt and depressing. A revulsion against war seized the peoples of the
West. The pressure to "bring the boys home," to "demob," was very
great. Labor grievances, pent up during the war, burst forth. Leftist agi-
tators and Wilsonian idealists made articulate vague feelings of dissatisfaction with the old order, though from different premises. To the East
the Bolshevist promise of a new order was being trumpeted; even liberals could sympathize with the aims, if not the practices, of the Bolshevik Revolution. All this created an atmosphere of confusion and turmoil,
of unrest and uncertainty, in which calm deliberation and wise decision-
making were virtually impossible.

The circumstance most directly affecting decisions of the peace conference respecting Russia was the poor morale of the Allied and American soldiers. After the Armistice discipline sagged in the democratic
armies of the West. The "boys," vociferously supported by public opinion, clamored to be brought home. No one wanted to fight any more,
least of all by intervening in Russia. The struggle was over. The citizen-
soldiers became citizens again, whatever their uniform. As Colonel
Freydenberg, with the French forces that landed in South Russia in December 1918, aptly expressed it: "No French soldier who saved his life
after the Marne and Verdun would want to lose it on the fields of Russia." [1] This attitude was prevalent among American and British troops
as well. In the great Folkestone riots of January 4, 1919, involving
thousands of British troops on leave who had been ordered to return to
France, demonstrating soldiers carried banners declaring "We Will Not
Fight In Russia" and demanding immediate demobilization.[2] Morale
among the American troops who had been sent to North Russia in the
spring and summer of 1918 sank rapidly after the Armistice, and in

[1] Quoted in A. I. Gukovskii, *Frantsuzskaia interventsiia na iuge Rossii, 1918–
19* (*French Intervention in the South of Russia, 1918–19*) (Moscow, 1928), 123.
[2] Oswald Garrison Villard, *Fighting Years: Memoirs of a Liberal Editor* (New
York, 1939), 382–83. See also Winston S. Churchill, *The Aftermath, 1918–28*
(Vol. IV of *The World Crisis*) (New York, 1929), 42, 50–53.

March 1919 an American company refused to go to the front.[3] The one major attempt by the Allies after the Armistice to intervene in Russia with their own troops, the French-led expedition to Odessa, ended in failure, partly because of growing disaffection among the French soldiers in the expeditionary force.

The unreliability of the troops available to fight the Bolsheviks was complemented by labor unrest on the home front. In February 1919 strikes and riots in England reached such proportions that Lloyd George hastened back to London from the peace conference to deal with the situation.[4] The labor movements in Britain and France were openly hostile to continued intervention in Russia. In England leftist elements organized a large-scale campaign of pressure and publicity under the slogan "Hands Off Russia." [5] There were veiled threats of resorting to "direct action" to put an end to British support of the anti-Bolshevik forces in Russia, while in France moderate socialist leaders protested against intervention to the American delegation to the peace conference and talked vaguely of a coordinated general strike in France and England if the Allies attempted further military action in Russia.[6]

The Specter of Bolshevism

The general postwar atmosphere, coupled with disquieting examples of military disaffection and social disorder, raised prominently in the minds of Western statesmen the threat of Bolshevism, not only to Russia and Germany, but even to their own countries. In retrospect, it is easy to point out that these fears were magnified, that there was no real danger of a Bolshevik upheaval in Western Europe. But such hindsight does not make sufficient allowance for the temper of the times, the utter fatigue of the Allied leaders, and the strain and pressure under which they were working. It was a "time of national shell-shock, exaggerated appearances, exaggerated fears," with the people in a "state of exhaustion and demoralization." [7] To the peacemakers the Bolshevik danger seemed real and imminent, and they acted on their impressions of the moment, not on what we may now calmly consider as the facts.

[3] Department of State, *Papers Relating to the Foreign Relations of the United States: 1918, Russia* (3 vols.; Washington, 1931–32), II, 567, and *ibid., 1919, Russia* (Washington, 1937), 620–23. Hereafter cited as *1918, Russia* and *1919, Russia.*

[4] Lord Riddell, *An Intimate Diary of the Peace Conference and After, 1918–23* (London, 1933), 21.

[5] See the interesting account of the "Hands Off Russia" movement by the British Communist Harry Pollitt, *Serving My Time* (London, 1940).

[6] These views of French socialist leaders were reported in a memorandum from William C. Bullitt to Colonel E. M. House, December 21, 1918, E. M. House Papers, Yale University Library.

[7] Baker, *Settlement,* I, 82–83.

Even before the Armistice, the Western leaders were apprehensive. On October 30, 1918, Colonel House reported to President Wilson that in discussing the danger of Bolshevism with Clemenceau and Lloyd George, the latter "admitted it was possible to create such a state of affairs in England, and both agreed anything might happen in Italy."[8] In the period before the peace conference opened, Colonel House surveyed the situation in England, noting the bitterness of political feeling and pointing out that labor was toying with the idea of a general strike. He concluded that "British public opinion is in a condition of nerves bordering almost on hysteria," owing to the strain of the war, relief at its end, and the excitement of a general election.[9] Immediately after the Armistice, in order to counteract the effects of revolutionary propaganda in England, the British government proposed an elaborate program, which was to include visits by the Prince of Wales to "large munitions factories employing women in order that his undoubted popularity might act as a check to the spread of anarchistic tendencies."[10] Reflecting the anxiety of the Allied leaders at the time, Ray Stannard Baker wrote a few months later: "Few people realize how tremendous and explosive was the situation throughout Europe during the conference. All the governments were shaky; a little misstep on the part of Lloyd George, Clemenceau, Orlando, and their ministries might have gone down."[11]

Although there was certainly no imminent danger of a Bolshevik revolution in America, even Wilson was troubled by what he interpreted as signs of future difficulty. On October 16, 1918, he told Sir William Wiseman, a confidential British representative in the United States: "The spirit of the Bolsheviki is lurking everywhere. . . . There is grave unrest all over the world. There are symptoms of it in this country—symptoms that are apparent although not yet dangerous."[12]

But the main focus of Western fears concerning the spread of Bolshevism was the defeated enemy: Germany and Austria-Hungary. British leaders were keenly apprehensive concerning the menace of a Bolshevized Germany, and the matter was discussed by Lloyd George and

[8] Charles Seymour, ed., *The Intimate Papers of Colonel House* (4 vols.; Boston, 1926–1928), IV, 118–19. Hereafter cited as Seymour, *House Papers*.

[9] In a cable to David Hunter Miller, legal expert with the preparatory commission for the peace conference in the United States. David Hunter Miller, *My Diary at the Conference of Paris* (21 vols.; privately printed, 1924–1928), I, 28. Hereafter cited as Miller, *Diary*.

[10] Report to Washington from London, November 20, *1918, Russia,* I, 126–27.

[11] Ray Stannard Baker, *What Wilson Did at Paris* (New York, 1919), 18.

[12] Notes of an Interview with the President by Sir William Wiseman, House Papers, Drawer 35. See also Wilson's comments on "danger signals" in the United States in a letter to Grant Squires of November 12, 1918, Woodrow Wilson Papers, Library of Congress, Series II.

Churchill on Armistice night.[13] American Secretary of State Lansing was particularly exercised at the possibility of Germany succumbing to radicalism, and forwarded to Wilson in the weeks just prior to the Armistice a number of telegrams, memoranda, and reports warning of this danger.[14] In a long confidential memorandum for his files dated October 26, 1918, Lansing summed up his fears:

> There are at work in Europe two implacable enemies of Individual Liberty and its guardian, Political Equality and Justice. These enemies are Absolutism and Bolshevism. The former is waning. The latter is increasing. . . .
> Its [Bolshevism's] appeal is to the unintelligent and brutish element of mankind to take from the intellectual and successful their rights and possessions and to reduce them to a state of slavery. . . .
> Bolshevism is the most hideous and monstrous thing that the human mind has ever conceived. It . . . finds its adherents among the criminal, the depraved, and the mentally unfit. . . . Yet this monster which seeks to devour civilized society and reduce mankind to the state of beasts is certainly spreading westward. . . . A Bolshevik Germany or Austria is too horrible to contemplate. It is worse, far worse, than a Prussianized Germany, and would mean an even greater menace to human liberty.[15]

In Allied and American circles several proposals for dealing with the Bolshevik danger in Europe were advanced. One idea, based on the premise that starvation and unemployment led to Bolshevism, was to provide food and economic assistance to Germany and Austria-Hungary. Lansing stated the case for this policy in its simplest form: "Food is the real problem. Empty stomachs mean Bolsheviks. Full stomachs mean no Bolsheviks. The feeding of Europe must take place as rapidly

---

[13] Churchill, *Aftermath*, 5. See also the views of Balfour, Lord Milner, and Lord Reading in Journal of Frank I. Cobb, October 31 and November 11, 1918, Wilson Papers, New Acquisitions, 32.

[14] These appear in the Wilson Papers for that period. In his desk diary Lansing noted that he discussed Bolshevism in Central Europe with the president on November 1. On the same date he directed Bullitt to prepare a daily file on the subject. On November 5 he again conferred with Wilson regarding the Bolshevik danger in Germany. Robert Lansing Papers, Library of Congress.

[15] *Ibid.*, Confidential Memoranda. He expressed similar views in a series of letters at that time, notably to Elihu Root on October 28 and to Charles E. Hotchkiss on November 13. *Ibid.*, Correspondence, vol. 39. Lansing recommended that the peace conference not be held in Switzerland on the grounds that Bolshevik revolutionaries and spies headquartered there might endanger President Wilson and the peace delegations. Letter to House, November 8, 1918, Ray Stannard Baker Papers, Library of Congress; Series IA.

as possible to defeat the chaos which threatens society." [16] In his address to Congress on the occasion of the Armistice, President Wilson declared that relief for the peoples of Europe "will set their minds and energies free for the great and hazardous task of political reconstruction. . . . Hunger does not breed reform; it breeds madness and all the ugly distempers that make an ordered life impossible." [17] Many British leaders favored giving Germany food, but the French were reluctant to do so. The latter feared it might help to revive Germany's economic power, and they wished to use the promise of food as a means of exerting pressure on Germany over the terms of peace. As a result, the issue of relief to Central and Eastern Europe was not settled until several months after the peace conference convened.[18]

The Allied leaders also sought to check the expansion of Bolshevism in Europe through the terms of the Armistice, by taking advantage of the presence in Russia of German troops, who, it was hoped, would serve as a barrier to the spread of Bolshevism westward.[19] Further military intervention in Russia—designated to eliminate Bolshevism at its Soviet roots—represented still another approach to the problem, one that was exemplified by the French-led expedition to Odessa in December 1918.

Many in the West, however, regarded peace itself as the best antidote to Bolshevism. A healthy world could probably resist the infection; a sick and disordered one might not. A return to stability and order, the restoration of economic life and trade, and the settlement of provocative boundary and minority conflicts would remove many of the grievances and uncertainties which nurtured Bolshevism. This conviction drove the peacemakers to their task. On Armistice Day, shortly before his address to Congress, Wilson talked briefly with Homer S. Cummings of the Democratic National Committee, speaking gravely of the deteriorating conditions in Europe and of the tremendous responsibility which the United States bore to see to it that the world did not fall into chaos.[20] Crossing the Atlantic to Paris in December 1918, Wilson gave an informal "pep talk" to a group of the senior experts attached to the American delegation to the peace conference. According to notes taken by geographer Isaiah Bowman, the president, speaking with great conviction,

[16] Memorandum of October 28, 1918, Confidential Memoranda, Lansing Papers.
[17] Ray Stannard Baker and William E. Dodd, eds., *The Public Papers of Woodrow Wilson* (8 vols.; New York, 1925–1927), v, 300. Hereafter cited as Baker and Dodd, *Wilson Public Papers*.
[18] See ch. seven.
[19] See pp. 25–26 below.
[20] Ray Stannard Baker, *Woodrow Wilson: Life and Letters* (8 vols.; Garden City, 1927–1939), VII, 581.

declared that for the first time decisions of a peace conference would reflect the opinion of mankind, not previous determinations and diplomatic schemes. If the conference failed to express the will of the people, the break-up of society might well result. Wilson added that Bolshevism was gaining acceptance because it was "a protest against the way in which the world has worked." The people wanted a new course, a cleansing process which would regenerate the world. The president concluded that the American delegation must fight for a new order based on justice.[21]

Thus, in Wilson's view, peace alone would not suffice. It had to be a just peace satisfying the aspirations of the peoples of the world. In his "Fourteen Points" and in subsequent addresses, Wilson had outlined the principles and ideals on which he believed a just peace should be based. But Wilson's plans for reordering the world did not stand unchallenged. Lenin had his own peace proposals, proclaiming objectives which had great popular appeal. From the moment the Bolshevik movement first came to the attention of the world, its peace program competed with that of the West for the support of peoples everywhere. In fact, this challenge, and particularly the declaration by the new Soviet government of a six-point peace program at the beginning of the Brest-Litovsk peace negotiations in December 1917, was an important factor leading to the restatement of Allied war aims by both Wilson and Lloyd George in early 1918.[22]

To be sure, there were points of similarity in the competing peace programs which Wilson and Lenin stood for. Both men were anti-imperialists and believed that only disaster awaited the world if international affairs continued to be conducted in the old way. They both sensed a widespread popular longing for new leadership and a better life. Both men tended to be messianic; each was convinced that he and he alone had the proper prescription for saving the world. But Wilson wanted reform and Lenin revolution.

The essence of Lenin's position became increasingly clear as the end of the war neared and his hopes for revolution soared. Genuine and lasting peace, he declared, could be secured only by the complete destruction of the old order and by the triumph of the socialist revolution

[21] Miller, *Diary*, I, 370.

[22] The impact of Bolshevik peace proposals on popular opinion in Germany and in the West, and on Allied war aims, is a fascinating and complex story in itself, lying beyond the limits of this study. See the careful examination of certain aspects of this question in Arno J. Mayer, *Political Origins of the New Diplomacy* (New Haven, 1959). Christopher Lasch's criticism of Mayer and Lasch's assertion that the peace programs of Lenin and Wilson were not competing but complementary are unconvincing and weakly supported. Christopher Lasch, *American Liberals and the Russian Revolution* (New York, 1962), 65 n.

throughout the world. The decree of the Soviet Central Executive Committee on November 13 annulling the Treaty of Brest-Litovsk declared: "The imperialist peace must be replaced by a socialist peace concluded by the toiling masses of Russia, Germany, and Austro-Hungary. . . . [It] would be more than a peace treaty. It would be an alliance of the toiling masses of all nations in their struggle to create and consolidate a socialist order upon the ruins of militarism and economic slavery." In a manifesto of November 3 to the workers of Austria-Hungary, the Soviet government warned them against submitting to a new "yoke" of the bourgeoisie in the guise of peace. The "toilers" were also cautioned against being deceived by bourgeois shouts of "Long Live Wilson." [23]

The latter admonition reflected the growing concern of the Soviet leaders over the appeal of "Wilsonism" to the European masses. Writing in *Izvestia* on October 8, 1918, Karl Radek, a prominent Bolshevik, labeled Wilson's Fourteen Points "a very deliquescent [*sic*] program of political rascality," and charged that Wilson was "the prophet of American imperialism." He predicted that despite Wilson's promises Lenin would prevail in the postwar struggle for a new order.[24] Lenin himself was disturbed by the attraction that the democratic ideals of Wilson had for European socialists and workers. One of the principal reasons for Lenin's decision to establish the Third International, later known as the Comintern, in March 1919, was to organize communist parties abroad to combat and counteract the influence of Wilson on the masses. Theses on bourgeois democracy and proletarian dictatorship drafted by Lenin and adopted by the Comintern at its first congress constituted in the main an attack on the principles of Wilson and the liberals. Lenin particularly stressed the danger of such "deceptive" concepts as democracy, freedom of speech, press and assembly, and parliamentarianism.[25]

These Soviet fears were by no means unjustified. German workers and their socialist leaders strongly urged the German government to make peace in October 1918, once they learned that Wilson had promised a peace based on the Fourteen Points. In the summer and fall of 1918, the French socialist press warmly endorsed Wilson's peace platform, and in December, on the occasion of Wilson's arrival in Europe, the French socialist Marcel Cachin wrote:

> . . . the passages of Wilson have touched most profoundly the sentimentality and the idealism of the proletariat. Alone amid the rulers

[23] Jane Degras, ed., *Soviet Documents on Foreign Policy* (3 vols.; London, 1951–1953), I, 124–25, 131–33. Hereafter cited as Degras, *Soviet Documents*.
[24] Cited in Alfred L. P. Dennis, *The Foreign Policies of Soviet Russia* (New York, 1924), 465.
[25] Jane Degras, ed., *The Communist International, 1919–1943: Documents* (London, 1956), I, 7–16. Hereafter cited as Degras, *Comintern Documents*.

he has known how to speak . . . the language of good will, humanity, of international justice. . . . He has formulated in chiseled terms the objectives of the odious war. . . . Because he has sustained these elevated ideals Wilson has conquered the generous hearts of the workers of the world.[26]

In February 1919 a socialist conference at Berne supported Wilsonian policies and backed the League of Nations, despite the opposition of its leftist participants. A careful student of the contest between "Wilsonism" and Leninism, Arno Mayer, concludes that Wilson's program played a significant role in thwarting Bolshevism in Europe: ". . . the attraction of Woodrow Wilson's vision for the coming peace and its contribution to civil reconciliation—strategically supported by American financial power and economic surplus—kept . . . many Socialists and Radicals from instantly joining the forces of Revolution." [27]

While "Wilsonism" made some headway among the peoples of Europe, Bolshevism remained a constant danger, both real and imagined, spurring the peacemakers on. A contemporary political cartoon showed the white dove of peace flying above the world, overshadowed by the great black vulture of Bolshevism.[28] The Western leaders viewed their efforts as a race with anarchy, a race they were in danger of losing at any moment. The pressure and strain were immense; delay or error, they feared, might lead to an upheaval from which the world would never recover. Lloyd George described the situation graphically before the House of Commons:

> We had to . . . work crowded hours, long and late, because, whilst we were trying to build, we saw in many lands the foundations of society crumbling into dust and we had to make haste. . . . I am doubtful whether any body of men with a difficult task have worked under greater difficulties—stones crackling on the roof and crashing through the windows, and sometimes wild men screaming through the keyholes.[29]

Harold Nicolson, a participant in the conference and one of the most acute and sensitive observers at Paris, characterized the atmosphere of the peace deliberations as follows:

[26] From an article in *L'Humanité,* cited in Sisley Huddleston, *Peace-Making at Paris* (London, 1919), 17–18. For the opinion of the French socialist press on Wilson, see George Bernard Noble, *Policies and Opinions at Paris, 1919* (New York, 1935), 42–43.

[27] Mayer, 392; see also 384–88, 390–91.

[28] By Fitzpatrick in the St. Louis *Post-Dispatch,* reprinted in Thomas A. Bailey, *Wilson and the Peacemakers* (New York, 1947), 312.

[29] Quoted in Baker, *Settlement,* II, 38.

It is not easy, when using the silent machinery of printed words, to reproduce the double stress of turmoil and time-pressure which in Paris constituted the main obstruction to calm thinking or planned procedure. . . . Only through the medium of a sound film could any accurate impression, that sense of riot in a parrot house, be conveyed. . . .

As a recurrent undertone throughout would run the rumble of Time's winged chariot; incessantly reiterant would come the motif of this time-pressure—newspapers screaming in headlines vs. the Dawdlers of Paris, the clamour for demobilization, "Get the Boys Back," the starving millions of Central Europe, the slouching queues of prisoners still behind their barbed wire, the flames of communism flaring, now from Munich, and now from Buda-Pesth.[30]

Thus from the very beginning the peacemakers were affected by the specter of Bolshevism. Consider it they must; deal with it if they could. Western society was under fire. Revolution threatened Central Europe and even their own countries. The men at Paris believed that they had to bring order to Russia, maintain stability in Germany and Austria-Hungary, and make a peace that would satisfy the aspirations of the masses. And all this had to be done quickly if they were to beat back chaos and anarchy.

Bolshevism and the Armistice

But even before the fighting stopped, Bolshevism began to play a role in shaping the pattern of the peace to follow. The fear that Bolshevism might triumph in Germany influenced to some degree Allied and German decisions concerning the timing of the German Armistice. The Germans used this fear, with some success, as a bargaining weapon in the Armistice negotiations themselves. Moreover, the provisions of the Armistice dealing with Eastern Europe were largely drawn with the threat of Bolshevism in mind. Issues and themes relating to Bolshevism that emerged at the time of the Armistice were to recur frequently during the peace conference.

Wilson's determination to have the Germans and the Allies accept his Fourteen Points as the basis for peace and his eagerness to begin the reconstruction of the world on that basis were undoubtedly the major reasons for his insistence, during October 1918, on an early and not too harsh armistice. He also feared, however, that if the terms of a truce were too severe, Germany might fall prey to Bolshevism. Commenting to Sir William Wiseman on the first German approaches suggesting an

[30] Harold Nicolson, *Peacemaking, 1919* (Boston, 1933), 152–53.

armistice, Wilson declared: "We should consider too the condition of Germany. If we humiliate the German people and drive them too far, we shall destroy all form of government there and Bolshevism will take its place." [31] House held a similar view of the situation. In late October he pointed out to Clemenceau and Lloyd George the danger of bringing about a state of Bolshevism in Germany if the terms of the Armistice were made too stiff and the consequent danger to England, France, and Italy.[32]

Even Clemenceau recognized that a Bolshevik Germany might be more of a menace than a Germany defeated but unconquered. On November 10, in final discussion of the Armistice provisions by the British Cabinet, Lloyd George twitted General Sir Henry Wilson, the British Chief of Staff, who had consistently argued for harsher terms for the Germans. The latter reported in his diary that the prime minister read two wires from Clemenceau: ". . . and Tiger [Clemenceau] is afraid that Germany will break up and Bolshevism become rampant. Lloyd George asked me if I wanted this or would rather have an armistice, and I unhesitatingly said 'armistice.' All the Cabinet agreed. Our real danger now is not the Boches but Bolshevism." [33] The Allies' fear of Bolshevism thus worked against delaying an armistice until Germany was completely vanquished, and for the inclusion of more lenient conditions in the document itself.

On the German side a similar fear influenced to some degree the final decision to give up the struggle and seek an armistice. This decision was later to become the subject of historical controversy and political manipulation. German generals and rightists vehemently claimed that the German army could have fought on to victory, had not subversive elements on the home front, including Bolsheviks, "stabbed it in the back." By the fall of 1918, war-weariness, lowered morale, and social discontent had undoubtedly diminished Germany's ability to resist. The German decision to sue for peace resulted, however, not so much from weaknesses on the domestic scene, and certain inroads of the Bolsheviks there, as from the military superiority of the Allies, General Ludendorff's panicky insistence in September on the necessity of an immediate

[31] Notes of an Interview with the President by Sir William Wiseman, October 16, 1918. House Papers.

[32] Reported in a telegram from House in Paris to Wilson, October 30, 1918. Wilson Papers, Series II. See also a discussion of this point between House and Joseph Grew, then a young State Department officer, in Joseph C. Grew, *Turbulent Era: A Diplomatic Record of Forty Years, 1904–1945* (2 vols.; Boston, 1952), I, 344.

[33] Major-General Sir C. E. Callwell, *Field-Marshal Sir Henry Wilson: His Life and Diaries* (2 vols.; London, 1927), II, 146. Hereafter cited as Callwell, *Wilson Diaries*.

cease-fire to stave off military disaster, and the army's inability later, after Ludendorff had changed his mind, to stop the momentum toward peace which the civilian government had generated under the impulse of Ludendorff's original demand.[34] At the same time German *fears* of Bolshevism did play a part in both the military and political calculations which led to the decision to seek an armistice.

Following the successful Allied offensive in the late summer and early fall of 1918, both civilian and military authorities in Germany recognized that if Germany were to continue the fight, the German armies on the Western Front would have to be reinforced. The German command, however, opposed any large-scale transfer of divisions from occupied Russia on the grounds that this would expose the East and eventually Germany itself to Bolshevism.[35] The German generals also feared that the transfer of soldiers from the East, some of whom were infected with Bolshevism, might weaken the morale of the forces in the West.[36]

Anxiety concerning the domestic situation also contributed to the German decision to bring the war to an end. Conservative forces in Germany were afraid that prolongation of the war might bring on a Bolshevik revolution. This, they feared, would sweep away the last remnants of their vested position, which might yet be partially preserved—and was —even in the face of an Allied victory and a dictated peace. According to the German socialist leader Scheidemann, Prince Max of Baden, the chancellor, for example, was so obsessed by fears that the German workers would fall under the sway of Bolshevism that he could think only of this in opposing a continuation of the war.[37]

The danger of Bolshevism in Germany became one of the main talking points for the German representatives at the Armistice negotiations. They argued, partly for effect but probably sincerely to a considerable extent, that unless the Armistice terms presented to them were ameliorated, Germany would be plunged into anarchy, famine, and Bolshevism. To prevent this, they maintained, was in the Allies' own interest. If Germany became a prey to Bolshevism, she would not be able to meet

[34] Harry R. Rudin, *Armistice, 1918* (New Haven, 1944), 393–94.

[35] On October 9 and October 19 Ludendorff warned the government against withdrawing troops from the Ukraine since food supplies from there were badly needed and since such an evacuation might open the door to Bolshevism. *Ibid.,* 111, 139. See also Erich Ludendorff, *Ludendorff's Own Story* (2 vols.; New York, 1919), II, 350–51.

[36] General Groener to Prince Max of Baden, the chancellor, on November 5. General Mordacq, *Pouvait-on signer l'armistice à Berlin?* (Paris, 1930), 98–99.

[37] Cited in Rudin, 218–19. Rudin, a careful historian of the Armistice period, concluded that such fears also helped convince Max of the necessity of securing the kaiser's abdication. Max hoped that the abdication of the kaiser would mollify the German Social-Democrats and encourage them to join fully in the fight against Bolshevism.

the obligations imposed on her or to pay reparations. Moreover, Germany was, they said, a bulwark against Bolshevism which the Allies could not abandon without endangering themselves. On November 9 House transmitted to Wilson a communication from Clemenceau on the progress of the Armistice negotiations: "Their [the Germans'] theme is to say that they will succumb to Bolshevikism [*sic*] if we do not help them to resist and that after them we ourselves will be invaded by the same scourge." [38]

The German delegates variously utilized the Bolshevik argument to plead against Armistice provisions requiring the evacuation of the left bank of the Rhine, setting a time limit for that evacuation, reducing the weapons of the German forces, and continuing the blockade.[39] Learning of the Allied demand for the surrender of large numbers of German arms, Erzberger protested: "How shall we defend ourselves against Bolshevism? You will destroy us but in doing so, also yourselves." [40] On most points the Allies turned a deaf ear to the German cries of alarm. Foch, however, was much concerned over the threat of Bolshevism, and on two issues made concessions to the German representatives: he reduced from thirty to twenty-five thousand the number of machine guns the Germans were required to hand over to the Allies, and he permitted the Germans to delay their evacuation from Russia. The latter decision, as we shall see below, was contrary to the policy of the Allied governments and was later to cause the Allies considerable embarrassment and difficulty.

Russia and the Armistice

The German Armistice contained two important and several miscellaneous provisions directly affecting Russia. Among the miscellaneous items were articles requiring the Germans to renounce the Treaty of Brest-Litovsk (Article XV), to surrender to the Allies the Russian Black Sea fleet and merchant marine, which the Bolsheviks had turned over to Germany in 1918 (Article XXIX),[41] and to deliver to the Allies, to be

[38] Telegram from House in Paris to Wilson and Lansing, November 9, 1918. Wilson Papers, Series II.

[39] For details of the German argument on these points, see Rudin, 113, 339–73.

[40] Mordacq, 28–33.

[41] Approximately half of the Russian Black Sea fleet was scuttled on Lenin's order before it could be surrendered to the Germans in the spring of 1918. After the Armistice the British interned the remainder of the fleet at Sebastopol, despite the demands of General Denikin, the White Russian leader in South Russia, that he be given the ships. At the time of Denikin's advance toward Moscow in the summer of 1919, the British gave him half of the interned fleet, as well as the Russian Caspian Sea flotilla. General A. I. Denikin, *Ocherki russkoi smuty* (*Sketches of the Russian Turmoil*) (5 vols.; Paris, 1921?–1926?), IV, 85 and 129; and see below ch. nine, p. 330.

held in trust for restitution to Russia following the conclusion of peace, Russian gold reserves paid Germany by the Soviet government under terms of the treaty of Brest-Litovsk (Article XIX).[42]

A significant provision of the Armistice was that requiring the Germans to open the Black and Baltic seas to the Allies (Articles XXV and XXIX). This provided the Allies with relatively direct and easy access to European Russia and to areas controlled or endangered by Bolshevism. Further intervention, for which certain British and French leaders were then pressing, could be carried out via the western and southern sea approaches to Russia with far greater facility than by the roundabout routes which the North Russian and Siberian expeditions of the summer of 1918 had had to utilize. The French-sponsored expedition to Odessa in December 1918 took advantage of the Black Sea route. In addition, supplies could now be shipped directly to anti-Bolshevik forces in South Russia and in the Baltic area.

The most important clause of the Armistice respecting Russia, a source of much subsequent confusion and controversy, was that calling for the delayed evacuation of the German forces occupying Russian territory:

> All German troops at present in any territory which before the war formed part of Austria-Hungary, Roumania, or Turkey, shall withdraw within the frontiers of Germany as they existed on August 1, 1914, and all German troops at present in territories which before the war formed part of Russia, must likewise return to within the frontiers of Germany as above defined, *as soon as the Allies shall think the moment suitable, having regard to the internal situation of these territories.* (Article XII) [43]

The question of what to do about the German troops occupying parts of Russia posed a perplexing problem for the Allies. It brought to the fore two fundamental and conflicting views of Germany's position vis-à-vis Russia, which were to clash and intermingle throughout the peace conference and, indeed, during the whole interwar period. Allied principles and policy called for the withdrawal of German forces from Russia. The sixth of Wilson's Fourteen Points had promised "the evacuation of

---

[42] For the Armistice terms, see Rudin, 429–31. In the fall of 1919 the White Russian representatives in Paris vainly asked the Allies to permit utilization of part of the Russian gold surrendered by the Germans under the Armistice as a guarantee for a loan of one hundred million francs. This sum, they claimed, was needed to subsidize Finnish participation in the White General Yudenich's second attack on Petrograd. Memorandum of November 3, 1919, Maklakov Papers, Part II.

[43] My italics. Rudin, 428–29.

all Russian territory," and in early consultations concerning the conditions for a cease-fire with Germany, the prime ministers of France, Great Britain, and Italy had recommended German evacuation of the Caucasus and the territory of prewar Russia.[44]

At the same time Western statesmen increasingly realized, as the war drew to a close, that the summary withdrawal of German forces from occupied Russian territory would create a vacuum in those areas which the Bolsheviks could be expected to fill rapidly. The idea of using these German troops as a temporary barrier against Bolshevism gained increasing currency. The concept of playing off Germany against Russia was not, of course, a new one, dating back, in British diplomacy at least, to the nineteenth century. In early 1918 some in the British government, such as Lord Milner, secretary of war at the time, were talking of the possibility of a negotiated peace in which "the gains of Germany on Russian soil" would compensate her for colonial and other losses.[45] On the eve of the Armistice, Lord Milner and General Sir Henry Wilson told Colonel House that they were disposed to object to German demobilization on the grounds that Germany might have to serve as a bulwark against Bolshevism.[46]

For their part the Germans were well aware of the advantages that might accrue to them from the role of defenders of Europe against Bolshevism. During his famous "funk" interview with Hindenburg on September 28, 1918, Ludendorff argued that the truce with the Allies he was urging should not mean giving up any German-occupied territory in the East since he "believed that the Entente were aware of the danger threatening them, as well as ourselves, from Bolshevism." [47] Moreover, the Germans did not hesitate to create conditions which would make their continued occupation of Russian territory more palatable to the Allies. On October 15 Lansing forwarded to Wilson an intercepted message from German Foreign Secretary Solf to General von Kress, a German commander in the East. Solf explained that the German government, in considering Wilson's terms of peace, felt constrained to comply with the general provision for German evacuation of occupied territories. He added, however, that Wilson's note had not made clear whether the Eastern areas were also to be evacuated; the government,

[44] In a meeting on October 5, *ibid.*, 92–93.

[45] Reported in a letter from William H. Buckler, attaché of the American embassy, London, to House, February 28, 1918, Buckler Papers, Yale University Library.

[46] Seymour, *House Papers*, IV, 116.

[47] Cited in Rudin, 49. See also a memorandum of a military representative at the German Foreign Office on why Germany should champion anti-Bolshevism, dated June 3, 1918, and described in *ibid.*, 4–5.

[25]

therefore, would object to withdrawal there. In a "very confidential" comment, Solf then pointed out that Germany's objections would be strengthened if the inhabitants of the occupied territories themselves opposed evacuation. He concluded archly that although the German commanders could not directly instigate this, he hoped that they would "give the best prospect that the local authorities will decide upon this step of their own accord." [48] Not surprisingly, a number of requests from "local authorities" for the maintenance of German troops in occupied Russia as a shield against Bolshevism were channeled to the Allies through Scandinavian capitals during October 1918.[49]

The fear that German evacuation of occupied Russia would pave the way for a Bolshevik advance into those areas was balanced, however, by another consideration. Many in the West, then as now, were concerned over the possible development of a Russo-German combination, which would bring together vast resources and which would represent an accretion of power capable of dominating all Europe. This anxiety was not new: prior to the revolutions of 1917 the Allies had feared extreme rightist intrigues within Russia for a separate peace with Germany; [50] after the Bolshevik seizure of power Western statesmen had become alarmed lest Germany either dominate and use to its advantage a weak Bolshevik Russia, or instigate the establishment of a pro-German reactionary government in Russia.[51] Ambassador Francis and Consul Poole, American diplomatic representatives in Russia, had not hesitated in the spring of 1918 to point to the latter possibility as a reason for immediate Allied intervention in Russia.[52] At the same time the Russo-German bogey had been used by opponents of intervention, who had maintained that Japanese landings in Siberia would drive Russia into Germany's arms.

On the eve of the Armistice, Western suspicions of German intrigues in Russia were stimulated by the publication, in September and October

[48] Baker and Dodd, *Wilson Public Papers,* VI, 151.
[49] For examples, see *1918, Russia,* II, 698–99, 838–39, 643.
[50] For a discussion of even earlier fears, among American liberals, of a Russo-German alliance, see Lasch, 13–15.
[51] The British historian E. H. Carr maintains that Western leaders feared co-operation either between the German right and Russian monarchists or between German and Russian Bolsheviks; they failed, as a result, to perceive "the real source from which the danger came," a combination of German right and Russian left, first evidenced in 1918 and developed in subsequent years. E. H. Carr, *German-Soviet Relations between the Two World Wars, 1919–1939* (Baltimore, 1951), 9. This is true to the extent that Allied statesmen did not foresee the relatively equal relationship between Germany and Soviet Russia subsequently established; however, as we shall see, Western diplomats were much concerned that a non-Bolshevik Germany could exploit and utilize a weak and helpless Communist Russia.
[52] *1918, Russia,* I, 528, 555.

1918, of the questionable "Sisson documents," purporting to show that the Bolsheviks were German agents.[53] Concurrently, earlier fears of a liaison between German rightists and Russian conservatives were revived. That there was some basis for these latter fears is indicated by reports of French agents that right-wing Russian groups abroad had proposed to the German High Command that Russian officers be permitted to organize Russian prisoners of war in Germany into an anti-Bolshevik army. According to these reports, some Russian monarchists were hoping to win German support for a restoration of the tsardom.[54] There was also some pro-German sentiment among the anti-Bolshevik forces inside Russia. In his diary for October 18, 1918, Vologodsky, one of the ministers of the Omsk government in Siberia, reported a discussion in the council of ministers concerning relations with Germany. One of the participants pointed out that by linking up with General von der Goltz, the German commander in the Baltic area, the anti-Bolshevik movement could gain forty thousand troops, although this would alienate the Poles and the Allies. Vologodsky noted that "several of the ministers rather favor rapprochement with Germany." [55]

The prospect that worried the Allies most, however, was of German economic domination of Russia in the postwar period. This anxiety, which troubled Lloyd George and Keynes throughout the peace conference, was epitomized in a letter from American Ambassador Page in Rome to Wilson on the eve of the Armistice. Page expressed his concern over German control of the Ukraine, western Russia, and the Baltic, concluding: "Unless something be done to oust Germany therefrom . . . Germany is likely to annex all of western Russia, at least commercially and financially, and to spread her influence gradually all over Russia and possibly once more become a menace to the world." [56]

Thus, as the Armistice approached, Western leaders were of two minds concerning the disposition of German troops in Russia. On the

[53] For a careful analysis of the authenticity of these documents, see George F. Kennan, "The Sisson Documents," *Journal of Modern History*, Vol. 28, No. 2 (June 1958), 130–54.

[54] Report of a secret agent in Berne, September 14, 1918, and of the French military attaché in Stockholm, November 2. Maklakov Papers, Part II, Packet I, File 8. These reports are from a typed summary of French dispatches, dated November 5, 1918. As we shall see later, relations between Maklakov and the French Foreign Office were very close, which explains the presence of these and other French documents in his files.

[55] Unpublished diary of P. V. Vologodsky, Hoover Institution, Stanford.

[56] Letter from Page to Wilson, November 5, 1918, Wilson Papers, Series II, Box 155. Unfortunately, Wilson's reply is lacking. For an expression of Lansing's fears along these lines, see his memorandum of September 21, 1918, on the peace settlement in Robert Lansing, *The Peace Negotiations: A Personal Narrative* (New York, Boston, 1921), 192–93.

one hand, they were anxious to utilize them as a bulwark against the advance of Bolshevism into Western Europe; on the other, they feared the use that Germany might make of her position in Russia. In an attempt to resolve this dilemma, and also to support the national aspirations of the Baltic peoples, the British government proposed, in September and October 1918, that indigenous defense forces be established along the Baltic littoral to supplant the Germans and to prevent the incursion of Bolshevism. The British recommended that in the interim between the German withdrawal and the organization of local forces, the Scandinavian governments should provide a protective cover of some two thousand troops to keep out the Bolsheviks. This suggestion was rejected by the Scandinavians, however.[57]

In an effort to save at least remnants of this plan, British Foreign Secretary Balfour proposed on November 2, when the Allied Supreme War Council was discussing the Armistice terms to be presented to the Germans, that German units withdrawing from Russia be ordered to leave one third of their arms "in the hands of local authorities to be designated by the Allies, in order to permit the population to defend itself against all disorders and aggressions." Pichon, the French foreign minister, argued that such arms would only fall into the hands of the Bolsheviks, and Marshal Foch declared coldly that the discussion was pointless since such a plan was not practicable of execution. In the face of these objections, Balfour withdrew his proposal.[58] French opposition was undoubtedly motivated in part by their belief that such a scheme would encourage and strengthen independence movements among the Baltic peoples. The French supported the White Russian objective of maintaining Russia's territorial integrity; they probably also feared that the Baltic states, if freed, would fall under British influence.

With the final rejection of the British proposal to arm the Baltic peoples, the problem posed by the German troops in Russia remained unresolved. In general the Allied civilian leaders seemed disposed to order the Germans out of Russia, despite the threat of Bolshevism. In discussing the Armistice terms on the Eastern Front, House pointed out to the Supreme War Council on November 1 that "the retreat of the German troops would be followed by a Bolshevist regime," but Sonnino, the Italian foreign minister, supported by Clemenceau, maintained: "The Bolshevist menace is old German strategy; we must not fall into the trap. The conclusion of an armistice . . . with Turkey reestablished our liaison with South Russia and Rumania and allows us to consider a re-

---

[57] *1918, Russia,* II, 838–849.

[58] General Tasker H. Bliss Papers, Library of Congress, Box 77, Minutes of the Eighth Session of the Supreme War Council, October 31–November 4, 1918.

organization." In the course of the discussion, Marshal Foch asked a question which indicated the direction his thoughts were taking: although Rumania might be able to recover control of her own affairs following the German evacuation, "what about the others? Are we to abandon them to themselves?" Apparently the Marshal was not convinced that there was no danger of Bolshevism in the occupied territories.

The next day Foch proposed clauses providing for the evacuation, within time limits, of Rumania and Poland, but significantly, not of Russia. After a brief discussion by the Council of the dangers of defining the territory of Poland in the Armistice, thereby prejudging the work of the peace conference, Balfour proposed a clause for the whole of the Eastern Front (presumably including Russia, although he did not specify so): "All the German forces in the East must return within their frontiers such as they were before the month of August 1914." The Council adopted this proposal, as well as Balfour's suggestion for a special provision guaranteeing Allied access to Poland and neighboring countries through Danzig or by the Vistula in order to convey supplies or to maintain order there (Article XVI of the final terms).

On November 4 Pichon and others pointed out that the clause agreed on concerning the Eastern Front was extremely vague and confusing, particularly the phrase, "German forces in the East." To rectify this, Lord Milner proposed the substitution, "German troops which are at present in the territories which, before the war, were a part of Russia, Rumania, or Turkey." This was approved, and became the wording included in Article XII of the draft terms which the Supreme War Council adopted on November 4, 1918.[59]

Thus, as matters stood one week before the Armistice, German troops were to evacuate Russia. But Article XII of the final terms signed on November 11, 1918, contained the significant additional provision that the German withdrawal would take place "as soon as the Allies shall think the moment suitable, having regard to the internal situation of these territories." Foch made this change during the Armistice negotiations, at the request of the Germans and without reference to the Allied civilian governments, who had earlier disapproved delayed evacuation.

On November 9, the day after the opening of the Armistice negotiations, the German delegation presented written observations on the Allied terms adopted by the Supreme War Council on November 4. Referring to Article XII, the Germans stated that the evacuation of Rumanian and Turkish territories could be carried out at once. They protested,

[59] All the foregoing, *ibid*. Excerpts from the minutes of the Supreme War Council are reproduced in Rudin, 290–318.

however, that "the immediate evacuation of former Russian territory now occupied by German troops would leave the inhabitants there defenseless against the horrors of Bolshevism." [60] Foch's reply on this point, delivered on November 10, stated that the German observation had been taken into account through a rewording of the article. This rewording consisted of the addition contained in the final text of Article XII.

Most historians of the Armistice period, including even as thorough a one as Rudin, have overlooked this significant concession won by the Germans, probably because neither Erzberger, the chief German delegate, nor Foch mentioned it in their memoirs.[61] Foch was disposed to accept the German position on this issue because, as we have seen, he was himself concerned about the Bolshevik threat to the areas in Russia held by the Germans.[62] Moreover, the Marshal was primarily interested in securing Armistice terms which would make it impossible for the Germans to continue the struggle. Knowing that the German armies in the East were weakened and demoralized and could pose no threat to France, he was willing to let them remain in Russia as a check to Bolshevism. In addition, the Turkish Armistice, signed ten days earlier, provided a precedent for the retention of occupying forces in Russia. Article II of that document called for partial evacuation of the Trans-Caucasus by Turkish troops, "the remainder to be evacuated if required by the Allies after they have studied the situation there." [63]

The Allied civilian governments were completely unaware of the change in Article XII until the Armistice was signed. On November 7 House referred to Wilson a request of the Austro-Hungarian government that, in view of the Bolshevism prevailing in the Ukraine, its troops be allowed to remain there until the arrival of Entente forces. House reported that Pichon and Clemenceau were opposed to granting the request on the grounds that it would "constitute a point which the

[60] The original terms, the German "observations," Foch's reply, and the final terms are printed in parallel columns in Herbert Kraus and Gustav Rödiger, comps., *Urkunden zum Friedensvertrage von Versailles vom 28 Juni 1919* (2 vols.; Berlin, 1920), I, 23–59. Article XII is on pp. 38–40.

[61] This episode is noted, however, in Titus Komarnicki, *Rebirth of the Polish Republic* (London, 1957), 233–37, and, more briefly, in Lionel Kochan, *The Struggle Over Germany* (Edinburgh, 1963), 10–11.

[62] It is also significant that in discussion of the Armistice terms in the Supreme War Council Foch objected to a draft proposal concerning the repatriation of Russian prisoners of war on the ground that to return them to the Bolsheviks would "run the risk of leading the whole world to Bolshevism." Apparently because of Foch's objections, no provision relating to Russian prisoners of war was included in the Armistice. The problem of their disposition was later to plague the peace conference.

[63] Rudin, 410.

Germans might make use of." House replied to Pichon that "we ought to make them no promises, but allow them to remain for the moment until we know more about the situation," a position similar to the one he had taken in the deliberations of the Supreme War Council on the issue of German evacuation of Russia. Wilson approved House's reply, indicating that the American leaders, at least, were in a frame of mind to accept the addition to Article XII.[64] In general, however, Western statesmen and diplomats were little interested in the conditions of the Armistice in the East. House, for example, described the changes in Article XII as "matters of detail." [65]

White Russian leaders, who in October had urged upon the Allies the necessity of providing in the Armistice for the unqualified evacuation of all Russian territory, were by the first week of November warning the Allied governments that too rapid a withdrawal by the Germans might open the door to Bolshevism.[66] They also were clearly in a mood to consent to the temporary retention of German forces on Russian soil.

As finally signed, Article XII failed to prescribe precisely and unequivocally the duration and conditions of the continued occupation of Russia by German troops. Foch was probably correct in judging that precipitate withdrawal would open the door to a quick Bolshevik advance westward, and his action may well have given Rumania, Poland, and the Baltic peoples a much-needed, though brief, period of security in which to organize their forces and get on their feet. Nevertheless, the vagueness of Article XII permitted the Germans to interpret it as they wished and left them in a position which they could easily turn to their own advantage. In areas where there was little to be gained by staying and acting as the Allies' "policemen," the Germans simply ignored Article XII and withdrew. Thus, by early 1919 the Germans had evacuated the Crimea and much of the Ukraine and Byelorussia, claiming that they had never undertaken an obligation to attempt to maintain order in Russia indefinitely.[67] They remained, however, in the Baltic region, which they hoped to dominate and perhaps later use as a base for the extension

[64] Wilson Papers, Series II, Boxes 153, 155.

[65] In transmitting the final terms to Lansing on November 11. File 763.72119/ 9131, Records of the Department of State, National Archives.

[66] Evacuation was called for in a memorandum of October 31 submitted to the State Department by Bakhmetev, the Provisional Government ambassador in Washington, and in a similar memorandum presented to Sonnino by de Giers, the ambassador of the Provisional Government in Rome. Maklakov Papers, Part II, Packet I, File 2. Reports of warnings to the Allies are in *ibid.*, Part II, Packet I, Files 5 and 6.

[67] Note from the German government transmitted by the Swiss and enclosed in a dispatch from the American legation in Berne to the American delegation in Paris, January 13, 1919. File 185.001/27, Records of the ACTNP, National Archives.

of German influence into Russia proper. It was only with great difficulty, and over a year later, that the Allies were able to get the Germans out of the Baltic. If, in delaying evacuation of Russia, Foch had specified the terms on which the Germans were to stay and had set a time limit for their eventual withdrawal, his anti-Bolshevik purposes would have been more effectively served, and a good deal of subsequent trouble avoided.

Thus, in the very act of ending hostilities, Western leaders were confronted by the complex and related issues of Bolshevism and Russia. At the periphery of their attention, the statesmen gave these questions relatively little thought, and what they did regarding them was insubstantial and inconclusive. This proved to be an accurate portent of the fate of these issues in the peace conference to follow. Yet in the two months that intervened between the Armistice and the opening of the peace conference the perplexities of Russia and Bolshevism persisted and increasingly were raised before Western statesmen. Unfortunately, the latter were ill prepared to grasp this nettle.

CHAPTER TWO

The Allies and Russia

A Difficult Problem

THE DECISION at the time of the Armistice to attempt to use German troops in Russia to dam the Bolshevik tide was a stop-gap solution to a question which had plagued Allied statesmen in the preceding months. During 1917 they had struggled with touchy issues arising from the downfall of the Tsarist regime, the waning ability and will of the Russian army to fight, the desire of Russian socialists and some Russian liberals for a redefinition of war aims, and the seizure of power by the Bolsheviks in November. With the Bolshevik withdrawal of Russia from the war by the Treaty of Brest-Litovsk in March 1918, and the subsequent Allied intervention in Russia in the summer of 1918, Western policy toward Russia had appeared to settle on the goal of reestablishing an eastern front against Germany. Allied intervention seems clearly to have been chiefly motivated by strategic considerations of the all-out struggle with Germany, no matter how chimerical and vain such calculations seem in retrospect.[1] Ill-disguised hostility to Bolshevism, which had made peace with Germany, and open support of those Russians who opposed both the Germans and the Bolsheviks had been natural corollaries of this decision.

Other motives were obviously at work, too. Japanese militarists, little interested in the war in Europe, saw an opportunity to extend their influence into the Russian Far East and Siberia. Some British statesmen, concerned for the future of the Empire, were anxious to develop spheres of influence in the Trans-Caspian and Trans-Caucasian regions, while French leaders dreamed of future economic domination of the Ukraine and South Russia.

On the other hand, the United States, without special economic, political, or strategic aspirations in Russia itself, had been most reluctant to intervene. American statesmen had doubted the military wisdom of intervention, and Woodrow Wilson had opposed the decision on prin-

---

[1] The two fullest studies are George F. Kennan, *The Decision to Intervene* (Princeton, 1958), and Richard H. Ullman, *Intervention and the War* (Princeton, 1961).

ciple. Although the president detested the Bolsheviks as violators of one of his most cherished principles, the democratic ordering of men's affairs, another sacred Wilsonian tenet, the right of peoples to determine their own fate without outside interference, militated against intervention. Only under relentless Allied diplomatic and personal pressure, and for the sake of unanimity and harmony in the anti-German camp, as he admitted at the time, had Wilson consented to the proposed intervention.[2] The reputed plight of the Czechoslovak forces in Siberia and the alleged German danger to them and to Russia had given Wilson a pretext for, and a way of rationalizing, the decision to intervene. Wilson had apparently also hoped, once the decision had been taken, that the participation of American troops in the Siberian expedition might act as a restraining influence on the Japanese.[3]

Here, as later during the peacemaking, Wilson compromised his ideals—but only in the face of what he regarded as inescapable political necessity and for the attainment of what he believed was a more important objective. In this case, he felt compelled to preserve unity and concord with his allies in order to ensure the rapid and successful completion of the joint struggle against Germany. At Versailles, Wilson accepted a peace he considered far from perfect, rather than further delays or no peace at all, in the conviction that his League of Nations could right the wrongs of the treaty. This decision and the one to intervene in Russia were realistic actions, dictated by the necessity of maintaining America's alliances, and calculated to control or ameliorate actions Wilson felt he could not prevent. Neither had a happy outcome, which should give pause to those who charge that Wilson's difficulties in international affairs stemmed from his impractical idealism in that realm.

[2] To Secretary of War Baker's objections regarding the Siberian intervention Wilson replied, according to Baker: "Baker, I wholly agree with all that you say from a military point of view, but we are fighting this war with allies and I have felt obliged to refuse to do so many things they have asked me to do that I really feel obliged to fall in with their wishes here." Wilson Papers, Supplement, letter from Newton D. Baker to Mrs. John B. Casserly, November 18, 1924. See also James W. Morley, *The Japanese Thrust into Siberia, 1918* (New York, 1957), 263–64; Kennan, *The Decision to Intervene,* 381–404; and Betty Miller Unterberger, *America's Siberian Expedition, 1918–1920* (Durham, 1958), 87–88.

[3] Morley (pp. 261–62) argues that although there is much indirect evidence to indicate the anti-Japanese character of the American intervention, a final conclusion can be reached only after the documents of the War Department for this period are opened to scholars. In a provocative and partially persuasive article, Christopher Lasch rejects completely the anti-Japanese thesis, maintaining that American intervention was based entirely on anti-German considerations, though of a wildly improbable and illusory sort. C. Lasch, "American Intervention in Siberia: A Reinterpretation," *Political Science Quarterly,* Vol. 77, No. 2 (June 1962), 205–23.

Perhaps American liberals, such as William Allen White and Louis Brandeis, were nearer the mark when they maintained that Wilson's downfall began the moment he abandoned his principles and, against his better judgment, consented to the Siberian intervention.[4]

Seizing upon Wilson's reluctant concurrence in limited intervention, the European Allies attempted to make the Siberian expedition the opening wedge for a large-scale military effort against the Bolsheviks. Almost before the first Allied troops had landed in Siberia, the British and French were urging that the expedition be reinforced with several more Japanese divisions.[5] The United States rejected this proposal, but Allied pressure to enlarge the intervention was steadily maintained. The French and British submitted a variety of plans—for linking up the North Russian and Siberian fronts, for supporting a Czech advance west of the Ural Mountains, for appointing Allied High Commissioners and establishing an inter-Allied political council in Russia, and, finally, for committing more American troops to the intervention. These Allied schemes thoroughly alarmed Wilson, who wrote to Secretary of State Lansing in late August: "The other governments are going much further than we and much faster—are, indeed, acting upon a plan which is altogether foreign from ours and inconsistent with it. . . . We do not think cooperation in *political* action necessary or desirable in Eastern Siberia because we contemplate no political action of any kind there, but only the action of friends who stand at hand and wait to see how they can help." [6] The president's unrealistic view of the situation reflects the dilemma he faced in trying to square American participation in intervention with his belief in the self-determination of peoples.

In September Allied pressure for an extension of military activity in Russia continued and even increased, but Wilson and his advisers steadfastly opposed any expansion of intervention.[7] In early October General Tasker H. Bliss, American military representative to the Allied Supreme War Council, rejected two draft proposals submitted to him by the French, one a plan for broadened military intervention in Russia in which the United States was allocated a specific role, and the other a

---

[4] Both White and Brandeis attributed Wilson's "surrender" on intervention to physical and spiritual exhaustion, which soon caused him to make other mistakes. William Allen White, *Woodrow Wilson: The Man, His Times, and His Task* (Boston, 1924), 427, 441; Ray Stannard Baker Papers, Firestone Library, Princeton University, Ser. 1B, interview with Louis Brandeis, March 23, 1929.

[5] *1918, Russia*, II, 341–42; Department of State, *Papers Relating to the Foreign Relations of the United States: The Lansing Papers, 1914–1920* (2 vols.; Washington, 1939–40), II, 376–77. Hereafter cited as *Lansing Papers*.

[6] Wilson's italics, *ibid.*, II, 378–79.

[7] *1918, Russia*, II, 393–95, 404.

recommendation to send American reinforcements to Archangel.[8] Bliss commented to Lansing that the Allies were anxious to obtain Wilson's approval of large-scale intervention in Russia since American resources in men, materiel, and money would be essential to such action.

At about this time President Wilson was again turning to the idea of relief and economic assistance to the peoples of Siberia as the best way to deal with the Russian situation. This approach had been widely discussed inside the American government in the early spring of 1918, when it had strongly appealed to Wilson. On September 24 Wilson told Colonel House that he had not pursued the policy of giving economic aid to Russia because "Redfield [Secretary of Commerce] had so 'messed the matter up' that it was impossible for him to do so; that he had now taken it out of his [Redfield's] hands and placed it in that of the War Trade Board and he hoped something would come of it." [9] On October 5 the Russian Bureau, Incorporated, of the War Trade Board was established with a capital grant of five million dollars from the President's National Security and Defense Fund. It later received an additional five million dollars from funds of the Department of State. The Russian Bureau was never very active, however. Most of its money was spent on supplies for the Czechs in Siberia and on food for North Russia, and in June 1919 the Russian Bureau was dissolved.[10]

[8] *Lansing Papers,* II, 161. The plan for further intervention in Russia was apparently the project to which Clemenceau, the French premier, was referring when he wrote to General Franchet d'Espérey, the commander of the Allied armies of the East, on October 27, 1918: "I enclose herewith a note sketching in general outlines a project for the economic isolation of Bolshevik Russia in order to bring about its fall. For the moment the project represents the views of the French government and to go into effect, an agreement with the Allies must be reached. In case this agreement is reached, intervention by the Allies in the south of Russia will be carried out according to the plan of operations of the Allied armies of the East." Despite failure to win British and American approval of the plan, the French went ahead with the proposed campaign in South Russia, landing an expeditionary force at Odessa in December 1918. Although the authenticity of this letter from Clemenceau to d'Espérey could not be verified, internal evidence suggests it is genuine. For example, Clemenceau also enclosed in the letter a copy of a draft proposal concerning the situation in North Russia—clearly the second proposal to which Bliss referred. Clemenceau's letter was published in the Paris *Le Matin,* June 17, 1919. The text cited here is given as Annex No. 1 in F. Kostiaev, "Interventsiia na iuge Rossii, Kavkaze, i v Turkestane, 1918–20" (Intervention in the South of Russia, the Caucasus, and in Turkestan, 1918–20), in *Kto dolzhnik? (Who Is the Debtor?)*, ed. A. G. Shliapnikov, R. A. Muklevich, and B. I. Dolivo-Dobrovolskii (Moscow, 1926), 377. Hereafter cited as *Kto dolzhnik?*

[9] House Papers, Diary, September 24, 1918. House claimed that he had engineered this revival of Wilson's interest in help for Russia, as well as the transfer of the aid program to Vance McCormick of the War Trade Board.

[10] For a review of United States economic aid to anti-Bolshevik Russia during 1918, and of the difficulties of securing Allied and Japanese cooperation in this

This flirtation with a policy of economic assistance failed to set Wilson's mind at rest in regard to Russia. As the war drew to a close, he continued to puzzle over the Russian problem, but began increasingly to relegate it to the category of problems which he hoped the peace conference would resolve. On October 16 Sir William Wiseman, the British confidential representative in the United States, reported an interview with the president:

> The question of Russia, he [Wilson] thought, should also be left to the peace conference. I protested that that would be too late; that the stage was even now being set by the Germans, and we should find forces and conditions had been created in Russia which it would be difficult, if not impossible, to alter at a peace conference. The President said there was a great deal in that view and the whole question was causing him great anxiety.[11]

Such was the state of Allied and American policy toward Russia in November 1918. The Allies were continuing to press vigorously for expansion of the limited intervention of the previous summer and favored a full-scale military effort against the Bolsheviks. The Americans refused to sanction the extension of the current intervention or to commit themselves to new interventionist plans, but they had no alternative to propose, other than a half-hearted attempt to organize relief and economic assistance for Russia.

In the two months between the Armistice and the opening of the peace conference in January 1919, the questions of how best to deal with the Russian situation and of how to meet the Bolshevik challenge pressed in upon Western leaders with increasing urgency. Large segments of public opinion opposed any further Allied military effort in Russia. Yet near chaos ruled in Central Europe, and there seemed a real danger that Bolshevism would burst out of Russia and flood westward. Of its own momentum, Western intervention in Russia continued, but the moral position of the Allies was weak, and their purpose uncertain. As Winston Churchill vividly described the situation: "Were they at war with Soviet Russia? Certainly not; but they shot Soviet Russians at sight. They stood as invaders on Russian soil. They armed the enemies of the Soviet government. . . . They earnestly desired and schemed its downfall. But war—shocking! Interference—shame! It was, they repeated, a

venture, see a memorandum of December 10, 1918, by A. A. Berle, Jr., "American Economic Intervention in Russia," *Peace Conference,* II, 471–75.

[11] Notes of an Interview with the President by Sir William Wiseman, October 16, 1918, House Papers, Drawer 35.

matter of indifference to them how Russians settled their own internal affairs. They were impartial—Bang!" [12]

Many Allied leaders believed that settlement of the Russian question was essential to the success of the peacemaking. If Europe were to enjoy a secure and lasting peace, the fighting in Russia had to be stopped and the challenge of Bolshevism had to be countered. Ideally, the Western statesmen would have preferred the formation of a representative government in Russia which could restore order, ensure stability, and speak for Russia at the peace talks. In fact, there was little immediate prospect of this, and everyone knew it. Thus it was up to the peace conference, many felt, to attempt the almost impossible task of putting an end to civil war and intervention in Russia.

As Western leaders faced the Russian problem in November and December 1918, they had open to them—in theory, at least—a wide range of policies. At one extreme, the Allies, predicating their action on the threat posed by Bolshevism to Europe and to the world, could intervene in Russia with their own troops, overwhelm the Soviet regime, and forcibly establish some type of "representative" government. At the other, they could withdraw their forces already in Russia, cut off aid to the anti-Bolsheviks, and let the Russians fight it out among themselves; if, as seemed likely, Bolshevism should triumph, the Allies could attempt to blunt its expansionist drive and to win Soviet acquiescence in their plans for the postwar world by offering the Bolsheviks relief, economic aid, and trade. Between these extremes were a number of variants of the two positions: indirect intervention through moral and material aid to the anit-Bolshevik forces in and around Russia; the isolation of Russia and the erection of a surrounding ring of buffer states to contain Bolshevism—a *cordon sanitaire;* mediation in an attempt to bring about a negotiated settlement of Russia's internal strife, which, in turn, might lead to her political self-determination under fair and peaceful conditions.

As we shall see, a number of factors prevented the unhampered selection and execution of any one of these policies. Instead, the Western statesmen moved suddenly and illogically from one position to another, sometimes attempting to combine several of these approaches and even on occasion pursuing two disparate courses of action simultaneously. Plans for further military intervention in Russia provided an insistent counterpoint to conciliatory gestures toward the Bolsheviks. It is no wonder that contemporary observers were bewildered and dismayed by the peacemakers' efforts to settle the Russian problem.

Conference policy toward Russia could not, of course, be written on a clean slate. Possible courses of action were circumscribed by previous

[12] Churchill, *Aftermath,* 243–44.

Allied commitments in Russia, as well as by the onrush of events, the resources available to the Western powers, and the restraints of public opinion. Moreover, there were sharp disagreements over Russian policy among, and even within, the Allied governments. Although all were alarmed at the menace of Bolshevism, the Western governments held varying views as to how best to deal with this danger, and each of them was pursuing different strategic, political, and economic objectives in Russia. To add to the confusion, the actions of individual governments were often inconsistent, reflecting, as they did, policy and personality conflicts among the leaders in each Allied country. Foch and Clemenceau differed on Russia, while Pichon and the French Foreign Office held still a third view. The Russian question placed Lloyd George and Churchill at odds, and found Lansing sometimes opposed to the views of Wilson and House.[13]

Views of the American Leaders

In attempting to ascertain Western policies and plans regarding Russia on the eve of the peace conference, the view of Russia and of Bolshevism held by Woodrow Wilson is of paramount importance. Wilson largely determined United States policy, and the position of the United States decisively influenced peace conference actions toward Russia. If Bolshevism were to be stamped out by force, the American army would have to supply most of the troops, and the American treasury would have to foot the bills. If democratic opinion were to support either a war against the Bolsheviks or a settlement with them, Wilson would have to lead it in the desired direction. His action (or inaction) proved to be a key factor in all major decisions of the conference respecting Russia. If Wilson had been able in his own mind to settle on a clear-cut policy to be pursued in Russia, and if he had had the time and inclination to press for the adoption of such a policy and to follow up its execution, it is possible, even granting the magnitude of the Russian problem and the relative inability of the Allies to control many of the factors involved in it, that the conference might have been able to develop a more effec-

---

[13] These inter-Allied and intragovernmental divisions on Russian policy pose a difficult dilemma for Soviet historiography when it is taking an anti-American and anti-Western line. In order to "prove" the existence of an American-inspired master plan of intervention against Soviet Russia in 1918–1919, Soviet historians have to gloss over these contradictions in Western policy, thus violating a basic Leninist tenet concerning this period—that the imperialist world was rent by rivalries and conflicts, which weakened its efforts to destroy Soviet Russia. See, for example, B. E. Shtein, *"Russkii vopros" na parizhskoi mirnoi konferentsii, 1919–20 ("The Russian Problem" at the Paris Peace Conference, 1919–20)* (Moscow, 1949), 23–25.

tive course of action than that of half-hearted intervention and support to the anti-Bolsheviks, the approach on which the peacemakers finally placed their hopes for a settlement in Russia.

To understand why Wilson acted as he did in regard to Russia and Bolshevism, it is necessary to know something of his basic philosophy and outlook. Wilson was a moralist; the Bolsheviks openly repudiated and scoffed at his moral standards. Wilson was a liberal; the Bolsheviks were radicals. Wilson believed in evolution; the Bolsheviks in revolution. Wilson supported nationalism under proper restraints; the Bolsheviks were avowed internationalists. Wilson was politically-minded; the Bolsheviks professed a program emphasizing economic and social principles. Yet with his intuitive grasp of political realities, Wilson, almost alone among the leaders at Paris, sensed the intensity and seriousness of the challenge Bolshevism presented to the West. At the same time he failed to understand fully the scope of that challenge, and his program of political reform did not take sufficient account of the economic and social grievances on which Bolshevism was attempting to prey.

William Allen White's disillusioned characterization of Wilson as "a canting Presbyterian moralist" [14] is certainly too harsh, but there is no doubt that Wilson possessed a fundamentally moral outlook upon life and society, based upon his Christian tenets and liberal philosophy.[15] As a result, Bolshevik philosophy, and particularly the elements of materialism in it, were repugnant to him. Wilson believed in a higher moral authority, of which nations as well as men were the agents. Thus, for Wilson, the principles derived from that authority—justice, equality, the rule of law—were immutable ones which individuals and countries were committed to uphold and which should guide conduct both among and within societies.[16] On this he based his dream of an ordered and peaceful world.

[14] William Allen White, *Autobiography* (New York, 1946), 557.

[15] The following summary of Wilson's basic philosophy is drawn in large measure from the following works: Richard Hofstadter, *The American Political Tradition and the Men Who Made It* (New York, 1948); Arthur S. Link, *Wilson: The Road to the White House* (Princeton, 1947), *Wilson: The New Freedom* (Princeton, 1956), and *Wilson the Diplomatist* (Baltimore, 1957); William Diamond, *The Economic Thought of Woodrow Wilson* (Baltimore, 1943); Harley Notter, *The Origins of the Foreign Policy of Woodrow Wilson* (Baltimore, 1937); H. C. F. Bell, *Woodrow Wilson and the People* (Garden City, 1945); Arthur Walworth, *Woodrow Wilson* (2 vols.; New York, 1958); Earl Latham, ed., *The Philosophy and Politics of Woodrow Wilson* (Chicago, 1958); and Edward H. Buehrig, ed., *Wilson's Foreign Policy in Perspective* (Bloomington, 1957). In addition, his public papers dealing with Russia and Bolshevism, and his private papers from November 1918 to June 1919 were consulted.

[16] Certain individual actions of the Bolsheviks particularly offended Wilson's sense of proper conduct. In the fall of 1918, Sir William Wiseman reported the president's view of the Bolsheviks as follows: "The Bolsheviki he agreed were im-

Wilson's intense conviction that the principles he believed in were right and universal and that their application to international and domestic problems was the world's only hope of salvation added a messianic overtone to much of his activity, particularly at the peace talks in Paris. His was a crusading spirit, which sometimes made him appear self-righteous and sanctimonious, prompting Clemenceau to remark that Wilson thought himself "another Jesus Christ come upon the earth to reform men." [17] In Wilson's view the system of democracy and free enterprise developed in America best embodied the principles to which he was dedicated; America, therefore, had a mission to convey its experience to the rest of the world, Russia included.

In accord with his belief in the moral agency of man, Wilson thought that not institutions or economic forces, but individuals, were the directing power within each society. Thus change and progress were generated through the actions of men upon institutions, taken in the light of experience and events, not through the eradication and replacement of basic institutions in accord with abstract theoretical principles. Only when revolution was necessary to establish self-government and liberty was it justified. Otherwise, Wilson believed, revolution led only to reaction and resulted in a setback to progress; consequently, he abhorred it. The Bolshevik revolution—directed against a democratic and duly constituted government—was particularly distasteful to him.

Wilson's "good society" was that of the nineteenth century liberal—a self-disciplined, ordered society adhering to moral principles and based on the consent of the governed. As a corollary to this view, he firmly believed that peoples everywhere possessed the inalienable right to determine their own fate and that, with sufficient training and experience, all could do so. Wilson felt strongly that this principle applied equally to the Russian people, and as early as the 1880's he reported optimistically that he saw the first signs of developing self-government among them.[18] He greeted the March Revolution of 1917 with elation and high hopes. The revolution seemed vindication of his belief in the capacity of the Russian people for self-determination, and he viewed the overthrow of the Tsar as another milestone in the orderly advance of humanity to-

possible. He had watched with disgust their treatment of Lockhart [his detention and expulsion], who had tried to help them." Notes of an Interview with the President by Sir William Wiseman, October 16, 1918, House Papers, Drawer 35.

[17] Cited by House as a comment made to the English journalist Wickham Steed, House Papers, Diary, April 2, 1919.

[18] Baker and Dodd, *Wilson Public Papers,* I, 76–77, 143; Woodrow Wilson, *The State: Elements of Historical and Practical Politics* (Boston, 1889), 601. For an interpretation of the importance of the Russian question to Wilson, see Kennan, *Russia and the West,* 121–23.

ward its democratic destiny. In his war address to Congress on April 2, 1917, the president commented:

> Russia was known by those who knew it best to have been always in fact democratic at heart, in all the vital habits of her thought, in all the intimate relationships of her people that spoke their natural instinct, their habitual attitude toward life. The autocracy . . . was not in fact Russian in origin, character, or purpose; and now it has been shaken off and the great, generous Russian people have been added in all their native majesty and might to the forces that are fighting for freedom in the world, for justice, and for peace.

Wilson, however, knew little about the history of Russia or about the real state of affairs there; as a result he was unprepared for the fall of the Provisional Government seven months later. Nevertheless, his dedication to the principle of self-determination of peoples was so great that, despite his detestation of the economic and political philosophy of Bolshevism and his dismay at Bolshevik actions in upsetting the democratic government of Russia, Wilson was most reluctant to intervene against the Bolsheviks, or even to sanction such intervention on the part of others. Even after intervention, in October, 1918, he remarked: "My policy regarding Russia is very similar to my Mexican policy. I believe in letting them work out their own salvation even though they wallow in anarchy for a while." [19] Reflecting the same point of view, as well as his continuing faith in self-determination by the Russian people, are Wilson's comments concerning Russia in an address to Congress on November 4:

> In the meantime, if it be possible, we must establish a peace that will justly define their [the Russians'] place among the nations, remove all fear of their neighbors and of their former masters, and enable them to live in security and contentment when they have set their own affairs in order. I, for one, do not doubt their purpose or their capacity. There are some happy signs that they know and will choose the way of self-control and peaceful accommodation. If they do, we shall put our aid at their disposal in every way that we can. If they do not, we must await with patience and sympathy the awakening and recovery that will assuredly come at last. [20]

At the same time there is no question that the Bolshevik seizure of power in Russia was a great shock to Wilson. Drawing his inspiration

[19] Notes of an Interview with the President by Sir William Wiseman, October 16, 1918, House Papers, Drawer 35.
[20] Cited in Herbert Hoover, *The Ordeal of Woodrow Wilson* (New York, 1959), 63.

from Spencer and Bagehot, Wilson believed in an organic society evolving inexorably toward the fulfillment of its ideals. For him, social change was a gradual and continual process, which could not be forced. Wilson viewed the progress of world society in a similar light, as the following excerpt from his address before the International Law Society on May 9, 1918, illustrates:

> One of the things that have disturbed me in recent months is the unqualified hope that men have entertained everywhere of immediate emancipation from the things that have hampered and oppressed them . . . we must see to it that those who hope are not disappointed by showing them the process by which hope must be realized, processes of slow disentanglement from the many things that have bound us in the past. You cannot throw off the habits of society immediately any more than you can throw off the habits of the individual immediately. . . . We must weave out of the old material the new garments which it is necessary that men should wear.[21]

Nothing could have been further from the Bolshevik view of how the world was to be transformed.

In proposing a solution for the ills of international society in 1919, Wilson did not envisage a really new order; rather he planned to patch up the old order, righting its wrongs by the application, through the treaty and the League of Nations, of his basic principles. He believed that Western institutions were basically sound, needing only a few repairs and adjustments to set them running smoothly again. Although many misconceived his purpose, fundamentally Wilson was a conservative, hoping to preserve the *status quo* by improving it.

Part of Wilson's difficulty, both in attempting to reform the world and in dealing with Bolshevism, was the predominantly political orientation of his thought. For him, "the economic man" did not exist. He saw man as a political creature above all else, and the solution to his difficulties as essentially political in nature. From an economically and socially secure background, Wilson had little conception of the complex social and economic problems emerging from the industrial revolution. Without any doubt, he rejected economic determinism and minimized the influence of economic forces in society. Thus his program for reordering the world was virtually devoid of economic concepts. Those it did contain—"the open door," freedom of the seas—were directed primarily toward ensuring the free play of competitive forces in the world economy, in accord with the precepts of his classical economic training and with his belief in

[21] Baker, *Settlement,* II, 108.

the efficacy of the free enterprise system when secured from abuse by governmental vigilance.

As we noted in the first chapter, Wilson was convinced that the peace must be a just one if it were to satisfy the longings of the people. But by this he meant only politically just. He sensed, but was uncertain how best to meet, the striving for status and security, the demand for economic betterment, and the yearning for social justice which agitated so many in the world, and on which fascism and communism were so brutally to capitalize in the subsequent decades. Revealing in this connection is the story related in the diary of William C. Bullitt, then a young and ardent liberal attached to the American Commission to Negotiate Peace, and later ambassador to Russia and France. En route to board the *George Washington,* the ship that carried the president and the American peace delegation to France in December 1918, Raymond Fosdick, a member of the delegation, met a crowd of "sweatshop" workers on their way to their usual fourteen-hour day. In the midst of complaining about their conditions, one of them pointed to the *George Washington* and said: "But do you see that boat? There's a man aboard her that is going to Europe to change all this." At Bullitt's urging, Fosdick told Wilson the story, using it to argue strongly for the inclusion of a bill of industrial human rights in the peace treaty. The president replied that it frightened him to think how much the common people of the world expected of him, but he did not consider it possible to take up such matters at the peace conference; rather he hoped that the international labor conference which he favored would press for such a bill.[22]

In short, as he sailed for Europe to make peace in the world, Woodrow Wilson perceived more clearly than most of his contemporaries the long-term appeal and challenge of Bolshevism, but he had little conception—other than a "just peace"—of how best to deal with this problem. Respecting Russia, one can summarize Wilson's views by saying that the president opposed further intervention and fervently hoped that the Russian people could work out their own salvation. The seeds of Russia's redemption, he was convinced, lay in a system of free enterprise and democracy like that the United States had developed. Consequently, in his view, America had a special responsibility to extend all possible sympathy to Russia, and to proffer economic assistance to her. Moreover, since the Bolsheviks had arbitrarily and violently cut short the promising beginnings in 1917 of a representative system of government,

[22] William C. Bullitt Papers, Yale University Library; Diary, December 10, 1918. Bullitt noted that the president was apparently opposed to international commissions in economic fields and had no inclination to fight for tariff reforms. *Ibid.,* December 12, 1918.

Wilson was anxious to do what he could to reestablish the conditions of peace and free choice necessary for self-determination; in fact, the need to assist in the restoration of such conditions was one of the arguments he had used to justify the Siberian intervention. Thus the president wanted to end the fighting in Russia, hoped the opposing factions might get together, and continuously sought a nucleus of self-government to which the Russians (and he) could rally.

The views on Russia of the other American delegates to the peace conference need detain us only briefly, since Wilson was seldom disposed to seek or accept their advice. House, who was probably more influential with the president on the Russian question than anyone else, was of the same liberal stamp as Wilson. The doctrines of Bolshevism repelled him, and he too believed that the ills of the world could best be resolved by moderate reform and a reaffirmation of moral principles in the ordering of society. Like Wilson, he was dedicated to the principle of self-determination. During 1918 he opposed intervention as a violation of that principle, as well as for the practical reason that it would only alienate the Russians. House felt strongly that the best course for the United States to pursue in Russia was relief and economic aid, and he so advised the president. This would assist the Russians to work out their own problems, and it would at the same time be an effective check to Bolshevism. In his diary on September 19, 1918, House noted: "I disagree almost entirely with the manner in which the President has handled the Russian situation [intervention], although I agree heartily with the objects he has in view. If he . . . had made the relief and economic end dominant, leaving the military merely to protect our civilians, I believe that everything could have been done that was possible in the circumstances." [23] House also firmly believed that the advance of Bolshevism into Europe could best be halted by giving food and economic aid to Germany and to Austria-Hungary, not by further intervention in Russia's affairs.[26]

Robert Lansing, Wilson's secretary of state, had little influence with the president on Russia, as on most matters. Lansing had an almost pathological fear and detestation of Bolshevism. While originally opposed to intervention on practical grounds, he was glad when it could be justified as aid to the Czechs, and he was, on the whole, more sympathetic to intervention as a method of dealing with the Russian situation than either Wilson or House. In addition, Lansing was closer than anyone else in the American government to the anti-Bolshevik Russians in

[23] House Papers, Diary, September 19, 1918.
[24] *Ibid.*, letter from House to Norman Hapgood, January 6, 1919.

Washington and in Paris, and he tended to be swayed by their appeals for assistance.

General Tasker H. Bliss, a fourth American peace commissioner, was not only a soldier and statesman, but a scholar and humanitarian as well. He was strongly antimilitarist in outlook and was opposed to intervention on both moral and practical grounds. Although Bliss had little positive impact on the deliberations of the conference respecting Russia, he did exert a strong restraining influence on his American colleagues and on the other delegates, constantly reminding them of the cost and difficulties of intervention, and working, quietly but with considerable success, to block the interventionist plans of Foch and Churchill.[25]

United States Policy

On the eve of the peace conference the United States government was committed to three basic positions respecting Russia: nonrecognition of the Soviet government, nonintervention in Russia's internal affairs, and preservation of the territorial integrity of Russia. These points had been formulated in late 1917 and early 1918, and they were to endure as cardinal tenets of American policy toward Russia into the 1920's and 1930's. As in Mexico, nonrecognition of the Soviet regime was based on the argument that no government should be recognized unless it represented the will of the people. Nonintervention and the commitment to Russia's territorial integrity stemmed from Wilson's conviction that the Russian people should be permitted to settle their own affairs and to determine their own future. In late 1918 the American government still stood technically on the principle of nonintervention, despite the presence of American troops in Siberia and North Russia. When these forces were landed, the United States had specifically disclaimed any intention of interfering in Russia's internal affairs, although it had offered "to steady any efforts at self-government or self-defense in which the Russians themselves may be willing to accept assistance."[26] It was stressed, however, that such assistance would be solely for the purpose of helping "the Russian people themselves in their endeavors to regain control of their own affairs, their own territory, and their own destiny."

The idea that the territorial integrity of Russia should be safeguarded had developed in American policy during 1918, but this position was not endorsed at all governmental levels. Point Six of Wilson's Fourteen

[25] Henry White, the other American delegate to the peace conference, played almost no role in conference consideration of the Russian question.

[26] Official statement of August 3, 1918, Cumming and Pettit, *Russian-American Relations*, 238.

Points, which dealt with Russia, referred to "the independent determination of her own political development and national policy." [27] This was interpreted by some as supporting Russia's territorial integrity.[28] In announcing the expedition to Siberia, the United States declared that it contemplated "no interference with the political sovereignty of Russia . . . and no impairment of her territorial integrity, either now or hereafter. . . ." [29] This was simply a reflection of Wilson's conviction, expressed to General Bliss on May 28, 1918, that in Russia's hour of travail the United States was obligated to maintain "unswerving fidelity to the principle of Russian territorial integrity and political independence." [30]

Colonel House, however, was inclined to favor the break-up of Russia. After discussing the Russian question with Wilson on September 19, 1918, House commented: "I am not in agreement with the President as to leaving Russia intact." [31] House went on to explain that Russia "is too big and homogeneous for the safety of the world. I would like to see Siberia a separate republic, and European Russia divided into three parts." A month later House noted that "if a great military figure should arise in Russia, she might become a menace to the world," little realizing that Bolshevik, not military, leadership would serve to make his prediction come true.[32]

There is some evidence that Lansing also looked to the division of the former Russian Empire into several states. On September 21, 1918, he expressed fears that the Germans were planning to penetrate and dominate prostrate Russia after the war, and he urged the erection of territorial barriers to prevent this. He suggested that the Baltic provinces and the Ukraine become autonomous states within a Russian confederation, with Poland and possibly Finland becoming independent.[33]

There was undoubtedly some public support for the position of Lansing and House within the United States, particularly from areas with large concentrations of Eastern European immigrants. Senator Lodge of Massachusetts, claiming to represent "the real feeling of the people of the United States and certainly the Senate of the United States," suggested that the peace conference consider the formation of an independ-

[27] *Ibid.*, 71.
[28] See, for example, Lansing's telegram to Ambassador Francis on January 15, 1918, *1918, Russia*, II, 743. The British interpretation of Point Six in this regard is discussed below on pp. 55–56.
[29] Cumming and Pettit, *Russian-American Relations*, 238.
[30] Baker, *Wilson: Life and Letters*, VIII, 175.
[31] House Papers, Diary, September 19, 1918.
[32] *Ibid.*, October 28, 1918.
[33] In a memorandum to be used as a guide in drafting instructions for the American peace delegation. Lansing, 192–93.

ent Ukraine and of separate Baltic states under American and Allied protection.[34]

The separation of the Baltic area, Poland, Finland, and perhaps the Ukraine from Russia, with the possibility of their later confederation with a Great Russian-Siberian state, was also envisaged by the American journalists Frank Cobb and Walter Lippmann, who undertook, in October 1918, to prepare a "commentary" on the Fourteen Points for Colonel House.[35] Wilson, however, responded in a rather lukewarm fashion to the work of Cobb and Lippmann as a whole, noting that their analysis was a satisfactory interpretation of the principles involved but that the detailed application of these principles should be reserved for the peace conference.[36] Wilson also commented that "the admission of inchoate nationalities to the peace conference" would be most undesirable, and there is no indication that the arguments of Cobb and Lippmann weakened his conviction that the territorial integrity of Russia should be preserved.

The right of self-determination, upon which Wilson based his support of Russia's territorial integrity, was, however, a two-edged sword when applied to the Russian question. On the one hand, it could be maintained that no Russian territory should be assigned without the consent of the Russian people as a whole. On the other, the right of the minority

[34] In a memorandum presented to Henry White, the lone Republican among the American delegates. Allan Nevins, *Henry White: Thirty Years of American Diplomacy* (New York, 1930), 354.

[35] Seymour, *House Papers,* IV, 195–96. The technical experts attached to the American delegation expressed similar views in a tentative report of January 21, 1919. Their recommendations, based on the work of the "Inquiry," a group of scholars assembled by House in 1918 to work out details of a peace settlement, provided for the separation of Georgia, Armenia, and Azerbaidjan as well, but with the proviso that this should be encouraged only if the Bolsheviks were still in power; otherwise, all of the border states except Finland, Poland, Armenia, and perhaps Lithuania should reunite with "a federalized or genuinely democratic Russia." Miller, *Diary,* IV, 219 and map on 221. For an evaluation of Soviet treatment of these recommendations in anti-American works, see George Kennan, "Soviet Historiography and America's Role in Intervention," *American Historical Review,* Vol. 65, No. 2 (January 1960), 302–22.

A minor but fascinating sidelight of American policy toward Russia is reflected in a memorandum of Admirals Evans, Hart, and Yarnell forwarded to Wilson on December 3, 1918. This proposed that Japan be compensated with eastern Siberia for the internationalization of the Caroline and Marshall islands on the ground that it would be better to provide an outlet for Japanese expansion than to thwart this strong pressure and sow the seeds of a future war between Japan and the United States. The admirals concluded that it was "of vital interest to the United States to turn Japan toward the continent of Asia." Wilson Papers, Series VIIIA, Box 1. There is no evidence that Wilson paid any attention to the suggestions of either his experts or his admirals.

[36] United States Department of State, *Papers Relating to the Foreign Relations of the United States; 1918 Supplement I* (Washington, 1933), I, 421.

peoples of Russia to determine their own fate could be argued. Nevertheless, Wilson's position, and therefore the American position, was that the territorial integrity of Russia should be safeguarded.

After the Armistice Wilson became increasingly skeptical of the value of having American troops in Russia and began to consider their withdrawal. Apparently he was considerably influenced in this regard by a long confidential letter to him from Secretary of War Baker, dated November 27, 1918. In this letter Baker aired his doubts concerning both the morality and the usefulness of the American position in Russia, and asked the president's guidance. The secretary of war pointed out that the original justifications for American intervention—to prevent supplies in North Russia from falling into German hands, and to assist the Czechs in Siberia—had lapsed with the end of the war, and that American forces "are now, I am afraid, being used for purposes for which we would not have sent them in the first instance." Baker then discussed the way in which Japan was making intervention serve her own designs. He suggested that the Russians ought to be left to work out their own problems; the United States might not like the result, but perhaps the Russians could resolve their affairs better and more speedily without "their primitive deliberations [being] confused by the imposition of ideas from the outside." He concluded that since the difficulty of securing a concurrent Japanese withdrawal from Siberia was growing hourly, the United States "ought simply to order its forces home by the first boat and notify the Japanese that in our judgment our mission is fully accomplished. . . ." Later, America could provide economic assistance to Russia. To support his letter, Baker the next day transmitted to the president a telegram from Siberia outlining Japanese intrigues there, as well as a report from North Russia on the low morale of United States forces in that area, which referred to the possibility that American troops might refuse to move up to the front when ordered to do so.[37]

Wilson was sufficiently concerned by Baker's letter to discuss the matter fully with him on November 29, 1918. Unfortunately, there is no record of the decision they reached—only a tantalizing letter from Baker to Wilson of November 30, referring briefly to the Russian question and stating that "the solution of this problem really lies in the direction which you pointed out to me verbally yesterday." Baker added: "I think I know your views and wishes and will be able to act understandingly upon any cabled instruction . . . from abroad."[38] The most likely supposition is that Wilson reminded Baker of the necessity of consulting the Allies before withdrawing American troops, but promised

[37] Letter and telegram in Wilson Papers, Series II, Box 157.
[38] *Ibid.*

that he would attempt to secure approval of American evacuation, at least from North Russia. Apparently Wilson was less anxious to withdraw from Siberia, fearing that this would give the Japanese a free hand there.[39] In a résumé to the British Cabinet of his meeting with Wilson on December 26, Lloyd George reported that Wilson was not in favor of the Bolsheviks, but was much opposed to armed intervention and would probably withdraw American forces from North Russia. According to Lloyd George, Wilson was far from enthusiastic about the Siberian expedition as well, but there "his principal anxiety was as to the conduct of the Japanese, who were apparently taking the whole of Eastern Siberia into their own hands. . . ."[40]

At the same time Wilson was already beginning to consider Russia in the category of questions that the League of Nations might resolve. In mid-December 1918 Sir William Wiseman noted prophetically that Wilson was increasingly envisaging the League as the key to the work of the peace conference, believing that the really great problems, such as colonies, freedom of the seas, the Balkans, Russia, and disarmament, could satisfactorily be settled only through the League.[41] Thus the end of 1918 found Wilson disposed to end intervention and to seek a peaceful settlement of Russia's difficulties through the mechanism of the peace conference or the League. His opportunity was not long in coming.

Policies and Plans of the European Allies

Most of the British leaders, and those in France and Italy as well, took a pragmatic and short-range view of Bolshevism. They saw its Russian expression as primarily a political force and a nucleus of sovereign power to be dealt with by means of traditional techniques of diplomacy and power politics. In weighing the merits of intervention, for example, they seldom considered whether troops could, in fact, suppress the revolutionary ideas Bolshevism espoused. None of the Allied leaders sensed, as Wilson did, the powerful ideological and emotional challenge Bolshe-

[39] At this time American–Japanese relations in Siberia were at a low ebb, as the Japanese were resisting an American plan for joint operation and control of the Chinese Eastern and Siberian railways. Wilson's reluctance to leave the Japanese in Siberia is suggested in a letter he wrote on November 27 to Grenville MacFarland, who had protested to the president against the continued presence of American soldiers in Russia. Wilson said: "My mind is not clear as to what is the immediate proper course in Russia. There are many more elements at work there than I conjecture you are aware of, and it is harder to get out than it was to go in." *Ibid.*

[40] David Lloyd George, *The Truth About the Peace Treaties* (2 vols.; London, 1938), I, 188–89. For a full discussion of the decision to withdraw from North Russia see ch. six, pp. 212–20.

[41] Sir Arthur Willert, *The Road to Safety: A Study in Anglo-American Relations* (London, 1952), 177. This book is basically a biography of Wiseman.

vism presented to the West, nor did any of them take seriously the Bolsheviks' claim to be the vanguard of a supranational class movement.[42] They were little concerned with the essentials of Bolshevism—its origins, its theories, its psychological appeal, its demands for new relationships among peoples and states. Rather they remembered what Bolshevism had meant for them. The Soviet rulers, in defiance of the Allies, had made a separate peace with Germany, thereby disrupting the wartime coalition and the European balance of power and bringing the Allies to the brink of defeat. Moreover, by publishing the wartime secret treaties, the Soviet government had embarrassed the Allies and created skepticism concerning the latter's professed war aims. At the same time Bolshevik propaganda incessantly attacked the very institutions on which Western society—and the position of its leaders—were based.

By the fall of 1918, however, the Allied statesmen were chiefly interested in the direct and immediate effect Bolshevism might have on their plans for the political and territorial reordering of Europe. To the extent that it impinged on or interfered with these plans, they took cognizance of it and attempted to deal with it. While recognizing, as we saw in the first chapter, that Bolshevism posed a threat to Central Europe, and even to their own countries, many Allied statesmen believed that this danger sprang largely from the immediate postwar dislocation, with its accompanying hunger and unrest. Some, like Balfour, felt that food relief and the settlement of political and territorial questions which were exciting popular passions would suffice to eliminate the danger of Bolshevism in Russia by building up a cordon of new states in Central and Eastern Europe. Others, such as Foch and Churchill, believed that Bolshevism should be forcibly suppressed.

In some respects Lloyd George's attitude differed from that of the other European leaders. As a liberal, he believed that the aspirations of the Bolsheviks were not entirely unworthy, whatever their practices. The revolutionary spirit abroad in Europe could not be met by force, he felt; instead, it should be dealt with by improving conditions and satisfying the just demands of the people.[43] He did not fear Bolshevism, as his

[42] In a meeting of the Imperial War Cabinet on December 24, Lloyd George scoffed at the suggestion of Prime Minister Hughes of Australia that Bolshevik "internationalism" was viewed in many quarters as an attempt to eliminate one of the causes of war—"racial feeling" (i.e., nationalism). Lloyd George noted, perhaps prophetically, that the Bolsheviks would be beaten if they tried to suppress "racial feeling" either in their own country or outside. Lloyd George, I, 631–34.

[43] In a campaign speech reported in the London *Times* on November 15, 1918, Lloyd George declared that the revolutionary spirit in the air needed wise direction, and concluded: "Revolution I am not afraid of. Bolshevism I am not afraid of. It is reaction that I am afraid of. Yes, reaction and disunion."

European colleagues did. Nor, unlike Wilson, did he morally detest it.

Lloyd George was convinced, furthermore, that the Russian people should be allowed to settle their own affairs. If they preferred the Soviet regime, it would be wrong to force a different government on them. At the same time, also with the principle of self-determination, he justified British aid to the anti-Bolsheviks, maintaining that these groups should be given enough arms and supplies to permit them to engage in an equal test of strength with the Soviet forces; then whichever side had the most popular support would win, and the will of the people would be clearly affirmed.[44] But Lloyd George also distrusted the White Russian leaders, fearing that they represented reactionary forces and trends in Russia.

As a humanitarian, the British leader was genuinely anxious to bring peace to Russia. He wanted to help the Russian people and to extend a hand of friendship to them in their difficulties. Moreover, as a practical man, Lloyd George believed that intervention was fruitless. It only antagonized patriotic Russians, thereby strengthening the Bolsheviks. In addition, he doubted that foreign troops could quench the revolutionary fire. Drawing on the lesson of the French Revolution, Lloyd George argued that the best course would be to accept the revolution in Russia, either attempting to temper its crusading spirit or letting that spirit burn itself out within Russia. Furthermore, intervention was very costly. The Allies had neither the men nor the money to undertake a full-scale attack on Soviet Russia. On the other hand, Lloyd George believed, under conditions of peace lucrative Western trade and economic concessions in Russia, Red or White, could easily be developed.

Finally, as a politician, the British prime minister was quick to adapt his Russian policy to the prevailing political winds. In the fall of 1918, when liberal and labor opposition to intervention was at a height, and when the voters were demanding rapid demobilization and the return home of the conscript armies, Lloyd George could give rein to his personal view that intervention was wrong, urging upon his government a conciliatory policy in Russia. In the spring of 1919, when Tory members of his own coalition, representing conservative opinion in England, strongly protested his "soft" policy on Bolshevism, Lloyd George came out in favor of continued intervention and further aid to the anti-Bolsheviks.

In sum, Lloyd George's Russian policy was capricious and inconsistent, reflecting the conflict between his personal preferences and his political calculations. He sincerely believed in helping the Russians, ending intervention, and working out an accommodation with the Bolsheviks —peace and trade in Russia were his objectives—but he was always

[44] Lloyd George, I, 315–19.

quick to temper his beliefs in the face of political attack. As a result, on this as on other issues, neither his colleagues nor the public were quite sure at a given moment just where Lloyd George stood, or that the next moment he might not be on the other side of the question.

It was some time before Lloyd George's opposition to intervention after the Armistice began to take effect within the British government. Consequently, in November and December 1918 official British policy toward Russia still favored the continuation of intervention and of substantial aid to the anti-Bolsheviks; at the same time, it endeavored to advance British strategic and economic objectives in Russia. The proponents of intervention, led by Lord Curzon, Lord Milner, and Winston Churchill, maintained that Britain was morally obligated to help those forces in Russia which had originally been organized, with British encouragement and assistance, as instruments against the Germans (and also against the Bolsheviks, who had helped the Germans by making peace with them). It was now impossible, they argued, to abandon these people to the Bolsheviks. Lord Milner publicly defended this position in a letter published in the London *Times* on December 19, 1918:

> . . . in the course of this Allied intervention [against the Germans] thousands of Russians have taken up arms and fought on the side of the Allies. How can we, simply because our own immediate purposes have been served, come away and leave them to the tender mercies of their and our enemies. . . . It would be an abominable betrayal, contrary to every British instinct of honour and humanity. . . . If the Allies were all to scramble out of Russia at once, the result would almost certainly be that the barbarism, which at present reigns in a part only of that country, would spread over the whole of it. . . . The ultimate consequences of such a disaster cannot be forseen. But they would assuredly involve a far greater strain on the resources of the British Empire than our present commitments.[45]

Lloyd George and Balfour were critical of intervention in Russia, either direct or through the anti-Bolsheviks. General Wilson noted caustically that in a Cabinet meeting on November 10 Lloyd George the politician spoke: "Then we discussed Russia, and Lloyd George wanted to come away from Murmansk because he thought our occupation there

---

[45] Cited in W. P. and Zelda K. Coates, *Armed Intervention in Russia, 1918–1922* (London, 1935), 135–37. In reply to a note from Constantine Nabokov, the Provisional Government chargé d'affaires in London, congratulating him on the above letter, Milner wrote that he personally favored much stronger Allied intervention against the Bolsheviks, but he feared that this might rally patriotic elements in Russia to the side of the Bolsheviks. Maklakov Papers, Part II, Packet I, File 2.

was unpopular. Again, all votes." [46] Several weeks later Balfour expressed doubts as to how practical the policy of intervention was. In a memorandum of November 29 he noted that British public opinion would oppose any attempt to dispatch large British forces to Russia; in any case, the extent of Western support to the anti-Bolsheviks "must largely depend upon the course taken by the associated Powers [principally the United States], who have far larger resources at their disposal than ourselves." Another factor militating against intervention, Balfour felt, was that the Russian people should have the right to choose their own government without outside interference. Balfour concluded, however, that despite these considerations the British should fulfill their obligation to those groups they had helped call into being; they should use what troops were available to this end, also sending arms and money into Russia, and protecting the nascent nationalities in the Baltic with the British fleet. [47]

Steps of this kind had actually been initiated earlier, when, immediately after the Armistice, the War Cabinet had decided to send supplies and munitions to the anti-Bolsheviks in South Russia and in Siberia. At the same time British officers were dispatched to both fronts to serve in an advisory capacity. [48] The position of the British government was summarized in an instruction sent its representatives in Archangel and Vladivostok on November 30, 1918: "To remain in occupation at Murmansk and Archangel for the time being; [49] to continue the Siberian Expedition; to try to persuade the Czechs to remain in Western Siberia; to occupy the Baku-Batum railroad [in the Caucasus]; and to supply the Baltic states with military material." These courses of action were based on an understanding that the British would be active in the Caucasus and the Trans-Caspian areas, leaving the Ukraine to the French, in accord with the agreement between the two governments of December 23, 1917, dividing their respective spheres of possible military action in

[46] Callwell, *Wilson Diaries*, II, 155.

[47] Balfour's memorandum is cited in Churchill, *Aftermath*, 166.

[48] *Ibid.*, 165. British aid to the White Russians was facilitated by the availability of considerable surplus war materiel, the result of a government decision to complete production of munitions and supplies more than 60 percent processed at the time of the Armistice. *Ibid.*, 21.

[49] Later, defending British actions in North Russia before the House of Commons, Churchill and General Wilson claimed that British troops in North Russia could not be evacuated after the Armistice because of the closing of the ports by ice. Great Britain. Parliament, House of Commons, *Accounts and Papers, 1920,* Vol. 2, Cmd. 818: "Evacuation of North Russia, 1919" (London, 1920), 4–5. Hereafter cited as British Parliament, *1920,* Cmd. 818. In fact, Churchill, a strong advocate of further intervention in Russia, was not anxious to remove them; see pp. 214–19 of ch. six.

South Russia along these lines.[50] The policy decision reflected in this instruction represented something of a triumph for the pro-interventionists in the Cabinet, since, as Churchill conceded in his memoirs, it was a far-reaching program, extending existing British commitments with new actions in various parts of Russia.

The course pursued by the British after the Armistice was motivated in part by anti-Bolshevik considerations and in part by their traditional political and commercial interests. For at least two reasons the British were not anxious to see a powerful and united Russia after the war. With all too vivid memories of Russian expansion into Asia in the nineteenth century, and the subsequent clash of Russian and British interests in the Far East, Central Asia, and Persia, those who thought in terms of the Empire did not relish the possibility of a strong Russia renewing its drive eastward and southward. A weak and divided Russia would be no threat to British hegemony in the Asiatic borderlands. Referring to the Anglo-French spheres of influence in South Russia, General Wilson noted with some satisfaction that "from the left bank of the Don to India is our preserve and interest," and Churchill, listing British gains from the war, commented that in Russia "a revolutionary government which had renounced all claims to Constantinople . . . could not be a serious military danger to India." [51]

In Europe, the British diplomats feared that a strong and united Russia facing a defeated Germany too weak to counter her might well develop a position of unquestioned preponderance, either by herself or in consort with her French ally, thus upsetting a prime objective of British policy—maintenance of a balance of power on the continent.[52] As a result, the British favored the detachment from Russia of Poland, Finland, the Baltic states, and perhaps other areas in Eastern Europe, as well as the Caucasus and South Russia. In such an event the British hoped that some of these new states, particularly Finland and the Baltic and Caucasian nations, would come under British political influence and would

[50] Churchill, *Aftermath*, 167. According to Churchill these French and British "zones" were reaffirmed by the War Cabinet on November 13. See also the summary of the British instruction cabled the State Department from Archangel on December 3, which specifically refers to the Anglo–French division of action and responsibility in South Russia. Telegram from Polk, acting secretary of state, to Lansing in Paris, December 7, 1918, transmitting the cable from Archangel. Wilson Papers, Series VIIIA, Box 1.

[51] Callwell, *Wilson Diaries,* II, 148, and Churchill, *Aftermath,* 1–2.

[52] As early as the fall of 1916, a Foreign Office memorandum on the future peace settlement had proposed the independence of Poland on the grounds that it and other states emerging in Eastern Europe would be a barrier to Russian domination of Europe and to German expansion eastward, and would help keep a balance of power in Europe. Lloyd George, I, 34–35.

be outlets for British commerce and investment, while Poland and the Ukraine would fall to the French. At the same time the British envisaged the possibility of developing profitable trade with a truncated and weakened, perhaps even with a Bolshevik Russia.[53]

It followed naturally that the British government, while paying lip service to the Wilsonian principle of self-determination for all the people of Russia, was particularly concerned that this right should be exercised first of all by the non-Russian peoples on the borderlands of Russia. As a result, the British objected to Point Six of the Fourteen Points, noting in early October 1918 that "it treats these territories merely from the point of view of Russia and no mention is made of them as districts, the population of which has a claim to consideration quite apart from their former position as part of the Russian Empire." [54] Consistent with the policy of encouraging the independent development of the border minorities, the British Foreign Office suggested to Wilson a draft agenda for the peace conference which placed Russian problems last, noting that this would give the nationalities time to organize themselves, to present their desires to the conference, and to enter into agreements with other ethnic groups.[55]

British action in the Baltic best exemplified this line of her Russian policy. In May 1918 the British government granted *de facto* recognition to the Estonian constituent assembly pending settlement by the peace conference of the fate of the Baltic peoples on the basis of self-determination. On November 11, 1918, the British took similar action respecting the Lettish (Latvian) National Council.[56] In November and December 1918, following their abortive attempt to provide in the Armistice for interim Scandinavian protection of the Baltic provinces, the British continued to support the aspirations of the Baltic peoples, furnishing them aid and maneuvering British warships off the Baltic coast.

---

[53] See pp. 356–60 of ch. ten.

[54] Foreign Office memorandum of October 12, 1918, Miller, *Diary,* II, 62.

[55] Transmitted to House for Wilson on January 5, 1919. Wilson Papers, Series VIII, Box 7. In fact, the conference never did have a firm agenda, but took up matters on an *ad hoc* basis.

[56] Malbone W. Graham, *The Diplomatic Recognition of the Border States* (3 parts; Berkeley, 1935, 1939, 1941), 245–52, 406–07. On October 31, 1918, the British government raised the Baltic question with the United States, which throughout the summer of 1918 had turned a deaf ear to all Estonian overtures and appeals. The British argued that provisional recognition of the Baltic peoples was in accord with the principle of self-determination and that there were advantages to supporting their full independence as buffer states against both Germany and a restored Russia. Lansing replied that United States declarations of friendship and loyalty to Russia and the Russian people caused it to feel "in honor bound" to await the peace conference for a settlement of these questions. *1918, Russia,* II, 841–42, 851–52.

In one sense, French policies toward Russia were the clearest and simplest of those of all the Allies: the French were the most consistent and vigorous foes of Bolshevism, and they resolutely opposed any negotiation or compromise with Soviet Russia. At the same time, under this general concept, French policies were the most difficult to identify and follow, partly because there was considerable disagreement within the French government itself as to how best to fight Bolshevism and at the same time protect French interests, and partly because France pursued, often simultaneously, at least three major lines of action in regard to Russia. Thus the French position at any given moment could easily appear confused and inconsistent, if not downright contradictory.

The most important French objective in Eastern Europe, the one which was most insistently and unwaveringly striven for and on which French policy ultimately came most firmly to rest, was the creation of a string of buffer states in that area—especially Poland, Rumania, and Czechoslovakia—closely allied to France and with sufficient viability and combined strength to replace Russia as an eastern counterweight to Germany and to serve as a barrier, both against possible German expansion eastward and against any future intrusion of Russian power into Europe.[57] Next among French goals was the restoration of a strong Russia to include most of the former empire but not Bessarabia and the Polish territories. A Russia reconstituted in this way would be intimately linked to France and would again play its former role of balancing Germany in the East. Finally, the French considered off and on during 1918 and early 1919, but rejected by the spring of 1919, the possibility of supplementing their basic cordon of East European allies with a few small, French-dominated states carved out of Russia, such as the Ukraine and the Crimea.[58] These, it was believed, would not only serve French political interests, but would also provide a fertile field for French economic and commercial activity. However, Clemenceau, whose mind was fixed on the creation of a powerful pro-French Poland, never evinced much interest in or support for this objective. Moreover, the claims of Poland and Rumania tended to conflict with those of the Ukraine, and the main French interest lay with the former states.

The policies of supporting a major East European cordon and of re-

[57] See, for example, Clemenceau's declaration to the conference along these lines on February 7, 1919. *Peace Conference*, III, 904.

[58] See the review of French policy toward the Ukraine by Pichon in a telegram from Paris to the French legation in Berne on November 7, 1918. Maklakov Papers, Part II, Packet I, File 6. Pichon indicated that the French considered supporting Ukrainian independence in December 1917 but had not pursued this policy because of the pro-German activities of the Ukrainians. While adding that the French did not currently favor the creation of an independent Ukraine, Pichon did not completely rule this out as a future course of action.

creating a largely intact Russia were not necessarily contradictory, and might even, with Polish restraint and Russian acquiescence in certain territorial losses, have become complementary and reinforcing.[59] But the creation of a secondary ring of French satellites on former Russian territory appeared to exclude the possibility of a regenerated Russia, although, on occasion, the French attempted in vain to reconcile the two. In general, the French, to their loss, were never able to bring about any real cooperation among the various anti-Bolshevik forces they supported—White Russians, separatists, Rumanians, and Poles.

The effort of the French government to keep several strings to its bow was clearly reflected in the major French action in Russia in the weeks between the Armistice and the peace conference, the French-directed expedition to Odessa in December 1918, and in the subsequent parliamentary debates over this action. French intervention at Odessa was designed to seal off South Russia from the Bolsheviks, thereby protecting the flank of Rumania and Poland and giving those nations time to consolidate themselves and to build up their forces. It was a step in the development of France's East European alliance system, and also marked the beginning of the implementation of Clemenceau's policy of the *cordon sanitaire*. As Clemenceau himself stated, the expedition was part of a larger project "for the economic isolation of Bolshevik Russia in order to bring about its fall." [60]

But the French landing at Odessa also provided indirect assistance to those anti-Bolshevik elements who stood for the reconstitution of a Great Russia; the French-led expeditionary force covered the western flank of Denikin's Volunteer Army and initially supported Denikin's forces against those of the Ukrainian separatists. At the same time, however, some French officials continued to toy with the idea of encouraging the establishment of an independent Ukraine under French tutelage, even entering into abortive negotiations with the government of Petliura.[61] Not surprisingly, the French attempt to deal with both the separatists and those who believed in a unitary Russia, and, on occasion,

---

[59] See the evaluation of French efforts in this direction by R. H. Lord, a Harvard professor and the expert on Eastern Europe for the American delegation, in E. M. House and Charles Seymour, eds., *What Really Happened at Paris* (New York, 1921), 70. In his memoirs Arnold Margolin, a member of Petliura's Ukrainian government, claimed that Clemenceau was pro-Polish, while Pichon and others in the Foreign Office favored orienting French policy on a restored Russia again allied to France. The two lines were often pursued separately and simultaneously, according to Margolin. Arnold Margolin, *From a Political Diary: Russia, the Ukraine, and America, 1905–1945* (New York, 1945), 45.

[60] See n. 8 above.

[61] Gukovskii, 11–13, 41. Gukovskii also gives an excellent account of the strained relations between the French and Denikin. *Ibid.*, 113–32.

to bring them together failed completely. French policy appeared vacillating and indecisive and succeeded only in antagonizing both groups.[62]

On December 27 and 29, 1918, the French government was called upon to defend its intervention in South Russia before the Chamber of Deputies. Through these debates ran the various strands of French policy. Right-wing deputies attacked the government action as half-hearted and inadequate and urged full-scale military intervention in support of the White Russians. Some of the socialists argued for a political, nonmilitary intervention to help the moderate elements in Russia find a democratic solution to the country's troubles. Franklin-Bouillon, the Radical Socialist chairman of the committee on external affairs, maintained that the government should both support the White Russians and encourage the aspirations of the national minorities, who could form states that would be "a most solid barrier against Germany" and "foyers from which a converging action will be made for the rebirth of Russia. He failed, however, to explain how opposing separatist and unitary views of Russia's future could be reconciled.[63]

In defending the government's position, Pichon shied away from an outright renunciation of further intervention in Russia, but depicted French policy as essentially defensive, in accord with Clemenceau's concept of the *cordon sanitaire*. Pichon then quoted excerpts from the instructions sent by Clemenceau to General d'Espérey, commander of the Allied forces in the East. On December 13 Clemenceau wired that the intervention was "not of an offensive character, but it simply interdicts to the Bolsheviks access to the Ukraine, the Caucasus, and western Siberia, which are economically necessary to them . . . and where the elements of Russian order are being organized. . . . If an offensive effort is necessary to reduce Bolshevism, it should be executed later by Russian forces."[64]

This "defensive" policy undoubtedly commanded majority support in France. The expedition to Odessa was unpopular. The French public was opposed to further sacrifices and to the dispatch of more French troops to Russia. Pressures for demobilization and a "return to normalcy" were almost as great in France as in England and the United States. Even the right-wing press, while urging intervention, suggested that it should be carried out by Allied volunteers and "The young

[62] John S. Reshetar, Jr., *The Ukrainian Revolution, 1917–1920* (Princeton, 1952), 239–45.

[63] République Française. Chambre des Députés, *Débats, 1918* (Paris, 1918), 3712–13. Hereafter cited as Chambre des Députés, *Débats*.

[64] Pichon's statement, with the quotations from Clemenceau's instructions, is given in Cumming and Pettit, 273–74.

American army." [65] In an interview in December with Kokovtsov, a leading Russian émigré, Paul Cambon, the French diplomat, summed up the prevailing sentiment, declaring that France could not support all-out intervention because she was too weakened by the war and because she needed all her resources to defend French interests at the peace conference. [66]

The Italian government, facing a radical social movement and serious economic problems at home, was quite naturally thoroughly anti-Bolshevik in outlook. Moreover, the Italians did not hesitate to use the threat of a Bolshevized Italy to press their claims at the peace conference. At the same time the Italians were half-hearted in their support of intervention, although later, in the spring of 1919, they were willing, almost anxious, to take a hand in events in the Caucasus, apparently seeing an opportunity to intrude Italian influence into that oil-rich area. [67] The Italian leaders favored the destruction of Bolshevik Russia, but they were reluctant to commit any Italian resources to intervention, recognizing that such a venture would be expensive, as well as unpopular among their people, and that they could supply no reliable troops.

Like the United States, Italy supported the preservation of Russia's territorial integrity, accepting only the separation of a Poland formed along the ethnic boundary recognized by Kerensky. [68] Although Italy, in the early summer of 1918, gave *de facto* recognition to the Estonian National Council, she stated that this was not to be construed as changing her basic policy of supporting the territorial integrity of Russia. [69] Since there was in 1918 little prospect that any of the pieces that might be broken away from the former Russian Empire would come under Italian influence, Italy had little interest in the dismemberment of Russia; in addition, she may have feared that too much emphasis on the right of self-determination for minority nationalities would jeopardize her claims in the Tyrol and Dalmatia.

As this brief review of the Allies' attitude toward Russia on the eve of the conference suggests, there was more improvization than far-sighted planning, more disparity than unity of purpose, and more inconsistency than steadfastness in the various policies and plans of the Western statesmen. Underlying much of their thinking were two important but

[65] Noble, 273.

[66] Count V. N. Kokovtsov, *Out of My Past* (Stanford, 1935), 533–34.

[67] See pp. 317–18 of ch. nine.

[68] Temperley, VI, 238–39. See also the assurances of de Giers, the Provisional Government ambassador to Italy, on this point in a telegram to Maklakov on November 1, 1918. Maklakov Papers, Part II, Packet I, File 2.

[69] Graham, 245.

seldom voiced assumptions: that the wicked Soviet regime could not last, and that Allied power could shape the course of affairs in Russia. Both were, of course, utterly false, as the Western leaders gradually learned to their dismay. Nevertheless, they approached the peace negotiations with considerable optimism, quite confident that the Russian problem could be resolved there, as a sideline to the main business of making peace with the Central Powers. But, first, the difficult question of whether Russia should be represented at the conference had to be settled, and it was not without its own complexities and challenges.

CHAPTER THREE

Should Russia be Represented at the Conference?

The Russian Anti-Bolsheviks

AFTER THE Armistice anti-Bolshevik Russians were a prey to both high hopes and disheartening fears. On the one hand, they calculated that the Allies could now turn their attention and their great power to the task of defeating the Bolsheviks. White Russian generals dreamed of Allied soldiers, supplies, and money pouring into Russia. On the other hand, some of the more farsighted anti-Bolshevik leaders realized that the coming of peace would create serious difficulties for the cause of intervention. It could not then be justified as anti-German and essential to the war effort, and cries of moral indignation against intervention from labor and liberal circles would be intensified and would have a wider hearing among a war-weary public. The Allied peoples would be preoccupied with problems of postwar readjustment and of peacemaking and would be little interested in supporting a crusade against Bolshevism.[1]

Moreover, the growing power of Bolshevism—both in the form of the Soviet state and as a revolutionary idea—frightened the anti-Bolshevik leaders. After a year's precarious existence, the Soviet regime seemed to be getting stronger. Popular resistance to Bolshevism appeared to be lessening. The Red Army under Trotsky was becoming a fighting force to be reckoned with. Bolshevik ideas were gaining currency abroad, particularly among the defeated peoples of Central Europe.

[1] See, for example, telegrams from Maklakov of October 5, 1918, to the anti-Bolshevik government in Omsk, and of November 5 to B. A. Bakhmetev, the Provisional Government ambassador in Washington. Maklakov Papers, Hoover Institution, Stanford, Part II, Packet I, Files 2 and 4. For the same reasons Churchill believed in retrospect that the Armistice sounded the death knell of the White Russian cause. Churchill, *Aftermath,* 285.

In addition, things were not going well within the White Russian camp. In North Russia the apathy of the Allied soldiers and lack of popular support for the anti-Bolsheviks had prevented any substantial advance toward Moscow. In the south the fortunes of the Volunteer Army were at their lowest ebb. In the east the Czechs were falling back, and the goal of an offensive across the Urals to effect a junction with North Russian forces seemed remote. The situation in Siberia was complicated by dissension among the anti-Bolshevik groups, which culminated in Admiral Kolchak's *coup d'état* at Omsk in November 1918.

Under these circumstances White Russian appeals to the Allies took on a desperate, almost threatening tone. Anti-Bolshevik leaders sternly pointed out that Bolshevism was a serious danger to the whole world, not merely to Russia; if tolerated in Russia, it would some day destroy the Allies themselves. Furthermore, they argued, the disorder and confusion in Russia were hardly conducive to a general peace settlement. A typical plea was that of the anti-Bolshevik government in Omsk to President Wilson on November 7, 1918:

> The problems of the future of Russia should be considered by governments and nations of the universe as a problem of their own future. Russia will not perish. . . .
>
> Moreover, the reconstruction of powerful and prosperous Russia presents itself as a condition necessary to the maintenance of order and international equilibrium. . . . [The Omsk government] expects to receive [Allied] aid, and considers itself in the right to demand such help insistently. . . .
>
> All aid already extended to Russia by the Allies would be in vain if the new help should arrive too late, or in insufficient quantity. Every hour of delay threatens with innumerable calamities Russia, the Allies, and other nations.[2]

In the weeks following the Armistice White Russian leaders increasingly recognized that, both to secure further aid and to protect Russia's interests in the postwar settlement, anti-Bolshevik Russia must somehow be represented at the forthcoming peace conference. Yet the legal problem of whether Russia should be represented was a complex and difficult one. Among the questions which puzzled the diplomats, both White Russian and Allied, were the following: since the Allies had not recognized the Soviet government or the Treaty of Brest-Litovsk, was not Russia still a cobelligerent in the war? If so, was she not entitled to sit at the peace conference to protect her interests and to claim her rights? On the other hand, the Provisional Government of 1917 no longer existing,

[2] Cumming and Pettit, 257.

what group or individual of the many struggling against the Bolsheviks could represent Russia? In any case, had not Russia as a sovereign entity defaulted her claims growing out of the war and the secret treaties when the Bolsheviks deserted the Allied cause and published those treaties? Moreover, what of the Fourteen Points on which the peace was to be based? They referred to a future Russian government representing the will of the Russian people and seemed to supersede the secret treaties. Finally, had not consideration to be given, under the principle of self-determination, to the desires and interests of the minority peoples of the former Russian empire?

As so often happens in diplomacy, it was not such intricacies of international law but the current distribution of power and the political atmosphere of the moment that ultimately determined the question of Russian representation at the conference. Reflecting this, the discussion of representation, both among the Russians and among the Allies, was not cast in legal terms, but focused primarily on practical considerations. The key to the issue lay in the absence of a functioning, all-Russian, anti-Bolshevik government. (There was no chance of the Soviet government being recognized or seated.) The Allies based their policies on this fact, and the White Russians bent every effort to alter it. As a consequence, the issue of representation took on considerable significance for peace conference treatment of the Russian question as a whole. The position of the Allies on representation and the struggle of the White Russians to form an all-Russian government which could represent Russia at the conference helped lead to the later decision of the Big Four, in May 1919, to assist the government of Admiral Kolchak.

During 1918 a number of individuals and associations, representing the whole spectrum of anti-Bolshevik Russian opinion, from monarchist to socialist, were active in the West, each claiming to speak for all of Russia and each attempting to win support for a particular interest, group, or scheme. Kerensky spent some time in England and met with a number of British leaders, but the memory of his paralyzed inaction in the face of the Bolshevik conspiracy and his arrogant attitude as a suppliant tended to discredit him with the Allies and to estrange him from his fellow Russians. Prince L'vov, the first premier of the Provisional Government, was sent to America in the fall of 1918 to plead the cause of the anti-Bolshevik government in Siberia. There were many others, usually without any clear authority or mandate and often acting individually and without relation to each other's efforts.

Similarly, within Russia, from the kaleidoscopic turmoil of civil war and intervention had emerged a number of anti-Bolshevik "governments," many of them pretending, or hoping, to represent the wishes of the Russian people. Under the double pressure of a desire for recognition and the need for aid, a first step toward unification of these governments took place in the summer and fall of 1918, when the Samara government, claiming to represent the authority of the All-Russian Constituent Assembly elected in December 1917, merged with the Siberian government at Omsk to form an "All-Russian Provisional Government," originally at Ufa, later moving to Omsk. In turn, this government, popularly known as the Directorate, was superseded in November 1918 by a quasi-dictatorial government headed by Admiral Kolchak. A nominal tie between the Directorate and the local anti-Soviet government established in North Russia in 1918 had existed in the person of Nicholas Chaikovsky, who was premier of the latter and also, as a member of the Constituent Assembly, had been given a titular role in the Directorate.

Virtually all the Russian anti-Bolsheviks agreed on the urgency of persuading the Allies to recognize one Russian government. There were, however, two opposing schools of thought as to how recognition could best be achieved. One view, espoused by Kerensky among the politicians and by de Giers, ambassador of the Provisional Government in Rome, among the diplomats, called for immediate recognition of some anti-Soviet Russian government, which might then be able to rally the others to it. A second position, supported first by Ambassadors Maklakov in Paris and Bakhmetev in Washington, and later accepted by other diplomats and some politicians, maintained that the White Russian governments must first unite and prove their cohesion and strength; recognition and representation at the peace talks would then follow quickly and easily. In a letter to Kerensky on October 12, 1918, Maklakov reviewed his reasoning, pointing out that premature recognition of one government would raise a storm of protest from other Russian factions and from all the national minority groups and might result in disaster. If the government nominally recognized by the Allies proved to be weak and was discredited or overturned by a change in the fortunes of the civil war or by the jealousy and noncooperation of the other governments, the whole anti-Bolshevik cause would be set back, future recognition might be impossible to obtain, and the representation of Russia at the peace conference would be jeopardized.[3]

At this juncture the government which seemed to have the best chance of being recognized by the Allies was the newly formed Directo-

[3] Maklakov Papers, Part II, Packet I, File 4. (All subsequent references in this chapter are to Part II of the Papers.) Kerensky's reply is lacking. See also Maklakov's correspondence with Nabokov on October 11, with Bakhmetev on November 5, with de Giers on November 5, and the latter's reply of November 8, still pressing for quick recognition.

rate in Siberia, and it quite naturally was pressing its case vigorously. On October 25 the Directorate asked the ambassadors of the Provisional Government to transmit its desire for recognition to the Allies, and, as we saw in the preceding chapter, the British government was on the verge of recognizing the Directorate when the latter was overthrown by Admiral Kolchak's *coup d'état*. Maklakov passed on the request of the Directorate to the French, but at the same time he began a long, difficult struggle to persuade the Siberian government, and later that of Admiral Kolchak, that it should reach an agreement on unification with the other governments in Russia before seeking recognition.[4] In telegrams to Omsk, Maklakov emphasized two points: that the Siberian government must unite with that in South Russia in order to give substance to its claims to recognition and representation as an all-Russian authority, and that such a broadened government would be better able at the peace conference to counter the demands of the nationalities striving for separation from Russia.[5] Maklakov was encouraged in his policy by indications from Pichon in mid-November that France would recognize the Siberian government if it could reach agreement with General Denikin, the anti-Bolshevik leader in South Russia.[6] The latter, however, rebuffed the first overtures of the Siberian authorities.[7]

The Russian Political Conference

After the Armistice the White Russian diplomats became convinced that the question of Russian representation at the peace conference was an urgent one, whose resolution probably could not await the outcome of Maklakov's attempts to bring the various Russian governments together. Consequently, a temporary alternative was proposed, based on the previous experience of the diplomats of the Provisional Government. Following the Bolshevik seizure of power in November 1917, the Western governments had continued to consider the diplomatic representa-

[4] Telegram from Omsk to Washington, London, Rome, Paris, October 25, 1918; Maklakov to the Ministry of Foreign Affairs, Omsk, October 31, 1918. *Ibid.*, Packet I, Files 2 and 6

[5] Telegrams of November 3, 19, 22. *Ibid.*, Packet I, Files 4 and 2. This also marked the beginning of Maklakov's efforts to secure some modification of the unitary outlook of the Siberian government. On November 3 he commented: "You must weigh the limits of possible concessions to the Baltic areas. . . ." Maklakov's attitude toward Kolchak's seizure of power is not reflected in the documents; apparently he accepted it, but subsequently much of his effort was directed toward persuading Kolchak to espouse a more liberal political program.

[6] Reported to de Giers on November 19. *Ibid.*, Packet I, File 2.

[7] Reported to Miliukov by Denikin on November 11, 1918. Diary of Paul N. Miliukov, 1918–1920, pp. 207–08, Archive of Russian and East European History and Culture, Columbia University. For the subsequent history of efforts to establish one all-Russian government, see pp. 268–77, ch. eight.

tives of the Provisional Government as the legal representatives of Russia, since no power, except the Central Powers and their allies, recognized the new Soviet government. In December 1917 an inter-Allied conference was held to discuss, among other things, Soviet Russia's imminent defection from the war. Anti-Bolshevik Russian representatives, though not officially invited, were permitted to attend certain sessions of the conference that touched on Russian affairs as observers. At about the same time some of the European ambassadors of the Provisional Government met in Paris, under Maklakov's aegis. This group decided to exchange information and views on a regular basis in order to coordinate their actions and policies and to avoid giving conflicting advice to the Allies. The Russian embassy at Paris became the center of this activity, and the ambassadors informed the Allies of the creation of this informal body, which existed in a tenuous way throughout 1918.[8]

It was natural, therefore, that at the conclusion of the war the group of ambassadors involved should decide to meet to discuss Russia's interest in the peace and the position they should take before the Allies. Such a meeting was broached at least as early as November 4, when Maklakov mentioned it in a telegram to Nabokov. Pichon tried to discourage the holding of this meeting, telling Malakov that if it produced a collective approach to the Allies which the latter could not accept, future cooperation between the Allies and the anti-Bolsheviks might be inhibited.[9] Actually, Pichon probably feared that the meeting would strongly insist on Russia's rights in the peace settlement, whose validity in many cases France was not willing to recognize.

The concept of the proposed conference of ambassadors was broadened on November 6, when Bakhmetev suggested that, in the absence of a recognized Russian government, the senior diplomats of the Provisional Government might be the most logical group to represent Russia's interests in the preparations for the peace talks and at the conference itself. Bakhmetev indicated that the selection of the members of such a body could be made in cooperation with the Omsk government, and that several outstanding Russian political figures might be added to it. He concluded that this group need not insist on full representation, but could act in a consultative capacity if there were any difficulty over the extent of its participation in the conference. Two days later Bakhmetev sent Maklakov a draft note to the Allies along these lines.[10]

On November 17 Maklakov replied cautiously to Bakhmetev's pro-

---

[8] Letter from V. A. Maklakov to Professor H. H. Fisher, March 31, 1934. Hoover Institution, Stanford, p. 2.

[9] Maklakov Papers, Packet I, File 6.

[10] *Ibid., Packet* I, Files 2, 10.

posal, stressing that formation of an all-Russian government that the Allies could recognize would be the best way to ensure the full and equal participation of Russia in the conference. He conceded, however, that in the interim it might be worthwhile to utilize a body such as Bakhmetev suggested to represent Russia's interests in the preliminaries to the conference; in any case, plans for the peace conference should be made, proposals drafted, and experts gathered.[11] Maklakov's hesitation stemmed in part from the opposition of several conservative White Russians in Paris and in Europe, who preferred that Russia not participate in the conference but keep her hands free. They feared that representation by a weak and unofficial group might lead to unfortunate commitments on behalf of Russia, particularly the surrender of territorial claims and concessions to the national minorities. They urged postponing the settlement of all questions affecting Russia except those of Polish and of Finnish independence and the issue of the Straits, which they reluctantly recognized the Allies would want to discuss.[12] However, as the opening of the peace conference rapidly approached and efforts to unify the Russian governments made little progress, Maklakov moved toward full acceptance of Bakhmetev's plan. On December 4 he reported that he had agreed with de Giers and Nabokov on the necessity of creating a collegium of both diplomats and "leading and authoritative representatives of all the chief tendencies and shades of political thought" to represent Russia in the peace negotiations, if the Allies admitted her.[13]

The criteria and difficulties of selecting such a representative group were recalled by Maklakov fifteen years later:

An anti-Bolshevik Russia could be divided in two political groups. The first one the camp of old pre-revolutionary Russia, and the camp of the New Russia, which accepted the February [March] Revolution of 1917. . . . The Conference of Ambassadors decided to invite to

[11] *Ibid.*, Packet I, File 2. Maklakov added that the money for such preparatory activities would have to come from Bakhmetev, and it largely did, the State Department releasing to Bakhmetev for use in Paris funds held in the Treasury for the account of the Provisional Government. For example, on December 5, Ughet, chargé d'affaires in Washington, wired $50,000 to Paris for Bakhmetev. *Ibid.*, Packet I, File 10. See also Diary of Frank Polk, December 2, 1918, Frank Polk Papers, Yale University Library. Polk was under-secretary of state. The French, while apparently unwilling to finance the activities of the White Russian diplomats, agreed to facilitate their coded communications with various parts of Russia. Letter from Pichon to Maklakov, January 4, 1919, Maklakov Papers, Packet II, File 9.

[12] Conversation between Maklakov and Miliukov in mid-December. Miliukov Diary, 468–71.

[13] Maklakov Papers, Packet I, File 10. On the same date he wired Omsk that "as long as there is no generally recognized government, Russia cannot be officially represented. . . . We must reconcile ourselves to this for the present."

take part in the new body the representatives of both camps—considering that in case of their solidarity, Europe will be convinced that their opinion will be the opinion of Russia, with no difference which of the camps may take the direction of Russia. On this basis was organized the body which was surnamed the Russian Political Conference. . . .

The political front of this organization was a very large one going from Revolutionary Socialists [i.e., Socialist Revolutionaries]—as Savinkov and Ivanov—to ministers of the Government of the Tsar [Izvolsky and Sazonov]. . . . At the beginning of the work, members of the Conference were invited by the ambassadors, further on the members were invited by the conference itself.[14]

The first requirement in forming the Russian Political Conference (*Soveshchanie*) was to secure the participation and support, or at least the acquiescence in it, of the Siberian government. Despite some suspicion of the original plan for a meeting of ambassadors, out of which the idea for the Conference had emerged, the Omsk government itself paved the way for future cooperation with the Conference by requesting on November 25, when it realized that the peace talks might begin before recognition could be gained, that Maklakov represent the interests of Russia.[15] At the same time the Omsk government asked Prince L'vov, its unofficial representative in the United States, to go to Paris to work with Maklakov on the problem of Russian representation.[16] From then on Omsk cooperated with the developing Conference although, on occasion, not without certain qualms as to its role and political orientation.[17]

The next step was to secure the backing of Denikin's government in South Russia. This proved to be a delicate matter. As early as October 27, Neratov, who was acting as an adviser on foreign affairs to Denikin, had proposed that there be a single Russian representative at the peace talks, implying that such a person should represent Denikin's govern-

[14] Letter from Maklakov to Fisher, March 31, 1934, pp. 3–4.

[15] Omsk's irritation at the proposed ambassadorial meeting is voiced in its telegram of November 9; the request to Maklakov reached him November 29, after a delay in transmission. Maklakov Papers, Packet I, File 2.

[16] Omsk to Maklakov, December 3, transmitting an undated copy of its request to L'vov. *Ibid.*, Packet I, File 10. Maklakov was probably not too pleased at the addition of Prince L'vov, since in replying earlier to a suggestion of Bakhmetev that a figurehead such as L'vov was needed for the Conference, he had expressed doubts that L'vov was a generally recognized national leader and had stated that a political front, not a personage, was required. *Ibid.*

[17] On December 20 Omsk warned Maklakov not to be content with unofficial representation, which would have no juridical force for the future, adding that the regeneration of Russia depended on its representation at the peace talks. *Ibid.*

ment.[18] Hampered by limited political contact and poor physical communications with the South Russian government, Maklakov nevertheless began a campaign in mid-November to win Denikin's backing for the emerging Russian Political Conference. On November 21 he wired Ambassador Demidov in Athens, asking that Denikin be informed that the presence in Paris of Sazonov and of other representatives of the South Russian government was urgently required. Simultaneously with his organizing of the Political Conference, Maklakov continued his efforts to unite the Kolchak and Denikin governments as the first step toward the recognition of an all-Russian government, warning Denikin that the "outcome of the [peace] conference, and possibly our participation in it, depends on the degree of unity of Russia and the recognition of a general Russian authority." [19]

Maklakov was particularly anxious to bring Sazonov into the picture: as a former Tsarist foreign minister, he would both add prestige to the Political Conference and represent a certain political coloration; he was also well known to Allied leaders and could establish close contacts with them. Maklakov's task was considerably lightened by the decision of the Kolchak government at about this time to offer Sazonov the post of its foreign minister.[20] On December 5 Maklakov wired Sazonov through the French Foreign Office:

> Am happy to enter contact with you. . . . Urgent question is that there is no government recognized by all anti-Bolshevik Russia and the other Powers. . . . Am in contact with Government of Omsk presided over by Kolchak and warmly supported by Allies. This government very well intentioned and serious; it reserves post of Foreign Minister for you personally. Hoping to enter communication with you and to work out union of South and Siberia. . . .
>
> But if reconstruction of Russia operates too slowly, it may be necessary at the time of the [peace] conference for a group of competent and popular political leaders of various parties to meet here in order to represent Russia officially. It is only a national bloc which will have authority in eyes of Entente. . . .[21]

At first, however, Sazonov showed some reluctance to recognize the position of the embryonic Political Conference and to accept the coordi-

[18] *Ibid.*, Packet I, File 5.
[19] *Ibid.*, Packet III, File 11.
[20] First mentioned in a telegram of November 22. *Ibid.*, Packet I, File 2. Kolchak had no senior diplomats with him in Omsk, and there was considerable friction among those directing foreign affairs for him, notably between Kliuchnikov and Sukin. Vologodsky Diary, December 29, 1918, and January 2, 1919.
[21] Maklakov Papers, Packet III, File 11.

nating role of Maklakov. On his arrival in Europe from South Russia, Sazonov spoke only in terms of the interests of Denikin's Volunteer Army and announced that he planned "the unification in my person of the representation of Russia at the peace congress." [22] In some alarm, Maklakov wired Sazonov, urging him not to make any declarations concerning representation until the agreement of Omsk could formally be obtained.[23] According to a report from Rome, where Sazonov stopped en route to Paris, he held a rather inflated view of Russia's role and position:

> Sazonov has little idea how much the world has moved. He sees things from the viewpoint of before the war and talks of Russia as though it were unchanged, still an Ally and powerful member of Entente. . . . Russia must be one great country under one government with free access to sea. He scouts idea of a free Finland or free Baltic State which he says would practically bar Russia from the sea, and he says "We will fight before we give up. . . ." [24]

However, after reaching Paris and talking with Allied and Russian leaders, Sazonov apparently realized that as an individual he had no chance of being seated at the peace conference or of exerting much influence on it. Consequently, he decided to accept the alternative of joining the almost completed Russian Political Conference, becoming a senior member of it in his joint capacity as foreign minister of the Omsk government (which post he accepted in mid-January, after securing the permission of Denikin) and as chief diplomatic representative of the government in South Russia.

With the Omsk and South Russian governments cooperating with the Political Conference, there remained unrepresented, of the major anti-Bolshevik groups in Russia, only the government of North Russia. Its adherence to the Conference also posed some difficulties for Maklakov. In the first place the head of the North Russian government, Chaikovsky, wanted very much to be the person representing Russia at the peace talks. On November 18 he asked Noulens, the French ambassador to the Provisional Government who was then in Archangel, the seat of the North Russian government, to be invited to the conference.[25] Second, Chaikovsky, representing a moderate political viewpoint and nominally

[22] Telegrams from Sazonov to Maklakov via Athens, December 25 and December 26. *Ibid.*, Packet I, File 10.
[23] *Ibid.*
[24] Telegram from Ambassador Page in Rome to Paris, January 16, 1919. ACTNP Files 861.00/127.
[25] Joseph Noulens, *Mon Ambassade en Russie Soviétique, 1917–19* (2 vols.; Paris, 1933), II, 108. Noulens gave a noncommittal reply.

a member of the Omsk Directorate, was critical of Admiral Kolchak's action in overthrowing the Directorate and of what he suspected was Kolchak's reactionary political orientation.[26] Consequently he was little disposed to subordinate himself to the Political Conference which aspired to represent Russia at the peace conference and which had the blessing of Kolchak.

Conversely, the Omsk government did not think highly of Chaikovsky and was reluctant to have him join the Conference. But Maklakov pressed for his participation, not only as representing the North Russian government but because he would broaden the political spectrum of the Conference, adding a democratic hue that would particularly appeal to liberal sentiment among the Allied leaders and public. Maklakov's position was supported by a personal plea from Prince L'vov to Kolchak; L'vov argued that since the committee in Paris was working for both recognition and representation, there was an urgent need to give it a broad and nonpartisan character.[27] Maklakov's efforts to make the Conference more politically representative were crowned with success; when it was at last officially constituted in January 1919, the Russian Political Conference included not only Chaikovsky but other representatives of supposedly "democratic" or "leftist" viewpoints: Ivanov, a Socialist Revolutionary, Dolgopolov from the Kuban area, and Savinkov, the noted terrorist.

Savinkov, well liked by the British and in close touch with them, was undoubtedly the most colorful figure of the Russian Political Conference; in fact, of all the flamboyant personalities who flocked to Paris during the peace negotiations, he was one of the most striking. In proposing his participation to Omsk, Sazonov noted that he stood well with French public opinion, and that he claimed influence in Russia among both democratic radical elements and the officer corps.[28] Sazonov added that the Conference planned to entrust him with "agitation" among democratic elements in Europe.[29] He was well suited to this task

[26] *1918, Russia*, II, 563, 573–74.

[27] Telegrams to Omsk of December 24, 26, and 28. Maklakov Papers, Packet I, File 10. Since Chaikovsky had spent a good deal of time in the United States, it was also hoped he might be a good liaison with the American delegation.

[28] This must have been a difficult proposal for Sazonov to make. Churchill reported asking the former foreign minister in the summer of 1919: "How do you get on with Savinkov?" Sazonov, making a deprecating gesture with his hands, replied: "He is an assassin. I am astonished to be working with him. But what is one to do? He is a man most competent, full of resource and resolution." Winston Churchill, *Great Contemporaries* (London, 1937), 125.

[29] Telegram of January 15 cited in I. Subbotovsky, *Soiuzniki, Russkie reaktsionery i interventsiia* (*The Allies, Russian Reactionaries and Intervention*) (Leningrad, 1926), 66. This work is based on the archives of the Kolchak government, seized when the Red Army captured Omsk in late 1919.

if, as seems reasonable to assume, it was to include intelligence and "undercover" operations. A former bomb-throwing revolutionary implicated in the assassination of Tsarist ministers, Savinkov had been active in an allegedly Allied-inspired revolt against the Soviet government during the summer of 1918. In the 1920's, after a series of adventures as an anti-Bolshevik mercenary, he was caught and tried by the Soviet government, reportedly escaping the firing squad by committing suicide in his prison cell. In Paris he made a dashing figure, twirling a cane, sporting a gardenia in his buttonhole, and invariably sitting with his back to restaurant walls to forestall possible assassination attempts.[30]

Despite the remarkable achievement of Maklakov and his colleagues in bringing together such a disparate group of Russian political figures, there were, nevertheless, some important names absent from the rolls of the Conference. Nabokov, the chargé in London, who had worked with the council of ambassadors during 1918 and who had participated in the early formulation of the idea for the Conference, refused finally to join. Nabokov's differences with the Conference were largely personal, although these were aggravated by a disagreement over policy. He resented Maklakov's prominent role in the Conference and the necessity of becoming subordinate to both Maklakov and Sazonov in policy direction and execution. In addition, he believed that it was unwise for the Conference to accept anything less than full representation at the peace talks; he felt that its ultimate role of informally and unofficially representing Russia—"sitting in the anteroom," as he described it—was degrading and a sign of weakness.[31]

On the other hand, Miliukov, the Cadet leader and former foreign minister in the Provisional Government, while somewhat skeptical of the composition of the Conference, might have been persuaded to join it and would undoubtedly have been acceptable to its members. However, when he reached Paris in December 1918 at the head of a delegation from the Jassy Conference, commissioned, with the blessing of Denikin, to seek aid from the Allies, Clemenceau and the French press raised such a storm over Miliukov's alleged collaboration with German forces in the Ukraine earlier in 1918 that Maklakov felt it prudent to send Miliukov on to London, where he remained until February.[32]

Kerensky, as we have seen, had so irritated both the Allies and the

[30] This description of Savinkov from Stephen Bonsal, *Suitors and Suppliants: The Little Nations at Versailles* (New York, 1946), 20.
[31] Nabokov, 202, 285–90, and Kokovtsov, 533. In defiance of Sazonov, Nabokov continued sending his reports directly to Omsk instead of through Sazonov in Paris. As a result, Sazonov finally had him transferred from London to Oslo.
[32] Miliukov Diary, 467–95; telegram from Maklakov to Omsk, December 28. Maklakov Papers, Packet I, File 10. Maklakov, however, co-opted two members of

Russian diplomats during 1918 that his participation in the Conference was never seriously considered. For his part, Kerensky viewed the Conference as unrepresentative and dominated by reactionary elements.

In view of its disparate membership and the tenuous bonds holding it together, the Conference worked remarkably well. There were, of course, disputes within the Conference, as well as between it and the White Russian governments in Russia. Maklakov noted: "All its decisions were adopted in unanimity; certainly this unanimity was not attained without friction and sometimes only after long debates, But a perfect union before the foreign powers was considered as absolutely necessary." [33] The relationship between the Conference and Kolchak and Denikin was a special and unusual one. The two anti-Bolshevik leaders were naturally reluctant to subordinate themselves to a group of diplomats and politicians gathered together hastily in Paris for a special purpose. At the same time, they realized that this group provided the only reasonable opportunity for Russia to be represented at the peace conference, pending formation of a unified government that the Allies would recognize, and that its location and prestige made it a useful intermediary in advancing their interests at the conference and before the Allies in general.

For their part, the diplomats did not wish to jeopardize their acknowledged position as the legal representatives of the last duly constituted and recognized Russian government by subordinating themselves to the authority of provisional and loyal governments in various parts of Russia. They feared that such action might sever their official and juridical link with established Russian governments of the past and break the legal continuity of the Provisional Government as represented in their persons, an inheritance which was essential to their management of Russia's interests and assets abroad and which might prove of the greatest value in the reconstruction of Russia after the expected fall of the Bolsheviks. As a result, both the White Russian leaders and the Conference acknowledged the latter's special and independent position, beholden only to a past and, they hoped, future authorized all-Russian government.[34] As Maklakov later described it: ". . . the Political Conference

Miliukov's delegation, Tretiakov and Titov, for the Russian Political Conference. On Miliukov's criticism of the Conference, see the report of the British postal censor, transmitted by Leland Harrison, a junior member of the American Commission to Negotiate Peace, to Joseph Grew, February 28, 1919. Leland Harrison Papers, Division of Manuscripts, Library of Congress, Acquisition 9611, Box 102.

[33] Letter from Maklakov to Fisher, March 31, 1934, pp. 5–6.

[34] Interview of May 9, 1949, with the late Professor Michael Karpovich, private secretary to Bakhmetev in 1918–1919. See also a long and interesting telegram from Omsk on November 22, which outlined in detail the unique position which the Conference later was to hold. Maklakov Papers, Packet I, File 2.

was not an elective body, but it neither was nominated by some higher authority. . . . The Political Conference did not consider that it depended from Koltchak, and Koltchak did not consider the Political Conference as his subordinated body. . . . On the other hand, the Political Conference never made any attempt to place itself higher than Koltchak." [35]

While this delicate and unusual arrangement seemed to work out fairly well with Admiral Kolchak, it was not as successful in the case of General Denikin. On the whole, the latter felt that the Conference adopted a superior, haughty attitude toward him and that it considered itself *the* all-Russian body, which should determine and direct the actions of the anti-Bolshevik governments. In particular, Denikin was piqued at the refusal of the Conference to receive the Don and Kuban minority delegations to Paris and by what he considered as the political corruption of Sazonov by the Conference. Commenting on the work and expense of the Conference in his memoirs, Denikin remarked: "For the South, at any rate, there was little result." [36]

The original aim of the Russian Political Conference was to secure official admission to the peace talks as the fully empowered representative of Russia. But, as we shall see in the next few pages, the Allies, viewing the disordered and confused scene in Russia and mindful of the embarrassing claims Russia might make under the secret treaties, were not anxious to seat Russia at the peace table. As a result, the Political Conference was forced to undertake the representation of Russia unofficially and informally, working where and how it could among the delegations and commissions of the peace conference. This also contributed to Denikin's disappointment and annoyance with the Political Conference, as he continued to insist on Russia's right to full participation in the peace conference. On February 15 the Ekaterinodar government wired Sazonov that even if the Allies should admit a Russian delegation with a consultative vote, such a concession would be "absolutely inadmissible" and that "Russia can be represented at the conference only on an equal footing with the other powers." Sazonov, however, now fully aware of Russian weakness and Allied strength, saw, perhaps wishfully, certain advantages in the off-stage role of the Political Conference. In his reply, he agreed with the South Russian government but remarked: "It is better for us to preserve our freedom of action in the future than to tie ourselves to participation in taking decisions unfavorable for us. . . ." [37]

[35] Letter from Maklakov to Fisher, March 31, 1934, p. 5.
[36] Denikin, IV, 238–44.
[37] Telegrams of February 15 and 17 between Ekaterinodar and Sazonov in Paris. "Vneshniaia politika kontrrevoliutsionnykh 'pravitel'stv' v nachale 1919 g." ("The

In its unofficial capacity the function of the Russian Political Conference was threefold: to represent the interests of Russia in the peace settlement, to help direct the foreign policies of the White Russian governments and promote the unification of those governments, and to organize and coordinate the determined efforts of all émigrés to persuade the Allies to send more aid to the anti-Bolshevik movement.[38] In order to carry out these responsibilities, the Conference developed an elaborate organization.[39] The Conference elected Prince L'vov as chairman. This was, however, largely a titular role, since the guiding spirit of the group was Maklakov, chiefly assisted by Sazonov and Bakhmetev. The directing organ of the Conference was the Russian Political Delegation Abroad, often referred to as *"chetverka"* (the four), since it consisted of L'vov, Sazonov, Maklakov, and Chaikovsky (Savinkov was added later in 1919). In addition to supervising the overall activity of the Conference, the Political Delegation was the medium of communication with the peace conference, speaking on behalf of the Russian Political Conference and signing all memoranda and papers addressed to the peace conference. On a few occasions, members of the Political Delegation were invited to appear before various commissions of the peace conference to present their views in person.

The work of the Conference and of the Delegation was supported by a series of commissions, each of which had the dual function of proffering advice to the peace conference on problems pertaining to its jurisdiction and of representing the White Russian governments in that field. Bakhmetev was president of the Political Commission; General Shcherbachev chaired the Military and Naval Commission; General Hermonius handled supply; A. Raffalovich was president of the Financial and Economic Commission; and Sablin, later Savinkov, headed a press bureau. Conference members met daily and busied themselves with the preparation of memoranda and leaflets on various issues. These were often pre-

Foreign Policy of the Counterrevolutionary 'Governments' in the Beginning of 1919"), *Krasnyi Arkhiv* (*Red Archives*), Vol. 37 (1929), 81, 83. Hereafter cited as "Vneshniaia politika," *Krasnyi Arkhiv*. This article contains copies of a number of telegrams from a file book of the Russian embassy in Paris, which was found when the Soviet government took over the embassy in 1922. The file book was apparently left behind when Maklakov moved the documents now deposited in the Hoover Institution.

[38] Letter from Maklakov to Fisher, March 31, 1934, pp. 4–5. Maklakov added, and his files reflect, that the Conference also dealt with a number of miscellaneous matters affecting Russia's interests abroad: e.g., preservation and management of Russian assets abroad and of supplies bought with credits of the Provisional Government, and the fate of Russian prisoners of war.

[39] Details of the organization and functioning of the Conference lie beyond the scope of this study, but abundant materials on this subject are available in the Maklakov archive.

sented to the peace conference and distributed through the press and mails.[40] Conference members also met, both in formal interviews and on informal or social occasions, leaders and staff members of the various Allied delegations to the peace conference. It is difficult to judge the success of the Russian Political Conference in affecting peace conference decisions affecting Russia. Its impact was certainly not large, but the Allies respected a number of its individual members and the latter's representations did play some part in the shaping of peace conference policies toward Russia, particularly in the decision in May 1919 formally to support Admiral Kolchak. Moreover, the Conference undoubtedly had some influence on territorial recommendations affecting Russia. In the territorial commissions and among the delegations (especially the French) the pleas of the Conference served to stiffen the backs of those who supported the preservation of Russia's territorial integrity. Thus the Conference probably helped block early recognition at Paris of the independence of the Baltic states and may have had some effect on peace conference decisions concerning Poland's eastern frontiers.

In presenting their case for admission to the Paris deliberations, the White Russian diplomats argued vigorously that only representatives of a democratic and united Russia should be seated—certainly not the criminal Bolsheviks who had betrayed the Allied cause, and, preferably, none of the national minority groups. White Russian leaders stressed the huge sacrifices made by Russia in the first three years of the war, maintaining that Russia's desperate, if unsuccessful, struggle on the Eastern Front, though it had helped prevent a German victory in France, had led directly to the Bolshevik Revolution, the cause of Russia's withdrawal from the war.[41] The possibility that national minority groups would be seated troubled the Russian Political Conference a good deal. Within the Conference there was considerable conflict over what position the nationalities should occupy in a reconstituted Russia, and this issue was to remain a source of disagreement among the members of the Conference and between it and the White Russian governments through-

[40] For a list of the notes, memoranda, and pamphlets presented to the peace conference by the Russian Political Conference, see Appendix 1. In addition to the Maklakov Papers and the letter from Maklakov to Fisher previously cited, Denikin's memoirs and Bulletin No. 93, March 20, 1919, of the American Commission to Negotiate Peace (Miller, *Diary*, XVII, 233) contain information on the structure and activity of the Russian Political Conference.

[41] The inside cover of one of the dozen or so pamphlets printed by the Russian Liberation Committee, the White Russian propaganda outlet in London, was entitled "What Russia has done for the Common Cause," and listed 18,450,000 mobilized; 1,700,000 killed; 4,950,000 disabled and wounded; 2,500,000 taken prisoner; and 3,500,000 enemy prisoners captured. Maklakov Papers, Packet II, File 1.

out the peace talks. Some, like Maklakov, maintained that in the interests of unifying and strengthening the anti-Bolshevik cause and of making it more acceptable to the Allies, concessions would have to be made to the minorities: independence for Poland and Finland and autonomy for other areas. Moreover, it might even be necessary to allow deputations of non-Russians to present their views to the peace conference, although they certainly should not be admitted as official delegations.[42] Others were unwilling to go farther than the recognition of Polish independence, and defended a unitary organization of the rest of prewar Russia.

Like so many other special-interest groups all over the world, the national minorities in Russia sent their representatives to Paris. As might be expected, the Finns, the Baltic peoples, and the Ukrainians were there, but more remarkable was the appearance of delegations from such areas as Circassia and Daghestan in the Caucasus, and even from the Pontine Greeks, whose last government was destroyed by Caesar in 47 B.C.[43] Since many of the groups from Russia were invited to present their cases before various delegations and commissions of the peace conference, they were a source of constant anxiety to the Russian Political Conference.

The Allies and Russian Representation

Allied handling of the question of Russian representation directly reflected the various strands of Allied policy toward Russia outlined in the previous chapter. The French were the first to raise the issue. On November 21, perhaps as a result of the arguments of Maklakov, who at that time was developing the concept of the Russian Political Conference, the French proposed that Russia's interests "could be defended by an invitation to [an] Allied committee with which Russian advisors could be associated." At the same time the French suggested that the Allies announce that participation of the state in the peace conference would act as a waiver of its rights under the secret treaties. The French commented: "Such a declaration has the advantage of freeing the Allies from any previous imperialist aims: the necessity of abolishing the agreements with Russia (which would comprise the cession of Constantinople to that power) would in itself [recommend] the adoption of such

---

[42] See n. 5 above. Also telegram from Maklakov to de Giers, November 26, 1918, Maklakov Papers, Packet I, File 2.

[43] Such groups were a drain on the time and energy of the peacemakers. Wilson particularly seems to have gone to extreme lengths to give them a hearing. His appointment book for April and May 1919 reveals that he received delegations of Assyrian-Chaldeans, Daghestan-Circassians, Kuban Cossacks, Carpatho-Russians, and Azerbaidjani. Wilson Papers, Series VIIIA, Box 37.

a measure." [44] The French clearly were not anxious to seat the Russians, or to give them an opportunity to press their claims under the secret treaties. Moreover, the presence at the peace table of France's former ally, Russia, would almost certainly have embarrassed French efforts to secure territorial gains along Russia's western border for France's new eastern allies, Poland and Rumania.

Meanwhile, in the United States, Prince L'vov, Bakhmetev, and other anti-Bolshevik leaders were pressing the case for Russian representation. Commenting on the issue, President Wilson wrote Lansing on November 20: ". . . is it feasible, in view of the present at least temporary disintegration of Russia into at least five parts . . . to have Russia represented at the peace table, or to admit a part of her by recognizing and receiving delegates from the Omsk government?" In reply, Lansing, apparently swayed to some extent by the representations of Bakhmetev, who called on the secretary of state several times in October and November, recalled Russia's heavy sacrifices in the war and her role in helping prevent an early German victory, and warned that to settle Russia's affairs without her participation was a heavy responsibility. He proposed that since the United States had consistently evinced an independent and sympathetic attitude toward Russia, it should take the lead in safeguarding Russia's interests in the peace and in ensuring that the Russian problem were considered as a whole, and not on the basis of her temporary disintegration. Lansing then stated that only delegates from a democratic government in Russia could be signatories of the peace and suggested that "in the interim approved representatives from existing elements of order in Russia" should be welcomed and heard.[45] The arguments of Lansing and of Prince L'vov, who saw the president on November 21, left Wilson unconvinced, however. In late December Lloyd George told the Imperial War Cabinet that the president did not favor Russia being represented at the conference, but had suggested that Maxim Litvinov, a Bolshevik representative in Stockholm and later Soviet foreign minister, who had addressed a conciliatory message to Wilson on Christmas Eve, should be asked what his proposals were.[46] Wilson apparently considered the question of Russian representation as part of the overall Russian problem, toward whose peaceful resolution his mind was already turning.

In London, Nabokov was persistently urging upon the British the necessity of having Russia represented at the peace talks, pointing out that

[44] *Peace Conference*, I, 352, and Miller, *Diary*, II, 11.
[45] *Peace Conference*, I, 268–71. Wilson sailed for Europe within a week, and there is no record that he replied to Lansing.
[46] Lloyd George, I, 189. For Litvinov's message and its impact on Wilson and the British, see pp. 90–92 of ch. four.

otherwise decisions of the conference would not be binding on any future Russian government. Piqued at Balfour's rejection of his arguments, Nabokov concluded that denial of Russian representation was part of a scheming British policy for keeping Russia weak and divided in order to give British imperialism a free hand in the Middle and Far East.[47] In the light of Nabokov's contention, it is significant that at an inter-Allied conference in early December, Balfour, supported by Lord Curzon, proposed that the border areas, but not Soviet Russia, be allowed to present their case to the peace conference. Sonnino, seizing upon the implications of Balfour's proposal, replied that dismembering Russia would only lead to German interference in the area and would create another trouble spot like the Balkans; moreover, he opposed any further contribution to "the centrifugal contagion" of the times. Clemenceau declared that the border states should be allowed "to cook"; when they were ready, they could be recognized and later worked into the peace settlement. Furthermore, Clemenceau said, he objected strongly to any representation of Russia, "which had betrayed the Allied cause during the war." He added that "the peace which was to be settled did not concern her." [48]

In reply, Lloyd George recalled Russia's great sacrifices in the early part of the war and the necessities which had forced her to make peace. In arguments which he was to reiterate often during the peace conference, Lloyd George maintained that the Russian dilemma had to be faced and that "the affairs of nearly two hundred million people could not be settled without hearing them." The British prime minister, backed by Borden of Canada and Hughes of Australia, then proposed that the only sensible course was to let all sides to the Russian controversy, including the Bolsheviks, state their case. The meeting adjourned, however, without a decision, pending presentation of the views of the United States. Lloyd George, under domestic pressure to end intervention and attracted by the conciliatory tone of recent Bolshevik appeals, was clearly ready to attempt peacefully to resolve the Russian situation, and in this meeting he first broached the essence of his later proposal for a conference of the various Russian factions on the Prinkipo Islands. The question of Russian representation was next formally considered

---

[47] Nabokov, 280. Nabokov's view is of interest since Soviet historians, drawing on Lenin's theory of imperialism, have often made a similar analysis of certain aspects of British foreign policy in 1918–1919. See John M. Thompson, "Allied and American Intervention in Russia, 1918–1921," in *Rewriting Russian History*, ed. C. E. Black (New York, 1956), 364.

[48] Lloyd George, I, 320–23. Clemenceau and many other Frenchmen were bitter over Russia's withdrawal from the war, believing that it had imposed untold additional burdens on the French. See, for example, Noulens, 279.

by the Allies on Sunday, January 12, 1919, in a meeting of the Supreme War Council at the Quai d'Orsay office of Pichon, dubbed "Pichon's Room of Head Frocks" by British General Sir Henry Wilson—"frocks" was Wilson's epithet for civilians. This was actually the first working session of the peace conference, which did not convene officially until January 18.[49] One of the first problems to be taken up was that of the representation of Russia. Pichon suggested that Russia should not be represented officially, but that the peace conference should hear the émigrés in Paris. Lloyd George retorted that "they represent every opinion except the prevalent one in Russia" and maintained that hearing them would give the public the impression that they were official representatives. It was finally decided to hear the émigrés by means of memoranda or by private interviews.[50] While representing a minor concession to the views of the White Russian diplomats, this was much less than the Russian Political Conference had hoped to achieve. On January 13 discussion of the question of Russian representation, which was to have been continued that day, was postponed, and on January 18 the *Rules of the Conference,* presented to the first plenary session, stated that "the conditions governing the representation of Russia shall be settled by the Conference when Russian affairs come up for discussion." [51] At this juncture the issue of Russian representation became merged with that of a general settlement of the Russian problem, to which the peace conference was then turning its attention. Out of conference discussion of this larger issue emerged the Prinkipo proposal, but it must be remembered that the Prinkipo policy had its origins in Lloyd George's (and later Wilson's) belief that all parties to the controversy in Russia should be given an opportunity to present their views to the Paris Conference.

[49] The first plenary session was held January 18, but the major decision-making bodies of the conference were the Supreme War Council, a group carried over from the war; the Council of Ten, a body based on the Supreme War Council but with the military advisors not present and consisting of two plenipotentiary representatives—usually the head of government and the foreign minister—from each of the major powers (England, France, Italy, Japan, and the United States), and the Council of Four (Clemenceau, Orlando, Lloyd George, and Wilson).

[50] *Peace Conference,* III, 490–91.

[51] *Peace Conference,* III, 173.

CHAPTER FOUR

The Prinkipo Proposal

THE FIRST major decision of the peace conference respecting Russia, the proposal for a conference of all parties to the Russian civil war on the Prinkipo Islands, was of particular significance. With the conclusion of the World War, both Allied and Soviet leaders had to take stock and subsequently to readjust their policies toward each other. The Prinkipo project represented a new, though abortive, approach to the Soviet revolution on the part of the West and presaged two later attempts by the peace conference to end civil war and intervention in Russia. Although all three efforts ended in failure and although the policy of intervention was to hold sway over that of conciliation for at least another year, the basic factors which evoked the Prinkipo experiment in *rapprochement* continued to affect Western policies toward Russia in subsequent months and eventually led to the uneasy *modus vivendi* established between the European Allies and Soviet Russia in the early 1920's. On the Soviet side the Prinkipo episode foreshadowed the NEP in foreign relations—an attempt by the Soviet government through diplomacy to mitigate or forestall capitalist attacks on the young revolutionary state, to obtain economic assistance necessary for its development, and to win time until the "inevitable" world revolution broke out in Europe.

The Soviet "Peace Offensive"

Since Soviet efforts to persuade the West to end intervention played such a significant role in the origins of the Prinkipo proposal, it is necessary first to examine briefly the development of Soviet policy in the period from the Armistice to the opening of the peace conference. Among the Bolshevik leaders the end of the war aroused mingled hopes and fears. Lenin was afraid that the conclusion of hostilities among the "imperialists" would free them to turn on and destroy the Soviet regime, their class and international enemy and the spark of the imminent "world revolution." [1] The Germans, some of whom had already

[1] V. I. Lenin, *Sochineniia* (*Works*) (30 vols.; 2nd ed., Moscow, 1926–1932), XXII, 317–19, XXIV, 458–59. The second edition is used unless otherwise stated. See

proffered their services for a European crusade against Bolshevism, Lenin declared, could be expected to join in the Allied offensive.[2] On one occasion, just before the Armistice, Lenin even struck a definitely pessimistic note: "We also know that while the imperialists cannot stop the international revolution, the defeat of individual countries and even more dreadful losses are quite possible." [3] Lenin's fears concerning the effect of the end of the war on Soviet fortunes were epitomized in a remark he made at this time to Chicherin, the Soviet foreign minister: "Now world capitalism will advance against us." [4]

Lenin's view of the nature of capitalism also gave him grounds for hope, however. His predictions that the imperialists would be compelled by class interest to band together to crush Soviet Russia were balanced by equally firm pronouncements that world capitalism was rent with divisions and decay, which undermined its ability to attack revolutionary Russia. On May 14, 1918, after analyzing at length the characteristics of world imperialism, Lenin concluded: "There are two tendencies; one makes inevitable an alliance of all the imperialists; the other pits one group of imperialists against the other." [5] In Lenin's opinion, imperialist rivalry between Japan and the United States reflected the latter tendency and reduced the effectiveness of anti-Soviet intervention in the Russian Far East. Lenin also counted on support and sympathy for the Bolsheviks among Western soldiers and workers to weaken any capitalist offensive against Moscow.[6]

But what raised the hopes of the Soviet leaders most was their expectation that defeat followed by disorganization and despair in Central Europe would lead to the outbreak of proletarian revolutions there—the first step in the development of the world revolution, predicted and dreamed of for so long, and the beginning of the end of Soviet Russia's struggle in isolation. As early as late August 1918 Lenin announced excitedly that there were signs of developing revolutionary activity in Austria and Italy, and that the demoralization of the German army was proceeding apace.[7] The prospect of a socialist revolution in Germany could

also V. I. Lenin *Collected Works* (New York, 1927–1945), XXIII, 16–17, 83, 93–95, 243–45. At this time Lenin consistently maintained that the primary motive for Allied intervention was world imperialism's fear of the effect the Bolshevik example would have on the crisis-ridden capitalist system. He argued that the imperialists' interest in dividing and exploiting Russia was only a secondary factor. I. I. Mints and A. I. Gukovskii, eds., *Lenin ob interventsii* (*Lenin on Intervention*) (Moscow, 1931), 42 n. 7.

[2] Lenin, *Collected Works,* XXIII, 256–60, 278–79.
[3] *Ibid.,* XXIII, 286.
[4] Cited in Fischer, I, 150.
[5] Lenin, *Collected Works,* XXIII, 19.
[6] Lenin, *Sochineniia,* XXIII, 272.
[7] Lenin, *Collected Works,* XXIII, 213–14.

not but buoy the spirits of the Bolsheviks, who had always considered highly industrialized Germany, with its advanced proletariat and its rich resources, the key to the world revolution. In an editorial typical of this period, *Pravda* confidently declared on November 5: "The time is not far off when the first day of the world revolution will be celebrated everywhere."

Lenin, however, even in his most optimistic moments, never overlooked the danger of additional and strengthened capitalist attacks on Soviet Russia, once Allied forces were freed by the impending victory over Germany. On October 22 he spoke sanguinely of the prospects of world revolution, but summed up the dual outlook for Soviet Russia in these words: "The Soviet power stands in a peculiar position: on the one hand, we have never been so close to the international proletarian revolution as at present; and on the other, we were never in such a dangerous situation as now." [8] These two calculations largely determined the course of Soviet policy abroad during late 1918 and 1919. The Soviet government did what it could to incite proletarian revolutions in Europe; it also made every possible effort to prevent, or at least to weaken, further intervention against it. The two objectives were, of course, not unrelated since revolutionary unrest among European peoples undermined the ability of the Western powers to launch an all-out offensive against the Soviet regime.

Although the attempt to stave off armed attack from the West through negotiations and compromise was the predominant concern of Soviet foreign policy during the winter of 1918–1919, revolutionary tactics played an important secondary role in Soviet strategy. In Lenin's view there were various ways in which Soviet Russia could assist the development of proletarian revolutions in the West. It could furnish money, supplies, and in some cases, as later in Poland, military aid to the revolutionaries. In October 1918 Lenin actually began to stockpile grain for the German workers and to strengthen the Red Army in hopes of being able to aid directly the expected revolution in Germany.[9] Lenin also believed that revolutions abroad could be fostered by revolutionary propaganda and agitation directed from Moscow. To the Eighth Party Con-

[8] Lenin, *Sochineniia*, XXIII, 238–39. Lenin apparently liked this formulation of the duality of the Soviet position, for he reiterated it several times in this period. *Ibid.*, XXIII, 228, 231, 232, 269. Contemporary accounts of Lenin's attitude at the time of the Armistice also refer to his mixed feelings concerning the end of the war. See those cited in E. H. Carr, *The Bolshevik Revolution, 1917–23* (3 vols; New York, 1951–1953), III, 96 n. 1.

[9] Lenin, *Sochineniia*, XXII, 320; *Collected Works*, XXIII, 238. Following the Armistice and formation of a new German government, the Soviet authorities actually offered two trainloads of scarce grain to Germany, but were rebuffed. Carr, *Bolshevik Revolution*, III, 98.

gress on March 18, 1919, he stressed the importance of training revolutionary cadres for work abroad, and reported that "hundreds of thousands of war prisoners . . . who are being removed to Hungary, Germany, and Austria are spreading the germ of Bolshevism, so that it is completely infecting these countries." [10] A key instrument for fomenting revolution, Lenin maintained, was the network of communist parties abroad. On January 23, 1919, only one day after the Western statesmen had invited the Russian factions to discuss peace on the Prinkipo Islands, Lenin called for the organization of the international communist movement into the Third International, or Comintern. In early March it held its first meeting in Moscow to plan the intensification of revolutionary propaganda and agitation around the world. Later in March revolutions broke out in Hungary and in Bavaria, where Soviet-type governments were established.

Lenin was also convinced that the very existence of the Soviet regime in Russia was of incalculable assistance in promoting the world revolution. He saw Soviet Russia as a model and inspiration to the workers of the world. It provided tangible proof that the proletariat, directed by its vanguard, the party, could seize and hold power. On one occasion Lenin referred to the Bolshevik Revolution in Russia as a torch "scattering sparks to add to the growing flames of socialist revolution," and in early 1918 he declared: "A living example . . . in some single country is more effective than manifestoes and conferences; this is what inflames the masses of the toilers in all countries." [11]

It therefore followed logically, in Lenin's view, that extraordinary efforts must be made to protect and defend Soviet Russia, to preserve this revolutionary example of a guide and spur to the world proletariat. Lenin believed that the Bolsheviks must somehow hold power in Russia until the outbreak of proletarian revolutions in the advanced capitalist countries, which would save the Soviet state by eliminating the danger of imperialist attack. The Bolsheviks could also then draw upon economic assistance from industrial Europe, without which socialist construction in Russia could not be completed.[12] In May 1918 Lenin wrote:

> . . . we must remain at our post until our ally, the international proletariat, comes to our aid . . . we must stick to our tactics of waiting and taking advantage of the conflicts and antagonisms among the imperialists, and of slowly accumulating strength—the tactics of

[10] Lenin, *Sochineniia*, xxiv, 128, 753–54 n. 41.
[11] *Ibid.*, xxii, 217.
[12] For an elaboration of Lenin's views on the necessity of "holding on" in Russia, see John M. Thompson, "Lenin's Analysis of Intervention," *American Slavic and East European Review*, Vol. 17, No. 2 (April 1958), 156–58.

maintaining the island of Soviet power intact amidst the raging sea of imperialism, of maintaining intact that island to which the eyes of the working people of all countries are even now turned.[13]

According to Lenin, there were several things the Bolsheviks could do, while awaiting succor from the world revolution, to help preserve "the island of Soviet power" in the face of threatened or actual imperialist attacks. One, mentioned in the quotation above, was to maneuver and tack in such a way as best to capitalize on the contradictions and rivalries which Lenin believed to be inherent in world imperialism. In Lenin's view such contradictions seriously hampered the efforts of capitalist states to cooperate in a concerted, all-out offensive against Soviet Russia; consequently, one of the chief tasks of Soviet policy was to attempt to exacerbate and to utilize these antagonisms.[14]

At the same time Soviet propaganda should unmask the crude imperialistic designs of the great powers, thereby attracting to the Soviet program the masses of all countries.[15] Thus Soviet appeals to the Western peoples in 1919 charged that the peace conference was a device for dividing the territorial and financial spoils of the imperialists' war under the hypocritical cloak of Wilsonian justice, while the League of Nations was depicted as an international concert of reaction dedicated to suppressing the world revolution.[16]

Lenin believed that the Soviet regime should go to almost any lengths to avoid an open, and clearly unequal, struggle with the capitalistic powers: "For until the international socialist revolution breaks out . . . and becomes strong enough to overcome *international imperialism,* it is the bounden duty of the socialists who have conquered in one country *not* to accept battle against the giants of imperialism. Their duty is to try to avoid war, to wait until the conflicts among the imperialists weaken them still more, bringing the revolution in other countries still nearer."[17] And on the eve of the Armistice Lenin stated: "Even now we are weaker than international imperialism . . . and must do everything to avoid battle with it."[18] If battle became unavoidable, Lenin urged a vigorous defense of Soviet Russia, but he also recommended

---

[13] Lenin, *Sochineniia,* XXIII, 16.

[14] *Ibid.,* XXIII, 16; XXV, 236, 485–86.

[15] *Ibid.,* XXIV, 61.

[16] See, as examples, point fifteen of the proposed party program, *ibid.,* XXIV, 693; and Lenin's letter to the workers of Europe and America, January 24, 1919, Lenin, *Collected Works,* XXIII, 520.

[17] Lenin's italics. Lenin, *Sochineniia,* XXII, 506.

[18] In his report to the Sixth Congress of Soviets on November 8, 1918. *Ibid.,* XXIII, 264.

making every effort to halt or to mitigate the imperialist attack with offers of compromise and negotiation.[19]

In the fall of 1918 Lenin was particularly anxious to avoid further armed conflict with the capitalist world. The Soviet regime was in a difficult position, struggling with serious internal problems of famine, economic collapse, and counterrevolution, and simultaneously fighting off external attacks from separatists, White Russians, and Allied forces already in Russia. Six separate offensives were being launched against the Bolsheviks on as many different fronts. The transportation system had largely broken down, and the supply of food and fuel to the cities was endangered.[20] As Lenin himself remarked the following spring, in December 1918 the Soviet regime could not have withstood a concerted Anglo-French attack.[21]

A respite in terms of even a temporary cessation of civil war and intervention was desperately needed. Such a "breathing spell" promised a number of advantages, from the Soviet point of view. Not only would a final, and undoubtedly successful, Allied attack be forestalled, but Soviet Russia would gain an opportunity to regroup its forces and to consolidate its internal position. Menshevik and Socialist-Revolutionary elements who had broken with the Soviet regime following what they branded as "the treason of Brest-Litovsk" began, in the period after the Armistice, to swing back to the Bolsheviks. They became convinced that the Soviet government, in opposing Allied intervention, was defending Russia and the revolution against foreign attack.[22] Lenin hoped to rally these forces behind the constructive work of the regime. He also believed that greater peasant adherence to the Bolshevik cause might be won.[23]

Moreover, the Soviet leaders were convinced that in several respects time was on their side. Every moment brought nearer the "inevitable" world revolution, with its promise of rescuing Soviet Russia from her difficulties.[24] At the same time, as the policies of the counterrevolution-

---

[19] *Ibid.*, XXII, 17, 18; XXIV, 116–18; XXV, 498–99; M. I. Trush, *Vneshnepoliticheskaia deiatel'nost' V.I. Lenina: 1917–1920, den' za dnem* (*The Foreign Political Activity of V.I. Lenin: 1917–1920, Day by Day*) (Moscow, 1963), 28–29.

[20] See the graphic eyewitness account of conditions in Soviet Russia in the winter of 1918–1919 in Arthur J. Ransome, *Russia in 1919* (New York, 1919), 65 *passim*.

[21] Lenin, *Sochineniia*, XXIV, 235.

[22] See pp. 173–74 of ch. five for Menshevik and Socialist Revolutionary statements in this regard.

[23] Lenin, *Collected Works*, XXIII, 305–13, 317, 320–46, 438–49.

[24] *Ibid.*, XXIII, 26–27; see also the report of Chicherin, the Soviet foreign minister, to the Fifth Congress of Soviets on July 4, 1918, in Degras, *Soviet Documents*, I, 83–85.

ary governments were put into effect in the territories they held, the people would quickly realize what a return to the old regime meant and would turn to and support the Bolsheviks. Furthermore, Lenin in his speeches during the fall of 1918 repeatedly found hope, not only for the world revolution but also for the successful defense of Soviet Russia, in the growing demoralization of the Allied armies and peoples. He believed that troops of the Entente in contact with the Bolsheviks were rapidly assuming a revolutionary attitude, while, by intervention and their predatory actions at the conference table, the French and British imperialists were revealing their greed to their own peoples and to the peoples of the world. They were, thus, in Lenin's phrase, "digging their own graves." [25]

Consequently, the first task of Soviet diplomacy in the fall of 1918, as six months earlier during negotiation of the Treaty of Brest-Litovsk, was to buy time, no matter what the cost, and to forestall further attacks on Soviet Russia. To do this the Soviet government launched a persistent, full-scale "peace offensive." The post-Armistice mood of war-weariness and disillusionment described in the first chapter provided a receptive setting for this effort; at the same time Soviet peace proposals contributed to the widespread unrest by increasing the popular longing for peace and by stirring up liberal and labor discontent with the Russian policies of the Allied governments.

From October 1918 through January 1919 the Soviet government officially proposed peace to the Western powers on at least seven different occasions. The form of these proposals was usually a diplomatic note sent through neutral channels or an open proclamation broadcast by radio and printed in radical newspapers abroad. With the exception of an extremely caustic and insulting letter of October 24, 1918, from Soviet Foreign Minister Chicherin to Wilson, in which Chicherin noted that Eugene Debs had not yet replaced Wilson as President and asked what ransom and tribute the West demanded of the Russian people, the Soviet peace appeals were uniformly well-written and conciliatory, with a conspicuous absence of revolutionary rudeness.[26] Moreover, the Soviet government consistently indicated that it was willing to pay a high price for peace. Most of the messages offered substantial economic and finan-

[25] Lenin, *Sochineniia*, XXIII, 272, 436, 449.

[26] Chicherin's letter is printed in Degras, *Soviet Documents*, I, 118–19. Lenin requested that it be prepared "in order to stop the bloodletting and to open the eyes of the masses." Trush, 28–29, 168. According to Fischer (I, 147 n. 1), Radek prepared the original draft. Litvinov later said the note was a "mistake," being "propaganda journalism, discourteous in tone and calculated to repel rather than to conciliate." Notes by William H. Buckler of a conversation with Mr. Litvinov, Wilson Papers, Series VIIIA, Box 11.

cial concessions to the Allies, and some also spoke of Soviet readiness to surrender Russian territory.

The concept of appealing to the West in the name of economic advantage which, in Chicherin's words, "became one of the most outstanding [ideas] in Lenin's foreign policy," and which was to remain a central premise of Soviet diplomacy into the 1920's, was adumbrated in a preliminary and unofficial plan for Russian-American commercial relations, submitted by Lenin to Raymond Robins, the American Red Cross representative in Russia, on May 14, 1918.[27] In his report to the Fifth Congress of Soviets on July 4, 1918, Chicherin referred to elements in the imperialist camp who, instead of robbery, preferred trade, concessions, and economic conquest.[28] The first official Soviet attempt to lure the West with the bait of future profits in Russia came in the previously cited sarcastic note from Chicherin to Wilson. The Soviet foreign minister concluded his letter by demanding "precise and business-like replies" to his questions concerning the economic and territorial concessions required by the Allies as the price of peace and concerning the terms and conditions prescribed by the French for repayment of Russia's debt. This insulting inquiry, with its insinuation of the baseness of Allied motives, was followed on November 5 by a more straightforward statement. In a note to Lansing, sent through neutral channels, Chicherin said that the Bolsheviks were "prepared to make far more concessions to the Entente powers in order to arrive at an understanding" and asked for an opportunity to enter into negotiations with the United States. Commenting on this proposal, Lansing said that there would be no answer and no negotiations.[29]

In early December the Soviet government sent Maxim Litvinov to Stockholm as its plenipotentiary representative to the West. He was charged with establishing direct contact with the Allies in order to sound them out on the prospects of ending intervention and making peace in Russia. Litvinov was empowered to offer concessions on behalf of his government, and in an interview with the London *Daily News* shortly after his arrival, he hinted that the Soviet regime might be willing to grant commercial and economic concessions to the Allies in return for a moratorium on Russia's war debts.[30] On December 23 Litvinov ad-

---

[27] The plan is printed in Cumming and Pettit, 204–12. Chicherin's words are quoted in Fischer, I, 353.

[28] Degras, *Soviet Documents*, I, 84.

[29] United States Department of State, *Papers Relating to the Foreign Relations of the United States: 1918, Supplement I* (Washington, 1933), I, 471, 484, 488.

[30] Fischer, I, 156; see Henry L. Roberts, "Maxim Litvinov" in Gordon A. Craig and Felix Gilbert, eds, *The Diplomats, 1919–39* (Princeton, 1953), 344–77, for an excellent analysis of the aims and style of Litvinov's diplomacy.

dressed a letter to the ministers of the United States, England, France, and Italy in Stockholm, officially proposing negotiations in these words: "I have been authorized by the Soviet government to enter into preliminary peace negotiations with representatives of the Allied countries should their governments reciprocate the desire of the Russian Republic for a peaceful settlement of all the outstanding questions which may give rise to a continuation of hostilities between the countries concerned." [31] The British immediately responded to this offer, the Imperial War Cabinet deciding on the following day "to enter into formal negotiations with an alleged Bolshevik representative to hear his proposals." [32] In the resulting *pourparlers* Litvinov suggested to the British that negotiations be undertaken on the basis of the following proposals: no indemnities, no regulation by the Allies of Russia's frontiers, qualified compensation to be paid by the Soviet government for foreign holdings it had nationalized, no Soviet reprisals against Russians who had cooperated with the Allies, introduction in Soviet Russia of nearly universal suffrage and of freedom of the press as soon as conditions permitted, and noninterference by the Allies in Russia's internal affairs.[33]

The biggest success of Litvinov's peace campaign, however, was a Christmas Eve appeal he addressed to President Wilson. This letter was persuasively written and cleverly timed (not only on Christmas Eve but at the very moment when Wilson was being given an enthusiastic reception in Europe and when popular acclaim of him as the world's hope for a just and democratic peace was at its height).[34] Litvinov's message was undoubtedly an important factor in persuading Wilson to endeavor to make peace in Russia, although, as we saw earlier, the president, even before he sailed for Europe, was a prey to increasing doubts concerning the wisdom of continued intervention.[35] Wilson showed the letter to Lloyd George, who was deeply impressed, and it was later circulated among the leaders of the peace conference.

Litvinov's appeal was an effective piece of work; its wording, content,

---

[31] *1919, Russia,* 1.

[32] Henry Borden, ed., *Robert Laird Borden: His Memoirs* (New York, 1938), II, 886. Hereafter cited as *Borden Memoirs.*

[33] British Foreign Office, *Documents,* III, 440.

[34] Fischer notes that in June 1918 Litvinov became convinced, from his observations in London, that the British and French were determined to intervene against the Bolsheviks; consequently, he planned to go to America, believing that Wilson's attitude was more reasonable. The United States, however, refused him a visa. Fischer, I, 300–01.

[35] At about the time of Litvinov's appeal Wilson also received several official American reports and messages opposing intervention; e.g., a telegram from Chief of Staff March suggesting the withdrawal of American troops from Russia and memoranda on the anti-intervention mood of British labor and liberal circles. Wilson Papers, Series VIIIA, Box 5.

and tone were all conciliatory and reasonable.[36] Litvinov began by stating that the Soviet government was prepared to enter into peace negotiations on the basis of Wilson's principles of justice and humanity. He pointed out that Russian workers and peasants had been the first to declare in favor of self-determination and against militarism and secret diplomacy. They were now "prepared to go to any length of concession . . . if they can secure thereby conditions enabling them to work out peacefully their social schemes." Litvinov maintained that Allied attacks had forced the Bolsheviks to rearm and to suspend the task of reconstruction and that intervention had been responsible for "terrible privations, bordering on starvation." Furthermore, the Red terror had been "not the cause but the direct result and outcome of Allied intervention."

In conclusion, Litvinov emphasized that there were only two possible courses for the Allied statesmen at Paris to follow: one was to continue open or disguised intervention, which, if successful, would lead to a White terror, a military dictatorship or the restoration of the monarchy, and the paralyzing of the economic development of the country; the other was to withdraw their troops and conclude peace, with all the benefits which this would bring. Litvinov urged the president to lift the blockade, "to help Russia to regain her own sources of supply, and to give her technical advice as to how to exploit her natural resources in the most effective way, for the benefit of all countries badly in need of foodstuffs and raw material." Litvinov objected that "representatives of the accused side have never been allowed to put fully their case and to answer the charges made against them"; and he closed with a most effective entreaty: "I venture to appeal to your sense of justice and impartiality. I hope and trust, above all, that before deciding on any course of action, you will give justice to the demand of *audiatur et altera pars* [let the other side be heard]."

This reasonable argument was well calculated to appeal to Wilson's liberalism. It was based on the same theory that Lloyd George had propounded at the inter-Allied conference in early December and that ultimately produced the Prinkipo proposal—that all sides to the Russian controversy should be heard before the peace conference determined its policy toward Russia. Litvinov's letter was unquestionably a significant factor in preparing the ground for the Prinkipo plan, helping to win Wilson over to the position toward which Lloyd George was already moving. And it was not long in taking effect: only a few days after Christmas Wilson suggested to Lloyd George that they ask "Litvinov formally and definitely what his proposals are"; and on New Year's Day, immediately after his return to Paris from London, the president decided to send Wil-

[36] For the complete text of the letter, see Degras, *Soviet Documents*, I, 129–32.

liam H. Buckler, a special assistant at the American embassy in London and a half-brother of Henry White, to hear what Litvinov had to say.[37]

After brief consultation in Paris, Buckler left for Stockholm on January 9.[38] From January 14 to 16 Buckler was closeted with Litvinov. The latter declared that the Soviet government was prepared to compromise on all points, including Russia's foreign debt, protection for existing foreign enterprises, and the granting of economic concessions.[39] As confirmation, Litvinov showed Buckler a wire from Chicherin, officially offering a number of issues for negotiation and pointing out that Russia sorely needed technical and financial advice and Western imports. In addition, Litvinov promised that, with peace, revolutionary propaganda abroad and terror at home would cease, since they were both purely defensive measures. As final bait, undoubtedly intended for Wilson, he hinted at Soviet support of an antiwar, nonreactionary League of Nations.

Litvinov's proposals included almost every concession contained in the Soviet reply to the Prinkipo invitation a month later. The Soviet leaders were desperately consistent in their offers of compromise. Buckler expressed his view that the prompt opening of negotiations and the granting of fair terms by the Allies would win concessions and fair terms in return. Buckler concluded that "the conciliatory attitude of the Soviet government is unquestionable."

Buckler's report of the concessions offered by Litvinov had a significant impact on the deliberations at Paris. President Wilson introduced the report just as the first conference debate over Russia was reaching a climax. On January 20 and on the morning of January 21, the Council of Ten heard oral presentations from Noulens, the French ambassador to Russia, and Scavenius, the former Danish minister to Russia, urging intervention against the Bolsheviks.[40] After their appearance Wilson read Buckler's report to the Council. The Council then discussed the Russian question again and finally authorized Wilson to draw up the Prinkipo proposal. Later Bullitt testified: "The Buckler meeting with Litvinov was what eventually swung the meeting in favor of Prinkipo." [41]

[37] On the suggestion to Lloyd George, see p. 79 of ch. three; on the January 1 decision to send Buckler to Stockholm, House Papers, Diary, January 1, 1919.

[38] *1919, Russia,* 4. Several books on early Soviet foreign policy (e.g., Fischer) state that Buckler departed in the first few days of January, confusing his trip from London to Paris for consultation with his journey to Stockholm a week later. Fischer also incorrectly links Buckler's mission with the British proposal of January 2, described below. Fischer, I, 159.

[39] Buckler's telegraphic reports of his conversations with Litvinov are in *1919, Russia,* 15–18, and *Peace Conference,* III, 643–46.

[40] *Ibid.,* III, 643. See pp. 102–04 below for a résumé of their reports.

[41] *The Bullitt Mission to Russia: The Testimony of William C. Bullitt before the Committee on Foreign Relations, United States Senate* (New York, 1919), 6. Hereafter cited as *Bullitt Mission.*

Although the Litvinov campaign was by far the most successful aspect of the Soviet "peace offensive," other efforts of the Soviet leaders to obtain peace continued at an unabated pace in this period. In a note to the State Department on January 12, 1919, Chicherin refuted a press statement, picked up by the Bolshevik radio, in which Senator Hitchcock, chairman of the Senate Foreign Relations Committee, had listed five reasons justifying intervention. Chicherin ended by summarizing the many Soviet attempts to obtain peace through diplomatic channels and requested a time and place for the opening of negotiations.[42] On January 17, having learned that the French General Confederation of Labor and the administrative committee of the French Socialist Party had taken a stand against intervention, the Soviet government sent an open radiogram to the Entente asking when negotiations to end intervention could be begun.[43]

But by this time events were moving rapidly at Paris, and the steady pressure of the Soviet campaign for peace was on the verge of bearing fruit. While now shifting our attention to the origin and formulation of the proposal for a Russian peace conference on the Prinkipo Islands, we must not forget the general situation which fostered the birth and growth of this concept. Without the Soviet "peace offensive" and the war-weariness and political and social discontent on which it played, the Prinkipo idea would never have been developed into a concrete proposal.

Origin of the Prinkipo Proposal

In discussing the question of Russian representation at the peace talks, Lloyd George had suggested at an inter-Allied conference in early December that all parties to the Russian conflict, including the Bolsheviks, should be heard.[44] On December 30, in a meeting of the Imperial War Cabinet, this idea was picked up and expanded by Sir Robert Borden, the Canadian prime minister. Borden pointed out that it was hardly an end of war if the peace conference left five or six nations and governments still fighting in Russia. He proposed, therefore, that "in lieu of forcible intervention, the Governments of the various states in Russia should be induced to send representatives to Paris for conference with the Allied and Associated Nations." The Allies could then exert pressure on the Russian factions to get them to stop their fighting and to agree on the creation of one stable government under the protection of the

[42] *1919, Russia,* 9.
[43] G. Chicherin, *Two Years of Soviet Foreign Policy* (New York, 1920), 30.
[44] See p. 80 of ch. three.

League of Nations.[45] This was the first expression of the Prinkipo idea, which was to develop rapidly in the succeeding three weeks.

On December 31 the Cabinet resumed its consideration of the Russian problem.[46] There was general agreement that past Western policy had been one of "drifting" and had had the effect of "merely poking with sticks into the kennel to infuriate the dog." However, Lord Robert Cecil, who spoke of British promises to the Czechs and of the dangers of Bolshevik expansion westward, and Churchill, who argued that while he was all for negotiation and joint action, any settlement with Russia would have to be imposed on her by force, opposed an outright renunciation of intervention. Lord Curzon supported them: in general he did not favor intervention because of the strain it imposed on British resources; it was, however, like "walling off a fire in a mine" and should be continued, at least in the Caucasus.[47]

In discounting intervention, Lloyd George stressed the immensity of the undertaking, the Germans with a million men not having been able to succeed in it. "Where were we to find troops with which to march into the heart of Russia and occupy the country? We already had to find troops for Germany, Palestine, Mesopotamia, and the Caucasus. . . . No British troops could be found for the purpose [of occupying Russia] without conscription, and if Parliament endorsed conscription, he doubted whether the troops would go." Pointing to the lesson of the French Revolution, Lloyd George added that intervention only strengthened the Bolsheviks by stirring up patriotic feelings on their behalf and that it would be better to let Bolshevism fall of itself. These were all arguments Lloyd George was later to present to the peace conference. At length the Cabinet agreed on a compromise: it supported Borden's proposal for conferring with the various Russian factions and disapproved further intervention, but it also decided that aid to existing governments threatened with Bolshevik aggression should be continued and that no troops should be withdrawn from Russia, pending the outcome of Borden's plan and of the deliberations of the Paris Peace Conference, where, it was agreed, Russia should be one of the first subjects of discussion.

The decision of the Cabinet was implemented on January 2, 1919, when the British government sent identical diplomatic notes to the prin-

[45] *Borden Memoirs,* II, 889–90, and Lloyd George, I, 199–200.

[46] *Ibid.,* I, 325–30. See also the accounts of this important meeting in *Borden Memoirs,* II, 889–90, and Callwell, *Wilson Diaries,* II, 158–59.

[47] In his memoirs Lloyd George commented caustically that Churchill and Curzon were the most powerful British advocates of intervention; Churchill, because "his ducal blood revolted against the wholesale elimination of Grand Dukes in Russia," and Curzon, because he had a special affection for the Caucasus as a result of a visit there some years before. Lloyd George, II, 325–30.

cipal Allied and Associated Powers, suggesting that the Allies call for a cease-fire in Russia, after which they would agree to confer with representatives of the various groups in Russia concerning a permanent settlement of the Russian problem. The British proposed a draft note to the Soviet and other Russian governments as follows:

> One of their [the Powers at Paris] first tasks will be an endeavor to bring about peace in Russia, to reconcile conflicting national parties and peoples both in Russia and in adjacent states and territories, and to bring succor to the suffering population. . . .
>
> The Great, Friendly Powers call upon all the governments, parties, and peoples . . . to abstain from further aggression, hostilities, and reprisals, and require them to keep the peace both at home and with their neighbors.
>
> If the aforesaid governments and parties will immediately suspend hostilities on all fronts for the duration of the Peace Negotiations, then if they or any of them should desire to send representatives to Paris to discuss with the Great Powers conditions of a permanent settlement, the Great Powers would be prepared to enter on such a discussion with them.[48]

In elaborating Borden's suggestion, the British Foreign Office framed the proposal in such a way that it took on anti-Bolshevik overtones and also served British plans for establishing spheres of influence in Russia. Borden had recommended consultation, during which measures for ending hostilities could be worked out. The Foreign Office proposed a cease-fire, then consultation. At that time Bolshevik forces were moving rapidly westward in the wake of the Germans, who, despite the injunction in the Armistice that they stay in Russia, were withdrawing from Byelorussia and the Ukraine. As a result, the Red Army was beginning to exert pressure on the Baltic areas. The British were much concerned by this threat. In commenting on the proposed appeal for a cessation of hostilies in Russia, the British note declared that action should be taken at once in view of the plight of the Baltic peoples, "who are in danger of being exterminated within the next few weeks." The Foreign Office apparently felt that an immediate cease-fire would halt the Bolshevik advance and might lead to recognition of the nascent Baltic states.

French reaction to the British *aide-mémoire* was hostile and uncompromising. On January 11, in a violation of diplomatic etiquette, French Foreign Minister Pichon issued a press statement on the confidential British note, in which he minced few words. He flatly rejected the pro-

[48] *1919, Russia*, 2–3. Although the British proposal was presented in Washington on January 3, it was dated January 2.

posal, although he announced with considerable sarcasm that he rendered "full homage to the generous spirit of universal reconciliation with which the British government was inspired in making this proposition." Pichon asserted that he was quite willing to hear other Russian groups, but to invite the Bolsheviks implied their recognition and was therefore insufferable. In conclusion, he made the well-known declaration: "The French government, so far as it is concerned, will make no contract with crime." [49] The action of the French in revealing the contents of a diplomatic note and in taking a dogmatic position before consultation with their allies boded ill for the success of the British proposition. The note had been circulated as a basis for discussion, yet the French had unilaterally announced a policy. Pichon's statement clearly foreshadowed the difficulties of attempting to formulate a joint Allied policy toward Russia at the peace conference.

Within the American government efforts were meanwhile being made to persuade Wilson to enunciate a definite policy toward Russia. These efforts were spurred by mounting public and congressional opposition to intervention. In the United States the campaign against intervention produced strange bedfellows; isolationists like Senators Johnson and Borah found themselves joined with liberal journalists like Oswald Garrison Villard of *The Nation* in protesting the presence of American troops in Russia.[50] Partisan critics of Wilson and congressmen and editors from Michigan and Wisconsin, the home states of most of the soldiers in North Russia, joined in the hue and cry. In early January Acting Secretary of State Polk was called before the Senate Foreign Relations Committee to explain United States policy regarding Russia. Subsequently, he privately "briefed" Senators Swanson and Hitchcock so that they could defend American actions in Russia in the Senate and before the public.[51] On January 7 Governor Sleeper of Michigan wired President Wilson concerning the plight of American troops in Russia. General Bliss, to whom the telegram was referred, was not sympathetic to continued intervention and avoided drafting a reply. On January 27 Wilson finally answered, enclosing a not entirely accurate report from General Pershing to the effect that the morale, discipline, and health of the troops were excellent, but saying nothing concerning their future disposition.[52]

The State and War departments were by no means agreed as to what should be done concerning the Russian situation. In December General

---

[49] *L'Humanité,* January 11, 1919, quoted in Cumming and Pettit, 280–81. See also a British summary of the official French reply in *1919, Russia,* 7.

[50] For a report on the agitation against intervention, see Polk's telegram to Lansing, December 31, 1918, *Peace Conference,* II, 483.

[51] *Ibid.,* II, 485, and Polk Papers, Diary, January 15, 1919.

[52] Wilson Papers, Series VIIIA, Boxes 8, 15.

March threatened to withdraw American troops from Siberia, but was rebuked by the president, who wired from Europe that he trusted nothing of this sort would be done until he had been fully consulted about the matter. On January 1 Secretary of War Baker wrote Wilson, reporting the restlessness of the soldiers in Russia and referring to the agitation at home against intervention.[53] On the other hand, Polk was urging issuance of a United States declaration against the growing menace of Bolshevism, and by cable discussed with Lansing the feasibility of further American support to Kolchak, short of recognition. Moreover, Polk was opposed to the British proposal of January 2, calling it "a very bad plan, as the Bolsheviks would not stop and it would merely have the effect of discouraging the liberals [in Russia]." [54]

At this time House, who was opposed to intervention, was again urging that the answer to Bolshevism lay in food relief and economic assistance. On January 6 he wrote:

> . . . Bolshevism is steadily creeping westward. Intervention would only aggravate it. . . . Not only would it aggravate it, but . . . it would be impossible to realize even if it were advisable and just. There is not a western country that could safely send troops into Russia without creating labor troubles at home. It seems to me therefore that a barrier should be raised by helping the Central Powers to bring about stable, democratic governments of the right sort. To do this it is necessary to send food there and lift the blockade and other restrictions.[55]

On January 8 House discussed the problems of Russia and Bolshevism with Clemenceau and Orlando. House noted in his diary that they both agreed with him that military intervention was impossible. It seems probable, however, that the two veteran politicians, both of whom wanted to keep in House's good graces in order to use him later as a lever of persuasion on Wilson, merely acquiesced in House's vigorous exposition of his idea for checking Bolshevism with food instead of arms.

Wilson, having decided to dispatch Buckler to hear what Litvinov had to say, was at this time increasingly attracted to the possibility of dealing with the Bolsheviks and making peace in Russia. He wrote Lansing on January 9, in reference to Polish attempts to find recruits in the United States for a crusade against Bolshevism: "It is clearly out of the ques-

[53] *Ibid.*, Series VIIIA, Boxes 7–9. Wilson's reply, if he made one, is lacking.
[54] *1919, Russia*, 3, 323–26; Polk Papers, Diary, January 3, 1919.
[55] House Papers, letter to Norman Hapgood, January 6, 1919. House was strongly supported in this position by General Bliss, Bliss Papers, Box 65, Diary, January 2, 6, 7, 1919.

tion to allow Poles to be enlisted in the United States to fight against peoples with whom the United States is at peace and whose affairs the United States is trying to compose. . . ." [56] And on January 10, when Lansing referred Polk's suggestion of an official declaration against Bolshevism to him, Wilson commented: "I must say that I still see no great advantage to be derived from words and public statements in the matter of Bolshevism. What I am at present keenly interested in is in finding the interior of their minds, and I hope that you have been able to get hold of Buckley [sic] and get him started to the interviews . . . which I regard as of capital importance." [57]

While the American leaders were weighing various approaches to the Russian problem and the British were developing their proposal to hear the Bolsheviks and other Russian groups, the French, in concert with their Polish ally, were busy working out a scheme to form an anti-Bolshevik base of operations in Poland, supported primarily by American soldiers. In the latter part of December several Polish agents approached General Bliss. They proposed that in order to save Poland from Bolshevism and to help establish a *cordon sanitaire* against this scourge, seventy thousand American troops should be sent to Poland to guard the railway lines and to restore order. On January 2 Marshal Foch broached a similiar plan to Bliss. As he had done with the Poles, Bliss replied that America would not contribute troops to such a venture. He urged instead that the westward advance of Bolshevism could best be halted by giving economic assistance and relief to Germany.[58]

On January 7 Foch took up with House another version of the Franco-Polish proposal. In a memorandum of that date Foch argued that it was essential to erect a barrier of stable and cooperating states in Eastern Europe against the menace of Bolshevism. To strengthen Poland, the key member of such a coalition, an Allied contingent, composed chiefly of American troops and commanded by an American, should be sent to Poland to guard the Danzig-Thorn railway line. According to Foch, this would permit the safe and rapid return to Poland of Polish troops in France and Italy and would ensure the maintenance of order in Poland.[59] This plan had certain obvious advantages for the French: its realization would have been an important step in the establishment of Clemenceau's *cordon sanitaire*; it would have strengthened Poland,

[56] Wilson Papers, Series VIIIA, Box 8.
[57] Note to Lansing of January 10. *Ibid.*, Series VIIIA, Box 9.
[58] Bliss Papers, Box 65, Diary, December 22, 29, 1918, and January 2, 3, 1919.
[59] Conversation between Colonel House and Marshal Foch, January 7, 1919. House Papers, Drawer 29, File 26. The same day the American delegates considered Foch's proposal. Bliss opposed it and felt that Wilson and the others agreed with him. Bliss Papers, Box 65, Diary, January 7, 1919.

France's new eastern ally; and it would have associated the United States with French plans for Eastern Europe and committed America to action against Bolshevism.

When the working sessions of the peace conference began on January 12, Foch advanced essentially the same scheme before the Council of Ten, but with its anti-Bolshevik objectives minimized, perhaps in deference to the known desire of Lloyd George and Wilson to make peace in Russia. Although Foch only uttered the word Bolshevism once, discussion quickly focused on this issue. Wilson, who was awaiting the outcome of Buckler's talks with Litvinov, suggested that they postpone a decision on Foch's proposal, "since it formed part of the much larger question of checking the advance of Bolshevism to the west. There was room for great doubt as to whether this advance could be checked by arms at all." [60]

Foch then submitted a second plan, avowedly anti-Bolshevik in purpose. He suggested that Russian prisoners of war in Germany be repatriated to non-Soviet areas of Russia for use against the Bolsheviks. This time it was Lloyd George who objected that such a proposal was also an aspect of the general policy toward Bolshevism, as yet undecided. No decision was reached on Foch's two schemes, pending consideration of the British proposal for a cease-fire in Russia followed by consultations with the Russian parties. The contrapuntal pattern which was to mark discussion by the peace conference of the Russian question was thus established at the outset: plans for the forcible suppression of Bolshevism balanced by efforts at conciliation and peacemaking in Russia. The policy of the conference toward Russia constantly wavered between these alternatives.

On January 16 the peacemakers turned to the task of attempting to thrash out a common policy toward Russia.[61] Lloyd George opened the discussion by remarking that the French had certainly misunderstood the British proposal of January 2, judging by Pichon's outcry to the press. The British had no intention of recognizing the Soviet government, and the proposal was not meant as even an implied recognition of the Bolsheviks; nor were the British considering the seating of Bolshevik delegates at the conference on an equal basis with the Powers. Rather it was

[60] Minutes of this meeting are in *Peace Conference*, III, 471–81. The proposal was discussed again on January 22 as part of the general question of conference policy toward Poland (*ibid.*, III, 670–75), and on February 25 as part of a larger anti-Bolshevik scheme of the French. See pp. 183–85 of ch. six.

[61] Minutes of January 16. *Ibid.*, III, 581–84, 589–93. Until January 22 two sets of minutes were kept, one an American report, the other a joint American-British version. The two records correspond on the major points although there is some discrepancy in detail.

an attempt to get at the facts and to face reality. Bolshevism had to be dealt with, for it was getting stronger—this report was from the British military authorities in Russia, who could hardly be suspected of leanings toward Bolshevism! [62]

After this attempt to appease the French Lloyd George analyzed three possible policies open to the Allies. The first, military intervention, he rejected as "sheer madness." Admittedly Bolshevism was a great danger, but who was to crush it? It had taken the Germans a million men to garrison just the fringes of European Russia, while the dispatch of only a thousand Allied troops would result in mutiny. "If a military enterprise were started against the Bolsheviki, that would make England Bolshevist and there would be a Soviet in London." The second solution, a *cordon sanitaire,* would be a death cordon, not a health cordon; it would be too inhuman. Besides, even if the Soviets were weakened by blockade and siege, who would overthrow them? Lloyd George expressed little faith in any of the White leaders: Kolchak was a monarchist at heart and the Czechoslovaks were now refusing to fight for him, while Denikin "was occupying a little backyard near the Black Sea" and was separated from Kolchak by a huge expanse of territory. The British prime minister concluded that "if the Allies counted on any of these men, he believed they were building on quicksand."

As a final possibility, Lloyd George proposed calling Russian representatives to Paris in much the same way that the Roman Empire had summoned tributary chiefs for an accounting of their actions. (The leading Soviet history of diplomacy wryly commented on this analogy: "Lloyd George omitted only one trifling circumstance: Russia had not entered into the makeup of the British Empire." [63]) The British leader declared that the last solution was the only possible one, and at the same

---

[62] Lloyd George was armed with a remarkable document entitled "Appreciation of the Internal Situation in Russia, January 12, 1919." Wilson Papers, Series VIIIA, Box 10. This report, prepared by the General Staff of the War Office, brilliantly analyzed the Soviet position, outlining the theoretical and practical reasons for the Bolsheviks' eagerness to conciliate the Allies and make peace, and describing growing support for the Soviet regime from those disillusioned with White Russian policies or repelled by foreign intervention. The paper also discussed the dilemma of the White Russian leaders in attempting to adopt liberal policies in the face of reactionary support and their difficulties in dealing with the national minorities. The report contrasted vividly with many reports from Russia and much of the current opinion—that the Bolsheviks were on the verge of collapse. On January 20 Lloyd George sent it to Wilson. The latter also had a memorandum on the Russian situation from his technical advisor on Russia, Prof. R. H. Lord, dated January 16. Lord's report, while full of accurate data, tended to stress Soviet weakness in its interpretations. *Ibid.,* Series VIIIA, Box 11.

[63] V. P. Potemkin, ed., *Istoriia diplomatii* (*History of Diplomacy*) (Moscow, 1941–45), III, 57.

time endeavored to quiet French fears of having the Bolsheviks in Paris by stating his conviction "that an educated democracy can always be trusted to turn down Bolshevism."

The French were certainly not pleased with Lloyd George's plan and remained unconvinced by his arguments. But instead of definitely rejecting the British proposal, Pichon merely suggested that the conference had better hear Noulens, French ambassador to Russia, who had just returned to France, before making such an important decision. President Wilson immediately took up the cudgels on Lloyd George's behalf and began to remonstrate with the French. In a long, idealistic exposition, which probably appealed little to the practical, hard-headed Clemenceau, Wilson set forth some of his fundamental beliefs about social progress.[64] The president argued that because of general world revulsion against large vested interests, both political and economic, Bolshevism had a certain appeal and won support among some people. Even though reform was being carried out through discussion and evolution, the world was becoming impatient and some men of the finest temper were in sympathy with the aspirations of Bolshevism. For example, in the United States there were vital capital-labor grievances which needed to be speedily solved if they were not to provide fertile soil for the seeds of Bolshevism.

By the same token, the president declared, British and American troops were unwilling to go to Russia for fear of restoring the old order. Moreover, foreign intervention facilitated Bolshevik control of Russia; if it were ended, the Bolsheviks might lose the support of those who were now backing them from patriotic motives. Wilson concluded by urging the adoption of Lloyd George's proposal, with the added condition that the Bolsheviks should first be required to withdraw from Poland and Lithuania.

He was accorded exactly the same reception as Lloyd George: Pichon suggested that they hear Noulens. Baron Sonnino, the Italian foreign minister, then proposed that they also listen to Scavenius, a Danish diplomat recently returned from Russia. Since Wilson and Lloyd George had been insisting on the importance of hearing all sides of the Russian question, there was nothing they could do but agree to hear Noulens and Scavenius. The meeting adjourned without the British and American leaders having made any apparent headway.

In the meeting itself French opposition to conferring with the Russians had been expressed only by a stony silence. Outside the conference

---

[64] Later Lansing commented: "The President favored it [Lloyd George's proposal] in a long but, I did not think, convincing speech. He is by no means at his best in these conferences." Lansing Papers, Desk Diary, January 16.

room, however, the French lobbied against Lloyd George's proposal. This provoked an outburst of bad feeling between Lloyd George and Clemenceau and nearly split the British delegation. At a small dinner on January 19, given by Lloyd George and attended only by Bonar Law, the leader of the House of Commons, Sir William Wiseman, and a few intimate friends and relatives of the British prime minister, the latter held forth at length on the Russian problem.[65] According to Wiseman's account of the conversation, Lloyd George stated that the French wanted to make war on the Bolsheviks, a war with American money and American troops to suit French purposes. Clemenceau had therefore opposed the British proposal for hearing the various Russian factions.[66] Despairing of being able to dissuade Lloyd George from this course, Clemenceau had gone to see Balfour; the latter had thereupon written a note to Lloyd George proposing that the Bolsheviks not be recognized but that a food commission should be sent to Moscow, nominally to deal with the Bolsheviks on the question of relief, but also to sound them out politically. Lloyd George said that he had disapproved of this proposal. He expressed his annoyance with Clemenceau for seeing Balfour and accused the French premier of attempting to divide the British delegation. In great excitement, the British leader then told the dinner group that he would see Clemenceau and put a stop to such activities; if Clemenceau demurred, he (Lloyd George) would return to England, leaving Balfour in charge at Paris without authority to make final decisions. After Bonar Law pointed out that such action would also constitute implied criticism of Balfour for seeing Clemenceau, Lloyd George calmed down but insisted that he was still going to speak to Clemenceau about the incident. Bonar Law then told Lloyd George that the Conservative Party strongly disliked Bolshevism, and if the prime minister made an issue of his proposal for a meeting with the Russians, it would "break up your Government." At this, Lloyd George flared up again, declaring that "if that is the case, the Government had better be broken," and adding: "The old man [Clemenceau] must be taken by the scruff of the neck!"

After this behind-the-scenes contretemps, the French continued their campaign to forestall a meeting with the Bolsheviks by having Noulens appear before the peace conference on January 20. He was one of the most colorful characters to appear on the peace conference stage. Noulens had a striking appearance, possessing a mammoth head adorned by a great walrus mustache. He represented the extreme interventionist point of view. An ardent French patriot, he despised the Bol-

[65] House Papers, Wiseman Diary, January 19, 1919.
[66] Wiseman noted parenthetically that Clemenceau had reportedly threatened to resign if the proposal were pressed to adoption.

sheviks for taking Russia out of the war. At the same time he was outraged and frustrated by the weakness and ineffectualness of the White
Russian governments. In later years Noulens sympathized with fascism
and declared in his memoirs that "firm" policies, such as those of
Mussolini in Italy, could have crushed the Bolsheviks.[67]

In opening his remarks, Noulens denied that his report was designed
to serve French interests or to influence the conference to adopt policies
recommended by the French.[68] Yet his entire statement was devoted to
depicting Bolshevism as so weak that only a token Allied intervention
force would be needed to destroy it. He had apparently been warned
that neither Wilson nor Lloyd George believed the troops necessary for
large-scale intervention were available. Noulens' report was widely at
variance with the facts and is significant only as indicating the caliber of
the information on which the French were basing their policies.[69]

Throughout the session Lloyd George was antagonistic to Noulens
and continually interrupted him to challenge his statements. For example, in attempting to show how little effort would be required to defeat
the Bolsheviks, Noulens claimed that in North Russia the Allies and
White Russians were standing off the Red Army, even though outnum-
bered two to one. Lloyd George at once countered with official British
figures, reporting that sixteen thousand British were opposing only five
thousand Bolsheviks. Noulens retorted that this only proved that the
Red Army was very small! In his memoirs Lloyd George asserted that
Noulens "was inclined to be pompous, sententious, and not informative.
He was a shallow and unintelligent partisan rather than a witness." [70]

On the night of January 20 the question of policy toward Russia was
thrashed out in a meeting of the British Empire delegation.[71] After
commenting disparagingly on Noulens' testimony, Lloyd George reported that in a private meeting in Pichon's office with General Franchet
d'Espérey, the latter had urged formation of a *cordon sanitaire* against
the Bolsheviks, utilizing White Russian forces supported by Allied volunteers and money. Lloyd George told his colleagues that the Americans
would not support such a scheme and asked whether Australia and
Canada would contribute to it. The prime ministers in question replied

[67] Noulens, I, xiii.
[68] *Peace Conference,* III, 623–28, 629–33.
[69] Noulens repeated a number of atrocity stories about the Bolsheviks, ranging
from the torturing of Uritsky's assassins by tearing out their fingernails to denying
naval officers the exclusive use of their cabins.
[70] Lloyd George, I, 338.
[71] *Ibid.,* 344–53. The senior American delegates, except House, who was sick at
the time, met the same evening to discuss Russia, among other things. There are
no minutes of the meeting, but Lansing commented that it was "of no real value
in determining policy." Lansing Papers, Desk Diary, January 20.

negatively. Smuts, South Africa's premier, suggested that when the League of Nations was established, it could send an investigating commission to Russia. After further discussion the meeting decided that in the future the British should undertake in the conference: first, to oppose a continuation of intervention or of subsidies to other Allied forces in Russia; second, to work for a withdrawal of Allied forces in Russia, with the proviso that such withdrawal would be temporarily postponed if the Russian factions agreed to come to Paris for a hearing; third, to recommend, at the same time, guarantees against the threat of Bolshevik invasion for any independent state in the process of formation. The last stipulation suggests that the British were not anxious to let their anticipated protégés in the Baltic and in the Caucasus fall into Bolshevik hands.

The next morning, January 21, the Council of Ten met to continue its gathering of evidence on the Russian situation. This time the witness was the former Danish minister to Petrograd, Scavenius, who presented a less emotional and more accurate report than that of Noulens. Again, however, the witness had evidently been carefully coached, for Scavenius also stressed the weakness of the Red Army. In addition, he recommended that, in order to meet the objections of Allied public opinion, intervention be undertaken with volunteer troops only. Sounding a note of urgency, he maintained that if intervention were to succeed, it must be launched at once. According to Scavenius, starvation made an excellent recruiting sergeant for the Red Army, and the longer the Allies delayed, the stronger the Bolsheviks would become. Scavenius suggested that the negative effect of foreign intervention—the stirring up of Russian patriotism on behalf of the Soviet regime—could be counteracted if the Allies clearly indicated the nonimperialist character of their actions and if they organized elections to a constituent assembly as soon as possible.

In pressing for intervention, Scavenius outlined a grand strategic plan which was a constant among interventionist schemes throughout 1918 and 1919. It envisioned crushing the Bolshevik center by a four-pronged attack: the Allies and Russians from the north, the Czechs and Kolchak from the east, Denikin from the south, and the Poles from the west. Scavenius estimated that a force of 150,000 volunteers would be sufficient to bolster the White Russian legions and ensure the defeat of the Red Army—the exact figure which the Jassy Conference had proposed in calling for intervention the previous November.

After Scavenius had finished his statement and withdrawn, Wilson read the Council Buckler's telegram from Stockholm reporting the attitude of the Soviet government, as expressed by Litvinov. While the meeting was recessed for lunch, this telegram was translated and circulated among the members of the Council of Ten. As already noted, Buckler's report was instrumental in securing the adoption of the Prinkipo proposal. It largely erased the effect of the previous statements by Noulens and Scavenius and helped dispel the interventionist atmosphere that had been built up. As the statesmen entered the afternoon meeting, the most recent evidence before them was an account of Litvinov's conciliatory proposals, which suggested that it might yet be possible to make peace in Russia.

Formulation of the Prinkipo Proposal

Before the session resumed, Clemenceau privately told Wilson and Lloyd George that it would be impossible to allow Bolshevik representatives to come to Paris.[72] Clemenceau's position was indeed a difficult one. The British proposal to hear Bolsheviks and other Russians in Paris had evoked bitter protests from right-wing papers and politicians in France: the Bolsheviks had not only betrayed France but, once in Paris, would undoubtedly resort to revolutionary propaganda and agitation. Consequently, when the Council of Ten reconvened on the afternoon of January 21, Wilson proposed a modification of Lloyd George's original plan: the Allies would hear the Russian factions at Salonika, not Paris. In an implied reference to French fears of Bolshevik propaganda and activity, Lloyd George noted that one advantage of Wilson's proposal "would be that they [the Bolshevik delegation] could be brought straight there from Russia through the Black Sea without passing through other countries." [73]

Wilson and Lloyd George continued to insist, however, that the essence of the plan was to hear *all* parties to the Russian controversy, preferably in one room. Sonnino argued stubbornly that since the Bolsheviks were avowed enemies of the Allies, there was no need to hear them at all. Lloyd George retorted that "the Bolshevists were the very people some of them wished to hear." He added that Sonnino's proposal meant that they would hear a string of individuals all with the same opinion and striking the same note, while they would not hear "the people who at the present moment were actually controlling European Russia."

President Wilson reverted to one of the theses he had advanced during the earlier discussion on January 16: while they were all repelled by Bolshevism, armed intervention merely strengthened the hold of the Bolshevik government on the Russian people. On the other hand, fair

[72] Lloyd George, I, 353.
[73] *Peace Conference*, III, 647–53, 663–68.

dealing "would bring about a marked reaction against Bolshevism."

Clemenceau then stated his views at length. He underscored the great danger facing Europe as a result of the spread of Bolshevism. It had begun to infest the Baltic countries, and that very morning he had received disturbing news of its growing strength in Budapest and Vienna. Italy and even France were in danger. Something had to be done to stop Bolshevism. "In principle, he did not favor conversation with the Bolsheviks; not because they were criminals, but because we would be raising them to our level by saying that they were worthy of entering into conversation with us." [74] Besides, he feared that the Litvinov proposals were a clever Bolshevik trap. The Bolsheviks promised debt payments and concessions; but if the Allies accepted, they would say to their own people: "We offered them great principles of justice and the Allies would have nothing to do with us. Now we offer money, and they are ready to make peace."

Clemenceau admitted that his remarks did not offer a solution and that a speedy one was urgently needed—the Allied "populations could stand no more." Personally, he favored the idea of a *cordon sanitaire* to check the spread of Bolshevism; he would, however, accept the proposal of his colleagues since "there should not be even the appearance of disagreement amongst them." He added that it was easier for him to make this concession because of President Wilson's suggestion that the Russians come to Salonika; therefore, he would ask the president to draft the final proposal.

The Tiger had yielded! After almost three weeks of debate and controversy, the Anglo-American position had won out, and the Allies were prepared to hear the Bolsheviks, as well as other Russians. It was a dramatic moment, for the Russian question had aroused intense feeling on all sides. According to an eyewitness, at the end of the meeting Clemenceau came into the antechamber for his coat. A French official rushed up to ask him the outcome of the discussion on Russia. "Battu!" replied the old statesman explosively.[75]

The long speech in which he gave in to Wilson and Lloyd George was Clemenceau's only real participation in the debate on the British proposal. In it he outlined his attitude with great clarity. In this skirmish

---

[74] This quotation is taken from the joint Anglo-American record of the meeting. The second set of minutes, the American version, is in direct contradiction on Clemenceau's remarks: it quotes him as saying that he *did* consider the Bolsheviks as criminals. But from the sense of the rest of his statement and from other internal evidence, the second set of minutes must be rejected as less accurate. All quotations in this account are from the first (British–American) version.

[75] Related by C. T. Thompson, an Associated Press correspondent, in his *The Peace Conference Day by Day* (New York, 1920), 132–33.

Clemenceau had felt constrained to make a reluctant surrender for the sake of agreement with his allies; he believed that it was of the utmost importance to present to the world at large, and especially to the Germans, an appearance of unanimity among the victors. Moreover, Clemenceau, a shrewd politician, undoubtedly recognized that later in the peace negotiations there would be a number of issues, of more immediate and pressing significance for France than the question of Russia, on which he would have to make a stand. It would be better to yield gracefully early in the game, thereby obligating his opponents to him, than to begin the conference with a record of disagreement and intransigence. Finally, his acquiescence did not mean that he had altered his fundamental view of how best to deal with Bolshevism; Clemenceau and the French considered their agreement to the Prinkipo proposal as only a temporary setback, and they continued to struggle throughout the peace conference for the adoption of stern measures against Bolshevism.[76]

Clemenceau's grudging adherence to Lloyd George's plan did not end the discussion, although the opposition was now fighting only a rearguard action. Baron Sonnino said that the problem for France and Italy was a fundamental one—a question of self-defense. If all the anti-Bolshevik governments in Russia were to coalesce and if the Allies supplied sufficient aid, then the elements of order could easily triumph and Bolshevism would be eliminated. Lloyd George, however, wanted to know the answers to one or two practical questions. Scavenius had estimated that 150,000 Allied troops would be needed to bolster the anti-Bolsheviks, but Canadian troops were being withdrawn because they refused to fight Bolsheviks, and British troops would mutiny if ordered to Russia. Who was to do the job? Sonnino suggested volunteers. In a dramatic gesture Lloyd George turned to the other heads of government and asked each of them how many troops their respective countries could contribute to such a volunteer army. President Wilson said none from the United States, Clemenceau replied none from France, and

[76] According to General Mordacq, his confidant, Clemenceau was more preoccupied than usual on January 23, the day following the formal adoption of the Prinkipo proposal. Clemenceau said that "over the past few days he had no longer found in Monsieur Wilson the conciliatory man that Wilson had seemed to be during their first interviews. He saw now that the head of the American government in fact understood Europe and its real political situation very badly. . . ." General Mordacq, *Le Ministère Clemenceau: journal d'un témoin* (3 vols.; Paris, 1930–31), III, 95. While there were other points at issue between Clemenceau and Wilson during the first days of the conference—publicity, whether English should be an equal language with French for the conference, support to the Poles—Clemenceau's growing disillusionment with Wilson undoubtedly stemmed primarily from his disagreement with Wilson over how to deal with Russia and Bolshevism.

Orlando ruefully admitted Italy could not contribute. Then Lloyd George asked again who would back the fight against Bolshevism— above all, who would pay for it? There was no reply.

Now only the assent of Orlando and of Baron Makino for Japan was needed. The former immediately linked the question at issue with the Italian position at the conference, stating that Bolshevism could never triumph among the Italian people except through "profound patriotic disappointment in their expectations as to the rewards of the war." This was only the first of a number of occasions on which the Italians endeavored to use the danger of Bolshevism in Italy to advance their claims. Orlando concluded, however, that he would support the proposal, now that Lloyd George had raised unanswerable objections to the use of force.

Baron Makino then backed Lloyd George's plan on the ground that the anti-Bolshevik objectives of the intervention in Siberia had already been attained. The Japanese probably believed that the proposal would lead to evacuation of the American troops in Siberia, thus giving the Japanese a free hand in that area. With the Japanese accession, the major powers had now approved Lloyd George's proposal. Balfour insisted, however, that "abstention from hostile action against their neighbors" be a precondition to the participation of Russian factions in the proposed meeting, and this was accepted. It later became one of the most controversial points in the plan. President Wilson was asked to draft the proclamation calling the Russians together.

According to an eyewitness, President Wilson lost no time in executing his commission. He sent at once for his own typewriter, and as dusk fell, Wilson sat in a corner of the conference room, composing the Prinkipo proposal on his old, battered machine.[77] The next day, January 22, the Council of Ten considered, amended only slightly, and unanimously accepted President Wilson's draft.[78] The site finally chosen for the proposed meeting with the Russians was the Prinkipo Islands, a cluster of nine islands in the Sea of Marmora only a few miles from Constantinople. In Byzantine times these islands had been a place of banishment; in 1919 the islands were a resort and were selected as a meeting place because of the number of large hotels available for housing the prospective participants.[79]

The Prinkipo proposal contained a number of idealistic and highflown phrases; in fact, the introduction stating the humanitarian purpose

[77] Riddell, 13.

[78] *Peace Conference*, III, 686.

[79] The Prinkipo Islands were to figure again in Russian history. In 1920 White Russian refugees from South Russia were harbored there, and in 1929 the islands became Trotsky's first place of exile after his expulsion from Russia.

and the altruistic motives which prompted the Allies to call the Russians together formed the bulk of the document.[80] Wilson's genuine anxiety that the Russians be permitted an unhampered determination of their own fate was apparent throughout the declaration. The Prinkipo proclamation began with the affirmation that the sole aim of the Powers was "to help the Russian people, not to hinder them, or to interfere in any manner with their right to settle their own affairs in their own way." The difficulties and privations under which the Russian people were suffering showed how acute was the need for the restoration of order and the creation of normal conditions of labor, trade, and transportation.

The declaration continued:

They [the Powers] do not wish to exploit, or make use of Russia in any way. They recognize the revolution without reservation, and will in no way and in no circumstances aid or give countenance to any attempt at a counterrevolution. It is not their wish or purpose to favor or assist any one of the organized groups now contending for the leadership and guidance of Russia as against the others.

Even if one assumes that the overthrow of the Tsar in March 1917 and not the Bolshevik seizure of power eight months later was the revolution recognized, this was an astonishing paragraph in the light of the facts. It reflected Wilson's inability at times to distinguish between what was and what ought to be. It must have astounded every knowledgeable Russian, whether he was fighting with or against American, French, British, and Japanese soldiers and supplies. The proposal went on to assert that the Allies, who were engaged in making peace for the world, hoped "to bring Russia peace and an opportunity to find her way out of her present troubles. . . . They recognize and accept it as their duty, therefore, to serve Russia in this great matter as generously, as unselfishly, as thoughtfully, and as ungrudgingly as they would serve every other friend and ally."

The declaration then passed to the actual calling of a conference:

They [the Powers] invite every organized group that is now exercising, or attempting to exercise, political authority or military control anywhere in Siberia, or within the boundaries of European Russia as they stood before the war just concluded (except in Finland), to send representatives, not exceeding three representatives for each group, to the Princes' Island, Sea of Marmora, where they will be met by representatives of the Associated Powers, provided, in the meantime, there is a truce of arms amongst the parties invited. . . . These represent-

[80] For the complete text, see *Peace Conference,* III, 676–77.

atives are invited to confer with the representatives of the Associated Powers in the freest and frankest way, with a view to ascertaining the wishes of all sections of the Russian people, and bringing about, if possible, some understanding and agreement by which Russia may work out her own purposes and happy cooperative relations be established between her people and the other peoples of the world.

The date set for the meeting was February 15, 1919.

The next morning, January 23, the Council of Ten decided to appoint two representatives from each of the five major powers to attend the Prinkipo meeting. Several days later President Wilson named George D. Herron and William Allen White as the American members of the Prinkipo commission. The appointment of Herron, a former socialist and preacher who had played a prominent role in the Armistice negotiations, aroused a storm of abuse from the American press and pulpit, based chiefly on his alleged support of free love and his socialist background, but Wilson stood by his choice.[81]

Reaction to the Prinkipo Proposal

The Prinkipo plan created a great stir at the peace conference and throughout the Western world.[82] Although it was generally known that the conference was considering the British proposal to hear the Bolsheviks and other Russian groups, almost everyone expected that French opposition and the testimony of such "experts" as Noulens and Scavenius would put an end to the idea. Few anticipated that the conference would go as far as it did in treating with the Bolsheviks. First comments of astonishment and incredulity were soon followed by expressions of doubt concerning the wisdom of the proposal or of pessimism as to its chances of success.[83] Press reaction was generally unfavorable. While *The Times* of London and *The Manchester Guardian* endorsed the Prinkipo suggestion, several papers in England and the conservative

[81] Mitchell Pirie Briggs, *George D. Herron and the European Settlement* (Stanford, 1932), 141 n. 20. In 1901 Herron had married Carrie Rand in a ceremony wherein each chose the other as companion. See also letter from Tumulty, Wilson's press secretary, to Wilson, February 9, 1919, Wilson Papers, Series VIIIA, Box 19. Wilson stated on February 13 that Herron was "much the best man we could use," and "we shall just have to let the comments [concerning his appointment] pass." Letter to Lansing, *ibid.*, Series VIIIA, Box 20.

[82] Noble called it one of the major sensations of the peace conference, and the British journalist Huddleston stated that "no decision taken by the Conference created so much surprise." Noble, 277; Huddleston, 49.

[83] See, for example, the reaction of Harold Nicolson, then a junior member of the British delegation. Nicolson, 247–50.

press in France bitterly attacked it. H. Wickham Steed, managing editor of Northcliffe's *Daily Mail,* who was in close touch with Colonel House during the peace conference, strongly opposed the Prinkipo plan. In France the press campaign against the Prinkipo proposal was led by *Le Temps,* an organ close to the French government. The French papers of the right castigated Wilson and declared that dealing with the Bolsheviks was unthinkable. They played upon French chauvinism by recalling the thousands of heroic French lives lost as a result of the Bolshevik decision to take Russia out of the war. They also printed every imaginable type of anti-Bolshevik report: stories of revolts in Soviet Russia, communiqués of Red Army defeats, "objective" dispatches detailing atrocities of the Red Terror, and eyewitness accounts by émigrés.[84] Ray Stannard Baker, press secretary for the American delegation, complained that "the French government press was instructed to emphasize chaotic conditions in Russia." [85] The French government also lent direct support to attacks on the Prinkipo invitation by issuing statements to the press discounting the plan.[86]

Although they criticized the vagueness of the proposal, liberal and socialist elements in the West greeted the Prinkipo plan with considerable enthusiasm. In a memorandum of January 27 to House, Bullitt stated: "Today the President has enormous prestige with European labor. His proposal in re Russia and his address on the League of Nations have completed his hold on leaders of the labor movement. For example, Cachin [French socialist leader] said in my presence . . . that the Russian decision had given him the first happy moment he had had since the war broke out. . . ." [87] Liberal papers in the United States supported the idea of meeting with the Bolsheviks and other Russians; there was, however, considerable opposition to this policy among conservative circles.[88]

Within the American delegation itself there was some uneasiness concerning Lloyd George and Wilson's handiwork. Colonel House, who had been sick when the proposal was discussed and formulated, was annoyed that the conference had wasted so much time on it; his criticism obviously reflected a certain pique that the Prinkipo idea had been worked out without consulting him and without consideration of his own

[84] Noble, 277–79.
[85] Baker, *Settlement,* I, 297.
[86] Noble, 281–84.
[87] House Papers, Correspondence Files, Bullitt.
[88] See Tumulty's summary of American reaction to the original British proposal of January 2 in wires to Wilson on January 13 and 14, Wilson Papers, Series VIIIA, Boxes 10 and 11.

pet project for countering Bolshevism—food and economic relief.[89] Lansing attempted to rationalize the Prinkipo decision, explaining to Polk that it "was the direct consequence of a recognition of the impossibility of military intervention," and that it represented a compromise with the British desire to treat directly with the Bolsheviks. Lansing concluded: "I hate the idea of even investigating those assassins. We know enough about them already. But what other course had we but to seek to bribe them to stop murdering by suggesting an investigation on condition that they stop fighting? Will it work? I don't think so. But no one had anything better to suggest." [90] In reply Polk suggested that recognition of the Omsk government be considered as a way of counterbalancing the discouragement the Prinkipo proposal could be expected to generate among anti-Bolshevik Russians.[91]

The call for a conference on the Prinkipo Islands was an open and general invitation, announced publicly for the benefit of all the parties concerned, but not transmitted formally by the peace conference to any of the Russian governments.[92] The Allies were concerned lest direct communication with any of the Russian groups, particularly the Bolsheviks, be interpreted as recognition of them by the peace conference. When Chicherin in a message to Wilson complained that the Soviet government had heard of the proposed Prinkipo conference but had not received an official invitation, Wilson noted that "to send an official communication would be tantamount to a recognition of the Bolshevist government," and Lloyd George commented with some annoyance that Chicherin "had received his notice like everybody else." [93]

Soviet reaction to the Prinkipo proposal was a mixture of surprise, suspicion, and cautious optimism. Having learned of the proposal from monitored radio reports, the Soviet government bent every effort to con-

[89] See Wiseman's report of his discussion of the Prinkipo plan with House, House Papers, Wiseman Diary, January 22, 1919; see also the comments of Gordon Auchincloss, House's son-in-law, House Papers, Auchincloss Diary, January 20 and 21, 1919, and a telegram from Auchincloss to Polk of January 23, 1919.

[90] Telegram to Polk, January 27, 1919, *1919, Russia*, 35, and letter to Polk, February 11, 1919, Polk Papers, Drawer 78, File 9. In a similar vein, see the letter from Henry White to William Phillips, a senior State Department officer, January 24, 1919, cited in Nevins, 366.

[91] *1919, Russia*, 38–39.

[92] Some writers, such as Louis Fischer, have suggested that elements in the Allied camp who opposed the invitation deliberately failed to transmit it to the Bolsheviks. Fischer, I, 167. This is incorrect; the Soviet government received the invitation in the same manner as the other Russian factions—through the public media of press and radio. Although some of the White Russian governments were notified directly by wireless, these messages were sent either by the Russian Political Conference or by the French government on its own authority.

[93] *Peace Conference*, III, 835.

firm the invitation as an official one. In addition to the message to Wilson mentioned above, the Bolsheviks asked their representative in Stockholm, Vorovsky (Litvinov having been forced to move to Norway), to verify the proposal and to attempt to ascertain whether the Allies were sincere in making it. A similar request was sent to Jean Longuet, editor of the socialist *Populaire* in Paris, and on January 31 the Soviet government wired Pichon directly.[94]

At the same time the official Soviet press was questioning the aims of the Allies in convening such a conference. A front-page editorial in *Pravda* on January 25, entitled "the Modest Proposal of the Allied Benefactors," sounded a note of skeptical sarcasm. The editorial ridiculed Allied claims of disinterestedness and altruism, pointing out that the fine words of the proposal hardly corresponded to the facts of the situation or to other Allied policies and pronouncements. Besides, how fair could arbitration be when the arbitrators were to be from one side to the dispute? Nevertheless, the editorial concluded: "It would be nonsense under all conditions to refuse *pourparlers* with these, our worst enemies. . . . The proletarian revolution goes by zigzags, and we should not pass over an opportunity to strengthen our position and to weaken the position of our class enemies."

Not all the Soviet leaders agreed with the conclusions of *Pravda*, however. According to British correspondent Arthur J. Ransome, who was in close contact with a number of prominent Bolsheviks in this period, the concerted Soviet "peace offensive" launched in the fall of 1918, which had borne fruit in the Prinkipo invitation, had been opposed by left extremists among the Bolshevik leadership on the ground that further intervention would result in strikes, riots, and mutinies in the Allied countries, thereby promoting a revolutionary situation and accelerating the outbreak of the world revolution.[95] Thus when news of the Prinkipo invitation reached Moscow, a lively debate ensued as to whether it was theoretically correct and practically advantageous to accept the invitation and to make peace with the bourgeois world. Nevertheless, throughout the succeeding weeks Lenin continued to advocate, in the face of considerable opposition within the Bolshevik party and in Soviet Russia as a whole, his policy of a "second Brest." He maintained

[94] For a summary of these Soviet efforts, see Potemkin, III, 58–59. Pichon forbade Longuet to answer over the French government wireless, but Longuet's reply was received by the Bolsheviks via the uncensored American news services. As a result, the French press and Foreign Office assumed that Wilson had connived in the flouting of the wishes of the French government by a French citizen and bitterly attacked him on this score. Huddleston, 55–56.

[95] Ransome's observation is contained in an appendix to Buckler's report, *Peace Conference*, III, 645. See also Bullitt's report on his mission, p. 173 of ch. five below.

that events had completely justified the correctness of the Soviet action in accepting the Brest-Litovsk peace, and that the Brest experience should now be applied to Soviet relations with the Allies.[96] As we shall see presently, Lenin also applied the Brest formula to the Bullitt mission.

On February 4 the Soviet government replied formally to the Prinkipo proposal, stating that although it had not received an invitation to the conference directly, it was nevertheless accepting the Allied offer in order to prevent the absence of a definite Soviet answer from being interpreted as a refusal.[97] In its reply the Soviet government declared that it was prepared to offer the Allies four major concessions as the price of the peace it so earnestly desired and as a basis for the proposed negotiations at Prinkipo. These concessions were: (1) to recognize Russia's foreign debts and, in view of the financial difficulties of the Soviet government and its poor credit rating abroad, to guarantee interest payments on these debts with Russian raw materials; (2) to grant mining, forest, and other concessions to Allied interests; (3) to discuss a territorial settlement, including possible Soviet cession of all territories then held by Entente troops; and (4) in the light of widespread complaints against Bolshevik propaganda, to agree not to interfere in the internal affairs of the Allies.

The Soviet government qualified its offer, however. On three different occasions in the note it warned that the nature and extent of the concessions finally agreed upon would depend on the military and internal position of the Soviet Republic at the time of the negotiations, which was improving rapidly with each passing day. To demonstrate the growing strength of Soviet Russia, the Soviet reply included a long list of towns recently captured by the Red Army. It also reported that the Menshevik party had taken a stand against intervention, and that a group of right Socialist Revolutionaries, former members of the Constituent Assembly, were about to come out in support of the Soviet regime because of their opposition to Allied intervention and to Kolchak.[98] As further evidence of the improved situation within Soviet Russia, the So-

[96] Lenin, *Sochineniia*, xxiv, 116.

[97] For the complete text in an official Soviet translation, see *The Nation*, Vol. 110, January 17, 1920. See also a Soviet note of the same date to the Italian government, proffering peace and friendship, defending Russia's withdrawal from the war, and confirming the concessions proposed in the Prinkipo reply. Degras, *Soviet Documents*, i, 139–45.

[98] Three weeks later the Soviet government amnestied the right Socialist Revolutionaries and accepted their support. In January and February 1919 the Mensheviks were permitted to publish their own paper, *Vsegda Vpered*, but on February 25, after the appearance of an article calling for an end to the civil war, the Soviet Central Executive Committee closed the paper. The Socialist Revolutionaries fared no better; their paper, *Delo Naroda*, lasted just one week, March 20–28. Lenin, *Sochineniia*, xxiv, 771, and Ransome, 164–69.

viet reply claimed that the local Chekas had recently been abolished.

This effort to represent Soviet Russia as an increasingly formidable opponent was rather belied, however, by the far-reaching concessions offered the Allies. Despite their bold front the Soviet leaders were clearly ready to go to almost any lengths to win some relief from the pressure of intervention. They neglected, however, to accept, or even to mention, the precondition of the Prinkipo proposal—a cease-fire by all the warring parties in Russia—perhaps believing that this was a technicality to be settled when the conference had been agreed on. This omission was later used as a pretext for charging that the Soviet reply was in fact a refusal.

On the whole the tone of the Soviet note was business-like and conciliatory; there were, however, several phrases which were offensive and insulting, whether by design or inadvertence. At one point the note stated that mining and forest concessions were being offered "in view of the great inclination which foreign capital has always displayed to exploit Russia's natural resources for its own advantage." The Soviet answer also implied that the anti-Bolshevik Russians were simply creatures of the Entente. Finally, the note declared that the Soviet government was ready to negotiate "and even—as it has often said—to purchase such agreement at the price of important sacrifices."

The clear inference that the Allied leaders could be "bought off" and that they could be bribed to make peace in Russia was a psychological blunder; both Lloyd George and Wilson, who believed that they represented the highest ideals of the democratic world and who conceived of the Prinkipo plan as a liberal and humane effort to help Russia and to stop the fighting there, were angered and repelled by the Soviet reply. There is, unfortunately, no record of Wilson's immediate reaction to the Soviet note of February 4. On February 14, however, he told the peace conference that the Bolsheviks had offered a number of concessions which had not been asked for. "This answer was not only uncalled for, but might be thought insulting. What the Allies had in mind was the establishment of peace in Russia as an element of the world's peace." [99] And on February 28, in an informal talk to the Democratic National Committee after his return to the United States, Wilson denounced the Soviet reply: "The Bolsheviks had accepted, but had accepted in a way that was studiously insulting. . . . [Their concessions] meant: 'We are dealing with perjured governments whose only interest is in striking a bargain, and if that is the price of European recognition and cooperation, we are ready to pay it.' " [100]

[99] *Peace Conference*, III, 1042.
[100] Joseph P. Tumulty, *Woodrow Wilson as I Know Him* (Garden City, 1921), 374–75.

In the same talk Wilson presented a graphic picture of Lloyd George's reaction to the Soviet reply, and further described his own sense of affront:

> I never saw anybody more angered than Mr. Lloyd George, who said: "We cannot let that insult go by. We are not after their money or their concessions or their territory. That is not the point. We are their friends who want to help them and must tell them so." We did not tell them so because to some of the people we had to deal with the payment of the foreign debt was a more interesting and important matter, but that will be made clear to them in the conference, if they will believe it. But the Bolsheviks . . . are the most consummate sneaks in the world. I suppose because they know they have no high motives themselves, they do not believe that anybody else has.

The caustic comments of the conservative French press may also have contributed to the righteous indignation and air of offended altruism with which Wilson and Lloyd George reacted to the Soviet acceptance of the Prinkipo invitation. Several French papers charged, for example, that the Soviet concessions were proof that selfish Anglo-American financial interests had inspired the proposal.[101]

Within Soviet Russia the government's reply to the Prinkipo invitation aroused widespread comment and discussion.[102] The opposition parties to the right, the Mensheviks and the right Socialist Revolutionaries, supported the Soviet reply. They were strongly opposed to intervention, believing not only that it was an offense against the Russian nation but that it facilitated Bolshevik control of the country. Many Bolsheviks and the opposition on the left, the left Socialist Revolutionaries, criticized the Soviet acceptance, arguing that it was a betrayal of the revolution and that the offer to discuss Entente annexations of Russian territory was nothing but unconditional surrender before the imperialist enemy. The possible territorial concessions, which might involve the loss of huge blocs of Russian territory, aroused the strongest criticism and the greatest opposition.

On February 10, however, at a joint meeting of the Moscow Soviet and the All-Russian Soviet Central Executive Committee, Bukharin, conceding that he had been wrong in opposing the Brest peace, approved the Soviet reply. Kamenev reluctantly joined him, finding solace in the fact that peace negotiations would force the Allies, as well as the

---

[101] Noble, 298 n. 87; E. J. Dillon, *The Inside Story of the Peace Conference* (New York, 1920), 158.

[102] According to Ransome, this was the main topic of conversation in Moscow in early February. Ransome, 48.

counterrevolutionaries, to recognize Soviet strength and the national authority of the Bolshevik regime. The meeting then unanimously adopted a resolution approving every effort of the Soviet government to obtain peace.[103]

It has been argued that the Soviet reply was insincere, designed only to trick the Allies into halting military operations.[104] In this view, the Soviet government would have dragged out the proposed negotiations and would finally have refused to make peace on the terms outlined in its note of February 4. In the light of the difficult economic and military situation confronting the regime, its urgent need for a reasonably secure respite, and the long duration and consistency of Soviet attempts in 1918 and 1919 to buy peace with substantial concessions, this contention must be rejected. It seems likely that the Soviet leaders would have gone to Prinkipo and would have agreed to most of the humiliating conditions set forth in their acceptance of the invitation. It was a high price but, as at Brest, Lenin was prepared to pay it in order to preserve the Soviet regime and to gain time while the "inevitable" world revolution developed. In March 1918 his enemies had been military expansionists; now they were greedy imperialists. Consequently, he changed the bait, offering economic concessions in the hope of enticing the capitalists to give up intervention. This, however, was just what Wilson and Lloyd George found repugnant in the Soviet reply. Here, as on a number of occasions since, reliance on the validity of the Marxist-Leninist view of the world led the Soviet rulers to oversimplify and, to some extent, to miscalculate the purpose and policies of the Western governments, to the detriment of the Bolshevik cause itself, and at great cost to the Russian people.

Lenin also believed that the mining and other economic concessions tendered the Entente could, under proper controls and safeguards, be used to Soviet advantage. Such concessions would help attract and pay for machinery, as well as foreign capital and technicians, all urgently needed to help restore the economic life of the country and to support "socialist construction" in Soviet Russia. The Prinkipo reply foreshadowed the determined Soviet effort in 1920 and under the NEP to lure economic assistance from abroad with concessions.[105]

[103] *Ibid.,* pp. 44–49, 57–61.

[104] On the other hand, Soviet historiography since World War II has claimed that the Soviet reply was a clever trap, aimed at unmasking the real purposes of the Allies in Russia and at fomenting imperialist conflicts among the Great Powers. See, for example, Potemkin, III, 60; Shtein, 410–11.

[105] See Lenin's report on concessions to the Eighth Congress of Soviets on December 21, 1920, when he reviewed the origins of this policy in the Brest and the Prinkipo periods. Lenin, *Sochineniia,* XXVI, 8. See also Ransome's interviews in February and March 1919 with Soviet economic officials who were urging the granting of concessions. Ransome, 104–05, 132, 161–64.

Most important, however, the Soviet leaders believed that the losses entailed in the Prinkipo concessions would be only transitory, as those suffered at Brest had been. On January 2 Litvinov told Dr. Davison of the American Red Cross that even if Western recognition of the Soviet government should mean concurrent recognition by the Allies of the counterrevolutionary governments, this would not be a high price to pay for peace; once these governments were deprived of Allied aid, they could be easily overthrown by the Soviet government.[106] The Soviet leaders were also convinced that the outbreak of proletarian revolutions in Western Europe, expected momentarily, would sweep away any unfavorable peace concluded with the Entente. Lenin, in his report to the Eighth Party Congress on March 18, 1919, declared that the Party Central Committee had known that the reply to the Prinkipo proposal had meant "consenting to a peace of an extremely irksome character." But this decision had been taken with an eye on the developing revolutionary situation in Europe and on the growth of a world, Soviet proletarian movement.[107]

Diplomatic efforts to secure "a second Brest" did not in any case mean an abandonment of the other, revolutionary arm of Soviet policy. In fact, one of the chief advantages which the Soviet leaders saw in a settlement with the Allies, no matter what the price, was an opportunity to regroup their forces for an intensified world revolutionary drive. Writing in *Izvestia* on January 18, Rakovsky pointed out that temporary peace in Russia would be "extremely useful and profitable to us since it would allow the Soviet government to consolidate its position in anticipation of the struggle of the Allied imperialists against their own revolutions." On February 2, Zinoviev spoke in a similar vein: "We are willing to sign an unfavorable peace with the Allies. . . . It would only mean that we should put no trust whatever in the bit of paper we should sign. We should use the breathing space so obtained to gather our strength in order that the mere continued existence of our Government would keep up the worldwide propaganda which Soviet Russia has been carrying on for more than a year." [108] Thus, while the Soviet leaders were prepared to make peace under almost any conditions, they planned simultaneously to continue their revolutionary activities, counting on a world revolutionary triumph to expunge whatever losses they might suffer in diplomatic negotiation.

[106] *1919, Russia*, 26.
[107] Lenin, *Sochineniia*, XXIV, 118.
[108] Quoted in United States Senate, 1919 (66th Congress, 2nd session), Document 172, *Memorandum on Certain Aspects of the Bolshevist Movement in Russia* (Washington, 1920), 20.

The Failure of the Prinkipo Proposal

The failure of the Prinkipo proposal is generally ascribed to the refusal of the White Russian governments to attend the conference. This is an oversimplified and, to some extent, misleading explanation. As the evidence below suggests, the White Russians, while violently opposed to the idea of meeting with the Bolsheviks, recognized their utter dependence on Allied aid and would probably have accepted the Prinkipo invitation if the Allies had exerted pressure on them to do so. The Allies could have threatened to cut off assistance to the White Russian governments or to make a separate peace with the Bolsheviks. The Allies, however, were divided on the advisability of the Prinkipo plan. The French characterized the Prinkipo plan to the anti-Bolsheviks as a temporary aberration of Allied policy and urged them to refuse the invitation. Churchill, who disagreed with Lloyd George on Russia, promised the White Russian governments continued British help. Wilson and Lloyd George, preoccupied with urgent conference and domestic concerns, made no effort to counteract this opposition to their plan or to persuade the White Russians to accept the invitation. As a result, the Prinkipo proposal died of maltreatment and neglect only a few weeks after its birth.

The immediate White Russian reaction to the Prinkipo announcement was a mixture of incredulity and indignation. This was soon followed by anger, despair, and in some quarters resignation. The anti-Bolshevik leaders were genuinely amazed and resentful that they, friends of the Allies, recipients of Allied support, defenders of decency, order, and property in Russia, should be expected to sit down at the same table with the Bolsheviks, the avowed enemies of Western principles, who had betrayed the Allied cause in the war, who had usurped power in Russia, and who were known terrorists and assassins. It was both unbelievable and unthinkable.[109] The day after announcement of the Prinkipo plan, Sazonov, in a press interview, denounced the whole concept and said that the invitation itself was unacceptable and insulting. At noon that day a mass protest rally of the Russian colony in Paris was held before the embassy.[110]

Within anti-Bolshevik Russia reaction to the Prinkipo project was also hostile and bitter. On February 1 General Denikin dispatched a

[109] Nabokov, for example, characterized the Prinkipo proposal as "the most pitiable act that has ever disgraced the pages of world history." Nabokov, 286. See also the editorial of the Paris émigré paper *Obshchee Delo* on January 28, 1919.

[110] H. Wilson Harris, *The Peace in the Making* (London, n.d.), 132; Nabokov, 287–88.

[119]

personal protest against it to Marshal Foch.[111] In Archangel pictures of President Wilson were removed from shop windows, and General Miller, head of the North Russian government in Chaikovsky's absence, promptly presented a note of rejection to the Allied representatives. The note, dated January 27, declared that the invitation was "morally unacceptable" since the Bolsheviks were "venal traitors in international affairs and brigands, robbers, and murderers in internal affairs." [112]

In Omsk news of the proposal created consternation. A few days later a British officer there noted, "Kolchak is said not to have slept a wink since he heard about Prinkipo." [113] On January 28 the government wired Paris that the Prinkipo plan had seriously undermined the morale of anti-Bolshevik groups and the army. Reports had begun to circulate that the Allies were abandoning the White Russians and that Allied aid would be cut off; disaster threatened the Siberian movement. As a result, Admiral Kolchak had issued an order of the day to the troops, declaring that rumors of an armistice with the Bolsheviks were unfounded and that on the contrary he was preparing an offensive.[114] As a further counter to the news of Prinkipo, Kolchak circulated a story in Omsk that the proposal was a sly diplomatic maneuver by the Allies to discredit the Bolsheviks before world opinion, after which the Entente would launch a program of all-out aid to the anti-Bolsheviks.[115] Protests against any negotiations with the Bolsheviks were voiced by a number of secular groups and religious organizations in Siberia and were transmitted abroad.[116] A letter from Omsk to Paris, dated January 29, 1919, reflected the atmosphere created by the news of Prinkipo:

> Now . . . there is this shocking, this impossible declaration of Wilson about the Prinkipo Islands. This was a thunderclap. . . . Today every editorial was a cry of indignation. . . . They say there was a case of hissing of English officers today. Poor fellows, they, that is all the Allies in Omsk, are as indignant about this misunderstanding of the Russian role as we are. . . .

[111] Maklakov Papers, Part II, Packet II, File 9.

[112] Cited in Leonid I. Strakhovsky, *Intervention at Archangel* (Princeton, 1944), 144–45.

[113] Cited in Peter Fleming, *The Fate of Admiral Kolchak* (New York, 1963), 126.

[114] On February 3 Basily, the Russian counselor of embassy in Paris, transmitted two telegrams reporting this information to Auchincloss, for House. House Papers, Drawer 31, File 225.

[115] George K. Guins, *Sibir', Soiuzniki, i Kolchak* (*Siberia, the Allies, and Kolchak*) (2 vols.; Peking, 1921), II, 89; John Ward, *With the "Die-Hards" in Siberia* (London, 1920), 158.

[116] For an example of these appeals, see "Vneshniaia politika," *Krasnyi Arkhiv*, 85. See also a telegram from Omsk to the Russian chargé in Washington, *1919, Russia*, 71.

They [the Allies] spit on us, we spit on ourselves, but Prinkipo is the last straw. . . . You cannot imagine the despair here—all the missions and representatives feel abashed and silly.[117]

As this letter indicated, the Allied representatives in Russia were as angered and dismayed over Prinkipo as the White Russians. Harris, the American consul general in Omsk, inveighed against the proposal in three messages to Washington, noting that a recent White Russian defeat had been largely due to disaffection among the troops caused by the Prinkipo proposal.[118] Poole, representing the United States at Archangel, threatened to resign in protest against the Prinkipo policy.[119] French General Janin, the supreme Allied commander at Omsk, noted that the Prinkipo proposal had lowered the morale of the anti-Bolshevik forces and had made more difficult the already arduous task of restoring order in Russia.[120]

Moreover, news of the Prinkipo plan led to a marked decline in Anglo-American prestige and a corresponding swing to the formerly unpopular Japanese among military and political circles in Omsk.[121] To meet this development Maklakov sent a long wire to Omsk on February 8, urging that nothing be done that might antagonize the Western Allies, and particularly warning against Omsk turning for assistance to Germany or to Japan in anger over the Prinkipo plan.[122]

The first reaction of the White Russians in Paris and Russia was quickly tempered by more cautious second thoughts. On January 23, the day following the call to Prinkipo, the Russian Political Conference met. After lengthy discussion it was decided that the Conference "should abstain from hasty conclusions, await developments and, in particular, ascertain the intentions of the French government, whose previous attitude . . . tended to show that the French themselves realized the impossibility of any compromise with the Bolsheviks." [123] On January 27 Maklakov sent a circular telegram to the White Russian capitals: ". . . Political Conference requests delaying any categorical answer to the proposal of the Powers. Please communicate your answer to us, entrusting us with right to use it at the opportune moment. The decision of the

---

[117] Maklakov Papers, Part II, Packet II, File 1.
[118] *1919, Russia,* 44–46, 54, 197.
[119] *Ibid.,* 42–43, 46–47, 51.
[120] General Pierre Janin, *Ma mission en Sibérie, 1918–20* (Paris, 1933), 73.
[121] Ward, 158; Vologodsky Papers, Diary, February 5, 1919. British correspondent Dillon claimed that because of the Prinkipo proposal the Omsk government was ready to conclude an economic agreement with Japan, but was dissuaded from doing so by Allied pressure. Dillon, 360–61.
[122] Maklakov Papers, Part II, Packet III, File 1.
[123] Nabokov, 287–88.

peace conference is not unanimous; there are opponents of the proposal, the French in particular." [124]

Meanwhile, in Omsk the government had tentatively agreed, on January 25, to send an indignant refusal to the Allied invitation. The next day, however, Kolchak and several of his aides met with the French and British high commissioners in Siberia, who urged Kolchak not to refuse before detailed explanations arrived from Paris.[125] In a day or two Maklakov's circular telegram from Paris brought similar advice. A reply, therefore, was delayed, pending clarification of the aims and motives of the Allies.[126]

If at this moment the Western powers had unanimously supported the Prinkipo plan and had threatened to cut off aid to the anti-Bolsheviks, the White Russian governments would have been forced to accept the proposal and attend the conference. In fact, at the end of January the Omsk government was even resigned to this eventuality. On February 4 Consul General Harris reported that although the Cadet party "bitterly disapproved the Allied suggestion, the other parties are acquiescing." He added that the Omsk government, while opposed to the Prinkipo plan, was willing to accept the invitation and send delegates, not from conviction but from a desire to comply with the wishes of the Allies.[127]

But Allied pressure to bring the White Russians to the proposed conference was not forthcoming. Instead, just the opposite occurred; from all sides the anti-Bolshevik governments received intimations that Allied aid would continue and that the Prinkipo plan would fail. On January 31 Admiral Kolchak told Colonel Ward: "While the British government advises an arrangement with the Bolsheviks, they continue to furnish me with generous supplies for the Russian Army." [128] On February 5 Nabokov wired Omsk from London: "Churchill told me in a confidential meeting that the War Ministry will continue to provide the Russian military forces struggling against Bolshevism with all necessary supplies. 'I will continue this supplying unless I receive categorical instructions to cease.' " [129]

[124] Cited in I.I. Mints, *Angliiskaia interventsiia i severnaia kontrrevoliutsiia* (*English Intervention and the Northern Counterrevolution*) (Moscow, 1931), 152.

[125] Guins, II, 88–89.

[126] This decision was reported in a telegram to the Russian chargé in Washington, dated February 19, which the latter passed to the State Department, *1919, Russia*, 71.

[127] *Ibid.*, 44–46.

[128] Ward, 159.

[129] E. Adamov, "Rol' Anglii v interventsii" ("The Role of England in Intervention"), *Vestnik NKID* (*Journal of the People's Commissariat for Foreign Affairs*), No. 6–7, August 25, 1920, 5. Nabokov also reported his interview with Churchill to Maklakov, Maklakov Papers, Part II, Packet III, File 1. Similar assurances from Lord Curzon to Chaikovsky on February 4 are reported in Miliukov Diary, 511.

On February 2 General Briggs, the British military representative with Denikin, was informed that the War Ministry would continue to aid the Volunteer Army. His instructions made clear that this decision had been taken in London during the end of January—at the very moment when Lloyd George and Wilson in Paris had broached a plan designed to end the fighting in Russia. The telegram to Briggs added: "Since the question of Russia is still being discussed by the Paris Conference, we cannot definitely decide on the request of General Denikin for the sending of troops." [130] This was indeed a generous concession on the part of War Minister Churchill to his superiors sitting in Paris—it was all right to send supplies, which were on hand, to the anti-Bolsheviks in contradiction of the purposes of Lloyd George and Wilson, but when it came to the dispatch of soldiers, which the Americans would have to furnish, then the peace conference would have to be consulted!

The French government was not to be outdone by Churchill. It hastened to reassure White Russian leaders concerning Prinkipo and the continuation of French aid to the anti-Bolshevik cause. On February 5 Sazonov wired Kolchak: "I have learned that the proposal for a conference on the Prinkipo Islands is being regarded as doomed to failure. France intends to continue to support us with supplies and will not withdraw her military units in Russia." [131] On February 11 Vologodsky replied to Sazonov's wire: "We, in our turn, received a communication from Pichon in the spirit of the first part of your telegram; i.e., about the apparent failure of the Prinkipo Islands meeting." [132] And on February 24, after the White Russian leaders had officially rejected the Prinkipo invitation, but evidently referring to a document some days old, the Omsk government wired Maklakov:

Martel [the French high commissioner in Omsk] has just translated a communication of the French government which stated that in view of the indefiniteness of the results that one can expect from the Prinkipo Islands conference, the French government cannot suspend its support of the Omsk government. The aid, which it formerly gave Omsk, and the fulfillment of measures already begun for the support of Admiral Kolchak and the organization of an army in Siberia will continue henceforth until some new decision, which can be reached only upon the full examination of policy.[133]

[130] The instructions to Briggs are quoted at length in a wire from Neratov in Ekaterinodar to Sazonov in Paris, dated February 21. "Vneshniaia politika," *Krasnyi Arkhiv*, 93.

[131] Quoted in Subbotovsky, 230. See also a telegram from Maklakov to Omsk on February 8, 1919. Maklakov Papers, Part IV, Packet III, File 1.

[132] "Vneshniaia politika," *Krasnyi Arkhiv*, p. 71.

[133] *Ibid.*, 95.

As further proof of the activity of the French in undermining the Prinkipo policy, there is a letter of February 13 to House from George Herron, one of the American delegates to the proposed meeting:

> These representatives [of various Russian groups that Herron had contacted] explained that officials of the French government persuaded or commanded them not to go. It has become clear to me that the refusal of all the parties except the Bolsheviks to participate is due to French intervention. Where persuasion has not answered, this intervention has taken the part of moral coercion. Even two delegates from the Caucasus yesterday told me that the French agents in the East told them to have nothing to do with the conference. I have tried to show these parties and nationalities their mistake, and tried to get them to consider their former decision even at this date and send representatives to Prinkipo . . . but, somehow, they are all under the fear of France and of French objection.[134]

All this evidence is even more damning of the French role in sabotaging the Prinkipo plan than the similar, better-known, but more partial testimony of Bullitt before the Senate Foreign Relations Committee later in 1919.[135] There is, thus, little doubt as to what led the White Russian governments to refuse the Prinkipo invitation. Their formal reply was delayed, however, until they were convinced that there was no chance of the conference being held, even with only the Bolsheviks in attendance. As a result, the first official White Russian statement in Paris concerning the Prinkipo plan dealt not with the original proposal but with the Soviet reply. A few days after Chicherin's note of February 4 the Russian Political Conference issued a declaration designed to give pause to those Western interests that might be attracted by the Soviet offer of concessions: "The representatives of Russia deem it their duty to declare, in order to avoid all misunderstandings, that no agreement made with Bolshevik authorities in regard to concessions or privileges will be recognized by the national authorities, and that all transactions concluded by foreigners with representatives of the Soviets will be considered null and void." [136]

In deciding on a formal reply to the Prinkipo invitation, the three major White Russian governments—in North Russia, South Russia, and Siberia—and the Russian Political Conference in Paris worked in close

---

[134] George D. Herron Papers, Hoover Institution, Stanford, Verbatim copies, Volume x, Document vi, p. 1. See also Herron's letter to Hugh Wilson, February 12, 1919. *Ibid.*, Document v, p. 2.

[135] *Bullitt Mission*, 32. Bullitt's allegations were based on a memorandum by A. A. Berle, Jr., of February 21, 1919. Files of the ACTNP, 861.00/287.

[136] *The Russian Almanac, 1919*, ed. N. Peacock (London, 1919), 23.

coordination. The first draft reply was apparently drawn up early in February, for on February 9 Vologodsky wired Sazonov from Omsk referring to a draft based on the assumption that the White Russian answer would precede that of the Bolsheviks. Vologodsky urged that in the light of the Soviet acceptance a new draft be prepared which would make clear that the White Russian governments regarded any meeting with the Bolsheviks as morally inadmissible. He assigned Sazonov the task of delivering the official White Russian reply to the peace conference.[137] On February 14 Maklakov dispatched a circular telegram to Omsk and Ekaterinodar, enclosing the text of the note which the Political Conference planned to present.[138] This note, although dated February 12, was delivered on February 16, one day after the Prinkipo conference was supposed to have met.

The delay in presenting the official White Russian reply was probably due in part to the necessity of securing agreement on the final text within the Political Conference and from the White Russian governments. At the same time there is some evidence that delivery of the White Russian rejection was held up until Lloyd George and Wilson, the sponsors of the proposed conference and the only ones who might have pressed for its convocation even in the face of a White refusal, had left Paris for London and Washington (on February 8 and 14, respectively), and until Churchill had arrived from London with new interventionist schemes to lay before the peace conference. On February 14, the day of Churchill's arrival in Paris, Maklakov wired Omsk: "There is even a basis for thinking that some powers are disposed to defeat the proposal [Prinkipo] after the departure of Wilson for America." [139]

The official White Russian reply was signed by Sazonov and Chaikovsky on behalf of the unified governments of Siberia, Archangel, and South Russia.[140] It opened with a lengthy, conciliatory introduction, expressing appreciation for the desire of the powers to help Russia restore order and reviewing the struggle of "democratic" Russia against the tyranny of the Bolsheviks. The note conveyed the readiness of the anti-Bolshevik Russian governments "to acquaint the Allied Powers with the present situation in Russia" and to cooperate with the Allies in "remedying this situation." The note concluded: "However, there cannot be any question of an exchange of ideas on this subject with the partici-

[137] "Vneshniaia politika," *Krasnyi Arkhiv*, 74.
[138] *Ibid.*, 75–76.
[139] *Ibid.* On Churchill's proposals, see ch. five, pp. 134–39.
[140] For the complete text as received by the peace conference, see *1919, Russia*, 53–54. At this time these governments were not formally united; they were linked only through the persons of Chaikovsky and Sazonov—the latter was foreign minister of both the Kolchak and Denikin governments.

pation of the Bolshevists, whom the conscience of the Russian people sees as traitors. . . . Between them and the national Russian groups, no conciliation is possible. Any meeting would not only remain without effect, but might possibly cause the Russian patriots as well as the Allied nations irreparable moral harm."

The White Russian leaders were particularly relieved to be able to refuse the Prinkipo invitation, not only because they fervently wanted to continue the anti-Bolshevik struggle and to prevent any Allied accommodation with the Bolsheviks, but also because they feared that the proposed conference might lead to the encouragement, even recognition, of the various separatist and nationality groups who were striving to break away from Russia and establish their independence. These groups were included in the Prinkipo invitation; all of them, except the Georgians, accepted the invitation, stressing that they did so not as part of Russia but as independent states. The replies from Petliura's government in the Ukraine and from the Baltic groups also stipulated that their participation in the proposed conference was conditional on the withdrawal of Bolshevik troops and the enforcement of a cease-fire.[141] The White Russian leaders, their hands full endeavoring to counter the lobbying of the separatist groups at the peace conference itself, were most anxious to avoid having to meet with them at Prinkipo.

It has been argued that the White Russian governments refused the Prinkipo invitation because they were winning the civil war; conversely, the Soviets accepted because they were losing. There is little foundation in fact for this statement. Although Kolchak's forces had recently retaken Perm, they were retreating elsewhere on the Siberian front. The Red Army was advancing in the Ukraine and in the Baltic area on the heels of the retreating Germans. It has also been suggested that the White Russian governments rejected the Prinkipo proposal because the preparation of Kolchak's spring offensive had already begun. According to General Janin, however, an offensive was impossible in December because Kolchak's troops were ragged and demoralized, while throughout January there was continued unrest in Kolchak's army, followed by a mutiny at the front on January 30 and 31.[142]

A curious historical aberration has arisen concerning the replies to the Prinkipo proposal. It has often been stated that the plan failed because the Bolsheviks refused to attend.[143] This distortion began to gain

[141] *Ibid.*, 49–50, 52–53, 69–70; Firuz D. Kazemzadeh, *The Struggle for Trans-Caucasia* (New York, 1951), 273, erroneously dates the Prinkipo invitation in 1920.

[142] Janin, 47–48, 74.

[143] See, as examples, the editor's comments in Seymour, *House Papers*, IV, 347; and Lord Hankey, *The Supreme Control at the Paris Peace Conference* (London, 1963), 54.

currency shortly after the Soviet reply was received. The White Russian representatives and the leading interventionists among the Allies emphasized, in discussing the Soviet note of February 4, that the Bolsheviks had not explicitly accepted the precondition of the proposal, a truce among the warring parties in Russia; therefore, it was argued, the Soviet reply actually amounted to a refusal of the invitation. This line of reasoning was set forth in a memorandum Bakhmetev presented to House in mid-February, and was stressed by Churchill and Sonnino in peace conference discussions on February 15, during which they advocated the replacement of the Prinkipo plan by a military crusade against Bolshevism.[144] This misconception took firm root, for on May 26 when the peace conference gave partial recognition to the government of Kolchak, the Big Four stated: "This proposal [Prinkipo] . . . broke down through the refusal of the Soviet government to accept the fundamental condition of suspending hostilities. . . ."[145]

This is an inaccurate statement since the Bolsheviks did not refuse a truce; rather they said nothing about it either way. It can, of course, be argued that the Bolsheviks would never have agreed to a cease-fire. However, given the difficult position of the Soviet government, its consistent efforts to secure a respite, and Lenin's statements concerning the Prinkipo proposal, it must be assumed that the Bolsheviks would have acceded to an armistice. In general, one of the major weaknesses of the Prinkipo plan was its vague reference to the necessity of a cease-fire in Russia as a precondition of the conference, without any indication of how such a truce should be arranged and enforced.

In this, as in many other respects, the Prinkipo affair was one of the most curious episodes of the peace conference. It was born of a paradoxical mixture of practical and idealistic considerations. On the practical side, the conclusion of the war made it impossible any longer to depict intervention as an anti-German measure, and its justification on other grounds was difficult. Much of public opinion opposed its continuation, and Allied soldiers objected to fighting in Russia. At the same time, there was a growing conviction among many British and American officials, including Lloyd George and Wilson, that the existing, halfhearted intervention was ineffectual, and served only to arouse Russian patriotism against the West and to strengthen the hand of the Bolsheviks. Moreover, these observers distrusted the politics and principles of

[144] The memo to House was undated, but was probably presented on February 19, when Bakhmetev had an interview with House. House Papers, Correspondence Files, Bakhmetev. On the meeting of February 15, see *Peace Conference*, IV, 18–21 and pp. 134–39 of ch. five.

[145] *Ibid.*, VI, 35. Lloyd George made a similar reference in his speech on Russia before the House of Commons on April 16; see pp. 245–46 of ch. seven.

the anti-Bolshevik leaders and governments and doubted the ultimate success of the White Russian cause.

In the light of these considerations and under the pressure of active liberal and labor agitation against intervention, Lloyd George—and later Wilson—sought a way to end intervention on terms permitting attainment of some of the purposes for which they had originally sanctioned such action. Lloyd George and many British statesmen felt an obligation of honor toward those anti-German Russians whom the Allies had encouraged and "who had remained true to the Allied cause and had thereby compromised themselves with the Soviet government." [146] They were therefore attracted by Litvinov's offer of an amnesty for such Russians. British policy-makers also wanted to preserve areas of influence they had marked out for the Empire in the Baltic region, the Caucasus, and Central Asia, and saw advantages in a cease-fire based on existing battle lines. Wilson, for his part, saw an opportunity to get the Japanese out of Siberia.

Yet the Prinkipo proposal was clearly as much motivated by idealism as by these many practical considerations. Lloyd George and Wilson wanted to help the Russian people out of their difficulties. They were genuinely anxious to make peace in Russia and to secure a just settlement of the Russian problem in accord with the liberal principles they espoused. They believed that the Bolsheviks were entitled to a fair and equal hearing in which the Soviet government would have an opportunity to state its case and to demonstrate the sincerity of its peaceful professions. Wilson, in addition, was opposed on principle to interference in Russia's internal affairs.

The views of Wilson and Lloyd George were widely supported among liberal and socialist elements in the democracies. There were many who sympathized to some extent with the aims, if not the practices, of the Bolsheviks, who objected to the White Russian governments as reactionary, and who espoused the principles of nonintervention and self-determination. Articulate segments of public opinion in the West had been captivated by the ideals which Woodrow Wilson symbolized and demanded that the tenets of the "new order" be applied to Russia as well.

The Soviet "peace offensive" described in the beginning of this chapter was well calculated to take advantage of both the practical and idealistic consideration which were leading to British and American reappraisal of the policy of intervention. Soviet peace appeals played upon

[146] Memorandum from General Sir Henry Wilson, chief of the Imperial General Staff, to the House of Commons, December 1, 1919; British Parliament, 1920, Cmd. 818, p. 3

the longing of citizens and soldiers for an end to bloodshed, separation, and sacrifice. The peaceful posture of the Soviet government made it even more difficult to justify intervention to the Western public and provided ammunition for the critics of intervention in the legislative assemblies and in the press. At the same time the Bolshevik proposals seemed to hold out to the politicians and diplomats the hope that existing zones of military and political control in Russia might be stabilized, at least temporarily, that fairly substantial political and economic concessions could be wrung from the Soviet government, and that Bolshevik-inspired propaganda and revolutionary activity abroad would be curtailed.

Most important, however, the Soviet peace offers appealed strongly to the liberalism of Lloyd George and Wilson. For virtually the first time since their seizure of power the Bolsheviks appeared to be reasonable and sensible people, speaking not their strange and frightening ideological tongue but the polite, civilized, and familiar language of Western society. The Soviet request to be heard seemed no more than simple justice, and the fair terms proposed by the Bolsheviks and their willingness to negotiate seemed to provide an opportunity for Wilson and Lloyd George to carry out their desire to assist the Russian people and to make peace in Russia. In this way, as we saw earlier, the Soviet "peace offensive" contributed significantly to the formulation of the Prinkipo policy.

In a sense, the Prinkipo plan was also an attempt to draw Russia into the peace settlement, thereby establishing a basis for future cooperative relations between Russia and the West, and for Russian participation in the reordered world of which Wilson dreamed. But even if the Prinkipo conference had met, the Western statesmen would soon have discovered that the aspirations of the Bolsheviks and, indeed, of some of the anti-Bolshevik forces in Russia, were in fact far removed from the ideals and values of the West.

The Prinkipo episode revealed clearly how limited was Western understanding of Russian life and politics. There was little appreciation at Paris of the nature and complexity of the struggle taking place in Russia. To expect that the welter of revolutionary, counterrevolutionary and separatist factions fighting in Russia would immediately cease hostilities at a word from the peace conference was unrealistic in the extreme. Russia was the scene of a violent and merciless civil war in which long pent-up social and nationalistic passions had been given vent; more than altruism and expressions of good will were needed to end the bitter struggle.

At the same time, the failure of the Prinkipo project provides a good example of some of the basic difficulties of both "personal" and coalition diplomacy as practiced in the twentieth century. The inherent weaknesses of the Prinkipo plan arising from its vagueness, impracticality, and naïveté might have been overcome had it not been for the political and technical defects in the project. It was supposed to represent a unanimous decision of the major powers; in fact, the French publicly criticized it and privately worked against it, thus making a farce of the attempt to reach and to put into effect a unified Allied policy toward Russia. In addition, no provision was made for implementation of the proposal. In this regard, the plan reflected the pressure and sense of urgency under which the peacemakers worked and the personal and often haphazard way in which major decisions of the conference were made and carried out. Lloyd George's impulsive good feeling toward the Bolsheviks and Wilson's intuition and sense of fair play were not enough; expert consideration of the details involved and a rigorous follow-up were needed to make the Prinkipo policy work.

If the peace conference had set up an armistice commission to establish and enforce a cease-fire, certainly necessary in view of the difficulties inherent in securing any armistice, especially in a civil war where the battle lines are vague and fluctuating, and if Wilson and Lloyd George had followed up their proposal, counteracting French sabotage of the plan and exerting pressure on the White Russian governments to participate, Prinkipo might have had some chance of success. As it was, this well-intentioned gesture remained only that. Even worse, however, it left a residue of hard feeling between the French and their Anglo-American allies, doubt and uncertainty concerning Allied intentions on the part of the White Russians, and heightened cynicism and distrust of the capitalistic world in Soviet Russia. The failure of Prinkipo was an ill omen for future efforts of the peace conference to settle the Russian question.

CHAPTER FIVE

The Bullitt Mission

⊞⊞ By the middle of February rejection of the Allies' invita-
⊞⊞ tion of January 22 by the White Russian governments and the
⊞⊞ unfavorable impression the Soviet acceptance had made on
Wilson and Lloyd George made it seem unlikely that the proposed
Prinkipo conference would ever convene. As a result, a new struggle over
Russian policy developed at the peace conference. Proponents of further
intervention advanced a plan, sponsored by Churchill, looking toward
military action in Russia. Their opponents, those who were seeking to
make peace in Russia and to work out some sort of accommodation
with the Soviet government, resisted Churchill's proposals and, in turn,
launched a new effort to bring an end to intervention. The pendulum of
conference policy toward Russia was once again in motion, swinging un-
certainly, as it did throughout the Paris negotiations, between conciliation and intervention.

Churchill's February Plan

In the three weeks between the tender of the Prinkipo invitation and
Wilson's departure for America on February 14, the president was
largely preoccupied with drafting the Covenant of the League of Nations, which he was anxious to take home with him. There is no indication that he gave much time or thought to the Russian problem. The
other senior statesmen at Paris were similarly engaged. In addition, the
Council of Ten discussed such major issues as the third renewal of the
armistice with Germany, disarmament, colonial questions and the mandate system, and territorial issues in the Balkans and Eastern Europe.
The Russian question receded into the background.

At lower levels, however, the American and British delegations continued to work for the success of the Prinkipo idea and to prepare for
the proposed conference. On January 30 Bullitt sent an urgent memorandum to Colonel House proposing the immediate evacuation of the
American troops at Archangel. Among other things, Bullitt argued, such
action would serve as proof that the Prinkipo proposal had been made

in good faith.[1] On January 31 William H. Buckler, on instructions from the American peace commissioners, reported the substance of his conversations with Litvinov to Philip Kerr, Lloyd George's private secretary (later Lord Lothian). In return, Kerr provided, unofficially, Lloyd George's current assessment of the Prinkipo policy: that a main purpose of the proposed conference should be to arrange for a cessation of the civil war and for an all-Russian assembly, and that the British government was "prepared to meet at Prinkipo, or anywhere else, the Soviet government's representatives, even if no other Russian representatives should accept." [2] This was a strong stand, indicating that the British prime minister was still determined to hear the Bolshevik side of the story—and within two weeks he grasped the chance to put his intention into practice.

The call to Prinkipo had set the date for the conference as February 15. On February 13 the American commissioners in Paris were still taking steps looking toward convocation of the conference, even though the White Russian governments had not yet answered the invitation. On that date they authorized a telegram instructing Consul General Harris in Omsk to urge Kolchak to attend the Prinkipo meeting and to offer as bait a hint that recognition might be accorded him afterward. Two days later they recommended that Professor Herron, the senior American delegate selected to go to Prinkipo, be called to Paris from Geneva.[3] As late as February 22 younger members of the American delegation, unaware that Bullitt had secretly left Paris for Russia that day, were still attempting to persuade anti-Bolshevik and separatist groups to attend the proposed conference.[4] Herron indignantly maintained later that Bullitt, while en route to pick up the orders for his trip to Russia, assured Herron of his fidelity to the Prinkipo plan. Herron himself was not informed that the Prinkipo proposal had been dropped until February 28, when a clerk, instead of one of the American delegates, gave him the news.[5]

---

[1] *Bullitt Mission,* 15–17.

[2] *Peace Conference,* XI, 5, 9

[3] *Ibid.,* XI, 35, 42.

[4] On that date Adolf A. Berle, Jr., Samuel Eliot Morison, and J. V. Fuller lunched with Lithuanian leaders in Paris. *1919, Russia,* 72. Also working for Prinkipo in Paris were William Allen White, the other American delegate to the proposed conference, and American labor leaders Samuel Gompers and William Walling. White, 562. In Geneva, Herron was actively lobbying for the Prinkipo plan. He later claimed that a number of Cadet leaders, some representatives of the Omsk government (but not Sazonov), and Chaikovsky had all either agreed to go to the Prinkipo conference or else had promised to put no obstacles in the way of the meeting. Herron, 220.

[5] *Ibid.,* 221. See also *Peace Conference,* XI, 84, 87; and House Papers, Diary, March 1, 1919.

In early February a dispute over Russian policy developed within the British government. When Lloyd George returned to England on February 8 to deal with mounting labor difficulties and to mend his political fences in the House of Commons, he found considerable criticism of his conciliatory policy toward the Bolsheviks among Tory members of his coalition, and outright opposition to it on the part of his minister of war, Churchill. Throughout the peace conference Lloyd George's position on many of the issues discussed at Paris was circumscribed to a considerable degree by the pressures of domestic politics—the necessity of keeping his coalition together and of appeasing the more conservative, vindictive, and vociferous representatives of public opinion in Parliament and in the press. Nowhere was this more evident than in the matter of policy toward Russia. In a sense Lloyd George's difficulties with Parliament in 1919 were ironic retribution for the low intellectual and high emotional level on which the prime minister had pitched his electoral campaign of December 1918. Lloyd George had not hesitated to appeal to popular passions with such slogans as "make the Germans pay down to the last ha'penny." The not unforeseeable result was what Harold Nicolson characterized as a most illiberal, short-sighted, and emotional House of Commons, seemingly "guided by pure hysteria and war-nerves." [6] As regards attitudes toward Russia, Nabokov reported gleefully to Omsk in early February that in the new Parliament "adherents of Russian Bolshevism are absent, and it has a quite significant contingent of friends of Russia. . . ." [7]

On February 11 Lord Curzon, who, like Churchill, opposed any sort of dealing with the Soviet government, stirred up Parliament with a vigorous speech attacking the Bolsheviks. The next day, in a reply designed to mollify the growing criticism of his Prinkipo policy, Lloyd George explained his position on Russia to Commons. The speech was somewhat equivocal: on the one hand, Lloyd George condemned the undemocratic and terroristic nature of the Bolshevik regime and indicated that there was no thought of recognizing it; on the other, he stressed that armed intervention in Russia, because of the tremendous cost it entailed, was out of the question.[8] Nevertheless, Lloyd George achieved his purpose to a considerable extent; Nabokov, reporting the speech to Omsk, noted that the press the next day gave the impression that the prime minister had partially dispelled public and parliamentary anxiety over his Russian policy.[9]

[6] Nicolson, 63, 263.
[7] Cited in Subbotovsky, 31.
[8] Great Britain, House of Commons, *Debates,* fifth series, CXII, Cols. 189–98.
[9] Nabokov to the Ministry of Foreign Affairs, Omsk, February 13, cited in Subbotovsky, 26–27.

Having placated his parliamentary critics for the moment, Lloyd George had then to face his ministers. In a meeting of the War Cabinet on February 12 the whole Russian problem was aired again. Military intervention against the Bolsheviks was once more voted down, but further action in regard to Russia was postponed, pending a decision on this issue by the peace conference.[10] This did not satisfy Churchill, the chief British advocate of intervention, who was anxious to find some way of helping the White Russians and whose penchant for energetic action was increasingly frustrated by the indecisiveness of the statesmen in Paris. He continued pressing Lloyd George for a definite policy toward Russia until the latter, undoubtedly desperate for some way of diverting Churchill's importunity, finally suggested that Churchill go to Paris himself to see if he could persuade the conference to adopt a firm stand on the Russian question.[11]

Churchill's general attitude toward Bolshevism at that time is well known; in his memoirs he called Lenin "the Grand Repudiator," and commented about Soviet Russia: "There ruled 'the nameless beast' so long foretold in Russian legend." [12] In January 1919 Churchill told Lord Riddell that military intervention, using British, French, and American volunteers, was the only solution to the Russian problem. When Lord Riddell replied that the British public opposed armed intervention in Russia's affairs, Churchill agreed, but added that their view might change.[13] This comment foreshadowed Churchill's later efforts to stir up press and parliamentary circles against conciliation in Russia and to rally them behind intervention.

On January 27 Churchill wrote Lloyd George in Paris, setting forth his dissatisfaction with the way the Russian question was being handled, and during the next two weeks he discussed the matter several times with General Wilson, Imperial chief of staff.[14] Wilson was strongly anti-Bolshevik, but he had lost confidence in Denikin and Kolchak. He was also concerned that the British would become dangerously overextended if they accepted substantial commitments in Russia, in addition to garrisoning duties in Europe and their normal responsibilities for order and security throughout the Empire. As a result, General Wilson proposed the withdrawal of British troops from Siberia and North Russia, although at the same time he recommended maintaining British forces in the Caucasus and Transcaspia. Wilson's views were supported by the

---

[10] Callwell, *Wilson Diaries,* II, 169.
[11] Churchill, *Aftermath,* 173.
[12] *Ibid.,* 61.
[13] Riddell, 15.
[14] Callwell, *Wilson Diaries,* II, 167–69.

British military representatives in Paris. In a memorandum drawn up in early February, they advised evacuation from Russia, arguing that half a million more men would be needed to ensure victory over the Bolsheviks; moreover, intervention, even if successful, would not settle the question of the future status of Russia and might have to be followed by a prolonged period of Allied occupation.[15]

Churchill himself, as well as others in British military circles, opposed evacuation from Russia. He believed that sending conscript British troops to Russia was out of the question, but he urged instead the recruitment of volunteer forces, the arming and equipping of the anti-Bolshevik armies from surplus British war materiel, the dispatch of British officers and instructors to help train these armies, and the combination of all the White Russian and separatist governments into "one system of war and diplomacy" directed against the Bolsheviks.[16] To this view, Churchill subsequently won over General Wilson. As we saw in the previous chapter, Churchill began, without authorization from Lloyd George, to put part of this plan into effect in late January and early February by sending supplies and a military mission to Denikin, actions which helped undermine the Prinkipo policy Lloyd George was pursuing at the peace conference. But, unable to get a decision from the Cabinet on the question of raising volunteers for Russia, Churchill departed for Paris to present his case to the peacemakers.

On February 14, just hours before President Wilson was to depart for America, Churchill dramatically appeared before a special meeting of the Supreme Council hurriedly called for six-thirty that evening. Lloyd George was in London and Orlando had just departed for Rome while President Wilson had actually risen from the table in order to leave when Churchill obtained the floor.[17] The latter announced that he represented the British Cabinet, which was most anxious to know what the policy of the conference toward Russia would be: Was the original Prinkipo plan to be followed? Was it peace or war in Russia? Was Wilson departing with the question unanswered?[18] Churchill declared that he believed little good would come of the Prinkipo meeting if only the Bolsheviks attended, but, in any case, there could be no further delay; a definite decision on the Prinkipo project must be made. The morale of the troops, of their families, and of the anti-Bolshevik forces was disintegrating because of the uncertainty.

Surprisingly, Clemenceau at once objected to Churchill's tactics,

[15] This memorandum is summarized in Beadon, 93–96.
[16] Churchill, *Aftermath*, 171.
[17] *Ibid.*, 173; Hankey, 69.
[18] *Peace Conference*, III, 1041–43.

[135]

claiming that the Russian question was too important for decision at such a hurried, unexpected meeting. Apparently the French, expecting the official White Russian refusal of the Prinkipo invitation at any moment, were afraid that an agreement to pursue the Prinkipo policy might be rushed through at the meeting. Wilson, obviously tired and preoccupied, nevertheless reaffirmed his position on the Russian problem. He again rejected military intervention as a solution, and urged the withdrawal of all Allied forces. In the first place, these troops were doing no good in Russia; they did not know "for whom or for what they were fighting," and they were not assisting in "any promising common effort to establish order in Russia." Second, there were in any case not enough Allied troops to defeat the Bolsheviks, and no one was able to furnish reinforcements. Finally, these forces would have to be withdrawn some day, and further delay did not seem to promise any betterment of the situation.

Turning to the question of the Prinkipo proposal, Wilson declared that its purpose had been fact-finding, not a *rapprochement* with the Bolsheviks. The Bolshevik answer had offered, instead of peace, things the powers had not requested—the repayment of debts and economic and territorial concessions—and it "might be thought insulting." Therefore, in order to obtain the information desired, the Allies might have to imitate Mahomet and go to the Russian governments. Wilson added: "As far as he was concerned, he would be quite content that informal American representatives should meet representatives of the Bolsheviks." The Bullitt mission, which Wilson had discussed with House that morning, was clearly much on his mind; and he appeared somewhat resigned to the failure of the Prinkipo plan in its original form.[19]

Churchill then turned to the attack. Complete withdrawal from Russia would be "pulling out the linch-pin from the whole machine," and would mean sentencing half a million non-Bolsheviks to death. Therefore, if Prinkipo failed, would the Supreme War Council approve the sending of volunteers and experts to Russia, as well as the arming of the anti-Bolshevik forces? Wilson replied that he doubted volunteers could be obtained and he feared that arms would only strengthen the reactionaries in Russia, but that he really had no dogmatic opinion on the question. If he were acting alone, he would get information first; but now he would defer to the majority opinion. Since Wilson had to leave for his train, the meeting broke up at this point.

To some extent Churchill's last-minute approach had succeeded. Wilson was hurried and harried, and his words suggest that he did not take an adamant stand against Churchill—as he later did by telegram—

[19] On the decision to send Bullitt to Russia, see pp. 151–52 below.

partly because he was anxious to get away. At the same time, since he had already given House permission to send Bullitt to Russia on an informal and unofficial fact-finding mission, he probably did not feel that it was of such urgency to defend and carry through the Prinkipo plan.

Churchill's appeal for a resolute Russian policy once again brought the Russian question to the forefront of conference deliberations. During the following week much time and attention, both in the meetings of the Council of Ten and behind the scenes, were devoted to this issue. The next day, Saturday, February 15, discussion of the Russian problem was resumed in the Council of Ten.[20] Wilson having departed, Lansing and House now represented the United States, while Churchill and Balfour spoke for England. The meeting opened with a long report on the military situation by General Alby of the French General Staff. He painted a black picture of advancing Bolshevism, but concluded that a small task force of regular Allied troops, well led and equipped with planes and tanks, could rout the Red Army at little cost. This set the stage attractively for the interventionist presentation of Churchill, who advanced two proposals. First, he pointed out that the Prinkipo plan had been hanging fire for almost a month and urged that some definite policy be adopted at once. The Bolsheviks were continuing to attack, while Allied offensive operations had been suspended pending the outcome of the Prinkipo plan. There was therefore a serious danger that the anti-Bolshevik forces would begin "to melt away." Churchill then suggested that the conference send the Bolsheviks a wireless message whose effect "would be either to bring about a discussion at Prinkipo and a cessation of fighting in Russia," or to leave the field clear for such other action as the Allies might wish to take.

The draft message which Churchill submitted began by denying the insinuation of the Soviet reply to the Prinkipo invitation that a desire for economic and territorial concessions motivated Allied policy toward Russia. Peace was the powers' supreme objective in Russia; therefore, essential to the Prinkipo proposal was its precondition of a cessation of hostilities. But the Bolsheviks had continued offensive operations and were stepping up their military preparations. Consequently, the message continued, unless within ten days the Bolshevik troops ceased attacking and withdrew five miles, the Prinkipo invitation would lapse. If the Bolsheviks complied with this stipulation, the Allies would then address a similar request to the anti-Bolshevik forces. Churchill's draft amounted to an ultimatum. Its one-sidedness is apparent. The Bolsheviks would either have to withdraw their troops (stop where they were winning and

[20] *Ibid.*, IV, 10–21; Churchill, *Aftermath*, 175–76.

keep on retreating where they were losing), without a similar commitment from the opposing forces, or they would be blamed for the failure of the Prinkipo project and for the dashing of hopes for peace in Russia.

Churchill's second proposal to the Council of Ten revealed his basic purpose—to prepare the way for a military crusade against the Bolsheviks. He suggested that the conference establish an inter-Allied council on Russian affairs, whose military section should begin to examine, at once, even before the ultimatum on Prinkipo had expired, what concerted action against the Bolsheviks was possible in case the ultimatum were refused. Thus, as Churchill himself pointed out, at the end of the time limit set in the ultimatum, the Supreme War Council would have ready an operations plan for military intervention in Russia. The Council could then make its choice: "either to act, or to withdraw their troops and leave everyone in Russia to stew in their own juice." Churchill argued against the latter alternative by raising the bogey of Russo-German cooperation. While before the war Russia had served as a counterpoise to Germany, after the war, if the Allies left Russia to her own devices, she would become the servant and abettor of German ambitions, Churchill warned.

In his memoirs the secretary of the Council, Maurice Hankey, describing this meeting, noted that everyone was mesmerized by Churchill's eloquence and enthusiasm. The statesmen all hastened to repudiate the Prinkipo project, which they had approved three weeks earlier, and were "all very brave and downright in the absence of Lloyd George and Woodrow Wilson." [21] Clemenceau, the first to speak, approved the idea of preparing military plans, but opposed the proposed message to the Bolsheviks. He recalled that he had been against the original proposal of Lloyd George, but had accepted it to preserve unanimity. Now it had failed—the White Russians had refused and the Bolsheviks had offered money—and the best way to get out of such awkward situations gracefully was to say nothing. Why send a message announcing to the whole world that the plan had failed? Clemenceau then returned to his pet theory of the *cordon sanitaire,* arguing that this was the best policy since, after being cut off from the rest of the world for a while, "the Russians would ask the Allies to intervene." At the same time he agreed with Churchill as to the danger of German domination of Russia and the consequent urgency of making a military decision regarding the Russian situation. In typical fashion Clemenceau concluded: "He did not court defeat in Russia, after having been victorious on the Rhine."

Sonnino supported Clemenceau at every point, and recalled *his* oppo-

[21] Hankey, 70.

sition to the Prinkipo plan. Somewhat gratuitously, he reminded his colleagues that he had predicted that the Bolsheviks would be the first to accept. He objected to any new message being sent to the Bolsheviks since it would only enhance their prestige and lower White Russian morale further. Since the Soviet government had obviously not complied with the original Allied demand for a cessation of hostilities, the conference would be justified in letting the whole matter drop. Why give the Bolsheviks another chance?

Colonel House then reviewed his position. Not to be outdone he noted that he had never favored the Prinkipo plan. Once the Allies had embarked on it, however, they should follow it through, he believed. He warned that unless tact were exercised, all the peoples east of the Rhine might be driven to turn against the Allies. If the Allies wished to take action in Russia later, House concluded, they would be in a stronger position before public opinion if they had pursued the Prinkipo policy as far as they could.

Taking up this theme, Churchill argued, in defense of his proposed ultimatum, that if the conference sincerely pressed the Prinkipo plan, then no one could say that the proposition had been a "false step" and that because the Bolsheviks had accepted, the Allies had withdrawn their invitation. At this juncture, just as it seemed that Churchill might carry the day, Balfour raised an important and embarrassing point, which brought discussion to a halt; he wanted to ask the military authorities a question of fact—it was being said that the Bolsheviks had not complied with the Allied condition of a cease-fire, "but had the Allied troops abstained from the hostilities? Or, to put his question in another way, had all the Allied military operations been defensive in their character?" Churchill made no attempt to answer the question or to deny its implication, commenting only that the Bolsheviks had made heavy attacks recently. The discussion thus far had indicated that only House and Balfour entertained doubts about Churchill's proposals; nevertheless, on Balfour's motion, further consideration of them was adjourned until Monday.

Although no decision had been reached, the groups in Paris working against the Prinkipo plan and for further Allied intervention in Russia felt that victory was at hand. On February 16 Maklakov wired Omsk: "The conception of a meeting on Prinkipo is apparently definitely abandoned. Judging from confidential information I have received, there is some hope for a turn in the attitude of the Powers on the Russian question in a direction more favorable for us." [22] And in his weekly

[22] "Vneshniaia politika," *Krasnyi Arkhiv,* 81.

press conference on February 16, Pichon stated that the Prinkipo question was no longer of interest.[23]

The opponents of intervention were by no means beaten, however, and they began at once to rally their forces. On Sunday, February 16, House discussed Russian policy with Lansing. He also met with Balfour to plan and coordinate the position Britain and America should take when discussion of Churchill's proposals was resumed the next day.[24] Following these consultations, Auchincloss for the American side and Wiseman representing the British together drafted an outline memorandum suggesting a modification of Churchill's first proposal. They recommended that instead of sending a message to the Bolsheviks, the Allies make a general statement to all the Russian factions and to the world at large. This public declaration would have two parts: in the first, the Allies would announce that negotiations for peace in Russia had not been broken off, but that the Bolsheviks had not complied with the conditions for the Prinkipo meeting and had misinterpreted the Allied proposal. The second part, designed to clarify the situation, would contain a statement that if the Russian parties came to a conference, the Allies would favor the peasants receiving land, would explain that the question of foreign loans and concessions was not their chief interest in Russia, and would serve Russia without any thought of interfering in her affairs; if, however, the Russian factions did not come, the Allies would be compelled "to protect neighboring states from *terrorist* armies (1) by sending forces to these states (2) [by] drawing an economic cordon around Russia *BUT* . . . [would] at any time be ready to meet Russian delegates . . . seeking peace and the free development of peoples under democratic principles." [25] This remarkable memorandum is an excellent illustration of the well-meant liberalism which guided the thinking of many in the West concerning Russia.

The next morning, February 17, the American commissioners approved the Auchincloss-Wiseman memorandum, which House had submitted to them as a basis for the position to be taken by the United States in further conference discussion of Churchill's proposals. Only one change of significance was made: on House's recommendation, an offer was added to send food and other supplies to Russia on condition that the Russian factions attend the proposed conference.[26] The com-

[23] Noble, 286.

[24] House Papers, Diary, February 16, 1919; Auchincloss Diary, February 18, 1919, containing a telegraphic report from Auchincloss to Polk on developments relating to the Russian question.

[25] Italics in original. House Papers, Auchincloss Diary, February 16, 1919.

[26] *Ibid.,* February 17, 1919, and *Peace Conference,* XI, 42–43.

missioners asked Secretary Lansing to prepare a new statement to the Russians based on the recommendations of the memorandum. After the meeting Lansing and House discussed the text of this statement, the latter noting in his diary that he excised an implied threat of military action in Russia which Lansing had included in his draft.[27]

After the commissioners had considered the Auchincloss-Wiseman memorandum, General Bliss suggested that the American delegation be ready with a complete answer in the event that the question of using armed force in Russia were raised in the Council of Ten. In a lengthy statement which he had prepared for use in such a contingency, and which he read to the commissioners, Bliss declared categorically that the government and people of the United States would never support hostile action in Russia as long as peace had not been made with the Central Powers and as long as the situation in the rest of Europe remained so confused and discouraging.[28] To Americans, the frightful conditions in Russia did not stand out from the general European turmoil. They were, therefore, little disposed to take action there. The immediate conclusion of peace in Europe would both throw into glaring relief the misery of Russia and "go a long way in removing or diminishing the menace of Bolshevism," which thrived on confusion and strife.

The other commissioners warmly endorsed Bliss' declaration and decided that it should be read to the Council of Ten that afternoon before submission by the American delegates of a new Allied statement on Russia along the lines of the redrafted Auchincloss-Wiseman memorandum. If this were done, the commissioners felt, Churchill's "proposal of referring the matter to a military commission . . . would of itself fall through." Although House drew on the Bliss statement in his remarks before the Council that afternoon, neither he nor Lansing actually read it to the Council of Ten, prompting General Bliss to remark tartly: "They lost their sand." [29]

While the Americans were mapping plans for renewal of the struggle with Churchill and the French and Italians, those in the British delegation who opposed Churchill's views and favored an effort to make peace in Russia were also busy girding for battle. After the meeting of February 15, at which Churchill had advanced his two proposals on Russia, Philip Kerr, Lloyd George's private secretary, received permission from Balfour to wire the prime minister the gist of what Churchill wanted the

[27] Lansing Papers, Desk Diary, February 17, 1919; House Papers, Diary, February 17, 1919.
[28] *Peace Conference*, XI, 44.
[29] Quoted in Grew, I, 378.

conference to undertake.[30] Lloyd George immediately replied in two vigorous cables of instructions to Churchill. The prime minister expressed great alarm at the idea of plans for a war against the Bolsheviks. He pointed out that the Cabinet had not authorized action of this kind, but had only contemplated sending supplies to the anti-Bolshevik forces. Lloyd George viewed Churchill's proposals as possibly leading to a costly commitment in men and money, and warned: "A war against a continent like Russia . . . is the direct road to bankruptcy and Bolshevism in these islands."

The British leader then took up a theme to which he was to recur with increasing regularity in subsequent months: Russia must save herself. He argued that the Russian people should be given an opportunity to throw off Bolshevik rule. If they were really anti-Bolshevik, they would need only supplies and equipment with which to fight. This the Allies should furnish. Failure, even with such help, to defeat the Bolsheviks would show that the people were not strongly opposed to Bolshevism. It would then be completely wrong to intervene with Allied troops and to attempt to force a decision on the Russian people. Moreover, this would strengthen the Bolsheviks in Russia and lead to grave difficulties on the domestic scene.[31]

Lloyd George's "peevish wire," as General Wilson described the instructions from the prime minister, was discussed at a meeting of the British Empire delegation on Monday morning, February 17. Although Kerr reported to Lloyd George that the latter's views had carried the day, the delegation actually decided on what amounted to a compromise between the position of Lloyd George and that of Churchill. Everyone agreed that war against the Bolsheviks was impractical because of public opinion in England and undesirable since it would arouse patriotic sentiment in Russia on behalf of the Bolsheviks. It was also the consensus, however, that it would be disastrous to let the Bolsheviks overrun Siberia and the border states; an inquiry should therefore be made as to the cost of maintaining the anti-Bolshevik forces in their present position.[32]

After lunch Kerr, as requested by Lloyd George, showed Colonel House the prime minister's instructions to Churchill. Kerr made the mis-

---

[30] Lloyd George, I, 264. Lloyd George dates this incident after the signing of the Treaty of Versailles, but from his description of it and from other evidence respecting the affair it is clear that his reference is to Kerr's report on Churchill's schemes.

[31] *Ibid.*, I, 371–72; Churchill, *Aftermath*, 177. Churchill summarizes only one of Lloyd George's messages. See also Riddell, 21, and Callwell, *Wilson Diaries*, II, 170.

[32] Lloyd George, I, 372–73. See also *Borden Memoirs*, II, 913.

take, however, of telling Churchill what he had done. Needless to say, this infuriated Churchill, who knew, as he entered the afternoon meeting of the Council of Ten, that House was aware that Lloyd George did not endorse the position Churchill was advocating.[33] Moreover, House had made clear to Kerr that he planned to oppose Churchill in Council debate, believing that the French would seize upon the formation of a commission of military inquiry respecting Russia as the occasion for proclaiming an anti-Bolshevik crusade and that such a war would only drive Germany and Russia together.[34]

The debate over Russian policy in the Council of Ten on the afternoon of February 17 was so acrimonious, and the point at issue—authorization to draw up a military plan of operations against the Bolsheviks—was considered to be so delicate, that the participants agreed to delete the record of their discussions from the minutes of that session.[35] Minutes of Council meetings were circulated to the delegations of the major powers, and although the proceedings of the Council were supposed to be secret, there had been consistent leaks. Fortunately, from memoir accounts and archival materials a fairly complete picture of this important and stormy meeting can be pieced together.[36]

When discussion of the Russian question began, Churchill submitted a resolution directing the Allied military representatives at Versailles "to examine and report at an early date as to the practical possibilities of joint military action by the Associated Powers to enable the Russian armies called into being by those Powers during the war with Germany to maintain themselves against Bolshevist coercion, and as to what measures and precautions may be necessary or possible to safeguard Finland, Esthonia, Livonia, Poland, and Rumania." [37] Churchill added that he believed it desirable for the Council, if it adopted his resolution, to make public its decision.

House at once opposed Churchill's resolution on the ground that the proposed study by the military representatives would be fruitless since the United States could not in any case support a military venture against the Bolsheviks. Under existing legislation the American govern-

[33] Lloyd George, I, 373–74; House Papers, Diary, February 17, 1919.

[34] Lloyd George, I, 373.

[35] *Peace Conference*, IV, 28; House Papers, Diary, February 17, 1919. Hankey, 72, erroneously reports no discussion took place, as does Seth P. Tillman, *Anglo-American Relations at the Paris Peace Conference of 1919* (Princeton, 1961), 147.

[36] Churchill, *Aftermath*, 178; Callwell, *Wilson Diaries*, II, 170; House Papers, Diary, February 17, 1919; *ibid.*, telegram from House to Wilson, February 17, 1919; *ibid.*, Auchincloss Diary, February 17, 1919; and *ibid.*, telegram from Auchincloss to Polk, February 18, 1919.

[37] Full text of the proposal in House Papers, Drawer 34, File 124. See also the extract in *1919, Russia*, pp. 68–69.

ment had no authority to fight the Bolsheviks since the United States was not at war with Russia. Moreover, House added, public opinion in America did not favor intervention in Russia. House then proposed a substitute resolution providing for informal consultation among the Allied military representatives, who would report separately to their respective governments, so that at a later date the delegates could discuss what course of action was feasible in Russia in the light of advice from their military experts. Why House failed to submit a proposal along the lines of the Auchincloss-Wiseman memorandum, as recommended by the American commissioners at their meeting that morning, is not clear; perhaps he felt it would have no chance of adoption in the face of the interventionist bent of Churchill and the French.

According to House, Balfour, piqued at Churchill being sent over from London to propose a new Russian policy, had planned to let the latter speak for the British.[38] After House had introduced his substitute resolution, however, Balfour joined in the discussion, opposing Churchill's plan and warmly endorsing House's position. Balfour insisted in particular that no press announcment of any kind concerning the discussion or the eventual decision taken should be made.

Clemenceau then delivered what Balfour described in an aside to House as "a brilliant but very offensive speech." Clemenceau declared that since America would furnish neither troops nor material to help fight the Bolshevik scourge, the other representatives "would discuss the Russian question without America." He added caustically that "it was a pitiful thing to see the victors of the Boches afraid to refer the Russian problem to Versailles."[39] This led Balfour, who, in Auchincloss' phrase, "was mad clean through," to answer Clemenceau tartly, and House to ask the French premier whom he was criticizing. Clemenceau replied that he was not criticizing anyone, and he apologized for any implications his remarks might have had.

Once this sharp exchange had shown that House and Balfour were not to be bullied into accepting Churchill's proposal, Clemenceau and Churchill backed down and accepted House's counterproposal that each government confer privately and informally with its military advisers, after the latter had consulted with their colleagues at Versailles. According to Auchincloss, House and Balfour insisted on this procedure because they feared that news of a formal directive from the conference to prepare war plans against the Bolsheviks would leak out, placing the American and British governments in an awkward position.

The outcome of the three days of Council debate on Russia was a

[38] House Papers, Diary, February 17, 1919.
[39] General Wilson quoting Clemenceau, Callwell, *Wilson Diaries,* II, 170.

stalemate between the interventionists and their opponents. The compromise reached meant that while Churchill's plan to prepare a military crusade against the Bolsheviks was sidetracked, at least temporarily, no action to carry out or renew the Prinkipo proposal was taken either. Conference policy toward Russia remained at dead center, and a definite decision on this important matter had once more been put off. Churchill and General Wilson were disgusted at the result, the former returning immediately to England, and the latter commenting: "I think this is the greatest depth of impotence I have ever seen the Frocks fall to." [40] Churchill, however, lost no time in carrying his case to the English public. In a speech at Mansion House on February 19 he reiterated his plea that the Russian armies fighting "the foul baboonery of Bolshevism" be aided with arms, equipment, and volunteers, although, in a bow to Lloyd George's views, he also declared that Russia must be saved primarily by Russian exertions. [41]

Immediately after the tempestuous meeting of February 17, both parties to the struggle over Russian policy hastened to prepare themselves for new clashes on this issue. The Americans informed President Wilson of what had taken place in two cables, one from the American Commission and the other from House to Wilson in their private code. [42] In his replies Wilson strongly supported the stand taken by House on February 15 and 17. He stressed that "we are not at war with Russia and will in no circumstances that we can now foresee take part in military operations there against the Russians"—overlooking the fact that American troops in North Russia were doing just that. Wilson added: "It would be fatal to be led further into the Russian chaos." [43] Wilson also expressed surprise at the direction Churchill's proposal had taken and dismay that his own agreement on February 14 to abide by the wish of the majority had apparently been interpreted as acquiescence in Churchill's scheme. [44]

House and Lloyd George were meanwhile planning a new effort to make peace in Russia based on the Prinkipo plan. On instructions from Lloyd George, Kerr called on House February 18 to discuss what should next be done in regard to Russia. Unfortunately, there is no record of

[40] *Ibid.*

[41] Churchill, *Aftermath,* 164.

[42] *1919, Russia,* 68–69; House Papers, telegram from House to Wilson, February 17, 1919.

[43] First quotation from Wilson's telegram to House of February 20, 1919, Wilson Papers, Series VIIIA, Box 21; the second from Wilson's telegram to the American Commission of February 19, 1919, *1919, Russia,* 71–72.

[44] For the reply of the American Commission to Wilson on February 23, 1919, assuring him that Churchill's project was dead and that the president's position had been made clear, see *ibid.,* 73.

this conversation, but Bullitt later testified before the Senate Foreign Relations Committee that it was agreed that House and Lloyd George would meet as soon as the latter returned from London. At that time "they were to prepare a renewal of the Prinkipo proposal, and they were both prepared to insist that it be passed against any opposition from the French." [45] On the basis of subsequent correspondence between Kerr and House it is probably more accurate to describe the policy which was being worked out between House and Lloyd George through the intermediary of Kerr not as a direct renewal of the Prinkipo proposal, but a fresh attempt to get in touch with the Soviet government and to persuade the Bolshevik and other Russian factions to enter into some sort of negotiations looking toward a cessation of hostilities in Russia, with an Allied promise, if this were done, of relief, recognition of all the Russian governments, noninterference in Russia's affairs, and eventual withdrawal of Allied forces. [46]

In reply to a report from Kerr on his conversation with House on February 18, Lloyd George once again set forth his views on the Russian question. [47] They differed but little from the stand he had taken a few days before in opposition to Churchill's project. He opposed foreign intervention in Russia, but favored the dispatch of equipment and supplies to permit the Russians to save themselves, if they so desired. "If . . . they are either indifferent, or very divided, or lean toward Bolshevism, although they must collapse, I see no reason why, if this represents their attitude toward Bolshevism, the Powers should impose on them a government they are not particularly interested in or attempt to save them from a government they are not particularly opposed to." The only new point Lloyd George made was his assertion that "we are bound to give moral, political, and, if necessary, material support to protect Finland, Poland, and other states carved out of Russia . . . against Bolshevik invasion." He added, however, that he saw no evidence of Bolshevik intention or desire to invade these areas.

On February 17, the day before these "long-distance" consultations between House and Lloyd George began, House took the first step to prepare a separate course of action regarding Russia, one which he had discussed with Wilson before the president's departure for Washington.

[45] Kerr's call on House is noted, without a résumé of the conversation, in House Papers, Diary, February 18, 1919; Bullitt's account of what transpired is in *Bullitt Mission*, 33–34. See also Bullitt Papers, Datebook, February 18, 1919.

[46] This is the tenor of a memorandum on policy toward Russia, unsigned but apparently prepared by Wiseman, which was attached to a letter of February 21 from Kerr to House. House Papers, Drawer 31, File 209.

[47] Kerr's report is not available. For Lloyd George's views, see House Papers, letter from Kerr to House, February 21, 1919, transmitting them, and Lloyd George, I, 376–77.

On that date House asked Bullitt if he would go to Russia on an unofficial mission for the American government. The next day the orders authorizing Bullitt's trip were drawn up, but Bullitt was not yet dispatched.[48]

While the Americans and British were busy with these consultations and plans, the French and General Wilson hastened to reap whatever benefit they could from the compromise decision of February 17. On the morning of February 18 General Bliss reported to the American commissioners that the informal conferences among the military representatives at Versailles called for in the resolution adopted by the Council of Ten had already been scheduled; he was to meet General Wilson and his colleagues that very day.[49] Bliss added that he planned to present to Wilson the memorandum he had discussed with the commissioners the previous morning and to declare firmly that "from a military point of view it would be a piece of criminal folly to start another war . . . until the present war had finished."

At this time Clemenceau was personally taking a particular interest in the Russian question. According to Auchincloss, no sooner had the contentious meeting of February 17 broken up than "Clemenceau rushed up to the Colonel [House] and Balfour and told them how much he loved them, and they arranged to meet for a private conference on Wednesday at ten o'clock."[50] On Tuesday, February 18, in the Council of Ten, after an unsuccessful French attempt to persuade House and Balfour to hear the views of a "liberal" Russian, Chaikovsky, sponsored by the Russian Political Conference, Clemenceau reinserted the Russian problem on the future agenda of the conference. He then moved that the Council not meet the next day, Wednesday, February 19, since "he wished to devote the whole day to thought on the Russian question."[51] What Clemenceau planned to propose to House and Balfour in their private meeting scheduled for Wednesday at ten, and what Clemenceau's devoting "the whole day to thought on the Russian question" would have led to, we may never know, for early on Wednesday morning Clemenceau was wounded by a fanatic gunman.[52] This dramatically changed the status of the Russian question at Paris. The attempt on Clemenceau's life brought to a halt not only his own, but most other,

---

[48] Bullitt Papers, Datebook, February 17, 1919; *Bullitt Mission,* 34; and see below, p. 152.

[49] *Peace Conference,* XI, 49.

[50] House Papers, Auchincloss Diary, February 17, 1919.

[51] *Peace Conference,* IV, 53–54, 56.

[52] When the archives of the French Foreign Office for the period of the peace conference are opened to scholars, clues to Clemenceau's plans and state of mind may be found.

developing plans for action regarding Russia, and suspended for over a week further formal consideration by the conference of how best to deal with the Russian problem.

The interventionists in Paris quickly spread the rumor that the shooting was the work of the Bolsheviks.[53] Lloyd George at once telephoned from London to say that as long as Clemenceau was wounded, the French premier was "boss of the roost" and could veto anything. It would be no use putting forth new proposals for peace in Russia because Clemenceau "would simply have to hold up a finger and the whole thing would drop to the ground."[54] Actually, Lloyd George may not have been too disturbed by this turn of events; he may well have found the wounding of Clemenceau a convenient excuse for delaying implementation of a policy of conciliation in Russia, to which he was rather heavily committed before his colleagues in Paris, but which was increasingly proving to be a political liability in Parliament. In any event, House and Kerr decided that no further conference action respecting Russia could be taken until Clemenceau recovered and until Lloyd George returned to Paris on February 28.[55] They did agree, however, on an important step falling outside the jurisdiction of the conference—the sending of Bullitt to meet the Bolsheviks. On February 20, following Lloyd George's phone call and in view of the suspension of conference consideration of new proposals respecting Russia, Bullitt was told to leave for Russia as soon as possible; he departed in secrecy two days later.[56]

In the events leading up to the dispatch of the Bullitt mission, and in the final demise of the Prinkipo project, chance—or historical accident as some prefer to call it—played a role of some significance. The absence of Lloyd George and Wilson weakened the hand of those in Paris urging a peaceful solution to the Russian problem. Then, at the very moment when Lloyd George and House had finally decided to attempt to press the Prinkipo policy of conciliation to a conclusion despite French opposition, Clemenceau was shot. If Wilson and Lloyd George had been in Paris, if Clemenceau had not been wounded—the always tantalizing "ifs" of history—some further effort akin to Prinkipo to stop the fighting in Russia and to reach agreement with the Bolsheviks and other Russian factions might well have been made, and Bullitt might never have set out on his controversial journey to Moscow. Or, examin-

[53] Vernon Bartlett, *Behind the Scenes at the Peace Conference* (London, 1919), 176. The gunman was actually a half-crazed anarchist.

[54] *Bullitt Mission*, 34.

[55] House Papers, letter from Kerr to House, February 21, 1919, and reply from House to Kerr, February 22, 1919. See also House's telegram to Wilson of February 23, Seymour, *House Papers*, IV, 348.

[56] Bullitt Papers, Datebook, February 20, 1919; *Bullitt Mission*, 34.

ing the possibilities in another light, one can speculate that if Clemenceau had not been attacked, he would have developed a new and more forceful approach to the Russian problem, and would have carried it through against the protests of House and Balfour.

The Origins of the Bullitt Mission

The impasse over Russian policy reached in the Council of Ten on February 17, and the suspension of consideration by the conference of new approaches to the Russian question that resulted from the wounding of Clemenceau led directly to House's final decision to send Bullitt to Moscow. The idea of a mission to Soviet Russia was, however, of long standing and had been actively discussed in Paris for at least six weeks before the departure of Bullitt. In fact, a year earlier, in February 1918, Bullitt himself had broached the idea to Colonel House, proposing, in the course of a plea for the recognition of Soviet Russia, that if recognition were not feasible, at least an emissary should be sent "to understand what the Bolsheviki are about." [57] In the summer of 1918 the head of the "Inquiry," S. E. Mezes, had suggested, in a memorandum on Russia's place in the peace settlement, that ignorance of conditions in Russia could be overcome by providing at the peace conference for a commission to visit "the territories of the former Russian Empire to hold hearings [and] to study local situations." [58] In addition, it must be remembered that the Prinkipo project grew out of Lloyd George and Wilson's desire to hear all sides to the Russian controversy, but particularly the Bolsheviks.

Thus the concept of an on-the-spot investigation of Bolshevik attitudes and of conditions in Soviet Russia was not a new one when it was first raised among those attending the peace conference. The immediate proposal, however, from which the idea of the Bullitt mission developed was not made, as has frequently been assumed, by Bullitt himself.[59] In fact it is a delightful touch of irony well suited to this curious episode that the seed which germinated into the Bullitt mission was apparently

[57] House Papers, letter from Bullitt to House, February 3, 1918.

[58] Memorandum from Mezes to the Executive Committee, June 14, 1918. Ingram Bander, ed., "The Inquiry Papers of S. E. Mezes" (American Documentation Institute), a microfilm copy of a typescript collection.

[59] Stated by Bullitt in an interview with the author on February 25, 1953, and confirmed by the evidence presented in the following pages. The claim of Steffens, backed by his journalist friend, Frederick C. Howe, that he first suggested the idea cannot be substantiated. Joseph Lincoln Steffens, *The Autobiography of Lincoln Steffens* (New York, 1931), 790; Frederick C. Howe, *The Confessions of a Reformer* (New York, 1925), 302. Steffens' claim is accepted, for example, in Unterberger, 147, and George F. Kennan, *Russia and the West*, 130.

first planted in the minds of members of the American delegation by the British publisher Lord Northcliffe, who was probably responsible, more directly than any other single individual, for the failure of the mission after Bullitt's return from Russia. On January 9, 1919, Gordon Auchincloss, House's aide, called on Northcliffe: "We talked for some time about the present situation, particularly in Russia and Germany. He [Northcliffe] suggested that a commission should be sent to Russia after securing the approval of the present government. The commission would simply find out what the facts of the situation were." [60] Four days later, Auchincloss, substituting for House, who was sick, went to see Wilson on a number of matters: "I told the President that the Colonel [House] suggested that the President propose that a Commission be sent to Russia to ascertain the facts of the situation there before they had been refused representation at the peace conference and that the President should appoint as American members of this Commission Radicals. The President said that this procedure was also in his mind." [61]

By mid-January, therefore, both House and Wilson were considering the possibility of sending a fact-finding body to Russia. This idea was not well received by Lansing, however. On January 18 he discussed it with Henry White and Bliss and noted his opposition to the plan.[62] On the other hand, Bliss was quite enthusiastic; he believed that if the French blocked Lloyd George's proposal for a conference of Russian factions, a mission of inquiry should be sent to Russia.[63] At this stage Bullitt began to push the idea, discussing it with House on January 19 and recommending the appointment of Learned Hand, Raymond Fosdick, William Allen White, A. R. Williams, and "not forgetting Bullitt as general bootblack," to a mission to Russia.[64]

The desirability of an investigation at first hand of conditions in Soviet Russia was also being discussed among the journalists in Paris, as well as within the British delegation. Lincoln Steffens, who was later to accompany Bullitt, wrote his brother-in-law on January 14 that he had heard a commission would go to Russia. "How I would like to be upon that commission. Some people are urging me for it, but I doubt that they

[60] House Papers, Auchincloss Diary, January 9, 1919. This seems to be the first reference by those at the peace conference to a mission to Russia. An undated memorandum from William Allen White to House making a similar proposal appears, on the basis of its contents, to have been drawn up at about the same time, but probably a few days later, in the period January 12–21. House Papers, Memorandum from White to House.

[61] House Papers, Auchincloss Diary, January 13, 1919.

[62] Lansing Papers, Desk Diary, January 18, 1919.

[63] Bliss Papers, Box 65, Diary, January 19, 1919.

[64] House Papers, memorandum of conversation from Bullitt to House, January 19, 1919.

can put me on. . . ." [65] In mid-January Balfour proposed to Lloyd George that a food commission be sent to Moscow, which would also take political soundings.[66] None of these various suggestions and proposals for a mission to Russia was developed further at that time, however, for on January 21 the Council of Ten finally agreed to accept Lloyd George's plan for a conference of the Russian parties, and the Prinkipo invitation was made public the next day. The idea of sending a mission to Moscow receded into the background, although the desire to get in touch with the Bolsheviks was not entirely forgotten, as Lloyd George's expression on January 31 of a willingness to deal directly with the Soviet government indicated.[67]

In February, as hopes for the success of the Prinkipo project dimmed, interest in a mission to Russia revived. It seems likely that Bullitt was largely responsible for renewed consideration of such a mission. With the blessing of House, Bullitt attended, from February 4 to 12, the congress of the Second International in Berne, Switzerland, at which it was decided to send a commission composed of leading socialists to inquire into conditions in Soviet Russia. Two days after Bullitt's return to Paris, on the morning of Wilson's departure for Washington, the president and House conferred, the latter reporting that "we settled all the important questions I had on my mind to take up with him before he left for America." [68] Although direct evidence is lacking, it seems almost certain that at this time House asked for, and received, discretionary authority to send a fact-finding mission to Russia, if and when such a course of action should seem desirable. In the later controversy over the Bullitt mission, Wilson never denied having prior knowledge of the mission. Moreover, as we saw earlier, that evening, in the debate in the Council of Ten over Russian policy, the president stated that the Allies might have to imitate Mahomet and go to the Russian governments, adding that he personally had no objection to American representatives meeting informally with those of the Soviet government—clear references to the idea of sending a mission to Russia. After Wilson's departure, House, apparently speaking with authority, talked with Lansing "about sending Bullitt to Russia to cure him of Bolshevism," as Lansing put it.[69]

[65] Letter to Allen Suggett, January 14, 1919, *Letters of Steffens*, eds., Ella Winter and Granville Hicks (2 vols.; New York, 1938), I, 457; hereafter cited as *Steffens Letters*. See also C. T. Thompson, 92.

[66] House Papers, Wiseman Diary, January 19, 1919.

[67] Kerr voiced this and other views of the British prime minister in a meeting with Buckler and Bullitt. See Buckler's report in *Peace Conference*, XI.

[68] House Papers, Diary, February 14, 1919.

[69] Lansing Papers, Desk Diary, February 16, 1919.

Up to this point the proposed mission had been thought of as only an investigative one, an effort to ascertain at first hand the views of the Soviet leaders and to study conditions in Soviet Russia. On February 17, however, House broadened the concept of the mission to include the conduct of negotiations with the Soviet government as well. After lunch that day House told Kerr that he feared the interventionist policies of Churchill and the French would only serve to drive Germany and Russia together.[70] He favored instead "keeping in touch with the Bolsheviks with the aim of arranging terms and restoring Allied influence and peace." [71] And that night Bullitt noted in his datebook: "Talk of methods and reviving idea of negotiating with the Soviet government."

On the same day—February 17—House asked Bullitt to go to Russia.[72] Just when during the course of the day he did so is not clear from the evidence, but it seems likely that the request was made that evening, after the stormy discussion of Russian policy in the afternoon meeting of the Council of Ten. During the preceding few days House had been actively considering sending Bullitt to Moscow; once he saw that a stalemate on Russian policy had been reached in the conference, he apparently decided that the time was ripe to put into effect the idea of an unofficial American mission, outside the authority of the conference.

At this juncture House, Bullitt, and Kerr, the three who planned and organized the mission, apparently considered it an alternative to the moribund Prinkipo proposal; for on the following day, February 18, after arrangements had been made for Lloyd George and House to attempt to renew the Prinkipo proposal, the dispatching of Bullitt to Russia was delayed, although his orders were prepared and signed. Only after the attempt to assassinate Clemenceau and receipt of Lloyd George's message that the planned renewal of the Prinkipo project would have to be postponed as a result, was it decided, on February 20, to send Bullitt at once.[73] At the same time it would be making too fine a distinction to assert that the Bullitt mission was a clear alternative to the Prinkipo plan. To some degree, at least, it was considered as a preparatory step leading to the tender of a new proposal similar to that of Prinkipo. As Bullitt himself put it: ". . . I was instructed to go in and bring back as quickly as possible a definite statement of exactly the terms the Soviet Government was ready to accept. The idea in the minds of the British and the American delegation were [sic] that if the Allies made another proposal it should be a proposal which we would know in

[70] See pp. 142–43 above.
[71] Reported to Lloyd George by Kerr in a memorandum of February 17, 1919, cited in Lloyd George, I, 373.
[72] Bullitt Papers, Datebook, February 17, 1919.
[73] Ibid., February 20, 1919; Bullitt Mission, 34.

advance would be accepted, so that there would be no chance of another Prinkipo proposal miscarrying."[74] Bullitt's implication that the Soviet government did not accept the Prinkipo proposal was inaccurate, as we saw in the preceding chapter.

To prepare for his mission, Bullitt met on February 20 and 21 with Lansing, House, and Kerr. From Lansing he received his credentials and orders, as well as instructions to attempt to obtain the release of an American diplomat, Consul Treadwell, who was being detained in Tashkent by the local Soviet authorities.[75] From Colonel House, Bullitt received, in the form of answers to questions Bullitt propounded, assurances that the American government would declare a cease-fire and stop attacking if the Bolsheviks did so, and that the United States was prepared to insist that its allies accept such an armistice. Second, House agreed that following an armistice the United States would reestablish economic relations with Russia and would furnish aid, provided food and relief supplies were equitably distributed to all classes of the population. Finally, it would press its allies for a joint announcement that all foreign troops would be withdrawn from Russia as soon as practicable, given a Soviet promise not to retaliate against those Russians who had cooperated with the Allies. This, Bullitt felt, gave him a clear idea of what terms might be proposed to the Soviet government. Bullitt and House failed, however, to take account of such issues of vital concern to the opponents of Bolshevism as Bolshevik propaganda abroad and the security of the states bordering Russia. On the other hand, House did express the opinion that although a Soviet promise to repay Russia's debts was not an essential precondition to a settlement, such an assurance would help overcome French opposition to making peace with the Soviet government, which, he felt, arose from the Bolshevik repudiation of Russia's debts to France.[76]

House's analysis of the motivation of French anti-Bolshevism was far from the mark. Most of all, the French wanted a moderate non-Bolshevik Russia, which would ally with France against Germany. As we saw in the second chapter, France's postwar economic objectives in Russia were to secure markets for French goods and capital and to gain control of Russian resources; the French were at first interested in the

[74] *Bullitt Mission,* 38. At about this time President Wilson also apparently still entertained hopes of arranging a conference of the Russian factions. In commenting on the Russian problem during a talk to the Democratic National Committee on February 28, he referred optimistically to the possibility of being able to explain his desire to help Russia directly to the Bolsheviks across a conference table. Tumulty, 375.

[75] *Bullitt Mission,* 4–5, 33. Bullitt succeeded in getting Treadwell released. Records of the State Department, File 184.02202/7.

[76] *Bullitt Mission,* 34–45.

recovery of loans made to Russia primarily as a vehicle for the achievement of these long-range objectives. It was only later, in the early 1920's, when there was no chance of direct economic penetration by the French and when Soviet Russia was finally recognized, that the Russian debt became a significant issue in Franco-Russian relations. On two occasions in early 1919—in its reply to the Prinkipo invitation and in the proposals it handed to Bullitt—the Soviet government formally offered in principle to pay Russia's debts, although it was implied on both occasions that negotiations to that end should take into account Bolshevik Russia's limited capacity to pay and possible Soviet methods of payment—such as concessions in Russia and the export of Russian raw materials. Since the French government strongly opposed acceptance of either of these offers, the thesis that French intervention in Russia in the period from 1918 to 1920 was primarily based on a desire to exact payment of those debts cannot be accepted.[77]

From Kerr, Bullitt received a suggestion of eight points that should be included in a settlement with the Soviet government.[78] In addition to issues covered by House's replies to Bullitt—a cease-fire, an amnesty for pro-Allied Russians, restoration of trade, and an equitable distribution of relief supplies—Kerr recommended the following terms: *de facto* governments to remain in control of the territories they occupied, regulation of railways and ports in accord with international agreements, right of free entry and full security for Allied subjects in Soviet Russia, amnesty to all political prisoners on both sides, separate consideration of the debt question following the establishment of peace, and the withdrawal of Allied troops after the demobilization of Russian armies to a limit to be defined.

According to Bullitt, Kerr stated "that he had discussed the entire matter with Mr. Lloyd George and Mr. Balfour. . . ."[79] Nevertheless, in a letter forwarding his proposals to Bullitt, Kerr wrote: "I inclose a note of the sort of conditions upon which I personally think it would be possible . . . to resume once more normal relations with Soviet Russia. You will understand, of course, that these have no official significance and merely represent suggestions of my own opinion."[80] Although this might well be discounted as the disclaimer of a cautious man, it seems more likely that submitting the terms as his personal views was the only condition under which the British were willing to have the matter discussed at all. Lloyd George was in London, and Kerr trans-

[77] This thesis is accepted, for example, in Unterberger, 141.
[78] *Bullitt Mission,* 37.
[79] *Ibid.,* 36–37.
[80] *Ibid.,* 36.

mitted his memorandum of terms to Bullitt on February 21, only one day after it had been decided to dispatch the mission. Nevertheless, in view of the delicacy of the affair, Kerr probably had had to "clear" his proposals with Lloyd George, at the same time informing the prime minister that an American mission was going to Russia.

It is not certain that Kerr discussed his recommendations in detail with Balfour. We do know, however, that Kerr informed Balfour in general terms of the mission and its purpose, and that the latter sounded a note of caution. On February 21, in a letter to House devoted primarily to reporting Lloyd George's reaction to the idea of renewing the Prinkipo project, Kerr incidentally noted Balfour's recommendation that if negotiations with the Bolsheviks were undertaken, the Russians who were cooperating with the Allies should also be consulted.[81] Kerr then appended his own outline of notes that might be sent to the pro-Allied Russians, as well as to the Bolsheviks. The draft note to the Soviet government regretted that the Bolsheviks, while accepting the Prinkipo invitation, had ignored the condition of a cease-fire; it then proposed as a basis for negotiations the eight points Kerr had forwarded to Bullitt. The draft note to the anti-Bolshevik governments declared that the Allies could not undertake a war of conquest against Soviet Russia if the latter agreed to a peace which would free her neighbors from the threat of military aggression. An armistice and the same terms for negotiation were proposed, with the promise that if the Soviet government accepted such an offer, the anti-Bolshevik governments would also be invited to the ensuing talks.

Overall, it seems clear that in Paris only House of the American delegation and Kerr and Sir Maurice Hankey of the British delegation knew what terms Bullitt was planning to propose to the Soviet leaders. President Wilson certainly did not; in fact, he was probably even unaware, until after his return to Paris from Washington, that House had empowered Bullitt to negotiate, as well as to investigate. In July 1919, when *The Nation* published, as part of the liberals' continuing attack on American policy in Russia, a lead (and very accurate) story on the still secret Bullitt mission, the president wrote in a memorandum to Tumulty:

> This is an amazing article. I know of no such "Allied terms" as are here quoted, and do not for a moment believe that it is true that "The Nation itself is in a position through information received direct from Paris, to state . . . that Messrs. Bullitt and Steffens did take a memorandum into Russia and that memorandum was in the handwriting of Philip Kerr, Private Secretary to Mr. Lloyd George." . . . my in-

[81] House Papers, letter from Kerr to House, February 21, 1919.

clination is to have its statement challenged in some way and a demand made for the evidence which the editor alleges to be in his hands.[82]

Happily for Wilson, Tumulty recommended taking no action; two months later Bullitt made public Kerr's memorandum in his testimony before the Senate Foreign Relations Committee.

The capacity in which Bullitt went to Russia and the amount of secrecy which surrounded the affair have always been confusing issues. They subsequently became important points of dispute and criticism concerning the mission, and it is well here to set the record as straight as the evidence will allow. When the mission was first decided on, House apparently did not tell Lansing that Bullitt was to discuss terms of a settlement with the Soviet government, for Bullitt's orders from Lansing referred only to his "studying conditions, political and economic," in Russia.[83] Whether this was a sin of omission or commission on the part of House is not clear, although the latter seems more likely. The moment when Lansing first learned of the negotiating aspect of Bullitt's mission is also obscure, but it was probably not until Bullitt cabled from Helsingfors that he was about to enter Russia and expected to "have definite propositions from the Soviet government to transmit within a week or ten days." In any case, Lansing was sufficiently alarmed, upon receipt of this telegram, to send a brief memorandum to Balfour and Pichon on March 10, informing them that an American mission had arrived in Helsingfors: "They had my permission to enter Russia, if they could make the necessary arrangements, in a purely unofficial capacity, for information purposes solely. It has been desired to give no notoriety or newspaper publicity to this affair lest its significance be exaggerated. . . . I hope to receive from Mr. Bullitt valuable information which will help us to understand the Russian situation." [84] In this way the French were officially notified of the mission two weeks before Bullitt arrived back in Paris.

The other American commissioners, Henry White and General Bliss, went on record, subsequent to Bullitt's testimony in the Senate hearings,

---

[82] First ellipsis contained in the memorandum, which was dated July 17, 1919. Wilson Papers, Series II, Box 169. The article in question was published in *The Nation*, XIX (July 12, 1919), 34. It would be interesting to know who *The Nation*'s source in Paris was, but it is useless to speculate on this since by then the story of the mission was quite widely known among American journalists and officials.

[83] *Bullitt Mission*, 4.

[84] Telegram from Lansing to Washington on March 10, 1919, summarizing Bullitt's cable and reporting that Lansing had transmitted a memorandum to Balfour and Pichon. *1919, Russia*, 76; copy of the memorandum in Henry White Papers, Acquisition 9736, Box 65. One author asserts Lansing informed the French much earlier, but this is apparently a mistake in dates. William A. Williams, *American-Russian Relations, 1781–1947* (New York, 1952), 168.

that "at no time was the mission of Mr. Bullitt discussed—much less acted upon—in our presence . . . nor did we know anything of Mr. Bullitt's intended journey until after his departure." [85] Although it is true that the proposed mission was not formally discussed by the commissioners, and although White and General Bliss were undoubtedly not officially informed of Bullitt's trip, Lansing did, in fact, mention it in a meeting of the American commissioners, and in a context which ought to have caught the attention of White and Bliss. On the day Bullitt left Paris for Russia, February 22, Samuel Gompers of the American Federation of Labor made a rather contentious presentation of his views on the peace negotiations at the regular daily meeting of the commissioners, who were all, with the exception of the president, in attendance. Among other things, Gompers referred to rumors that "faddist parlor socialists" were in closer touch with the American Commission than were the representatives of American labor, citing as an example the sending of a representative from the commission to the socialist conference in Berne. Lansing retorted sharply that "this was absurd, that a Mr. Bullitt had gone to Berne as an observer . . . and in no way as a representative to the Conference, that in the same way Mr. Bullitt was now going to Russia as an observer." This led Gompers to attack Bullitt and others supposedly influential with the American Commission as reportedly in sympathy with the Bolsheviks or of Bolshevik leanings, charges which Lansing heatedly denied and which were only cut off by the interruption of one of Gompers' assistants.[86]

In the excitement this passing reference to Bullitt's mission may well have escaped the notice of White and General Bliss. In any case, the next day they might well have wondered and asked about the absence of Bullitt, one of whose duties was to provide each commissioner with an oral intelligence "briefing" every morning. White, at least, was apparently not curious as to Bullitt's whereabouts, for on March 18 he wrote to Sazonov:

> On Saturday . . . you asked me whether the American Peace Commission had sent someone to Russia to negotiate with the Bolsheviki, to which I replied in the negative, having no knowledge of any such mission.
>
> I find on inquiry, however, that Mr. Lansing permitted two Americans, who were anxious to go to Russia, to do so in a purely unofficial capacity and for information purposes only . . . but in no way as representatives of our Peace Commission.[87]

[85] Letter of White and Bliss to Grew on November 19, 1919. *1919, Russia*, 97. White wrote to Senator Lodge in a similar vein. Nevins, 463.
[86] *Peace Conference*, XI, 70–71.
[87] Henry White Papers, Acquisition 9736, Box 11.

After they had learned about the mission, White and General Bliss were undoubtedly considerably nettled that they had not been consulted in any way as to its desirability or purposes; and when, from Bullitt's testimony, they discovered that Bullitt's credentials had referred to authorization from the American commissioners, it is not surprising that they were sufficiently annoyed to attempt to correct the record.

Technically, Bullitt, as a member of the State Department attached to the American Commission to Negotiate Peace, and assigned by the latter to go to Russia, was on an official mission. He needed this status both to secure the full cooperation and assistance of American diplomatic posts and officers en route and to aid him in getting into Russia and obtaining an attentive hearing from the top Soviet leaders. His orders from Lansing referred to his studying conditions "for the benefit of the American commissioners," and his credentials from Grew, the secretary-general of the American Commission, stated that he had been "authorized by the American commissioners" to go to Russia; but, as Grew pointed out in his reply to White and General Bliss, this was simply the form ordinarily used when someone was dispatched on a mission for the American delegation at Paris.[88] Actually, it is doubtful if anyone, from Wilson and House down, ever considered the mission as anything more than an exploratory effort, with the possible exception of Bullitt himself, who was reluctant to acknowledge its informal status even after Lloyd George had repudiated the mission in the House of Commons following Bullitt's return. It was thought of as an attempt to sound out the Bolsheviks, which might later lead to official negotiations in the form of an Allied proposal or of a conference of the Russian parties. Thus, subsequent denials from all sides that the mission was a formal negotiating effort, no matter how painful they were to Bullitt, were correct in substance.[89]

The American Commission reported Bullitt's trip to the State Department on February 24.[90] Very few in the British government knew about the mission, however. The Foreign Office itself did not, and, in fact, it did not learn details of the affair until four months later. After publication of the Soviet proposals to Bullitt in an English newspaper in mid-June, the Foreign Office asked the British delegation in Paris what the mission had been all about. Kerr replied, giving a short summary of its

[88] *Bullitt Mission*, 4–5; *1919, Russia*, 97. It is interesting to note that copies of Bullitt's orders and credentials were not found in the files of the Department of State. *Ibid.*, p. 74 n. 67.

[89] See, for example, in the New York *Herald*, September 19, 1919, the report of the State Department's denial that Bullitt went to Russia in an official capacity, following Bullitt's testimony before the Foreign Relations Committee. Clipping in Lansing Papers, Correspondence File, Vol. 47.

[90] *1919, Russia*, 74.

origins. He stressed that the suggested terms of a settlement with Russia had been discussed with Bullitt unofficially and had represented only his own opinions.[91] Nor was the British War Office notified of Bullitt's trip when he departed; it learned of the mission in mid-March through a report from Stockholm.[92]

Finally, news of the departure of the mission was kept from the press. Members of the mission had been instructed to forego "good-byes" and, in any case, not to disclose their destination.[93] The effort to avoid newspaper publicity met with considerable success. The first dispatches reporting that Bullitt had gone to Russia were not published until March 20 and 21, only a week before Bullitt's return.[94] After their publication Lansing discussed the mission with a group of journalists, but gave few details and, according to one newsman, adopted an attitude of "apparently polite curiosity" concerning it.[95]

According to Bullitt, the mission was clothed in secrecy "because of fears that the French Foreign Office and the conservative wings of the French, British, and American press would raise such an outcry as to prejudice in advance the success of the peace negotiations which the mission hoped to arrange." [96] These fears were certainly well founded. At the same time House's failure, whether deliberate or unthinking, to inform at least the senior members of the American delegation and his own subordinates about Bullitt's journey and its purpose substantially reduced the chances that Bullitt's report would be well received and favorably acted upon following his return.[97] These individuals, who might have helped put Bullitt's recommendations across at Paris and before public opinion, felt left out; as a result, many of them, instead of backing Bullitt, resented and criticized the mission.[98] Moreover, the

[91] Letter to Sir Ronald Graham, July 11, 1919, British Foreign Office, *Documents*, III, 425–26.

[92] Note by Leland Harrison, undated. Harrison Papers, Acquisition 9611, Box 102, Bullitt File; telegram from London to Paris, March 18, 1919, Records of the ACTNP, 184.02202/6½.

[93] Interview by the author with Mr. Walter W. Pettit, a member of the mission, May 10, 1953; Steffens, *Letters*, I, 460. Pettit, a captain in army intelligence, was to wear civilian clothes and to leave behind "any papers which would tend to establish his military status." Letter from Grew to General Marlborough Churchill, chief of army intelligence, February 21, 1919, Bullitt Papers.

[94] Letter from Leland Harrison to Edward Bell, March 22, 1919, Harrison Papers, Acquisition 9611, Box 102; Lansing Papers, Desk Diary, March 20, 1919.

[95] *Ibid.*, March 21, 1919; Hansen, 252.

[96] Author's interview with Bullitt, February 25, 1953.

[97] Judging from the diary of Auchincloss for the period between mid-February and mid-March, for example, one concludes that House did not even let his own aide in on the secret. House Papers, Auchincloss Diary, February 15–March 18, 1919. See also letter from Grew to William Phillips, March 18, Grew, I, 383.

[98] For an illustration of this attitude, see Harrison's letter to Bell, cited in n. 94, and a suggestion to House from two junior members of the American delegation,

storm of press criticism of the mission which broke in late March and early April, and which helped to defeat Bullitt's proposals, might have been mitigated, or at least countered to some extent, if House had quietly, and on a pledge of secrecy, given friendly journalists what is to-day called a "background" story on the mission. As it was, newspapermen who favored making peace in Russia were caught unawares by the violent reaction in the conservative press to the idea of an agreement with the Bolsheviks.

Criticism of the composition of the Bullitt mission also seems justified; no conservative was included, nor was there anyone with diplomatic experience. Officially attached to Bullitt were R. E. Lynch, a stenographer, and Captain Walter W. Pettit of the intelligence section of the peace conference. Pettit, a liberal in outlook, had done relief work in Russia in 1916 and 1917. Upon entering the army, he had been assigned to work on Russia in the military intelligence division of the War Department. In Paris he continued this work for the American delegation to the peace conference.[99] Pettit, however, did not accompany Bullitt from Petrograd to Moscow, and took no part in the negotiations with the Soviet leaders. Lynch was left behind in Helsingsfors. Accompanying the Bullitt party, but not an official member of the mission, was Lincoln Steffens, the journalist.

Bullitt wanted to keep the mission small.[100] He apparently felt that this would help prevent unwanted publicity, and he probably was anxious to keep direction of the mission in his own hands. (Bullitt, only twenty-eight years old, was a junior member of the American delegation; almost anyone accompanying him would have outranked him.) The result, however, was not entirely fortunate. Although Steffens went to Moscow with Bullitt, he did not participate in the negotiations with Lenin and Chicherin. Responsibility for working out terms of a settlement with the Soviet government thus fell on Bullitt alone. And Bullitt was not a trained diplomat, having been a newspaperman before entering the intelligence section of the State Department. He was not experienced in the art of negotiation, and, worst of all, he had no one accompanying him with such experience to whom he could turn for advice and with whom he could consult, checking his own procedures and conclusions as he went along. The proposals Bullitt brought back were certainly reasonable ones, but, as we shall see, there were several serious shortcomings in them and in the position Bullitt had taken, both from

Dresel and Dolbeare, that the mission be abandoned in favor of an inter-Allied one. Records of the ACTNP, 184.022/11.
[99] Author's interview with Pettit, May 10, 1953.
[100] Author's interview with Bullitt, February 25, 1953.

the point of view of reaching a workable agreement and from the standpoint of protecting Allied interests. If a diplomatic officer such as Joseph Grew or Allen Dulles, both junior members of the American delegation in Paris, had accompanied Bullitt, these difficulties might have been avoided.

More serious, however, was the absence of anyone with a conservative political viewpoint. The idea of a mission to Russia had been advanced by various circles in Paris, but most vigorously by the liberals, who were opposed to intervention and who believed that some accommodation should be reached with the "Bolshevik experiment." There were plenty of anti-Bolshevik reports available in Paris, circulated by Allied diplomats stationed with the anti-Bolshevik armies and by the French and White Russians, and exemplified by the testimony before the peace conference of Noulens and Scavenius. As a result, Wilson and Lloyd George had clearly indicated their interest in hearing the other side of the story. It was therefore quite natural, in view of the origins of the mission and of the type of information existing in Paris, that those selected to go were individuals known not to have closed minds on the subject of Bolshevism. House may even have shared to some extent Steffens' opinion that it should be "a mission that understood the Bolshevik point of view, that could talk its language." [101]

Bullitt was well known as an active liberal, an opponent of intervention, and a person who wanted to see the Bolsheviks given a fair chance. Steffens, who had made his reputation as a "muckraker," had been to Russia in 1917 with the Crane mission. He had backed the Provisional Government and supported a just war for the achievement of Wilsonian principles. Later, however, he had welcomed the Bolshevik seizure of power with considerable enthusiasm, viewing it as a progressive break with the past. In 1918 he had written an introduction to a tract by Trotsky published in New York and entitled *The Bolsheviki and World Peace;* in the public mind this tended to associate him with the Bolshevik cause. At the peace conference Steffens opposed intervention, arguing that the Bolsheviks would give up the class war which they were waging—and which he deplored—if intervention were ended.[102] According to Bullitt, Steffens was asked to accompany the mission for a very practical reason. Bullitt believed that since Steffens was known to the Bolshevik leaders, he could vouch for the sincerity of the mission

[101] Steffens' characterization of the mission quoted in Howe, 302.

[102] For an excellent account of Steffens' involvement in the Russian question, see the chapter "Lincoln Steffens and Russia," in Irving G. Cheslaw, "An Intellectual Biography of Lincoln Steffens," unpublished dissertation, Columbia University, 1952, pp. 204–41.

and could assure Lenin and Trotsky that Bullitt meant what he said.[103]

Although the composition of the mission undoubtedly helped assure Bullitt a sympathetic reception from the Soviet leaders, it had just the reverse effect on many individuals at the peace conference and on conservative legislative and press circles in England and America. This reaction, as we shall see in chapter seven, helped block the adoption of Bullitt's recommendations. When Lloyd George met Bullitt on the latter's return from Russia, he commented incisively, if belatedly, on the mission's composition, declaring, according to Bullitt: ". . . we have got to send in somebody who is known to the whole world as a complete conservative, in order to have the whole world believe that the report he brings out is not simply the utterance of a radical." [104] After mentioning Smuts and others for such a mission, Lloyd George settled on the Marquis of Salisbury as "respectable enough and well known enough so that when he came back and made the same report [as Bullitt's] it would go down with British public opinion." Lloyd George never acted on these musings, but it is clear that the Soviet proposals to Bullitt would have had a better chance of being adopted by the conference if the mission had included at least one individual who could have vouched for its disinterestedness and reliability, not to the Soviet leaders, but to those groups opposed to any sort of dealings with the Bolsheviks.

Bullitt's Trip to Russia

Bullitt and his party left Paris on February 22 and arrived in Petrograd on March 8. The trip took two weeks because the destroyer that was to have taken them from England to Scandinavia broke down, forcing them to travel by commercial vessel, and because it was necessary in Stockholm to contact agents of the Soviet government to arrange permission for the group to enter Russia. With the assistance of the American minister to Sweden, Ira Morris, these arrangements were satisfactorily completed, apparently through leaders of the Swedish Communist Party, and Bullitt left Stockholm in a most optimistic frame of mind, wiring House: "There is every indication that Lenin is in a thoroughly conciliatory mood. . . . It looks as if my end of the job was going to be easy and as if the hardest fight . . . will be in Paris, but you have

---

[103] Author's interview with Bullitt, February 25, 1953. According to Bullitt, Steffens served this purpose well; Steffens was, however, less useful to him as an informant on Soviet conditions and policy since Steffens seldom left his room in Moscow.

[104] *Bullitt Mission*, 66. In his testimony Bullitt did not indicate that he was offended by this remark or annoyed because Lloyd George had not thought of this consideration earlier.

got to put it across." [105] Bullitt's comment was indeed a prophetic one.

In Petrograd, Bill Shotoff, head of the city police and a former member of the radical American labor movement, the IWW, cared for the party. Shotoff was not without a sense of humor; noticing Pettit's rather khaki-looking clothes under his civilian overcoat, Shotoff suggested, with a twinkle in his eye, that Pettit might like to visit the northern front to observe the operations of the American army from the Bolshevik lines.[106]

Also in Petrograd to greet the mission were Chicherin and Litvinov, with whom Bullitt talked on March 9. Following these conversations, Bullitt sent Pettit to Helsingfors to dispatch a report to Lansing and House. Bullitt stated that the two Soviet leaders were "most favorably disposed toward the cessation of hostilities and a peace conference," but were concerned over how a cease-fire could be enforced on the various anti-Bolshevik armies and wondered whether the American government would be able to restrain the French from using an armistice to reinforce existing anti-Bolshevik groups and to raise new anti-Bolshevik forces. Bullitt added that the Soviet government was willing in principle to pay Russia's foreign debt, but special methods of meeting immediate payments would have to be worked out because of the Bolsheviks' difficult financial position. The Soviet attitude in general seemed reasonable, Bullitt concluded, and he expected to have in a few days "an exact detailed statement of the position of the Soviet government on all points." [107] On March 10 Bullitt proceeded to Moscow for further talks with Chicherin and Litvinov and a meeting with Lenin.

Bullitt had not misjudged the stance of the Soviet leaders. Their situation had improved only slightly, if at all, since Lenin's decision in the fall of 1918 to attempt to secure peace with the Allies at almost any cost and since the conciliatory reply of the Soviet government to the Prinkipo invitation a month earlier, when substantial concessions were offered the Western governments. Soviet Russia stilll faced a ring of external enemies. The Red Army had achieved some successes in the Ukraine and was advancing into the Baltic area; on the other hand, Denikin had improved his position in south Russia. The economic crisis was, if anything, worse, the supply of food and fuel to Moscow itself being reduced to a trickle. In his report Bullitt described, apparently with little exag-

[105] Telegram from Bullitt to House, March 4, 1919, House Papers. On arrangements for the mission, see telegram from London to American Mission, Paris, February 25, 1919, *ibid.*, Bullitt Correspondence; telegram from Morris to House, March 6, 1919, *ibid.*, Morris Correspondence; and several telegrams in *1919, Russia,* 75.
[106] Author's interview with Pettit, May 10, 1953.
[107] *1919, Russia,* 76–77.

geration, the conditions of economic stagnation and virtual starvation which prevailed. The sight of corpses on the street was commonplace, and two children were found frozen to death on Chicherin's doorstep while Bullitt was in Moscow.[108]

In these circumstances Lenin was most anxious to make peace with the Allies, to secure a respite, no matter how brief, from foreign attack. On March 9, in an interview with British journalist Arthur Ransome, Lenin "spoke of Chicherin's last note [of February 4], and said they based all their hopes on it." Lenin added that he thought that America and England were ready to reach an agreement with the Soviet government, but that the French were opposed to this.[109] On March 13, two days after meeting Bullitt, Lenin, as he had done earlier in the winter, affirmed the policy of "a second Brest." In a speech to a public meeting in Petrograd, Lenin said:

> . . . that policy, which led us to accept the Brest peace, the most atrocious, outrageous, humiliating peace, turned out to be entirely correct. I think that it is not without value to recall this policy just now, when the situation in reference to our relations with the Allies is similar, when they in raging fury want to use Russia's debts to crush her in poverty and ruin, to pillage her so that they may drain her of the growing might of her toiling masses.[110]

The same day Chicherin reported to Rakovsky in the Ukraine on Bullitt's mission: "The decision is very important. If we do not reach an understanding, the policy of blockade will be pressed with vigor. They will send tanks, etc., to Denikin, Kolchak, Petliura, Paderevski, etc." [111]

In Lenin's view, the Bullitt mission, like the Prinkipo proposal, was motivated by the desire of the Allied governments, representing the interests of the imperialists, to secure economic and financial concessions from Soviet Russia. In his report to the Seventh Congress of Soviets on December 5, 1919, Lenin reviewed the history of Soviet efforts to make peace with the capitalist world and urged their continuation. As an example, he recalled the Bullitt mission, pointing out that the Soviet proposals to Bullitt had now been published in the Allied countries: "As a result, they [the Allies] have exposed themselves to the whole world as either swindlers or infants—let them choose! And the sympathies of everybody, even the middle classes . . . are on our side, for we signed most onerous terms of peace in a most businesslike manner, and said:

[108] Author's interview with Bullitt, February 25, 1953. See also Bullitt's report on his trip in *Bullitt Mission,* 49–65.

[109] Ransome, 224.

[110] Lenin, *Sochineniia,* XXIV, 59–60.

[111] Quoted from Rakovsky's private files in Fischer, I, 171.

'The blood of our workers and soldiers is too dear a price to pay; we shall pay you, like the merchants you are, a heavy tribute as the price of peace. . . .' " [112]

The formal Soviet proposals to Bullitt did include an offer to pay a share of Russia's foreign debt. No mention was made of economic concessions to the Allies, although the Soviet government informally expressed to Bullitt its desire to grant concessions in order to secure the foreign credits it needed to pay for essential imports.[113] The question of concessions had not been included in the draft terms Bullitt discussed with House and Kerr before his departure. The Soviet government's offer of concessions in its reply to the Prinkipo invitation had been considered "insulting" by Wilson and Lloyd George. It had also been used by the conservative French press as the basis for charges that those who wanted to deal with the Bolsheviks were motivated by avarice and selfishness. As a result, Bullitt and the others apparently felt that the less said about this matter the better. Lenin, however, believed in retrospect that it had been a mistake not to offer Bullitt tempting economic concessions:

> These gentlemen, these merchant-capitalists, . . . cannot judge matters otherwise than as merchants, and when our diplomacy makes noncommercial proposals, when we say that for us the life of our Red Army men is dearer than huge losses of territory, they, judging purely as merchants, cannot understand this other than as a sign of weakness. If the Bolsheviks agreed to such a peace [the proposals to Bullit], it meant that they were on their last gasp and all the bourgeois press was full of glee, all the diplomats clapped their hands, and millions of pounds of sterling were advanced to Kolchak and Denikin.[114]

In any case, Lenin was convinced that concessions granted to the capitalist world, whether economic, political, or territorial, would be only transitory, being shortly canceled by the extension of Soviet power in Russia and by the spread of proletarian revolutions abroad.[115] In an exposition of Soviet foreign policy the following year, Lenin recalled: "When we proposed a treaty to Bullitt a year ago, a treaty unusually

[112] Lenin, *Sochineniia,* XXIV, 602–03. Lenin added in an amusing aside: "And he [Bullitt] assured us (how these gentlemen love to brag) that America was everything—and who considered France in view of the might of America? And when we had signed that treaty, the French and British ministers made this kind of gesture. (Lenin makes an expressive movement of the foot. Laughter.) Bullitt was left with a scrap of paper."
[113] Recounted in Bullitt's official report on the trip. *Bullitt Mission,* 64–65.
[114] In a speech on June 12, 1920. Lenin, *Sochineniia,* XXV, 296.
[115] *Ibid.,* XXIV, 35, 207, 217–20.

advantageous for them and unusually unprofitable for us, which left tremendous amounts of territory to Denikin and Kolchak, we proposed this treaty with the knowledge that if peace were signed, those governments [of Denikin and Kolchak] could never hold out." [116]

Nor were the Soviet leaders neglecting at the time of the Bullitt mission the other arm of Soviet Russia's dual foreign policy—the promotion of world revolution, with its promise of the fall of the capitalist governments themselves. Only two days before Bullitt's arrival in Moscow, the founding meeting of the Third International had concluded with a call "to the Workers of All Countries" to assist the Soviet regime against its foreign enemies. The "toiling masses" abroad were exhorted to attempt by all possible means, "including, if necessary, revolutionary means," to force the Allied governments to give up intervention, to withdraw their armies from Russia, and to cease giving aid to anti-Bolshevik forces. Foreign workers were also urged to exert pressure on their governments to recognize the Soviet regime and to seat its representatives at the Paris Peace Conference, to lift the blockade and establish commercial relations with the Soviet government, and to send to Russia engineers and technicians needed in the work of reconstruction.[117] Thus, from its very inception, the Bolshevik leaders began to use the organization of the international communist movement to further the interests of the Soviet state.

In his interview with Ransome on March 9 mentioned above, Lenin declared frankly that while he feared the governments of England and France would use establishment of the Third International as a pretext for further intervention, the leaders of those countries should realize that the struggle between Soviet Russia and the capitalist powers was, in fact, war. The Soviet government intended, therefore, to use whatever measures it could to weaken its opponents, just as England had endeavored during the World War to foment revolution in Germany, and Germany had tried to stir up trouble in Ireland and India. Already the Allies were inhibited from sending more troops to Russia, Lenin added, because they knew it was "the same thing as sending them to a Communist university." [118] Significantly, Bullitt's telegraphic reports to Paris did not mention the establishment of the Third International. That he was, however, well aware of its founding is indicated by a reference in his later formal report to his attending a meeting of the Petrograd Soviet to celebrate the creation of the Comintern, at which, Bullitt felt, an almost religious fervor prevailed.[119]

[116] *Ibid.*, 603.
[117] Degras, *Comintern Documents*, I, 29–31.
[118] Ransome, 224–25.
[119] *Bullitt Mission*, 60.

According to Bullitt and Steffens, some of the Soviet leaders disagreed with Lenin and Chicherin on the question of making peace with the Allies. Trotsky and others believed that the continued advance of the Red Army would provoke more vigorous Allied intervention, which, in turn, would cause the peoples of Western Europe to rise against their governments.[120] Steffens, in his autobiography, reported that Zinoviev was one of three officials appointed to negotiate with the mission (presumably in addition to Chicherin and Litvinov, and perhaps because of his new responsibilities as president of the executive committee of the Comintern). Zinoviev refused, however, to deal with Bullitt because he doubted the purpose, credibility, and usefulness of the mission.[121] The existence of opposition within Soviet Russia to a negotiated peace with the Allies is also indicated in Bullitt's statement, on his return, that the reason the Soviet leaders preferred to have the Allies make the peace proposal discussed with him was their fear that if they made such an offer, this would cause misunderstanding in Russia.[122]

In some respects Bullitt proved to be a hard bargainer. He told the Soviet officials that only if they made maximum concessions, and the Allies received very favorable terms, would Wilson and Lloyd George have a chance of convincing the French and other proponents of intervention at Paris that peace should be made with Soviet Russia.[123] When the negotiations were completed, Bullitt believed that he had secured all he could from Lenin and Chicherin, reporting to Paris that the Soviet proposals represented the maximum that the Bolsheviks would yield.[124] And, indeed, struggling to preserve their regime, the Soviet leaders gave up a good deal, the terms proposed containing more concessions than the West has been able to extract from the Soviet government from that day to this.

The proposals agreed on were delivered to Bullitt on March 14, after five days of negotiating; they were approved by the Bolshevik Central Committee that same day.[125] The proposals were in the form of an offer to be made by the Allies.[126] The Soviet government agreed to ac-

[120] *Ibid.*, 52, 53.

[121] Steffens, *Autobiography,* 793.

[122] Bullitt's statement is reported in a letter of July 11, 1919, from Kerr to the British Foreign Office, explaining the Bullitt mission. British Foreign Office, *Documents,* III, 426.

[123] Steffens, *Autobiography,* 793; letter from Chicherin to Rakovsky cited in Fischer, I, 171.

[124] *1919, Russia,* 78. See map on p. 168, which shows the small area of central Russia that would have remained under Soviet control.

[125] Trush, 29, 190.

[126] For the text of the proposals, see Degras, *Soviet Documents,* I, 147–150. The versions given in *Bullitt Mission,* 39–43, and U.S.S.R., Ministerstvo Inostrannykh Del, *Dokumenty vneshnei politiki SSSR (Documents on the Foreign Policy of the*

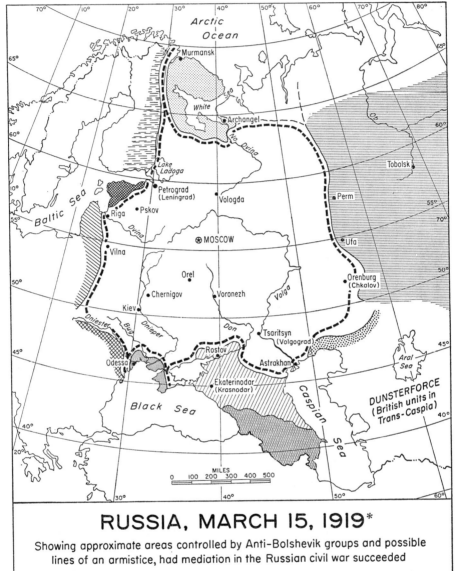

RUSSIA, MARCH 15, 1919*

Showing approximate areas controlled by Anti-Bolshevik groups and possible
lines of an armistice, had mediation in the Russian civil war succeeded

- - - - Approximate boundaries of Soviet Russia

	Omsk government of Admiral Kolchak
	Government of North Russia (General Miller assisted by Allied and American forces)
	Anti-Bolshevik ("White") Finns led by General Mannerheim
	Northwestern army led by General Yudenich assisted by anti-Bolshevik Estonians
	Anti-Bolshevik Poles, Lithuanians and Germans (under General von der Goltz)
	Rumanians and anti-Bolshevik Ukrainians (under Petliura)
	French led expeditionary force in South Russia
	Volunteer army under General Denikin
	Independent republic of the Trans-Caucasus
	Anti-Bolshevik Ural Cossacks

*Based on fighting fronts in George Stewart, The White Armies of Russia (N.Y.,1933), pp. 130, 267.

cept this offer provided it were made not later than April 10. The major provisions of the offer followed rather closely the outline terms given Bullitt by Kerr.[127] The Allies were to propose a two-week armistice on all fronts to take effect one week from the date of the proposal. A peace conference would then be convened in a neutral country, but preferably not on the Prinkipo Islands, within a week after the inception of the armistice. Soviet fears of the build-up of anti-Bolshevik forces were reflected in the preference of the Soviet government, expressed in a footnote, that the conference begin three days, not a week, after the armistice went into effect. The Soviet negotiators apparently also pressed for a minimum period between the tendering of the proposal and the taking effect of the armistice, for an earlier draft of the terms provided for a lapse of three weeks, instead of one, between the Allied offer and the armistice.[128]

At the proposed conference peace was to be discussed on the basis of seven principles, which would not be subject to revision by the conference. These principles were:

(a) The retention by all *de facto* governments in Russia of control of the territories they occupied unless the conference decided on territorial changes or the peoples therein determined to change their government. No attempts were to be made by any government concerned, including that of Germany, to upset by force any other government.

(b) The lifting of the Allied economic blockade, and the restoration of trade relations between the Allies and Soviet Russia, with the proviso of equitable distribution of Allied supplies in Russia and of Allied inspection of this distribution.[129]

(c) The guaranteeing of unhindered transit for the Soviet governments on all railways and through all ports in Russia.

(d) The right of free entry and full security for Soviet citizens in Allied countries and in all Russian territories, provided they did not interfere in domestic politics; a reciprocal right in Soviet Russia for Allied citizens and for all nationals of the territories of the former Russian

USSR) (8 vols. to date; Moscow, 1957–   ), II, 91–5, have only minor variants, though the latter is dated March 12.

[127] See p. 154 above.

[128] This earlier draft is in the Bullitt Papers. It also stated that the date for the conference should be set within a week, rather than that the conference itself meet within a week. The only other difference from the final draft was omission of the provision for mutual repatriation of prisoners of war and other nationals contained in point (e) of the summary of terms given below.

[129] The right of the Allies to send inspectors into Russia to oversee the relief work was an oral understanding not specified in the written proposals. See *Bullitt Mission*, 45.

Empire.[130] Also, the mutual right of sending official agents with immunity, but not diplomatic representatives, into each other's countries.[131]

(e) A mutual general amnesty of political opponents and prisoners, including Allied nationals who aided Soviet Russia and Russians who aided the anti-Soviet armies, and mutual repatriation of prisoners-of-war and other nationals.

(f) Following the signing of peace at the conference, the withdrawal of Allied armies from Russia and the cessation of Allied military assistance to the anti-Soviet governments in Russia. The demobilization of Soviet and anti-Soviet Russian armies to a peace footing under methods of inspection and control to be determined by the conference.

(g) Recognition by the Soviet and other Russian governments of their joint responsibility for Russia's debts; detailed arrangements for payment to be determined by the conference, with the understanding that Russian gold seized by the Czechs and that delivered to Germany by the Bolsheviks under the terms of the Brest-Litovsk Treaty, and now held by the Allies, to count as part of the share to be paid by the Soviet government.[132]

Bullitt was also given a separate statement, which he refused to accept as part of the formal proposal, but which he agreed to transmit to his superiors; in it the Soviet government asked for a semiofficial guaranty from the Amerian and British governments that they would do their utmost to ensure France's adherence to the conditions of the proposed armistice.

The only significant change from the outline terms discussed between Bullitt and Kerr was addition of the provision that the Allies should cease to furnish assistance to the anti-Bolshevik governments. According to Soviet historians, this change was made at the insistence of Lenin, who believed that the anti-Soviet governments would soon fall if Allied aid were withdrawn.[133] Acceptance of this provision would certainly

[130] Commenting a number of years later on this provision for noninterference in domestic affairs, Pokrovsky, the leading Soviet historian in the 1920's, wryly declared: "This we yield. We are not beasts; we are shorn lambs, and we will sit in Moscow and eat our vegetable soup because we have no other." M. N. Pokrovsky, *Vneshniaia politika Rossii v XX Veke* (*The Foreign Policy of Russia in the Twentieth Century*) (Moscow, 1926), 89.

[131] The understanding that such officials would not be diplomatic representatives was an oral one. *Bullitt Mission,* 45.

[132] Neither this Soviet offer to pay at least part of Russia's debts nor that contained in the Soviet reply to the Prinkipo invitation dealt with the important issue of compensation for foreign investments nationalized by the Soviet government.

[133] Potemkin, III, 63; A. V. Berezkin, *SSHA—aktivnyi organizator i uchastnik*

have been a significant concession on the part of the Western powers. Since continuation of aid to the anti-Bolsheviks had been a major tenet of the policy toward Russia which Lloyd George had proposed to House on February 21, it is questionable whether the British government could have been persuaded to agree to this provision of the Soviet proposals, even if the Bolshevik offer had been seriously considered at Paris and among the Allied governments.[134]

Another provision which the Western powers might have been reluctant to accept was that which obliged them to pardon their own nationals who had been prosecuted for abetting the Soviet cause. Bullitt foresaw this difficulty, however. When he wired the Soviet proposals to Paris, he commented that this provision was not of vital importance, and could be modified without making the terms as a whole unacceptable to the Soviet government.[135]

There were, in addition, several aspects of the proposals which would have been difficult to enforce and which the Soviet government might have used to its advantage. In part, these provisions reflected Bullitt's inexperience in diplomatic negotiations, as well as the hasty nature of the *pourparlers* resulting from House's request that Bullitt bring back an answer quickly, if possible before President Wilson returned from America. They also stemmed in part from the difficulties inherent in trying to reach an understanding with a revolutionary government which considered itself engaged in an all-out, international class war, and which therefore did not feel bound in its activities by state borders or by the sanctity of diplomatic agreements. These are, of course, difficulties which many others have encountered in dealing with the Soviet government.

The terms Bullitt brought back provided that Soviet nationals granted free entry and full security in Allied countries would not interfere in domestic politics. The Germans, however, had found a similar provision in the Treaty of Brest-Litovsk of little protection against Bolshevik propaganda. It certainly would have been difficult for the Allies to define "interference in domestic politics" strictly enough to inhibit the activities of Bolshevik agents, especially since many of the individuals and much

voennoi interventsii protiv Sovetskoi Rossii, 1918–1920 gg. (USA—Active Organizer and Participant in Armed Intervention against Soviet Russia, 1918–1920) (Moscow, 1949), 82. No evidence for this assertion is given.

[134] Lloyd George's position was outlined in a letter to Kerr for House and was summarized in a telegram from House to Wilson. See p. 146 above.

[135] *1919, Russia*, 78. According to Bullitt's testimony before the Senate hearings, the Soviet negotiators had declared that it was necessary to include such a provision in order to get the draft terms through the Soviet "executive committee." *Bullitt Mission*, 43.

of the propaganda would have been "domestic" in origin, the Soviet government simply supplying the impetus and inspiration and, covertly, some of the funds and materials. Bullitt himself later realized this, although perhaps only after members of the American delegation in Paris had criticized the Soviet offer for its inadequate safeguards against Bolshevik propaganda.[136] At any event, in the formal report he submitted a week after his return, Bullitt argued that the provision authorizing the admission of Soviet nationals into Allied countries could be modified to protect Allied rights to control such admission and "to exclude definitely all possibility of an influx of propagandists." [137]

Similarly, the statement that the existing *de facto* governments in Russia should not be changed by force or other than by a decision of the proposed conference or of their own citizens provided no real guarantee against Bolshevik propaganda and subversion or against what later came to be known as "indirect aggression"—a change in status accomplished by external threats and pressure and by the internal manipulation of parties and "front" groups. Even without direct attacks by the Red Army, it would probably have been a relatively easy matter for the Bolsheviks to arrange the overthrow of the White Russian governments, as well as those of the minority nationalities, once Allied material and moral support to them had been withdrawn.

Finally, as with the Prinkipo project, the offer negotiated by Bullitt contained no provision for arranging and enforcing a cease-fire. Under the confused conditions existing and with so many fighting fronts involved, more detailed arrangements for an armistice, including the establishment of an armistice commission, were clearly needed.

Despite these difficulties, the terms certainly furnished a basis for serious negotiations and represented an offer from the Soviet government which contained a number of advantages for the Allies. The most important was an opportunity to extricate themselves from an illogical and increasingly unprofitable situation on honorable terms, a chance to end intervention and to withdraw Allied forces from Russia without completely disavowing their obligations to the anti-Bolshevik Russians, about which the British claimed to feel so keenly. Withdrawal under the terms brought back by Bullitt would certainly have been more graceful and advantageous than the disorderly and awkward evacuation, at no profit, which the Western powers were compelled to undertake in any case later in 1919 and in 1920.

Bullitt believed strongly that the Soviet offer was sincerely made and that the Soviet government would have accepted the terms agreed to with him. As with the Soviet reply to the Prinkipo invitation, there is no

[136] See p. 234 of ch. seven.
[137] *Bullitt Mission*, 54.

reason to doubt this. When Bullitt reached Helsingfors on March 16, he at once cabled the Soviet offer to Wilson, House, and Lansing in Paris. He stressed that he had found Lenin, Chicherin, and Litvinov "full of a sense of Russia's need for peace," and that he had "no doubt whatever of the desire of the Soviet government for a just and reasonable peace, or of the sincerity of the proposal." [138]

The next day Bullitt wired to Paris a summary of his general impressions of the situation in Soviet Russia, which his later formal report closely followed.[139] The difficulty with Bullitt's appraisals lay not in what he reported about Soviet conditions—he was quite accurate and informative—but in the enthusiastic and sympathetic tone in which his account was couched, and in what he failed to say about the Soviet regime. His two main themes were "the acute economic distress" existing, which he ascribed entirely to the Allied blockade and to the holding of key agricultural areas and mineral resources by anti-Soviet forces, and the moderate policies and political strength of the Soviet government. Bullitt reported that the inhabitants of Petrograd and Moscow were slowly starving because lack of transportation had seriously impaired the supply of food to the cities; they were also suffering from the cold because of a shortage of fuel, and from a variety of diseases, which sometimes reached epidemic proportions because no medicines were available. Since foreign trade had been cut off and since the factories still operating were largely engaged in producing supplies for the army, few goods were obtainable in the stores.

Despite these privations the people as a whole supported the Soviet government and disapproved of intervention, Bullitt asserted. The left Socialist Revolutionaries and anarchists who opposed the Soviet government were a destructive force, drawing strength only from the current terrible conditions; they favored further intervention because they believed that it was the surest way to bring about revolutions throughout Europe. On the other hand, the constructive opposition, represented by the right Socialist Revolutionaries and the Mensheviks, stood against intervention and for that reason temporarily supported the Soviet regime. If intervention were ended, they would work against Bolshevik policies and for their own, more moderate programs.[140]

In the face of the difficult economic situation, the Soviet government

[138] *1919, Russia,* 77–80. The telegram was not received in Paris until the evening of March 17. Although Bullitt subsequently adopted a conservative political outlook and became one of the severest American critics of the Soviet regime, he still believed in 1953, when the author talked with him, that the Soviet leaders would have made peace on the terms proposed and that this would have been a reasonable basis for a settlement between Soviet Russia and the West at that time.

[139] *Ibid.,* 81–84. For his formal report, see *Bullitt Mission,* 49–65.

[140] Bullitt brought with him statements along these lines from the right Socialist Revolutionary leader Volsky and from the Menshevik, Martov. *Ibid.,* 60–62.

was promoting industry and education, was encouraging sound management, had halted the terror and restored order, and had raised moral standards by, among other things, eliminating prostitution. (Bullitt, incidentally, was perhaps one of the first to aver that in a totalitarian society the trains "run on time.") [141] In the process, Bullitt reported, the Soviet regime, under the dominant and moderating influence of Lenin, had been forced to alter a number of basic Bolshevik principles in the direction of less extreme tenets. The Red Army, though without heavy munitions, was growing in strength and was high-spirited. The soldiers no longer had the "beaten, doglike look" of the Tsarist recruits but carried themselves "like free men and very like Americans."

Bullitt's emphasis on the economic ruin and near starvation of Soviet Russia, on the one hand, and on the reasonableness and stability of the Soviet government, on the other, was well calculated to support the conclusion Bullitt wished the statesmen at Paris to draw: that the time had come to end intervention and to stabilize Western relations with the Soviet regime. Judging from Bullitt's reports, it was clearly inhuman to continue to blockade and to make war on Soviet Russia; it was also fruitless, since the Soviet government enjoyed popular support and since any anti-Bolshevik government would have to be propped up by Allied armies. Finally, on the basis of Bullitt's evidence, one could hope for a moderation of Bolshevik policies as the Soviet government consolidated its position.

In his telegraphic report to Paris Bullitt warned that although it might be possible to overthrow the Bolsheviks by force, the resulting famine, riots, and anarchy would drive Russia leftward, not to the right. It would mean intervening "over the dead bodies and dead hopes of the simple Russian people to set up a form of government they do not want and against which they will revolt whenever the strength returns to them." Bullitt declared that the Soviet government was prepared to meet the Allies half-way because it realized that otherwise it would "go down with the rest of the Russian people into anarchy." Moreover, the Soviet leaders were hopeful that Wilson was "beginning to see through the lies against them to the very simple truth that a dull, inexperienced, a young people were trying, rudely but conscientiously, and at the cost of great suffering to themselves, to find a better way to live for the common good than the old way."

This fervent and rather unquestioning attitude on the part of Bullitt is also reflected by the omissions in his reports. He said nothing, for example, about Lenin's "dictatorship of the proletariat" and the ways in which this affected civil and political rights, or about what was happen-

[141] *Ibid.*, 50.

ing to such principles as freedom of speech, press, and assembly. Although Bullitt accurately reported that some managers were working for the Bolsheviks at high wages, he gave no indication of the fate of those "bourgeois" who did not cooperate with the Soviet government, nor of what the nationalization of industry and trade meant to the artisan and consumer. In his telegraphic report there was not one word, as we saw earlier, concerning the founding of the Third International. Neither of his reports dealt with the central issue of Bolshevik revolutionary expansion.

Thus, to a considerable degree, Bullitt's reports were one-sided in content, stressing what was important to his case, and something less than dispassionate in tone. The latter fact was probably the more damaging to his purposes; those at Paris who were jealous of Bullitt, who were suspicious of his liberalism, or who were opposed to any sort of dealings with the Bolsheviks, were able to seize on this to discredit the significant truths of his report and to discount the advantages for the West contained in the Soviet offer to negotiate peace on reasonable terms.

Steffens also prepared a report on the trip, but this need detain us only briefly since, submitted separately from Bullitt's, it had little or no influence on the eventual disposition of the Soviet offer brought back by Bullitt.[142] Steffens, to be sure, was hardly an impartial witness. He was sympathetic to what he believed were the humanitarian aspirations and goals of the Soviet system, and he judged the revolutionary events in Russia in unrealistic terms. Although a journalist, Steffens was not necessarily a good reporter, often describing, as he explained to Bullitt, not things as they were, but as he wanted them to be.[143] His trip to Russia with Bullitt, as reflected in his letters and in his report, certainly had an air of fantasy and self-deception about it. While en route to Petrograd, Steffens described in a letter his excitement and enthusiasm over the mission: "I feel as if I were going to see a good play . . . at a good theater." [144] Moreover, according to Bullitt, Steffens thought up the famous phrase in which he later characterized his impression of the So-

---

[142] It is interesting that a copy of Steffens' report was read by Lenin sometime in April and is now in the archive of the Institute of Marxism-Leninism in Moscow. How the Bolsheviks received the report is not clear. Trush, 30, 193. In early April, following his return to Finland from Petrograd, Captain Pettit, the other member of the mission, also submitted several reports. Bullitt had recommended that Pettit remain in Petrograd as an observer and point of contact, but Lansing disapproved this recommendation. Pettit's reports were made separately from those of Bullitt. On the whole, Pettit was impressed with what the Soviet regime had achieved and seemed to have been naïve and uncritical in his inquiries. For Pettit's reports, see *Bullitt Mission*, 131–151; *1919, Russia*, 95–96.
[143] Author's interview with Bullitt, February 25, 1953.
[144] Steffens, *Letters*, I, 460.

viet regime to all who would listen—"I have seen the future and it works!"—on the train to Stockholm, long before he entered Russia.[145]

As might be expected, therefore, Steffens reported glowingly that the destructive phase of the revolution was over, that a new order was being built.[146] He was impressed with the egalitarianism and "economic democracy" of the Soviet system, and with the strength and stability of the Bolshevik party and of the Soviet form of government. He touched on many of the same points Bullitt did, but in a more impressionistic and idealized fashion. Unlike Bullitt, however, Steffens remarked on aspects of Soviet life which he did not like, although he always softened his criticism with a rationalization or justification. He pointed out, for example, that the Soviet government was an absolute dictatorship, that it suppressed discontent, and that Lenin was, if anything, farther removed from the will of the people than even the Tsar had been; he added, however, that the Soviet leaders themselves realized this and planned to modify their dictatorship as soon as the economic revolution had been carried through.[147] Steffens also commented portentously on the all-embracing nature of party control, with its reach into every aspect of the people's lives, but he saw the aims of such control as benevolent and desirable ones. Finally, Steffens cautioned that the Bolsheviks were prepared to foment revolution throughout Europe. At the same time, he declared that they would abandon this course if the Allies made peace on the terms brought back by Bullitt; the Soviet rulers would then turn all their energies to the tasks of peaceful construction, fomenting revolution only by inspiration and example, not by propaganda and force.

The Soviet proposals and Bullitt's telegraphic report on conditions in Soviet Russia reached Paris on March 17. The next day Bullitt wired House, asking him to show these cables to Kerr. (House did even more, sending copies directly to Lloyd George and Balfour.) Bullitt then concluded: "You must do your utmost for it [the Soviet offer], for if you had seen the things I have seen during the past week and talked with the men I have talked with, I know that you would not rest until you had put through this peace." [148] What House did, and how the other Western leaders reacted to the Soviet offer, were much influenced by events

[145] Author's interview with Bullitt, February 25, 1953. Among journalists in Paris in 1919, another of Steffens' favorite characterizations of Soviet Russia—"And can you believe it, they've abolished prostitution!"—was met with "But, my God, Steffie, what did you do?"

[146] His report, dated April 2, 1919, is in *Bullitt Mission*, 111–27.

[147] Steffens was later disillusioned on this score, writing in September 1919 that he opposed the class war as "too fierce, too expensive, too atrocious." Steffens, *Letters*, I, 486.

[148] *1919, Russia*, 84.

that had been taking place at Paris and in the world during Bullitt's journey. We must now examine these events, considering later, in its chronological place, the fate of the proposals Bullitt brought out of Russia.

CHAPTER SIX

Plans for a Crusade Against Bolshevism

SHORTLY AFTER Bullitt left for Moscow to investigate the possibility of working out an accommodation with the Bolshevik government, proponents of intervention placed before the peace conference grandiose schemes for an all-out attack against that same government. In a series of proposals presented between February 25 and March 27, Marshal Foch endeavored to win conference approval and Anglo-American support for a crusade designed both to eliminate Bolshevism in Russia and to ensure French hegemony in Eastern Europe. The alternating pattern of treatment of the Russian problem at Paris was demonstrated once more: proposals for conciliation countered by plans for further intervention.

Foch's Proposal of February 25

Marshal Foch was a determined and dogmatic man, single-minded in purpose and tenacious in the execution of that purpose. For him, the security of France was the paramount consideration of the peacemaking, and he worked steadfastly toward that goal. French security, he believed, was threatened by a strong Germany and by Bolshevism, either as separate forces or combined in some form. In mid-February he thought he saw a way to destroy these two menaces at a single stroke, thus insuring the safety of France for a long time to come. If Germany could be compelled, in its current weakness, to accept crushing preliminary terms of peace, the Allies would then be free to support and supervise the creation of a coalition of East European forces to be directed against the Soviet regime; if necessary, the Allies might even enlist German assistance in this struggle. In this way the plague of Bolshevism would be eradicated at its source, and a ring of states under French domination would be securely established to surround and contain Germany in the East.

This bold plan was compounded of a number of disparate considerations, which Foch ingeniously linked together. As far back as the Jassy Conference, a meeting of Allied diplomats and Russian émigrés in mid-November 1918, there had been talk in anti-Bolshevik circles of the formation of a grand coalition against Bolshevism consisting of Russians and East Europeans, strengthened by contingents of regular or volunteer Allied troops. In mid-January 1919 the commander of Allied forces in the East, French General Franchet d'Espérey, broached a project of this kind to Lloyd George.[1] During the same month negotiations for the establishment of such a force were actually undertaken among the White Russians, some East Europeans, and the French. At that time Savinkov, the former terrorist and member of the Provisional Government, who was working with the Russian Political Conference, proposed to the French government that it support a volunteer army of 250,000 men to be sent against the Bolsheviks.[2] The army was to be composed of Russian prisoners of war and of Czech and Yugoslav troops; the French were to finance and command it. Tardieu, the French high commissioner to the United States during the war and a close associate of Clemenceau, approved the plan, provided Savinkov could obtain assurances from the Czech and Yugoslav governments that they not only would permit but would tacitly support recruiting of their nationals for such an army. When Savinkov approached Beneš, the leading Czech representative in Paris, the latter replied that he could not make such a commitment without consulting Masaryk, who had always opposed intervention in Russia and was therefore unlikely to agree to the plan. Prince Regent Alexander of Yugoslavia, though strongly opposed to Bolshevism, indicated that although Yugoslav volunteers might be recruited, he could not formally endorse the project.

Faced with these rebuffs, Savinkov in early February proposed the creation of an all-Russian anti-Bolshevik army. It was, however, to be formed, trained, and based in Bohemia. The French promised to supply the money and equipment; they also offered to lead it if the Czech government would exercise general supervision and control of the undertaking. Masaryk refused to consent to this, but the plan collapsed of its own impracticality before Beneš could deliver Masaryk's negative answer.[3]

Reports of Savinkov's proposals reached Lloyd George's ears through

[1] Lloyd George, I, 344.
[2] For a general outline of the plan, see *ibid.*, I, 369. For details see K. Kramař, *Kramářuv Soud nad Benešem* (Prague, 1938), 29, 92; translation kindly supplied by Dagmar Horna Perman.
[3] *Ibid.*, 30, 96.

the French. On February 20, in the course of a letter transmitting his views on Russia to House, the prime minister wrote from London:

> The military in France, as well as here, frankly like intervention. They would like to make war on the Bolshevists, and I hear of fantastic French schemes to organize an army of Russian prisoners in Germany, supported by Czecho-Slovaks and other odds and ends, to invade Russia. The French military staff have gone so far as to suggest even using German units that have been left in Esthonia. . . . Who is to pay these mercenary armies? How much will France give? I am sure she cannot afford to pay; I am sure we cannot. Will America bear the expense? Pin them [the military] down to the cost of any scheme before sanctioning it.[4]

Foch, aware of these projects, was at the same time becoming increasingly concerned over the slow pace of the peace negotiations. Little progress was being made on what Foch considered to be the important issues—the demilitarization of Germany, her confinement behind the Rhine, and heavy reparations. On these points the French and the Anglo-American positions were still far apart, while, in Foch's view, much time had been wasted on such irrelevancies as the Covenant of the League of Nations. Moreover, Foch was convinced that it was essential to conclude peace with Germany as quickly as possible. Because of mounting public pressures for demobilization and in view of declining morale in the Allied armies, Foch feared that by spring or summer the Allies might not have the military strength to compel Germany to accept the severe terms which he felt were necessary to preserve French security. The Germans might refuse to sign and might even take up arms again. At the moment, however, the Germans were weak, Foch believed. They were going through a difficult winter of semiprivation and were facing the threat of serious social unrest and disorders. Although they had protested vigorously, on February 16 the Germans had at once knuckled under and signed a renewal of the Armistice when confronted by an ultimatum from Foch implying that if they did not sign, hostilities might be resumed on February 17. Foch felt sure that at the moment the Germans would accept almost any terms. Finally, Foch was worried that every passing day increased the danger that Bolshevism would spread through Europe. This scourge had to be dealt with at once.

Others besides Foch were concerned over the dragging out of the peace talks. In mid-February the delegates began to consider the possibility of immediately drawing up preliminary peace terms covering the

[4] Letter from Kerr to House transmitting Lloyd George's views, February 21, 1919, House Papers. See also Lloyd George, I, 377.

main issues; these could then be presented to the Germans, leaving detailed and less significant points to be worked out later. Taking account of this sentiment, Foch began to see a way in which his several interests and purposes might be combined. In a conversation with General Wilson on February 18, Foch argued that if the Allies could settle among themselves three main points of the German treaty—the strength of Germany's armed forces, her boundaries, and the indemnity she must pay—the Germans would have to accept whatever terms in this regard were presented to them.

> If the conditions of a preliminary peace treaty can thus be imposed on Germany, the Allies can then turn their attention to the Russian problem, which must take time to solve. The Marshal thinks the Allies may lose the war if they fail to arrive at a satisfactory solution of the Russian question, either by Germany settling it in her own interests, or by the spread of anarchy. He favors the solution of helping all the anti-Bolshevik elements in Russia and all the neighbors of Russia who are resisting Bolshevik encroachment. He would go so far as to accept German cooperation after the signing of his preliminary treaty of peace, and thinks it might be very valuable.[5]

Commenting on Foch's views, President Wilson saw only the marshal's interest in French security, overlooking Foch's genuine concern with the Bolshevik danger. Wilson cabled House on February 20 that Foch and the French were simply attempting to pressure the United States into hasty acceptance of French proposals for depriving Germany of the left bank of the Rhine, and that House was in no case to accede.[6]

Wilson also failed to note Foch's curious willingness to draw upon German assistance for the proposed crusade against Bolshevism. This suggestion indicated the extent to which Foch was alarmed over the Bolshevik danger; the marshal was prepared to sublimate his national pride and his hatred of the Germans in a common effort to preserve the established political and social order of Europe. Two weeks later Foch brought to the attention of the Council of Ten a request from the German High Command, transmitted through the German Armistice Commission, that German forces in East Prussia and Latvia be permitted to receive supplies and reinforcements, despite the blockade, so that they could continue to oppose the westward expansion of Bolshevism. The

---

[5] General Wilson's memorandum of conversation with Foch was transmitted to House by Sir Maurice Hankey, secretary-general of the British delegation, on February 19, and cabled to President Wilson by House the same day. House Papers, Correspondence Files, Hankey; Seymour, *House Papers*, IV, 333–34.

[6] Telegram from Wilson to House, February 20, 1919, House Papers.

Germans asked bluntly: "Are the [Allied] Governments interested, yes or no, in having our troops fight Bolshevism?" [7] Foch brought up this question despite the Council's approval two days earlier of a recommendation of its military advisers that a similar request from the Germans be denied. The military advisers opposed the German request because its approval would tend to involve the Allies in the support and financing of German and anti-Bolshevik Russian operations in the Baltic area and might also provide the Germans with a means of pressure on the peace conference.[8] The conference leaders took no action on the German offer to fight Bolshevism, and, in fact, they did not squarely face the issue of the role the German army in the Baltic provinces should play until much later in the spring, when the plight of the Baltic peoples and the high-handedness of the German forces there brought it forcibly to their attention.[9]

Foch's interview with General Wilson clearly indicated the direction in which his thoughts were turning. There is one bit of evidence to suggest that about this time Foch even alerted his commanders to the possibility of extended operations in Russia. Reporting on February 19 to the conference's Commission on Rumanian Affairs concerning the possibility of Allied troops garrisoning a proposed neutral zone in Transylvania between clashing Hungarian and Rumanian forces, General Alby, the French chief of staff, declared that French troops would not be available for such duty, in part because General Berthelot's army had numerous assignments ahead of it and "must be kept ready and available for eventual employment in South Russia." [10]

In any event, a few days later Marshal Foch found a peg on which to hang his developing plans. In late December and early January Foch had proposed to the American government and to the peace conference that Polish troops in France be returned to Poland to help keep order there and to check the spread of Bolshevism. To ensure their safe return, Foch had suggested that a contingent of Allied units under American command precede the Poles. The Allied force would occupy the port of Danzig and the Danzig-Thorn railway line, key facilities which

[7] *Peace Conference*, iv, 207, 212. This issue had first been raised earlier, on February 17, a day before Foch's talk with General Wilson, but in a much less direct fashion. *Ibid.*, 27.

[8] *Ibid.*, 190, 191–92. For German General Groener's willingness to fight Bolshevism in exchange for milder peace terms, see Klaus Epstein, *Matthias Erzberger and the Dilemma of German Democracy* (Princeton, 1959), 296.

[9] See pp. 336–40, ch. nine.

[10] *Recueil*, Part iv, C (4), 46. See also mention of Alby's statement in a memorandum sent to President Wilson by Bliss on March 28, in which Bliss accused the French military of planning an extensive war against both the Bolsheviks and the defeated Central Powers. Baker, *Settlement*, iii, 242–43. On the neutral zone in Transylvania, see pp. 194–95 below.

the Germans held but which were needed for the disembarking and transporting of the Polish troops.[11] The matter had been shelved, but as a result of later discussion of this and other issues relating to the situation in Poland, the conference had decided in late January to dispatch an inter-Allied mission to Poland to establish contact with the Polish government and to report on local conditions. It is interesting and significant that this mission was headed by Noulens, the former French ambassador to Russia and a strong anti-Bolshevik—as his testimony before the Council of Ten in January had indicated. In mid-February this mission sent several messages to Paris urging that Polish troops in France be returned at once in order to bolster the stability and morale of Poland.[12] The Commission on Polish Affairs of the conference approved this recommendation and on February 24 referred it to the Council of Ten for final action.[13] Foch declared before the Council that if passage of the troops to Poland were to be assured, the conference would either have to establish a provisional eastern frontier for Germany west of the Danzig-Thorn line and compel the Germans to withdraw behind it, or the Allies would have to send troops to guard the port and railway and to prevent clashes between the Germans on the spot and the Polish forces in transit. At this point the matter was adjourned to permit the delegates to consult their military advisers.

The next day, February 25, when discussion was resumed, Foch presented a remarkable project which, starting from the insignificant question of returning the Polish troops in France to Poland, unfolded with startling rapidity and seeming logic into a complete design both for the settlement of the German treaty and for the elimination of Bolshevism.[14] And Foch's line of reasoning was not tortuous. He argued that it would be expensive and difficult for the Allies to occupy Danzig and the railway line; therefore, it would be better to adopt the alternative solution he had suggested the day before, namely, the definition of Germany's eastern frontier, thus freeing the port and railway from German control. But it would be fruitless to attempt to settle Germany's eastern boundaries until the issues affecting Germany in the West had been resolved. He therefore recommended the prompt imposition on Germany of preliminary peace terms delimiting all her frontiers and fixing the sum of her reparations payments.

... since the Armistice has been signed, the Allies had been marking time in the West, and they had lost ground in the East. Consequently, the situation on the Western Front should forthwith be set-

[11] See pp. 98–99 of ch. four.
[12] *Recueil,* Part IV, C (2), 699.
[13] *Peace Conference,* IV, 104–06.
[14] *Ibid.,* 112–17.

tled so that all the resources in men and materials thus set free could be made available for the solution of the Eastern problem.

In Russia at the present moment Bolshevism and complete anarchy reigned, and sooner or later these Russian questions must be solved; otherwise the fruits of victory would be lost, either through the cementing of an alliance between Germany and Russia, or through the spread of Bolshevism in Germany. On the other hand, if carefully considered, the Eastern problem would not be more difficult to solve than the Western problem. . . .

The difficulties which the Allies had to face in Russia were due not only to the enormous distances . . . but also to the nature of the enemy that had to be dealt with. The enemy might be badly organized, but he was scattered over an enormous territory, acting like a violent virus. Now to fight against such an enemy, troops . . . need not be strongly organized or of superior quality. . . . But great numbers were required, which could be obtained by mobilizing the Finns, Poles, Czechs, Rumanians, and Greeks, as well as the Russian pro-Ally elements still available. . . .

If this were done, 1919 would see the end of Bolshevism, just as 1918 had seen the end of Prussianism. But in order to attain that object, just as the Allies had a base on the Western front, the Rhine, which enabled them to impose their will on Germany, so would it be necessary to constitute a similar base on the Eastern side, consisting of a chain of independent states—the Finns, the Estonians, the Poles, the Czechs, and the Greeks. . . .

Finally, to enable the Allies to transfer their resources from the Western base to the Eastern base, an end would have to be put to all further discussions in the West by imposing on Germany the Preliminaries of Peace, which she would be bound at the present moment to accept.

Q. E. D.! Foch's astonishing presentation is quoted almost in full so that its character and flavor may be directly savored; sweeping, grand, and ingenious in conception, precise, direct, and forceful in purpose, the plan would solve with one bold stroke what Foch believed were the two major problems facing the conference. Needless to say, his hearers were somewhat taken aback. The first to recover, Balfour, made a fitting reply:

. . . everybody must admit that Marshal Foch had made a speech covering a wide field and of far reaching importance. On the other hand, the proposition . . . moved yesterday was that the Polish division now in France should be sent to Poland: a small and modest suggestion involving no particular question of principle at all. On that narrow foundation Marshal Foch had started out to build a great plan stretching from the Rhine to Vladivostok. . . .

Balfour went on to point out that while he was one of those most anxious to conclude preliminaries of peace with Germany as soon as possible, it was not reasonable to suppose that this could be accomplished until President Wilson's return from America permitted settlement of three or four of the most basic issues. Thus, five or six weeks could be expected to elapse before the preliminary terms were prepared; it would make no sense to delay a decision on the transfer of the Polish troops that long. Moreover, the suggestion that a great anti-Bolshevik East European army be mobilized to invade Russia raised policy issues of the greatest importance. The conference could hardly be asked to settle these before making up its mind whether or not to send a few troops to Poland.

After this rebuke Foch returned to the point under discussion, not referring again to his larger scheme. The Council finally decided to ask the inter-Allied mission in Poland to ascertain what the attitude of the Germans would be toward the disembarkation of the Poles at Danzig, and whether it would be necessary to send Allied troops to secure such an operation.

The revelation before the conference of Foch's plan to undertake a crusade against Bolshevism thoroughly alarmed General Bliss, who saw in it one more indication of a profound misunderstanding by European authorities of the fundamental position and attitude of the United States. Accordingly, Bliss drafted a long letter to the American commissioners, which he presented to them on February 28.[15] Bliss emphasized his conviction that the European Allies were planning military operations following the conclusion of peace with Germany, evidently, as Foch's proposal indicated, in the form of an offensive against Russia undertaken by an East European army under French direction. In their planning the Allied generals must be counting on assistance from the United States in the form of troops or supplies or money, or perhaps all three, since France and England were certainly in no position to support and finance such a venture. In Bliss's view, this explained the desire of Foch to involve the United States in Poland; even if only one American officer were sent to Danzig, this would make the United States a party to the larger plan of establishing an anti-Bolshevik base of operations in

---

[15] *Ibid.*, XI, 83–84, where the letter is summarized. See also the full text in Bliss Papers, Box 70.

Poland. Bliss then criticized the aggressive attitude and military activity of the governments in Eastern Europe and warned that American aid to these countries might well be helping to prepare another Thirty Years' War in the area. The time had therefore come, Bliss concluded, for the United States to declare, politely but positively, that it would not support any postwar military efforts in Europe, that it planned the immediate withdrawal of its troops upon the signing of peace, and that it would give no further assistance to nations engaged in aggressive operations in the East.

Although Bliss perhaps overstated the case, he was undoubtedly correct in believing that many European leaders were disposed to assume continued American involvement in and support to Europe after the peace, little realizing the strength of the flooding isolationist tides in American domestic politics. After some discussion, Lansing and White approved Bliss's letter and authorized him to prepare a telegram to the president along the same lines. Bliss did so but was unable to obtain the approval of House, who was absent from the meeting of the commissioners that day, in time for the cable to reach Wilson before the president sailed back to France.

The Design of March 17 and the Polish-Ukrainian Question

Shortly after his return to Paris from London in early March, Lloyd George himself took a hand in attempting to squelch the expansive schemes of Marshal Foch, reports of which had reached him in London. The British prime minister believed that one of the quickest and most effective ways to discredit the ambitious schemes of the military authorities for intervention in Russia was to demand to know how much such a venture would cost and who would pay for it, and, as we saw earlier, he so advised House. Putting into practice this tactic, Lloyd George, "nettled," in Churchill's words, "by repeated War Office requests" for decisions of policy on Russia, asked Churchill in late February for an accounting of the cost of intervention to date, as well as exact estimates of the expense of various proposed courses of action in Russia.[16] Armed with these figures, Lloyd George took Clemenceau to task on March 7, in the course of a private meeting with the French leader and House at which a number of major issues before the conference, including Russia, were discussed. The British prime minister declared that while Foch had "great plans for invading Russia," the marshal never submitted any estimates of the expense of such an undertaking. Lloyd George then showed Clemenceau the War Office figures on what even the present limited operations in Russia were costing the Allies. The

[16] Churchill, *Aftermath*, 179.

French premier was astonished. Pressing his advantage, Lloyd George announced that the British planned to withdraw their forces from North Russia and Siberia; they would, however, agree to furnish Denikin and Kolchak with surplus munitions and supplies to enable the White Russian leaders to defend their territories against Bolshevik aggression. According to Lloyd George, both Clemenceau and House approved such a policy, and both were "hostile to any plan for the invasion of Russia." [17]

Lloyd George was clearly moving toward endorsement of a policy of containment—not so very different from Clemenceau's *cordon sanitaire* —which the prime minister's reaction to Churchill's February plan and his letter to House on February 21 had adumbrated and which later became, in the spring and summer of 1919, settled British policy toward Russia.[18] Foch, however, was not content with a simply defensive posture. Despite his rebuff by the conference on February 25, Foch had not given up his plan for an offensive against the Bolsheviks.[19] During the first part of March he continued to seek opportunities for putting this plan into effect. His next chance came when the inter-Allied mission in Poland wired the conference that the Ukrainians under Petliura had launched a successful offensive against the Poles and were about to capture the key city of Lemberg (Lvov) in Eastern Galicia. This territory was in dispute between the two groups, with the Eastern Galicians themselves adding a third complicating factor, and its final disposition had not yet been decided on by the conference. By this time, with the expedition to Odessa faring badly, the French government had lost whatever slight interest it had earlier had in the possibility of establishing an independent Ukrainian state under French and Polish domination as an added member of the projected East European cordon against both Bolshevism and a revived Germany and as an arena for postwar French investment and trade.[20] The pro-Polish policy of Clemenceau was dominant, although the alternative of relying on a strong, reconstituted Russia was still being held in reserve.

[17] Lloyd George, I, 291–92. Lloyd George unfortunately did not reveal the figures with which he confronted Clemenceau. Later, in May, he told his colleagues on the Council of Four that intervention and aid to anti-Bolshevik Russia had cost the British more than £100,000,000.

[18] On Lloyd George's earlier stand, see p. 146 of ch. five; for his later position, see pp. 245–46 of ch. seven.

[19] An indication of this is contained in a telegram from Maklakov in Paris to General Miller in Archangel on March 6. Maklakov reported that the official public policy of the Allies toward the anti-Bolsheviks was to send the latter arms, supplies, and volunteers, but not troops. Maklakov added: "It is known to us that the real intentions of influential governments go much farther than this, but they could not be stated publicly." Cited in Mints, 60–61.

[20] See, for example, Maklakov's telegram to Omsk of March 29, reporting that the French had no intention of supporting Ukrainian separatism and that agree-

Consequently, on March 17 Foch, seizing on the reportedly imminent defeat of the Poles at Lemberg, proposed an elaborate plan for assisting Poland which would have been a first step toward his dreamed-of East European crusade against Bolshevism and which was, in fact, simply a variant of the extensive project he had advanced on February 25, as he himself indicated at the conclusion of his presentation.[21] This time the pivot of the plan was the situation in Eastern Galicia, rather than the transport of Polish troops through Danzig. But the purpose was the same, and it did not disconcert Foch in the least that the Ukrainians opposing the Poles were themselves fighting the Bolsheviks alongside the French soldiers at Odessa. Foch first stressed the gravity of the danger to Poland and the necessity of getting assistance to the Poles with all possible speed. The Polish government, Foch warned, would fall if Lemberg did; as a consequence, this important nation, which the Allies had reconstituted, assisted, and put under their special protection, would dissolve into anarchy at its birth and would fall prey to the enemies surrounding it on three sides: Germans, Bolsheviks, and Ukrainians.

In referring the crisis over Lemberg to the Council of Ten, the Commission on Polish Affairs had recommended four possible courses of action for consideration: the transfer of Polish troops at Odessa to Lemberg; the immediate transport by rail through Austria of a part of General Haller's Polish divisions in France; the dispatch to Lemberg of units of the Rumanian army; and the enjoining of an armistice between the Poles and Ukrainians.[22] Carefully omitting any mention of the last suggestion, Foch reviewed the first three. He placed greatest emphasis, however, on the third, the employment of Rumanian troops, pointing out that the Rumanian government had agreed "to participate in the prepared operations" if the Allies supplied the necessary equipment and food. In concluding, Foch declared:

> . . . Poland and Rumania, with whom the Allies were tied, offered sufficient forces for the purpose required, provided that these troops received guidance and material assistance. Their combined action

ments between the local French command and Petliura's Directory had been solely for the purpose of furthering joint military action against the Bolsheviks. Maklakov Papers, Part II, Packet II, File 5. After the evacuation of Odessa the French agreed, in a meeting with the British in Paris on April 4, 1919, that there was no possibility of forming an independent Ukraine and that Denikin's claim to control in that area should, therefore, be supported. Reported in a memorandum on Russia, June 6, 1919, British Foreign Office, *Documents*, III, 366.

[21] *Peace Conference*, IV, 379–85. See a discussion among the American commissioners on February 10 for earlier suspicions of Foch's actions regarding Galicia, in *ibid.*, XI, 28.

[22] Notes of March 12 and 14 from the Commission on Polish Affairs to the Council of Ten, Miller, *Diary*, XVII, 179–82.

would constitute a most solid barrier against Bolshevism, which would otherwise triumph. The object in view would be realized as soon as the Allied governments decided on a resolute policy, affirming their resolve to stop the progress of Bolshevism, and constituting for the purpose an Allied High Command, charged with the duty of supplying to Poland and to Rumania (and eventually to the other governments in a position to act, such as Finland, etc.) the necessary material aid, and with the duty of coordinating the action of these various governments.

The pattern was clear; it was the old scheme of a great coalition of the states bordering Russia in an offensive against the Bolsheviks under the supervision of the French high command. Lloyd George retorted at once and categorically. He declared that to support Foch's recommendations would mean "the perpetration of a great mischief. The proposal at bottom merely meant the setting up of a great army for the eventual invasion of Russia." The Rumanians had, in fact, nothing whatever to do with the problem of Lemberg, Lloyd George continued, but it was obviously hoped in some quarters that once they were there, they would be available for operations against Russia. Lloyd George then returned to a favorite theme: even if the policy proposed were correct, it would have to be carried out at the expense of the Allies since surely neither the Rumanians nor the Poles could pay for the operations envisaged.

Turning to the question of Lemberg itself, Lloyd George pointed out that by transferring troops from the anti-Bolshevik front in Odessa "to take part in some quarrel at Lemberg," and by attacking Petliura, who opposed the Bolsheviks, the Allies would simply be aiding the Red Army. Moreover, the British leader asked, what right had the conference to support the Poles over Lemberg when no decision had yet been reached as to whether the city should be included in the future Poland? Lloyd George concluded by urging the rejection of all Foch's proposals and by recommending instead some means of persuasion on the Poles and Ukrainians to bring about a temporary settlement between them.

In some heat Foch renewed his proposition, hinting darkly that, as the experience of previous years had shown, March was the month "in which the enemy generally prepared his offensive." He then argued, somewhat petulantly, that his proposals were, after all, primarily a reaffirmation of the recommendations of the Polish Commission of the conference itself, and that they were designed only to support and to ensure the execution of a fixed policy of the Allies—the reconstitution of Poland. The plan was, according to Foch, "a very moderate and restricted one," and it could be successfully implemented with small military forces, without great expense, and "without undertaking any imprudent engagements." He simply favored the creation of a nucleus of resistance against the Bolsheviks to prevent the center of the anti-Bolshevik front from being pierced (he failed to explain how fighting the anti-Bolshevik Ukrainians would accomplish this), and he had only suggested that an inter-Allied staff be constituted to study how the question might be solved in the light of all available means.

At this point Pichon, who was probably not, in any case, in favor of Foch's grand design because of its anti-Russian overtones, brought up the fourth approach recommended by the Polish Commission—the enjoining of an armistice—and remarked that this seemed to accord with Lloyd George's position. He maintained that if the Ukrainians were given the oilfields in the region, they would probably accept an armistice. He added pointedly that this was also the view of the French generals attached to the Polish Commission, and it was an opinion "accepted by all the experts, except Marshal Foch."

After the Council members had agreed that the conference should attempt to secure an armistice at Lemberg, Foch proposed that, in addition, an Allied staff be appointed to study the transporting of Polish troops overland from France and Odessa, as well as the possible utilization of Rumanian troops in Poland. Clemenceau, perhaps remembering Lloyd George's lesson on March 7 on the high cost of intervention, objected that since the use of Rumanian forces would entail considerable expense, the question was primarily financial, rather than military. Lloyd George then declared that he would accept the first proposition of Foch—to study the transfer of Polish troops—but that he could under no circumstances approve the second: he was adamantly opposed in principle to having the Allies encourage the Rumanians to attack the Ukrainians, with whom the Allies were cooperating in the defense of Odessa. President Wilson, who had returned to Paris a week before, had been strangely silent on the substance of the issue during the discussion; at this point, however, he indicated his agreement with Lloyd George's position, and on that note the meeting adjourned. All that was left of Foch's scheme was permission for him to study the possibility of transporting Polish troops from France and Odessa to Poland.[23]

Foch was angry and frustrated. As he and Lloyd George left the conference room, he continued to remonstrate vigorously with the British

[23] At the next meeting of the Council, March 19, the decision to endeavor to obtain Ukrainian agreement to an armistice was emended, on the recommendation of Professor Lord, the American specialist on Poland, to include a direct appeal by the Council to the Ukrainian and Polish forces for an immediate cease-fire, with subsequent armistice negotiations to take place in Paris under the supervision of the Conference's Commission on Polish Affairs. *Ibid.*, IV, 405–12.

prime minister over the failure of the Council to take decisive action, and to emphasize the importance of sending Rumanian troops to Poland. In reply Lloyd George kept repeating: "The great necessity is to give them food that will keep them from Bolshevism." But Foch always added: "Yes, and an army." [24]

Though defeated, Foch did not give up his dream of establishing the Poles firmly in Eastern Galicia and of linking the Polish and Rumanian armies together at that point to provide a continuous front for either offensive or defensive action against the Bolsheviks.[25] After two months of fruitless attempts to secure Polish adherence to an armistice with the Ukrainians, Wilson and Lloyd George, outraged at the Poles' defiant attitude and at their continuing aggression in the area, agreed on May 21, with the reluctant assent of Clemenceau, that a strong telegram should be sent to Pilsudski, the Polish chief of state, threatening to terminate aid to Poland unless the armistice terms in Eastern Galicia were promptly complied with. The message also expressed the displeasure of the conference at the Poles' alleged attempt to settle a boundary question by force.[26]

The fate of this telegram is significant for the outcome of the affair but must remain a matter of speculation until the French archives are opened. It was widely believed in peace conference circles that the French, who were charged with sending the telegram, deliberately delayed it until Haller's army had reached Galicia and had driven out the Ukrainians and until a junction with the Rumanians advancing northward had been effected. In any case, in a stormy session among the Big Three on May 27 Lloyd George accused the French of intriguing with the Poles to evade execution of the conference's decision.[27] He recalled that the heads of government had been asked to delay action "from day to day, and almost from hour to hour" because they had been told Paderewski was due to arrive in Paris momentarily. Now it turned out Paderewski was in Prague, and there was no evidence that the telegram

[24] Recounted in Riddell, 35. See also on the meeting of March 17 Callwell, *Wilson Diaries*, II, 174–75, and letter of March 21 from Bliss to Major General Kernan, American representative on the inter-Allied mission to Poland, Bliss Papers, Box 72.

[25] For a detailed and careful analysis of the conference's treatment of the Polish position in the East, see ch. four of Piotr Wandycz, *France and Her Eastern Allies, 1919–25* (Minneapolis, 1962), 104–31. For a pro-Polish view, see Komarnicki, 373–428.

[26] Mantoux, I, 247, 312, 505. See also letter of Bliss to Wilson, April 18, and Wilson's reply of April 22. Wilson Papers, Series VIIIA, Box 39; *Peace Conference*, V, 676, 711–14, 754–55, 778–82, 800, 859–60.

[27] *Peace Conference*, VI, 60–62. Some support for Lloyd George's accusations is contained in a telegram from Gibson to Wilson on May 15 cited in Wandycz, 112 n. 36.

of reprimand to Pilsudski had ever been sent. Wilson referred to "the old plan of the so-called sanitary cordon which the Military Authorities had proposed to establish against the Bolsheviks, and which had been rejected." He then commented, probably correctly, that "it was possible that the Military Authorities were, nevertheless, trying to carry out this plan in fact." That afternoon Clemenceau explained lamely that the telegram had been sent on May 22, but that because of delays in transmission and the use of the wrong code in attempting to decipher it, it had not been delivered in Warsaw until May 26.[28]

Nevertheless, on June 3 the Council of Four meekly accepted Pilsudski's reply of May 31, in which he promised to suspend hostilities now that the Polish objective of linking up with the Rumanians had been achieved. In other words, the heads of government had to acknowledge a *fait accompli,* which was apparently carried out with the connivance of at least some of the French authorities. Moreover, toward the end of June the Big Four, on the advice of the Council of Foreign Ministers, turned the wheel full circle by endorsing Poland's right to occupy all of Eastern Galicia in order "to protect the peaceful population . . . against the dangers to which they are exposed by the Bolshevik bandits." [29]

On June 27 the heads of government followed up this decision by eagerly agreeing to send whatever supplies and equipment the Polish army required, admonishing themselves—like neglectful parents—for having been so inattentive to Poland's vital needs.[30] Apparently the Big Three had decided that if the Poles were to agree to the newly proposed plebiscite in Upper Silesia and if Poland were to serve as an effective buffer force against both Germany and Bolshevism, they had best, like the three monkeys, hear no evil and see no evil regarding Polish policy in the east. To some extent Foch had thus finally had his way.[31]

---

[28] *Peace Conference,* VI, 69–70.

[29] *Ibid.,* 352, 667–68, 731. Temperley (VI, 272) asserts that this about-face occurred because of unfounded reports that the Ukrainian army had collapsed and unless the Poles were supported the Bolsheviks might drive through this gap in the southeastern cordon in an effort to reach Bela Kun in Hungary. Wandycz (113–14) supports this general view, referring vaguely to reports of the Allied military advisers in Warsaw. Wilson was certainly influenced by an extremely pro-Polish report from an American observer in Poland, Lieutenant Foster. See letter from Lord to Wilson of May 29 enclosing and warmly endorsing the report, and Wilson's hearty reply of June 3. Wilson Papers, Series VIIIA, Box 54. Wilson read extracts of the report to his colleagues on the Council of Four on June 3, *Peace Conference,* VI, 118.

[30] *Peace Conference,* VI, 726–27.

[31] For later developments concerning Poland, see ch. ten, pp. 343–46.

Revolution in Hungary

Returning now to the events of March and Foch's *idée fixe,* we find that despite being rebuffed by the Council of Ten a second time Foch had by no means abandoned his hope of organizing a crusade in the east against Bolshevism. With his plan to make Poland the base of operations for such an offensive temporarily sidetracked by Lloyd George's opposition and by German reluctance to agree to the passage of General Haller's troops,[32] Foch turned his attention to the possibility of building up the Rumanian army and of launching the attack from that country. His opportunity was not long in coming. In fact, the timing of events in Paris and Eastern Europe was such as to lead General Bliss and others in the American delegation to conclude that Foch and the French military authorities had conspired to precipitate the communist revolution in Hungary as a pretext for mounting a war against Bolshevism, and perhaps also as an excuse for renewing hostilities against the Central Powers, with the aim of immediately imposing severe terms of peace on the enemy.[33] The sequence of events that preceded and followed the outbreak of the Hungarian revolution is certainly suggestive, and the opinion of American observers closely following the situation cannot be entirely discounted despite their obvious emotional bias against the policies of the French. On the other hand, there is no direct evidence of French intrigue or of a conscious French effort to foster Bolshevism in Hungary.[34] Until official French documents for this pe-

[32] In reply to inquiries from the inter-Allied mission in Poland, the local German authorities indicated that the transport of Polish troops from France through Danzig was a matter to be taken up with the German Armistice Commission at Spa. Two entire sessions of the Council of Ten, on March 21 and 22, were devoted to discussion of this issue and to attempts to persuade Marshal Foch personally to present the Allied request to the Germans at Spa. Foch stubbornly maintained that this would place him in the position of entreating the Germans to permit something the Allies had every right to do under Article XVI of the Armistice. *Peace Conference,* IV, 423–42, 449–58. Pointless and time-consuming sessions such as this contributed to the decision of Wilson, Lloyd George, Clemenceau, and Orlando to meet alone in what came to be known as the Council of Four, beginning March 24. Foch eventually raised the matter directly with the Germans and arranged for the Polish troops to be transported to Poland by rail through Germany.

[33] Bliss's views are in a letter and memorandum of March 28 to President Wilson, cited in Baker, *Settlement,* III, 238–45, and discussed below. For the views of other American officials see below.

[34] Karolyi, the head of the post-Armistice democratic government in Hungary, suggested in his memoirs, written in 1953, that the French representative in Budapest, Lieutenant-Colonel Vyx, conspired with reactionary and Germanophile elements in Hungary against Karolyi's government, with the aim either of restoring a conservative regime directly or of bringing about a Bolshevik revolution, which would serve as a pretext for the seizure of power by the landowners and aristocrats.

riod are opened to historians, it is impossible either to confirm or to refute Bliss's charges.[35]

The circumstances on which Bliss based his allegation can be summarized briefly. The territory of Transylvania, possessing a mixed population, was in dispute between Rumania and Hungary. In January and February 1919 Rumanian troops advanced into Transylvania beyond the armistice line laid down the preceding fall. The Rumanians claimed that the Hungarians were committing atrocities in the area and were encouraging the spread of Bolshevik propaganda among peoples who might eventually be under Rumanian jurisdiction. In an effort to prevent clashes between Rumanian and Hungarian forces and the prejudging of conference decisions respecting this territory, the Commission on Rumanian Affairs of the conference recommended on February 19 the delimitation of lines of occupation for each side separated by a neutral zone in which, the Commission suggested, Allied troops might be stationed "to prevent the spread of Bolshevism, which was prevalent in Hungary." After Council discussion on February 21 and subsequent review by the military advisers at Versailles, this proposal was approved by the Council of Ten on February 26, when Wilson and Lloyd George, who might have objected, were both away.[36] Provision for occupation of the neutral zone by Allied forces was made, but the lines of demarcation established were distinctly unfavorable for the Hungarians. The decision permitted the advance of the Rumanians and required the further withdrawal of Hungarian forces to a point considerably behind the original armistice line. In a memorandum of March 8 to Lan-

Karolyi offers no proof of this assertion, however. Michael Karolyi, *Memoirs* (London, 1956), 147, 152–53. For a detailed account of this situation in Hungary and of Bliss's allegations see Alfred D. Low, *The Soviet Hungarian Republic and the Paris Peace Conference* (Transactions of the American Philosophical Society— New Series, Vol. LIII, Part 10; Philadelphia, 1963), chs. 4, 5.

[35] The truth of the matter is further obscured by evidence indicating the existence of Italian intrigues in Hungary at this time. The Italians, anxious to find an ally in the Balkans to help them block Yugoslav ambitions, believed that Hungary could play this role. They supported and encouraged the government of Karolyi and were subsequently friendly to the regime of Bela Kun, suggesting it be recognized. According to one report, Italian officers even sold Bela Kun arms. Letter from T. N. Page, American ambassador in Rome, to House, March 9, 1919, House Papers; memorandum of Captain Nicholas Roosevelt dated March 26, Wilson Papers, Series VIIIA, Box 29; Weekly Report on the Political Situation in Central Europe, April 5, 1919, from Professor Robert J. Kerner, an expert with the American delegation, Bliss Papers, Box 257, File 907; and, charging the sale of arms to Bela Kun, letter to Hoover from T. T. C. Gregory, relief representative in Central Europe, June 4, 1919, Wilson Papers, Series VIIIA, Box 60, which is referred to in Herbert Hoover, *My Memoirs* (3 vols.; New York, 1951–1952), I, 399. Hereafter cited as Hoover, *Memoirs*.

[36] *Peace Conference*, IV, 59–61, 145–47.

sing, on which no action was taken, General Bliss pointed this out. He added that he had been absent when the military advisers had worked out the zones. The American representative present had not been cognizant of all the facts, although he had made clear that his concurrence in no way committed the United States to military action in Southeastern Europe.[37]

The decision of the Council of Ten was transmitted to General d'Espérey the next day.[38] Yet not until March 19, over three weeks later, and two days after the rejection of Foch's plan to hinge his anti-Bolshevik crusade on the relief of Lemberg, did the Allied military representative in Budapest, Lieutenant-Colonel Vyx, inform the Hungarian government of the action taken in Paris. Bliss believed that the French military authorities deliberately delayed transmitting the decision of the conference to the Hungarians until after it had become clear that the conference would not, as things then stood, support an offensive against the Bolsheviks.

The official Allied note was delivered to the Hungarian government of Count Karolyi on March 20. Believing that acceptance of this latest in a long series of demands on Hungary could not be justified before the Hungarian people, Karolyi resigned the following day. His government was replaced by a coalition of socialists and communists led by Bela Kun, who installed a Soviet-type regime in Hungary. That such a denouement would follow presentation of the Allied note was not unpredictable at the time in the light of the political situation in Hungary; therefore, some contemporary observers argued that the French generals provoked the coming to power of a radical regime in Hungary in the hope that this would force the Allies to take action against the Bolsheviks. On March 28 the French socialist leader Cachin made this charge in a conversation with Buckler. Calling attention to Cachin's allegation, Bullitt told House the next day that Professor Archibald Cary Coolidge, one of the experts with the American delegation and the head of a mission to Austria, had supported Cachin's view.[39]

In any case, there is some evidence to suggest that at least the French did nothing to reverse the trend of events in Hungary. Just before the transfer of power to Bela Kun representatives of the bourgeois parties

[37] Bliss Papers, Box 70. See also Baker, *Settlement*, III, 243.
[38] *Peace Conference*, IV, 172.
[39] Memorandum of conversation between Buckler and Cachin, March 28, 1919, with Bullitt's notation of March 29, House Papers, Drawer 30, File 218. See also the memorandum of Captain Nicholas Roosevelt, a member of the Coolidge mission, who was in Budapest at the time of the revolution. The memorandum, dated March 26, was transmitted to Wilson on March 27. Wilson Papers, Series VIIIA, Box 28.

proposed to the French military authorities a Hungarian alliance with the Entente against the Russian Bolsheviks, on condition that the existing lines of occupation in Transylvania be maintained and that the Allies send fifteen thousand troops to restore order in Budapest; otherwise, they said, they would be forced to compromise with Bela Kun.[40] No response was made to this offer.

The news from Hungary created deep-seated apprehension, but little surprise, among conference circles. Throughout the winter everyone had been talking about the danger of Bolshevism spreading westward and infecting Western Europe. Now it had happened; the threat so long and familiarly discussed as to become a little unreal and unconvincing had materialized. The work of the conference, the social order in Europe, the Allied governments themselves seemed endangered. Moreover, the Hungarian revolution preceded by only a few days the greatest crisis of the conference. Even the resort to private meetings of the Big Four had not brought a break in the deadlock between the French and Anglo-American positions over the German terms. Neither side was prepared to yield, and it seemed that the alliance against Germany might break up, with a resumption of hostilities almost certain to follow. An atmosphere of alarm, almost of panic, hung over the peace deliberations.

In this situation the threat of Bolshevism became a pawn in the struggle between Clemenceau on the one hand, and Lloyd George and Wilson on the other. Hoping to persuade the French to yield, Lloyd George presented to his colleagues on March 25 his well-known "Memorandum of Fontainebleau." [41] This document was a plea for the imposition of moderate terms of peace on Germany. The British prime minister warned prophetically that an unjust peace could survive only the generation that itself had experienced the horrors of war; after thirty years it would lead to new wars. No matter how much the Allies weakened Germany, the Germans would find ways to exact retribution if they felt unfairly treated. But, Lloyd George went on, an even more telling argument against a harsh peace was the existence throughout Europe of a spirit of revolution:

> There is a deep sense not only of discontent, but of anger and revolt amongst the workmen against pre-war conditions. The whole existing order in its political, social, and economic aspects is questioned by

[40] Reported to Foch in a telegram from d'Espérey on March 22. Miller, *Diary*, XVII, 281–82.

[41] Formally entitled "Some Considerations for the Peace Conference Before They Finally Draft Their Terms," and prepared while Lloyd George was conferring with his advisers at Fontainebleau. For the text, see Baker, *Settlement*, III, 449–57, where its authorship is erroneously attributed to General Bliss. For the circumstances of its drafting, see Hankey, 98–101.

the masses of the population from one end of Europe to the other. In some countries, like Germany and Russia, the unrest takes the form of open rebellion; in others, like France, Great Britain, and Italy, it takes the shape of strikes and of a general disinclination to settle down to work. . . .

After reviewing the course of events in Russia, Lloyd George warned that "the greatest danger . . . in the present situation is that Germany may throw in her lot with Bolshevism and place her resources, her brains, her vast organizing power at the disposal of the revolutionary fanatics whose dream it is to conquer the world for Bolshevism by force of arms." If this happened, all of Eastern Europe might be "swept into the orbit of the Bolshevik revolution, and within a year we may witness the spectacle of nearly three hundred million people organized into a vast red army under German instructors . . . equipped with German cannon . . . and prepared for a renewal of the attack on Western Europe. . . . The news which came from Hungary yesterday shows only too clearly that this danger is no fantasy." According to Lloyd George, such a danger would be realized, however, only if an unjust peace drove Germany into the arms of the Bolsheviks and if the Allies did not offer Germany an alternative to Bolshevism in the form of a fair settlement.

If the terms were too harsh, Lloyd George continued, the Germans would refuse to sign; the Allies would have to reimpose the blockade, which could lead only to Bolshevism throughout Central and Eastern Europe. If the terms were just, if the Allies proffered relief to Germany and promised her admission to the League of Nations, the German people would have a powerful inducement to resist the lures of Bolshevism.

The British leader concluded by reminding his colleagues that the peace, if it were to be complete and lasting, must include not only a reasonable settlement with Germany but some resolution of the situation in Russia itself and some answer to the threat of Bolshevism in Eastern Europe; he failed to explain, however, how the latter objectives might be accomplished. When it was finally accepted, the Treaty of Versailles met none of these goals, and proved to be neither complete nor lasting. As it turned out, however, the yearning for better conditions and the reaction to an unjust peace took forms in Europe other than Bolshevism, though with consequences hardly less fateful for the world.

On March 27 the Council of Four, formed a few days previously and consisting of only the heads of government—Lloyd George, Wilson, Clemenceau, and Orlando—discussed Lloyd George's memorandum.[42]

[42] Paul Mantoux, *Les délibérations du Conseil des quatre* (2 vols.; Paris, 1955), I, 41–46. When the Council of Four first began to meet on March 24, no minutes were kept; the sessions were designed to be completely private and secret and to give the statesmen a chance to speak frankly. The interpreter, Professor Paul Man-

Supporting the British statesman, Wilson urged Clemenceau to accept moderate terms in order to avoid provoking a spirit of revenge in Germany and sowing the seeds of future wars. Wilson did not touch on the problem of Bolshevism. Clemenceau, in a lengthy reply, proved that he was not to be outdone by Lloyd George, or by the many others at Paris and throughout Europe who threatened the conference with Bolshevism in an attempt to gain their ends. The French leader chided Lloyd George with being too afraid that the Germans would not sign the peace treaty. The Germans would argue, would delay, and might even endeavor to use incidents "like that in Budapest," but if met with firmness, the only language they understood, they would sign. Clemenceau declared that the terms must be just, not in the eyes of the Germans, who would never be persuaded that the Allies had acted fairly no matter what was offered them, but in the eyes of the Allied peoples, who had undergone terrible sacrifices and who were not to be denied the fruits of victory and the assurance of future security from German depredations. Clemenceau added:

> We have reason to fear Bolshevism in Germany and to avoid provoking its development there; but it should not therefore be necessary to propagate it among ourselves. There is a sentiment of justice among the Allied populations which must be satisfied. If this sentiment is violently contradicted, be it in France, or in England, a great danger may result. It is all right to wish to lead the vanquished, but we must not lose sight of the victors. If a revolutionary movement must be produced somewhere because our solution appears unjust, let it not be among us.

To Lloyd George's threat that too harsh terms would lead to Bolshevism in Germany, Clemenceau had posed the danger that too lenient terms might lead to Bolshevism in France or England. Lloyd George retorted that he knew something of the Bolshevik danger in his own country; he had recently been engaged in fighting it—a reference to his efforts in February to deal with strikes and growing labor unrest in England. "I combat Bolshevism," continued Lloyd George, "not by force but by seeking ways to satisfy the legitimate aspirations which have

toux, kept rough notes, published in the work cited above. At some early meetings of the Council of Four, Sir Maurice Hankey, secretary-general of the British delegation, was present and kept a record. Beginning April 19, Hankey was charged with preparing regular minutes so that the Four could review and keep track of their deliberations and decisions. All of the minutes prepared by Hankey are included in *Peace Conference*, v, vi. Evidence of what occurred in the meetings of the Council of Four can also be gleaned from the resolutions published in the official *Recueil* of conference acts and from accounts given in memoirs, diaries, letters, and memoranda.

allowed it to be born." This approach, he claimed, had been successful, and the danger of "an explosion of Bolshevism in England will not come from the reproach of having asked too little of the enemy but from that of having asked too much."

Clemenceau remained unconvinced, however, at least as far as the relation of Bolshevism to the peace terms was concerned. Although that day there was no further discussion on this point, Clemenceau, in his subsequent written reply of March 28 to Lloyd George's memorandum, renewed his charge that failure to satisfy the demands of the Allied populations might stimulate the growth of Bolshevism in Western Europe. Moreover, he argued, if moderate terms were imposed, leaving too much to the Germans and depriving the new states created on Germany's eastern borders of their national and territorial rights, this would dangerously weaken these new states and expose them to Bolshevism. As a result, "the only barrier which at the present moment exists between Russian Bolshevism and German Bolshevism will be shattered," and Germanic Bolshevism will dominate all of Eastern and Central Europe.[43]

The talk of Bolshevism on both sides was chiefly talk, however; despite their expressed fear of Bolshevism—partly genuine, partly for bargaining purposes—they were unable to develop a program to meet this challenge or even to agree on a practical plan for dealing with its immediate manifestations. At this time they had before them an elaborate project of Foch to rid Europe of Bolshevism by force and, at the other extreme, proposals brought back by Bullitt from Moscow to make peace with the Soviet government and to attempt in this way to draw it into a European settlement based on Western principles. The conference leaders rejected both approaches and continued to pursue a confused and ineffective course somewhere between the two, a policy whose purpose was obscure and which helped neither the Russians nor the peoples of the West, contributing, on the contrary, to the poisoning of future relations between them.

Others, however, believed that they knew how to handle Bolshevism. Shortly after the Hungarian revolution, General Berthelot, whom Bliss accused of being the chief proponent of intervention in Russia among the French military leaders in Eastern Europe, and who a month earlier had reported that his troops would not be available to garrison the proposed neutral zone in Transylvania because they were being held in

[43] Baker, *Settlement*, III, 249–52. Clemenceau also strongly implied that Lloyd George was proposing a temporary and inadequate settlement for France while obtaining all the advantages that England desired—destruction of the German fleet, seizure of Germany's colonies, and the opening of Germany's foreign markets.

readiness for eventual deployment in Russia, told an American relief official in Rumania, Captain Green, that he could guarantee the occupation of all Hungary within nine days.[44] In Paris journalists and junior officials of the conference were discussing what ought to be done, and there was much talk, particularly in the French press, of imposing the French terms on Germany by force and of undertaking a holy crusade against the Bolshevik menace.[45]

Taking advantage of this atmosphere, Foch renewed his efforts to win the support of Britain and the United States for operations against the Bolsheviks in Eastern Europe. On March 12 General d'Espérey had reported to Paris that if clothing were supplied to the Rumanian army, ten Rumanian divisions could be placed on the line of the Dniester to hold back the Bolshevik tide; only two Allied divisions would be needed to support them, in d'Espérey's judgment. Two days later the Rumanian representative in Paris, Brătianu, asked the Allies for equipment and supplies.[46] These developments were apparently what led Foch to include in his design of March 17 provision for employment of Rumanian troops in support of the Poles at Lemberg. He also encouraged the Rumanians to seek from the British government and the French civilian ministers a definite commitment for the supply and financing of a Rumanian army of a quarter of a million men. Tentative agreement on such support was apparently reached at lower levels, but Foch was aware that the concurrence of the heads of government would be needed to implement it.[47] The Hungarian revolution and the deteriorating situation in Odessa gave Foch the opening he needed.

On March 25 the Council of Four, meeting for the second time, considered telegraphic reports on the plight of the Allied expedition to Odessa, which urgently needed reinforcements and supplies to maintain itself; this led to a discussion of the general problem of combating Bolshevism.[48] The military advisers, headed by Foch, were called in to

[44] Report of Captain Green dated April 11 and transmitted to House by Hoover on April 21. House Papers, Correspondence Files, Hoover.

[45] See, for example, Thompson, *Conference Day by Day,* 268; House's diary for this period; and summaries of the French press prepared by George Bernard Noble for the American delegation, March 26–28. Bliss Papers, Intelligence Reports.

[46] See a report to the Council of Four on March 25 by General Alby, French chief of staff. Mantoux, I, 19.

[47] On March 25 Norman Davis, one of the American financial experts, told Bliss that Bratianu had inquired some five days previously about the possibility of Rumania purchasing surplus American railroad equipment in France. When Davis asked about the supplying of the Rumanian army itself, Bratianu replied that this was being taken care of by the French and British. Memorandum from Bliss to Wilson, March 26, Wilson Papers, Series VIIIA, Box 28.

[48] Mantoux, I, 18–23; Resolution 200 of March 25 in *Recueil,* Part I, Division II,

provide expert advice. Lloyd George and Wilson recommended the evacuation of Odessa, especially in view of the reportedly hostile attitude of the population. The president, in fact, sounded almost like Clemenceau, like a believer in the *cordon sanitaire:* "This [the situation at Odessa] confirms me in my policy, which is to leave Russia to the Bolsheviks—the Russians will stew in their own juice until circumstances have restored them to greater sanity—and to limit ourselves to preventing Bolshevism from invading other parts of Europe."

The British generals testified that Odessa had little strategic importance; the only reason to endeavor to hold it would be to avoid a serious blow to Allied prestige and to the morale of the anti-Bolshevik movement. Of greater importance than saving Odessa, they concluded, would be reinforcement of the Rumanians. Foch, though agreeing as to the intrinsic value of Odessa, urged that the Allies "cling fast to it" and also support the Poles at Lemberg. He admitted, however, that Odessa was virtually a lost cause, and he placed greatest emphasis on the necessity of assisting the Rumanian army and of developing a coordinated plan of action which would take account of all factors in the situation.

Lloyd George maintained that it would be foolish for the Allies to squander their resources to bolster a precarious, if not hopeless, position at Odessa; it would be better to redeploy their forces from Odessa to Rumania, establishing there a defensive barrier against Bolshevism. He then suggested that since the French were primarily responsible for matters in that area, just as the British were for the area in which Denikin was operating, the French government should state what it was able to furnish the Rumanians and what in addition would still be needed. In advance of such a calculation, Lloyd George offered to divert from Denikin to Rumania enough of Britian's war surplus arms and supplies to equip 100,000 men. Foch was delighted with this suggestion and declared candidly, to the undoubted annoyance of the British present: "What one sends to Denikin is lost. I do not attach great importance to the army of Denikin, because armies do not exist by themselves. . . . They must have behind them a government, legislation, and an organized country. It is better to have a government without an army than an army without a government. That is why I say: build on Rumania. . . ."

It was finally agreed that the British would send supplies, originally destined for Denikin, to the Rumanians and that the Allied military representatives would "elaborate a military plan to fit the situation." This

89. See also memorandum from Bliss to Wilson, March 28, in Baker, *Settlement,* III, 244; and Bliss's memorandum of conversation with Wilson, March 26. Bliss Papers, Box 175.

was, of course, a great victory for Foch and the French. A necessary preliminary step to an anti-Bolshevik crusade had been taken, and Foch had been authorized to work out and present the whole project. In addition, General Denikin, who was under British influence, had been weakened. Clemenceau felt, however, that Lloyd George and Wilson had gone along with the French most reluctantly and that they did not really understand the danger. That night the French leader discussed the meeting with his confidant, General Mordacq, who reported:

> . . . our allies did not want to adopt a clear position and hesitated to take openly all the measures necessary to support the patriots who were struggling against Lenin, Trotsky, and company and who needed money, war materiel, munitions, and supplies. . . . He [Clemenceau] had great difficulty in making his colleagues understand that if they resorted to half measures, and especially if they did not take a clear stand at once, they might later have to atone for their error in blood.[49]

In accord with the decision of the Four, President Wilson asked Bliss to ascertain how American supplies could best be furnished to the Rumanian army. Bliss did so, but the decision of March 25 and the president's request provoked a memorandum from Bliss to Wilson on aiding Rumania.[50] In his memorandum Bliss strongly disapproved assisting the Rumanians on the grounds that this would commit the United States, militarily and financially, in a situation which might evolve into "a series of wars for the purpose of throttling the revolutionary movement in Europe." In some ways Bliss saw the situation more clearly than Wilson, although the general did not have the difficult experience of dealing daily with Clemenceau.

The Grand Crusade—March 27

Foch wasted no time in following up the advantage he gained on March 25. The next day he called Bliss and the British military advisers to a conference to discuss the recent decision of the Four. But instead of arrangements to supply the Rumanians, which Bliss had assumed would be the subject under consideration, the topic was a great plan of military operations in Eastern Europe. Unprepared, Bliss and the British were taken aback and confused. Foch gave the impression it was a plan already endorsed by the Four and proceeded to expound on it. Assuming

[49] Mordacq, III, 183–84.
[50] The memorandum, dated March 26, is in Wilson Papers, Series VIIIA, Box 28.

that the president had already approved the project, Bliss made little objection.[51]

The next day, March 27, Foch submitted to the Council of Four "a military plan to fit the situation," as called for on March 25.[52] And a grandiose plan it was. Foch began: "The situation is known: between Rumania and Poland through the breach of Lemberg, Bolshevism had just penetrated into Hungary, thus creating a redoubtable menace on the very rear of the barrier which we must oppose to it, and having, via Vienna, an open field for its march toward Western Europe." Consequently, Foch continued, the advance of Bolshevism must be checked by supporting Rumania and Poland, by "closing up the breach of Lemberg," by "extinguishing the blaze alight in Hungary," and by occupying Vienna with an inter-Allied force under American command. According to Foch, the greatest danger lay in Rumania, threatened by Bolshevism on two sides. He therefore recommended the formation of two armies in Rumania: one of three French, three Greek, three Rumanian, and one Polish division against Russia; and another of two French, three Serbian, and four Rumanian divisions against Hungary.

President Wilson at once objected that the plan went far beyond the scope of the question originally posed and discussed on March 25—the situation at Odessa and the request of the Rumanians for aid.[53] In suggesting that the "breach" at Lemberg be closed, Foch was in effect proposing that the Allies take the Polish side in the dispute, even though they did not know the merits of the case and had not yet determined their position. Wilson went on to point out that the plan also raised the fundamental question of military intervention in Russia; the heads of government had examined this issue "more than once, and each time have arrived at the conclusion that one cannot consider military intervention." Wilson recommended therefore that the Council stick to the point immediately at issue—whether Rumania should be assisted.

The Four then asked for the comments of their military advisers. The Italian, General Diaz, stressed the urgency of occupying Vienna and declared that an Italian force should undertake this task.[54] British General Sir Henry Wilson supported the military aspects of the plan, though

[51] Draft memorandum from Bliss to Wilson, March 27, Bliss Papers, Box 70. This memorandum was not completed and sent, since House suggested Bliss submit a condensed version, which Bliss did on March 28.

[52] An English carbon copy of Foch's proposal is in Wilson Papers, Series VIIIA, Box 29. It has marginal question marks penciled beside all operational aspects of the plan; these may well be Wilson's.

[53] Mantoux, I, 52–57. See also Callwell, *Wilson Diaries*, II, 176.

[54] Orlando, after the military men had withdrawn, disavowed Diaz and said that an inter-Allied force should occupy Vienna. Italian interest in acquiring this means of pressure on Austria was, however, clear.

warning it might lead to larger commitments. But as to the question of policy—whether military action was the answer to Bolshevism—that was up to the heads of government.

Bliss, still believing that the plan had the sanction of the Four and reluctant to contradict the position of the president, criticized it cautiously. Bliss argued that if they were going to fight Bolshevism, they should know just what it was they were undertaking to combat. According to Bliss, Bolshevism was simply one more terrible aspect of widespread revolutionary stirrings. It was therefore not possible to deal with it by force or to bottle it up in Russia with a military cordon. "It is true that you can prevent an army of Bolsheviks from coming out of Russia by posting on its borders a sufficiently large military force, but you cannot in this way prevent Bolshevism from coming out." [55] Revolutions, Bliss went on, are likely to erupt behind the cordon imposed, and then new cordons will have to be formed. Bliss concluded that if the conference wished to fight Bolshevism with military means, Foch's plan was perhaps as good as any other. Personally, however, he would prefer to exhaust every other way of combating it first, and he saw at least two alternatives: the prompt conclusion of peace, including the definition of national frontiers, and the lifting of the blockade and the restoration of production and trade.

Foch simply reiterated the basic points of his plan, adding that it was not, however, "a question of an offensive, but rather of a defensive barrier, behind which one can undertake the necessary cleansing." The generals then withdrew.

President Wilson began the private discussion among the Four by repeating his assertion that they were on familiar ground. Once again it was a question "of knowing if it is possible to organize armed resistance against Bolshevism, which means: have we not only the troops necessary, but also the material means, and the support of public sentiment?" Taking up Bliss's line of argument, the president declared:

> The word "Bolshevism" covers a variety of different things. In my opinion, to try to stop a revolutionary movement by a line of armies is to employ a broom to stop a great flood. The armies, moreover, can be impregnated with the Bolshevism they are charged with combating. A germ of sympathy exists between the forces which we wish to oppose to each other. The only way to act against Bolshevism is to make its causes disappear. This is, however, a formidable enterprise; we do not even know exactly what its causes are.

[55] Quoted from an undated memorandum by Bliss of his remarks at the meeting, which corresponds closely to the notes published by Mantoux. Bliss Papers, Box 175.

As on previous occasions, Wilson clearly sensed that force was not an effective way to deal with Bolshevism, and that to some degree there was a bond between the professed goals of the Bolsheviks and the aspirations of much of mankind; as always, however, he was perplexed and unsure as to what Bolshevism really represented and, therefore, as to how best to counter it.

The American leader concluded by directing the attention of the Council once more to the limited problems at issue—Odessa and Rumania. Despite an effort by Orlando to win approval for the occupation of Vienna, Clemenceau and Lloyd George agreed that these were the chief questions to be decided. The Four thereupon instructed Foch "to limit his recommendations to measures necessary for the reinforcement of the Rumanian army, which is understood to include the evacuation of Odessa and the sending to Rumania of supplies destined for Odessa." [56]

Foch was beaten again. His third and most extensive scheme for a great crusade to destroy Bolshevism had been vetoed, and, in fact, a withdrawal before Bolshevism had been ordered. Foch was incensed, alleging, in General Wilson's words, that "it was the four Frocks [civilians] who gave the order for Odessa to be evacuated, that he had refused to send it, and that it had been sent by Clemenceau, the real author being [President] Wilson because he won't fight the Bolsheviks." [57] In fact, however, the action of the Four did not force the evacuation of Odessa. On April 2 the Council of Four had before it a telegram from the local commander at Odessa, General d'Anselme, reporting that he had ordered a withdrawal because of lack of food for the civilian population. Clemenceau remarked that d'Anselme's decision apparently predated receipt of the Council's order, "which proves how necessary was the decision was reached." [58]

Foch had been unable to overcome the opposition of Lloyd George and Wilson to costly military adventures in Eastern Europe, which they disapproved in principle. Clemenceau, concerned over the expense of Foch's schemes and undoubtedly alarmed at the prospect of committing five French divisions to a struggle of uncertain duration and intensity, did not put up much of a fight in support of Foch. In any case, he believed not in offensive operations, but in the defensive *cordon sanitaire;*

[56] Resolution 204, *Recueil,* Part I, Division II, 90.
[57] Callwell, *Wilson Diaries,* II, 182.
[58] Mantoux, I, 117. In his memoirs Herbert Hoover denies charges allegedly made by French military authorities that Odessa could have been held if Hoover had supplied the necessary food; Hoover maintains that he offered the French shipping with which to obtain wheat from Denikin, but the offer was not taken up. Hoover, *Memoirs,* I, 419.

support to the Rumanians would further that end even though Odessa had to be given up. At the same time Clemenceau may not have been above using Foch's reckless military schemes to exert pressure on Wilson, as a way of showing the president what lay in store for Europe if Clemenceau were not given enough concessions on the German issue to enable him to maintain himself in power against the extremists.

Even the limited decision to aid Rumania was too much for Bliss, however. He was concerned lest this lead to the dispatch of American troops to that country to assist in the enforcement of a decision—on the neutral zone in Transylvania—which Bliss considered completely unjust. Consequently, he prepared another memorandum for the president on March 28, explaining that his remarks before the Council the preceding day had been made under the misapprehension that the Four had already sanctioned Foch's plan. He urged that the conference revise the neutral zone decision and reassure the Hungarian people that they would be dealt with justly on the basis of the Fourteen Points. Finally, he warned against letting the United States be dragged into a military adventure in Eastern Europe.[59] The president sent Bliss word through Colonel House that "under no circumstances would he send a man to Southeastern Europe, but that he might have to let the Rumanians have some military supplies." [60]

The decision to shore up Rumania made, the question then arose of what measures could be taken to deal with the situation created in Hungary itelf by the coming to power of Bela Kun. The economic weapon was ready at hand. On March 12 the Supreme Economic Council had approved the lifting of the blockade against Austria and Hungary, but on March 28 the Council of Foreign Ministers decided, "in view of the events that had lately taken place in Hungary," to maintain the blockade of that country pending further study of the question by the Economic Council.[61]

On March 29 the Council of Four considered a memorandum from Count Borghese, an Italian diplomat who had been in Budapest at the time of the revolution.[62] Borghese reported favorably on the new gov-

---

[59] Baker, *Settlement*, III, 238–45. See also *Peace Conference*, XI, 134–35.

[60] Penciled notation signed "THB" on the first draft of the memorandum dated March 27. Bliss Papers, Box 70.

[61] *Peace Conference*, IV, 522–24. See also Herbert Hoover, *The Ordeal of Woodrow Wilson* (New York, 1958), 135; hereafter cited as Hoover, *Ordeal of Wilson*. The Supreme Economic Council was the top economic body of the conference. The Council of Foreign Ministers was formed after the heads of government had decided to meet privately in the Council of Four; it dealt with subsidiary issues and also screened problems for the Council of Four.

[62] For the meeting of the Council of Four, see *Peace Conference*, V, 16, 18; Mantoux, I, 80–81. For Borghese's memorandum, see Wilson Papers, Series VIIIA, Box 28.

ernment. National indignation against the Allied demand for new withdrawals in Transylvania, he indicated, had played a significant part in precipitating the revolution. The government of Bela Kun, still in relatively moderate hands, was maintaining order and genuinely wanted to avoid a break with the Allies. As evidence of this desire, Borghese attached an *aide mémoire* from Bela Kun, which the Italian diplomat had agreed to transmit unofficially to the peace conference. Bela Kun declared that his government recognized the continuing validity of the armistice despite its refusal to accept the new demand presented by Colonel Vyx on March 20. Hungary's proclaimed alliance with Soviet Russia was simply an expression of "natural friendship" and of an identity of interests; it was not aggressve in intent and should not be interpreted as a desire to break relations with the Entente. Bela Kun concluded by offering to discuss all territorial issues on the basis of the principle of self-determination, and by suggestion that the Allies send a mission to Budapest. This suggestion met with the immediate approval of Wilson and Lloyd George, the latter commenting: "Let us decide not to deal with Hungary as we have with Russia—one Russia is enough for us." Clemenceau was doubtful, however, and the Four finally agreed that the matter should be considered with their foreign ministers at the next session of the Council.

At this session, on March 31, Pichon strongly opposed sending a mission to Budapest on the ground that it would mean discussing territorial issues with an enemy behind the back of a friend—Rumania.[63] Lansing, clearly influenced by Bliss, asserted that since the conference, by its unfair action in regard to the neutral zone demarcation, had helped to bring on the revolution, it had a responsibility to repair the injustice done and to help clear up the resulting situation. In any case, Lansing added, it was a mistake for the conference to adopt a peremptory attitude toward the former enemy countries. "The result is that we are turning all these people into Bolsheviks. Today we are the best friends Bolshevism has. In my opinion, the hard, brutal military way is the wrong way unless we wish to see all Central Europe turn Bolshevik."

Clemenceau retorted that unless the Allies insisted on fulfillment of their orders, they would lose the respect of the enemy peoples. The Bolshevik government of Hungary should be dealt with sternly. This was a favorite theme of Clemenceau, who insisted on several occasions that if the victorious Allies appeared weak and conciliatory in carrying out the armistice terms or in negotiating the peace settlement, the defeated nations would be encouraged to resist "just" Allied demands. German

---

[63] Mantoux, I, 98–101. See also a memorandum by Lansing reporting, among other things, on this meeting: "The French Spirit of Militarism and its Consequences, April 1, 1919," Lansing Papers, Confidential Memoranda.

reaction to the Versailles peace would hardly seem to validate Clemenceau's contention.

Sonnino agreed with Pichon and Clemenceau, declaring that "Bolshevik blackmail ought not to procure for Hungary any advantage; this would be a dangerous precedent." Wilson, Lloyd George, Orlando, and Balfour supported Lansing, however. Pichon became silent, and Clemenceau finally shrugged his shoulders, raised his eyebrows, and gazed at the ceiling, according to Lansing. It was finally agreed that although the Allies could not have any official relations with the government of Bela Kun, an unofficial fact-finding mission should be dispatched. General Smuts was selected to head the mission. He was authorized to study the question of the neutral zone in Transylvania, to explain to the Hungarians that this demarcation was not intended to prejudice in any way final settlement of the Rumanian-Hungarian boundary, and, if necessary, to make any adjustments in the neutral zone he deemed desirable. General Wilson commented laconically in his diary: "A curious business. A Welshman sends a Dutchman to tell a Hungarian not to fight a Rumanian." [64]

There was some speculation in Paris that the Smuts mission had the additional secret purpose of ascertaining whether Bela Kun might not serve as a channel of communication between the peace conference and Lenin. In the discussion of the mission before the Council of Four on March 31 Pichon had asked whether contact with Bela Kun might not be a preface to negotiations with Soviet Russia. He received a negative reply. However, Harold Nicolson and Allan Leeper, British aides who accompanied Smuts, entertained similar suspicions.[65] There is no evidence that the Four ever considered the Smuts mission in this light; the rumors may have stemmed from Bela Kun's own suggestion that he serve as an intermediary between the Allies and Soviet Russia. Shortly after the Hungarian revolution he proposed to Philip Marshall Brown, a member of the Coolidge mission to Austria who was then in Hungary, that negotiations for peace with Soviet Russia be undertaken in Budapest. He repeated the suggestion several weeks later.[66]

In view of the limited channels of communication between Budapest and Moscow, it seems likely that these proposals were made on Bela

[64] Callwell, *Wilson Diaries,* II, 179.
[65] Mantoux, I, 98–99; Nicolson, 293, 307.
[66] Memorandum of Conversation with Bela Kun, April 15, 1919, from Philip Marshall Brown to Archibald Cary Coolidge, Bullitt Papers. According to Brown, Kun also declared that he was attempting to mediate between the Polish and Ukrainian forces fighting in Galicia. In addition, there is evidence of negotiations between Kun and the Ukrainian Directory. Reshetar, 278–79. An agreement with the Ukrainians would have provided a route for the passage of Soviet Russian aid to the Hungarian revolution.

Kun's own initiative rather than at Lenin's prompting. The latter greeted the Hungarian revolution with great enthusiasm, both as a harbinger of the developing world revolution and as proof to the proletariat of Europe that power could be seized without the bloody struggle which the Russian Bolsheviks were being forced to undergo. Anxious to extend military support to Bela Kun, Lenin nevertheless recognized the virtual impossibility, because of Soviet Russia's own difficulties and her physical separation from Hungary, of providing direct assistance to the Hungarian revolution. He also warned that since Hungary was a small and isolated country, the imperialists could crush the Soviet regime there almost at will, a prediction that was fulfilled three months later.[67]

On his return to Paris Smuts recommended to the peace conference a moderate program for dealing with the Hungarian situation—Allied occupation of a neutral zone revised somewhat in Hungary's favor; relief for Hungary and the lifting of the blockade; and a central commission in Paris, on which Hungary and Austria would be represented, to consider all financial, economic, and territorial questions resulting from the dissolution of the old Austro-Hungarian Empire—but these proposals were not carried out.[68]

In April the Rumanians, apparently on their own initiative, resumed their advance against Hungary. On April 26 President Wilson suggested that the Rumanians should be forced to stop, but no action was taken.[69] At about this time Hoover began to develop the idea that if the Allies promised to lift the blockade of Hungary, provided order were restored there, this might put a good deal of pressure on the Bela Kun government and perhaps bring about its overthrow. At Hoover's urging the Council of Foreign Ministers approved this plan on May 9, and the Council of Four endorsed it on May 22, announcing that the blockade would be removed as soon as a government was formed in Hungary "which gives some assurance of settled conditions." [70]

At the same time, despite pleas for action from some of their advisers, the Big Four were not prepared to go further and recommend direct intervention in Hungary. They recognized the dangers and difficulties of such a course, and they feared endorsing in this way extreme Rumanian claims, which might prejudice a fair and acceptable territorial settlement in Eastern Europe.[71] On May 19 Wilson read to his colleagues a rec-

[67] Lenin, *Sochineniia*, xxiv, 157, 170, 176–78, 218–20.
[68] Memorandum from Lansing to Wilson enclosing Smut's recommendations, April 17, 1919. Wilson Papers, Series viiia, Box 37. For details of the Smuts mission and subsequent conference policy toward Soviet Hungary, see Low, 50–57, 62–89.
[69] *Peace Conference*, v, 291–92.
[70] *Ibid.*, iv, 693–94; v, 813.
[71] Low, 65–66.

ommendation from an American expert who had recently returned from Hungary that the only solution was for Allied forces to occupy Budapest. Although Clemenceau offered to have his staff study the possibilities of French action in concert with the Rumanians, and the Rumanians ten days later offered to march on Hungary, no one favored intervention and the matter was dropped.[72] By early June Hoover had swung over to favoring direct intervention and urged this course on the president in a letter of June 9. Wilson refused to be swayed, replying the following day that the heads of government believed "it might be very imprudent to send the forces of neighboring countries into Hungary." [73]

At this juncture a new complication arose when hostilities broke out between the Hungarians and the Czechs along their disputed boundary. At Bliss's suggestion the Council of Four decided on June 10 that they should immediately make a final delimitation of Hungary's frontiers with Rumania and Czechoslovakia and then demand that all fighting cease and that the forces of the three combatants withdraw behind those boundaries and respect them scrupulously. After urgent and hurried consultations by the foreign ministers with the Rumanian and Czech representatives in Paris, this was accomplished on June 13, and the three governments were notified of the conference's decision.[74] The Hungarians promptly complied, the Czechs delayed action, and the Rumanians continued to advance. This was the situation at the end of June, when the heads of government departed for home.

No sooner had the Big Four left Paris than Hoover again proposed intervention in Hungary, arguing that the existence of a Bolshevik regime there interfered with relief operations and the restoration of economic activity throughout Southeastern Europe.[75] It remained, however, for Foch to supply the pretext on which subsequent conference action against Bela Kun was based. On June 25 he had charged that the Hungarians had not disarmed to the extent required by the armistice of 1918 signed at Belgrade.[76] Picking up this idea, Balfour asserted to the Council on July 5 that the Hungarians had violated the 1918 armistice by increasing their army beyond the limit of six divisions imposed on them at that time. Although Bliss later pointed out that this increase had

[72] *Peace Conference,* v, 706–07, vi, 130, xi, 188.

[73] Wilson Papers, Series viiiA, Box 60.

[74] Letter from Bliss to Wilson, June 10, *ibid.,* Box 63; *Peace Conference,* vi, 246–7, 289, 352, 399.

[75] For Hoover's position, see Hoover, *Ordeal of Wilson,* 136–44; *Peace Conference,* xi, 259–60; vii, 20–28. For a detailed summary of conference policy toward Hungary in July, see Low, 73–87.

[76] Cited in Francis Deak, *Hungary at the Paris Peace Conference* (New York, 1942), 95–96.

occurred because of conditions that had arisen long after the armistice had been signed, namely Rumanian attacks on Hungary, Balfour, supported by the other heads of delegations, remained unshaken. The chief charge against the Hungarians—who had scrupulously complied with the June 13 demands of the Allies—now became their alleged violation of the armistice.

Nevertheless, Clemenceau, who still sat occasionally at the conference sessions, was most reluctant to sanction intervention. On July 5, in a long speech delivered in the vein of an elder statesman, he reminded the Council that the Big Four had considered and rejected a policy of intervention many times, and he recalled that the only plan presented to them had been that of Foch, which had proved to be "more ambitious than . . . Napoleon's march on Moscow." Adding that the French people and parliament would not provide the men or money needed, Clemenceau recommended the application to Hungary of his favorite strategy for dealing with Russian Bolshevism: he counseled his colleagues to erect a cordon around Hungary and then "hold the issues and wait." [77] This did not satisfy the advocates of intervention, however, and it was finally agreed that the military representatives at Versailles should be asked to study what force was available with which to threaten the Hungarians.

After Foch recommended on July 17 that military action was quite feasible provided a unified command were established and the Rumanians supplied the troops they had available, the peacemakers began to have second thoughts and finally decided to send a military investigating mission to Budapest first.[78] But on July 20 Bela Kun attacked the Rumanians, who soon launched a counteroffensive.[79] Nevertheless, the Council of Heads of Delegations, still puzzled about what to do, turned with relief to a proposal by Hoover that food, relief, and economic assistance be promised anyone who could overturn Bela Kun. On July 26 the Council published a statement which promised the Hungarians food and an end to foreign occupation as soon as a responsible government representative of the wishes of the Hungarian people were formed. The invitation was clear, and the statesmen concluded their Council discussions by prophesying, quite correctly as it turned out, that the military pressure already being exerted on the Hungarians, combined with

[77] *Peace Conference*, VII, 20–28.

[78] *Ibid.*, 60–61, 177, 198–200. Although there is no direct evidence on this point, Bliss's letter to his wife of July 17 suggests that his warnings and advice may have had a restraining influence on the heads of delegations; the letter is quoted in Palmer, 409.

[79] *Peace Conference*, VII, 236, 248–49; XI, 312–22.

Hoover's blandishments, would accomplish the Allied objective of deposing Kun without the need for open military intervention.[80]

A few days later the plan worked—under the inducements of Hoover's announcement, and in the face of a continuing advance by the Rumanian armies, the regime of Bela Kun was overthrown on August 1.[81] Hoover was as good as his promise and shipped in food on August 2, though he soon objected to it being seized by the Rumanians, who had quickly occupied Budapest, and he later cut off aid in an attempt to force the Rumanians to withdraw. In any case, indirect intervention had succeeded. But with what results? To be sure, Bolshevism had been eradicated from Hungary, but it was replaced by a Rumanian occupation and a reactionary government. The statesmen at Paris struggled for many months to get the Rumanians out and to establish a representative government in Hungary; these largely futile attempts to deal with the Pandora's box they had opened lie outside the scope of this story. Nevertheless, the Hungarian case, almost more than the Russian, presents an instructive example of the dilemma of intervening in modern revolutions.

Evacuation of North Russia

The question of evacuating North Russia was formally discussed in the councils of the peace conference only once, and then very briefly. Nevertheless it is indirectly a part of the story of conference action toward Russia. The preliminary decision to withdraw Allied forces from Archangel and Murmansk was made in Paris, where the policies of the individual Allied countries toward Russia were largely determined throughout the first half of 1919. Moreover, subsequent efforts by Churchill and the British War Office to postpone or to evade the execution of this decision influenced to some degree conference consideration of the question of supporting Kolchak.[82]

Discussion among opponents of intervention of the desirability of evacuating North Russia had begun as far back as the eve of the Armistice. In a cabinet meeting on November 10 Lloyd George proposed withdrawing British forces on the ground that intervention in North Russia was unpopular with the British public.[83] No decision was taken, however. At the end of November Secretary of War Baker discussed

---

[80] *Ibid.*, xi, 254–58, 304–08, 317–22; Hoover, *Ordeal of Wilson,* 136–44; Hoover, *Memoirs,* i, 399–400.

[81] Whether the Rumanian counteroffensive was launched on Foch's orders will remain unclear until the French archives are opened; in any case, the hints from Paris to the Rumanians were clear enough to lead them to act.

[82] See ch. eight.

[83] Callwell, *Wilson Diaries,* ii, 155.

with the president the disadvantages of continued intervention in Russia in general; the latter apparently promised to raise with the Allies, when he reached Europe, at least the question of withdrawing from North Russia.[84] In any case, during talks with Lloyd George in London just after Christmas, Wilson expressed a desire to withdraw American troops from North Russia.[85] At this time pressure for evacuation of the American forces in Russia was rapidly increasing in the United States, as senatorial and public demands to bring "the boys" home from Russia mounted.[86] Wilson, however, was not yet ready to take a final decision on this question and turned all his attention to the Prinkipo project.

A successful Bolshevik offensive in North Russia during the latter part of January and alarming reports of a critical military situation around Archangel as a result brought the issue of evacuation to the fore once more. On January 30 Bullitt addressed an excited memorandum to Colonel House urging the immediate withdrawal of American troops from Archangel to prevent their destruction; Bullitt added that in any case they were serving no useful purpose there. Bullitt made a similar oral representation to Lansing, and the latter transmitted to the president several telegrams reporting the serious situation at Archangel.[87]

At about the same time two opposing policies respecting North Russia were being developed within the British government. One view, entertained by Lloyd George and supported by some British military and civilian officials, was that the British forces should be withdrawn at the earliest practicable moment; that moment could not possibly come, however, until spring, after the North Russian rivers and ports were free of ice.[88] A conflicting opinion, advanced by the British commander at Murmansk, General Maynard, and backed by other generals and Churchill, held that the situation was by no means hopeless; the dispatch of reinforcements would permit the launching of a successful offensive against the Red Army. If such reinforcements were not forthcoming, however, the only alternative was withdrawal, which would expose the loyal Russian population to massacre at the hands of the Bolsheviks.[89] General Wilson vacillated between these two positions, endorsing the

[84] See p. 49 of ch. two.

[85] See p. 50 of ch. two and Callwell, *Wilson Diaries,* II, 158.

[86] See pp. 96–97 of ch. four and letter from Secretary of War Baker to Wilson, January 1, 1919, Wilson Papers, Series VIIIA, Box 7.

[87] Bullitt's memorandum to House is in Wilson Papers, Series VIIIA, Box 16, with House's penciled notation: "This is worth considering—you may wish to take it up with L. G. this morning." See also Lansing Papers, Desk Diary, February 1, 1919, and Wilson Papers, Series VIIIA, Box 19.

[88] Miller, *Diary,* I, 15, and Kerr's report of Lloyd George's views, contained in Bullitt's memorandum to House cited in n. 87.

[89] British Parliament, *1920,* Cmd. 818, pp. 9, 19–20.

latter when his anti-Bolshevik feelings were strong and the former when concern over meeting British commitments around the world was uppermost in his mind.[90]

Churchill, however, cleverly saw a way to bring the two positions together in a rationalization of policy which he felt would ensure maintenance of British troops in North Russia at least through the summer and which at the same time would place the anti-Bolshevik forces there in a position to undertake an offensive if the changing fortunes of the civil war should later make this possible and desirable. His argument was very ingenious: in view of the difficult military situation in North Russia and of the Allies' obligation to protect or evacuate those Russians who had supported them, the withdrawal of Allied forces would be a very delicate matter; reinforcements were therefore urgently required to back up a last-minute preventive offensive designed both to cover the withdrawal and to ensure the security of the whole operation—in short, reinforce in order to evacuate. It is a testimony to Churchill's persuasiveness and charm that he was able to get his colleagues in the British government and even some Americans to accept the logic of this line of reasoning.

Churchill's plan was apparently first broached to the military representatives at Versailles in early February through the intermediary of General Wilson. On February 5 the latter told General Bliss that the British had asked for an American contingent to join reinforcements which the British were planning to send to Murmansk in response to urgent appeals from General Maynard.[91] According to General Wilson, President Wilson had agreed on February 4 to the inclusion of a few American troops in the British force, provided General Bliss also approved. Whether the matter was first raised with the president by Lloyd George or by General Wilson is not clear; nor is it possible to determine whether President Wilson endorsed American participation in the operation because he was concerned about the critical military situation at Archangel or because he was led to believe that this was the first step in the eventual evacuation of all Allied forces from North Russia. In any case, General Bliss, under pressure from General Wilson and undoubtedly influenced by the president's acquiescence in the plan, grudgingly

[90] Callwell, *Wilson Diaries*, II, 171.

[91] The British request was apparently the outgrowth of a recommendation to General Wilson and Churchill from the British General Staff on January 31 that since the venture in North Russia was a joint Allied operation, the British should attempt to persuade the French and Americans not to withdraw any strength and to add at least token forces to the contemplated British reinforcements. British Parliament, *1920*, Cmd. 818, pp. 21–22.

gave in, but only after receiving assurance as to the purpose of sending reinforcements. In a memorandum of February 8 to the president, Bliss expressed his doubts concerning "the political or military wisdom of sending any more troops to North Russia." On February 12, however, Bliss reported to President Wilson that the British had now requested only the immediate dispatch of some seven hundred American railroad service troops to ensure the smooth operation of internal lines of communication and supply during the winter, when river and sea routes were closed by ice; for this immediate purpose and for the ultimate aim of preparing "for prompt withdrawal as soon as the season permits," Bliss recommended acceding to the British request. He added that the president should stress the latter objective to the American people, concurrently making it clear to his colleagues on the Council of Ten that the sending of additional American troops to North Russia was solely for these two purposes. Wilson endorsed Bliss's memorandum, "Entirely approved." [92]

For the moment at least the United States appeared to be playing Churchill's game. Within a week, however, growing senatorial criticism of American intervention in Russia forced the administration to adopt a less equivocal position in relation to the situation at Archangel and Murmansk. On February 15 Senator Hiram Johnson's resolution calling for withdrawal of American troops from Russia came to a vote. It was defeated only by the vice-president breaking the resulting tie. Two days later Secretary of War Baker informed the military affairs committees of the Senate and House of the decision reached by the president and Bliss in Paris, and this information was released to the press. Baker's statement, however, contained a promise of "prompt withdrawal" from North Russia "at the earliest possible moment that weather conditions in the spring will permit." Baker also declared that at the direction of the president he had communicated this decision to the Allied governments.[93] Poole, the American diplomatic representative at Archangel, reported a week later that the announcement had vastly improved morale among the discontented American troops in that area, but he noted: "Neither the British nor French diplomatic or military authorities have received any information of the withdrawal of their forces." [94]

The British and French representatives had not received any instructions for the very good reason that their governments had not decided

[92] Bliss Papers, Box 70. See also Diary, February 5, Bliss Papers, Box 65.

[93] *1919, Russia*, 617–18, and *Peace Conference*, XI, 45. Bliss cabled from Paris authorizing Baker to make this statement, but it was apparently also cleared with Wilson, then en route home.

[94] *1919, Russia*, 618–19.

on evacuation. The French, in fact, continued to send reinforcements, despite such widespread disaffection among their troops that they had to be employed largely for rear echelon duties. At the same time, despite intimations from the British that they would withdraw in the spring, the British government had taken no definite action concerning the matter. On the contrary, within a few weeks Churchill was able to convince the British Cabinet of the worth of his plan for sending reinforcements to North Russia. To be sure, on March 4 the Cabinet agreed to press the peace conference to approve the early evacuation of North Russia; but they simultaneously authorized Churchill to take necessary measures to prepare the evacuation and to ensure the safety of the troops in position until the withdrawal could be carried out. These measures were the immediate dispatch of a relief force of four thousand men, to be followed by a similar complement at a later date.[95] The first step in evacuation was therefore to increase by almost one third the Allied forces in North Russia.

With this decision in hand Churchill turned his attention to ways in which the reinforced armies in North Russia could best contribute to a coordinated offensive against Bolshevism. Attack, not withdrawal, became the topic of discussion, and little was heard of the promised evacuation. Since the opposing Bolshevik forces were sufficiently strong to rule out a frontal attack on Moscow from the north, Churchill planned instead to extend the two flanks of the North Russian battle line, linking up with the anti-Bolshevik forces of Kolchak to the southeast and joining with the Finns to the southwest for an offensive against Petrograd. In conjunction with the latter strategy, Churchill toyed with the idea of using the German forces still in the Baltic area.[96] He also contemplated sending British warships to Petrograd and even the dispatch of British troops to Finland to assist the proposed offensive.[97] These plans did not materialize because no troops were available and because the British Foreign Office was unwilling to take responsibility for involving the Finns in a war with the Bolsheviks. For their part the Finns demanded political support and substantial loans from the British as the price of their participation in an attack on Petrograd, but the British refused.[98] An attempt to push southwest from the Murmansk front toward Finnish

[95] British Parliament, *1920,* Cmd. 818, p. 24.

[96] *Ibid.,* p. 26, and Riddell, 50. On April 11 Lloyd George commented to Lord Riddell concerning Churchill: "He has Bolshevism on the brain. Now he wants to make a treaty with the Germans to fight the Bolsheviks."

[97] Bartlett, 55–56; article in the London *Times,* April 17, 1919, cited in Coates, *Armed Intervention,* 182; and author's interview with Bullitt, February 25, 1953. In April, when Bullitt visited London, Churchill outlined to him plans for a joint Finnish-British attack on Petrograd.

[98] See ch. ten, pp. 331–33.

forces advancing into Eastern Karelia was undertaken, however. General Maynard's offensive in this direction met with considerable success, but he was not encouraged to link up with the Finns, the British fearing, with some reason, that the Finns were as much interested in extending their own borders with Russia, particularly in Eastern Karelia, as they were in a general campaign against Bolshevism.[99]

Plans for a push southeast from Archangel to link up with Kolchak were developed during the end of March and the beginning of April. Included were provisions for reinforcing Kolchak's forces with additional British troops. In mid-March Kolchak launched an offensive which enjoyed considerable initial success. By the end of March tenuous contact had been established between advance units of the Archangel forces and outposts of the Siberian armies. Consequently, on April 9 Churchill issued a special call in London for volunteers to go to North Russia, and on April 15 a British General Staff paper proposing operations in North Russia to effect a junction with Kolchak's forces was submitted to the British Cabinet, which approved this course of action.[100]

Because of the ice, however, the first contingent of British reinforcements did not reach Archangel until the end of May. By that time Kolchak's drive westward had been turned back, and his forces were in retreat across Siberia. Nevertheless, Churchill, in the vain hope that some of the Czech units with Kolchak might still be able to fight their way out and link up with the Archangel forces, persuaded the Cabinet on June 27 to approve the launching of the proposed offensive southeastward; he used the old argument that such a sally was a necessary preventive action to cover the evacuation from Archangel.[101] Churchill's plan to use the Czechs to save the northern front against Bolshevism was bold and simple. The Czechoslovak troops who had been trapped in Russia by the Bolshevik seizure of power and who had played an important role in the Siberian intervention and counterrevolution of 1918 had been clamoring to go home ever since the Armistice and were displaying a growing reluctance to fight for Kolchak, whom they considered reactionary. The tentative plan was to take them out through Vladivostok and then by ship across the Pacific and the Atlantic, but few vessels were available for this task.[102] Seizing on this fact, and apparently encouraged by a report from Omsk on June 3 that Kolchak's right or

---

[99] Telegram from Poole to Washington, May 3, 1919, *1919, Russia,* 630; Memorandum from R. H. Lord to Bullitt, May 8, 1919, Bullitt Papers; British Parliament, *1920,* Cmd. 818, p. 35.

[100] *Ibid.,* pp. 10, 25–33.

[101] *Ibid.,* pp. 13, 38–39.

[102] *1919, Russia,* 273–74, 279, 283.

northern wing under the Czech General Gaida was faring somewhat better than the rest of the army, Churchill daringly proposed that thirty thousand Czech troops, or about half of the total force in Siberia, be evacuated by having them fight their way out to Archangel, whence they would be transported home.[103]

Apparently through his enthusiasm and persuasiveness, and by a subtle threat that if his plan were not adopted it might take two years to repatriate all the Czechs by way of Vladivostok, Churchill secured the grudging assent of Beneš, the chief Czech representative in Paris.[104] But the whole idea soon foundered on objections from various quarters. Both General Janin, the senior Allied military representative in Siberia, and Kolchak doubted the ability of the demoralized Czechs to fight their way out; the British government refused to promise to have its troops wait in Archangel for the Czechs; and President Wilson, advised by General Bliss and Lansing, declined to provide American troops to replace the Czechs on the Siberian railway.[105]

Finally, the Council of Heads of Delegations abandoned the idea of an evacuation through Archangel, and turned its efforts to arranging repatriation of the Czechs through Vladivostok. In the face of difficulties in finding the necessary shipping and delays caused by British and French reluctance to share the costs of repatriation, the Americans took the initiative and pressed the matter vigorously; repatriation was finally begun through Vladivostok at the end of November.[106] Although the war minister's scheme was impractical and unlikely to succeed from the beginning, one cannot help admiring Churchill's daring and ingenuity.[107]

In the meantime it proved impossible to mount Churchill's proposed "evacuation" offensive in North Russia because of mutinies and desertions in the anti-Bolshevik Russian units and problems of transport. Finally, in mid-July, when it was clear that there was no hope of salvaging anything from the situation in North Russia, the War Office gave a final and definite order to evacuate. The last British troops left North Russia in October 1919.

As these various schemes of Churchill unfolded, the Americans be-

[103] British Foreign Office, *Documents*, III, 339; *Peace Conference*, VI, 635, 674, 684–86.

[104] *Ibid.*, 708–09; VII, 63–65.

[105] *Ibid.*, VII, 63–65, 211–12; *1919, Russia*, 284, 285–86, 287–88, 295; July 11, Diary, Bliss Papers, Box 65; Memorandum from Bliss to Baker, referred by the latter to Wilson, Wilson Papers, Series II, Box 159; Lansing Desk Diary, July 25.

[106] *Peace Conference*, VII, 211–12, 556–57, 652–53; VIII, 307; *1919, Russia*, 298, 309, 310–11, 312, 314.

[107] Churchill himself, not one to dwell on failures, makes only a passing reference to the idea. *Aftermath*, 250.

came increasingly distrustful of British intentions in North Russia.[108] They were proceeding in good faith with plans for the ostensibly agreed withdrawal of Allied forces as soon as weather conditions in the spring permitted, and late in March an American general was dispatched to North Russia to oversee evacuation of the American troops.[109] The announcement in early April that the British were dispatching reinforcements and Churchill's public appeal for volunteers on April 9 alarmed American officials in Paris and Washington. As a result, Chief of Staff March promised publicly on April 10 that all American soliders in North Russia would be evacuated by June 30.[110]

A week later General Bliss, disturbed by reports from Archangel that an offensive to link up with Kolchak was being planned, wrote to the president: "This matter of playing fast and loose with the plans for the North Russian expedition is becoming very serious. I think that you should request from Mr. Lloyd George to see the exact orders which have been issued to the British Commander at Archangel. . . . [The latter] may make plans which may so tie up the American forces that they cannot be withdrawn when navigation opens, notwithstanding the practical pledge which has been given to the American people." [111] The president was sufficiently concerned by this warning from Bliss to raise the matter with Lloyd George in the Council of Four on April 22. Lloyd George, perhaps unaware of Churchill's real intentions in North Russia, replied that the reported offensive operation was either the result of a misunderstanding or was an attempt to preserve the secrecy of the decision to withdraw by pretending that no withdrawal was intended. He promised to look into the matter.[112] The same day President Wilson reported to Bliss that Clemenceau and Lloyd George were "quite of our mind and purpose" regarding the situation in North Russia and were "anxious to cooperate with us in getting the troops out." [113]

[108] This suspicion was not only of British Military operations; early in March the American government received a report that a British Major Shackleton was negotiating with the North Russian government for substantial economic, mining, and forest concessions. The American commissioners at Paris were much concerned at what they considered this display of selfish commercial policy on the part of the British. Letter from Grew to White, March 10, 1919, White Papers, Box 65. Grew referred to a discussion of this question at the meeting of the American commissioners on March 6. This discussion is omitted from the minutes of the meeting published in *Peace Conference,* XI, 97–99.

[109] *1919, Russia,* 622.

[110] Polk Papers, Diary, April 8, 1919; *New York Times,* April 11, 1919, p. 1.

[111] Letter from Bliss to Wilson, April 18, 1919, Wilson Papers, Series VIIIA, Box 38.

[112] *Peace Conference,* V, 114–15. According to General Wilson, he subsequently convinced Lloyd George of the value of the plan to effect a junction with Kolchak. Callwell, *Wilson Diaries,* II, 185.

[113] Letter from Wilson to Bliss, April 22, 1918, Bliss Papers, Box 70.

In spite of this seeming clarification of policy, British military authorities continued to urge their American counterparts, if the United States decision to evacuate at once were indeed irrevocable, to keep at least limited forces in North Russia, now gunboats to support both the evacuation and operations along the Dvina River, later railway service troops, without which, according to the British, their own evacuation later in the summer would be impossible.[114] General Bliss, Secretary Lansing, and President Wilson steadfastly resisted these pressures, as well as the urgent recommendations of the American diplomats in North Russia that the evacuation be postponed or that token American forces be left behind.[115] As a result, all the American troops were brought out on schedule before the end of June, and the remaining diplomatic and other American personnel in North Russia withdrew by early fall.

By the end of March those who favored intervention in Russia and proposed countering Bolshevism with force had apparently lost much ground. Foch's several schemes to launch an offensive against Soviet Russia from Poland or Rumania had been decisively vetoed. In spite of an outbreak of Bolshevism nearer home, in Hungary, the Allied statesmen had rejected Foch's plan to use this as the pretext for mounting a grand crusade against Bolshevism in Europe and Russia; instead, they had sent an emissary peaceably to discuss matters with Bela Kun. The American and British governments had decided to evacuate North Russia, although Churchill was able to delay and evade this order well into the summer as far as the British forces were concerned. The Allied force at Odessa, unsuccessful and demoralized, had had to be withdrawn. On the military side a more propitious moment for Bullitt to return from Moscow with a reasonable offer of peace from the Soviet government could hardly be imagined. Yet, as we shall now see, British domestic politics, the preoccupation of conference leaders with other matters, and conservative influences in the American delegation acted together to prevent the proposals Bullitt had obtained from being adopted. At Paris new personalities were at work on the Russian problem, and fresh approaches were being devised. When Bullitt's recommendations were

[114] On the gunboats, see letter from Admiral Benson to Wilson, May 1, 1919, and Wilson's reply of May 2. Wilson Papers, Series VIIIA, Boxes 43, 44. On the railway service troops, see Lansing Papers, Desk Diary, May 26; letter from Bliss to Wilson, May 29, Bliss Papers, Box 70; reply from Wilson, June 10, Wilson Papers, Series VIIIA, Box 60.

[115] In the face of insistent British appeals, Bliss and Wilson finally agreed to leave the railway troops if they volunteered to stay; they did not and were withdrawn. Letter from Bliss to Wilson, June 26, and Wilson's reply, June 28, *ibid.*, Box 67 and *1919, Russia*, 638–39. For the recommendations of the American diplomats, see *1919, Russia*, 619, 637.

dropped, an alternative Russian policy was available, quickly to be clutched at by the Allied heads of government who were tired of the baffling and discouraging Russian question and who were at the same time deeply immersed in their intramural quarrels over the treaty with Germany.

CHAPTER SEVEN

Relief as the Antidote
to Bolshevism

Feeding Germany and Central Europe

▚▚▚ AMERICAN LEADERS were convinced of the necessity of
▚▚▚ promptly furnishing food relief to Europe after the Armistice,
▚▚▚ as we saw in the first chapter.[1] They were motivated both by
humanitarian considerations and by a belief that "full stomachs mean
no Bolsheviks," as Lansing expressed it. An additional factor was their
desire to dispose of large agricultural surpluses accumulated in the
United States as a result of America's intensive food production effort
during the last summer of the war.

On the eve of the Armistice House wired Wilson from Paris urging,
despite provision in the draft Armistice terms for the continuation of the
blockade against the enemy powers, the immediate dispatch of food and
other relief supplies to Central Europe "if serious disturbances are to be
averted." House recommended the formation of an international relief
organization to be headed by Herbert Hoover. Wilson cabled back his
assent, adding that he was taking the matter up with Hoover at once.[2]

A relief program for Europe under American direction was subsequently drawn up by Hoover, House, Hurley and others and was submitted to the European Allies. The latter, fearing American use for political
and commercial ends of the economic power represented by relief, opposed this plan. They demanded instead inter-Allied control of the program, a proposition unacceptable to the Americans, who were to supply
most of the food. There was also disagreement over the proposed use of
German merchant ships to carry supplies. The British, while recognizing
the necessity for relief measures, wanted most of the food to be carried

---

[1] See pp. 15–16 of ch. one. This chapter will discuss relief only in terms of its
consideration by Western statesmen as a check to Bolshevism. There will be no
attempt to treat the large-scale relief effort in Europe after World War I.

[2] Telegram from House to Lansing for Wilson, November 8, 1918, *Peace Conference,* II, 628–29; Wilson's reply in *ibid.,* I, 128.

in British bottoms; they were also anxious to participate fully in the opening of channels of trade containing undoubted commercial advantage for the future. The French, on the other hand, were reluctant to supply Germany at all until the latter had accepted a peace which the French were satisfied would guarantee the future security of France. French financial experts also objected to food payments by Germany from liquid assets on which they claimed first priority for reparations.[3]

In view of the negative position of the European Allies, House and Hoover, with the blessing of President Wilson, decided in mid-December to proceed with American distribution of relief supplies to the most stricken areas in Europe outside Germany, simply inviting the Allies to join the United States in this emergency operation, if they so desired. Loans from the American treasury to pay for food were arranged for Yugoslavia and Rumania, and money for relief to Austria, a former enemy, was made available from the President's National Security and Defense Fund. There still remained the problem of financing supplies to neutral countries, to liberated nonbelligerents, and to newly formed states. For this purpose the president, strongly backed by the other leaders of the American delegation, requested in early January an emergency relief appropriation by Congress of one hundred million dollars. In support of his request, Wilson cabled Congressional leaders on January 10: "Food relief is now the key to the whole European situation and to the solutions of peace. Bolshevism is steadily advancing westward . . . and is poisoning Germany. It cannot be stopped by force but it can be stopped by food. . . . I do not see how we can find definite powers with whom to conclude peace unless this means of stemming the tide of anarchism is employed." [4] The president's plea was vigorously endorsed by Henry White, the Republican member of the delegation, who wired Senator Lodge on January 8:

> Feel I should no longer delay laying before you condition . . . which now dominates entire European situation above all else, namely steady westward advance of Bolshevism. . . . Only effective barrier now apparently possible against it is food relief, as Bolshevism thrives only on starvation and disorder. Consensus of opinion is that joint

[3] See a report on relief embodying the objections of the European Allies to the American proposal in *ibid.*, II, 654–61. See also discussions of the relief issue in Baker, *Settlement*, II, 322–23, and Hoover, *Ordeal of Wilson*, 91–99. In January the Allies finally accepted the major principles of the American plan for organizing the relief effort.

[4] Telegram from Wilson to Tumulty for Senator Martin and Representative Sherley, January 10, 1919, Wilson Papers, Series VIIIA, Box 9. The same day Wilson wrote Lansing in response to Polk's request for a public statement against Bolshevism: "The real thing with which to stop Bolshevism is food." *Ibid.*

military occupation which has been suggested by French for Poland, even if practical, would not solve problem. . . . I consider it therefore of utmost importance the President's request for hundred million appropriation for relief be granted at once.[5]

House and Bliss were also of the same mind, the former telling a British journalist that the Allies must assist the Central Powers in order to erect a "barrier of continental self-respect" against encroaching Bolshevism, and the latter writing Mrs. Bliss on January 14: "An empty stomach feeds on nothing but Bolshevism feeds on empty stomachs." [6]

The president's request for emergency funds for the neutrals and others was granted. Relief for Germany was, however, another and more complicated problem. Arrangements for a partial lifting of the blockade, as well as for means of payment and for the supply of transport by the Germans, had to be made. On December 20, when it had become clear that working these matters out would take some time, Hoover wrote Wilson recalling the president's statements at the time of the Armistice as to the desirability of feeding Germany "not only out of humanity but out of its fundamental necessity to prevent anarchy." Hoover went on to urge, in effect, that the promise of food and relief to Germany be used as a political weapon against the growing danger of Bolshevism there. Hoover suggested an immediate Allied-American statement that the powers "could only hope to solve the food difficulties in Germany until next harvest through the hands of a stable and experienced government based on an expressed popular will." If this were done, Hoover added, and if a hint were given "that the Allies cannot anticipate furnishing the food assistance to Germany through the hands of Bolshevist elements, it would at once strengthen the whole situation in Germany and probably entirely eliminate the incipient Bolshevism in progress. . . ." [7]

At the same time Hoover was endeavoring, with the full backing of the president, to persuade the Allies to relax the blockade against Germany sufficiently to permit essential foodstuffs and supplies to reach Germany, first through the neutrals and eventually by direct purchase. Meeting Allied objections and, in one instance, the reversal of a prior favorable decision on loosening the blockade, Hoover, Vance McCormick of the War Trade Board, who had come to Paris to handle blockade matters, and General Bliss persuaded Wilson to raise the ques-

---

[5] Cited in Nevins, 363.

[6] For House's views, see Willert, 175; also House Papers, Diary, January 8, 1919, and his letter to Norman Hapgood, January 6, 1919, quoted on p. 97 of ch. four. Bliss's letter to his wife is cited in Palmer, 365.

[7] *Peace Conference*, II, 680–81.

tion of relief for Germany at an early session of the peace conference.[8] On January 13 the president broached the issue to his colleagues in the Council of Ten during a discussion of renewing the Armistice. In response to a French proposal that the unresolved issue of how Germany should pay for food relief be turned over to a committee for further study, Wilson categorically declared:

> . . . any further delay in this matter might be fatal, as it meant the dissolution of order and government. They were discussing an absolute and immediate necessity. So long as hunger continued to gnaw, the foundations of government would continue to crumble. Therefore food should be supplied immediately, not only to our friends, but also to those parts of the world where it was to our interest to maintain a stable government. . . . He trusted the French Finance Department would withdraw their objection, as they [the Allies] were faced with the great problem of Bolshevism and the forces of dissolution which now threatened society.

Klotz, the French minister of finance, continued to object to the possibility of German payments for food taking priority over reparations payments, which led Wilson to assert that if food were not supplied, "there would be no Germany to pay anything." Despite Wilson's strong stand, it was finally left that while the supplying of food to Germany might begin, the order of priority of Germany's financial obligations would be studied further with a decision to be reached by the peace conference within two months.[9] In fact, this was no solution at all since the issue of payment was crucial. Moreover, the French, sometimes supported by the British, continued to obstruct American efforts to have the blockade partially lifted to permit food to reach Germany.[10] As a result, the Allies' implied promise at the time of the Armistice to provision Germany remained unfulfilled for four months, provoking justifiable cynicism and bitterness within Germany.

The matter was finally resolved only when Lloyd George took a personal interest in the problem early in March. At that time General Plumer, commander of the British occupation forces in Germany, reported to the British prime minister that the German people were on the verge of starvation and that Germany would embrace Bolshevism unless the population were fed. He added that "the rank and file of his army were sick and discontented and wanted to go home because they just could not stand the sight of hordes of skinny and bloated children pawing

[8] Hoover, *Ordeal of Wilson*, 155–59.
[9] *Peace Conference*, III, 515–17.
[10] Hoover, *Ordeal of Wilson*, 160–63.

over the offal from British cantonments." [11] Aroused by this report, Lloyd George raised the question of feeding Germany in an informal meeting with Clemenceau and House on March 7, at which a number of major unresolved issues before the conference were discussed. Clemenceau scoffed at the idea that the Germans would succumb to Bolshevism from lack of food, treating it as a German invention "circulated with a view to intimidating the Allies into giving favourable terms to Germany." In a memorandum reporting that meeting Lloyd George commented that Clemenceau was "anxious to preserve the demeanour of a conqueror towards Germany"; it would therefore be difficult to induce the French to assent to a reasonable plan for feeding Germany.[12]

Nevertheless, that evening Lloyd George called in Hoover to find out why the Germans had not been receiving the food supplies authorized for them by the conference almost two months earlier on January 13. Hoover reviewed the obstructionist tactics of the French and of some British officials and agreed to prepare a memorandum on the question for Lloyd George.[13] The next day, March 8, the issue was squarely joined in the Council of Ten, with Lord Robert Cecil presenting proposals aimed at an immediate resolution of the financial, shipping, and other problems which had been holding up the supply of food to Germany.[14] In the course of the long and acrimonious discussion that followed the French once again set forth their objections to feeding Germany. A principal complaint, expressed most plainly by Marshal Foch, was that the proposed commitment to provision Germany until the full harvest "had the effect of disarming the Allies, who would be obliged to start hostilities should any difference arise with Germany, since . . . pressure could not be exerted by the fear of withholding food." The French also renewed their opposition to German payments for food from liquid assets suitable for prompt reparations payments, and indicated that the Germans should pay for the food by the export of raw materials and by credits from neutral countries and others (presumably the United States).

In rebuttal, Lloyd George pointed out that Allied action against the Germans would be necessary only if the latter either failed to carry out the terms of the Armistice or refused to sign the peace treaty; in either case the agreement to supply food would lapse and pressure against the

[11] Quoted in *ibid.*, 164. General Wilson was also alarmed at the situation in Germany and was urging on Lloyd George at this time the necessity of feeding the population to avert the spread of Bolshevism in Germany. Callwell, *Wilson Diaries*, II, 172.

[12] Lloyd George, I, 291.

[13] Hoover, *Ordeal of Wilson*, 164–65.

[14] *Peace Conference*, IV, 274–93.

Germans could be exerted by the stoppage of relief shipments. Lloyd George then made a typically eloquent and emotional appeal to the conference for the feeding of Germany. First, he maintained that the Allies had an obligation of honor to fulfill the implied promise of Article XXVI of the Armistice that Germany would be provisioned. Second, he warned:

> The Allies were now on top, but the memories of starvation might one day turn against them. . . . [These] constituted far more formidable weapons for use against the Allies than any of the armaments it was sought to limit. The Allies were sowing hatred for the future: they were piling up agony, not for the Germans, but for themselves.

Finally, the British statesman asserted that lack of food was driving the German people to Bolshevism:

> . . . the Allies by their action were simply encouraging elements of disruption and anarchism. It was like stirring up an influenza puddle, just next door to one's self. . . . If Germany went . . . who would feel safe? As long as order was maintained in Germany, a breakwater would exist between the countries of the Allies and the waters of Revolution beyond. But once the breakwater was swept away, he could not speak for France, but trembled for his own country. . . . He was there that afternoon to reinforce the appeal which had come to him from the men who had helped the Allies to conquer the Germans, the soldiers, who said that they refused to continue to occupy a territory in order to maintain the population in hunger. . . . Unless this people were fed, if as a result of a process of starvation enforced by the Allies, the people of Germany were allowed to run riot, a state of revolution among the working classes of all countries would ensue with which it would be impossible to cope.

Clemenceau at once turned to the attack, declaring that while he was prepared to revictual the Germans, "his information tended to show that the Germans were using Bolshevism as a bogey with which to frighten the Allies" and that conditions inside Germany were not nearly as black as had been pictured.

> It was essential that no signs of weakness should be displayed on the eve of the settlement of other large territorial, military and economic questions. The Germans must not be given any advantage today that might give them the impression that the Allied Powers could be intimidated and made to yield. . . . As soon as the Germans recognized this fact, he felt sure his colleagues, M. Loucheur, M. Klotz,

and M. Clementel, who were ever ready to be guided by feelings of humanity, would easily arrive at an agreement in regard to the supply of food to Germany, and the payment therefor.

To mollify Clemenceau, Lloyd George and the others finally agreed that before Allied representatives undertook to work out with the Germans procedures for the supply of food, the Germans would have to state formally that they were prepared to hand over their merchant ships to the Allies in accord with the terms of the first renewal of the Armistice.[15] Discussion then turned to means of payment for the food to be supplied, and Klotz and Loucheur reiterated their objections to the use of German liquid assets for this purpose. This provoked another outburst from Lloyd George, who, after reading excerpts from the minutes of the meeting of January 13 and listening to Klotz's rejoinder, chided:

> Nothing had, however, been done during those two months and now the question had been brought up for discussion with all the old arguments. He would not have raised the matter, but for the fact that during the past two months, in spite of the decision reached by the Supreme War Council in January last, obstacles had continually been put in the way. . . . He appealed to M. Clemenceau to put a stop to these obstructive tactics, otherwise M. Klotz would rank with Lenin and Trotsky among those who had spread Bolshevism in Europe.

House supported Lloyd George, but Clemenceau retorted sharply, virtually charging the British and Americans with coveting Germany's assets at the expense of France.

> . . . his country had been ruined and ravaged; over two million men had lost their lives; mines had been rendered unworkable; and yet what guarantee had France that anything would be received in payment for all this destruction? She merely possessed a few pieces of gold, a few securities, which it was now proposed to take away in order to pay those who would supply food to Germany; and that food would certainly not come from France. In a word he was being asked to betray his country, and that he refused to do.

[15] In meetings with the Germans at Brussels on March 13–14 this instruction was technically adhered to, but, according to Lansing, the British representatives secretly told the Germans in advance that they would receive food if they accepted the commitment demanded of them. Memorandum, "The French Spirit of Militarism and Its Consequences," April 1, 1919, Lansing Papers, Confidential Memoranda. See also the caustic and detailed discussion, "Dr. Melchior: A Defeated Enemy," in John Maynard Keynes, *Two Memoirs* (New York and London, 1949), 11–74.

This heated exchange seemed to clear the air; after some further discussion the Council finally agreed to proceed with the immediate supply of food to Germany.[16] Arrangements with the Germans were settled a few days later at a meeting in Brussels, and Germany subsequently received more than a million and a quarter tons of food and medical supplies.[17] Hoover, McCormick and other Americans pressed through the remaining months of the conference for a further lifting of the blockade to permit the revival of trade and the partial restoration of production in Germany and throughout Europe on the grounds that unemployment and economic stagnation only bred Bolshevism and, in the case of Germany, weakened her ability to pay reparations. The French, however, refused to give up this means of pressure on Germany, and the British were reluctant to lose the commercial advantage provided by the exclusion of Germany from world markets.

Once the battle over food for Germany had been won—and to those advocating relief as a weapon against Bolshevism it must have seemed in the nick of time, as revolutionary disturbances broke out in Bavaria in mid-March, followed by the establishment of a short-lived Soviet-type government there—it was only natural that the Americans concerned with relief should turn their attention to the possibility of supplying other areas in Europe not yet included in the relief program. On March 15 McCormick, the United States representative to the Superior Blockade Council, proposed that Poland and the Baltic provinces be freed "from further blockade restrictions owing to the importance of resuming normal life to discourage Bolshevism." [18] The British objected, however, McCormick commenting in his diary that he was "afraid some trade advantage [is] hoped for by Great Britain." Despite continued British opposition, the Supreme Economic Council, acting on the recommendation of the Blockade Council, finally decided on March 24 that the blockade should be lifted for Poland and Estonia as long as suitable precautions were taken to prevent the reexport of goods to Bolshevik Russia or to Germany. On March 28 the Council of Foreign Ministers approved this decision, with the additional recommendation that the lifting of the blockade be extended to Lithuania and Latvia as soon

[16] Commenting on French stubbornness over this issue, Lloyd George wrote in his memoirs: "Mr. Hoover, who organized the distribution, seemed to have ruffled French susceptibilities by his manner of extracting money from them. . . . It needed tact to handle any appeal for help to those who had been the perpetrators of . . . [French] misery. Mr. Hoover has many great qualities, but tact is not one of them." Lloyd George, I, 302.

[17] Hoover, *Ordeal of Wilson*, 172.

[18] McCormick Diary, 53.

as the political and military situation in those areas permitted.[19] In addition, Hoover continued to press for the maintenance and expansion of relief operations in Central Europe. In letters to Wilson, Hoover argued that feeding the population of Austria had prevented a Bolshevik revolution there and that food could be used as a weapon against Bolshevism in the remainder of Central Europe and, specifically, as a means of pressure on Bela Kun's regime.[20]

The Origins of the Hoover-Nansen Plan and the Fate of Bullitt's Proposals

A logical next step was the extension of relief to Bolshevik Russia itself. As we saw in earlier chapters, American leaders had actively considered relief and economic assistance as a method of dealing with the Russian problem during the spring of 1918 and again in September and October of that year. For various reasons, this approach had not been vigorously pursued, and little had been done in this direction through the winter of 1918–1919. Some American officials and junior members of the peace delegation had continued to argue the advantages of a policy of economic intervention in Russia, but their recommendations were not taken up at higher levels.[21] The most consistent champion of relief for Russia and, indeed, it is fair to say, the "father" of the Hoover-Nansen plan for feeding the population of Soviet Russia, was Vance McCormick, formerly a newspaper publisher and chairman of the Democratic National Committee, a leading organizer of the American war effort and a close friend of President Wilson. In the fall of 1918 McCormick, as head of the War Trade Board, had been given responsibility for economic aid to Russia, but he had had little opportunity to inaugurate a program of assistance before coming to Paris as a member of the American peace delegation.[22] McCormick knew little about Russia, but he was convinced that relief was an important prerequisite to a solution of the problem.

Once in Paris, McCormick began to urge the adoption of a relief pro-

---

[19] *Ibid.*, 55, 57; *Peace Conference*, IV, 524–25, 535; Hoover, *Ordeal of Wilson*, 174–75. On general policy toward the Baltic states, see pp. 336–43 of ch. nine.

[20] Letter of March 31, Wilson Papers, Series VIIIA, Box 30; of April 15, Hoover, *Ordeal of Wilson*, 135–36.

[21] See, for example, a memorandum of November 14, 1918, from Bullitt to Lansing, one of a series prepared by Bullitt for the secretary of state on the Bolshevist movement in Europe, Bullitt Papers; a relief plan for Russia advocated to David Hunter Miller by Butler Wright, counselor of the American embassy in London, on December 4, 1918, Miller, *Diary*, I, 29; and a memorandum on "American Economic Intervention in Russia" by A. A. Berle, Jr., dated December 10, 1918, *Peace Conference*, II, 471–75.

[22] See p. 36 of ch. two.

gram for Russia. He was an inveterate party-goer, thoroughly enjoying the social side of the conference and turning up regularly at receptions, dinners, and other functions which attracted both conference delegates, when they could find time, and the "hangers-on" of the conference, those with a special interest which they fervently, and usually unsuccessfully, hoped would find favor at the conference table. As early as January 30, at a dinner attended by Lloyd George, McCormick advanced a plan for feeding the citizens of Petrograd, but he received little encouragement from the British prime minister. Undismayed, McCormick continued to advocate this plan, raising it with Hoover around the first of March after the demise of the Prinkipo project. On March 4 Oscar Straus, a lawyer and former American ambassador to Turkey, who was in Paris as an unofficial lobbyist for the League and for the rights of Jewish minorities in Europe, arranged a dinner, attended by Bakhmetev, Sazonov, and Hoover, at which McCormick presented his "scheme for [the] economic relief of Russia by joint Allied and neutral action, [with] distribution under proper military protection." [23] At about the same time the feasibility of basing a solution to the Russian dilemma on relief was also being discussed in House's entourage, Auchincloss and Wiseman going over the possibilities at length on March 7.[24]

At this juncture McCormick received support from an unexpected quarter: American Vice-Consul Imbrie stationed in Viborg, Finland. In a telegram to the Department of State early in March Imbrie transmitted alarming information on conditions in Petrograd and Moscow. Although a number of the reports he cited were clearly exaggerated or fabricated, the picture of virtual starvation and rapid depopulation that emerged was sufficiently disturbing to lead the Department of State to raise with the American delegation in Paris on March 11 the "question of how long the Allied governments can properly delay some organized attempt to remedy conditions of distress such as those described in this report [Imbrie's]." [25] Acting Secretary of State Polk recommended immediate action by the International Red Cross, with a number of country agencies of the Red Cross cooperating in a joint emergency operation in Russia.

On March 20 Lansing, White, and Bliss considered the issue posed by Polk on the basis of a memorandum prepared by Fred R. Dolbeare, a junior diplomat in the delegation secretariat.[26] This memorandum

[23] McCormick Diary, 36, 48; Oscar S. Straus, *Under Four Administrations: From Cleveland to Taft* (Boston, 1922), 411.
[24] House Papers, Auchincloss Diary, March 7, 1919.
[25] *1919, Russia,* 98–100.
[26] Records of the ACTNP, 861.00/364.

asserted that the proposed relief of Russia was too big and expensive a job for the Red Cross to handle and recommended that it should be a governmental project undertaken as part of a definite American policy and program toward Russia covering not only relief but other matters as well. Dolbeare went on to urge immediate economic assistance to the states bordering Russia, in addition to Soviet Russia itself, and to suggest a declaration of policy calling for an armistice on all Russian fronts. He predicted that these measures would serve to defeat Bolshevism, though not necessarily the Soviet form of government (whose democratic form always held a strong fascination for American liberals). The American commissioners agreed in principle with the memorandum, but doubted whether the United States had sufficient funds to finance a large-scale relief program for Russia. They also questioned how, in practice, an armistice could be secured and food supplies equitably distributed in Russia and neighboring states.[27] The evening of March 24 Lansing wired Polk the gist of the commissioners' views. He added, however, that since the commissioners were anxious to find a way to assist the Russian population, Hoover was being consulted as to whether any relief measures were possible.[28]

The decision to call in Hoover may have been an outgrowth of a meeting between Lansing and McCormick on March 24. The latter's efforts to arouse interest in a relief plan for Russia were, of course, greatly strengthened by Polk's raising of the issue and by subsequent discussion of it within the American delegation. Taking advantage of these developments, McCormick presented his plan to Lansing in meetings with the secretary of state on March 24 and 25; as a result, the latter asked McCormick to prepare for the president a telegram to Washington on the relief question.[29]

On March 26 McCormick sent Wilson a note asking for an interview to discuss the whole matter, but unfortunately, at just this crucial point, direct evidence on the development of the idea for feeding Russia runs out, and one has to resort to speculation.[30] In his diary McCormick does not mention meeting with the president on Russia at this time, nor is there in the Wilson papers any proof of such a meeting, such as the draft telegram that Lansing requested McCormick to prepare for the president. There is, however, one telling bit of circumstantial evidence: on March 27, as we shall see, when House discussed with Wilson the proposals brought back by Bullitt in the context of the general problem

[27] *Peace Conference,* XI, 126–27.
[28] *1919, Russia,* 100.
[29] McCormick Diary, 57; Lansing Papers, Desk Diary, March 25, 1919.
[30] McCormick's note is in Wilson Papers, Series VIIIA, Box 28.

of policy toward Russia, the president suggested that House consult Hoover concerning the possibility of getting food to Russia, a suggestion which led directly to the formulation of the Hoover-Nansen plan.[31] Since there is no indication that Wilson himself was thinking about relief to Russia at this time, it seems not unreasonable to assume that some-time on March 26 or early on March 27 McCormick planted the idea with the president, perhaps not even at a formal appointment, but in a brief conversation held in the corridors, or in Wilson's quarters.[32] The president in turn passed the idea on to House, who promptly took it up with Hoover. Although from this time on the proposal for relief to Russia was taken over by Hoover and House, and McCormick faded into the background, it is clear that McCormick, not Hoover, was the inspirer of the plan for feeding Russia subsequently adopted by the peace conference, notwithstanding the impression left by Hoover in his memoirs that he originated it, a view also widely found in historical studies of the period. McCormick had most consistently advocated such a plan in the preceding months and weeks, and in March he urged it on Hoover and Lansing, and, in all probability, on the president.

At this moment—just when many in the American delegation had be-come interested in, and even excited at, the prospect of helping the starving Russian people and when some felt that they had perhaps at last found a key to the baffling Russian puzzle in food relief, which re-quired neither intervention nor recognition of the Bolsheviks—Bullitt returned from Moscow, bringing the Soviet proposals for peace. Pre-occupation in the American delegation with relief to Russia would not in itself have been enough to sidetrack Bullitt or to bring his recommenda-tions to grief, but when House lost interest in pushing Bullitt's proposals further, the relief program then under discussion did provide a con-venient and plausible alternative.

Bullitt left Russia on March 16 and reached Paris on the evening of March 25. As we saw in the preceding chapter, he arrived at an appar-ently propitious time: impending withdrawals from Odessa and North Russia and rejection two days later of the last of Foch's grandiose schemes for intervention in Russia and Eastern Europe clearly indicated that further Allied military action against the Bolsheviks was highly un-likely and that an alternative policy was urgently needed. On the other hand, Bullitt had the misfortune to arrive on the eve of one of the most severe crises of the conference, what Ray Stannard Baker called "The

[31] See p. 238 below.

[32] As a friend and confidant of Wilson, McCormick, like House, often discussed matters with the president on an informal and personal basis. McCormick's diary records a number of instances of this kind. See, for example, the entry for April 3.

Dark Period," when Wilson and Lloyd George felt that they had yielded all they could to inflexible French demands for security, and when the conference appeared on the verge of breaking up. The Allied leaders were heavily preoccupied with German issues and were deeply concerned as to whether peace in the West could be achieved at all; the question of peace in Russia seemed for the moment a relatively insignificant and secondary problem.

As we noted in chapter five, the Soviet proposals to Bullitt and his impressions of conditions in Bolshevik Russia were cabled to Paris as soon as Bullitt arrived in Helsingfors. They reached Paris on March 17 and 18. Immediate reaction to these messages within the American delegation was mixed. On March 19 in the daily meeting of the American commissioners, hard on the heels of a sobering report by House concerning the impasse that had been reached with the French, Bullitt's messages and the Soviet proposals were discussed.[33] Lansing noted: "House seems favorable. White opposed. I think that I must oppose." [34] David Hunter Miller was also present at this meeting to discuss possible changes in the Covenant of the League to meet French wishes. Miller, a conservative, who became one of the staunchest opponents of Bullitt's recommendations, commented: "I thought the message [the Soviet proposal] was very artfully drawn and that Bullitt had been completely fooled by it. . . . One of the terms of the Russian message was that the Russians should have full right of access to other countries." [35] House suggested a cable to Bullitt asking him to be sure to get the Soviet proposals in writing and congratulating him. According to Miller, this suggestion did not appeal to either Lansing or White. Later, they apparently worked together to block dispatch of the cable proposed by House and also to reverse a decision of the commissioners approving Bullitt's recommendation that Pettit remain in Petrograd as an observer.[36] Not only was the reception accorded Bullitt's efforts by the commissioners something less than enthusiastic, but, in addition, no one seemed to know what the next step should be, Grew commenting that neither the commissioners nor he "have any idea of action, if any, to be taken on

[33] *Peace Conference,* xi, 124–25.
[34] Lansing Papers, Desk Diary, March 19, 1919.
[35] Miller, *Diary,* i, 189.
[36] *Ibid.;* Lansing Papers, Desk Diary, March 19, 1919; and letter from Grew to A. C. Kirk, Lansing's private secretary, March 21, 1919, *ibid.,* Correspondence, Vol. 42. For House's draft cable to Bullitt, see Bullitt Papers. According to Bullitt, the cable was not sent because of an objection on the technical point that the telegram was incorrectly signed, but it seems likely that this was simply a pretext and that actually Lansing and White never intended that the telegram should go out. *Bullitt Mission,* 46.

the proposed agreement with the Soviets." [37] Consequently, the matter remained in abeyance until Bullitt himself returned on March 25.

That night Bullitt reported at length to House on the mission. House was interested and enthusiastic, confiding in his diary: ". . . at last I can see a way out of that vexatious problem [Russia], that is, if we can get action by the Prime Ministers and the President. . . . While Bullitt was talking, I was maturing plans which I shall begin to put in execution tomorrow." [38] The same night House telephoned Wilson that Bullitt had arrived with proposals of the utmost importance, which seemed to promise an opportunity to make peace in Russia.[39] The president agreed to see Bullitt in House's office the next evening at six, but Wilson did not keep the appointment because of a headache. This headache may of course have been a "diplomatic indisposition"; Wilson may have wished to avoid Bullitt, perhaps feeling that he had neither the physical strength nor intellectual stamina to resist the vigorous and impassioned plea for a settlement with the Bolsheviks that Bullitt would certainly have made to him. It should be remembered that the president, over-worked and under a great strain, was physically and emotionally exhausted. A few days later he became ill, an illness which lasted for some days and which may have been a precursor of his later stroke. He may well have had a headache the night of his scheduled meeting with Bullitt. Whatever the reasons, the president did not deal with Bullitt directly.

Nor did Steffens have better luck in reaching Wilson. Disturbed at the president's failure to see Bullitt, Steffens recalled a promise Wilson had made to him several years earlier—that Wilson would always receive Steffens if he sent in his name with the words, "It's an emergency." Steffens followed this procedure, but Wilson refused to see him.[40]

The day after hearing Bullitt's oral report—March 26—House, faithful to the plan of action outlined in his diary, began to lobby for the adoption of a new policy toward Russia. He first approached Orlando, giving the Italian premier the gist of certain parts of Bullitt's report.[41] In line with a belief expressed in his diary that fear, not pity, was what would eventually induce the European Allies to reach an agreement with the Bolsheviks, House emphasized Bullitt's description of the strength of the Red Army and asserted that if peace were not made with the Soviet government, "Russia and Germany would link up together, thereby

[37] Letter to William Phillips, assistant secretary of state, March 18, 1919, Grew, I, 383.

[38] House Papers, Diary, March 25, 1919.

[39] *Bullitt Mission,* 73.

[40] Steffens, 800.

[41] House Papers, Diary, March 26, 1919, and Memorandum of Conversation with Orlando, Drawer 29, File 31.

realizing my prophecy that, sooner or later, everything east of the Rhine would be arrayed against the Western Powers." House said little about the deplorable conditions of economic stagnation and near starvation in Soviet Russia reported by Bullitt, apparently for fear that evidence of Bolshevik weakness would encourage the Allies to undertake further intervention. At the same time he told Orlando that the Soviet leaders were anxious to make peace with the West and that a settlement on reasonable terms could be reached. Without mentioning that Bullitt had actually brought back such a draft treaty, House urged that the Allies "proceed to draw up a treaty with Russia, practically on our own terms, provided they were just, and send this treaty to Moscow for their signatures, promising to sign it ourselves in the event it was agreed upon there." To bolster his case, House added that such a procedure would obviate the necessity of meeting the Bolsheviks "at some place such as Prinkipo." He concluded with the argument that while ideally the Western leaders might prefer some other plan, no other approach was practicable in view of the lack of reliable troops and of money necessary to undertake large-scale intervention; consequently, the Allies would either have to face up to the unpleasant reality of dealing with the *de facto* government in Russia, no matter how much they disliked it, or else remain in a state of semiwar with that country. According to House, Orlando accepted these arguments and agreed to support House's proposal for an accommodation with the Bolsheviks.

Having lined up Orlando, House telephoned the president only to find that "as usual . . . his 'one-track mind' is against taking up this question at present." House nevertheless decided to push ahead with his plan: "I would have preferred to have taken it up first with the President, but since he is not in a frame of mind to do so, I shall take it up with Lloyd George and see whether I cannot commit him as I have Orlando. If peace is to come to the world, the Russian settlement must be a part of it." [42]

In the meantime House asked his aide, Gordon Auchincloss, and David Hunter Miller, legal expert for the delegation, to work out details of an agreement with the Soviet government along the lines of the proposals obtained by Bullitt.[43] Miller, already critical of the Soviet terms, as we have seen, noted in his diary his opposition to this course on the ground that the Bolsheviks, while reaping the benefits of an agreement with the Allies, would not live up to their part of the bargain. It is not clear, however, whether Miller voiced these objections to House. The point is of some importance, as we shall learn in a moment.

[42] *Ibid.*, Diary, March 26, 1919.
[43] *Ibid.*, Auchincloss Diary, March 26, 1919; and Miller, *Diary,* I, 206.

The next link in the chain of circumstances that squeezed the life out of Bullitt's plan was forged that afternoon. Foolishly and recklessly, Auchincloss leaked the news that an agreement with the Bolsheviks was being considered to H. Wickham Steed, editor of Lord Northcliffe's *Daily Mail*.[44] It is clear from Steed's memoirs and Auchincloss's diary that the latter frequently passed on information of this type to Steed, but Auchincloss's purpose in doing so is obscure. Perhaps Auchincloss, a conservative himself, felt that the conservative, anti-German, anti-Bolshevik line taken by Steed in his editorials would help support policies at Paris that Auchincloss believed in, and would help produce the kind of peace settlement that Auchincloss desired. Perhaps Auchincloss simply enjoyed a sense of power and importance from transmitting secret information to an influential publicist. In any case, Auchincloss's activities in this regard did not escape the notice of the man for whom they caused the most trouble. On April 4 Auchincloss and House met with Lloyd George on another matter, and Auchincloss reported in his diary: "[Lloyd] George referred to Steed's attacks and said that Steed had been using matter that we (looking at me) had no doubt given him in confidence and that he thought that was the worst thing a newspaper man could do. I did not comment but just stared George back. He is playing a slick game and is getting nervous on account of the attacks in the Daily Mail and London Times. . . . Of course, I realize that I am playing with fire also but I may be able to escape getting burned."

In dealing with Steed, Auchincloss was indeed playing with fire. Steed, clever and unscrupulous, was virulently anti-Bolshevik. Though without evidence to support his contention, Steed maintained that powerful international financial interests, among them Jewish bankers such as Schiff and Warburg, "were at work in favor of the immediate recognition of the Bolsheviks," from whom they hoped to receive lucrative financial concessions in Russia. Steed maintained that the Soviet reply to the Prinkipo proposal, with its offer of concessions, reflected the commercial motives which inspired that proposal, as well as all efforts to deal with the Bolsheviks.[45] On the basis of the "tip" from Auchincloss on March 26, Steed prepared a strong editorial opposing any sort of recognition of the Bolsheviks, which was printed on March 27 under the title "The Intrigue That May Be Revived." The intrigue was, of course, the Prinkipo plan. "Lenin," Steed fulminated, "who is a sinister fanatic, would promise any price to secure the recognition he needs in order that his agents . . . [might] encompass the ruin of ordered democratic

[44] Steed, II, 302; House Papers, Auchincloss Diary, March 27, 1919.
[45] Steed, II, 301–02.

civilization." [46] This, it should be noted, was the editorial which Lloyd George had before him the morning of March 27 when Bullitt talked with him at breakfast, and which, as we shall see, he waved in front of Bullitt on that occasion.

The morning Steed's editorial appeared House went to see the president concerning Russia. It is important to remember that on the preceding day House had been enthusiastic about Bullitt's plan and had worked vigorously to secure support for it, at the same time initiating staff action to put it into effect. His diary entries for March 25 and March 26 were full of optimism and conviction concerning it. But by the evening of March 27 House's mood and point of view had changed, and he wrote in his diary: "I have taken up actively with the President today the Russian Question. I am trying to think something out that is workable. It is very difficult because no one wanted to deal with such as Lenine and Trotsky. The President suggested that I talk to Hoover and Robinson of the Shipping Board and see whether we could get ships and food to Russia in the event we wished to do so." After noting Hoover's optimism and Robinson's pessimism, House went on: "I shall try and enlist Hoover actively in the Russian Question and together I hope we may be able to reach some sort of solution." Thus, the Hoover-Nansen plan was born. But what had led to House's change of attitude and opinion? Who had not "wanted to deal with such as Lenine and Trotsky" and had persuaded House of the difficulties of carrying out his original plan? Who, in short, had taken the wind out of House's sails?

A definite answer cannot be found, but three possibilities exist, on the basis of the evidence available. The first is that Miller and Auchincloss talked House out of his original commitment to the Bullitt approach. As we know, Miller strongly opposed an agreement with the Bolsheviks, both in principle and on the terms Bullitt brought back. This explanation is also the one Bullitt himself advanced at the time. On April 18 he wrote Pettit recounting his failure to get the Soviet proposals accepted in Paris. After reporting that both the president and Lloyd George had left the matter to House, who was prepared to put the Soviet proposals through, Bullitt asserted: "At the last moment, however, David Hunter Miller, who, as you know, is the blackest reactionary we have here, and in addition, is Auchincloss' partner, and therefore the legal expert of the Commission, persuaded Auchincloss that such a proposal was excessively bad, and Auchincloss in turn persuaded House that something milder should be done first." Bullitt then goes on to describe House's support of the Hoover-Nansen plan as an alternative and indirect approach to the Bolsheviks.[47]

Another explanation for House's change of mind is that Steed's editorial in the *Daily Mail* that morning alarmed him. House, well versed in English politics, may have recognized the import of the attack for Lloyd George's position, and concluded that he could never hope to drive the idea of an agreement with the Bolsheviks through the conference without the whole-hearted backing and cooperation of the British prime minister, the sort of support Lloyd George was not likely to give him in the face of Steed's criticism.

Finally, it is possible that Wilson himself put a damper on House's plans. Wilson probably did nothing actively to discourage House, and, in fact, the president told House that he was leaving the Russian problem entirely in House's hands, as the latter later informed Bullitt.[48] At the same time it seems clear that Wilson showed no enthusiasm for the Soviet proposals or for House's efforts to get them accepted, suggesting as an alternative the relief approach. On March 27 or March 28 the president asked for a written report from Bullitt, which was duly prepared and delivered to him.[49] Wilson, however, did not submit this report to the Council of Four, nor would he permit it to be released.[50]

Because of the timing involved, it can be argued that Wilson shied away from Bullitt's proposals in deference to American public opinion and for domestic political considerations. At this time the Overman Committee was raising a great anti-Bolshevik hue and cry, and March marked the beginning of the "Red Scare" of 1919. In addition, when news of the dispatch of the Bullitt mission became public on March 21, press reaction in the United States was distinctly unfavorable. For example, a headline in the New York *Tribune* of March 24 declared: "Wilson Sees Russia By Steffens' Eyes." [51] There is, however, no evidence in the Wilson papers that the president's attitude toward Russia was affected at this time by the rising hysteria at home, which in any case was largely directed against Bolshevism in America itself. Moreover, Wilson was apparently not even aware of the press attacks on the Bullitt mission until April 2, when Tumulty wired: "The proposed rec-

[47] Bullitt Papers, letter to Walter Pettit, April 18, 1919.
[48] *Bullitt Mission*, 73.
[49] *Ibid.*, 48.
[50] *Ibid.*, 67–68, and Baker Papers, Notebook Series II, Box 46, No. 22, entry for March 29.
[51] Cited in Cheslaw, 235–37, where this and other press attacks on the mission and on the allegedly pernicious influence of Bullitt and Steffens on Wilson are summarized.

ognition of Lenin is causing consternation here." [52] This was several days after Wilson had clearly made up his mind not to encourage further discussion or action on the Bullitt recommendations.

Another supposition—that Wilson's lack of interest in the Soviet proposals brought back by Bullitt reflected an increasingly hostile attitude toward Bolshevism on his part—must also be rejected. On March 27 and April 1, as we have already seen, Wilson strongly opposed intervention against Bolshevism in Hungary and backed a conciliatory step, the sending of General Smuts to talk with Bela Kun.

The explanation of Wilson's failure to support Bullitt's recommendations would seem rather to lie in his attitude toward the Russian question at the time. The bits of evidence available indicate that insofar as Wilson had a policy on Russia at that moment, it was to do nothing. This meant opposing Foch's plans for further intervention, but it also meant not encouraging efforts to reach a settlement with the Bolsheviks. (Immediate practical measures, however, such as evacuation of American forces from North Russia and maintenance of the American position in Siberia vis-à-vis Japan, had to be, and were, taken.) Wilson was still confused and baffled by the Russian problem, which had troubled him for many months and the solution of which had escaped him for so long. He had placed great hopes in the Prinkipo project, but this had not worked out, largely, he felt, because of the cynical attitude of the Soviet leaders. If they were not turning out to be the moderate and reasonable men his liberal faith had led him to hope they might become, there was then little chance of engaging their participation in self-determination for Russia, in the reestablishment of representative government there, and for the moment nothing more could be done. The president still opposed intervention, but he had no alternative to offer. On March 25 he told his colleagues in the Council of Four that his policy was to let the Russians "stew in their own juice," at the same time "preventing Bolshevism from invading other parts of Europe." Two days later Wilson warned that trying "to stop a revolutionary movement by a line of armies is to employ a broom to stop a great flood," but he admitted that he was at a loss to know what to do: "The only way to act against Bolshevism is to make its causes disappear. This is, however, a formidable enterprise; we do not even know exactly what its causes are." [53]

These last words, however, do provide a further clue to Wilson's thinking about Russia at this time. Deeply preoccupied with the German settlement, Wilson had little time or energy to devote to the Russian

[52] Wilson Papers, Series VIIIA, Boxes 30, 31.
[53] See p. 204 of ch. six.

problem and its resolution, and, as he told House, he did not wish to divert his one-track mind from the treaty with Germany. Yet, in Wilson's view, a connection existed between the two issues. Although he believed that the settlement in the West had first priority, he was also convinced that a just peace there would remove much of the discontent and uncertainty on which Bolshevism fed. The League of Nations could then give full and considered attention to the solution of the Russian problem. Wilson outlined this point of view in a talk to the Democratic National Committee on February 28, 1919, during his mid-conference trip home.[54] He declared that, as a result of the war, the peoples of the world had lost faith in their own governments and leadership, and he warned that the West must support the peoples' aspirations for a world order of justice and peace:

> . . . if we can confirm that belief we have steadied the whole process of history in the immediate future; whereas, if we do not confirm that belief, I would not like to say what would happen in the way of utter dissolution of society.
>
> The only thing that that ugly, poisonous thing called Bolshevism feeds on is the doubt of the man on the street of the essential integrity of the people he is depending on to do his governing. . . . [Some people] are in a temper to have anything rather than the kind of thing they have been having; and they say to themselves: "Well, this may be bad but it is at least better and more immediately in touch with us than the other, and we will try it. . . ."

Wilson then discussed the confused situation in Russia and the complexities of the Russian problem, adding: "And yet we may have to go home without composing those great territories, but if we go home with a League of Nations, there will be some power to solve this most perplexing problem." [55] Because he himself could not see a clear path to a solution, Wilson was disposed to postpone the Russian issue, leaving it to the League in much the same manner as he had left it, in the fall of 1918, to the peace conference.

It is, of course, quite possible that none of the factors discussed above—Miller's opposition to an agreement with the Bolsheviks, Steed's

---

[54] Tumulty, 367–79.

[55] In a related vein, see a letter from Wilson to William Allen White on April 2, 1919. Wilson Papers, Series viiiA, Box 31. Commenting on White's suggestion that an impartial commission be sent to Russia for a serious, long-term study of the situation, Wilson asked: "I would very much like to have your idea . . . as to whether investigation should go on irrespective of the peace conclusions and in the meantime leaving Russia out of the settlement." See also a letter from Wilson to Ambassador Francis, April 18, 1919, *ibid.*, Box 38.

attack on such a course of action, or Wilson's apparent lack of enthusiasm for this alternative—influenced House to drop Bullitt's plan for a less bold policy; some other person or event, of which no record appears in the evidence, may have caused House to change his mind. This is not probable, however, and one is forced to conclude that one, two, or perhaps all three of these factors led House to abandon his original position. In any case, the consequences were fateful for the Bullitt mission; from March 27 on House refused, despite steady pressure from Bullitt, to support the policy he had at first endorsed, turning instead to the more cautious course of approaching the Bolsheviks indirectly through a relief program.

House's defection need not have been decisive for the Bullitt plan, however. If Lloyd George had fully backed the Bullitt recommendations, they might still have carried the day; Lloyd George's advocacy of them would probably have won back House and swept Wilson along with him. But this was not to be. On March 26, the day after he returned, Bullitt met all morning and part of the afternoon with Lansing, White, and Bliss. Bullitt felt that he had secured the support of the commissioners, and, with the approval of House and the help of Philip Kerr, he then arranged a breakfast interview with Lloyd George on March 27.[56] According to Bullitt's testimony before the Senate Foreign Relations Committee, both Lloyd George and Smuts, who was also present, declared that the Soviet proposals were of the utmost importance and should be carefully considered. Lloyd George added, however, that "he did not know what he could do with British public opinion." Holding the copy of the *Daily Mail* in his hand which contained Steed's editorial, the British leader asked rhetorically: "As long as the British press is doing this kind of thing, how can you expect me to be sensible about Russia?" [57] After Lloyd George had expounded, rather belatedly, the advantages of sending a conservative observer to Russia,[58] it was finally agreed that Lloyd George would leave preparation of a definite course of action to House, and that the British prime minister would follow and support the lead of the Americans on the matter.

The same day Bullitt, with the assistance of Whitney Shephardson, an aide on House's staff, prepared a draft public statement to be issued by the Allies. House had requested such a document, apparently before his

[56] *Bullitt Mission,* 65; Bullitt Papers, letter to Pettit, April 18, 1919; author's interview with Bullitt, February 25, 1953. For an indication that Lansing was not entirely convinced, see Lansing Papers, Desk Diary, March 26, 1919.

[57] *Bullitt Mission,* 66.

[58] See p. 162 of ch. five.

change of heart.[59] The statement, entitled "A Declaration of Policy . . . and an Offer of an Armistice," first reviewed the Prinkipo project and expressed, lest there be misunderstanding in Russia and the world, the intention of the Allies not to interfere in Russia's internal affairs and their desire to assist the Russian people. It warned, however, that the Allies would not tolerate aggression by any government in Russia, and that assistance could not be rendered Russia as long as fighting continued in that area. Apparently hoping to draw support from those who were interested in a relief program for Russia, Bullitt indicated in the statement that relief would follow a settlement. He then proposed an armistice and a subsequent conference to discuss peace on the basis of a set of principles which were identical with those enumerated in the proposals he had brought back from Moscow.[60] No action was taken on this draft statement, however, for by the afternoon of March 27 House had already decided to substitute a relief plan for the direct negotiations with the Bolsheviks recommended by Bullitt.

Unaware of this, Bullitt continued his efforts to win support for the latter course of action, talking with Balfour that afternoon and reportedly gaining his endorsement.[61] But, with House already retreating from Bullitt's plan, the only one who could rescue it was Lloyd George. The next day, March 28, House invited the British leader to lunch to discuss the Russian question. That morning, however, the Council of Four was the scene of a major clash between Wilson and Clemenceau over the Saar. As a result, discussion at lunch revolved around this crisis, House reporting: "We scarcely touched upon the Russian Question except that I told him what I was doing and asked him to postpone any action on his part until I could get a more matured plan for our consideration. He is sympathetic toward a settlement with Russia, and I think will meet me half way." [62]

Even if House and Lloyd George had had a chance to talk about Russia, it would probably have been of little help to Bullitt's position. As Lloyd George had indicated to Bullitt, it was politically awkward for him to espouse a moderate course toward Russia in the face of violently anti-Bolshevik British opinion, such as that represented by Steed's editorials in the *Daily Mail*. On March 28, the day of the House–Lloyd

[59] *Bullitt Mission,* 68. The text of the draft statement is given on pp. 69–73; another copy with minor variations is in the Bullitt Papers.

[60] The version in the Bullitt Papers added that the proposed conference would discuss the relief of Russia, as well as peace. In addition, a specific date and place for the conference was inserted—April 25 in Oslo.

[61] *Bullitt Mission,* 67.

[62] House Papers, Diary, March 28, 1919.

George luncheon, Steed printed another diatribe against those who wished to deal with the Soviet government. This editorial, entitled "Peace With Honor," argued that the Bolsheviks' crude economic bait certainly could not appeal to the idealism of Wilson, but only to the crass commercialism of profitseekers willing to betray Western civilization for financial gain.[63] It was hardly the sort of thing to encourage Lloyd George to take up the cudgels on Bullitt's behalf.

This editorial was also the result of a "tip," probably from Auchincloss. The previous afternoon House had seen Steed and had mildly reproached him for having attacked a policy the conference had not yet decided on in his editorial "The Intrigue That May Be Revived." Steed, in turn, had warned House of the dangerous influence of certain Jewish bankers. House, already pursuing the relief alternative, had pointed out that to distribute supplies in Russia with proper safeguards did not mean recognizing the Bolsheviks but provided an opportunity both to prevent the ruin of Russia and to gather reliable information about the situation.[64] Steed, unconvinced, received word that evening that Wilson and Lloyd George were to act favorably on Bullitt's proposals the next day. He immediately penned "Peace With Honor."

Much annoyed, House sent for Steed the morning of March 28. House told Steed that the latter should have consulted him before writing such an editorial. He asked Steed to stop his attacks until a policy had been worked out; Steed could then endorse it or oppose it as he thought best. Steed agreed provided that no major decision on Russia were taken before he was informed.[65] For a few days thereafter Steed indeed remained quiet, but the French press, taking its cue from Steed's earlier editorials, carried on the campaign against any sort of dealings with the Bolsheviks. On March 29 Le Temps, reflecting the viewpoint of the French Foreign Office, virtually accused Wilson and Lloyd George of betraying Russia to the Germans through the Bolsheviks. Le Journal du Peuple published information on the Bullitt mission and charged Lloyd George with having endorsed the trip in order to pave the way for a business deal with the Bolsheviks.[66]

Steed's truce did not last long. On April 3 the London Times carried a scathing editorial attack by Steed on those in Paris who proposed reaching an accord with the Soviet government. This marked the be-

[63] Steed, II, 303.

[64] Ibid., II, 302.

[65] Ibid., II, 304; House Papers, Diary, March 28, and Auchincloss Diary, March 28.

[66] Noble, p. 289; Memorandum of Conversation between W. H. Buckler and Marcel Cachin, March 28, 1919, House Papers, Drawer 30, File 218; ibid., Auchincloss Diary, March 29, 1919.

ginning of a vigorous press and parliamentary campaign in Great Britain against a conciliatory policy toward the Bolsheviks. This campaign, directed at Lloyd George primarily, was led by Lord Northcliffe, the press baron and Steed's publisher, and by Winston Churchill, who stirred up the Tory members of Lloyd George's own coalition.[67] It coincided with mounting public and parliamentary criticism of the conference for its delay in making peace and of Lloyd George for allegedly taking a "soft" line on Germany and for not extracting the largest possible reparations form the defeated enemy. On April 8 a Tory bloc in Parliament wired Lloyd George challenging his position on the reparations issue. To meet this parliamentary revolt and to counter Northcliffe's attacks on Russian policy and other issues, Lloyd George returned to London in mid-April.[68]

On April 16 Lloyd George reviewed British policy toward Russia before the House of Commons.[69] Like his address to Parliament on this subject in February, it was an equivocal speech, in which the British leader attempted to appease the interventionists without entirely disavowing his own views. The position Lloyd George took became the basis for British policy in Russia until the fall of 1919. He began by arguing that it was impossible to recognize either the Soviet or the White Russian governments in view of the civil war, the fluctuating zones of control in the area, and the inability of either side to establish its authority over all Russia. He rejected a policy of intervention on principle and because of its impracticality and cost. On the other hand, Lloyd George maintained that the British government was bound to give assistance to the White Russians, both from an obligation of honor and in order to give the anti-Bolsheviks an opportunity to see if they did, in fact, represent the will of the majority of Russian people.[70] Lloyd George concluded, with somewhat obscure logic: "Therefore, I do not in the least regard it as a departure from the fundamental policy of Great Britain not to interfere in the internal affairs of any land that we should support General Denikin and Admiral Kolchak."

The policy of allegedly not interfering but at the same time giving aid to one side in the Russian struggle failed to win the support of some Laborites; in the subsequent debate Lloyd George was asked about the Bullitt mission. In an evasive fashion, he denied any knowledge of peaceful approaches made by the Soviet government or initiated by the Allies. Af-

[67] Callwell, *Wilson Diaries*, II, 181; Nicolson, 59–62, 307; and Harris, 137.
[68] Lloyd George, I, 562–64.
[69] *Ibid.*, I, 569–82; Great Britain, House of Commons, *Debates*, fifth series, 1919, CXIV, cols. 2936–84.
[70] See p. 142 of ch. five for a fuller summary of this last argument, also advanced by Lloyd George in February.

ter being pressed, he finally had to admit that "there was some suggestion that a young American had come back from Russia with a communication." Then, attempting to shift the onus to Wilson, Lloyd George asserted in a statement which, though perhaps literally correct, was certainly misleading: "It is not for me to judge the value of this communication, but if the President of the United States had attached any value to it he would have brought it before the conference, and he certainly did not." [71]

Needless to say, this enraged Bullitt. On April 18 he sent Wilson a clipping of Lloyd George's remarks with the inquiry: "I should greatly appreciate it if you would inform me whether the last sentence of this statement of Mr. Lloyd George [quoted above] is true or untrue." [72] Wilson did not reply. Churchill in his memoirs commented: "The Soviet proposals to Mr. Bullitt, which were, of course, in themselves fraudulent, were treated with general disdain; and Bullitt himself was not without some difficulty disowned by those who had sent him." [73]

Bullitt, angered and discouraged by the treatment afforded the Soviet proposals, as well as himself, and subsequently dissatisfied with the treaty presented to the Germans, resigned from the American Commission in mid-May. It is evident that throughout the affair he seemed not to realize that anyone undertaking an informal diplomatic mission runs the risk of being disavowed by his superiors when they find it politic to do so.

Why did Bullitt fail, and why was this chance for the Allies to get out of the Russian tangle on reasonable terms not taken? It is not true, as it is sometimes asserted,[74] that the Soviet proposals were rejected because of a belief, engendered by news of Kolchak's spring offensive, that the Bolshevik government was about to be overthrown. Reports of Kolchak's victories did not begin to reach Paris until the very end of March and early in April. By then Bullitt's recommendations had already been shelved. The explanation of Bullitt's failure lies in part in the circumstances surrounding the mission and in the situation at Paris when Bullitt returned, factors which have been discussed in chapter five and earlier in this chapter. But primarily Bullitt failed because, on the one hand, the Western leaders, and especially Wilson, were too preoccupied to give Bullitt's proposals the careful consideration they deserved, and, on the other, they, and especially Lloyd George, were so influenced by conservative opinion in the press and among the public that they were

[71] The exchange with Lloyd George's interlocutor, Labour M. P. Clynes, is quoted in full in *Bullitt Mission*, 94.
[72] Wilson Papers, Series VIIIA, Box 38.
[73] Churchill, *Aftermath*, 176.
[74] For examples, see Unterberger, 148, and Fischer, I, 153.

prevented from taking a bold step, which, though undoubtedly unpopular in some circles, would probably have been in the best interests of the West. The Bullitt story illustrates the pitfalls of "personal" diplomacy as it has developed in the twentieth century, as well as the difficulties of "democratic" diplomacy—the formulation and execution of foreign policy under the pressure of an often uninformed or emotional public opinion.

The Hoover-Nansen Plan

On March 27, as we saw, Wilson suggested that House consult Hoover and Robinson concerning the availability of food and ships for a relief program to Russia. House did so and found Hoover enthusiastic about the possiblities of sending food to Russia, viewing it primarily as an anti-Bolshevik measure, according to Auchincloss:

> Hoover recognized that we must have some dealings with the present authorities [in Russia]. . . . He feels that as soon as the fighting stops the Bolshevik army will disintegrate and the distribution of food to the people of Russia will make them less eager to continue their policy of agitation. . . .
>
> Hoover suggested further that we get Nansen or some neutral to start an organization for the relief of Russia. . . . There is much to be said for this plan which could be carried through without the co-operation of the French.[75]

The next day Auchincloss noted: "At the present time we are working on a scheme to set up a neutral organization similar to the Belgian relief organization to act as an intermediary between the Allies and the Russian governments." [76]

The same day, March 28, Hoover wrote the president a long letter commenting on the Russian problem.[77] Hoover pointed out that in part Bolshevism represented a reaction against past tyranny in Europe and was based on genuine social grievances. Americans could not but sympathize to some degree with those who had been oppressed for generations and with their "blind gropings for better social conditions." On the other hand, Hoover asserted, Americans, with a system "about as near perfection as human nature permits," clearly recognized the "foolishness of Bolshevik tenets," and they could only be repelled by the negation of democracy embodied in the Bolshevik dictatorship and by the terror,

[75] House Papers, Auchincloss Diary, March 27, 1919.
[76] *Ibid.,* March 28, 1919.
[77] Full text of a copy in House Papers; extracts printed in Hoover, *Ordeal of Wilson,* 117–19; *1919, Russia,* 100–02; and H. H. Fisher, *The Famine in Soviet Russia, 1919–1923* (New York, 1927), 11–14.

violence, and bloodshed which were the instruments of Bolshevik rule. Hoover warned, however, that the emotional impulse behind Bolshevism made it a powerful and dangerous movement and might lead the Bolsheviks to undertake large military crusades in an attempt "to impose their doctrines on other defenseless people."

Despite this danger, Hoover declared, military intervention in Russia was not the solution. It would do more harm than good, since Bolshevism would simply ferment and spread under repression. Moreover, intervention might mean American involvement in years of police duty in Russia and would make the United States a party to the restoration of reaction in Russia. Finally, Hoover opposed intervention because the United States should not "insist that any given population must work out its internal social problems according to our particular conception of democracy."

Hoover then made three recommendations: first, the United States should not recognize the Bolsheviks because "we cannot even remotely recognize this murderous tyranny without stimulating actionist radicalism in every country in Europe and without transgressing on every National ideal of our own." Second, a well-known and respected neutral person should be encouraged to create a relief commission for Russia, like that which operated in Belgium during the war. This individual could draw on the Scandinavian countries for assistance, perhaps even on Germany. He would act as an intermediary between the Allies and the Bolsheviks, and the Allies should agree to cooperate with him and to aid him provided the Soviet government ceased hostilities and put an end to its subversive and propaganda activities abroad. The equitable distribution of food supplies would also have to be assured. According to Hoover, such a plan had the advantage of not involving "any recognition or relationship by the Allies of the Bolshevik murderers." In addition, "it would at least test out whether this is a militant force engrossed upon world domination"; it would provide a temporary stabilization of the situation in Eastern Europe, and it would win time in which to see "whether the Russian people will not themselves swing back to moderation and themselves bankrupt these ideas."

Third, Hoover urged Wilson to make a public statement recognizing the legitimate popular aspirations on which Bolshevism capitalized, but emphasizing the prospects for continued social betterment through democratic processes and repudiating the tenets and methods of the Bolsheviks. Such a stand, Hoover felt, would rally the forces "for orderly progress against anarchy" and would give heart to those opposing the Bolshevik attempt at world domination. This last suggestion, however, was not adopted by the president, and a later attempt by Hoover to carry it out in his own name was rebuffed.[78]

In a sense the relief program outlined in Hoover's second proposal represented a compromise between a policy of further intervention and the idea of reaching an accommodation with the Bolsheviks. While Hoover rejected intervention, partly on principle and partly because of the dangers and embarrassments accompanying it, his relief recommendation did not go far toward a settlement with the Bolsheviks; in fact, it is clear that Hoover hoped that once the Russians were well fed and warmly clothed, they would repudiate Bolshevism. If they did not, at least time would have been gained, Europe would have had a chance to recover its equilibrium, and world opinion could then be marshaled for a fight against the militancy of Bolshevism. In the meantime, his plan permitted an investigation at first hand of Russian conditions and made it possible to save the lives of many innocent Russians.

For House, the attractiveness of Hoover's proposal was that it involved no recognition of or direct dealings with the Bolsheviks; at the same time it held out hope of ending hostilities in Russia, and it seemed to open up an indirect route to a settlement there.[79] On April 5 House, complaining about the difficulty of getting the Council of Four to act on the plan, characterized it as follows: "without recognizing the Soviet government or doing anything to which the conservatives could reasonably object, an arrangement might be made now by which fighting on the Russian fronts could be immediately stopped and the advance of Bolshevism westward checked." [80]

During the next few days House, Hoover, Miller, and Auchincloss worked to develop the relief idea into a detailed proposal. Although Hoover discussed the suggestion with Lord Cecil, his colleagues on the Supreme Economic Council, and Auchincloss sounded out Kerr and Hankey of the British delegation, no one consulted the senior British statesmen nor the French delegation, Balfour later complaining to House that neither he nor the French Foreign Office knew anything about the plan to feed Russia until they saw it announced in the

[78] See pp. 257–58 below.
[79] *Bullitt Mission*, 75.
[80] House Papers, Diary, April 5, 1919. Although he was enthusiastic about the possibility of checking Bolshevism through an armistice and through food relief, House also believed that the Poles at least should be given military assistance to help them fight off the Bolshevik advance. On April 8 he advised E. B. Parker, chairman of the commission for disposing of American surplus material in France, to sell munitions to the Poles, who were attempting to check "advances in two directions from Russia [presumably House meant the Bolsheviks and the Ukrainians]." *Ibid.*, April 8, 1919.

papers.[81] Fridtjof Nansen, whom Hoover had mentioned to House on March 27 and with whom Hoover had become acquainted during the war when Nansen purchased food for Norway in the United States, was asked to head the proposed relief organization for Russia. At first Branting, a Swedish socialist, was to be associated with Nansen in the relief effort, but after a few days he dropped out of the negotiations.[82]

Nansen, a renowned Norwegian explorer of the Arctic, had been active in a number of humanitarian enterprises before and during the war. Later, in the 1920's, he served with the League of Nations in connection with the repatriation of prisoners of war and the resettlement of refugees. Although unsophisticated in political matters and diplomacy, Nansen was highly respected throughout Europe and America, and he seemed an ideal choice for the Russian relief project. He was dedicated to the idea of bringing peace and succor to the suffering peoples of Russia. Moreover, while Nansen had little comprehension of either the ideological or the practical aspects of Bolshevism, he believed firmly that in general it was a tragic error to leave Russia out of the comity of nations; Russia, he was convinced, had much to contribute to European civilization, and her destiny was inextricably linked with that of the West.[83]

Nansen had come to Paris in the winter of 1919 with an interest in the Russian question, as well as in the plight of prisoners of war.[84] Early in March the leaders of the Russian Political Conference apparently attempted to persuade Nansen to become the figurehead of an international movement to raise money for the fight against Bolshevism, but Nansen felt that he did not have enough information about the Russian situation.[85] In any case, his reputation, interests, and presence in Paris made him a logical person for House and Hoover to turn to. At first Nansen was reluctant to undertake the job, feeling that the resources he could draw on in Scandinavia would be inadequate to carry it out successfully. Nansen accepted, however, after Hoover had assured him that initial relief supplies would be furnished by the United States on credit, that the Allies would assist him in various ways, and that the Bolsheviks would be expected to pay for the relief goods with gold and

[81] *Ibid.*, March 29, April 20, 1919; *ibid.*, Auchincloss Diary, March 29, April 4, 1919.

[82] *Ibid.*, March 29, March 31.

[83] Fridtjof Nansen, *Russia and Peace* (London, 1923), 7–10.

[84] According to Hoover, he telegraphed Nansen to come to Paris, but the intervention of the Norwegian prime minister was needed to persuade Nansen to accept the invitation. Hoover, *Ordeal of Wilson*, 119–20. From evidence in McCormick's diary and from other references, however, it is clear that Nansen was already in Paris in March 1919; e.g., McCormick Diary, March 18, 1919.

[85] Reported in an account of a conversation with Nansen, *ibid.*

exportable raw materials. Hoover also promised that American relief specialists would handle the purchasing and transport of foodstuffs if Nansen and his organization would supervise equitable distribution of the supplies in Russia.[86]

On April 3 a letter, signed by Nansen but drafted by House, Hoover, and their subordinates in the preceding few days, was sent to each member of the Council of Four.[87] The letter proposed the organization of a neutral relief commission for Russia in order to help remedy the tragic conditions of starvation and disease prevailing there. The letter stressed that the endeavor would be solely humanitarian and entirely nonpolitical in character. "If thus organized upon the lines of the Belgian Relief Commission, it would raise no question of political recognition or negotiations between the Allies with the existing authorities in Russia." The letter concluded by inquiring under what conditions the leaders of the peace conference would approve such an undertaking. There was no reference to outside control of Russia's transportation facilities, nor was anything said about the cessation of hostilities, issues which were introduced into the scheme later and which led to much criticism of the plan and, eventually, to its rejection by the Soviet leaders.

As President Wilson had left the whole matter in House's hands, the latter asked Bullitt to draft a reply from the Four to Nansen's letter. House also asked Miller and Auchincloss to prepare a draft reply.[88] Bullitt had been making no headway in his efforts to persuade House to pursue the original plan negotiated in Moscow. On April 2, in a memorandum to House, Bullitt had brusquely declared: "May I remind you that the pledge of the Soviet government to accept a proposal similar to the one handed to me will expire in 8 days."[89] House did nothing, however. Consequently, Bullitt, though opposed to the Hoover-Nansen plan as against his own, decided to try to use the relief project as a cloak for his original proposals. A disguised approach, he concluded, was better than none. Bullitt's draft reply to Nansen on behalf of the Four, dated April 4, drew heavily in language and in content on the proposed declaration of policy implementing his recommendations prepared for House on March 27.[90] Bullitt incorporated *in toto* his proposal for a cease-fire to be followed by a conference at Oslo to discuss peace on the

[86] Fisher, 15. According to Hoover, pressure from the Norwegian government was also needed before Nansen would agree to undertake the relief project. Hoover, *Ordeal of Wilson*, 120; Hoover, *Memoirs*, I, 414.

[87] House Papers, Auchincloss Diary, March 31, April 1. For the text of the letter, see *1919, Russia*, 102.

[88] *Bullitt Mission*, 75, 79; House Papers, Auchincloss Diary, April 3, 1919.

[89] House Papers, Correspondence Files, Bullitt.

[90] See pp. 242–43 above for this draft policy declaration; Bullitt's draft reply to Nansen is in *Bullitt Mission*, 79.

basis of the principles agreed to by the Soviet leaders in Moscow, simply inserting an introductory paragraph referring to the necessity for relief and to Nansen's project and adding that the suggested conference would have the purpose of discussing the provisioning of Russia, as well as peace.

According to Bullitt, House, when he received Bullitt's draft, stated that he would like Miller and Auchincloss, as legal experts, to go over it before he presented it to the president.[91] In fact, as we have seen, House had already commissioned Miller and Auchincloss to prepare a separate draft reply. Their draft was totally different from Bullitt's.[92] Emphasizing the difficulties of transporting and of distributing relief supplies in Russia in view of "the existing situation" there, Miller and Auchincloss proposed that the neutral relief commission have full control over the necessary transportation facilities within Russia, which should therefore "to the necessary extent be freed from any governmental or private control whatsoever." In addition, they recommended that under the general supervision of the relief commission, local distribution of the supplies should be managed by the Russian people themselves, with each community advising the commission concerning the methods and personnel to be used in its area. Given the violent struggle taking place in Russia and the inexperience of the Russian people in self-government, a more impractical and politically oriented approach can hardly be imagined. Nevertheless, Auchincloss and Miller solemnly stated: "Under no other circumstances could it be believed that the purpose of this relief was humanitarian and not political, and still more important, under no other conditions could it be certain that the hungry would be fed." Finally, they demanded a cessation of hostilities on all fronts as a prerequisite to relief. Nothing, however, was said about how such an armistice might be arranged, nor about a peace conference.

Bullitt, understandably outraged, promptly addressed a caustic memorandum to Auchincloss, dated April 4.[93] In it Bullitt, with more heat than exactness, asserted that the proposal that the relief commission control Russia's railroads could "hardly be accepted by the Soviet government which knows that plots for the destruction of railroad bridges were hatched in the American consulate in Moscow. You are asking the Soviet government to put its head in the lion's mouth." Bullitt also complained that the Auchincloss-Miller draft failed to call for the cessation of hostilities by Allied forces, "a number of whom, you may recall, have

[91] *Ibid.*
[92] *1919, Russia,* 103–04. I have found no evidence to support Kennan's assertion that Hoover himself drafted this reply. Kennan, *Russia and the West,* 140.
[93] *Bullitt Mission,* 83–84.

invaded Russia," or for the withdrawal of Allied troops and the prohibition of further Allied aid to anti-Bolshevik groups in Russia. Bullitt concluded: "As it stands, your armistice proposal is absolutely unfair, and I am sure that it will not be accepted by the Soviet Government."

The next day, April 5, Bullitt caught Auchincloss just as the latter was taking the Auchincloss-Miller draft to the president for approval. Bullitt at once appealed to House and succeeded in persuading him that the Soviet leaders would never accept such terms. House thereupon asked Bullitt to revise the Auchincloss-Miller draft so that it might be acceptable. Bullitt was told to follow the original text as closely as possible and he was instructed not to make any substantial changes.[94] He was nevertheless able to cut out some of the phrases that he felt were most likely to antagonize the Soviet leaders and to eliminate direct reference to commission control of the Russian railroad system. In addition, he inserted a statement that a cessation of hostilities would also mean a suspension of the movement of troops and supplies within and to the area.[95]

At this point Bullitt, who had fulfilled under protest House's request to rework the Auchincloss-Miller reply, became sufficiently disgusted with the whole affair to draft a personal appeal to Wilson.[96] This letter, dated April 6, was never sent, however. In it Bullitt lectured the president, warning him that the Russian events were symptomatic of a growing European-wide movement of protest against the old order and that if the peace conference could not help the peoples to find "a better way to live for the common good of all," they would turn to Moscow, even though they did not believe in the theories of communism. In fact, Bullitt went on, the European populations, believing that Wilson had not fulfilled their hopes, were already beginning to look to Lenin for guidance. Therefore, Bullitt maintained, it was essential to establish a *modus vivendi* with the Bolsheviks and to attempt to win their cooperation in the establishment of a new order: "Draw the Russian Revolution into the paths of peaceful and constructive work and the remainder of the European Revolution will follow it." Bullitt concluded by appealing to the president to take action on the original Soviet proposals, due to expire in four days.

Calmer, second thought may have led Bullitt to decide not to dispatch this letter to Wilson. In addition, he was perhaps somewhat mollified by

[94] *Ibid.,* 84.

[95] For Bullitt's redraft, see *ibid.,* 85–86. Auchincloss particularly objected to this insertion on the ground that it would prevent the transfer of Haller's Polish army to Poland. House Papers, Auchincloss Diary, April 6, 1919.

[96] Draft letter to Woodrow Wilson, April 6, 1919, Bullitt Papers. Lasch (pp. 200–01) mistakenly states the letter was sent.

the acceptance later in the afternoon of April 6 of his redraft of the Auchincloss-Miller reply to Nansen. Meeting at the bedside of the president, who was still recovering from his illness, the American commissioners discussed the Hoover-Nansen plan and approved the reply as revised by Bullitt, with Lansing supporting it in preference to the original version by Auchincloss and Miller.[97] Wilson agreed to sign the reply to Nansen's letter and to submit it to his colleagues on the Council of Four for their signature. The same day House took advantage of a meeting with Orlando and Cecil on another matter to present briefly the plan to them. According to House, they promised to support it.[98]

Two days later the Council of Four referred the Hoover-Nansen plan to an *ad hoc* committee of economic experts composed of Hoover, Cecil, Clementel, the French commerce minister, and Crespi, the Italian minister for supply.[99] The next day, April 9, the Four discussed the plan briefly. Wilson raised the relatively minor question of finding the necessary shipping for the Russian relief program, a problem about which Hoover had written the president that morning.[100] Clemenceau, going to the heart of the matter, asserted that the most important question was that of distributing the supplies in Russia. Since there was no organization in Soviet Russia except the Bolshevik government that could be charged with the distribution of relief goods, was it intended to give Lenin power over the allocation of food to the Russian people? Wilson and Lloyd George hastened to assure the French premier that distribution would be in the hands of a neutral relief commission. Wilson added that he thought the Soviet leaders would accept this; the neutrals, for their part, were interested since "they can establish for the future very interesting commercial relations with Russia." No decision was taken, however.

The same day the *ad hoc* committee appointed by the Council of Four met to consider the American-sponsored draft reply to Nansen. Although agreement in principle was reached, concern was expressed over the shipping problem. The committee also pointed out that the boundaries of Soviet Russia would have to be determined before armistice lines could be established.[101] In general, the French objected to the

[97] House Papers, Auchincloss Diary, April 6, 1919; Lansing Papers, Desk Diary, April 6, 1919. Auchincloss, whose objections were not taken into account, commented irritatedly: "The casual way in which they decide these questions is astounding." The minutes of this meeting are not included in the collection of minutes of meetings of the American commissioners published in *Peace Conference,* XI; it is likely that at this meeting, as at a number of others, no formal minutes were kept.

[98] House Papers, Diary, April 6, 1919.

[99] Resolution 239, April 8, *Recueil,* Part I, Division II, p. 103.

[100] Mantoux, I, 207. For Hoover's letter, see Wilson Papers, Series VIIIA, Box 34.

[101] Second letter from Hoover to Wilson, dated April 9, *ibid.*

phrase "the territory of the former Russian Empire" as defining the area in which hostilities were to cease, presumably because this would have embraced regions along Russia's western borders, such as Bessarabia, which the French believed had already been permanently removed from Bolshevik, or for that matter from Russian, jurisdiction.[102] Bullitt's revision of the Auchincloss-Miller draft reply to Nansen was thereupon amended slightly. The phrase to which the French objected was changed to read "within definite lines in the territory of Russia," and a sentence stating that payment for the relief supplies would be the responsibility of "the Russian authorities" was inserted in the third paragraph.[103] Despite these changes, however, Clemeneau refused to sign the proposed reply to Nansen.

The following day, April 10, marked the expiration of the period during which the Soviet authorities had agreed to accept a peace offer based on the terms discussed with Bullitt. As a result, Bullitt, in desperation, called this fact to the attention of the American commissioners, warning that the Bolshevik leaders might interpret the silence of the conference as a rejection of the Soviet proposals.[104] Bullitt then asked the commissioners to authorize the dispatch of a message to Chicherin through reliable sources apprising him that a neutral relief plan was under consideration. This, Bullitt argued, might forestall belligerent statements or the launching of offensive operations by the Soviet government, actions which could only make more difficult the implementation of the Nansen plan if it should be approved by the Council of Four. After inserting a phrase placing responsibility for the message directly on Bullitt, the commissioners approved its transmission to Chicherin.[105]

After several more days had passed without any indication that the French would ever agree to the relief plan, both Hoover and Nansen became very much disturbed.[106] Finally, on April 14 House approached Clemenceau directly on the issue. House argued that a relief effort in Russia would help to expose the evils of Bolshevism to the world and

[102] *Bullitt Mission,* 89, 91.

[103] Hoover's letter to Wilson cited above. To compare Bullitt's revision of the Auchincloss-Miller draft with the final reply of the Four, which contained only these two changes, see *Bullitt Mission,* 85–86, 87–89.

[104] *Ibid.,* 90–92.

[105] Bullitt a week earlier had apparently endeavored to get some sort of a message to the Soviet leaders through communist agents in Stockholm. On April 15 Minister Morris in Sweden, referring to a letter from Bullitt dated April 4 (not found in the records), cabled cryptically but not in code: "Your friend is pleased to place himself entirely in hands of the person you mention in your letter and also agrees entirely with his plan." As might be imagined, this aroused a good deal of annoyed curiosity among the American secretariat. Harrison Papers, Acquisition 9611, Box 102, Bullitt file.

[106] Their concern is reported in Lansing Papers, Desk Diary, April 13, 1919; McCormick Diary, April 14.

thereby weaken the Bolshevik cause: ". . . if Russia could be opened up in some way to give the people a chance to look at conditions there, no one would desire to bring about similar conditions in their own countries." [107] Clemenceau agreed and promised to sign the reply to Nansen. House commented in his diary, with some justification, if not much modesty:

> The reason I get along with Clemenceau better than the President does is that in talking of such matters as this Russian Question, the President talks to him as he would to me, while I never think of using the same argument with Clemenceau as I use with the President. One is an idealist, the other a practical old-line statesman. When I told him [Clemenceau] about Russia and the good it would do the French and the rest of us to open it up, he saw it at once and was willing. If I had told him it was to save life in Russia and to make things easier there for the sick, for the weak and the helpless, it would have had no effect.

The morning of April 16 House asked Auchincloss to deliver to Wilson the proposed reply to Nansen so that Clemenceau could sign it at the meeting of the Council of Four that day. Wilson agreed to get Clemenceau's signature but suggested that the reply not be released "until Hoover had had a talk with Pichon and had told Pichon that he, Hoover, would not have any direct dealings with the Bolsheviks." [108] Clemenceau duly signed the reply that day, but it is unlikely that Hoover ever had the suggested discussion with Pichon, who continued to oppose the plan even after Clemenceau had agreed to it.

French suspicions concerning the relief project had already been widely publicized in the French press. Early in April, when news of the proposed plan first leaked out, several French papers charged that in essence the project was simply another attempt to appease the Bolsheviks. In addition, *Le Temps* and the right-wing journals depicted it as a thinly veiled scheme of American, British, and, worst of all, German financial circles to establish their domination of the Russian market and to secure railroad and other concessions from the bankrupt Soviet authorities. Even the liberal and socialist press in France expressed some doubts concerning the motives and feasibility of the plan.[109]

On April 16, the day Clemenceau finally signed the reply to Nansen, Pichon issued a defiant statement to the press which supplied valuable

---

[107] House Papers, Diary, April 14, 1919.
[108] House Papers, Diary, April 16, 1919; Auchincloss Diary, April 16.
[109] Noble, 290–91; Fisher, 18; Bartlett, 194.

ammunition for the campaign in France against the plan.[110] Pichon's statement was ostensibly a clarification of the French decision to participate in the project; in fact, it was a long and intemperate attack on the whole idea. Pichon, while acknowledging the humanitarian objectives of the plan, declared: "On the other hand, the French government cannot give its support to any step which might invest this tentative with a political character, the result of which would be a moral and material reinforcement of the iniquitous Bolshevik Government, an evident support of its dangerous propaganda and finally, the abandonment and definite loss of the loyal parts of Russia and of the Russians who have remained faithful to the Allies." Pichon went on to pose a number of conditions for French support of the relief project: its limitation to a few large towns, no negotiations by or for the Allies with the Bolsheviks, Nansen to act only in his own name or on behalf of the neutrals, and equitable distribution of food among all social classes under the strict control of Nansen and his commission with the aid of the local population and Russian "cooperatives" and without the intervention of the Bolshevik government. Pichon added that the plan would not put an end to the Red terror, upon which the Bolsheviks relied to stay in power. He concluded by criticizing the idea of an armistice, maintaining that it would not be accepted in good faith by either side; moreover, it would weaken the position of the Russians faithful to the Allies and would result in delivering "the rest of Russia to massacre, oppression and Bolshevik anarchy in a short time."

Once Clemenceau had accepted the reply to Nansen, Hoover, stung by the attacks on the plan and on the motives of its sponsors by Pichon and by the French press, and perhaps anxious to protect himself before conservative opinion in Europe and at home, proposed that a public statement on Bolshevism be released simultaneously with the reply of the Four to Nansen. This statement was to be along the lines suggested by Hoover in the third recommendation of his letter of March 28 to President Wilson.[111] The statement Hoover drew up, however, contained a more outright denunciation of Bolshevism, as well as a clearer expression of the hope that relief to Soviet Russia would serve to undermine the Bolshevik regime.[112] While reaffirming the humanitarian objectives of the plan, Hoover emphasized that it would also give the states surrounding Soviet Russia a respite from Bolshevik aggression; would illuminate the real character of Bolshevik rule, thereby weakening

---

[110] For the text of the statement, see Fisher, 19–21.
[111] See pp. 248–49 above.
[112] For Hoover's draft statement, dated April 18, see House Papers, Correspondence Files, Hoover.

its appeal to peoples outside of Russia; would save the bourgeois classes from extermination; and would undercut recruiting for the Red Army, which, Hoover claimed, was based on the lure of food. Finally, Hoover argued, starvation existed in Russia because of the Bolsheviks' "fool idea that processes of production and distribution can be broken down in a country and the population still live." Hoover added that the Bolshevik experiment had been a total failure and concluded: "Under the plan of a Neutral Commission for feeding Russia there is no intention of recognizing the men whose fingers are even today dripping with the blood of hundreds of innocent people of Odessa."

House heard of Hoover's proposed statement the night of April 18. He was alarmed and annoyed by it, commenting in his diary the next day:

> It is the most foolish thing I have known Hoover to do yet, although I am somewhat accustomed to an occasional "brain storm" from him. We have been for several weeks trying to get this Russian matter in the shape that it now is and he has helped as much as anyone. Just as soon, however, as we have it signed by the President and the three Prime Ministers, Hoover gives out a statement which would absolutely destroy any chance of its success. Whether his action is because of his inordinate desire for publicity I do not know.[113]

The morning of April 19 House expressed his displeasure to Hoover; according to House, Hoover finally agreed not to put out such a statement. That afternoon, however, Hoover wrote House, enclosing an article from the morning edition of *L'Echo de Paris* which attacked the relief plan and which alleged that the French Foreign Office had refused to support it despite Clemenceau's acceptance of the reply to Nansen.[114] Hoover added: "I also learned that statements went out to the United States from French sources of the same import in an attempt to create an atmosphere that either I or the Americans were supporting the Bolsheviks. Our New York office also telegraphs over, apparently disturbed by the reaction that has been created." Hoover declared that although he did not object to making a personal sacrifice in order to obtain the larger objectives in view, he thought it only fair to the American people to "define our stand on Bolshevism. While I regard the parlor operators who are coquetting with this fire with contempt, I do realize that we stand to further the forces of disorder in the United States if we stand still." Hoover offered to make the proposed public statement in his own name, adding that he doubted that such a declaration would lead the

[113] House Papers, Diary, April 19, 1919.
[114] Letter from Hoover to House, April 19, House Papers.

Bolsheviks to oppose the relief plan since no enemy "resents a frank statement of opposition." After asking House to reconsider his opposition to issuing the statement, Hoover concluded:

I wrote the document in question after three days and nights of careful consideration as to all of its bearings and I have now again had an opportunity to think it over, also with a view of what has happened since and with a large knowledge of certain forms of publicity. I have made certain alterations in the text which relieves everyone else of responsibility. . . . It is possible that the whole mission will be driven into making a defensive statement within the next three days, whereas if I make an offensive statement now we will never have to do so. Even if this is not the case, unless we disarm the parlor operators we will have to answer for a stimulus to this clap trap over the next twelve months.

House did not change his mind, however, believing that Hoover had amended the proposed statement very little and that it would still be most damaging. House showed the statement to the other commissioners and to the president, "and they were unanimous in the opinion that it was a childish thing to do. The President asked me to say to Hoover that he hoped he [Hoover] would not make any statement at the moment because it would be impossible for him to disassociate himself either from our government or the governments of the Allies." In a letter of April 20 House conveyed the president's wishes to Hoover.[115] Nevertheless, the next day Hoover, paying no attention to the president, released a statement to the press in his own name.[116] It contained several paragraphs taken from his draft of April 18, although the most direct reference to the anti-Bolshevik results to be expected under the plan were dropped.

While this behind-the-scenes contretemps was taking place, efforts to implement the plan were going forward. On April 17 the reply of the Four to Nansen was released, and the same day Hoover and Nansen prepared a message from Nansen to Lenin, incorporating Nansen's letter of April 3 to the Four and their reply, and adding: "I would be glad to hear from you in this matter at your earliest convenience. I may add that the neutral organization which I propose offers its services in this cause without any remuneration whatever, but of course its expenditures in the purchase and transportation of supplies must be met by the Soviet

[115] House Papers, Diary, April 19, 1919; letter from House to Hoover, April 20, 1919.
[116] Text in Fisher, 21–22.

government." [117] The French, however, refused to dispatch the message on the ground that they could not communicate with a government which they did not recognize.[118] Lloyd George declined to send it through British channels, arguing that to do so would give it the appearance of a project sponsored by the Allies rather than by neutrals.[119]

After a delay of several days Hoover asked the Dutch government to transmit Nansen's message to Moscow, but the Dutch authorities pleaded that they were not in direct communication with Soviet Russia. Bullitt then urged that it be sent through the American consul in Helsingsfors; if necessary, Pettit, who was still in Finland, could take it to Petrograd himself.[120] Meanwhile Nansen had asked the Norwegian government to send the communication to Russia by courier, but, because of Finnish military operations along the Russian frontier, the courier was unable to reach Petrograd. In desperation Nansen decided on May 9 to go to Norway, intending, if necessary, to proceed on to Russia to deliver the message to Lenin personally. In the meantime the cable had been dispatched from Berlin at the request of the Norwegian government, and the Soviet reply, received by wireless through Swedish and Danish stations, was awaiting Nansen when he reached Norway.[121] The spectacle of the Allied heads of government solemnly endorsing a plan which, besides its humanitarian aspects, provided for considerable interference in Russia's economic and political life, and then being unable or unwilling even to transmit the message to the Bolsheviks reflected the illusory nature of the whole affair and boded ill for its success.

Reaction to the Hoover-Nansen Plan

The proposal for a relief effort in Russia met with a mixed reception. Even within the American delegation there was no unanimity, some endorsing the plan, others supporting Bullitt's position that the original Soviet proposals should be acted on, or at the very least that the relief approach should be considered as merely supplemental to the main objective of reaching a settlement with the Soviet government. As Grew noted at the time in a letter to Washington: "The Commission and personnel thereof has been considerably torn with dissension on this sub-

---

[117] Nansen, 26.

[118] *Ibid.;* Hoover, *Ordeal of Wilson,* 123.

[119] Undated memorandum from Close, one of Wilson's secretaries, to the president, containing Hoover's telephoned report of Lloyd George's views. Wilson Papers, Series VIIIA, Box 70.

[120] Bullitt Papers, Memorandum to Herter, April 24, 1919; letter to Ira Morris, American minister to Sweden, May 6, 1919.

[121] Nansen, 28; *1919, Russia,* 111; Lenin, *Sochineniia,* XXI, 792 n. 124.

ject." [122] Grew himself favored the Hoover-Nansen plan, believing that "Bolshevism feeds on hunger and armed opposition—food will lead it to a natural death, arms will make it grow."

Similar views were held among other circles at the conference and among the Anglo-American journalistic corps in Paris. In addition, some observers felt that Bolshevism bred on isolation, as well as hunger; a relief program would not only fill empty Russian stomachs but would also be an avenue for the introduction into Russia of outside influences and Western contacts, which would help to counteract or at least to ameliorate Bolshevik doctrine.[123] Even some of those strongly opposed to Bolshevism welcomed the plan, believing that at last an inexpensive and morally defensible method of putting an end to Bolshevism had been discovered, ". . . and the new proposal became immensely fashionable for a short time in peace conference circles. Everyone talked as if the real antidote to Bolshevism had been found." [124]

The White Russian leaders in Paris, though very much against any sort of dealings with the Bolsheviks, were at first reluctant to criticize the relief proposal. According to Nansen, he met with members of the Russian Political Conference several times in early April to discuss the plan. While far from enthusiastic about it, they felt "that they ought not to oppose an attempt of that nature to carry relief to their necessitous countrymen." [125] Their dislike of the plan gradually increased, however —undoubtedly under French prodding—and when news of Kolchak's victories began to reach Paris, and after the reply of the Four had laid down the precondition of a cessation of hostilities, the White Russian leaders undertook a vigorous campaign against the Hoover-Nansen proposal. They maintained that the plan would give moral and material assistance to the Bolsheviks just when the Soviet government was on the point of collapsing in the face of internal difficulties and of Kolchak's advance.[126] On April 23 Chaikovsky told Oscar Straus that the Bolsheviks would simply divert the food to the supply kitchens of the Red Army, at the same time propagandizing the program in such a way as to make people think that the Allies had recognized the Soviet regime.[127]

Finally, on May 4 the Russian Political Conference issued an official protest against the plan signed by L'vov, Sazonov, Chaikovsky, and

[122] Grew, I, 385.
[123] Huddleston, 164.
[124] Beadon, 98.
[125] Nansen, 27.
[126] See, for example, Bakhmetev's opposition reported in Lansing Papers, Desk Diary, April 19, 1919.
[127] Straus, 422–23. See also a public statement by Chaikovsky carried in the New York Times on April 23 and cited in Fisher, 18.

Maklakov.[128] The White Russian leaders, while expressing gratitude for the generous offer of the Allies to assist the Russian people and appreciation for the humanitarian purposes and brotherly spirit motivating the sponsors of the plan, warned that if, as seemed likely, the food fell into the hands of the Bolsheviks, the relief program would only serve to prolong the life of the Soviet dictatorship, thereby increasing the suffering of the Russian people. Feeding the Russian people, it was argued, was not a solution to the Russian question; what was needed was to liberate Russia from the Bolsheviks, and nothing should be permitted to interfere with the struggle for that goal.

In Omsk the Hoover-Nansen plan was greeted with hostility. Riding a wave of military success, Kolchak had no intention of agreeing to an armistice. On May 17 Kolchak and his ministers discussed a telegram from Sazonov in Paris—apparently sent in mid-April, before the Russian Political Conference had decided to oppose the relief program—which urged Kolchak "to meet halfway the proposal of Nansen to organize help to the starving Russian people." [129] All agreed that the plan would only strengthen the prestige of the Bolsheviks and that the supplies would probably be used to feed the Red Army. It was decided to send a negative response to Sazonov.

The first official Soviet reaction to the Hoover-Nansen plan, based on news reports of the proposal, was indirectly expressed, but was clearly hostile and defiant in tone. On April 18 Chicherin appealed by radio to the workers of the Allied countries to protest against the blockade of Russia.[130] After reviewing the history of foreign intervention in Russia, Chicherin referred to Lloyd George's speech of April 16 and declared that the Allies were pretending to renounce the policy of intervention, but, in fact, they were planning to pursue it by other, indirect means—by sending aid of every kind to anti-Bolshevik forces, both within Russia and along her borders. In addition, they were continuing and strengthening the blockade heedless of the suffering it caused the Russian people. "While all this is taking place, they would like to persuade us and to make you believe that they are so sincerely anxious to help us in our misfortune that they are preparing to send food to the hungry people of Soviet Russia." Despite the duplicity and intrigues of the Allied governments, Chicherin asserted, Soviet Russia would hold out. It needed help, however, from the Allied workers, who should compel their governments to stop attacking Soviet Russia and sending aid to its enemies.

[128] Text in *1919, Russia,* 110.
[129] Vologodsky Diary, 28.
[130] Degras, *Soviet Documents,* I, 150–54.

Chicherin concluded with the cry: "Lift the blockade! That is the only way to put an end to famine in Russia."

On May 4 Nansen's message to Lenin finally reached Moscow. Lenin asked Chicherin to draft a reply which would "unmask" the policies of the Allied leaders.[131] This reply, reviewed by Lenin, was dated May 7 but was not received in Paris until May 15. It was long and prolix, half florid propaganda against the Allies and the anti-Bolshevik movement, and half serious discussion of the relief proposal.[132] The note, addressed to Nansen, expressed appreciation for the humanitarian objectives of the plan and gratitude for the help proffered. However, Chicherin maintained, the terrible sufferings of the Russian people were solely the result of the Allies' inhuman blockade and of the wars forced on Soviet Russia against her will. Left in peace, the Soviet government could restore production and would soon not only not need aid but would be able to export foodstuffs. Moreover, Nansen's "benevolent intentions . . . have been mixed up by others with political purposes . . . [and] have been fundamentally disfigured by the governments of the Associated Powers." This, Chicherin explained, occurred when the Council of Four laid down the precondition of an armistice: ". . . military operations which obviously have in view the changing of external or internal conditions of the involved countries belong wholly to the domain of politics, and likewise cessation of hostilities which means preventing the belligerent who has every reason to expect successes from obtaining them is also a purely political act." Nevertheless, the note went on, the Soviet government was always ready to enter negotiations with the Allies for peace, as its reply to the Prinkipo proposal had shown.

After a long and bitter attack on the nature and policies of the White Russian governments, Chicherin finally returned to the point at issue, maintaining that there were really two separate aspects to the plan and, in effect, making two counterproposals. On the one hand, the Soviet government was prepared, and indeed anxious, to discuss directly in a conference with the Allied powers the cessation of hostilities in Russia and the general question of a peaceful settlement designed to end intervention and the civil war. "But it is of course impossible for us to make any concessions referring to these fundamental problems of our existence under the disguise of a presumably humanitarian work." On the other hand, Chicherin continued, the Soviet government welcomed the humanitarian side of the plan and was willing to facilitate Nansen's efforts and

[131] Trush, 197–98.
[132] Text in *1919, Russia*, 111–15.

to pay for relief supplies with Russian goods. Chicherin concluded by asking Nansen to name the time and place of a conference abroad at which Nansen and Soviet representatives could discuss the implementation of relief work in Russia.

Nansen favored meeting Soviet representatives to arrange a relief program, as the Soviet reply had proposed, and so informed Paris. He also telegraphed Chicherin that he was prepared to open discussions in Moscow, if that were desirable, but he would first have to learn the reaction of the powers to the Soviet answer.[133] In Paris Hoover found Chicherin's message not entirely unacceptable: "I believed the reply left a crack open and that much of it was for internal consumption." He attempted to pursue the matter further, discussing the Soviet reply with various members of the conference.[134]

On May 16 the *ad hoc* committee formed by the Council of Four in April to deal with the Nansen scheme met to consider Chicherin's note. The French representative was absent, but Hoover, Cecil, and an Italian representative agreed that Nansen should be instructed at once not to arrange any meeting with the Bolsheviks until the conference had considered the matter further. They also approved a memorandum to the Council of Four on Russian policy, which was apparently drafted by Hoover.[135] This memorandum realistically discussed the major alternatives confronting the Allies and set forth procedures which, if carried out, might have led to a peaceful settlement in Russia. It asserted that in view of the Soviet refusal to stop fighting as specified under the relief plan, but bearing in mind Chicherin's expressed willingness to enter negotiations for a general Russian peace, the Allies really had only two courses open to them: either to decide that, with the Bolsheviks in power, there was no hope for peace in Russia and that the Soviet regime must therefore be smashed, or to proclaim and enforce an armistice in Russia under international supervision, to be followed by a plebiscite. If the first course were elected, the Allies should do their utmost, short of sending troops, to support the anti-Bolshevik groups within and surrounding Soviet Russia, supplying materiel, money, and instructors to all of them. The powers should also break off all relations with the Bolsheviks, including Nansen's. Such a policy "may be the right one," the memorandum commented, "but it undoubtedly involves much further bloodshed and destruction of material wealth."

If the second alternative were adopted, the Allies should establish armistice lines in Russia, require the withdrawal of opposing forces ten

[133] *Ibid.*, 115; Nansen, 33.
[134] Hoover, *Ordeal of Wilson*, 123; see also letter from Hoover to Wilson in the same vein, May 16, 1919. Wilson Papers, Series VIIIA, Box 49, and Fisher, 27.
[135] *1919, Russia*, 115–17.

kilometers, and send an international commission to supervise and enforce the cessation of hostilities. The Allies should then furnish food and supplies to those groups that accepted and cooperated in the armistice, at the same time depriving those that did not of all assistance. The next step would be the election, under the auspices of the League of Nations, of a Russian constituent assembly to determine the future of the country. The memorandum concluded:

> I believe that either of these policies has a fair chance of success, and may be defended by powerful arguments. What is not defensible is a combination of the two: a suggestion that Lenin must cease fighting while we are supplying arms and equipment to Denikin and Koltchak; or, conversely, that Koltchak and Denikin should be encouraged to wage war against Lenin while we are negotiating with the latter to give him economic assistance. Compromises of this kind can only lead to a prolongation of hostilities in Russia, and the spreading in that country of the belief that the Associated Powers cannot be trusted.

On May 20 the Council of Four considered this memorandum and the Soviet reply to Nansen. In the month that had elapsed between approval by the Four of the Hoover-Nansen plan and their consideration of Chicherin's reply, however, news of a radical change in the military situation in Russia had reached Paris, and the attitude of the Allied leaders toward the Russian question had altered considerably as a result. Toward the end of March Kolchak had launched an offensive against the Bolsheviks; at first it met with substantial success. During April reports of Kolchak's victories, coupled with stories of peasant revolts, strikes, and other difficulties within Soviet Russia, led most observers in Paris to conclude that the Bolsheviks' days were numbered and that Kolchak would soon be in Moscow. For example, on April 21 Vance McCormick, the "father" of the Hoover-Nansen plan, referring to the growing strength of the Omsk government and to the complications this posed for the relief project, commented in his diary: "Lenine will not agree to stop fighting for food unless we get anti-Bolshevists to agree to stop also. This is hard on Kolchak as he is winning now. I am going to put this new situation to the President. Unfortunately almost impossible to have a satisfactory talk with the President on this matter on account of other pressing peace terms now concluding." [136] As we shall see in the next chapter, British and American officials actually began, during the latter part of April, to press for recognition of the Omsk government. This period included, however, two of the serious crises of the conference—those over the claims of Italy and of Japan. Only early in

[136] McCormick Diary, p. 72.

May, after compromises on these issues had been reached, after the Covenant of the League of Nations had been revised, and after the Germans had been called to Paris to receive the treaty, did the Council of Four have time to turn once again to the Russian question.

Well before receipt of the Soviet reply to Nansen the heads of government had begun to reconsider their relationship to Kolchak in the light of the widespread reports that the Bolsheviks were on the verge of collapse and that Kolchak might soon be in control of most of Russia. As a result, Chicherin's note and the memorandum of the *ad hoc* committee received only nominal attention when they were discussed on May 20.[137] Wilson and Clemenceau, in agreement on Russia for once, commented that Lenin obviously would not stop fighting unless the Allies cut off aid to the anti-Bolsheviks and forced them to cease hostilities at the same time. In view of Kolchak's successes, no one was disposed to support this course of action. Lloyd George recalled the Allies' obligations to the anti-Bolshevik Russian groups they had helped call into being. Wilson added that "at least pledges could be exacted for further support" to such groups. This turned the discussion to the conditions which should govern the powers' relations with Kolchak. The Council of Four never referred again to the Hoover-Nansen plan or to the Soviet reply to this offer.

One can speculate that if the reply of the Four to Nansen had been promptly dispatched to Lenin, and if, as a result, the Soviet answer had been received and considered two weeks earlier, the efforts of Hoover to pursue the matter further might have had more chance of success.[138] This seems highly unlikely, however. From the beginning, none of the Big Four had been very enthusiastic about the Hoover-Nansen plan; Clemenceau, who had strongly opposed it, apparently had finally acquiesced primarily because, as with the Prinkipo proposal, he wished to avoid any semblance of Allied disunity. It had been accepted by the Council of Four at the insistence of House and Hoover and because at that moment it had seemed a relatively harmless alternative to the extremes either of entering into direct negotiations with the Bolsheviks, as urged by Bullitt, or of giving all-out support to the anti-Bolsheviks, as the interventionists demanded. The Soviet reply aroused little interest because no one of the heads of government was prepared to endorse, in the face of conservative opinion in the West, a conference with the Bolsheviks, as proposed by Chicherin.

[137] *1919, Russia,* 351–52.

[138] Bullitt believed that some Allied officials deliberately obstructed the dispatch of Nansen's message to Moscow because of the news of Kolchak's advances. Letter to Ira Morris, May 6, 1919, Bullitt Papers. Although there is no direct evidence to support this, it is a not implausible supposition.

Despite its unrealistic aspects, the Hoover-Nansen plan, like previous proposals of the conference for dealing with the Bolsheviks, might have served as a first step toward some kind of uneasy accommodation between the Allies and the Soviet regime, with a consequent narrowing of the gulf of bitterness that was steadily forcing Soviet Russia and the West apart. However, when news of Kolchak's successes reached Paris, the Big Four were only too glad to drop the whole matter and to pin their hopes for a solution of the Russian question on the triumph of the anti-Bolshevik forces and the elimination of the Soviet regime.

After a brief, hesitant impulse toward an approach to the Russian problem through relief, the pendulum of conference policy was swinging once again to the anti-Bolshevik side, where it was to remain for many months. The Hoover-Nansen plan was the last attempt by the West to effect a settlement in Russia other than by force until the late fall of 1919, when their "White" hopes, Kolchak and Denikin, had finally failed. Soviet Russia was fully isolated and under siege; a fateful period of unrelieved hostility and rancor in Soviet-Allied relations had set in.

CHAPTER EIGHT

The Partial Recognition
of Kolchak

FROM THE FALL of 1918, when the Allies first seriously considered recognizing an anti-Bolshevik government in Russia, it was acknowledged on all sides, White Russian as well as Allied, that before such a government could be accorded formal recognition three basic questions concerning it would have to be satisfactorily answered: its nature and policies, its stability, and the scope of its authority in Russia. The Allied and White Russian policies discussed in the latter part of this chapter were largely directed to a clarification of the first question. As far as the Omsk government was concerned, Kolchak's military successes in March and April 1919 convinced Allied policy makers that the second question had been disposed of. At the same time the extension of Kolchak's authority as a result of his military advances helped to resolve the third question. There remained, however, two other major anti-Bolshevik centers in Russia, one in the south under General Denikin and one in the north under General Miller. Delicate political negotiations were required to unify these groups under Kolchak. Only when this had been accomplished could the Omsk government be presented to the Allies as deserving of recognition as an all-Russian government.

The Union of Russian Governments

Part of the third chapter related the efforts of Maklakov, in the fall of 1918, to bring the three major anti-Bolshevik governments together in order to strengthen the White Russian case, both for recognition and aid and for representation at the peace conference. Maklakov was partly successful; Denikin nominally recognized the supreme authority of Kolchak in mid-December, while Kolchak, at about the same time, appointed Denikin's adviser on foreign affairs, Sazonov, as concurrently foreign minister of the Omsk government. By then, however, it was too late for these first steps toward a merger of the governments to have any effect on the question of the representation of Russia at the peace talks.

Maklakov, abetted by Sazonov, nevertheless continued his efforts, looking to the day when circumstances might permit a unified White Russian government to make a strong plea for recognition. The Russian Political Conference encouraged negotiations on unification between Kolchak and Denikin and between Kolchak and General Miller in North Russia. A merger between Kolchak and Denikin proved to be the more difficult problem, and its achievement required greater time and effort. Morever, negotiations between these two leaders had begun with a serious setback. One of the most difficult points at issue was how military operations and strategy on their respective fronts should be coordinated. In October 1918 General Alexeev, who was highly respected by both sides, died as he was about to set out from South Russia to carry on negotiations in Omsk for the establishment of military and political cooperation between General Denikin and Admiral Kolchak.

In Paris in late 1918 Maklakov was initiating efforts to bring the two leaders together. At first it looked as if Sazonov himself would be a source of friction. In approaching the question of cooperation between Kolchak and Denikin, Sazonov seemed to assume that the latter would play the dominant role. On December 17 he wired Kolchak directly from Ekaterinodar, the seat of Denikin's government: "We recognize the supreme power assumed by Your Excellency, being convinced that you adhere to the essential principles of the political and military program of the Volunteer Army." [1] Sazonov listed these principles as the reconstitution of Russia, great and undivided, with its political organization to be determined later, but with acceptance of the principle of extensive autonomy for those areas entitled to it by historical or enthnographic reasons; continuation of the struggle against the Bolsheviks to the end; and concordance of the military operations of the Siberian army with the plan of campaign of the Volunteer Army, "and consequently, with that of the Allies, who share our viewpoint and give us great aid."

Subsequently, as we saw in the third chapter, Sazonov took a completely independent stand, declaring himself the sole Russian representative to the peace conference and singling out the Volunteer Army of Denikin as the force in Russia which the Allies should recognize and assist.[2] Much disturbed, Maklakov cabled Sazonov that it was of the utmost importance to avoid declarations which reflected conflict or which

[1] Maklakov Papers, Part II, Packet I, File 5. This message was also transmitted to the United States and apparently to the other Allies. See *1918, Russia*, II, 647.
[2] See p. 71 of ch. three and telegram of December 25, 1918, from Demidov in Athens to Maklakov transmitting Sazonov's declaration. Maklakov Papers, Part II, Packet I, File 10.

might lead to it.[3] He added that an open rift between Kolchak and Denikin would be disastrous for the future reconstitution of Russia. A few days earlier Maklakov had cabled Omsk emphasizing that if recognition were to be won, Kolchak had to strengthen his internal position and also arrange a union of his government with that of Denikin.[4]

After a delay occasioned by difficulties in communication between Ekaterinodar and Omsk, Kolchak wired Denikin on January 10, in response to the latter's nominal recognition of Kolchak's authority on December 17:

> Recognition by you of Supreme Authority which has grown up in Eastern Russia signifies a great step toward full unification, for the achievement of which we are bending all our energies. The basic principles of the political and military program of the Volunteer Army, set out in your telegram are completely shared by me and the government. The community of aims and the deep internal unity between us guarantees the success of our cooperation. Your communication strengthens in me faith in the quick resurrection of united Russia.[5]

This friendly and conciliatory message undoubtedly pleased Sazonov, who had arrived in Paris in early January. In mid-January he accepted, with Denikin's concurrence, Kolchak's offer of the post of foreign minister in the Omsk government and began actively to work for the further unification of the two groups.

He was encouraged in this regard by a telegram from Denikin, dated January 16, welcoming Sazonov's concurrent supervision of the foreign policy of both governments and declaring: ". . . with pleasure we affirm the community of interests and aims between us and Admiral Kolchak. The further development of ties with him under your aegis is our common task, as the Admiral has also recognized." [6] Moreover, only a few days later, in a telegram of January 19 to Sazonov, Kolchak also fully endorsed further efforts to bring the two governments together and went on to propose prompt and precise definition "of the character of the interrelations between the two state centers . . . with complete frankness and directness." Adding that he had already telegraphed Denikin that "the question of recognizing one of them as Supreme Ruler over the other should not present any difficulty," Kolchak declared:

[3] Telegram to Demidov for Sazonov, December 30, 1918, *ibid*.
[4] Telegram of December 20, 1918, to the Ministry of Foreign Affairs, Omsk, *ibid*.
[5] *Ibid.*, Part II, Packet II, File 4.
[6] *Ibid.*, Part II, Packet III, File 11.

This means that I would not hesitate to recognize Ekaterinodar as of leading significance if, upon consideration of the advantage to the nation of such a decision, it seemed preferable to the unification in Omsk of the supreme authority. . . . It seems to us that a declaration now about the unification of the supreme authority would be of the utmost importance. Nevertheless, before receiving exact clarification from you, we do not want to give a general interpretation to your communication concerning the recognition by Denikin of the authority of Kolchak. . . . Perhaps there should be an official act authorizing Denikin to act for the Supreme Ruler in South Russia.[7]

Sazonov, perhaps a little concerned that Denikin might resent being designated as Kolchak's agent in South Russia, replied on January 30, sending Denikin a copy of his reply. Sazonov stressed the importance of completing the unification of the two governments if the Allies were to be persuaded to recognize an all-Russian government. He then proposed that Omsk be the center of a unified government, and Denikin the leader of its armed forces: "Among the Allied governments the impression has been created that unification has already been completed around Omsk. A decision of the question in this way would have definite advantages in our international relations. . . . I have reason to suppose that in event of the establishment of a direct tie between the Omsk and Ekaterinodar centers, the latter would be inclined to recognize Kolchak as Supreme Ruler and General Denikin as Commander-in-Chief of the military forces."[8]

At the prospect of formal consummation of their marriage, however, both White Russian leaders began to draw back. On February 5 Kolchak replied to Sazonov that he recognized the value of unification and that he agreed in principle to the suggested appointment of Denikin as overall commander of the armies; there were, however, several practical difficulties. Military coordination, Kolchak argued, would be essential, both to the success of the unified government and to enable Denikin to fulfill the role of commander-in-chief. Yet this could be effectively realized only if each army kept the other fully informed and if operations were jointly planned—or, best of all, if the two armies could establish a direct link in southeastern Russia.[9]

Although there is no record in Maklakov's files that Denikin commented directly on Sazonov's proposal of January 30, two telegrams dispatched from Ekaterinodar to Omsk at about this time clearly reflected

[7] *Ibid.*
[8] *Ibid.*
[9] *Ibid.*

Denikin's reluctance to subordinate himself fully to Kolchak, as well as the difficulties involved in establishing military coordination between their widely separated forces. On January 16 Denikin reviewed the situation in the south of Russia for the benefit of Kolchak.[10] He reported that a week earlier the forces of the Don and Kuban Cossacks had placed themselves under his command; the Volunteer Army was now in control of all of South Russia from Byelorussia to Transcaspia, except for parts of the Ukraine. Denikin then proposed that to eliminate the possibility of conflicting claims to authority over areas in the southeast of Russia the two governments should agree on a demarcation of their respective zones of control in that region: for example, along a line running from Samara down the Volga to Astrakhan, thence across to the Aral Sea and the eastern border of Bukhara. On February 5 Denikin again wired Kolchak, referring to a telegram from the Siberian army command at Omsk, transmitted through the British, which had "outlined the position on your front, and expressed a desire to discuss coordination of our activities." Denikin said that he had heard through the British that General Miller's Archangel army was not very active and that Kolchak's Orenburg and Ural armies were not meeting with much success. "Under these conditions the conduct of operations by you in the north . . . ought to be changed and the center of power ought to be directed toward the south. . . . A concentration of forces in the south guarantees our quick junction, the rising of all the Cossack Hosts, and the rapid achievement of our common aims." [11]

There is no record of Kolchak's reply to this suggestion, but Denikin's appeal apparently carried little weight with him. Kolchak's spring campaign, planned in consultation with his French and British military advisers, was directed to the west and northwest, not to the south. Undoubtedly Denikin, who was not faring too well against the Red Army, wanted Kolchak to drive southward as much for the support this would lend to the operations of his own Volunteer Army as for any assistance it might be in the formal establishment of a unified White Russian government. But Kolchak and the Allied generals in Omsk were moved by other considerations; to some extent they were attracted to the plan, advocated by Churchill, for linking up the Siberian and North Russian forces as a prelude to a combined advance on Moscow supported and reinforced by the British. Kolchak was especially interested in a direct thrust toward Moscow, which, if successful, would settle decisively the question of who was to exercise supreme power and be recognized as an

---

[10] This cable was repeated to Paris through Athens on February 5. Mel'gunov Papers, Hoover Institution, Stanford, File B6, Part I.
[11] A copy to Paris in Maklakov Papers, Part II, Packet III, File 11.

all-Russian ruler. Even though Kolchak was turned back before Moscow, his early successes on that front led directly to his partial recognition by the Allies, as we shall shortly see.

By mid-February negotiations on unification between Kolchak and Denikin, directly and through Maklakov and Sazonov in Paris, had been going forward for almost three months. The results were negligible: chiefly, some fervent expressions of good intentions on both sides and a vague indication from Denikin that in principle he was prepared to acknowledge Kolchak's supreme authority. When it became clear in February that neither leader was willing to make a formal and definite commitment to unification and that a sharp difference of opinion relating to strategy and control of military operations existed between them, the negotiations were suspended.

As news of Kolchak's victories reached Paris in the beginning of April, however, and as the Allies began to consider the possibility of recognizing the Omsk government,[12] the leaders of the Russian Political Conference decided that the time had come to attempt a final resolution of the question of the unification of the White Russian governments, before it settled itself in the onrush of events. On April 23 Sazonov wired Denikin pressing for action:

> In view of the necessity of clearly strengthening before the Allies the unity of the Russian national movement, internally already unified on its basic aims, . . . the Political Conference invites the separate governments, while preserving the independence demanded by circumstances in the area of practical policy, officially to recognize the unified and supreme authority of the government in Omsk as a Provisional All-Russian National Government. Chaikovsky agrees and is telegraphing to Archangel.
>
> On my part, relying on the telegram sent to Kolchak in December by agreement with you . . . I expressed the conviction that such action would correspond to your views. I ask prompt affirmation considering this step as absolutely necessary in the present situation.[13]

Two weeks later Sazonov cabled Denikin the text of the decree the Archangel government had adopted on April 30 accepting the invitation of the Political Conference and officially recognizing the supreme authority of the Omsk government.[14]

At first these appeals from Sazonov seemed of no avail. On May 2

---

[12] See pp. 287–90 below.

[13] Maklakov Papers, Part II, Packet III, File 11. The first paragraph of the telegram was repeated to Omsk.

[14] Telegram of May 7 to Ekaterinodar, *ibid.*

Neratov, Denikin's foreign affairs adviser in Ekaterinodar, replied that the two leaders had already exchanged letters establishing their identity of interests and aims and had agreed on the necessity for coordinated action. Neratov said nothing about the invitation of the Political Conference and skirted the question of formal recognition, declaring:

> As soon as solid contact is established between the two armies, there will be a meeting between Admiral Kolchak and General Denikin to settle the questions of a single Power and Command and of the unification of their governmental bodies. This settlement will be based on the political importance which the Governments of the South and East of Russia represent at that time, the strategic situation of their armies, and the extent of their respective territories. . . . In other words, this decision will be inspired exclusively by the interests of the Russian state without any regard for personal interests.[15]

Several weeks later, however, apparently as a result of increasing pressure from Paris and perhaps also from his British advisers, Denikin officially recognized Kolchak as "Supreme Ruler of the Russian State and Supreme Commander of the Russian Army" in *prikaz* (order) number 145 of May 20, 1919.[16] Although news of this action did not reach Paris until after the Big Four had decided on May 26 formally to support Kolchak, Sazonov nevertheless warmly welcomed this development, apparently believing that it would help Kolchak win full Allied recognition. On June 22 Sazonov wired Denikin: "The high patriotism of the Volunteer Army had found a clear new expression, which serves as a lasting guarantee of the rapid achievement . . . of the reestablishment of our national unity. Your decision has produced here the very best impression. May the Lord aid you in your further undertakings." [17]

Persuading the North Russian government to subordinate itself to Kolchak proved to be an easier task than that of winning over Denikin, although not without difficulties of its own. Before Kolchak's *coup d'état* of November 1918, Chaikovsky, then the head of the government in North Russia, had expressed his willingness to recognize the Directorate at Omsk as an all-Russian authority. After Kolchak seized power, however, Chaikovsky, who opposed Kolchak's methods and suspected him of reactionary tendencies, refused to subordinate his government to

---

[15] *Ibid.*

[16] Transmitted to Paris in early June and cited in a subsequent *prikaz* of July 3, which ordered the continuation of governmental activity in South Russia on the basis of Denikin's previous decrees and policies, pending receipt of definite instructions from Kolchak. *Ibid.* Both orders are given in translation in United States Department of State, *Russian Series*, No. 3, 1919, pp. 4–5.

[17] Maklakov Papers, Part II, Packet III, File 11.

that of Kolchak.[18] The stand taken by Chaikovsky, who in December went to Paris to participate in the work of the Russian Political Conference, was endorsed in a proclamation of the North Russian government issued on February 2, 1919. It declared that the principal task of the representatives of the Russian governments in Paris was "the solution of the problem of an all-Russian political center." Until this problem were solved, however, the North Russian government reserved the right to continue "to direct the life of the Northern Region." [19]

There the matter rested for two months. As with Denikin's government, Kolchak's rapid advance westward in late March raised again the question of unifying the North Russian and Omsk governments. Moreover, the establishment of contact between North Russian outposts and advance units of the Siberian army in early April made prompt resolution of the issue a matter of some urgency. As a result, General Miller, head of the North Russian government in Chaikovsky's absence, cabled the latter in Paris on April 9, proposing that in principle the northern government agree to merge itself with the Omsk government. Miller pointed out that Kolchak exercized control over more territory in Russia and had greater economic and military resources than any other leader. Miller also suggested that Chaikovsky enter the Omsk Cabinet as soon as the proposed unification were affected. For the moment, however, pending a firmer junction with Kolchak's forces, which would permit the establishment of a common administration, the sovereignty of the North Russian government should be preserved.[20] In reply Chaikovsky urged, on his own behalf and as the opinion of the Russian Political Conference, that the northern government formally recognize Omsk as the provisional all-Russian authority. On the other hand, Chaikovsky strongly endorsed Miller's suggestion that the northern government retain its independent authority for the time being, and he went on to recommend that, even after unification, Omsk should be given only overall military command and the most necessary functions of a central power, with the North Russian government preserving full autonomy on matters of legislative initiative, taxation, and local administration. Finally, Chaikovsky declared that he personally would not enter the Omsk Cabinet, but would withdraw from the North Russian government upon completion of the merger.[21] In short, while Chaikovsky recognized the advantages of presenting a united front to the Allies and felt obliged to fall in with the unification program being advanced by the Political Conference, he

[18] See pp. 71–72 of ch. three.
[19] Cited in Strakhovsky, 304.
[20] Maklakov Papers, Part II, Packet III, File 3.
[21] S. P. Mel'gunov, *N. V. Chaikovskii v gody grazhdanskoi voiny (N. V. Chaikovsky in the Years of the Civil War)* (Paris, 1929), 212.

was reluctant to give up completely the independence enjoyed by the North Russian government, and he was still suspicious of the orientation of Kolchak's government.

As we saw earlier, the Political Conference decided at this time to invite the governments of Denikin and of North Russia officially to recognize Kolchak.[22] On April 30 the North Russian government decreed its recognition of the Omsk government, but reserved for itself "the liberty of action in practical matters demanded by present conditions until our complete merger." [23] In the middle of June Kolchak sent an acknowledgment welcoming "the wise and patriotic action of the northern government" and recognizing its "liberty of action in practical matters." Kolchak added that the decrees and laws of the local government would remain in force for the present and that detailed instructions would follow.[24] After receiving this message, the government of North Russia decided to issue all its orders and decrees in the name of the Provisional All Russian Government and to establish formal liaison with Omsk in the person of Prince Kourakin, who had departed for Siberia in April. A few days later Kolchak officially appointed General Miller commander-in-chief of all Russian forces on the northern front.[25] Formal unification of the two governments was complete although the prospect of an actual merger rapidly dimmed as Kolchak's forces were driven back across Siberia in the summer of 1919; in practice, General Miller ruled independently and increasingly autocratically.[26]

General Yudenich, the White Russian military leader who subsequently formed an anti-Bolshevik army and launched an attack on Petrograd from Estonia, was in early 1919 still in Scandinavia trying to raise money and to win support for his venture. Since he controlled no Russian territory and was without much political backing, he readily acknowledged Kolchak's supreme authority.[27] Thus, after prolonged

---

[22] For the invitation to the North Russian government, see telegram from Maklakov to Miller, April 26, 1919, in M. Svechnikov, "Soiuznicheskaia interventsiia na severe Sovetskoi Rossii" ("Allied Intervention in the North of Soviet Russia"), *Kto Dolzhnik?*, Annex 6, p. 469.

[23] Telegram of May 3 from Miller to Kolchak, Mel'gunov, 212–13.

[24] Kolchak's telegram is paraphrased in a cable from the American chargé at Archangel to Washington, June 20, *1919, Russia,* 633.

[25] Telegram from the American chargé to Washington, June 25, 1919, *ibid.,* 634.

[26] In the middle of July the North Russian Cabinet dissolved itself and handed over all power to General Miller, ostensibly for "a more uniform system of government and closer collaboration with the supreme authority." In reality General Miller was now virtually dictator in the north, a development which much alarmed Maklakov in Paris. Mints, 218–19, and telegram from Maklakov to Miller, July 29, in *Kto Dolzhnik?*, Annex 9, pp. 474–75.

[27] See a report from Peter Struve in Helsingfors, February 14, 1919, cited in Nabokov, 294.

discussion, and largely as a by-product of Kolchak's military successes, all the major Russian anti-Bolshevik centers had recognized the supreme authority of the Omsk government by the end of May 1919. The success of the unification effort, as we shall see, influenced the decision of the Big Four to assist Kolchak very little. The Allied statesmen wanted to know how soon Kolchak would be in Moscow and how democratic he was—not how many other White Russian groups acknowledged his rule. At the same time those Allied and White Russian leaders who were urging that Kolchak be recognized were now able to depict him as the head of an all-Russian anti-Bolshevik movement; if his military position had not been so sharply reversed, the unification of the White Russian governments around him would have significantly strengthened the case for his official recognition by the Allies at a later date.

The American Dilemma

By the end of May the Council of Four had decided to extend support to Kolchak short of recognition, on certain conditions. The path leading to this decision was long and tortuous, especially for the Americans. As far back as the spring of 1918 President Wilson had expressed an interest in finding a government in Russia which he felt he could encourage and assist. On April 18 of that year he wrote Lansing asking for full information on "the nuclei of self-governing authority" that were springing up in Siberia. "It would afford me a great deal of satisfaction to get behind the most nearly representative of them, if it can indeed draw leadership and control to itself." [28] In view of the number of weak and competing groups in Siberia, however, Wilson did not pursue the matter further at that time.

When, in the fall of 1918, two of the stronger anti-Bolshevik centers in Siberia merged to form the Directorate, the question of recognizing a Russian government began to be seriously considered in Allied and American circles. In late October the British Cabinet approved de facto recognition of the Directorate, but implementation of this decision was suspended when the Directorate was overthrown a few weeks later by Admiral Kolchak.[29] The French Foreign Office was sympathetic to the program of the Directorate and to its request for recognition, but believed that the stability of the government was not well enough established to permit official French recognition. Presenting its views in Washington, the French government suggested that if the Directorate were able to reorganize the anti-Bolshevik armies in Siberia and to establish a system of taxation, and if it showed signs of being based on

[28] Baker Papers, Series IA, Box 11.
[29] Churchill, *Aftermath*, 165; Nabokov, 276–77.

the consent of the people, the Allies might then consider its recognition.[30] In the interim, the Allies should keep in close touch with the Directorate and lend it moral and financial assistance. Lansing replied to the French, and also to Bakhmetev, who had presented the case for recognition of the Directorate to Lansing, that while the United States was sympathetic to Russian efforts to create a government protecting the rights of the individual and performing Russia's international obligations, the American government could not yet recognize the Directorate.[31] Lansing added to the French that the United States also wished to keep in touch with the Directorate, but that it could not join the French in promising moral and material assistance to that government. Although America was glad to render economic aid to the Russian people as a whole, "it is not yet in a position to lend definite support to any movement or group of leaders." This stand was in accord with Wilson's general policy on recognition, i.e., that no government should be recognized that was not based on the will of the people.

As Kolchak established his authority in Siberia and reorganized the government and army at Omsk, French and British diplomats increasingly urged that he be encouraged and concretely supported. With a slight time lag, the senior American diplomat in Siberia, Consul-General Harris at Omsk, followed their lead. In early December Harris reported that Kolchak was growing stronger and that the situation was much improved: "It would appear that the English and French representatives are inclined to favor Kolchak. It is possible [I] may eventually recommend recognition too, without committing ourselves, for the reason that an effort is actually being made to do the best possible under most trying and adverse circumstances." [32] In January the British sent a message to Kolchak intended to encourage his military efforts and to strengthen his hand politically in Siberia. The British high commissioner at Omsk, Sir Charles Eliot, declared: ". . . His Majesty's Government desire to express their warm sympathy with every effort to establish a free Russian Government on the basis of public confidence." [33] The French sent a similar assurance of sympathy and support and congratulated Kolchak on his nominal union with Denikin.[34]

A recommendation from Harris in late December that the United

[30] Letter from Jusserand, French ambassador to Washington, to Lansing, October 15, 1918, *1918, Russia,* II, 412–13.
[31] Letters from Lansing to Bakhmetev, October 17, and to Jusserand, November 5, 1918, *ibid.,* II, 413, 425.
[32] Undated telegram from Harris to Washington, received December 7, 1918, *ibid.,* II, 455–56.
[33] Cited in a memorandum on Siberia by J. D. Gregory, December 1919, British Foreign Office, *Documents,* III, 709–10.
[34] Reported in a telegram from Harris, January 24, 1919, *1919, Russia,* 327–28.

States join the European Allies in a publicly announced policy of friend-
liness and assistance to Kolchak, short of recognition, led to a telegraphic exchange between Polk and Lansing on the attitude the United
States should adopt toward the Omsk government.[35] At first Lansing
was sympathetic to Harris's suggestion; he proposed to Polk on January
9 that, without recognizing Kolchak or committing the United States to
an extensive military undertaking, the Allied and American governments
should declare that they wished, while refraining from interference in the
internal affairs of Siberia, to give the existing government economic and
financial assistance and military aid until all of Russia were united under
a central and representative government. In reply Polk renewed a suggestion he had made a few days earlier—that the president issue a declaration defining the United States attitude toward Bolshevism and toward
the Soviet government; he also asked Lansing how far the Allies were
prepared to go in assisting anti-Bolshevik groups and what funds the
American government could draw on to finance military supplies to
Kolchak.[36]

For the moment the matter died at this point. Wilson, engrossed with
the possibility of getting the Bolsheviks and other Russians together in a
conference and, in Siberia, with securing Japanese and British adherence
to the American plan for supervision of the railways, was not interested
in Polk's suggestion, and Lansing found little support elsewhere in the
American delegation for a program of encouraging and aiding Kolchak.[37] Moreover, at this time other circles in the American government were definitely opposed to assisting Kolchak. Arthur Bullard, who
had headed the operations in Russia of the Committee on Public Information and who was a friend of Colonel House, advised the latter several times in December and January against recognizing Kolchak.
Bullard feared that the admiral was surrounded by and dependent on
reactionary elements.[38] General Graves, commander of the American
expeditionary force in Siberia, had consistently interpreted the powers'
declaration of noninterference in Russian affairs issued at the time of the

[35] Harris's telegram of December 27 embodying this recommendation was transmitted to the American Commission in Paris for comment on January 2, 1919.
Ibid., 322.

[36] *Ibid.*, 323, 325; Polk's earlier suggestion is in a telegram to Lansing of
January 6, *ibid.*, 3.

[37] See p. 98 of ch. four.

[38] Memorandum of November 28, 1918, sent to House on December 7, Arthur
Bullard Papers, Firestone Library, Princeton University, Box 13; and telegram of
January 23, 1919, from Toyko, *1919, Russia,* 327. See also telegram from Washington to Paris, January 6, transmitting a report of the American journalist Carl
Ackerman, dated January 2, which opposed Kolchak's government as undemocratic and dominated by reactionaries. Bullard Papers, Box 13. On the telegram is
a penciled note by Auchincloss: "Colonel should read this."

Siberian intervention as strictly as possible. He refused to send American troops into western Siberia and was most distrustful of Kolchak's capabilities and intentions. For example, in a report to the War Department on December 28, 1918, which Secretary Baker forwarded to Wilson on March 3, 1919, Graves strongly criticized the autocratic nature of Kolchak's rule and doubted the ability of Kolchak to stand without the support of Allied troops.[39]

In the meantime, the leaders of the White Russian movement abroad continued to press for recognition of the Omsk government. In *aides-mémoire* to the Allies on January 6 and 10, the Russian Political Conference set forth the growing strength of Kolchak and urged that his government be recognized and its representatives be seated at the peace conference.[40] As we saw in the third chapter, the Russians were not seated, and within two weeks Wilson and Lloyd George dismayed the anti-Bolshevik groups by inviting them to meet with Soviet representatives on the Prinkipo Islands.

In mid-February, however, as soon as it was clear that the Prinkipo project was dead, the White Russian diplomats initiated fresh efforts to persuade the Allies that an anti-Bolshevik Russian government should be recognized. On February 19 Bakhmetev presented a memorandum to House which couched the White Russian argument in new terms designed to appeal to liberals in the West. After asserting that the investigation of Russian conditions envisaged under the Prinkipo proposal could just as well be carried out through the activity of the Allied representatives in Russia and through consultation with the agents of the anti-Bolshevik governments assembled in Paris, Bakhmetev suggested that the Allies should in any case not support a particular group or party in the Russian struggle; instead they should announce that the reconstitution of Russia could only be based on a clear program of democratic principles—such as the calling of a constituent assembly, distribution of land to the peasants, and liberal treatment of a minority nationalities. The Allies should then give their full backing to whatever Russian elements were willing to commit themselves to such a program.[41] In a letter to House on March 11, Bakhmetev further developed this argument. He added that such a stand on the part of the powers would serve to

[39] Letter from Baker to Wilson, March 3, 1919, enclosing Graves' report, Wilson Papers, Series VIIIA, Box 22.
[40] *Peace Conference*, I, 275–77.
[41] Memorandum from Bakhmetev to House, House Papers, Correspondence Files, Bakhmetev. The memorandum is undated, but on the basis of internal evidence and of a notation in House's diary of an interview with Bakhmetev on February 19, it seems likely that Bakhmetev presented the memorandum to House on that date.

eliminate reactionary or anarchic tendencies in Russia and would pave the way for cooperation between the Russians and the minority nationalities.

It is difficult to determine when the Russian Political Conference first decided on this new approach to the Allies. As early as the fall of 1918 the White Russian leaders had recognized the importance of reassuring the Allies on at least one point of special interest to the latter: on November 21 Kolchak's government had declared that it recognized and would fulfill all of Russia's domestic and foreign financial obligations as soon as a central Russian authority had been established.[42] This, however, was a fairly obvious point; more subtle and, in the long run, more effective was the idea that the anti-Bolshevik movement should associate itself with the democratic principles and aims espoused by the Western Allies. This concept undoubtedly emerged in part from the uneasiness Maklakov and Bakhmetev felt over Kolchak's political orientation and methods.[43] In part it probably stemmed from their awareness of the suspicion with which many at Paris, particularly some members of the American and British delegations, viewed the Russian Political Conference and the White Russian movement as a whole; most liberals were convinced that reactionary political forces were dominant among the anti-Bolshevik groups. As we saw in the third chapter, Maklakov did his best to make the Political Conference representative of a wide range of anti-Bolshevik opinion, and particularly to include in it those standing for "democratic" tendencies in Russian political life. Finally, the new strategy toward the Allies was probably partly the result of pressures exerted on the Political Conference by these same "democratic" elements in the emigration, both within and outside the circles of the Political Conference.

In any case, Bakhmetev's appeal to House in mid-February was soon followed by a policy recommendation from the Russian Political Conference to the White Russian governments that the whole anti-Bolshevik movement "democratize" itself. In a circular telegram of March 5 to Admiral Kolchak, General Denikin, and General Miller, the Political Conference warned that "democratic ideas" were significantly affecting the work of the peace conference in general and the questions of recognizing and giving aid to an anti-Bolshevik Russian government in particular.[44] According to the Political Conference, the Allies' attitude toward the Russian problem was much influenced "by the degree of democracy of our governments and of the Political Conference. . . .

[42] Telegram from Omsk to Bakhmetev in Washington, November 29, 1918, published in Department of State, *Russian Series, 1919,* No. 3, p. 2.

[43] See p. 66 of ch. three.

[44] Maklakov Papers, Part II, Packet IV, File 2. The copy in the Maklakov Papers is undated, but a copy cited in Mel'gunov, 103–04, is dated March 5.

Any shadow of the old Russia inspires distrust. The ghosts of social and political reaction tend to highlight and exaggerate doubts about the true democracy of the new national Russia." In these circumstances, it was essential to establish a democratic basis for the reconstitution of Russia as soon as possible, perhaps by promptly electing, in each anti-Bolshevik region, representatives to a future all-Russian constituent assembly. Granted the difficulties under present conditions of doing this, the Political Conference nevertheless wanted to know whether the various governments believed it possible to hold such elections, bearing in mind that the elections would be designed to strengthen the position of the governments, not to interfere with the prosecution of the struggle against the Bolsheviks nor to disturb existing lines of authority. In the interim, the Conference urged, the White Russian leaders should encourage participation in governmental activity by public organizations and social groups as a step in the development of local organs of self-government.[45]

At about this time the British Foreign Office began to urge that the Allies adopt a clear-cut and coordinated policy of supporting Kolchak. In a note presented to the American government on March 1, the British maintained that, with agreement reached on the supervision of the Siberian railroads, the position and purpose of the Allies in Siberia should now be more clearly defined.[46] While awaiting a decision in Paris as to the policy to be followed by the Allies respecting the Soviet government, and in the face of the disruptive tactics of certain Russian groups in Siberia, such as that led by Semenov, the Allies should do everything possible to increase the strength and efficiency of Kolchak's government. Would the American government accept and support such a policy?

In reply the State Department noted its sympathy with the Omsk government but declared that the United States was not "disposed to afford it formal recognition."[47] The United States would, however, continue to support the joint Allied effort to reorganize and to operate efficiently the Siberian railways, "which it is believed will make possible the transport of needed supplies." This equivocal answer did not satisfy those in the American government who favored outright support to Kolchak, if

[45] Miliukov held a contrary view of the situation. In a memorandum on Russian policy prepared at the request of Charles Crane and, according to Miliukov, delivered to Wilson by Crane in February 1919, Miliukov argued that the first job of Kolchak and Denikin was to restore order. They should not be asked to institute internal policies that might weaken their military efforts; a liberal regime could be established as soon as order had been restored. The text of the memorandum is given in Paul Miliukov, *Russia and England* (London, 1930), 45–51. Miliukov's memorandum was not found in the Wilson Papers.

[46] Text of the note in *1919, Russia*, 329–30.

[47] The American reply is cited in Unterberger, 151, from a telegram from Paris to Washington on April 1 found in the Department of State files in the National Archives.

not his formal recognition, and they continued to press his case.[48] At just this juncture, moreover, events in Siberia itself made it necessary for the American leaders to reassess their policies in Siberia and toward Kolchak.

In eastern Siberia reactionary Cossack leaders, encouraged by the Japanese, were acting as minor warlords and were taking repressive measures against local inhabitants who opposed their actions.[49] On March 8 the State Department instructed Consul-General Harris to tell the Omsk government frankly that such incidents might "have a most unfortunate effect upon public opinion in this country and very seriously embarrass the support which the United States is now lending the authorities in Siberia in the shipment of supplies, including military equipment, bank notes, and railway materials." [50] At the same time Polk asked the senior American diplomatic, military, and railway officials in Siberia to pool their views on the situation in that area.[51]

The disturbances in eastern Siberia also helped to bring to a head a growing conflict over policy between General Graves, on the one hand, and the Japanese military authorities and British General Knox, one of Kolchak's military advisers, on the other. General Graves had consistently adhered to a position of strict neutrality in Russia's internal quarrels, refusing to support any faction, including that of Kolchak, over any other, including the Bolsheviks. As a result, General Knox charged Graves with sympathy for the Bolsheviks and with failure to back the forces of law and order in Siberia, while the Japanese complained that General Graves not only would not support punitive actions by their own units and by the Russian authorities against those—allegedly Bolsheviks—who threatened the security of the region, but he even remonstrated against such actions. Finally, in early March both Roland S. Morris, American ambassador to Japan on temporary detail in Siberia, and General Graves himself reported that the issue was approaching a showdown and requested instructions as to what course the American government wished them to pursue. On March 13 Polk cabled Lansing and McCormick in Paris seeking their advice. Polk added that personally he believed that General Graves should be instructed to exert his influence against the forces of reaction and "to use his good offices to prevent armed conflict between factions." General Graves should at the

[48] Ibid., 151–52.
[49] See reports from General Graves and from American diplomats in Siberia at the end of February and beginning of March in 1919, Russia, 468–77.
[50] Ibid., 477–78. See also a telegram from Ughet, the Russian chargé in Washington, to Paris, March 8, reporting the State Department's concern over the situation in eastern Siberia. Maklakov Papers, Part II, Packet III, File 7.
[51] 1919, Russia, 478–79.

same time be authorized to use force, if necessary, to protect the Allied service troops and the local population along the railway.[52]

As a result of this inquiry from Polk, as well as of a growing awareness in Paris of the seriousness of the Siberian situation, first the technical experts and staff members, and then the leaders, of the American peace commission began seriously to consider, toward the middle and end of March, what the United States attitude should be toward the Japanese and toward Kolchak. On March 17 Colonel U. S. Grant, III, the American military representative in the peace conference secretariat, sent Wilson a memorandum suggesting that domestic public opinion would support assistance to the anti-Bolsheviks only if it were clear that the latter represented democratic, not reactionary, forces in Russia. There were, however, hopeful signs that the reconstruction of a liberal orderly Russia was being undertaken by the Russians themselves, and a "beginning has been made in Crimea [sic] under Admiral Kodchak [sic]." [53] At about the same time the American commissioners considered a memorandum on Siberian policy prepared by the delegation's technical experts, but deferred action on it pending clarification from Washington of the extent of American aid to Kolchak.[54] This question had been raised in their minds by Polk's reference to the shipping of military equipment to Siberia in his cable to Consul-General Harris on March 8, which was repeated to Paris.[55] In fact, since the first landings at Vladivostok in August 1918, the State Department had been facilitating shipment of various kinds of supplies to Siberia by the Russian embassy in Washington, which purchased the goods through credits the United States extended the Provisional Government in 1917. In reply to the commissioners' inquiry of March 23 respecting the shipping of supplies to Siberia, the State Department acknowledged this fact, adding: "As you are aware, in our efforts to aid the Czecho-Slovak armies it seemed proper to cooperate in measures to strengthen the Russians who were acting with them." [56]

At this juncture Lansing decided that matters had reached the stage at which the president should be consulted. On March 22 he wrote Wilson enclosing two reports on the policy conflict between Graves and the Japanese authorities in Siberia. One, a dispatch to the Navy Department

---

[52] Polk's telegram, which cites the reports from Morris and Graves, is in *ibid.*, 480–81.

[53] Wilson Papers, Series VIIIA, Box 24.

[54] *Peace Conference,* XI, 128.

[55] See p. 283 above.

[56] Telegram from Paris to Washington, March 23, 1919, and reply, March 27, *1919, Russia,* 331.

from the commander-in-chief of the Asiatic fleet, emphasized the mounting danger of incidents occurring between American and Japanese troops, and warned: "Increasing indications of Japanese intrigue leads to belief that Japanese military party willing to strain relations before sacrificing hope of retaining control of Chinese Eastern railroads and with it territory of eastern Siberia. Doubt whether military government wants war, but its action and reports as stated by Japanese press may arouse popular feeling beyond control of government." [57] The other report was a telegram from General Knox to the British War Office on March 8 criticizing Graves' conduct and asserting that American neutrality only served to increase Japanese influence in the area. During the next few days Lansing discussed the matter with Wilson and secured the president's approval of instructions to General Graves that "the United States favors economic rehabilitation of the country and feels strongly that a policy of political moderation among the several Russian factions is a necessary condition" for the achievement of this goal. General Graves was, therefore, authorized to establish a zone three miles wide on each side of the railways in which "he should exercize definite police power and prevent any disturbance that might interfere with the operation of the railways." [58] The latter instruction was opposed, however, by Polk and by Secretary of War Baker on the ground that it would require sending more troops to Siberia and that it might give the impression that the Allies were attempting to establish a "zone" of political control.[59] Subsequently, the issue of military control and protection along the railways became the subject of prolonged negotiations with the Japanese, lasting until the fall of 1919.[60]

Quite aside, however, from the question of cooperating with the Japanese in guarding the railroads, General Graves' stand in refusing to support repressive actions by various anti-Bolshevik groups against local citizens continued to be strongly criticized by the Japanese, by the British, and finally by Kolchak himself.[61] Moreover, pressures to induce the

[57] Quoted from enclosure in a letter from Lansing to Wilson, March 22, 1919, Wilson Papers, Series VIIIA, Box 27.

[58] These instructions were contained in a telegram from Paris to Washington, April 1, 1919, *1919, Russia*, 552–53. Wilson's approval, provided Secretary of War Baker also approved, was stated in a letter from the president to Lansing, March 28, 1919. Wilson Papers, Series VIIIA, Box 27.

[59] *1919, Russia*, 553–54.

[60] *Ibid.*, 551, 554–603.

[61] For the Japanese position, see Polk's summary of the representations of the Japanese ambassador to Washington, Viscount Ishii. Polk Papers, Diary, April 8, 1919. For British criticism of Graves, see Polk's summary of British complaints in a telegram to Paris, May 9, 1919, *1919, Russia*, 493–94; Lansing's notation of a meeting with Lord Curzon on May 15, when the secretary of state was visiting

American government to abandon its policy of noninterference in Siberia and to assist the anti-Bolsheviks grew steadily as the question of recognizing Kolchak began to be more actively considered in the Allied capitals and at the peace conference. There were suggestions that General Graves be replaced, and on April 19 Sukin, acting head of the Ministry of Foreign Affairs at Omsk, wired Sazonov in Paris that because of the neutral attitude of the Americans and because of their criticism of the government's methods of suppressing "Bolshevik" revolts, Kolchak wished Sazonov to raise with Lansing the possibility of withdrawing American forces from the Far East, "if their policy there is not more clearly and favorably defined." [62] Although Sazonov promptly replied urging Kolchak to proceed cautiously on this matter, since the evacuation of the Americans would stimulate leftist agitation in England for withdrawal of all Allied troops and would remove the restraint that the American presence placed on Japan, the Omsk government nevertheless proceeded to express its dissatisfaction with the American attitude directly to Graves, as well as to Lansing in Paris and to Polk in Washington.[63]

Polk replied sharply that the Omsk government should make every effort to remain on friendly terms with the American authorities in Siberia; its failure to do so might impair the effective operation of the railways and weaken the position of the Omsk government itself. Polk's

London for a few days, Lansing Papers, Desk Diary, May 15, 1919; a subsequent note to Lansing from Curzon, *1919, Russia,* 499–500; and March, 130. For Kolchak's stand, see below.

President Wilson strongly supported Graves. When Lloyd George raised the British objections to Graves in a meeting of the Council of Four on May 14, Wilson retorted that "General Graves was a man of most unprovocative character, and wherever the fault might lie . . . it was not with him." *Peace Conference,* v, 608. General March and Secretary of War Baker also endorsed Graves' policy of noninterference. Polk, who believed that Kolchak should be recognized, was critical of Graves. See his telegram of May 9 cited above and a letter to Lansing on April 17, in which Polk said: "Graves is a useless old woman . . . and so the result is that our men are not as effective as park policemen." Polk Papers, Drawer 78, File 10. For a description of the basic differences between the State Department and the War Department over Siberian policy, see Unterberger, 124–25.

[62] Maklakov Papers, Part II, Packet III, File 2. See also a memorandum from Kolchak's General Staff of April 27, 1919, charging that American interest in the Siberian railways was part of a plan to ensure American economic domination of Siberia to the exclusion of the Japanese. *Vestnik NKID,* No. 9-10 (December 15, 1920), 64–65.

[63] Sazonov's reply of April 29 in Maklakov Papers, Part II, Packet III, File 2; for the representations to Graves, see his report in a telegram to Washington and Paris of May 4, *1919, Russia,* 491–92; for the protest to Lansing, see Bakhmetev's letter to Lansing of May 10, enclosing a telegram from Omsk dated April 24, *ibid.,* 494–96; for the approach to Polk, see his comments in a telegram to Paris, May 9, *ibid.,* 493, and Polk Papers, Diary, May 8, 1919.

warnings were reinforced by those of Sazonov, who cabled Omsk on May 22: "Your message about the role of the American army produced a bad impression. It is extremely important at this time when the question of recognizing the government is being actively discussed not to antagonize the Americans, who are playing a leading role in shaping Allied policy." [64]

In the meantime Kolchak, flushed with victory, was becoming increasingly adamant that the American forces either help him or get out. In early May he declared that he no longer needed the assistance of any foreign armies except to guard the railway lines, and he censured both the Japanese and American armies in Siberia, the former for conducting itself as if it were in a conquered country and for encouraging separatist tendencies in the Maritime Provinces, and the latter because it "consisted of the dregs of the American Army—Jewish immigrants—with a corresponding command and has been only a factor of decay and disorder." [65] On May 17 the Omsk Cabinet discussed Graves' attitude. Sukin urged that they attempt to get along with Graves, but he was overruled by Kolchak, who declared that toleration of the "hands-off" attitude of the Americans was humiliating to Russian national dignity and only served to permit the spread of Bolshevism in Siberia. [66]

The mounting criticism of General Graves was closely connected with the campaign for the recognition of Kolchak being waged by the White Russian leaders abroad and by supporters of the anti-Bolshevik cause in French, British, and American official circles. As a result of Kolchak's successful offensive at the end of March, this campaign was stepped up considerably. At upper levels of the American government those most actively supporting the recognition of Kolchak were Acting Secretary of State Polk in Washington and Vance McCormick in Paris. Polk, who had expressed sympathy with the Omsk government as far back as the fall of 1918 and who had suggested its recognition in January 1919, told General March on April 8 "that the time had now come for recognition," and he reiterated this recommendation on April 10. [67] He was shortly encouraged in this view by a report from the senior American representatives in Siberia whom he had instructed to submit a joint evaluation of the situation there. In a message dated April 2, but which

[64] Maklakov Papers, Part II, Packet III, File 2.

[65] Telegram from Sukin to Sazonov, May 10, quoting a statement by Kolchak, *ibid.* It is not clear from the telegram whether Kolchak's statement was a public declaration or a policy paper for use within the government. Criticism of Jewish members of the American expeditionary force in Siberia as pro-Bolshevik was also made in a telegram from Omsk to Bakhmetev, April 24, 1919, which the latter transmitted to Lansing. *1919, Russia,* 495–96.

[66] Vologodsky Diary, 27–28.

[67] Polk Papers, Diary, April 8, 10, 1919.

apparently did not reach the State Department until April 20, Consul General Harris reported that he and his colleagues, although they did not believe Kolchak to be a great national leader, were convinced that the admiral was "sincerely committed to the good of Russia." [68] Noting that the Omsk government was growing stronger, they recommended that "the Siberian situation would be improved if, after enunciation of satisfactory liberal policies, some form of encouragement, yet not reaching formal recognition as [a] *de facto* government, could be given by the Allied powers to the liberal movement now headed by Kolchak." Although generally endorsing these views, Roland S. Morris, American ambassador to Japan, who had recently returned from a trip to Siberia, emphasized in a separate report that he opposed recognition of the Omsk government since he still entertained doubts as to the permanence of Kolchak's regime.[69]

In Paris, meanwhile, McCormick began to press for the recognition of Kolchak. Although, as we saw in the previous chapter, McCormick had been instrumental in initiating the Hoover-Nansen relief plan, House and Hoover had undertaken its development and execution, and McCormick had lost interest in it. He may have been influenced against the relief project and for Kolchak by members of the Russian Political Conference, with whom he was in close contact. In any case, as early as April 11 he raised with Lansing the question of recognizing Kolchak. At this time Wilson disapproved such a course of action, for Lansing noted that he and McCormick also discussed "the President's opposition to recognizing [the] Omsk government." [70] Ten days later McCormick commented in his diary that the growing sentiment to recognize Kolchak conflicted with the current policy of the peace conference toward Russia—that of organizing a relief effort in Russia following an armistice. McCormick mused that to enforce a cessation of hostilities on both sides in Russia would be "hard on Kolchak as he is winning now. I am going to put this new situation to the President." [71]

The last remark reflected a development which other evidence indicates took place at about this time. From the middle of April McCormick, not House, began to handle Russian affairs for the American dele-

[68] *1919, Russia*, 333–36.
[69] Telegram from Morris to Washington, April 12, 1919, *ibid.*, 331–32.
[70] Lansing Papers, Desk Diary, April 11, 1919.
[71] McCormick Diary, 72, and similar comments in entries for April 24, May 2, and May 7, pp. 74, 80, 82–83. In his entry for April 21 McCormick referred to a State Department proposal to recognize the Omsk government. In the documents published by the State Department covering this period, no message containing such a recommendation appears. McCormick may have been referring to an informal communication from Polk, or perhaps to the telegram from Consul General Harris described above urging support, though not recognition, for Kolchak.

gation and to consult with the president on Russia. After this House was seldom involved in the Russian question; he had, for example, very little to do with the decision of the conference to extend support to Kolchak. In his diary for late April and May House made no mention of any discussions with the president on Russia. Memoranda and letters to and from Wilson relating to Russia now passed through McCormick's hands, not House's. Polk began at this time to address his telegrams concerning Russian affairs to "the Secretary of State and McCormick." It is not clear whether this transfer of responsibility was due to Wilson's lack of enthusiasm for the Hoover-Nansen plan, which House had vigorously advocated, or whether it was a result of the growing estrangement between Wilson and House on all matters which began to develop at about this time.[72] In any case, it is apparent that McCormick was Wilson's principal adviser on Russia in late April and May, and that he was instrumental in persuading the president to support the Omsk government.

In the middle of April press reports appeared stating that the Allies were planning to grant *de facto* recognition to Kolchak immediately after the conclusion of peace with Germany.[73] These stories may have been inspired by supporters of the Omsk government in Paris, or they may have been based on knowledge of the growing sentiment in this direction within the British and American delegations. At any rate, they gave Polk new hope. On April 24 he cabled Lansing that in view of such press reports, he wished to review for the benefit of the American Commission the extent to which the American government had already assisted and supported the anti-Bolshevik forces in Siberia:[74] it had facilitated shipment to Siberia by the Russian embassy in Washington of rifles and locomotives purchased with British credits; it had helped the Russian embassy to secure "licenses and necessary tonnage space either in commercial vessels or in army transports for shipment of rouble notes, shoes, rifles, and railway equipment" bought with American credits; it had encouraged American diplomatic officials to keep in close touch, informally and unofficially, with the authorities at Omsk; and on occasion American units in Siberia, in conjunction with Japanese and Czech troops, had participated in "engagements with Bolshevik forces operating with prisoners of war in their ranks." Although Polk did not directly recommend recognition of Kolchak, he referred to the optimistic reports of Harris and Morris as to the growing strength of the Omsk government and concluded that in the past "this Government has mani-

[72] On the latter point, see Lansing's reports of House's loss of contact with the president in Lansing Papers, Desk Diary, April 25, June 10.

[73] See, for example, a story in the *New York Times*, April 18, 1919, cited in Schuman, 134.

[74] *1919, Russia*, 336–37.

fested a friendly disposition towards the Omsk authorities which must have had a direct result in strengthening the Omsk government."

In light of growing Allied interest in the possibility of recognizing Kolchak, the Russian Political Conference began at this time to lobby more actively for achievement of this long-sought end. In early April the Conference sent an emissary to London to press the case for recognition of the Omsk government.[75] After meetings with sympathetic British M.P.'s led by Sir Samuel Hoare, the representative of the Political Conference reported that it was very important for the Conference to proclaim a program based on democratic principles and to secure written declarations from "liberal" Russians abroad that they supported the struggle against Bolshevism and did not think Kolchak was a reactionary.

In accord with the first suggestion, the Russian Political Conference submitted to the peace conference and to the Allied governments on April 15 a declaration of the basic purposes of the anti-Bolshevik movement.[76] The Conference vehemently denied any intention on the part of the anti-Bolshevik governments of restoring the old regime or of taking the land away from the peasants. Their fundamental aim was depicted as the reestablishment of national unity and the regeneration of Russia on a democratic basis. The Conference declared that only the Russian people themselves could decide the future destiny of Russia; therefore, the anti-Bolshevik governments would sponsor prompt and free election of a constituent assembly as soon as the Bolsheviks were defeated. The proclamation concluded by asserting the desire of the anti-Bolshevik governments to conclude the civil war as quickly as possible; for this purpose they appealed to the Allies for aid, especially since "the national movement is struggling for the realization of the same principles of true democracy and social equality in the name of which the Peace Conference was assembled." The advantages of a similar declaration by Kolchak were recognized in several quarters, and on April 26 Ughet, the Russian chargé in Washington, proposed to Omsk that the government make clear its democratic aims, its liberal policies in regard to labor, land, and the national minorities, and its intention to call a constituent assembly.[77]

Similar questions were becoming of increasing concern to both the British and Americans. Part of Churchill's scheme in North Russia, as

[75] Unsigned report on this trip, April 18, 1919, Maklakov Papers, Part II, Packet IV, File 11. From internal evidence it seems likely the emissary was either General Hermonius or General Golovin.

[76] Text in *1919, Russia*, 332–33.

[77] Telegram from Ughet to Omsk, April 26, 1919, *Vestnik NKID*, No. 9–10 (December 15, 1920), 56–57.

we saw in chapter six, involved the strengthening of Kolchak and the linking up of his armies with those of the government in Archangel. A memorandum from the British General Staff to the Cabinet on April 15 emphasized that if such a plan were to succeed, it would be necessary to send Kolchak additional supplies and to recognize his government.[78] The British Foreign Office endorsed the recognition of Kolchak in principle, but raised several difficult questions. Should Kolchak be recognized as an all-Russian government, or only as a provisional government for Siberia? Was Kolchak insisting on restoration of the monarchy and reinstitution of centralized Russian rule giving no autonomy or independence to the minority nationalities? [79]

The nature and objectives of Kolchak's rule began to be discussed at about the same time within the American delegation at Paris. This concern with Kolchak's political orientation and aims stemmed, at least in part, from the activity and views of Kerensky. On May 4 Kerensky talked with an unidentified member of the American delegation, perhaps McCormick himself.[80] Kerensky expressed the fear that if, as seemed likely, Kolchak overthrew the Soviet government, the result would be a regime "hardly less sanguinary and repressive than that of the Bolsheviks." Kerensky urged that the United States take the lead in formulating a concerted Allied policy dedicated to the restoration of a genuinely democratic government in Russia. This objective, he felt, might be accomplished if the powers told Kolchak that they were prepared to recognize him "on condition that he give proof of his democratic principles" by taking certain specific measures, such as the restoration of civil liberties and the reestablishment of zemstvo and city organizations in Siberia, the reorganization of the Omsk Cabinet on a coalition basis, the issuing of a call for the convocation of a constituent assembly as soon as possible, and the granting of firm guarantees, until the meeting of the constituent assembly, of peasant land holdings and of the rights of workmen. On May 14 Kerensky and a group of "democratic" Russians in Paris, all members of the Constituent Assembly of 1917, presented a letter along similar lines to House for Wilson.[81] This letter, however, specifically opposed Allied recognition of Kolchak, maintaining that the Allies should instead proclaim a broad program of democratic principles

[78] British Parliament, *1920*, Cmd. 818, pp. 30–31.
[79] British Foreign Office, *Documents,* III, 710.
[80] Unsigned memorandum of conversation with Kerensky, May 4, *1919, Russia,* 337–38.
[81] House Papers, Diary, May 14, 1919. A summary of the letter, prepared by House, was sent to the president and may be found both in *ibid.,* Drawer 34, File 139, and in Wilson Papers, Series VIIIA, Box 69. The signers of the letter, in addition to Kerensky, were N. Avxentieff, A. Argounoff, V. Zenzinoff, G. Ragovsky, F. Minor, M. Slonim, and B. Sokaloff.

and practice for Russia and support any group which accepted this program.

Kerensky's ideas strongly influenced consideration by the Americans and by the peace conference of the question of recognizing Kolchak. The evening of the day on which Kerensky talked with someone in the American delegation, the American Commission sent a telegram to Polk: "There is a feeling here among some that it would be unworthy [unwise] to recognize the Omsk government even provisionally because it seems to be a military dictatorship. If Kolchak were to take steps at once to summon a Constituent Assembly it might lessen opposition to some form of recognition. What are your views as to the possibility of inducing such action by Kolchak?" [82] On May 20, when the Council of Four was discussing Russian policy, Wilson, in order to support his contention that assistance to Kolchak should be conditional on the latter accepting a program of democratic principles, read to his colleagues excerpts from Kerensky's letter of May 14.[83] Moreover, the attitude toward Kolchak which the Allies subsequently adopted was almost identical with that suggested by Kerensky on May 4. This was ironical on two counts: first, Kerensky in his letter of May 14 and in subsequent statements to the press was highly critical of Kolchak; second, partial recognition of Kolchak, so long worked for by the Russian Political Conference, was greatly assisted by Kerensky, whom the Conference had excluded from its councils.

Kerensky was, however, not the only one who maintained that Allied support to Kolchak should be dependent on his adopting a liberal political program. At about this time Ambassador Morris, whose judgment Wilson greatly esteemed, made a similar proposal. On April 29 Polk cabled Morris that the American Commission was "carefully considering the advisability of a provisional recognition of the Kolchak Government"; the commissioners wanted to know whether, in view of Kolchak's military successes, Morris had modified his earlier opposition to the recognition of Kolchak.[84] On May 3 Morris replied that unity of action among the Allies was a paramount need in Siberia; he would, therefore, recommend recognizing Kolchak if France and Great Britain decided to do so.[85] He added, however, that he "would prefer to see

[82] *1919, Russia*, 339. Word in brackets inserted by editors of the documents.

[83] *Ibid.*, 352–53, and see pp. 297–98 below.

[84] *Ibid.*, 337. Unfortunately, no evidence was found to indicate who in the American Commission was "carefully considering" Kolchak's recognition or who initiated the request for Morris's views. In both cases it was probably McCormick, although Wilson himself may have first suggested obtaining Morris's judgment.

[85] Morris's reply cited in a telegram from Polk to Paris on May 6, 1919. *ibid.*, 339–40. At about this time the Russian chargé in Tokyo noted with satisfaction that Morris was beginning to look somewhat more favorably on Kolchak. Tele-

recognition postponed until the Kolchak government shows more willingness to define its purposes and policy and less subserviency to reactionary influence." Moreover, Morris went on, if it were decided to recognize Kolchak, it would be important first to obtain a statement from him defining his views on democratic government and on the convocation of a constituent assembly.

When he transmitted Morris's views to Paris on May 6, Polk also cited several other judgments on the question of recognition. On April 30 John Stevens, head of the railway mission in Siberia, had reported his belief that recognition of Kolchak was the only alternative to anarchy. A telegram from Consul Caldwell in Vladivostok, sent with the approval of General Graves, also urged that the Omsk government be recognized, provided Kolchak agreed to certain reforms and to the calling of a constituent assembly as soon as possible. The alternative, Caldwell maintained, was withdrawal of the American troops in Siberia. Buttressed by these proposals, Polk then added his own strong recommendation that the Allies recognize Kolchak. Referring to the American Commission's inquiry of May 4 concerning the possibility of persuading Kolchak to call a constituent assembly, Polk commented that Kolchak would undoubtedly be willing to issue a satisfactory statement on this point, as well as to support publicly a broad program of democratic policies, if it were made clear to him that recognition depended on such assurances.[86]

The recognition movement was gaining momentum rapidly, but at this point Wilson himself was apparently still not supporting it. Now that the draft treaty with Germany had been completed, however, and the Germans had been called to Paris to receive it, Wilson and his colleagues on the Council of Four were able to devote considerably more attention to the Russian question than they had in the preceding two months. During May the Russian problem was frequently discussed; it received almost as much consideration then as it had had in the opening weeks of the conference. It was first raised briefly on May 7, when Lloyd George told the other heads of government that Kolchak's advance and the probable collapse of the Bolsheviks made it urgent for the powers to define their attitude toward Kolchak, and toward Denikin as well. Lloyd George, referring to the views of Chaikovsky and of Paderewski, the Polish premier, contended that Kolchak was primarily a

gram to Sazonov in Paris, May 8, 1919, Maklakov Papers, Part II, Packet II, File 2d.

[86] Telegram of May 6 to Paris, enclosing cables from Morris, Stevens, and Caldwell, *1919, Russia*, 339–41. See also Polk's telegram of May 12, citing a number of democratic utterances made by Kolchak and by other Omsk officals, *ibid.*, 347–48.

military man and that his political program was vague and indefinite; therefore, it might be desirable to impose "some conditions on Kolchak and Denikine [*sic*] before further supplies were furnished." Wilson agreed, suggesting "that we should demand a programme of reforms and insist that our continued support depended on its being adopted." [87] Unfortunately, there is no evidence to indicate whether Wilson supported this course of action—in essence the one approved by the conference a few weeks later—on the basis of his own estimate of the situation, or whether the views of Kerensky and of Morris influenced him to adopt this position.

For Wilson, the developing policy conflict in Siberia between Graves and the Japanese and Russian authorities came to a head on May 9, when he received a telegram from Secretary of War Baker enclosing a message from General Graves. The communication from Graves, dated May 4, candidly reviewed the deteriorating relations between the Omsk leaders and himself and reported the complaint of Sukin that "America is not yet convinced of the right and justice of our cause and so fails to sympathize with us." [88] Graves acknowledged that his policy of noninterference probably had the effect of weakening Kolchak, since those in Siberia who idealized American democracy took it as an indication of disapproval of Kolchak by the United States. He concluded gravely: "If we continue our policy here we will almost surely have armed conflict with Russian troops as they are determined we cannot remain in Siberia and continue the policy of noninterference. . . . We are now squarely up against the proposition of using force or getting out. . . ." In forwarding this telegram to Paris, Baker warned that "if Congress and the people want war to be made upon Bolshevism by force of arms," the United States should send a force to Siberia of sufficient size so that it could act independently of either Japanese or Russian allies; this, however, might lead to the Japanese sending an even larger force. Baker concluded: "Either General Graves should be directed to cooperate with the Kolchak government or he ought to be withdrawn." [89]

The dilemma facing Wilson was obvious. He was opposed to interfering in Russia's affairs. Yet the policy of neutrality he had set for Graves seemed to be leading to armed clashes with either the Russians or the

[87] *Ibid.*, 341–42.

[88] Graves' telegram, which is printed in *ibid.*, 491–93, was enclosed in a cable from Baker to Bliss for the president, May 8, 1919, Bliss Papers, Box 66.

[89] *Ibid.* Baker's telegram with the enclosure from Graves was transmitted to Wilson by Bliss on May 9. Wilson Papers, Series VIIIA, Box 46. The same day Polk wired Lansing and McCormick, reporting British criticism of Graves and adding his own opinion that Graves had been rigid and tactless and should therefore either be replaced or instructed to abandon the policy of noninterference and to support the Omsk authorities. *1919, Russia,* 493–94.

Japanese. On the other hand, if he took the course that most closely accorded with his principles—withdrawal of the American forces in Siberia, leaving the Russians to decide their own fate—this might strengthen the dictatorial grasp of the Bolsheviks on European Russia, and it would certainly give the Japanese a free hand in Far Eastern Russia, permitting them to shut the "open door" in that area. To send in larger American forces was not only against his principles but impolitic, since the Japanese might use it as a pretext for dispatching an even larger army to Siberia. The policy toward which Wilson felt his way in the next few weeks as a solution to this dilemma was adumbrated by a shorthand notation he made on the copy of Baker's telegram given to him: "Lend assistance." [90]

On May 9 President Wilson outlined his predicament to his colleagues on the Council of Four with complete frankness.[91] He acknowledged that the United States had not supported Kolchak and that the American attitude of neutrality tended to encourage criticism of the admiral's regime. He expressed openly his fears that if the United States withdrew its forces, the Japanese would have a clear field, while if the Americans were reinforced, the Japanese might send in even more troops. Wilson added that "he had always been of the opinion that the proper policy of the Allied and Associated Powers was to clear out of Russia and leave it to the Russians to fight it out among themselves." Lloyd George declared that the president's remarks underlined the importance of the powers agreeing on a policy toward Kolchak. Wilson concurred but suggested that they should first ask Kolchak what his program was. Lloyd George recommended that they hear the views of Chaikovsky before reaching any decision.

The next day the Four had a long session with Chaikovsky.[92] Wilson and Lloyd George questioned him closely concerning the attitude of the anti-Bolshevik governments toward land reform and toward the status of the nationalties in a reconstituted Russia. They also wished to know what sort of political influences surrounded Admiral Kolchak. In reply Chaikovsky first presented a report of a liberal program recently proclaimed by Denikin. It turned out, however, that the program had been suggested to Denikin by the Allied representatives in South Russia and that the general had simply endorsed it. Chaikovsky declared that the

[90] Since Wilson used his own system of shorthand, there is no certainty that this is the correct transcription of his notation. However, Miss Katherine Brand of the Division of Manuscripts at the Library of Congress, who is familiar with Wilson's system, and who kindly examined this notation for the author, believes that this is the most likely transcription.

[91] *Ibid.*, 345–47.

[92] *Peace Conference*, 544–52.

question of land reform would have to be decided by a constituent assembly to be convoked after the Bolsheviks had been overthrown. Discussing the future status of the nationalities, he avoided committing himself to a definite position, but argued in general that many of the nationalities were too weak to stand alone.[93] He denied that Kolchak was under reactionary influences and disputed a British report, read to him by Lloyd George, that Kolchak had been suppressing the cooperatives and other democratic organizations in Siberia. Chaikovsky indicated that at the moment some in the anti-Bolshevik camp favored establishment of a constitutional monarchy in Russia; he was certain, however, that a republic would be the form of government ultimately adopted.

After Chaikovsky had withdrawn, Wilson noted that Chaikovksy had been vague on some points and had not really clarified the question of what kind of men surrounded Kolchak.[94] Lloyd George agreed but declared that even if Kolchak's government turned out to be reactionary, public opinion might demand that the Allies support it as the only force capable of restoring order in Russia. This would certainly be awkward since the powers would be placed in the position of supporting a government they did not believe in. Wilson said he was still dissatisfied with the information they had on Kolchak; consequently, he planned to send Ambassador Morris to Siberia to make an independent investigation of the Omsk government.

The Decision Taken

Increasingly the attention of the peacemakers now focused on what guarantees could and should be extracted from Kolchak as a condition of his being either supported or recognized. On May 12 McCormick urged Bakhmetev to exert pressure on Kolchak to convoke a constituent assembly.[95] On May 15 Wilson, in accord with his declaration to the Council of Four on May 10, asked the State Department to instruct Ambassador Morris to proceed to Omsk for the following purposes:

> To obtain from that Government official and definite assurances as to the objects that they have in view with regard to the future Governmental regime in Russia and the methods by which they mean to set a new regime up, asking particular assurances with regard to the reform

[93] His equivocal position was in accord with a memorandum of the Russian Political Conference to the peace conference on March 9, which argued that none of the border areas, except Poland, should be granted independence without the consent of the Russian people as a whole, although, in the interim, the Allies might find it necessary to recognize as provisional governments some of the nationality groups fighting against the Bolsheviks. Miller, *Diary*, xviii, 433–35.

[94] *Peace Conference*, v, 560.

[95] McCormick Diary, 85.

in land tenure, and the extension and security of the suffrage, and the choice and projected action of a constituent assembly, and also [to] learn as definitely as possible the influences that Kolchak is under. The President states his object is to satisfy himself as to whether the Kolchak Government deserves the recognition, or at least the countenance, if not the support, of our government. . . .[96]

The next day McCormick pressed the case for Kolchak further, urging Wilson to offer Kolchak the hope of recognition in exchange for a democratic government. McCormick gave the president a draft telegram to Kolchak, which expressed the interest of the United States in the efforts of the Omsk regime to establish a government based on popular consent and asked whether conditions in Siberia might not now permit an expression of the will of the people in some form. In such an event the United States would give sympathetic consideration to the possibility of recognizing the resulting government.[97] Wilson wrote McCormick that he approved sending the telegram to Polk for transmission to Kolchak, but that Polk should "consider it in the light of my recent instructions to Morris at Tokio." With the concurrence of Lansing, McCormick, on May 17, "very confidentially" sent Polk the telegram and Wilson's comment on it.[98] Polk replied that in view of the detailed instructions the president had given Morris, this further telegram "might confuse Morris." McCormick concurred, and the message to Kolchak was not sent.[99]

On May 19 Wilson informed his colleagues on the Council of Four that he had ordered a direct American inquiry regarding Kolchak's program and policy.[100] He added that he had received a letter from Kerensky proposing that recognition and assistance to groups in Russia be made dependent on their adhering to a democratic course. Wilson concluded that "this seemed to provide the rudiments of a policy."

The next day the Four considered the Soviet reply to the Hoover-

[96] Telegram from Polk to Morris, May 15, 1919, *1919, Russia,* 349. The next day Wilson instructed Morris particularly to ascertain whether Kolchak was strong enough and liberal enough to control the men and influences surrounding him. Telegram from Polk to Morris, May 16, *ibid.*

[97] Draft in Wilson Papers, Series VIIIA, Box 49. In an earlier draft the vague phrase, "an expression of the will of the people," read "the holding of a representative constituent assembly." It is not clear, however, whether the penciled change was made by McCormick or by Wilson.

[98] *Ibid.,* Box 51.

[99] Telegram from Polk to McCormick, May 21, and reply, May 22, Records of the ACTNP, 861.00/658.

[100] *1919, Russia,* 350. It is not clear whether Wilson was referring to his instructions to Morris or to the telegram prepared by McCormick. He may have had both in mind.

Nansen proposal.[101] As we saw in the preceding chapter, they took no action on Chicherin's message, quickly passing on to a discussion of the question of recognizing Kolchak. After Wilson had proposed again that "at least pledges could be exacted" for further support to the anti-Bolshevik groups in Russia, and Clemenceau had agreed with him, Lloyd George declared that this could be done either by sending a formal dispatch to these groups or by summoning their representatives now in Paris to receive the conditions decided on by the Four. Wilson objected to the latter procedure on the ground that it violated the principle that had underlain the Prinkipo project—not to hear one party to the controversy without hearing the other. (Wilson overlooked the fact that Chaikovsky had recently appeared before them.) The president said he preferred sending a formal message to the Russian groups, and he then read the Council parts of Kerensky's letter suggesting democratic policies that should be required of an Allied-supported Russian government. The Four decided to have Philip Kerr, Lloyd George's secretary, draft the proposed declaration to the Russians. His instructions were based to a considerable extent on Kerensky's proposals, and he was told to make clear in the statement that if the anti-Bolshevik groups did not promise to institute democratic practices, they would receive no further support from the powers.

The next day, May 21, a telegram from Secretary of War Baker again called Wilson's attention to the difficult position which General Graves was in.[102] Baker defended Graves as an intelligent man conscientiously trying to carry out his orders under trying circumstances. Baker reported that he and Polk had conferred and had agreed that replacing Graves at this time would make a bad impression and might lead the Russians and the Allies to think that a radical change in American policy was to be made. They had concluded, consequently, that it would be best to await Morris's report from Omsk and a decision in Paris as to the policy to be pursued toward Kolchak before doing anything about Graves. If Wilson and the other Allied leaders decided to assist the Omsk government, Graves' instructions could be changed accordingly. Baker added that he was sure the General would faithfully carry out any new orders given him. On May 23 Wilson replied, concurring entirely with the conclusions of Baker and Polk.

The same day the Four resumed their consideration of the communication to be made to Kolchak.[103] Clemenceau favored recognizing the

[101] *Ibid.*, 351–54.
[102] Memorandum from Auchincloss to Close, enclosing Baker's telegram of May 21, Wilson Papers, Series VIIIA, Box 51.
[103] *1919, Russia*, 354–58.

Omsk government as an all-Russian government, but Wilson and Lloyd George insisted that it should be considered as only a regional government. They then turned their attention to the draft note Kerr had prepared.[104] The note, eventually adopted with only minor changes, referred to the "cardinal axiom of the Allied and Associated Powers to avoid interference in the internal affairs of Russia," and asserted that intervention had been undertaken only to assist those Russians who wished to continue the struggle against Germany and in order to rescue the Czechs. Reviewing the Prinkipo project and the Nansen relief plan, the note declared that these efforts "broke down through the refusal of the Soviet Government to accept the fundamental condition of suspending hostilities while negotiations or the work of relief was proceeding"—a not entirely accurate statement, as we have seen. According to the note, the Allies were being pressed, in view of the failure of intervention to produce a settlement, to withdraw their troops and to incur no further burdens in Russia; they were, however, prepared to continue their aid to the Russian groups they had encouraged, provided they believed such assistance would really help the Russian people to liberty, self-government and peace.

The note then declared that the Allies' basic objective in Russia was to restore peace by encouraging the establishment of a freely elected constituent assembly and by arranging for the definition of Russia's frontiers under the auspices of the League of Nations. Since they believed it impossible to attain these goals in cooperation with the Soviet government, the powers were prepared "to assist the Government of Admiral Kolchak and his Associates with munitions, supplies, food, and the help of such as may volunteer for their service, to establish themselves as the government of all Russia," if the White Russian leaders would first agree to certain conditions. In Kerr's draft Kolchak was asked to promise: first, to summon a freely elected constituent assembly upon reaching Moscow, or, if conditions did not permit elections to such a body, to summon the Constituent Assembly of 1917 to sit on an interim basis; second, "to permit" in the areas of his present control free elections for local assemblies, such as the zemstvos; third, to oppose any attempts to restore the old regime and to preserve the civil and religious liberties of all Russians, although the settlement of specific questions, such as that of land tenure, should be left to the constituent assembly; fourth, to recognize the independence of Finland and of Poland and to submit boundary disputes with these nations to the arbitration of the League of Nations; fifth, to settle Russia's relations with the Baltic and Caucasian territories under the auspices of the League if a solution

[104] Text in *ibid.*, 358–60. Text as finally approved in *ibid.*, 367–70.

could not be reached by agreement with the peoples concerned; sixth, to join the League and to abolish conscription in Russia; and seventh, to abide by Kolchak's declaration of November 1918 recognizing Russia's debts.

After a brief discussion during which Kerr pointed out, in response to an objection from Wilson, that the note would probably be acceptable to the governments of General Denikin and of North Russia since they both had recently indicated they were prepared to recognize Kolchak as provisional all-Russian ruler, Clemenceau and Orlando stated that they approved everything in the note except the proposed abolition of conscription.[105] After Clemenceau had raised this point several times, apparently fearing the loss of Russian manpower on Germany's eastern flank should a non-Bolshevik Russia be reconstituted, Wilson suggested substitution of the phrase "the limitation of armaments and of military organization," and this was accepted. The president urged that Kolchak be asked "to promote" local elections, not simply "to permit" them, but he was overruled by Lloyd George, who insisted that in view of the wartime conditions in the anti-Bolshevik areas and of the confusion that must naturally exist there, this was asking too much.

Wilson wondered if the note did not imply that the Allies would recognize Kolchak provided he met the conditions it set forth. Kerr replied that it did not, that the note did not mention recognition; the conditions governed only the continuation of Allied assistance. This, it should be noted, was in accord with the instructions Kerr had received on May 20. It also followed the view of the British Foreign Office that Kolchak's government should be considered as only a regional body and not as an all-Russian government.[106] President Wilson concluded that in any case, before approving the draft, he would like to consult Lansing concerning what assistance, if any, the United States had sent to Russia.

The next day Wilson reported to his colleagues that Lansing approved the draft note but wished to suspend action on it until the report from Ambassador Morris was received.[107] The president, however, was prepared to proceed with it at once. At the same time he urged the Council to approve an additional condition suggested by Lansing—that Kolchak be asked to recognize the autonomy of the Baltic and Caucasian territories, as well as existing relations between governments in those territories and the Allied governments, pending final settlement of their status. This was accepted at the morning meeting of May 24.

[105] This condition is not included in the draft note printed in the Department of State documents, but in the first draft Kerr prepared it apparently formed part of point six.
[106] British Foreign Office, *Documents,* III, 709–10.
[107] *1919, Russia,* 360–61. See also Lansing Papers, Desk Diary, May 23, 1919.

Up to this point no one had paid much attention to the position of the Japanese in Siberia or to how they might feel about the policy being discussed by the Four. The direction in which the Western leaders were moving was no secret; it had been discussed and warmly endorsed in the conservative French and English press beginning in the middle of May, and on May 23 *Le Temps* declared that the Allies had practically decided to recognize Kolchak.[108] Fearful that among the White Russians the Western governments might get all the credit for the recognition of Kolchak, the Japanese indicated at this time that they were also seriously considering his recognition.[109]

Consequently, at the afternoon meeting on May 24 the Big Four brought Viscount Chinda, one of the Japanese delegates to the conference, into their discussions. That the decision to include the Japanese was a hasty one is indicated by the absence from Paris at this time of Baron Makino, the Japanese foreign minister, and by Chinda's statement that he had only just received the draft note to Kolchak.[110] Chinda, while requesting time to consult his colleagues, stated as his personal opinion that the Japanese government would support the declaration to Kolchak. Chinda said that he assumed that the task of giving Kolchak aid, provided the latter replied affirmatively, would be divided among the powers according to their ability to furnish such assistance. Lloyd George remarked, in a half-joking and half-serious manner, that he welcomed this idea since then the United States, not Great Britain, would have to supply the bulk of the aid. Wilson replied that although this would be up to Congress, he hoped to persuade the lawmakers to help Kolchak. Chinda questioned the promise to send volunteers to Russia, and after brief discussion this phrase was dropped. It was also agreed that the specific notation in the message of the amount of British aid to Russia ("more than 100,000,000 pounds") had better be omitted. Subject to these changes and to formal approval by the Japanese delegation, the Council approved the note.

Discussion then turned to what should be done if Kolchak sent a

[108] Noble, 291–94; English press opinion is summarized in a telegram from Nabokov to Omsk, May 15, cited in Subbotovsky, 43. Right-wing papers expressed annoyance, however, with the delay in recognizing Kolchak and with the demand, attributed to Wilson, that Kolchak make democratic promises in advance. The socialist press, on the other hand, berated Wilson for betraying Russian democracy by dealing with Kolchak at all.
[109] On May 24 the Japanese ambassador to Washington, Viscount Ishii, presented an *aide-mémoire* to this effect to Polk. Polk Papers, Diary, May 24, 1919. See also Clemenceau's alarmed reference, in the meeting of the Council of Four on May 23, to the possibility that the Japanese might forestall the Allies on recognition. *1919, Russia,* 354.
[110] The minutes of the May 24 session are in *ibid.,* 361–66.

favorable reply. Lloyd George suggested that they would have to decide whether to limit themselves to assisting him, or whether to recognize his government as a regional or an all-Russian government. Wilson said that before these questions came up, he hoped to have a full report from Ambassador Morris.

The next day was a Sunday. Monday, May 26, the Japanese delegation approved the draft note to Kolchak with only minor changes, one being their substitution of the wording "some of the Allied and Associated Governments are now being pressed to withdraw their troops" for the original statement that all the governments were being so pressed. The Japanese obviously wanted it understood that they were under no pressure to evacuate Siberia. The Japanese also requested that the note not be published until Kolchak's reply had been received.[111] Although the Japanese representatives in Paris acquiesced in the decision taken by the Big Four, the Foreign Office in Tokyo was annoyed that the Japanese had not been consulted earlier and complained to Morris that the message to Kolchak "had been presented at a hastily called meeting in Paris and had been adopted without allowing sufficient time for consideration or discussion." [112]

On May 26 the communication to Kolchak, a slightly amended version of Kerr's original draft note, was signed by the five powers. The next day, however, before it was dispatched to Kolchak, the Council approved the addition of one more condition, stipulating that Kolchak should recognize "the right of the Peace Conference to determine the future of the Rumanian part of Bessarabia." [113] Although the minutes of this session of the Council of Four do not state from which quarter this suggestion came, it was undoubtedly the handiwork of the French, who strongly supported Rumania's claims to this territory.

For Wilson the decision to extend support to Kolchak on certain conditions represented at least a partial answer to the dilemma the president faced in regard to Siberia. If Kolchak accepted a program of democratic principles, Wilson felt justified in abandoning the policy of noninterference and neutrality and openly assisting the Omsk government against the Bolsheviks. This permitted him to keep American forces in Siberia and to prevent the Japanese from having a free hand there. For the moment, at least, Wilson was able to square his principles with the requirements of what he felt was America's national interest, although, as we shall shortly see, fundamentally he still believed in "nonintervention."

[111] *Ibid.*, 366.
[112] Telegram from Morris to Lansing, June 6, 1919, Records of ACTNP, 861.00/4647.
[113] *Peace Conference*, VI, 72.

On June 7 he read to the Council, with obvious relief, a telegram from Consul General Harris in Omsk reporting the gist of a proclamation Kolchak planned to make, in which the admiral promised to hand over all his power to a constituent assembly whose election was being prepared, and in which he guaranteed the rights of the peasants and workmen. Wilson "considered this a very good proclamation." [114]

Lloyd George, under pressure from Churchill and the interventionists in Parliament, was quite willing to accept the concept of assisting a "democratized" Kolchak. Moreover, Wilson's approval of such a policy held out the hope that the United States might now supply most of the aid to Kolchak, relieving the British of this burden. The French were, of course, delighted that the conference had at last taken a firm anti-Bolshevik stand, although outright recognition of Kolchak would have pleased Pichon even more.

The Next Step

As soon as the decision of the Four became known, Wilson's four colleagues on the American Commission to Negotiate Peace sent him a note urging that the president "obtain from the members of the Council of Four assurances that no special concessions for the benefit of the countries which they represent have been given or offered by the Kolchak Government and that there is no intention to accept such concessions in the future." Learning from Lansing that the American delegates' concern was not based on any specific information but only on "allusions in the air," Wilson accepted their suggestion but pointed out that "it is a very delicate matter to handle, and I shall have to await a favorable opportunity." [115]

First reaction among the anti-Bolshevik leaders to the note to Kolchak was not entirely favorable. Some were disappointed that the Allies had not taken the further step of granting Kolchak *de facto* recognition. Some, like Sazonov and General Miller, objected to the demands of the powers respecting the status of the border areas and to the suggestion that the Constituent Assembly of 1917 (which included Bolsheviks) might be reconvened.[116] Sazonov's strong criticism of the Allied note alarmed Lloyd George, who feared that Sazonov might dissuade

[114] For Wilson's comment, see *ibid.*, 233. For the telegraphic report from Harris, see *1919, Russia*, 371–72.

[115] Letter from Lansing, House, Bliss, and White, May 26, 1919, and from Lansing, May 28; Wilson's reply of May 27, Wilson Papers, Series VIIIA, Box 53.

[116] For Miller's views, see a telegram from Poole in Archangel to Washington, May 29, *1919, Russia*, 370–71, and Mints, 243–44; for Sazonov's, British Foreign Office, *Documents*, III, 360–61; on dissatisfaction within the Russian Political Conference with the action of the powers, see Dillon, 365–68.

Kolchak from accepting the conditions of the powers. Consequently, the British leader had Churchill telegraph General Knox "to urge Kolchak not to listen to Sazonov." [117] This intervention was unnecessary, however, since Sazonov advised Omsk on June 12 that Kolchak's reply, while safeguarding the chief interests of the White Russian cause, should be cautious and conciliatory in order not to offend liberal opinion in the West.[118] Moreover, the draft reply prepared by the Russian Political Conference, which crossed Kolchak's own answer, was mild and accommodating, although it, like Kolchak's response, disavowed the Constituent Assembly of 1917 and postponed to a future all-Russian representative body settlement of the status of Finland and Bessarabia and of Russia's relations with her minority groups.[119] White Russian anxiety over the nationality question was apparently considerably allayed by French assurances at just this time that they would not support the dismemberment of Russia and would urge the Allies to postpone final settlement of the Finnish and Baltic questions and of Poland's eastern frontiers until Russia was in a position to present her views and to protect her interests respecting these issues.[120]

In Omsk, meanwhile, there was apparently some debate over how best to respond to the Allied note, but a conciliatory answer was finally prepared.[121] Because of difficulties in transmission, Kolchak's reply, dispatched on June 4, was not received by the Four in final form until June 11.[122] Without committing himself on most of the detailed points in the note of May 26, Kolchak accepted the Allied conditions as a whole. He promised to convoke a constituent assembly as soon as the Bolsheviks were defeated, but he rejected the Allied suggestion that the Constituent Assembly of 1917, "elected," as he put it, "under a regime of Bolshevik violence," could be accepted as even an interim authority.[123] Kolchak recognized Polish independence and the *de facto* independence of Finland, but he maintained that final resolution of the Finnish problem, definition of the exact boundaries between Russia and

[117] Reported to his colleagues in the Council of Four on June 3, 1919. *Peace Conference,* VI, 158. See also Churchill, *Aftermath,* 255–56.

[118] Cited in Subbotovsky, 48.

[119] Draft is in Records of ACTNP, 861.00/862.

[120] Telegrams from Omsk of May 24 and 25 reporting an official reply from the French government to questions Kolchak had posed to General Janin, cited in Subbotovsky, 74–77.

[121] Fischer (I, 186) reports that Colonel John Ward told him that Kolchak's reactionary advisers urged a stiff reply, including rejection of Poland's independence, but Ward persuaded Kolchak to ignore them.

[122] Text of the reply in *1919, Russia,* 375–78.

[123] It is interesting that both the White Russian leaders and the Bolsheviks repudiated this body, which was, in fact, probably as nearly representative of articulate Russian political opinion as any group elected at that time could have been.

Poland, and the status of Bessarabia could only be determined by the future constituent assembly. He promised only autonomy to the other nationalities, although he expressed willingness to accept the good offices of the League of Nations in the settlement of possible conflicts between the Russians and these groups. He reaffirmed his previous acknowledgment of Russia's debts and disclaimed any intention of restoring the old regime. Finally, he assured the powers that he was protecting and encouraging the exercise of civil liberties and rights of self-government and that he fully supported a just solution of the land question.

Although the answer was rather vague, reserving the settlement of most issues to the constituent assembly, the Four considered Kolchak's reply quite satisfactory. They were particularly pleased that there would be no return to the old regime. On June 12 they agreed to send an acknowledgment in this sense and to inform Kolchak that they were now willing to extend him the assistance mentioned in their first note.[124] This decision was taken despite the fact that, in the interval between sending their original message and receiving Kolchak's reply, reports of military defeats suffered by Kolchak had reached Paris.[125]

There remained, moreover, the question of what they should do next. As Lloyd George had pointed out on May 24, the Allies must now decide whether to confine themselves to assisting Kolchak (which the French and British had been doing for some time anyway) or whether they should now proceed to recognize the Omsk government. Baron Makino advocated the latter course, but Lloyd George declared that they should not yet recognize Kolchak's regime as the government of all of Russia.[126] Moreover, as the British Foreign Office put it later in a memorandum on Siberia: "When Kolchak replied, however, his armies were in full retreat, and the moment was hardly propitious to confer a privilege which might easily have proved an empty one almost as soon as it was conferred." [127]

The leaders of the Russian Political Conference pressed the advantage gained, hoping that the Allies might extend formal recognition to the Omsk government. At the end of May Sazonov had visited England, where he had had an audience with the king and had met with

[124] *Ibid.,* 374, 378, 379. They also authorized the whole correspondence with Kolchak to be released. Their decision prompted the historian Samuel Eliot Morison, then an expert with the American delegation, to resign in protest. Records of the ACTNP, 861.00/721.

[125] See Lloyd George's reference to such reports on June 3, 1919, *Peace Conference,* VI, 158; see also Noble, 293–94.

[126] *1919, Russia,* 378–79.

[127] Memorandum on Siberia by J. D. Gregory, December 1919, British Foreign Office, *Documents,* III, 710.

members of Parliament and officials of the Foreign and War offices. He returned full of optimism.[128] On June 17, however, Sazonov wrote prophetically to Vologodsky in Omsk: "Further steps in the direction of official recognition . . . will doubtless directly depend on the military successes of the Siberian armies." [129]

At the same time Bakhmetev pleaded the case for recognition with McCormick, seeing him on June 5, 14, and 21.[130] Bakhmetev also urged that Morris, who was still in Tokyo, should proceed to Omsk and that the United States should now take concrete steps to assist the Kolchak government.[131] Both these recommendations influenced McCormick. On June 17 he suggested to Lansing that Morris now go to Omsk, and the secretary of state encouraged McCormick to raise the matter with the president.[132] On June 25 Wilson instructed Morris to proceed to Siberia "in view of the fact that the joint action taken here . . . still leaves open the question of his [Kolchak's] formal [recognition?] and the extent and nature of the support which should be given him." [133] Wilson added that Morris "should so utilize his visit to Omsk as to impress upon the Japanese Government our great interest in the Siberian situation and our intention to adopt a definite policy which will include the 'open door' to Russia, free from Japanese domination." At about the same time, however, to a number of specific inquiries as to how far the United States was prepared to go in interpreting the exchange of notes with Kolchak as recognition and in assisting his regime with credits—questions which McCormick submitted to Wilson on Bakhmetev's behalf—the president returned largely negative answers.[134]

From Washington Polk began to press the American leaders in Paris for an explanation of just what the decision of the Four meant, and he urged the speedy formulation of a program of concrete assistance to Kolchak.[135] On June 23 McCormick discussed the whole matter with

[128] Telegram from Sazonov to Omsk, June 1, in E. Adamov, "Rol' Anglii v interventsii" ("The Role of England in Intervention"), *Vestnik NKID,* No. 6–7 (August 25, 1920), 7.

[129] Maklakov Papers, Part II, Packet III, File 9.

[130] McCormick Diary, 97, 102, 110.

[131] Polk had decided on his own not to send Morris to Siberia, since the Allies were on the verge of recognizing Kolchak. Wilson was furious when he learned this. Wilson Papers, Series VIIIA, Boxes 53, 55, 57.

[132] McCormick Diary, 104.

[133] Letter from Wilson to Lansing, June 25, Wilson Papers, Series VIIIA, Box 66, and telegram from Washington to Morris, June 30, containing the president's instructions, which were drafted by McCormick. *1919, Russia,* 388. Second insertion in brackets is by the editors of the documents.

[134] *Ibid.,* 384–85.

[135] Telegrams to Paris of June 16, June 19 (two on that date), and June 20 (also two), *ibid.,* 379–80, 381–83.

the president. Wilson declared that, contrary to the interpretation the press had placed on the decision of the Four, the exchange of letters with Kolchak did not constitute recognition of his government, but only the setting of certain conditions for the continuation of Allied assistance to him. McCormick pointed out that it would be difficult to find money with which to finance aid to Kolchak as long as there was no legal government with which to deal. After further discussion McCormick and Wilson agreed that the only course was to tell "Congress the whole story and . . . appeal [to it] for funds." [136] At that moment Hoover entered the room, and the three men discussed the importance of giving Russia substantial economic aid; they agreed that to restore her economic life should be the first step in the eventual development of rational and stable self-government in Russia.[137] But Wilson declared that such aid would have to be channeled through an inter-Allied organization, and it would thus inevitably become entangled with the political purposes of the powers. The president then said: "The Russian people must solve their own problems without outside interference. . . . Europe had made a great mistake when they attempted to interfere in the French Revolution. It seems hard on the present Russian generation, but in the long run it means less distress for Russia."

Wilson was returning to his basic principle of noninterference, which, at heart, he had never really left. He had intervened reluctantly, against his better judgment. He had been alarmed by reports of German influence in Russia and had been repelled by the undemocratic nature of the Soviet regime. He had wanted to assist the Czechs, and he had believed that limited intervention might "steady efforts at self-government." Now, if he were to protect the American position in Siberia, Wilson found himself obliged to work with Kolchak. Although the president made some effort in the summer of 1919 to get assistance to Omsk, in principle he had washed his hands of the Russian mess—either it would have to settle itself, or perhaps the League of Nations could do something about it. The fact that there seemed no sane and practicable solution to the Russian question reinforced his natural inclination, based on his beliefs, to let the Russians determine their own fate, no matter what the cost.

[136] McCormick Diary, 110–11. And see telegram to Polk from Lansing and McCormick, June 25, *1919, Russia,* 386.

[137] This was the gist of a proposal Hoover made to the president in a letter of June 21, Records of the ACTNP, 861.00/786. During the summer McCormick attempted to develop a plan of economic assistance to Russia for the president to submit to Congress, but it fell by the wayside in the fight over ratification of the Versailles Treaty. The plan is referred to in a telegram from Lansing to Morris, August 25, *1919, Russia,* 421.

The outcome of six months' consideration of the Russian problem by the peace conference was the decision to extend moral and material assistance to the White Russian movement headed by Kolchak. This course of action, although it remained a fundamental policy of the West toward Russia until the late fall of 1919—and even later for the French —failed almost from the moment of its inception. Kolchak was unable to rally popular support in Russia to his cause and was defeated by the Red Army. Allied assistance to his government could not prevent these developments—nor would official recognition of his regime have significantly altered his fate. At the same time Allied support of Kolchak, and later of Denikin and Wrangel, outraged many patriotic Russians. How did the Western leaders at Paris arrive at a decision that proved to be so futile? The immediate reasons were Kolchak's ephemeral victories, which gave rise to the wishful belief that his forces might soon take Moscow—a prospect that spurred the Allies not only to assist him but also to attempt to obtain some control over his policies—and President Wilson's need to clarify the American position in Siberia, which he was reluctant to leave in the hands of the Japanese. More fundamental, however, was the fact that aiding Kolchak with money and supplies was virtually the only course of action that was both feasible and at the same time acceptable to all the major powers. Some things that the Allies might have done, such as negotiating a settlement with the Bolsheviks, they could not agree on. Others, such as all-out intervention, they could not carry out, even if they had all favored it. The half-hearted step taken on May 26 was really all that was left.

CHAPTER NINE

Russia and the Peace Treaties

▦▦ BEFORE EXAMINING the efforts of the peacemakers, during
▦▦ the remainder of the conference, from July 1919 to January
▦▦ 1920, to deal with the problems of Russia and Bolshevism, a
brief review is necessary of the clauses affecting Russia incorporated in
the peace treaties signed with the former Central Powers. This discussion will be limited to the pertinent articles of the Treaty of Versailles
with Germany, since these formed the basis for analogous sections of
the related treaties of St. Germain with Austria, Trianon with Hungary,
and Neuilly with Bulgaria.

Treaty Provisions Affecting Russia

The problem of Russia in the peace treaties, as throughout the conference, was an anomalous one. Under the terms of the Armistice Germany had renounced the Treaty of Brest-Litovsk; technically and legally
Russia was therefore both still at war with Germany and remained one
of the Allied and Associated Powers. Yet the last Russian government
recognized by the Allies was the Provisional Government of 1917,
which no longer existed. Thus there was not only no Russian representation at the peace conference but no Russian government either to adhere
to the proposed treaty or to make a separate peace with Germany. At
the time, given the civil war in Russia, her weakness, and her uncertain
future, this difficulty seemed of minor consequence, and the leaders of
the conference spent little time puzzling over it. Within a year, however,
the lack of Russian participation in the Versailles settlement helped lead
to the Soviet-Polish war of 1920, and three years later this circumstance
proved to be an important factor in the Soviet-German rapprochement
symbolized by the Rapallo Treaty. Moreover, leaving Russia out of the
European peace of 1919 had profound consequences throughout the interwar years and contributed to the fundamental instability of the Versailles system.

As Fritz Epstein has pointed out in his important article on this subject, the clauses of the Versailles Treaty respecting Russia were drafted
with two primary purposes in mind: to reserve the rights of a future

reconstituted, Western-oriented Russia, which in the spring of 1919 the Allies still hoped might emerge from the confused struggle within Russia, and to prevent German interference in or domination of the affairs of Russia either through the Brest-Litovsk and associated treaties or in the future.[1] There is, however, no evidence that the Western statesmen gave any thought to what might happen if the Soviet government consolidated its position and sought its own pattern of relations with defeated Germany. Moreover, the dangers of a marriage of convenience between beleaguered Russian Bolshevism and a revisionist German imperialism, later consummated in the Soviet-German Nonaggression Pact of 1939, were occasionally mentioned but seldom considered seriously.

The most important provisions regarding Russia were included in the political chapter of the Versailles Treaty, under Section XIV, "Russia and Russian States."[2] Of the two articles contained therein, Article 116 provided three things: first, Germany was required to recognize the independence of all territories that had been part of the prewar Russian Empire; second, the Treaty of Brest-Litovsk and all related and associated treaties were abrogated;[3] third, the Allied and Associated Powers reserved Russia's right to obtain reparations from Germany. Article 117 reinforced the first paragraph of Article 116 by compelling Germany to recognize all treaties and agreements that the Allied and Associated Powers had concluded or might conclude with present or future states on Russian territory, as well as all frontiers established in such treaties.

Three further clauses, paragraph 6 of Article 259 in the financial chapter of the treaty and Articles 292 and 293 of the economic chapter, confirmed and elaborated Section XIV. In addition, they required Germany to transfer to the Allies all assets and payments she had received under the terms of the Brest-Litovsk and associated treaties and to revoke all public concessions and privileges received by the German state or German citizens from Russia. No procedure was stipulated for the return of these assets to Russia, but it was assumed that the Allies were to hold them in trust pending the reestablishment of a recognized Russian government.

The last clause in regard to Russia was Article 433, which repeated the wording of Article XII of the Armistice by calling for the evacuation

[1] Fritz. T. Epstein, "Zur Interpretation des Versailler Vertrages: Der von Polen 1919–22 erhobene Reparationsanspruch," *Jahrbücher für Geschichte Osteuropas*, N.F., Vol. 5, No. 3 (1957), 315–35; Zitelman, 2.

[2] See Appendix 2 for the full text of all clauses respecting Russia; for a brief and sketchy annotation, see U.S. Department of State, *The Treaty of Versailles and After: Annotations of the Text of the Treaty* (Washington, 1947), 273–74, 540–41, 578–79. Hereafter cited as *Treaty Annotations*. The articles in the other treaties corresponding to Article 116 of the Versailles Treaty were 87 in St. Germain, 72 in Trianon, and 58 in Neuilly.

[3] For a list of all the treaties being annulled, see Zitelman, 77–91.

of German troops from the Baltic as soon as the Allies "shall think the moment suitable, having regard to the internal situation of these territories." New provisions were added: Germany was prohibited from sending reinforcements to the area, and, at the urging of the unofficial Baltic representatives in Paris, it was stipulated that the Germans should not carry out requisitions or interfere in any way in Baltic affairs.[4] With the withdrawal of the German forces in December, this article became inoperative even before the treaty went into effect.

In drafting the Russian clauses of the treaty most attention was paid to the question of reparations. It was clear to everyone that because of the confused situation in Russia little could be done concerning such immediate and concrete questions as Russia's territorial and diplomatic interests and aspirations, but the right to reparations was a more abstract claim, which Russia might later be able to assert. If the principle could be established in the treaty, Russia could endeavor to secure restitution from Germany, once order had been restored and a democratic government established.[5] It is interesting that apparently no one discussed how such a future Russian claim would relate to the prior Western claims against Germany or how Germany could be expected to pay heavy reparations to Russia, in addition to those already due the Western Allies.

The reparations issue was first raised on February 24 in the tenth meeting of the conference's Reparations Commission.[6] Klotz, the French delegate and president of the Commission, recommended that the Subcommittee on the Evaluation of Damages not neglect to estimate damages caused Russia by Germany. Despite objections by the Australian delegate, Hughes, who argued on March 6 that the issue should be decided by the Council of Ten, and attempts by the Polish delegate, Olszowski, to include in Polish claims most of the territory of Byelorussia and Lithuania on the ground that these areas would form part of the future Polish state, Klotz continued to press for Russia's rights.[7] As a result, on April 14 the Commission permitted Raffalovich, the financial expert of the Russian Political Conference, to submit, in an unofficial

---

[4] Miller, *Diary*, XVIII, 481; XIX, 489–90; *Peace Conference*, V, 451–52. For the problems connected with getting the Germans out of the Baltic, see pp. 336–40 of ch. ten.

[5] Telegram from Maklakov to Sebastopol, February 19, 1919, Maklakov Papers, Part II, Packet II, File 10.

[6] *Recueil*, Part IV, B(3), p. 63.

[7] *Ibid.*, pp. 71–72, 194, 309–13, 372–86. On March 28 Klotz proposed that states formerly part of Russia, e.g., Poland, should also have a right to reparations, but this wording was not included in the final draft of Article 116. An interesting sidelight was a brief Polish attempt to make the Germans legally liable for the outbreak of Bolshevism in Russia and the consequent damages to Poland. *Recueil*, Part IV, B(2), pp. 8, 474; B(6), pp. 237–38.

capacity, a long memorandum which outlined in a general way the bases of Russian claims, though no detailed figures or total amount was included.

This report was based in part on a note of April 9 from the Russian Political Conference to the peace conference entitled "Terms Affecting Russia in the Preliminaries of Peace with Germany." [8] The White Russians argued that Russia's contribution to the Allied cause before her betrayal by the Bolsheviks entitled her to equal treatment in the peace terms. Russia, though not a party to the treaty, should be guaranteed by a special clause the opportunity to exercise the same rights, advantages, and privileges that accrued to the Allies under the treaty. Russia should also be represented on all commissions for the execution of the treaty and in the League of Nations. The final form of Article 116, which was submitted by Clemenceau on May 2 and approved by the Council of Four on May 3 with a minor drafting change, did not go as far as the White Russians requested but did nevertheless establish the basis for a later reparations claim on the part of Russia. [9]

The question of preventing German influence in Russia was also treated cursorily and with little discussion among the leaders of the conference. In his Fontainebleau Memorandum of March 25 Lloyd George, after dwelling on the potential dangers of a German-Russian alliance, urged that the peace treaty provide for German recognition in advance of any arrangements the Allies had made or would make with regard to former Russian territory. [10] On April 7 the Council of Four asked the Council of Foreign Ministers to prepare such a clause. On April 17 the Foreign Ministers approved a proposed article along these lines, which, according to the Drafting Commission, was "not intended to prejudge anything concerning the future of Russia." [11] This became, with insignificant drafting changes, Article 117 of the treaty.

On May 29, in their observations on the draft treaty, the Germans, commenting on its Russian clauses, protested in particular against Article 117, claiming that it was unfair to force Germany to recognize in advance whatever arrangements the Allies might make respecting Russian territory and states. [12] The German delegation argued that Ger-

[8] Unfortunately, no copy of this note was found in the Maklakov Papers, but its main arguments are referred to in the Raffalovich memorandum and in later notes of the Russian Political Conference.

[9] Miller, *Diary*, XIX, 139–40; *Peace Conference*, V, 424, 451.

[10] Temperley, VI, 544.

[11] *Peace Conference*, V, 40, 580–81; Miller, *Diary*, XVII, 496–97, XIX, 138–39.

[12] *Peace Conference*, VI, 809, 845, 951; Alma Luckau, *The German Delegation at the Paris Peace Conference* (New York, 1941), 312, 343–44, 368, 433.

many could recognize such arrangements only if she knew what they were and could judge for herself whether they affected Germany's boundaries or interfered with Germany's peaceful relations with her eastern neighbors. In regard to Article 116 the Germans maintained that the first paragraph, requiring Germany's unconditional recognition of the independence of Russian territory, was superfluous since Germany claimed no Russian lands and had no intention of interfering in the political or other affairs of these areas. Concerning the rest of Article 116, the Germans declared that the second paragraph was also unnecessary since they had already abrogated the Treaty of Brest-Litovsk under the terms of the Armistice, and they concluded by flatly rejecting Russia's right to reparations. In addition, the German delegation opposed Article 292 on the grounds that its provisions would jeopardize Germany's reestablishment of normal economic relations with Russia. In their reply of June 16 to the German observations on the treaty the Allies refused to make any changes in the clauses affecting Russia. This was done without any comment on the German arguments, except to note in regard to Article 292 that it did not prevent Germany from restoring economic relations with Russia.

Despite the inclusion of Article 116 the Russian Political Conference was dissatisfied with the treaty, repeating in a note of May 22 the claims it had advanced on April 9.[13] The White Russian leaders added that they hoped the reference in Article 117 to "states part of the former Russian Empire" was intended to embrace only those states whose independence Russia would recognize. They also urged that the abrogations and restitutions called for in the financial and economic clauses be broadened to include private, as well as public, German assets and concessions in Russia. A month later, on the eve of the signing of the treaty, in a memorandum of June 25 submitted to each of the Allied governments, the White Russian diplomats reviewed the difficult position in which the peace terms placed Russia. Since the Versailles Treaty was not sufficiently satisfactory to Russia to permit her simply to adhere to it, she would be forced to end the state of war still existing with Germany by concluding a special treaty with Germany "under especially unfavorable conditions for herself." [14]

Nevertheless, in the succeeding months the White Russians attempted on several occasions to profit from their right to reparations under Article 116. Efforts were made to obtain German arms and supplies for Yudenich in this way, as well as German shipping for Denikin, but with

[13] Miller, *Diary,* XVIII, 444–48.
[14] British Foreign Office, *Documents,* III, 396–98. See also Sazonov's bitter comments in a telegram to Omsk on June 9, cited in Subbotovsky, 77.

little result.[15] The Poles also utilized Article 116, pressing reparations claims on this basis from December 1919 into 1923.[16]

Article 116 also played a role in the making of the Soviet-German agreement at Rapallo in April 1922. In 1921 the Germans, faced with further French pressures over reparations, had been concerned that Soviet Russia might attempt to claim reparations under that provision of the Versailles Treaty, even though the Bolsheviks had denounced and ignored the treaty. In the first days of the Genoa Conference of 1922, as secret negotiations between the Western leaders and the Soviet delegation proceeded in Lloyd George's villa, the Germans became increasingly alarmed that Soviet Russia and the Allies might decide to put into effect Article 116 and might also reach a general political agreement which would isolate Germany. These German fears—unfounded as far as Article 116 was concerned, since the Soviet diplomats apparently had no intention of using it to press claims against Germany—helped convince the German leader Rathenau to conclude the Rapallo agreement with Soviet Russia.[17] This treaty annulled the right reserved to Russia in Article 116 by establishing a mutual waiver of claims for war damages, a provision confirmed in subsequent German-Russian agreements.[18]

Thus the clauses affecting Russia in the Versailles Treaty, having received little attention from the peacemakers, met with little success. The effort to safeguard a right to reparations for a reconstituted anti-Bolshevik government in Russia was fruitless since no such government appeared. And the attempt to prevent German influence in Russia was soon undermined by the natural drawing together of the two "outcasts" of Europe, a process in which Article 116 played its part.

Russia and the League of Nations

To a considerable degree, as we shall see in the conclusion, Woodrow Wilson viewed the League of Nations in the abstract as a major alternative to and defense against Bolshevism. However, the interests of Russia as a nation were, because of her current distress, almost entirely ignored in the planning and foundation of the League of Nations. In two respects only—in regard to membership and to territories which might be mandates under the League—was the position of Russia briefly considered during discussions of the League at the peace conference.

---

[15] Maklakov Papers, Part II, Packet III, File 6; Polk Diary, September 10, October 8.

[16] For a full discussion of this Polish effort, see the article by Epstein cited in n. 1 above.

[17] Fischer, I, 337–40.

[18] *Treaty Annotations*, 274.

During the preparation of the Covenant the participation of a Bolshevik Russia in the League was definitely ruled out, but a British draft of January 20, 1919, which was largely the work of Robert Cecil, declared in an accompanying note: "Russia cannot probably be invited to adhere, but it may be advisable to state in a protocol the reasons for this omission." [19] On March 18 in a discussion with Wilson, House, and David Hunter Miller, the American expert on the Covenant, Cecil went further, arguing that since the Great Powers should be an essential element in the Executive Council of the League, Article III of the Covenant should be amended to provide for the eventual participation in the Council of Germany "and even of Russia." [20] Moreover, in a long, somewhat pessimistic letter of April 11, Hoover warned Wilson that exclusion of Germany and Russia from the League "will tend to drive the Central Empires and Russia into an independent League." [21] Later, the Russian Political Conference, in a memorandum on the peace terms dated May 22, maintained that Russia should be included as an original member of the League in order to ensure the latter's stability.[22] On June 3, during a discussion among the Big Three of the advisability of providing for Germany's later admission to the League, President Wilson noted in passing: "The most troublesome elements in Europe—Germany and Russia—were, at present, being left outside the League." [23] Nothing was done, however, to follow up these fleeting suggestions, and Russia was not included in the League when it was founded, nor was provision made for her eventual membership.

The possibility of applying the League mandate system to certain of the former territories of the Russian Tsardom received more extensive consideration. In a long proposal of December 16, 1918, which David Hunter Miller believed had "a profound influence on President Wilson," the South African statesman J. C. Smuts suggested that the League should become the heir to the former multinational empires of Russia, Austria-Hungary, and Turkey, serving as guardian for the politically unschooled and economically backward national minorities of these areas, not in the former spirit of centralization and repression, but in a spirit of justice and equality.[24] By holding these territories in trust until they were ready for full independence, the League could prevent annexations and a division of "spoils," which would only frustrate national

[19] Miller, *Diary*, IV, 42; see also a copy of Cecil's draft in the Bullitt Papers.
[20] Miller, *Diary*, I, 181.
[21] Wilson Papers, Series VIIIA, Box 35.
[22] Miller, *Diary*, XVIII, 445–46.
[23] *Peace Conference*, VI, 157–58.
[24] David Hunter Miller, *The Drafting of the Covenant* (2 vols; New York, 1928), II, 25–33; I, 34.

aspirations and drive the peoples to Bolshevism. Smuts felt that Poland and Finland were already capable of establishing their independence, but that the peoples of the Caucasus and of Transcaspia should be autonomous under the supervision of the League or its trustees. The latter, he suggested, might be states selected by the peoples themselves as mandatory rulers on behalf of the League. Miller commented that the Smuts proposal would lead to "intervention in Russia by all the world," and Wilson's draft of the Covenant on January 10, though including the general idea of mandates as suggested by Smuts, omitted any mention of Russia, adding instead the former German colonies as areas to be governed by mandate.[25]

Nevertheless, the idea of a mandate for the Caucasus was implicit in the discussions of the Council of Ten on January 30, when it was decided to study how best to police Turkey and the Caucasus pending a decision by the conference on the general assignment of mandates.[26] And on February 8, after it had become clear that there was little likelihood of getting the groups fighting in Russia, including the national minorities, to come together at Prinkipo, Wilson proposed to the conference's Commission on the League of Nations an additional clause on the mandate system "intended to extend the import of the [mandate] article to some territories which were formerly part of the Russian empire." But this proposal met with no support at all and was not included by the editing committee in the final draft of the article on mandates, which was approved on February 10.[27]

Behind these general discussions at the conference lay the specific idea that the United States, which unlike the European powers clearly had no special strategic, economic, or political interests in the area, might be persuaded on humanitarian grounds to accept a mandate for all of Armenia, including both its Russian and Turkish-ruled parts, and perhaps for Constantinople and the Straits as well.[28] It was hoped that the American public, which had often in the past expressed sympathy and concern for the plight of the Armenian people, might more willingly support a commitment in Armenia than in any other part of the world. Wilson himself was attracted to this idea but warned his colleagues that it would take some time for him to develop the necessary understanding and climate of opinion in the United States. Because of this consideration, among others, the drafting of a Turkish treaty was put off in the spring of 1919, to the disadvantage of the Allies. The Treaty of Sèvres with Turkey was completed only in the spring of 1920, after it had be-

[25] *Ibid.*, I, 34, 101.
[26] *Peace Conference*, III, 807–08.
[27] *Recueil*, Part IV, B(1), p. 45; Miller, *Drafting of the Covenant*, I, 186.
[28] Miller, *Diary*, I, 74; Lloyd George, II, 1259–60.

come quite clear that the American public would support no foreign obligations at all (and, also, after the emergence of a national movement in Turkey had made it impossible to enforce the treaty).

Though linked to some extent with the Turkish treaty, the situation in Russian Armenia, and in the Caucasus as a whole, had distinctive features which made it impossible for the peacemakers also to postpone action there. The area was impoverished and hungry, national movements of the Caucasian peoples were developing rapidly, which brought them into conflict with Denikin and the White Russians, and in the distance there lurked the danger of Russian Bolshevism. During the war, and after the Bolshevik seizure of power, the British had been anxious and concerned about the area, primarily because they feared German or Turkish expansion into the Caucasus, with a consequent threat to the British position in the East. The British had intervened early in 1918, but insisted after the Armistice that the fate of the Caucasus should be settled by the peace conference and that they were keeping forces there only to maintain order and to prevent bloodshed. By mid-January 1919, however, the British commander-in-chief, General Sir Henry Wilson, was increasingly worried that the British could not, in the face of the great pressures for rapid demobilization, support garrisons everywhere, and he decided that the Caucasus was one area from which the British ought to withdraw. He believed that if the Americans could not replace the British, the Italians might be persuaded to do so. After securing approval of the Cabinet and of Lloyd George, he worked out on March 26 with the Italian General Diaz a plan for eventual replacement of the British forces in the Caucasus by Italian troops.[29] The same day Orlando proposed to House that Italy, in order to secure much-needed coal and oil, should become a mandatory for the Caucasus, while the United States should accept a mandate for Armenia and share in the control of Constantinople. House seemed agreeable to this suggestion.[30]

Apparently either House and Lloyd George never informed President Wilson of these arrangements or the latter forgot, as the prime minister told General Wilson. In any case, six weeks later when Lloyd George mentioned to the American president and Clemenceau on May 3 that the Italians were going to the Caucasus, Woodrow Wilson was surprised and dismayed, and both he and the French leader opposed the plan.[31] The matter was raised again indirectly on May 14 and May 21, when Lloyd George suggested a provisional American mandate for all of the

[29] Callwell, *Wilson Diaries*, II, 163–64, 171, 176.

[30] Memorandum of conversation between Orlando and House, March 26, House Papers, Drawer 29, File 31.

[31] Callwell, *Wilson Diaries*, II, 180, 188; *Peace Conference*, v, 467–68.

Caucasus, as well as a regular mandate for Armenia and the Straits. President Wilson was doubtful of Senate approval but did not completely reject the possibility of an American mandate for Armenia alone.[32] A month later the president commented privately that although he personally wanted to see the United States take mandates for Armenia and Constantinople, it was up to the American people to decide.[33]

The Big Three took no further action on a mandate for the Caucasus and Armenia, though they approved on June 28, just before they broke up to go home, a proposal by Hoover for appointment of an American, acting on behalf of the Allies, to be resident high commissioner in Armenia. His task was to be supervision of relief operations there pending a final settlement.[34] To some, assignment of an American to this post seemed to be the first step toward an eventual American mandate in the area, but Hoover in his memoirs disclaims any such intention and maintains he consistently advised Wilson against accepting a mandate for Armenia because it would involve the United States in European power politics and would lead to eventual Russian or Turkish pressures to force the Americans out.[35] In any case, opposition in the United States to the Versailles Treaty and the League soon put an end to the idea of an American mandate for Armenia, the Senate formally rejecting a mandate for Armenia on June 1, 1920. In a last display of interest Wilson agreed a few months later to arbitrate the boundaries of the abortive independent Armenia called for under the Treaty of Sèvres.

Meanwhile, the Italians, whose desire to acquire a mandate for the Caucasus had never been supported formally by the Big Three despite Lloyd George's pleas, lost interest in the whole venture as soon as they began to calculate what it would cost in men, money, and future commitments as against what the potential gains might be. Finally, after Orlando's Cabinet fell in June, Nitti, the new premier, abandoned the whole idea, and the problem of the Caucasus was dumped back into the laps of the British. British attempts to settle matters in the Caucasus are closely related to later efforts at the peace conference to erect a defensive cordon against the Bolsheviks and will therefore be treated in the next chapter.

[32] *Ibid.*, 614, 622, 765–70.
[33] C. T. Thompson, 406.
[34] *Peace Conference*, VI, 712, 741, 743–44.
[35] Hoover, *Memoirs*, I, 455.

Soviet Attitudes toward the Versailles Treaty
and the League of Nations

In the fall of 1918, as we saw in the first chapter, the Soviet leaders viewed the Wilsonian peace proposals and the projected League of Nations with mingled scorn and anxiety. They both doubted the sincerity of Wilson's idealistic goals and feared the appeal that the latter might have for the war-weary masses of Europe, to the detriment of their own revolutionary program.[36] They considered the Communist, or Third, International, established in March 1919, an important weapon to counteract Wilsonian propaganda and to defend the revolution against the expected postwar concert of "imperialist" enemies. Among the reasons given for the founding of the Comintern was the necessity to combat "the danger that the alliance of capitalist states that are organizing themselves against the revolution under the hypocritical banner of the 'League of Nation's will strangle the [world] revolution." [37]

As the peace negotiations progressed, however, the Soviet leaders became increasingly optimistic that Wilson's program would not be realized and that the resulting settlement could serve their own ends. On January 24, and again on March 12 and 13, 1919, Lenin claimed confidently that the behavior of the peacemakers was confirming his analysis of the war as an imperialistic war fought for territory and profit; he observed that the victors were quarreling over division of the "spoils" and were thereby "digging their own graves." The statesmen's actions in Paris could not fail to open the eyes of the masses to the "predatory" character of the war and to the "plundering" nature of the so-called democratic governments, and would hasten the development of a revolutionary consciousness among the workers of Europe.[38]

The Bolsheviks were elated when they read the peace terms presented to Germany in May, and they promptly sent messages to the German workers denouncing the harshness of the treaty and expressing sympathy.[39] After the signing of the Versailles Treaty Lenin continued to view the peace as a stimulus to the revolutionary cause, commenting on July 4 that "this unworthy repressive peace . . . is winning us friends throughout the world every day and the imperialist victory reveals the true nature of English and French imperialism and is the beginning of

[36] *Istoriia diplomatii*, III, 28; letter from Chicherin to Wilson, October 24, 1918, in Degras, *Soviet Documents*, I, 115–18.

[37] *Ibid.*, I, 136.

[38] Lenin, *Collected Works*, XXIII, 520; *Sochineniia*, XXIV, 34–35, 61.

[39] Dennis, 92, citing Chicherin in *Izvestiia*, May 13; Jane Degras, *Calendar of Documents on Soviet Foreign Policy, 1917–41* (London, 1948), 26, referring to a note of May 19 from Rakovsky to the German workers' councils; Carr, *German-Soviet Relations*, 27, citing a message in German signed by Chicherin.

the end for them." [40] In one of the earliest and most interesting Soviet commentaries on the Versailles peace, Chicherin analyzed the treaty in an article of June 20, 1919, entitled "Four Congresses." [41] Comparing the Versailles conference to the congresses of Vienna, Paris, and Berlin in the nineteenth century, Chicherin stated that the current meeting was simply a continuation of the European concert of reaction, directed now against the world proletarian revolution. He likened Clemenceau to Metternich, and Wilson to Alexander I: "Wilson, the product of the still not completely decayed bourgeois world, recognizes with foresight the general interests of the bourgeois world, attempts to adapt them to the demands of the times and to the strivings of new awakening forces, and similar to Alexander I, gives first priority to the collective concerns, as he understands them, not only of Europe but of humanity." But, Chicherin continued, like the Russian tsar, Wilson had been unable to overcome the reactionary forces of his society and had been defeated by the new Metternich, Clemenceau. As a result, the principle of self-determination had been turned into an instrument for the imposition of reactionary governments on the peoples of Europe, while the League of Nations was destined to become a guardian of the acquisitions of the Great Powers, as well as a formidable alliance of oppressors against the masses and the proletarian revolution. Interestingly, Chicherin said nothing about Wilsonian democracy serving as a "mask" to conceal the aspirations to world domination of American imperialism, the main theme of attacks on Wilson in Soviet historiography since 1948.

Later, during the Soviet-Polish war of 1920, the Soviet leaders concluded that Poland was the key element in the Versailles settlement: Poland was the active weapon of the imperialists for crushing the Soviet state. Thus a Bolshevik victory in Poland would strike a death blow at the whole postwar imperialist structure and would quickly lead to the long expected European-wide revolution. Moreover, in mid-1920, in Lenin's fullest analysis of the Versailles peace, the Soviet leader took great comfort from Keynes' attack on the treaty in *The Economic Consequences of the Peace*. Citing Keynes' figures, Lenin concluded that the defeated nations were ruined and that this would soon lead to the bankruptcy of capitalism as a whole, thus paving the way for the world revolution.[42] Lenin added that the League of Nations had bitterly disillu-

[40] Lenin, *Sochineniia*, XXIV, 360–61; see also similar comments in speeches on July 15 and November 22. *Ibid.*, 400–01, 545–46.

[41] *Vestnik NKID*, No. 1 (June 20, 1919), 1–12.

[42] Report to the Second Congress of the Comintern, July 19, 1920, Lenin, *Selected Works*, X, 180–99. In early 1964 during a tour of Lenin's office, which is now maintained in the Kremlin as an historical museum, the author noticed on Lenin's bookshelf André Tardieu, *The Truth About the Treaty* (Indianapolis, 1921)

sioned the workers since it had proved to be nothing but an alliance of the rich against the poor and completely unworkable: "Every day of the existence of this Covenant is the best agitation for Bolshevism."

Subsequent Soviet attitudes toward the Versailles peace and the League of Nations lie beyond the limits of this study. Consideration must now be given to the final attempts of the statesmen in Paris to do something about the Russian question, first by assisting various anti-Bolshevik forces and blocking the expansion of Bolshevism, and then, a few months later, by endeavoring to work out some sort of *modus vivendi* with a beleaguered but undefeated Soviet state.

and E. M. House and Charles Seymour, eds., *What Really Happened at Paris* (New York, 1921).

CHAPTER TEN

Final Decisions of
the Conference

ON JUNE 28 the Treaty of Versailles was signed. A few days later President Wilson sailed for home, shortly to face the bitter disappointment of America's rejection of his labors at Paris and his beloved League, for which he had sacrificed so much. The other heads of government soon returned to their regular duties, although occasionally in the succeeding months Clemenceau and Lloyd George participated in the continuing sessions of the peace conference. Partly as a result of the departure of the Big Four, the conditions under which the peacemakers dealt with the Russian question in the period following the signing of the Versailles Treaty were paradoxical. On the one hand, there existed, for the first time since the failure of the Prinkipo proposal, a general Allied policy toward Russia to guide their efforts; on the other, their actions in Paris respecting Russia suffered from a lack of purpose and direction and were poorly coordinated with each other and with the policies of the individual Western governments.

The leaders of the conference in the summer of 1919 all seemed to share an implicit assumption that they should do everything possible to check and, if possible, to defeat Bolshevism. Such a common aim was seldom openly debated or expressly formulated, but it clearly underlay all their discussions and actions concerning Russia and Bolshevism. To a considerable extent the statesmen at Paris were guided by the conference's half-hearted recognition of Kolchak in May and June. This decision both symbolized and set the pattern of general Allied policy toward Russia up to January 1920. There was to be no direct intervention against the Bolsheviks, but every sort of comfort and succor short of troops was to be provided their enemies. Help was to be given to the White Russians, but also to the Baltic peoples, the Poles, the Rumanians, and the peoples of the Caucasus, even though the interests of the non-Russian anti-Bolsheviks often conflicted with those of Kolchak and Denikin. Nevertheless, the Allies took no direct responsibility for their chosen warriors, and little was done to organize and combine the disparate forces fighting Bolshevism. The struggle continued on many fronts, but no war was declared. At the same time there were to be no negotiations with the Bolsheviks and Soviet Russia was to be isolated, diplomatically, politically, and economically.[1] Only if Bolshevism should break out of its Russian enclave were more direct measures to be considered.

Nevertheless, attempts to implement this general policy were hampered by the altered nature of the conference itself. After June 1919 the peace conference was no longer, as it had been for six months, the government of Europe. This was true even though the machinery of the conference, elaborately built up in the preceding half year, continued to operate. There were still a "Supreme War Council" of top military advisers at Versailles, a Supreme Economic Council, a food council, a series of special territorial and substantive commissions, and reduced but still large delegations representing all the major powers. And at the apex, directing this complex of men and power, there remained a "Supreme Council," now called the Council of Heads of Delegations. Chiefs of government did not sit in this body, except on a few occasions, but the Council still theoretically represented the collective will of the victorious Allies on all matters pertaining to the peace settlements. The main business of the conference was the execution of the Versailles Treaty and the conclusion of treaties of peace with Austria, Hungary, Bulgaria, and Turkey, but the heritage of the previous months and the confused conditions in many parts of Europe inevitably led the Council into problems, such as that of Russia, which were only tenuously related to its main tasks.

At the same time the conference now formulated Allied policy less and less, and served increasingly as transmitter and executor of decisions made in the Western capitals. With the departure of the Big Four from the conference, each government, and its respective foreign office, began to reassert control over policy and to take independent action. As a result, there was often a lack of coordination between the conference and the individual governments, as well as among the Allied powers. Nowhere was the consequent uncertainty and confusion more apparent than in respect to policy toward Russia. In principle the conference had

[1] In the evidence used for this study only two instances were found of proposals in official quarters during the summer and fall of 1919 for peace with the Bolsheviks: on June 17, when the military advisers to the British delegation in Paris recommended talks with the Bolsheviks and other parties to the Russian civil war along the lines of the Prinkipo plan (Beadon, 103–07), and on July 28, when a memorandum by O. C. Harvey of the British Foreign Office proposed negotiations with Lenin (British Foreign Office, *Documents*, III, 464).

determined a joint Allied policy by its decision to support Admiral Kolchak. But in practice many questions remained: how was Kolchak's partial recognition to be implemented? Who was to bear the required burdens, and where? What did this imply for the peoples along Russia's western border? Not only did no one know any of the answers, but no one was sure how to proceed to find them. Were these matters to be placed before the already overburdened peacemakers in Paris? Or should each government make up its own mind and then try to win the cooperation and support of its allies through regular diplomatic consultations?

The diplomats, both in Paris and at home, were puzzled and distressed by the lack both of direction in Russian policy and of a mechanism to develop and execute specific courses of action. As early as July 7 a senior specialist on Russian affairs in the British Foreign Office advised Balfour of "the inconvenience which results from the present more or less dual control" over Russian matters; he recommended that since the peace conference did not seem to have the time or inclination to pursue the subject, Russian policy should be handled through ordinary diplomatic and military channels. Others in the Foreign Office suggested at about the same time establishment of a special inter-Allied council on Russia, but no action was taken.[2] Frank Polk, who headed the American delegation in Paris after Lansing and Henry White had returned home, noted several times in the late summer and fall the uncertainty over Russian policy at the conference and the confusion of responsibility which existed concerning this question.[3] Moreover, there was some feeling among those at the conference that Russia was not their affair and should be left to the individual governments. On September 19, in the course of a trip to Europe, Colonel House reported to President Wilson from Paris that "The Russian situation . . . in the opinions of all of us, is a matter which should be handled through the Foreign Offices since no decision is possible here with the heads of government no longer sitting." And in mid-November Sir Eyre Crowe, then head of the British delegation, reported to London that "we have here acted on the understanding that the peace conference was not the proper organ for treating" the Russian question.[4]

Lloyd George, however, believed otherwise. On three occasions in the fall and winter, as we shall see shortly, he appeared personally at the

[2] *Ibid.*, III, 419; and see Curzon's memorandum of August 21, discussed below, p. 365.

[3] Polk Diary, *passim.*

[4] Letter from House to Wilson, September 19, House Papers, Correspondence; British Foreign Office, *Documents*, III, 647–48; and see Polk's remarks to the conference in a similar vein, *Peace Conference*, IX, 101–02.

peace conference to plead, among other things, for a concerted Western policy toward Russia. It is clear that the British leader, ignoring proposals for a special Allied body to deal with Russia, saw the Council at Paris as the best instrument for endorsing and putting into effect on an inter-Allied basis the policies toward Russia which he favored.

On the other hand, in the periods between these high-level interventions the conference dealt with matters affecting Russia more or less haphazardly, though within the general framework of policy described at the beginning of this chapter. As a result, the various measures adopted in Paris to strengthen those opposed to Bolshevism were usually *ad hoc* decisions, related only in a vague way to any overall design. These actions will be summarized here to indicate both the overall pattern of Allied policy toward Russia as reflected at the conference and its disjointed operation and execution.

Containing Bolshevism

With the demise of the Hoover-Nansen relief plan and the decision to grant partial recognition to Kolchak, it was clear that the Western powers intended to isolate the Soviet regime as completely as possible. One of the first actions to this end was the decision in mid-June to continue the blockade of Soviet Russia, in fact if not in name. In the course of 1918 trade with the Bolsheviks had been quite completely interrupted, first by the British, who not only cut off their own exports but applied pressure to other states, both allied and neutral, to do so, and then established naval units in the Gulf of Finland to interdict shipping for Petrograd, and later by the Americans, who refused to grant export licenses for Bolshevik-dominated areas of Russia.[5] These restrictions were defended as measures designed to prevent vital supplies from reaching the Germans through the Bolsheviks, and the means of enforcement, including agreements with numerous neutral countries not to ship to Russia, were connected with the vast Allied blockade machinery against Germany.

In May 1919, as agreement on the terms of peace with Germany neared and in view of the Allied promise to lift the blockade against Germany once the treaty was signed, the leaders at Paris began to consider what to do about the supplementary blockade against Bolshevik Russia. Without explanation or discussion the Council of Four decided on May 9 that the planned raising of the blockade against Germany would not apply to Soviet Russia as well.[6] After the question of

[5] For these earlier measures in the blockade against Russia, see *1918, Russia,* III, 103–18, 170–82.
[6] *Peace Conference,* v, 522.

blockading Soviet Russia had subsequently been debated, without resolution, in the Supreme Economic Council and its Blockade Committee,
President Wilson declared in the Council of Four on June 17 that there
was no legal justification for continuing to blockade Russia.[7] Lloyd
George, foreshadowing his concern later in the year that British merchants have a chance to capture a part of the Russian market, warned
that the powers, by blockading Russia, might be opening the door to
German commercial and economic domination of Russia. Anxious to
prevent assistance reaching the Bolsheviks but puzzled as to how to accomplish this legally, the Council finally unanimously agreed on an ingenious compromise: no measures would be taken to continue the
blockade but there would also be no announcement or encouragement of
the resumption of trade with Soviet Russia.

This, however, did not satisfy the French and British, who in July and
August pressed for formal endorsement by the peace conference of a full
blockade against the Bolsheviks, despite the legal complexities raised by
the fact that the Allies were not at war with Soviet Russia. Even though
Balfour in Paris addressed a personal appeal to President Wilson in
Washington, the United States government, now thoroughly committed
to anti-Bolshevism but with a long history of concern for the rights of
neutrals on the seas, was not to be bullied into establishing in this case
what might be a dangerous precedent.[8] Wilson tempered his refusal with
the suggestion that the Allies might instead jointly request the neutrals
not to trade with Soviet Russia in view of the danger Bolshevism posed
to the whole world.

The French and British accepted this recommendation but wanted, in
addition, to tell the neutrals that Entente naval authorities, acting on behalf of all the powers, would turn back ships approaching Petrograd.
The Americans objected that this was tantamount to a blockade.[9] After
six weeks of wrangling, the conference finally agreed in October 1919
on a compromise: a joint note would be sent to the neutral nations and
also to Germany asking them to embargo trade, communications, and
financial transactions with Bolshevik Russia, while the naval warning
desired by the Entente would be delivered only in oral form. When the
note was sent, the Germans rejected the Allied request.[10] By that time,

[7] *Ibid.*, XI, 248, 325–26, 333–36; VI, 530–32. In a speech on May 15, 1922, Hoover
claimed he had opposed continuation of the blockade against Russia in 1919, but
the records of the conference give no evidence of his position then.

[8] *Ibid.*, VII, 131–34, 265–67, 312–14; *1919, Russia,* 155–56.

[9] *Peace Conference,* VII, 720–21, 724–27, 817; VIII, 8–10, 345–48, 365–68, 438–
40; and letter from Polk to Lansing, September 26, Wilson Papers, Addendum III,
Acquisition 9712, Box 19.

[10] The Soviet government strongly protested the Council's action in parallel
notes of October 20 to Germany and to the neutrals involved. *Dokumenty vneshnei
politiki SSSR,* II, 263–64.

however, a reversal of Russian policy was in the making, and Lloyd George was soon to advocate the resumption, not the blockading, of trade with Russia.

The action of the conference concerning the blockade of Soviet Russia is an excellent example of how difficult it was for the men at Paris to deal with the Russian question. In the first place, as so often happened, the decision, or half-decision, of the conference had relatively little effect on the issue itself. Regardless of the struggle around the council table and the Americans' firm defense of legality in this case, in fact very little trade was taking place between Bolshevik Russia and the outside world anyway.[11] This was less because the conference opposed it in general, whatever the quarrels about it in detail, than because individual Allied powers not only opposed it but took specific action to prevent it. Thus while the peacemakers debated, the Americans continued to refuse export licenses to Russia, and French and British warships continued to patrol the waters of the Baltic and Black seas. Moreover, the neutrals' fear of incurring Allied displeasure, the difficulties of establishing normal communications with Russia, and the absence of credit and exchange facilities operated to keep trade to a minimum.

Second, this case, as so many others affecting Russia, reflected the hazards and problems of coalition diplomacy. The position and policy of one power, in this instance the United States, no matter how much it accorded with that of the majority in its general outlook on Russia and Bolshevism, was sufficient to delay joint action for almost four months, or until long past the time when it could have had any effect. And unanimity, once reached, was almost at once easily overturned by a change of heart on the part of the prime minister of one of the major partners to the alliance.

All this is not to say that the will of the conference to blockade and isolate Russia meant nothing. It certainly had an important negative effect in that a contrary policy, a decision to lift the blockade, would undoubtedly have considerably hastened the reestablishment of normal intercourse and commercial exchange between Soviet Russia and the outside world. The Soviet government protested bitterly against the blockade, and the Russian people suffered grievously in the winter of 1919–1920 and in the great famine of the succeeding year. This is not the place to attempt to assess how much the continued Allied blockade was responsible for those sufferings and disasters.[12] The Allies were

[11] See the report of the Commissariat of Trade and Industry to the 7th Congress of Soviets, December 1919, *ibid.*, ii, 621–28.

[12] See, for example, the British Parliamentary report on the blockade prepared by the so-called Emmott Committee, which concluded in 1920 that the blockade was one factor contributing to the virtual economic collapse of Russia. British Parliamentary Papers, *1921,* Vol. 25, Cmd. 1240, pp. 106, 110.

waging an undeclared war against the Bolsheviks, and the blockade was one weapon in that struggle. Given their overall policy toward Russia, it is hard to see how the Allies could have eschewed this weapon. Perhaps what was wrong was not the weapon but the war.

Besides attempting to maintain the isolation of Soviet Russia, the men at Paris did what they could to assist that beleaguered country's manifold enemies. Following the partial recognition of Kolchak, the next natural step, and the one which would have furnished maximum assistance to the White Russian cause, would have been full recognition of Kolchak's regime as the *de facto* government of Russia. But by mid-June word had reached Paris that Kolchak's armies were in retreat, and his prospects looked bleak. In early fall, prompted by ephemeral victories of the White Russian armies and by the urgings and appeals of White Russian diplomats, there was brief reconsideration of the possibility of granting Kolchak full recognition.[13] Before a decision could be taken, President Wilson had his stroke and Kolchak's armies were again on the run.[14]

Most aid to Kolchak and other White Russian leaders was furnished directly by the individual Western governments in the form of advisers, surplus war materiel, and credits. There was little the peace conference could do. One possibility, however, was to reinforce the anti-Bolshevik armies with the several hundred thousand Russian prisoners of war in Germany who were now under Allied control.[15] This plan had been broached by Foch at the very beginning of the conference in mid-January, but the Council had not acted on it at that time. Instead, the peace-makers had decreed that these unfortunate souls, homesick, destitute, and of questionable military value, should not be repatriated at all, in order to prevent their falling into the hands of the Bolsheviks.[16] Follow-

[13] For British consideration of full recognition, see *1919, Russia*, 728–29; British Foreign Office, *Documents*, III, 711. For American views, letter from Phillips to Wilson, September 27, Wilson Papers, Addendum III, Acquisition 9712, Box 19; for Polk's interest see *1919, Russia*, 431, and Polk Diary, September 26, reporting on a meeting with Sazonov; for Lansing's position, Confidential Memorandum, "The Suggested Recognition of the Kolchak Government," October 9, Lansing Papers, and *1919, Russia*, 723–24, 447. For discussion in the American delegation, see S-H Bulletin 964 of September 20, Department of State Records, 184.611/1084.

[14] I could find no evidence to support Polk's sanguine statement to a Russian caller that "as a matter of fact, if it had not been for the President's illness, recognition would have been granted." Polk Diary, October 1.

[15] For details on the whole problem, see Edward F. Willis, *Herbert Hoover and the Russian Prisoners of World War I* (Stanford, 1951), who, however, greatly overrates the potential value of the POW's to the Red Army.

[16] For discussion on January 12 of the prisoners' fate, see *Peace Conference*, III, 472–73, 479–81; for the new clause covering the prisoners which was included in

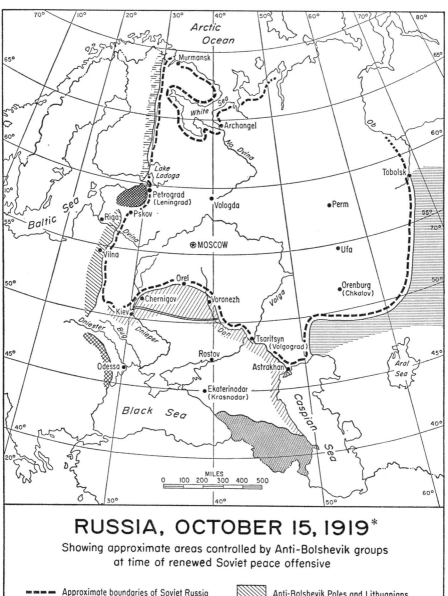

RUSSIA, OCTOBER 15, 1919*

Showing approximate areas controlled by Anti-Bolshevik groups
at time of renewed Soviet peace offensive

- – – – Approximate boundaries of Soviet Russia
- Omsk government of Admiral Kolchak
- Anti-Bolshevik ("White") Finns led by General Mannerheim
- Northwestern army led by General Yudenich

- Anti-Bolshevik Poles and Lithuanians
- Rumanians
- Volunteer army under General Denikin
- Independent Caucasian Republics

═══════ Battle line in South Russia, November 1, 1919, after General Denikin had begun to retreat

*Based on fighting fronts in George Stewart, <u>The White Armies of Russia</u> (N.Y., 1933), pp. 267, 282.

ing an abortive decision in April to let the Germans repatriate the Russian prisoners at will, the Council of Foreign Ministers attempted in mid-May to arrange repatriation of selected prisoners to anti-Bolshevik areas.[17] When this scheme failed for lack of organization and transport, the conference declared in late July that the Germans were henceforth responsible for the feeding and repatriation of the Russian POW's—in short, the powers were washing their hands of the whole affair, even though they were responsible for the fact that the prisoners were still in Germany and not home.[18] Foch's later proposal for an international repatriation commission was rejected by the Germans, and those prisoners who remained in Germany after the close of the conference either eventually returned home, with the assistance of the International Red Cross and of refugee organizations under the League of Nations, or settled in Western Europe. Although a few prisoners may have reached the White Russian armies during 1919, this meager assistance for the anti-Bolshevik cause hardly justified the human suffering that resulted from the delays in settling the prisoners' fate. The whole affair was indeed a sorry minor episode in the history of the peace settlement.

One of the few resources of military significance that the conference, as a collective Allied body, did control was surplus war materiel in the defeated countries. A number of efforts were made, usually at the instigation of the Russian Political Conference in Paris, to transfer some of this materiel to the White Russian fronts, but, as with the prisoners, little was actually achieved, except the delivery of a few ships to the Black Sea fleet of General Denikin.[19]

Efforts to give the White Russians material assistance, limited though they were, nevertheless were more successful than the few attempts the peacemakers made to encourage cooperation between the White Russians and the non-Russian anti-Bolsheviks. During the summer and fall the leaders of the conference several times urged the Estonians and the White Russians in the Baltic to bury their differences, but to little avail. And, when it was suggested that the conference act to stop friction between Denikin and the Ukrainians on one occasion, and between Denikin and the peoples of the Caucasus on another, the peacemakers almost

---

the January 16 renewal of the Armistice as a result of that discussion, see *ibid.*, II, 13. For a Soviet protest against the handling of the prisoners, see Degras, *Soviet Documents*, II, 132–33.

[17] *Peace Conference*, IV, 706–09, V, 40; *Recueil*, Part IV, C(2), 771–72; Miller, *Diary*, XVII, 453–55, XVIII, 129–31, 203–05.

[18] *Peace Conference*, VII, 208–10, 230–31, 486–88, 498–501; Palmer, 410.

[19] For White Russian requests, see Maklakov Papers, Part II, Packet III, File 6. For conference action, *Peace Conference*, VII, 792; VIII, 489, 501, 580–82; IX, 342–43, 391–93, 425–27, 531, 784–85, 796–97.

literally threw their hands in the air, admitting helplessly that they were unable to prevent such squabbles.[20]

The most significant failure in this regard occurred in connection with abortive schemes for a joint Finnish-White Russian attack on Petrograd. The design was an attractive and winning one; it envisaged an army of sturdy Finns advancing on the former Russian capital from the north, while White Russians and Estonians invested the city from the south. The Allies were to furnish guns, food, and money. Once the city was taken, a link could be made with the hard-pressed anti-Bolshevik forces in North Russia and the combined armies would sweep down on Moscow to destroy the Bolshevik menace forever.[21] There was an essential prerequisite, however. The Finns demanded recognition of their independence and territorial claims by both the Allies and the White Russians. The role of the peace conference in this endeavor was secondary to that played by the White Russian and Allied governments, particularly the British, but in the spring of 1919 some action was taken in Paris to support the scheme.

Spurred on by Herbert Hoover, the Allied foreign ministers at the peace conference decided in early May to recognize Finnish independence.[22] Wilson justified this apparent violation of Russia's territorial integrity, which he so consistently championed, as follows:

> I am pretty clear in my view that the case of Finland stands by itself. It never was in any true sense an integral part of Russia. It has been a most uneasy and unwilling partner, and I think that action in regard to the recognition of the Finnish government would not commit us or embarrass us with regard to the recognition of any other part of the former Russian empire that might be separately set up.[23]

A further proposal, that the Allies encourage the Finns to assist the White Russian General Yudenich, was blocked by the British.

Although Finnish participation in an offensive against Petrograd clearly depended now on White Russian recognition of Finland's inde-

[20] *Ibid.*, VIII, 766; IX, 606–07, 696–97; British Foreign Office, *Documents*, III, 613–15.

[21] For early discussions of this plan, see Journal of Outgoing Communications with the Allies, December 23, 1918, Denikin Papers, Archive of Russian and East European History and Culture, Columbia University; Tomilov Papers, same, pp. 38–40; *1919, Russia*, 670–71, 674; various telegrams in Maklakov Papers, Part II, Packet III, File 4.

[22] Miller, *Diary*, I, 239; Hoover, *Memoirs*, I, 365–66; and *Peace Conference*, IV, 662–68; V, 316, 352; XI, 82, 87, 112. I have found no evidence to justify Hoover's assertion in his *Memoirs*, I, 365, that "the French were the obstruction [to Finnish recognition], as they believed Communist Russia would collapse and that the question should be kept open to settle with the expected new Russian government."

[23] Letter to Lansing, May 13, Wilson Papers, Series VIIIA, Box 47.

pendence, Hoover proposed to the conference on May 23 that food and supplies be shipped to the vicinity of Petrograd in expectation of its capture.[24] Despite Lansing's opposition and the failure of the foreign ministers or the Big Four to act on his proposal, Hoover, on his own and independently of conference policy and of the position of the American delegation, went ahead and stockpiled during the summer of 1919 thousands of tons of foodstuffs at Viborg, earmarking it for the relief of Petrograd, when and if it should be occupied.[25]

Meanwhile negotiations between the Finns and White Russians were proceeding badly. Admiral Kolchak's government in Omsk urged full military cooperation with the Finns, but refused to go beyond granting the Finns autonomy until an all-Russian constituent assembly could be convened.[26] Driven to desperation by such shortsightedness, in mid-June General Yudenich finally reached an agreement with the Finns on his own.[27] Ignoring the agreement and British pressure to secure his endorsement of it, Kolchak sent vague and emotional appeals both to the Finns and to the Allies. But he promised only "Russia's sincere esteem for the freedom of the Finnish people," and that all issues between Russia and Finland would be settled with the assistance of the League of Nations.[28] On July 7, in response to Kolchak's message, the Council of Heads of Delegations decided that the Finns should merely be told that if they "felt able to grant the request to act made to them by Admiral Kolchak, the Allied Governments, without bringing any pressure on the Finnish Government, would have no objection to that operation." [29] Not surprisingly, such noncommittal support from the Allies did not satisfy the Finns.

Subsequent attempts by Finnish General Mannerheim to shake Kol-

[24] *Peace Conference*, IV, 753–57; for earlier reports on which Hoover based his proposal, see *1919, Russia*, 669–71, 674.

[25] British Foreign Office, *Documents*, III, 346; *1919, Russia*, 693–96, 698–99, 700–01; Hoover, *Memoirs*, I, 418–19. Moreover, Hoover, again on his own initiative, accepted payment for the food for Petrograd in 5 per cent notes of the unrecognized Russian government in Omsk; telegrams of July 15 to Omsk and July 20 to Washington reporting the financial agreement with Hoover, Maklakov Papers, Part II, Packet II, File 2.

[26] Telegram from Kolchak to Yudenich, May 2, cited in "Kolchak i Finliandiia," *Krasnyi arkhiv*, XXXIII, 52–54.

[27] British Foreign Office, *Documents*, III, 394–95 n. 1. Details of the subsequent complicated negotiations among Mannerheim, Kolchak, Yudenich, and the British, which lie outside the scope of this study, can be found in *ibid.*, III, 381–436, and in Maklakov Papers, Part II, Packet III.

[28] Subbotovsky, 245–46; *1919, Russia*, 681.

[29] *Peace Conference*, VII, 38–39. This was in general accord with recommendations to Lansing of his advisers Lord and Whitehouse on June 30, although they suggested the phrase "would welcome" rather than "would have no objection." Records of the ACTNP, File 861.00/813.

chak's adamant position and to secure British guarantees and financial assistance failed, and the whole scheme collapsed.[30] As an ironic footnote, on October 29 Sazonov in Paris, despite the protests of the faltering "Supreme Ruler" in Omsk, agreed to recognize the "factual" independence of Finland and even offered to pay Finnish expenses in a joint campaign against Petrograd.[31] Alas, it was far too late!

The whole episode had a fantasy-like yet tragic quality. It was quite clear, not only in retrospect but at the time, that the capture of Petrograd would deal a serious, perhaps mortal blow to the Bolshevik cause; it was equally clear that the city could be taken only with the help of the Finns and that they would assist only if their independence and territorial aspirations were recognized by the White Russian leaders. Only a few miles from Petrograd stood a willing, even eager General Mannerheim, the Finnish commander. Thousands of miles away in the heart of Siberia stood a proud and patriotic Russian admiral, the nominal ruler of Russia, whose armies were already in full retreat before the Bolsheviks. Blinded by national pride and oblivious to the realities of the situation, Kolchak refused to yield what the Finns asked, even when his own dreams were in ruins. Here, as in its relations with the peoples of the Baltic and the Caucasus, the White Russian leadership proved fatally shortsighted, contributing heavily to its downfall.[32]

The Baltic and Poland

A complicating factor in all the schemes and dreams for capturing Petrograd was the struggle of the Baltic peoples to assert their independ-

[30] Subbotovsky, 246–49; British Foreign Office, *Documents,* III, 411 n. 1, 435–36, 444. The refusal of the British Foreign Office and government to take responsibility for Finnish participation is clear throughout the episode. The White Russian military representative, General Golovin, reported to Omsk on June 21 that the chief of operations in the War Office had outlined to him a plan of attack against Petrograd which involved the use of Finnish troops under Allied direction. Maklakov Papers, Part II, Packet II, File 2d, printed under date of June 13 in *Kto dolzhnik?,* 343–44.

This single telegram, unreliable evidence at best, has been the chief basis of numerous Soviet charges that England tried to force Finland into attacking Petrograd; see, for example, E. Adamov, "Rol' Anglii v interventsii" ("The Role of England in Intervention"), *Vestnik NKID,* No. 6–7 (August 25, 1920), 18. Fischer (I, 200) concluded on the basis of similar evidence, but quite erroneously, that the Allies and the peace conference tried to pressure Finland to join Yudenich's effort against Petrograd.

[31] British Foreign Office, *Documents,* III, 620–21, and telegrams exchanged between Sazonov and Omsk in October and November. Maklakov Papers, Part II, Packet III, File 4.

[32] The story of White Russian policy toward the non-Russian nationalities of the former Empire, with its strange rationalizations, its reluctant compromises, and its divisive effect within the movement, has never been fully told but may be unraveled in the Maklakov Papers at the Hoover Institution.

ence of both Russia and Germany. Their efforts, coupled with Allied, Bolshevik, and German intrusions in the area, led to an extraordinarily confused situation within the Baltic territories in 1919. The Baltic question soon became one of the most persistent and complex problems relating to Russia that the peacemakers faced. Four important and closely linked issues were involved: first, the future status of these areas— Estonia, Latvia, and Lithuania; should they remain within a reconstituted Russia in some dependent or autonomous relationship, or should they be recognized as independent states in accord with the pleas of their unofficial representatives in Paris? Second, what assistance should the Baltic governments, whether recognized or not, receive to help them prevent famine and restore order, and to buttress them against the inroads of domestic or Russian Bolshevism? Third, what policy should be adopted toward the continuing efforts of the anti-Bolshevik Russian movement in the Baltic led by General Yudenich? And finally, what should be done about the German forces which had been permitted to remain in the area under Article XII of the Armistice but which were clearly attempting to establish a base for future German domination of the Baltic and perhaps of Russia? [33] In the absence of any clear-cut conference policy toward Russia or toward Bolshevism, it was manifestly impossible to supply definite answers. Moreover, with occasional exceptions, the Big Four were not directly concerned with the Baltic question, leaving its discussion to the second-level Council of Foreign Ministers, to the Commission on Baltic Affairs, and to the staffs of each delegation. The lower echelons, without clear guidance from the top, were naturally reluctant to make far-reaching decisions and found it difficult to determine a consistent course of action.

As a result, and as so often happened regarding issues that affected Russia, those at the conference concerned with Baltic affairs temporized, or developed *ad hoc* policies to meet immediate needs, and in the end were largely swept along by the tide of events in the area itself. These events, together with decisions made not at the peace conference but in the Allied capitals, largely determined, some time after the conference closed, the postwar settlement of the Baltic question.[34] Our concern here cannot be with these broader developments and policies; we will attempt only to see how the peace conference did act on the Bal-

[33] All of these issues were cogently raised in a memorandum of April 11, 1919, from the Food Section of the Supreme Economic Council to the Council of Foreign Ministers. The latter avoided these questions in their discussion of the memorandum. *Peace Conference,* IV, 589.

[34] Two studies of the general problem of the struggle of the Baltic peoples for independence are Graham and Alfred Senn, *The Emergence of Modern Lithuania* (New York, 1962).

tic question, from what motives, and the extent to which its decisions influenced the tangled affairs of that area. Nevertheless, from this "case study" certain generalizations can be drawn concerning the difficulties and handicaps which surrounded the whole effort at Paris to solve the Russian problem.

In the winter of 1918–1919 conditions in the Baltic area were chaotic. Indigenous Baltic governments were being hard pressed both by Bolshevik forces, which on the eve of the peace conference had captured Riga and established a Latvian Soviet Republic, and by German troops, who had remained in the area under the Armistice terms. The German forces, at first supported by the new German government but later disavowed by Berlin, were depicted as assisting in the establishment of a bulwark to protect Europe from the "Eastern" threat of Bolshevism, a task which some Germans insisted the Allies should aid and encourage.[35] At the same time the Germans in the Baltic often interfered with the newly established local governments and took measures designed to ensure German political and economic domination of the area in the future.[36] The British were assisting the Baltic peoples, while the French were torn between the desire of the Quai d'Orsay to support White Russian hopes for a reconstituted Russia "one and indivisible," and the anxiety of Foch and others to help anti-Bolshevik forces wherever they existed.[37] The Americans, though maintaining their insistence on the territorial integrity of Russia, were also attracted to the possibility of establishing the Baltic states as an anti-Bolshevik barrier. In addition, Herbert Hoover, primarily concerned with relief problems, was determined to aid the Baltic peoples regardless of the consequences for the general policy of the United States toward Russia.

Thus, to a considerable extent, all the major powers desired to help the Baltic peoples against Bolshevism. But how was this to be done? The statesmen all agreed that no Allied troops and very little money were available to support direct action in the area. Foodstuffs, supplies,

[35] For this argument, see an address of February 3, 1919, by Prince Max of Baden in the *Preussische Jahrbücher,* March 1919, translated in the German Press Summaries, 1917–June 1919, of the National Board for Historical Service, Box 4, Manuscript Division, Library of Congress.

[36] Graham, 254, 328, 407–08; Temperley, VI, 298–99. For a fuller discussion of German policy in the Baltic after the war, see the memoirs of the German high commissioner, August Winnig, *Am Ausgang der deutschen Ostpolitik, persönliche Erlebnisse und Erinnerungen* (Berlin, 1921). On the German war aims which lay behind this policy, see Fritz Fischer, *Griff nach der Weltmacht: Die Kriegszielpolitik des Kaiserlichen Deutschland, 1914–18* (Dusseldorf, 1961).

[37] See pp. 55–59 of ch. two on British and French policy and pp. 46–49 of ch. two on American policy. See also a suggestion in a British Foreign Office memorandum of June 6, 1919, that the Baltic was primarily an area of British influence and responsibility. British Foreign Office, *Documents,* III, 365.

and surplus war materiel could indeed be sent, but this course of action might produce some unpleasant consequences for the Allies. On the one hand, such assistance might permit the Baltic peoples to assert their independence, an accomplishment which neither French nor American policy favored. On the other, the aid might fall into the hands of the Germans, helping them to thwart the aspirations of the Baltic peoples and to establish German hegemony in the area. It is little wonder that the diplomats at Paris remained perplexed, and were in the end able to do little to shape events in the Baltic.

When the Baltic question was first raised at the conference in March 1919, the peacemakers decided on two steps. First, they permitted the German forces to remain in the Baltic but forbade the German government to reinforce them, a prohibition which was largely ignored.[38] Second, in order to open up normal channels of assistance, the Council of Foreign Ministers approved on March 28 a recommendation of the Supreme Economic Council that the blockade of Russian territories be lifted in respect to Estonia, provided no supplies were reexported to Bolshevik Russia or to Germany.[39] The initiative for this second step came chiefly from the American delegation, which in mid-March sent a mission of inquiry to the area and which at this time was actively discussing relief for Russia as a whole, the consideration of which led, as we saw in chapter seven, to the Hoover-Nansen plan.[40] The Council of Foreign Ministers at the urging of Lansing and McCormick, also agreed on the same day that the blockade could be lifted in regard to Latvia and Lithuania as well, as soon as the political and military situation in those areas had become more favorable.

Events in the Baltic soon cast doubt on the wisdom of these first halting and limited steps. On April 16 the German forces in the Baltic instituted the overthrow of the Latvian national government. This served to dramatize the dilemma of the powers: if they left the Germans there and sent in aid, as they had just decided, they ran the risk of turning the Baltic into a German province. If they forced the Germans to withdraw, while failing either to replace them with Allied contingents or to recognize the Baltic Governments, the whole area might fall prey to Bolshevism. Prolonged debate attempting to square this circle took place during April and May. French and American delegates rejected a tentative

[38] Council of Ten, March 3 and 5, *Peace Conference*, IV, 190–92, 207, 212. For a discussion of how German requests at this time to be permitted to supply and reinforce their troops in the Baltic were related to Foch's plans for a crusade against Bolshevism, see pp. 181–82 of ch. six, and Council of Four, March 29, Manfoux, I, 80.

[39] *Peace Conference*, IV, 524–26, 535.

[40] *Ibid.*, XI, 40, 62, 79, 112–14, 126–27; *1919, Russia*, 668–69, 672–74.

British recommendation to recognize at least the Estonian government, which had established itself more firmly than the others against both the Bolsheviks and the Germans.[41] Lansing, Hoover, and McCormick continued to press vigorously for sending aid under guarantees that neither the Germans nor the Bolsheviks would benefit from it; they also objected vehemently to the refusal of the British naval forces in the area to facilitate the landing of even emergency relief supplies. Heated exchanges occurred with Pichon and Balfour, who charged that assistance really meant helping and cooperating with the Germans, a morally distasteful and politically dangerous course.[42] The strength of Hoover's convictions about aid and his pique at the British attitude were revealed in his independent decision in early May, before the conference had decided on a policy, to send three relief ships to Estonia and Latvia and by the claim in his memoirs that he asked German General von der Goltz to occupy Riga so that order would be restored and supplies could be landed there.[43] Although this was not the only time Hoover acted rashly and without regard to conference policy, his impetuousness led on this occasion to especially unfortunate results; he acknowledges in his memoirs that after von der Goltz took Riga on May 22, a "White Terror" was instituted. He adds lamely that since he "had no particular authority in the matter," he could only protest to his relief agent in Riga.

A compromise policy for the Baltic, which in many respects was to guide conference actions in that area until the end of 1919, was finally adopted on May 23, when the Council of Foreign Ministers decided to send food, clothing, equipment, and arms to the Baltic states. It was also agreed that the Germans should evacuate the area as soon as local forces were organized, a vague provision which soon gave rise to difficulties, and that a military mission under British command should be sent to the Baltic to advise the local governments and to assist in the

[41] Council of Foreign Ministers, May 9, *Peace Conference,* IV, 687–93. On their own the British shortly accorded Latvia *de facto* recognition anyway. The British position was supported in a memorandum of April 29 from Lord and Morison, the American specialists on Russia and the Baltic; however, their recommendations were disavowed by Lansing, who insisted on preservation of Russia's territorial integrity, and they were apparently never discussed with President Wilson. *Ibid.,* 641–42, 655–56, 661–62. Morison later resigned in protest over the decision to support Kolchak and the failure to recognize the Baltic governments. *Ibid.,* XI, 511, and n. 124, ch. eight.

[42] Council of Foreign Ministers, April 19, May 9, and May 23, *Peace Conference,* XI, 589–93, 687–93, 752–57; McCormick Diary, May 7, pp. 82–83. Lansing called the debate on May 9 "a pretty violent discussion." Lansing Desk Diary, May 9.

[43] *1919, Russia,* 676; Hoover, *Memoirs,* I, 374–76. I found no evidence to support or refute Hoover's assertion; his own papers are not yet open to general scholarly use. In view of his beliefs and the availability to him, through his relief agents in the Baltic, of unofficial channels of communication to von der Goltz, the claim is not improbable.

organization of their defense.[44] A further recommendation which called for volunteers from Scandinavia, including Finland, to assist the local Baltic troops against the Bolsheviks as the Germans were withdrawn was never carried out.

As an example of the lack of coordination which often existed within the machinery of the peace conference, the Council of Four, quite independently and without reference to the Foreign Ministers, at least as far as the conference minutes show, discussed some of the same issues on several occasions during June. In general, the heads of government reached the same conclusions, adding only a prohibition of treasury credits to the Baltic states, which each leader argued his government could not afford, and going beyond the Foreign Ministers to demand on June 13 the immediate and complete evacuation of the Germans.[45] This last decision was prompted by reports that the Germans were advancing northward to join the White Russians in the liberation of Petrograd. This news raised vividly before the Big Four a specter just as menacing as that of Bolshevism, the danger of a reactionary Russo-German alliance which might come to dominate all of Europe east of the Rhine. Until then the Allies had been quite content to have the Germans act as a defensive buffer against Bolshevism in the Baltic, even though this meant closing their eyes to German transgressions against the Baltic peoples. Now, however, the risk seemed too great, or as the British Foreign Office later put it, "it would be better that Petrograd should not be captured at all than it should be captured by the Germans." [46]

The order to evacuate the Baltic, transmitted to the Germans on June 18, was easier to issue than to enforce. Despite a reiteration of the powers' demand on August 1 and August 24, the Germans stayed in the Baltic and continued to interfere with the efforts of both the Baltic governments and the various Allied missions to restore order and to establish local defense forces. At first the German government, to justify the failure to withdraw its forces in the Baltic, pointed to the general threat of Bolshevism in the area; its spokesmen also advanced various excuses for the delay, such as the necessity of a prior Allied guarantee of German

[44] *Peace Conference,* IV, 752–57, 762–63. Only ten days earlier, on May 13, in response to a German threat to withdraw from the Baltic without delay and regardless of the consequences for the Baltic peoples, Foch had urged that the Germans be reminded of their obligation under the Armistice to remain. *Ibid.,* 766–73.

[45] Council of Four, June 7, 12, 13, 20, 23, 25, *ibid.,* v, 243–44, 355–56, 373–74, 551–52, 621–22, 672–74.

[46] Memorandum on Germany and the West Russian Government, October 9, 1919, British Foreign Office, *Documents,* III, 140–43. For further details on intrigues in the Baltic between Russian reactionaries and German militarist and extreme right circles, see also Foreign Office Memorandum on the Baltic States and Germany, November 15, 1919, *ibid.,* 225–30.

property and subjects against Baltic retaliation, or the impossiblity of arranging the necessary transporation for the withdrawal. In early September the German authorities took a new tack, maintaining that they had given the order to evacuate but the local commanders had refused and the government was powerless to make them obey. (Later, the Germans admitted that the troops in the Baltic were paid by the Berlin government!) [47]

Finally goaded to action by the infuriating temporizing of the Germans and by their virtual defiance of the Allies' repeated requests, the Council of Heads of Delegations decided in mid-September to attempt to force the Germans out. Since no Allied troops were available for the task, the Council discussed the possibility of using Polish troops, which Paderewski had generously offered for a crusade against Bolshevism. [48] Though proposed by Lloyd George and supported by the French, this plan foundered on the objections of Polk, the American chief delegate. Polk had originally approved this somewhat desperate idea, but he argued after consulting his advisers that this might lead both to Polish annexation of Lithuanian territory and to renewed Polish-German hostilities in Silesia, which would endanger the coal supply of much of Europe for the coming winter. [49] Polk was strongly supported by Lansing in Washington, who cabled on September 30 that he feared Polish designs on Lithuanian territory. In the bitter debates in May the secretary of state had minimized the German risk in the Baltic, and he now added: "While we consented to making the demand for German withdrawal, we did so with the greatest reluctance as it seemed to be the British policy to obtain German evacuation because they feared economic advantage to the Germans, while the French were undoubtedly supporting the Poles' desire for an extension of their boundaries eastward." Polk replied proudly and reassuringly: "Much to the irritation of Lloyd George and Foch I blocked the plans for the use of Poles to compel the Germans to withdraw. . . . I think I have persuaded the British and the French to abandon for the moment all thought of coercive action as to using military force of any kind." [50]

After a good deal of backing and filling occasioned by the need of the

---

[47] *Peace Conference,* vi, 373; vii, 404–05, 428, 734–35; viii, 211–12. For details of most aspects of the effort to obtain German evacuation, see British Foreign Office, *Documents,* iii, Ch. i; for the Allied-German exchange of notes on this issue between May 24 and October 16, see F. C. Zitelman, *Russland im Friedensvertrag von Versailles: Kommentar Nebst einschlägen Noten* (Berlin, 1920), 99–117.

[48] See pp. 344–45 below.

[49] *Peace Conference,* viii, 211–12, 218–22; Polk Papers, Diary, September 15, 16.

[50] Lansing to Polk, September 30, Lansing Papers, Correspondence, Vol. 47; Polk to Lansing, October 3, Records of the Department of State, 761E.62/9A.

American and British representatives to consult Washington and London, the Council decided in late September to apply economic pressure by threatening to cut off the supply of essential foodstuffs and raw materials promised Germany once the Versailles Treaty was ratified, and by warning that the American government would block private credits the Germans were obtaining in the United States. The French also recommended threatening cessation of the repatriation of German prisoners of war, but this was not mentioned in the ultimatum finally sent the Germans on September 27. Stung to action by these threats, the German government proposed on October 3 establishment of a mixed German-Allied commission to supervise and assist the evacuation. The diplomats at Paris agreed, warning at the same time that the responsibility for evacuating was not theirs but Germany's and that measures to ensure compliance had not been abandoned but only suspended.[51]

Shortly afterward the remnants of the German forces in the Baltic were defeated by the Estonians and Latvians, a final attempt by General Yudenich to take Petrograd collapsed, and it became clear that the Baltic states would soon make peace with the Bolsheviks. No further purpose being served by attempting to retain their Baltic foothold, the Germans, prodded along by the supervising commission and the government in Berlin, finally withdrew from the Baltic by mid-December.[52]

Concurrently with the efforts of the conference leaders to clear the balky Germans from the area, attempts were being made in Paris to define a clearer policy toward the Baltic states than that enunciated on May 23 and confirmed on June 13 and June 25. But the obstacles were far too big. In the first place there was no coordination of policy making. During earlier conference discussions of Baltic affairs, as we have seen, there had been little communication between the Big Four and the Foreign Ministers. Moreover, neither group had paid much attention to the Commission on Baltic Affairs, which had been created by the Council of Four on April 16 and which had held its first session on May 15.[53] Although the Commission had been charged with studying the current Baltic situation, as well as the future of that area, the Council of Foreign Ministers had appointed on May 9 its own *ad hoc* commission to propose a policy in the Baltic and had adopted its recommendations

[51] *Peace Conference*, VIII, 233, 342–43, 505–06. Independently of the conference, British naval authorities imposed in mid-October a partial blockade on German shipping in the Baltic, which the Council at Paris subsequently confirmed. British Foreign Office, *Documents*, III, 190–91.

[52] For details of the work of the commission on evacuation, see the study by its head, General A. Niessel, *L'évacuation des pays baltiques par les Allemands* (Paris, 1935).

[53] Memorandum from Lord to Grew, April 8, Wilson Papers, Series VIIIA, Box 33; Mantoux, I, 257–58.

on May 23.[54] After the heads of government returned home, the Council of Heads of Delegations relied very little on the Commission on Baltic Affairs, using it chiefly in regard to the question of Memel.

Furthermore, as we have seen, after June the formulation of policy was divided among the conference, the Allied capitals, and various conference or governmental missions in the field. For example, the heads of delegations were outraged on August 20, when they learned that the military mission in the Baltic under British General Gough, originally dispatched by the conference but largely a British instrument, had forced the formation of a new White Russian government which recognized the independence of Estonia. The diplomats at Paris promptly repudiated that recognition.[55] Similarly, the heads of delegations were adamant that the commission under French General Niessel that they sent to the Baltic in late October to supervise the German evacuation should have no political authority or powers whatsoever. Polk warned that any action implying recognition of the Baltic governments would be disavowed by the United States.[56] Despite Foch's plea a month later that General Niessel be permitted to intervene with the Estonian government to arrange the reorganization and regrouping of Yudenich's army after its defeat before Petrograd in November, Polk and the British representative, Sir Eyre Crowe, absolutely refused to let Niessel act in what they considered to be a political affair.[57] Thus Baltic policy was sometimes made in the capitals and sometimes in the field, but seldom at the peace conference.

In the third place, the conference did not have the power to resolve policy conflicts among the individual Allied nations. In the second half of 1919 it became increasingly clear that the logical course would be for all the powers to follow the British lead and recognize, at least *de facto,* the existing Baltic governments. But pleas from the Baltic delegations and recommendations to this effect in the Baltic Commission were blocked by the firm commitment of Italy and particularly the United States to the territorial integrity of Russia, an obligation which the Russian Political Conference constantly buttressed with strong representations to Lansing, Pichon, and the delegations in Paris.[58] Even "black-

[54] See pp. 337–38 above, and *Peace Conference,* IV, 692–93, 752–57.
[55] *Ibid.,* VII, 730–34.
[56] *Ibid.,* VIII, 788.
[57] *Ibid.,* IX, 388–90, 407–08, 594–95, 604–05, 695–96, 770–71, 785–86.
[58] The United States position opposing Baltic independence was reaffirmed on June 30 by President Wilson; on July 2 by Lansing, *Peace Conference,* XI, 263; on October 11 by the American delegation, which disapproved a draft note on Baltic policy drawn up by the Commission on Baltic Affairs because the note spoke of the "internal independence" of the Baltic states, *Recueil,* Part I, (3), p. 423 n.; and on October 15 by Lansing, *1919, Russia,* 723–24. For examples of the pressure

mail," as Balfour called it, the threat by the Baltic states to make peace with Soviet Russia unless they were recognized, failed to shake Allied policy, the British replying that *de jure* recognition had to be decided in concert with its allies, or through the peace conference or the League of Nations.[59]

Finally, and perhaps most important, the conference was stymied in the Baltic situation, first by the absence of any clear-cut policy toward Russia as a whole and later by the action of the Big Four in partially recognizing Kolchak. As early as March Clemenceau had told Estonian representatives pleading for recognition that nothing could be decided concerning the future of the Baltic until the conference resolved the Russian question, which it would turn to after the German treaty had been settled.[60] Then, after Kolchak's assertion to the conference in June that the future of the Baltic area could be finally determined only by the action of an all-Russian constituent assembly, and the Allies' acceptance of this position, no one was able to set a policy going beyond this mandate. Consequently, the Commission on Baltic Affairs decided on July 17, after weeks of detailed and painstaking effort to work out a complete draft statute governing relations between Russia and autonomous states in the Baltic, that no solution could be reached in the face of the vague commitment to Kolchak, which seemed to leave the matter to an indefinite future settlement.[61] On July 26 the heads of delegations largely accepted this point of view and expressed their helplessness to establish Baltic policy under present circumstances.[62]

By the fall of 1919 events were unfolding in the area almost completely outside the control of the conference, with the exception of the evacuation of the Germans. At the end of the summer the British had begun to reduce their aid to the Baltic states and ceased it altogether in the fall. American food relief had come to an end.[63] The Baltic govern-

of the Russian Political Conference, see Bakhmetev to Bliss, Paris, July 8, *ibid.*, 686–87;*aide-mémoire* of the Russian embassy in Washington, August 29, *ibid.*, 705–06.

[59] Circular telegram of the Foreign Office, September 25, British Foreign Office, *Documents*, III, 569–70. See also a report on the British position in a telegram to Washington, October 23, *1919, Russia*, 728–29; report of the Estonian leader Piip, cited in Graham, 364 n. 66; and telegram from Sablin in London to Maklakov, October 4, Maklakov Papers, Part II, Packet II, File 2d.

[60] Graham, 268, 358 n. 22.

[61] Minutes of the 14th meeting of the Commission on Baltic Affairs, July 7, *Recueil*, Part IV, C(7), p. 149.

[62] *Peace Conference*, VII, 325.

[63] For the reduction of British aid, see Bakhmetev's report of this in a letter to Lansing, August 4, *1919, Russia*, 697; for its cessation, see telegram from Sablin in London to Maklakov, October 4, Maklakov Papers, Part II, Packet II, File 2d, and Curzon in the International Council of Premiers on December 12, *Peace Conference*, IX, 851. For the completion of American relief, totaling 27,700 tons of food, see *1919, Russia*, 698, 700–01.

ments had established themselves, and with the failure of Yudenich's last thrust against Petrograd, Allied interest in the area as an active anti-Bolshevik front faded away. From September on the conference leaders protested weakly against the tendency of the Baltic governments to seek peace with the Bolsheviks, but as the International Council of Premiers, which was the supreme body of the peace conference whenever it sat in December 1919 and January 1920, admitted on December 12, the West could hardly pressure the Baltic states not to make peace with the Bolsheviks unless the Allies intended to assist them against the Red Army. All agreed that no country was prepared to do this and that action would be necessary only if the Bolsheviks attacked again.[64] Lloyd George and Clemenceau also rejected at this time a plan advanced by Curzon and Churchill for formation of an anti-Bolshevik alliance of states surrounding Russia, including the Baltic governments.[65]

Thus the conference ended without a clear resolution of the Baltic problem. It was simply left that the new states there should be considered part of a defensive cordon against the expansion of Bolshevism, although Lloyd George, then in the midst of developing his new approach to the Russian problem as a whole, added optimistically that the Baltic states might "offer a means of peaceful penetration into Russia." [66] In the course of 1920 and 1921 the Baltic governments made peace with Bolshevik Russia and were recognized by most European states. In 1922, following Japan's withdrawal from Asiatic Russia, the United States finally accorded them recognition.

Although the Baltic region, in the view of many at Paris, might serve as a significant eastern outpost against Bolshevism, it was apparent that Poland would have to play the key role in checking Soviet expansion into Europe. Throughout the peace conference the Poles were in a powerful position in regard to "Eastern" questions. As long as the Red Army was heavily engaged with Kolchak, Denikin, and Yudenich, Polish troops, especially after the arrival in the spring of 1919 of Haller's army from France, were the main force in being in the area. The Poles could readily claim to be acting as the chief defenders of Europe against the Bolshevik scourge. At the same time if they were denied assistance or fulfillment of their territorial aspirations, they argued—with some credibility in view of nationalist sentiment in Poland and the country's political inexperience and instability—that this would mean the collapse of the Polish government and the delivery of the country to anarchy and probable Bolshevism.

[64] *Peace Conference*, IX, 851–52.
[65] See pp. 367–70 of ch. ten.
[66] *Ibid.*, 852, 898.

As we saw in chapter six, in June the Big Four agreed—though somewhat hesitantly—to support an enlarged Poland as a central bastion against Bolshevism. Foch and the French representatives in Poland seem to have been the chief proponents of this policy; Wilson and Lloyd George protested at first but soon acquiesced in the extension of Polish control eastward and accepted the idea of constructing a strong Polish buffer against Soviet Russia. For their part, the Poles, though undoubtedly anti-Bolshevik, seized the opportunity to attempt to extend their frontiers to the east and to recover what they believed to be part of the patrimony of a greater Poland.

During the summer of 1919 Poland was considered, with occasional reservations by the British, as a key fortress in the struggle against Bolshevism. Aid of all kinds was supplied, and French officers were sent to help build up and train the Polish army. At the same time the Allies were little inclined to support a direct frontal attack by the Poles on the Bolsheviks. At important Supreme Council sessions on September 15 and 16, called to discuss outstanding issues before the peace conference and attended by Lloyd George, Clemenceau, and Foch, as well as by the heads of delegations, the Allied leaders discussed an offer by Paderewski to invade Russia and to capture Moscow with an army of five hundred thousand men—if the powers were prepared to pay for the whole venture at a cost of a million pounds a day.[67] The alternative, Paderewski stressed, was for the Poles to make peace with the Soviet government. Somewhat staggered, Lloyd George and Polk doubted that the Allies were prepared to take on such a heavy financial commitment, while Clemenceau argued that a Polish invasion would simply rally all Russians to the Bolshevik cause. Even Foch warned that Poland had better secure her western frontier with Germany before embarking on forays to the east.[68] At the same time the Allied leaders declined to advise the Poles to make peace with the Bolsheviks. The plan for capturing Moscow was nevertheless soon dropped, although, as we saw above, discussion then turned to the possibility of using Polish troops to replace the German forces in the Baltic, a suggestion eventually killed by Polk's ob-

[67] Although the Poles were generally skeptical of the possibility of launching this attack in concert with the White Russian armies, at about this time they began negotiating secretly with Denikin, as well as with Maklakov and Shcherbachov in Paris, demanding political and territorial concessions from the White Russians as the price for an offensive against the Bolsheviks. Both Denikin and Kolchak, to whom the question was referred from Paris, welcomed Polish military cooperation but indignantly rejected the proposed concessions. Telegrams from Denikin to Sazonov, October 15, Sazonov to Denikin, November 27, and Kolchak to Sazonov, December 9, Maklakov Papers, Part II, Packet III, File 5. See also Piotr Wandycz, "Soviet-Polish Peace Talks in 1919," *Slavic Review*, xxIV (September 1965).

[68] *Peace Conference*, vIII, 204, 208–09, 211–13, 218–22.

jections. After this, peremptory demands from the Poles for increasing quantities of materiel and munitions began to be scrutinized more carefully, although the French continued to urge all-out support to their Polish protégés. In mid-October the United States firmly refused to supply more arms to the Poles, Polk asking pointedly whether they really needed such a big army, and in early January 1920 the British blocked a Polish request for authorization to buy arms from the Germans.[69]

At the same time the conference regularly overlooked Polish transgressions eastward. Little was done, for example, to restrain Polish incursions against Vilna and the Lithuanians, and a proposed Polish mandate over Eastern Galicia for twenty-five years, which had been worked out after months of painstaking discussion and compromise, was obligingly suspended in December 1919 in the face of violent Polish objections that the territory was indisputably Polish and because of fears that the mandate decision endangered Paderewski's government. Concurrently, the Allies promised to furnish defensive assistance to Poland.[70]

The conference also agreed in December to a provisional definition of Poland's frontier with Russia along a line (later known as the Curzon Line) which, though quite unsatisfactory to the Poles, was clearly labeled as a "minimum" line beyond which the Poles were free to negotiate wider boundaries with the Russians if they could. To be sure, as Wandycyz and Komarnicki argue, such a tentative settlement in the east amounted to no settlement at all, and in fact the Allies were attempting to use the Poles to contain the Bolsheviks without confirming Polish sovereignty in that direction. At the same time the Allies were genuinely, and rightly, concerned over the final allotment to Poland of territories to which the Russians had some claim as well.

Given the Allies' nonrecognition of the Bolsheviks and the absence of any official Russian representation at the conference, it is difficult to see how the diplomats in Paris could have acted differently. As Professor Lord pointed out, some of the Allied statesmen were anxious "to keep the aspirations of the new ally, Poland, within limits that would not irrevocably antagonize the old ally that might some day be won back—Russia." [71] The Allies, fearing the dangers to Poland of such a course and still hoping for the reconstitution of a democratic Russia, were not prepared at that time to support the dreams of Pilsudski for a Greater Poland, including much of the eastern borderlands of Lithuania, Byelorussia, and the Ukraine. As a result, the Poles acted on their own in

[69] *Ibid.,* 710–12, 722–23; ix, 787–89.

[70] See p. 369 below.

[71] In Charles Seymour and E. M. House, *What Really Happened at Paris* (New York, 1920), 70.

1920. The consequent Polish-Soviet war lies outside the scope of this study, but some of the issues involved were clearly a heritage of the inability of the Allies to develop a consistent policy in the east in 1919 and of the incompleteness of a European peace settlement made without Russia's participation.

The Resumption of Trade

As the brief summaries above have indicated, the peacemakers, under the general banner of anti-Bolshevism, planned or carried out during the second half of the Paris Peace Conference a number of separate measures designed to assist the opponents of the Soviet government and to prevent any expansion of Bolshevism. These efforts were partially successful: although the Soviet regime in Russia was not destroyed, it was temporarily checked from extending its control over the non-Russian areas on the western borders of the former Tsarist Empire. It is hardly surprising that the statesmen in Paris, hampered by insufficient authority, power, and popular support and frequently confronted with conflicting interests among the Allied powers and between the White Russians and the non-Russian border peoples, were unable to develop a clearer and more consistent policy toward Russia than the vague anti-Bolshevism the conference espoused or to coordinate effectively Western policy and the varied aspects of the anti-Bolshevik movement. Whether a better organized and more concerted effort might have toppled the Soviet regime is problematical. In any case, the result was a stalemate between the West and Soviet Russia. With the collapse of the forces of Kolchak, Denikin, and Yudenich in the late fall of 1919, it was clear that indirect intervention in Russia itself, as one strand of anti-Bolshevik policy, had failed. The Soviet government was isolated but undefeated. The border peoples seemed on the verge of securing a precarious independence. All parties to the struggle were exhausted and dispirited. The time was ripe for new policies and new approaches. Bolshevism had survived, and the Allied leaders now had to decide how the West could live with it.

As a result, during the closing weeks of the peace conference, in December 1919 and January 1920, the statesmen at Paris adopted an ambivalent policy toward Russia. On the one hand, they agreed to end military intervention against the Bolsheviks and to encourage resumption of trade with Soviet Russia; on the other, they decided to establish a defensive cordon against Bolshevism along Russia's western and southern borders. Both these measures, to be implemented concurrently, were the result of British initiative—though, to be sure, each came from a different quarter in the British government. Lloyd George and his personal advisers advanced the idea of trade, while Curzon, Churchill, and the Foreign and War offices supported the encirclement of Russian Bolshevism.

Several circumstances help explain why it was the British who took the lead in Russian matters in the latter part of 1919. In the first place, British interests, both commercial and strategic, were more directly affected than those of the other powers. Some British traders were anxious to gain entry to the Russian market before the Germans or others could establish themselves there. At the same time the potential threat to the Middle East of Bolshevism, or of Bolshevism combined with Islamic nationalism, alarmed those British statesmen whose chief concern was the "Empire." Moreover, in Russia itself the British were still carrying most of the financial and military burden of the anti-Bolshevik struggle.

There was also the personal factor; Lloyd George had supported aid to the White Russians in the spring when it seemed expedient and when political opposition at home and among his allies had defeated the Prinkipo and Bullitt plans, but he had never abandoned his hopes for some sort of peaceful settlement in Russia. He still believed that an accord with the Bolsheviks would both mitigate their radicalism by bringing them into contact with Western Europe, and would serve to prevent German domination of Russia.

Finally, leadership devolved on the British partly by default; neither the French nor the Americans were in a position to shape and direct Russian policy for the West. The French were primarily concerned with the German question and were content to leave the dilemma of Bolshevik Russia to the British as long as Allied support to Poland and Rumania was assured. The United States was chiefly interested in Siberia and the Far East. Moreover, although the American government continued to assist Kolchak and to endorse the territorial integrity of Russia, it was already beginning to develop the policy of withdrawal and nonrecognition which characterized its attitude toward Soviet Russia throughout the next decade.

Thus it fell to the British to initiate new approaches to the Russian problem. In order to understand what led them to propose the measures adopted by the peace conference near its close, we must examine briefly the evolution of British policy toward Russia after the conference's decision in May and June 1919 to accord partial recognition to the government of Admiral Kolchak. At first British diplomats were puzzled and disturbed. They were not sure how the decision to assist Kolchak should be implemented; they were perplexed by the conflict within the anti-Bolshevik camp between the White Russians and the border peoples; and they were distressed that neither a concerted Allied policy toward Russia nor a mechanism for developing such a policy seemed to exist.[72] On July 29, after the collapse of Churchill's scheme to evacuate the Czechs through North Russia, and with Kolchak still retreating across Siberia, the War Cabinet reaffirmed its earlier decision to withdraw all British forces from North Russia. At the same time, however, it reiterated its support for the general policy of anti-Bolshevism set forth in Lloyd George's speech of April 16.[73] It was agreed that in this effort British assistance should now be concentrated on Denikin, to whom a political representative would be sent. It was also decided that Lord Curzon should prepare a draft message to the Allies proposing a common policy toward Russia, but this was never done.

The decision to focus British aid to the anti-Bolsheviks on Denikin was based on several considerations. The heavy costs of the anti-Bolshevik struggle dictated some rationalization and curtailment of British aid, while British interests in the Caucasus, discussed in chapter nine and later in this chapter, made it more logical to support Denikin than Kolchak.[74] Moreover, as Kolchak's military position worsened, Denikin's improved. Finally, it was easier to assist Denikin, using the supply route through the Black Sea. Both Kolchak and the White Russians in Paris were soon told of this decision, although Churchill attempted to soften the blow by encouraging the admiral to seek aid from the United States.[75] Churchill wanted personally to lead a mission to Denikin, but was finally dissuaded from going by Lloyd George.[76] In the fall a British professor and politician, Sir H. J. MacKinder, was sent, but by the time he returned with detailed recommendations for assisting Denikin and making his government more democratic, Denikin had been defeated by the Bolsheviks. The French, whose withdrawal from Odessa and earlier support of Petliura and the Ukrainians had aroused Denikin's ire and Britain's suspicions, also sent a mission, accompanied by Maklakov, to Denikin in an effort to establish more cordial relations with him and to prevent his falling completely under British influence.[77]

Before very long, however, Lloyd George began to think not only of concentrating and curtailing aid to the anti-Bolsheviks, but of ceasing it altogether and making peace with the Soviet government. Unfortunately, he has not left in his memoirs any explanation or account of how he

[72] See Foreign Office Memoranda of June 6, July 11, and July 28 and Memorandum from the Director of Military Intelligence, July 4, in British Foreign Office, *Documents,* III, 5, 365–68, 460–64, 413–15.

[73] *Ibid.,* III, 464 n. 1; on Churchill's scheme, see pp. 216–20 of ch. six; on Lloyd George's speech, pp. 245–46 of ch. seven.

[74] *Ibid.,* III, 717.

[75] See telegram from Churchill in Annex No. 29, *Kto dolzhnik?,* 411–12.

[76] Riddell, 117–18, 175.

[77] British Foreign Office, *Documents,* III, 366; Maklakov Papers, II, Packet II, File 9.

reached this conclusion, but it is possible from other sources to reconstruct the sequence of events and the likely motivations for his action. It seems clear that, in the beginning at least, four considerations influenced the British leader: growing opposition in Britain to a policy of active anti-Bolshevism, the expense involved, the dimming prospects of the anti-Bolshevik armies, and his own predilection for a peaceful settlement with Lenin. Only later did the attractions of trade with the Bolsheviks play an important role in his thinking.

By the end of August Lloyd George had decided that intervention was a failure. He began telling associates that the anti-Bolshevik Russians had been given the chance to save Russia that he had promised them in his April 16 speech; now Britain could no longer bear the burden of supporting a war that seemed both indecisive and of doubtful utility.[78] Moreover, during the summer Labour and Liberal opposition to British intervention in Russia had continued to grow, and a session of the Trades Union Congress in September threatened to call a special meeting to decide what action the labor movement should take if the government did not change its Russian policy.[79] On the other hand, Churchill and influential Conservative politicians were still strongly advocating all-out support of the White Russians. As a compromise, Lloyd George first decided that future aid to the anti-Bolsheviks should be limited to a fixed amount and to a definite period. If the White Russians had not succeeded with that help and within that time in establishing themselves, that would be the end of the matter, and no further assistance would be given them.[80] Churchill accepted this decision grudgingly, and only after the prime minister on September 22 had written him a blunt but friendly letter, reminding the war minister that England had done all it could to keep faith with the anti-Bolshevik Russians but that "not a member of the Cabinet is prepared to go further. . . . We cannot afford it." Pleading with Churchill to abandon further schemes for intervention, Lloyd George admonished: ". . . I have found your mind so obsessed by Russia that I felt I had good grounds for the apprehension that your great abilities, energy, and courage were not devoted to [fulfilling my repeated requests for] the reduction of expenditure." [81]

Not content with this half-measure Lloyd George went to Paris in mid-September to try to persuade the peace conference to formulate a new

[78] Riddell, 117–18; Polk Diary, September 1; letter from Lloyd George to Churchill, August 30, cited in Frank Owen, *Tempestuous Journey: Lloyd George, His Life and Times* (London, 1954), 517–18.

[79] Coates, *Anglo-Soviet Relations,* 140–41.

[80] Polk Diary, September 1 and 13; telegram from Sablin in London to Sazonov, September 19, Maklakov Papers, II, Packet III, File 10.

[81] Owen, 519–21; Churchill, *Aftermath,* 261–63, 267–70.

Russian policy. He succeeded in raising the Russian question with the Council of Heads of Delegations on September 15 and 16, but the discussion was almost at once sidetracked into consideration of the Polish offer to send an army of half a million men against Moscow.[82] Nevertheless, Lloyd George issued a press statement that the Council had endorsed British plans to withdraw from Russia and to oppose future intervention there. This was completely untrue, but evidence is insufficient to show whether this was a deliberate "trial balloon" by the prime minister or whether the statement, prepared in advance in hopes that the conference would approve what Lloyd George had intended to propose, was released accidentally. In any case, the statement created a storm of protest and comment in England.[83] Conservative leaders and papers strongly criticized the statement, while Liberal and Labour circles applauded it.

Within a day or two Bullitt's testimony before the Senate Foreign Relations Committee was released, which occasioned another outburst of debate on Britain's Russian policy.[84] Although Lloyd George was widely criticized for lack of candor regarding his relationship with Bullitt, attention soon focused on Bullitt's betrayal of personal and governmental confidences and on the harm his testimony would do to Wilson's efforts to secure Senate ratification of the Versailles Treaty. Thus for a few weeks discussion of the Russian question subsided in the British press.

It revived quickly in mid-October, however, once Denikin's thrust toward Moscow had been turned back, and it had become clear that the Baltic states were likely to make peace with the Bolsheviks. Public opposition to continued intervention received new impetus from Labour's gains in recent municipal elections, from the declaration of a left-leaning Liberal M.P., Lieutenant Colonel Cecil Malone, who had just returned from Soviet Russia, that Lenin was still prepared to make peace with the Allies on the lines of the Bullitt proposal, and from the open questioning of Britain's policy toward Russia by Lord Robert Cecil.[85] Nevertheless,

[82] See p. 344 above.

[83] Polk was caught in the middle when he candidly told a journalist, in reply to a direct question, that the Council had taken no such action. Polk Diary, September 16 and 17; telegram from Polk to Wilson and Lansing, September 17, Records of the ACTNP, 861.00/1032A.

[84] See press reports in Lansing Correspondence, Vol. 47; telegram from Sablin in London to Sazonov, September 18, Maklakov Papers, II, Packet III, File 10; and Ann C. Gerhart, "The United States and the Problem of Russia at the Paris Peace Conference," unpublished honors thesis, Bryn Mawr College, 1956, 75–83.

[85] Dispatch from Sablin in London to Sazonov in Paris, November 4, 1919, Maklakov Papers, Part II, Packet III, File 10; Great Britain, House of Commons, *Debates,* 1919, Vol. 120, cols. 954–55, 1578.

Churchill and his supporters apparently scored a clear-cut victory on November 5 when the House of Commons considered a supplementary army appropriation which included a final allocation of fifteen million pounds for Denikin, to be expended in the period up to April 1, 1920. After over six hours of heated discussion in which Colonel John Ward, recently returned from Siberia, strongly defended the government against the attacks of Malone and other opponents of intervention, Churchill concluded the debate with a forceful summary of why Britain should continue to aid the anti-Bolsheviks. He stressed the international menace of Bolshevism, the danger of German domination of Russia, and British obligations of honor to the White Russians and the border peoples. When the vote was taken, the government won easily, 251 to 52.[86]

This victory for the interventionists was almost immediately undercut by the prime minister himself. On November 8, in a speech at the annual Guildhall banquet of the lord mayor of London, Lloyd George surprised his audience and took a daring political gamble by enunciating his doubts about intervention and by proposing new efforts to establish peace in Russia.[87] He declared that the Allies had paid their "debt of honor" to the Russian people by giving them a chance to win their freedom. Maintaining that "the world cannot afford a continuance of the struggle in Russia, which is devastating a country essential to the world's prosperity," Lloyd George recalled with regret the failure of the Prinkipo proposal and expressed his hope that in the near future "an opportunity may offer itself for the Great Powers to promote peace and concord in that great country." In a reply to Parliamentary questioning of these statements on November 13, Lloyd George endorsed *pro forma* Churchill's policy statement of November 5, but then went on to discuss the desirability of ending the Russian civil war both for humanitarian reasons and because Europe needed Russia's great resources of food and raw materials.[88]

True to form, the Labour and Liberal press expressed delight, while Conservative papers, led by *The Times,* bitterly criticized Lloyd George's speech as "a vicious proposal for a renewal of 'Prinkipoism.' " The progovernment French press was horrified, and, according to one report, Lloyd George's speech moved Clemenceau to characterize the

[86] *Ibid.,* cols. 1545–1642.

[87] The London *Times,* November 10, 1919, p. 9. This speech was made without the knowledge of Lord Curzon, the foreign secretary, according to a report by American Ambassador Davis to Washington, December 3, 1919, U.S. Department of State, *Papers Relating to the Foreign Relations of the United States, 1920,* III, 484.

[88] Great Britain, House of Commons, *Debates,* 1919, Vol. 121, cols. 470–75.

[351]

British prime minister as "a deserter in the face of the enemy." [89] Fuel was added to the flames when the House of Commons debated the Guildhall speech on November 17.[90] Lloyd George took an equivocal stand, strongly attacking Bolshevism and defending the policy of aid to the anti-Bolsheviks outlined in his April 16 speech, but at the same time repeating that Britain could not continue indefinitely to finance the White Russians, who had been given a fair chance, and asserting that he did not fear Bolshevism when it was confronted with confidence by a just and sympathetic government. This bit of fence-straddling failed to satisfy *The Times,* which labeled it the worst defense of foreign policy in decades, adding that the prime minister had done little to allay the anxiety aroused by his November 8 speech.

From this time through the spring of 1920 Lloyd George, with his usual dexterity, continued to pursue a two-sided policy. On the one hand, he lent his support to efforts by Churchill and Curzon to create an anti-Bolshevik cordon around Soviet Russia; on the other, he developed his interest in establishing contact with the Bolsheviks in order to reach a settlement with them. Politically, this was an astute maneuver. The first aspect of British policy appeased to some extent the strongest anti-Bolsheviks in the Conservative Party and press; the other accorded with the wishes of Labour and Liberal critics of intervention. Skillfully juggling both balls in the air, Lloyd George seemed little disturbed by the inherent contradictions in these two approaches to Russia, and managed to avoid, for a time at least, the political pitfalls strewn along the course of Anglo-Russian relations in these years.

For six weeks after the spirited Commons debate on November 17 the nimble prime minister played down his peace plans and seized upon the policy of a defensive cordon around Soviet Russia as a means of disarming and discomfiting his Conservative critics, who were then exerting heavy pressure on him.[91] This policy, to be discussed in the next section of this chapter, embraced, among other things, the calling of an anti-Bolshevik strategy conference, either of the Allied powers alone or together with the White Russians and the border peoples. Lloyd George vaguely supported the idea of such a conference, and, building on a reference in his November 17 speech to Disraeli's warning against the dan-

[89] Bonsal, 29, citing a letter from Clemenceau to House. A copy of this letter was not found in the House Papers.

[90] Great Britain, House of Commons, *Debates,* 1919, Vol. 121, cols. 682–738.

[91] For an account of the efforts of Conservative circles to influence Lloyd George in November, see the political report of Prof. D. D. Gardner to General Heroys, Denikin's military representative in London, December 3, 1919. Maklakov Papers, Part II, Packet III, File 10.

gers of a strong Russia, he also began to advocate recognition of the non-Russian peoples of Russia's borderlands and the breaking up of the old Russian Empire.[92] Tactically, these moves were extremely clever, since they exacerbated the main problem confronting the supporters of an anti-Bolshevik alliance—how to reconcile the contradictory aims of the White Russians and of the national minorities and how to get the two groups to sit down together and concert their efforts. Subsequently Lloyd George reduced the conference idea simply to a discussion of Russian policy during an already planned meeting of the Allied premiers in London.[93] But he permitted unofficial contacts with the Ukrainian separatists and encouraged Curzon's efforts to secure recognition of the independence of the Caucasian states, commenting laughingly to one of his confidants: ". . . Denikin is opposed to the new states [in the Caucasus] so that in protecting them you are fighting Denikin. That places Winston in an awkward quandary." [94]

In December and early January, however, Lloyd George also began to advance more actively his other policy—to establish contact with Soviet Russia.[95] The rout of Denikin, the collapse of Kolchak, the imminence of peace between the Baltic states and the Soviet government, and the Bolsheviks' renewal of formal peace offers to the Allies all helped to create a more favorable climate for the fruition of Lloyd George's hopes. The first three developments are self-explanatory, but the last deserves some attention.

The Soviet desire for peace was, of course, nothing new. Despite the failure of the Bullitt proposals and the Hoover-Nansen plan, Lenin in the summer of 1919 was as anxious as ever to end Allied intervention, direct and indirect; however, with the almost complete physical and diplomatic isolation of Soviet Russia and with the necessity of concentrating all Bolshevik efforts to repulse the attacks of Kolchak, Denikin, and Yudenich, the Soviet leaders had little opportunity to pursue their peace policy directly with the West. In this period revolutionary propaganda became a major feature of Soviet foreign policy, or as Foreign Minister

[92] See replies to questions in the House of Commons on November 20 and 25, *Debates,* 1919, Vol. 121, cols. 1109, 1594–95; reports of Lloyd George's views in a telegram from Polk to Lansing, November 29, Records of the ACTNP, 861.00/1175A, and in a telegram from Ambassador Davis to Washington, December 3, *U.S. Foreign Relations, 1920,* III, 484.

[93] See pp. 367–68 below.

[94] Margolin, 56–57; Riddell, 161.

[95] Report of the prime minister's views in a telegram from Polk to Lansing, November 29, Records of the ACTNP, 861.00/1175A, and telegram from Sablin in London to Sazonov in Paris, December 9, Maklakov Papers, Part II, Packet III, File 10.

Chicherin put it: "We write fewer notes to governments but more appeals to the working classes." [96] Thus on July 17 Chicherin sent a radio message to the workers of the Entente countries urging them to oppose intervention and the blockade against Soviet Russia.[97] This was followed by radio appeals of September 27 and October 30 calling upon the English and French workers to agitate against indirect intervention through the border states and to support peace between Soviet Russia and the Baltic governments.[98]

Indirect contact with the West was reestablished in October, when an August interview with Lenin was published in the *Manchester Guardian* under the headline, "Bullitt Peace Terms Still Hold Good." [99] Shortly after this Lieutenant Colonel Malone returned from Soviet Russia with confirmation that the Soviet leaders were still prepared to make peace on those terms. It was apparently in response to these "feelers" that Lloyd George commented in his reply to Parliamentary questions on November 13 that the Allies could not consider unofficial peace offers but only direct and official proposals from the Soviet government.[100]

The Soviet leaders were quick to take this hint and to follow up the change of British policy adumbrated in Lloyd George's Guildhall speech. Interpreting the November 8 speech as a tentative, cautious invitation to open negotiations, Chicherin sent a radiogram to the Allied capitals on November 10 protesting against continued Entente support of "counterrevolution" and a wireless message on November 19 offering to pay Russia's debts and to grant economic concessions to the West.[101] On December 1 the British Labour organ, *The Daily Herald,* published an interview with Chicherin.[102] The Soviet foreign minister expressed hope that Lloyd George's recent speeches would pave the way to a better understanding between England and Soviet Russia. He stressed that good relations were possible despite the differences in the two countries' systems, and he concluded by offering trade and economic cooperation in exchange for peace and the opportunity for the Soviet people to reconstruct their nation. Chicherin's remarks were devoid of propaganda or of revolutionary rhetoric.

At a conference of the Bolshevik Party on December 2, convened in

[96] Chicherin, *Two Years of Soviet Foreign Policy,* 35.
[97] *Dokumenty vneshnei politiki,* II, 208–11.
[98] Degras, *Calendar of Documents,* 6–7.
[99] *Manchester Guardian,* October 21, 1919, interview by special correspondent W. T. Goode; Trush, 204.
[100] Great Britain, House of Commons, *Debates,* Vol. 121, cols. 470–75.
[101] Report of the Narkomindel to the Eighth Congress of Soviets, December, 1920, *Dokumenty vneshnei politiki,* II, 662–65; Degras, *Calendar of Soviet Documents,* 7–8.
[102] Summarized in Coates, *Anglo-Soviet Relations,* 4–5, and in Dennis, 380.

order to prepare for the Seventh Congress of Soviets, Lenin drafted a resolution on peace to be presented to the meeting of Soviets.[103] This resolution was passed unanimously by the Congress of Soviets on December 5, after Lenin had argued that such offers of peace raised Soviet prestige throughout the world and that peace was worth heavy sacrifices.[104] It expressed the desire of the Soviet government to live in peace and to concentrate on reconstruction. After reviewing ten previous Soviet peace proposals, the resolution offered once again to enter peace negotiations with the Allied powers, jointly or individually.[105]

At almost the same moment an opportunity arose for the Soviet government to establish direct and official contact with the Allies—for the first time since Bullitt's departure from Moscow nine months previously. In the preceding spring, on May 7, the British government had proposed in a radiogram to Chicherin a general exchange of prisoners. The Soviet government agreed on condition that a Soviet representative be permitted to come to a neutral country in order to be able to communicate directly with Russian prisoners in Western Europe. After prolonged negotiations over the summer, agreement was finally reached in October for a meeting between a British and a Soviet representative in Copenhagen.[106] Both Chicherin and Lenin considered this a significant break in the isolation of Soviet Russia and a sign that British hostility was weakening. So did the White Russian diplomats.[107] On the other hand, Curzon, under pressure from the French, was determined that the talks in Copenhagen should be confined solely to the question of the exchange of prisoners and should rigidly exclude all political issues. The British representative, M. P. James O'Grady, was given strict instructions along these lines. The only qualification in his orders was that he could listen, and then cable London for instructions, if the question of raising the blockade were broached.[108]

From the moment he set foot outside Soviet Russia, however, the Soviet representative, Litvinov, made clear that he had no intention of limiting himself to the subject of prisoner exchanges. On his way to Den-

[103] Lenin, *Sochineniia*, XXIV, 818 n. 177. Unfortunately, Lenin asked during his speech to the conference that his remarks evaluating the significance of the apparent shift in Entente policy not be transcribed. *Ibid.,* 563.

[104] *Ibid.,* 602. Dennis suggests that "ultras" in the Bolshevik Party opposed this renewal of peace offers but gives no evidence. Dennis, 378.

[105] See text in *1919, Russia,* 131–32.

[106] The course of these negotiations, which were conducted by wireless, may be followed in British Foreign Office, *Documents,* III, 344ff. and in *Dokumenty vneshnei politiki,* II, 745, 750.

[107] *Ibid.,* 673; Lenin, *Sochineniia,* 4th ed., XXX, 256; on the anti-Bolshevik reaction, see reports from London, Copenhagen, and Irkutsk in Maklakov Papers, Part II, Packet I, File 18.

[108] British Foreign Office, *Documents,* III, 643, 663–64.

mark on November 25 he told a British representative in Reval that the Soviet government was prepared to offer concessions, such as payment of the Russian debt, in order to obtain peace. He raised the question of peace negotiations again as soon as he reached Copenhagen, and on December 10 he attempted to deliver to the Allied representatives in the Danish capital the peace resolution of the Congress of Soviets. The Western diplomats refused officially to accept this communication on the ground that Litvinov had been admitted to Denmark solely to negotiate an exchange of prisoners, but its contents were, of course, transmitted to their capitals. The same day, and again on December 19, Litvinov issued press statements deploring the Allied refusal to receive a direct offer from the Soviet government, which he asserted, Western leaders had asked for. He reiterated the Soviet desire to make peace and resume trade.[109] After lengthy negotiations an Anglo-Soviet agreement limited to the exchange of prisoners was finally signed on February 12, 1920; it followed by only ten days the first postwar Soviet agreement with a bourgeois government, a peace treaty with Estonia, and paved the way for subsequent agreements with other European powers on prisoner exchanges and minor political questions. For the isolated Soviet leadership this was indeed a major breakthrough.

Even more important, however, was the effect of Litvinov's activity on the developing plans of Lloyd George to establish some sort of relations with Soviet Russia. The Soviet peace proposal of December 5 evoked an immediate response from labor circles in England. On December 9 and 10 a special meeting of the Trades Union Congress, convened to decide what action to take should the government fail to alter its Russian policy, called for an end to intervention and the resumption of trade; it also determined to send a special labor delegation to investigate the situation in Soviet Russia.[110] Although the Soviet peace offer was not discussed at the conference of Allied premiers in London on December 10-13, which, pursuing the other tangent of British policy, decided to establish a cordon around Soviet Russia, and although the Conservative press and Churchill continued to campaign for forthright anti-Bolshevik action, the possibility of trading with the Bolsheviks now began to be discussed actively in British official circles.

Frequently Western and Soviet writers have asserted that Soviet trade was the bait that lured British diplomacy into a change of course toward Russia in late 1919; visions of the vast Russian market, it has been argued, permitted Lloyd George to win over influential business and finan-

[109] Degras, *Calendar of Soviet Documents*, 9–10.
[110] Coates, *Anglo-Soviet Relations*, 140–41. The delegation, headed by Arthur Henderson, visited Soviet Russia in the spring of 1920.

cial leaders, thereby counterbalancing emotional Conservative opposition to dealings with the Bolsheviks. As the preceding pages have indicated, the temptation of trade was in fact a relatively insignificant factor in the early development of Lloyd George's new policy, at least as far as the published Parliamentary and diplomatic records show.[111] A general British interest in commerce with Russia and a desire not to let the Germans dominate the postwar Russian economic scene had, of course, been manifest for a long time. Even after the Bolshevik revolution, the British had considered, in February 1918, sending a representative to Petrograd to negotiate a commercial agreement with the Soviet government. At the very time Allied intervention in Russia was beginning, in the early summer of 1918, a British representative initiated exploratory trade talks with Chicherin, although nothing came of them.[112] Later all the Allied powers expressed some interest in developing trade with those areas of Russia under White Russian control, but little was accomplished.

By the spring of 1919 some liberals in the West were advocating both relief and trade as antidotes to Bolshevism in Russia, and proposals were advanced for lifting the blockade and dealing directly with a national union of Russian cooperative societies, which was alleged to be independent of Bolshevik control.[113] At about this time the British government was exploring the possibility of opening large-scale trade with Siberia, North Russia, and South Russia through the medium of cooperative societies in those areas. During the summer, when it was decided to concentrate British aid on Denikin, plans were also broached for the dispatch of an extensive commercial and financial mission to the White Russian general as a preliminary to the establishment of credit and commodity exchanges.[114]

In September, as it became clear that Lloyd George was increasingly dissatisfied with the policy of intervention, rumors began to circulate that the British were thinking of trading with the Bolsheviks.[115] But the government continued to support and enforce the blockade, as we saw in chapter nine, and the first official hint of a possible change of course did

[111] Unfortunately, neither the papers of Lloyd George nor those of any members of his secretariat were available to me. These would undoubtedly clarify how important the consideration of trade was.

[112] Letter from Buckler to House, February 22, 1918, Buckler Papers; Fischer, I, 97.

[113] See, for example, letters from Norman Hapgood, American minister in Denmark, to Wilson on May 26, June 21, and June 30, 1919, Wilson Papers, Series VIIIA, Boxes 52, 67, 68. For the general interest of American liberals in the Russian cooperatives, see Lasch, 146–48.

[114] British Foreign Office, *Documents*, III, 384, 386, 399, 400, 673–78.

[115] *1919, Russia*, 155.

not appear until Lloyd George's Guildhall speech of November 8 and his Parliamentary statement of November 13, both discussed earlier. Throughout the rest of November, while Lloyd George was weathering the heavy Conservative counterattack, there was no mention of trade in official speeches, Parliamentary debates, or diplomatic papers. After Litvinov's appearance in Denmark, however, the question began to be discussed again. Sometime in December talks were apparently begun between the British Food Ministry and foreign representatives of the Russian cooperative societies, and on December 22 a Foreign Office memorandum submitted to Lord Curzon recommended establishment of "business relations" between British firms and the Russian cooperatives.[116] Curzon disapproved this suggestion and instructed O'Grady in Copenhagen not to reply to proposals submitted by Litvinov on December 22 for an exchange of Russian flax and other raw materials for British manufactured goods. Nevertheless, the idea of trade was in the air.

On January 6, 1920, E. F. Wise, the British representative on the Supreme Economic Council in Paris, submitted a memorandum to Lloyd George entitled "Economic Aspects of British Policy Concerning Russia." [117] Wise stressed the importance of prewar Russian exports, particularly of grain, timber, and flax, to the European and especially to the British economy. He asserted that the absence of these Russian products was contributing significantly to high world prices. The reopening of trade with Russia would force the United States to reduce its high prices on grains and fats and would mitigate Britain's monetary exchange difficulties with America. Wise also pointed out the general attractions of the Russian market and the danger of American and German competition there. He concluded by arguing that the blockade was awkward, troublesome, and a liability in domestic politics and that in any case the Bolsheviks could now break it by trading through Germany and the Baltic states; therefore, he recommended the lifting of the blockade and the resumption of trade through the Russian cooperatives, without either recognizing the Soviet government or permitting the sale of arms to the Bolsheviks.

At a meeting in Paris of the premiers of Britain, France, and Italy on January 14, Lloyd George submitted this memorandum to his colleagues. It is interesting that this meeting, which was a continuation of similar meetings held in London in December and which was considered part of the sessions of the peace conference as a sequel to the meetings of the Council of the Heads of Delegations, did not include either a representative of the United States or anyone from the British Foreign

---

[116] Dennis, 380; British Foreign Office, *Documents*, III, 735–40.
[117] *Ibid.*, 867–71.

Office. Moreover, the decision taken at this meeting and confirmed on January 16—to resume trade with Russia—was not communicated to the Foreign Office, which learned of it from a press report. According to a "Very Confidential" memorandum from Lord Curzon to his staff on January 22, Lloyd George defended this unusual procedure to his foreign secretary on the ground that the matter being discussed was under the jurisdiction of the Food Ministry and did not concern the Foreign Office.[118] More probably, the British prime minister, knowing perfectly well that both the United States and his own Foreign Office would raise strong objections to opening any sort of relations with Soviet Russia, simply wished to avoid argument and to present his opponents with a *fait accompli*.

In connection with Wise's memorandum, the Entente premiers heard Alexander Berkenheim, the head of the Russian cooperative societies abroad, and his colleagues present their case.[119] Berkenheim maintained that the cooperatives were apolitical but had a large membership and could effectively execute barter trade for the surplus raw materials that existed in Soviet Russia. He concluded that the Bolsheviks would be forced to permit the cooperatives to undertake such trade, though only a few minutes later, in reply to a direct question from Lloyd George, Berkenheim declared that the restoration of trade would be an effective way of undermining Bolshevism. After the representatives of the cooperatives had withdrawn, Lloyd George argued that not only would trade reduce prices in Europe but by provisioning the needy Russian peasants directly the Allies could also strike a telling blow at the Bolsheviks: "The moment trade is established with Russia, Communism will go." Nitti and Clemenceau acquiesced with little comment, and a committee was appointed to work out the details.

On January 16 the committee's report was submitted, with representatives of Japan and the United States present.[120] The arguments for reopening trade that had been previously advanced in the Wise memorandum and by Lloyd George were reviewed. The committee pointed out that the chief difficulty was to secure the assent of the Soviet government without entering into direct relations with it or seeming to recognize it. It was agreed that the cooperatives should serve as an intermediary and that their representatives should be asked to go to Moscow to secure the permission of the Soviet authorities and to make the necessary arrangements for trade and transportation. The decision to resume trade on this basis was then formally approved, with the American and Japanese rep-

[118] *Ibid.*, 911 n. 5.
[119] *Ibid.*, 867–75.
[120] *Peace Conference*, IX, 863–66, 868–71.

resentatives reserving their positions until they could consult their governments. A press statement was adopted, which stressed the humanitarian motives of the Allies, the role of the cooperatives, and the fact that this action did not mean any change in Allied policy toward the Soviet government. On January 19 the conference agreed to charge the Supreme Economic Council with putting the decision into effect.[121]

In all these discussions nothing was said about the failure of the Allied policy of supporting the White Russians or about the policy, being confirmed concurrently at the conference—and discussed below—of establishing a *cordon sanitaire* around Soviet Russia. One might have thought the Russian peasants and cooperatives existed in a fragile political vacuum, the seal of which everyone was afraid of breaking with frank talk about the realities of the situation. The Italians supported Lloyd George because, as Prime Minister Nitti indicated in his brief comments, the government was anxious to encourage trade with Russia. Also, Nitti had a generally less anti-Bolshevik outlook than his predecessor, Orlando, and he was under pressure from Italian socialist and labor circles to end intervention. The reasons for the French decision to go along with the lifting of the blockade are harder to discern, and will probably never be entirely clear until the French archives are opened. Apparently the French also foresaw some commercial advantage in the decision; moreover, as long as it did not involve any direct relations with the Bolsheviks or any danger to anti-Bolshevik Poland, they seemed unwilling to fight the matter out with the British prime minister.[122]

On January 20 the Allies dispatched a telegram informing the American government of their decision.[123] For the first time there was an admission of the bankruptcy of previous Allied policy. The Entente leaders depicted the advantages of trade—obviously not in terms of "beating down" high American prices—but as a means of alleviating a European food shortage which was creating conditions ripe for the growth of Bolshevism. The telegram argued, also for the first time, that the resumption of trade would force the Bolsheviks to restore normal conditions at home and to abandon terror and repression, which they had only been able to enforce as war measures. The Allies stressed that no recognition or direct negotiations with the Bolsheviks were involved, and concluded —perhaps with tongue in cheek—that since the United States had not supported the blockade of Russia, it should have no objection to the resumption of trade. The immediate American reaction, though directed

[121] *Ibid.*, 889–90.
[122] See, for example, Millerand's comments to the Chamber of Deputies on February 6, cited in Coates, *Anglo-Soviet Relations*, 15.
[123] *Peace Conference*, ix, 924–26.

more to a concurrent conference decision on the Adriatic question, was one of annoyance that the European Allies were deciding major issues without waiting to hear the views of the United States government.[124] On March 6, however, Washington telegraphed the Allied capitals that although it strongly opposed the establishment of any sort of relations with the Bolsheviks, it would soon end restrictions on private American trade with Russia and it would like to coordinate its action with that of the Allies.[125]

Public reaction to the conference's decision was clouded by a controversial press statement released the day before that concerning the resumption of trade. Drawing on parts of a speech by Churchill on January 3, a British War Office communiqué issued on January 15 warned of the menace to Europe and Asia if Bolshevism, unchecked, were allowed to join hands with the rising nationalism of Islam in the East and with the desperate nationalism of a defeated Germany in the West.[126] It implied that a new war with the Bolsheviks was imminent and that the Allies should begin their preparations at once. This release was accompanied by the hurried departure of War Minister Churchill and the British chief of staff, General Sir Henry Wilson, for Paris. Many observers naturally jumped to the conclusion that the conference was once more planning to intervene against Soviet Russia. Although Churchill subsequently denied that he had authorized this statement and, in fact, he and General Wilson went to Paris chiefly to discuss specific issues related only to the Caucasus, the clear effect was to undercut announcement of the decision to trade with Soviet Russia. Whether this was deliberate or accidental remains a mystery.

It has generally been assumed in Western accounts that the cooperative societies through whom trade was to flow between Soviet Russia and Europe were pliable instruments of the Soviet government; consequently, some have concluded, the Allies either were deceived, or knowingly planned to dupe the public, when they advanced the cooperatives as their intermediary for the restoration of trade. Actually, however, the cooperatives in Russia at this time were not all under strict Bolshevik control, while Berkenheim and his colleagues abroad occupied a somewhat independent and politically neutral position.[127] As a result, Lenin personally helped to draft decrees of the Council of Peoples' Commissars

[124] *Ibid.*, 999–1000 n.
[125] *U.S. Foreign Relations, 1920*, III, 703–04.
[126] Dennis, 8–9, 11–13; Riddell, 161.
[127] *Dokumenty vneshnei politiki*, II, 676, 749 n. 64; the latter footnote asserts that Berkenheim traded with areas under White Russian control and cites a Cheka report of April 28, 1920, attacking the cooperative leaders, some of whom were subsequently investigated.

of January 27 reorganizing the central cooperative organization and placing it under closer supervision of the Soviet authorities.[128] Moreover, the Soviet leaders, though not completely rejecting contact with Berkenheim, proposed on February 2 that trade arrangements be made through a Soviet delegation to be sent to Europe with Litvinov at its head.[129] Because of British objections to Litvinov, who had been expelled from England in 1918 for conducting revolutionary propaganda, Krassin subsequently chaired the delegation, whicth carried on trade talks with the British in the spring of 1920. After an interruption occasioned by the Soviet-Polish war, these negotiations led eventually to the Anglo-Soviet trade agreement of 1921.

Thus, though little came of the specific Allied proposal to establish commercial relations through the Russian cooperatives, the decision of the peace conference on January 16 did pave the way for later trade. It also marked the end of Soviet Russia's complete isolation. In the eyes of the Soviet leaders, the lifting of the blockade seemed at first to be a great triumph for their "peace policy." They believed it signaled the opening of a new era of commercial exchange and of less hostile relations with the West.[130] According to Chicherin, the Allied decision also strengthened the hand of Soviet diplomacy in negotiating peace with the Baltic states since the latter were no longer able to press for a privileged economic and diplomatic relationship vis-à-vis Soviet Russia.[131] As Polish hostility intensified, however, Lenin became somewhat puzzled and dubious about the meaning of the January 16 action. In an interview in early February he told an American journalist that the lifting of the blockade seemed to be "a move in the chess game of the Allies, the motives of which are still not clear—more unclear, for example, than the meaning of Foch's [proposed] visit to Warsaw (smiling)." He doubted the sincerity of the Allies and wondered why the Supreme Council in Paris had not notified the Soviet government directly if it wished to trade.[132]

As we have seen, the motives of Lloyd George, the prime mover in this event, were really not so obscure. Genuinely anxious to make peace with Russia and believing, perhaps somewhat naïvely, that the Bolsheviks, if they could not be vanquished, might perhaps be "civilized" by

[128] Lenin, *Sochineniia*, 4th ed., xxx, 283–84, 508 n. 61.

[129] *Dokumenty vneshnei politiki*, II, 327, 358, 391–92.

[130] Review of foreign policy by Chicherin on June 17, *ibid.*, 639; Lenin, *Sochineniia*, xxv, 13–16, 26–27.

[131] G. Chicherin, "Za piat' let," ("For Five Years"), *Mezhdunarodnaia zhizn'* (*International Life*), No. 15 (November 7, 1922), p. 5.

[132] *Dokumenty vneshnei politiki*, II, 379–83.

intercourse and commerce, the skillful Welsh leader also saw considerable political advantage in ending the military and financial burdens of anti-Bolshevism, once the White Russian cause appeared hopeless. Seizing upon prospective economic gains to make the reopening of relations more palatable and aided by a renewal of the Soviet "peace offensive," he was able to carry with him his European allies, as well as a considerable segment of British public opinion. Prudently, however, he kept another string to his bow—a defensive cordon around Soviet Russia in case the Bolshevik contagion should erupt toward Europe or Asia.

Russia Encircled

At about the time that Lloyd George was developing his plans to establish commercial relations with Soviet Russia the peace conference discussed and approved the second strand of British policy toward Russia in the fall of 1919—the encirclement of the Soviet republic with a ring of small, newly independent states, whose security against Bolshevik attack the Allies guaranteed. Like the resumption of trade, this policy followed naturally from the failure of Allied intervention and the collapse of the White Russian armies, but the idea had originated much earlier in the year and had evolved slowly during the summer of 1919. Its parentage was mixed—a crossing of the sweeping anti-Bolshevism of Churchill with the special interests of Lord Curzon and the national strivings of the non-Russian peoples of the Russian Empire. Prominent among its midwives were the colorful and controversial figures of Savinkov, the dashing Russian adventurer, and Karel Kramař, the embittered former Czech premier.

As far back as February, as we saw in chapter five, Churchill had urged coordination of the whole anti-Bolshevik effort through the formation of a special inter-Allied body on Russian affairs. Since neither Wilson nor Lloyd George was committed at that time to all-out anti-Bolshevism, nothing came of Churchill's proposal. The war minister continued, however, to press for some sort of overall planning and strategy and, also, for greater cooperation between the White Russian forces and those of the border nationalities.

In the summer of 1919 Churchill received support from an unexpected quarter—Lord Curzon, who had been in charge of the Foreign Office in London since January, when Balfour, the foreign secretary, had gone to Paris to attend the peace conference. The former viceroy of India had long been concerned about the security of the British Empire in the East. He dreamed of creating a chain of buffer states from India to the Mediterranean to protect the East against any possible threat from the north, whether German, Turkish, or Russian.[133] After Germany had defeated Russia, Curzon feared German expansion toward India through the Caucasus, whether Germany was beaten in the West or not. Thus, Curzon believed in the re-creation of a strong Russia to block German penetration eastward. In his social and political outlook, however, he was also a strong anti-Bolshevik. In 1919 these views forced some puzzling dilemmas on Curzon.

In the spring of 1919 Curzon opposed the planned British withdrawal from the Caucasus and strongly criticized the proposal that the Italians take over there. Otherwise, he had little to do at that time with Russian affairs, both because they were secondary to his main interests in the Empire and in a Turkish settlement and because Russian policy was being made primarily at the conference in Paris, and not in London. After the decision to support Kolchak, however, there was a good deal of talk in the Foreign Office, as we noted earlier, of the need to reassess and coordinate Allied policy toward Russia. On July 1 Curzon sent a long dispatch to Balfour in Paris, proposing that in accord with the fifth point of the peace conference's May 26 note to Kolchak (which called for the working out of future relations between Russia and the border areas by mutual agreement or through the League of Nations), the Allies should convene a conference between the White Russian diplomats in Paris and representatives of the border areas. At such a meeting the two sides would be urged to agree on the future status of Russia— Curzon preferred a federated state—and to develop plans for cooperating in the Allied policy of assisting Kolchak.[134] Curzon argued that the Allies could persuade the two parties to get together, despite their mutual suspicions, since the border peoples looked to the Allies for support of their aspirations to independence, while the White Russians were dependent on the Allies for aid. If no agreement were reached, the matter could still be referred to the League. Curzon's suggestion was one of the earliest expressions of the hope, discussed frequently later in 1919, that the Allies might arrange a conference, and eventually an alliance, of all the anti-Bolshevik parties to the Russian civil war. There was no direct reply from Paris, but a memorandum of August 2 within the British delegation at the peace conference noted that Balfour opposed the calling of such a conference because too little common ground existed between the parties.[135]

[133] This summary of Curzon's general views relies heavily on Earl of Ronaldshay (J. L. D. Lawrence), *The Life of Lord Curzon* (3 vols; London, 1928), III, 204–11, and Harold Nicolson, *Curzon: The Last Phase, 1919–25* (London, 1934), 55–60.
[134] British Foreign Office, *Documents,* III, 409–10.
[135] *Ibid.,* 410 n. 1.

Nevertheless, as the summer progressed, Curzon became increasingly alarmed at the confusion and inconsistency of Allied policy toward Russia. In a long memorandum for the Cabinet dated August 21 Curzon charged that the policy of intervention had failed and that no clear policy had replaced it.[136] Pointing out that at times the Allied governments acted on their own and at times through the peace conference, Curzon maintained that amid the general uncertainty refuge was often taken in inaction. He then reviewed the situation in Russia and its peripheral areas, alleging that both toward Kolchak and toward the peoples of the Baltic and the Caucasus the Allies had vacillated between recognition and polite indifference with a resultant loss of prestige and influence. Moreover, no effort had been made to bring the White Russians and the border peoples together. Asserting that the powers had individually dissipated their resources in various regions, Curzon called for a special conference in Paris at an early date to revise and coordinate Allied policy toward Russia. This revival of Churchill's February plan was approved by the Cabinet, but Balfour noted tartly: "Nobody is less disposed than I to overrate the qualities of statesmanship shown by the Allied powers in this connection—even in their individual capacity. But to attribute the apparent and real fluctuations of Allied policy in Russia merely to Allied stupidity and indecision is to misunderstand the situation." On August 27 Balfour disapproved the circulation of Curzon's memorandum to the other Allied governments but agreed to raise its substance with their representatives in Paris.[137] There is no evidence he ever did so.

With no action being taken on either an anti-Bolshevik conference or an inter-Allied conference on Russia, Churchill in September did what he could on his own initiative, congratulating Denikin on his military successes but urging him at the same time to put a stop to the anti-Jewish pogroms in the areas under his control and to improve his relations with the Ukrainians on his left flank and the peoples of the Caucasus in his rear.[138] Denikin acknowledged Churchill's felicitations and ignored his advice. In a memorandum to the Cabinet on September 22 Churchill strongly recommended further support to Denikin. He admitted that the White Russian general's relations with the Ukrainians and Caucasians were bad but suggested that the Allies try to resolve these conflicts by pressuring all sides to accept the solution of a federated Russia of autonomous states. Rejecting the Polish offer, recently tendered to the Supreme Council in Paris, of an army of half a million

[136] *Ibid.*, 519–26.
[137] *Ibid.*, 530.
[138] Churchill, *Aftermath*, 265.

men to capture Moscow on the ground that it would antagonize Russian nationalist feelings and Western public opinion, the war secretary urged instead that the Allies keep up pressure on Soviet Russia's western borders by providing material and moral support to the Baltic states and to Poland.[139]

This renewal of the idea of an anti-Bolshevik alliance was followed up in the Foreign Office by further proposals that the peace conference undertake to work out a coordinated Allied policy toward Russia and some method of collaboration between the White Russians and the border peoples. Lord Curzon approved but noted despairingly his doubts that "this moribund conference is capable in its death throes of producing a Russian policy." [140]

At this juncture the White Russian diplomats in Paris, aware of the growing British concern over coordination of all anti-Bolshevik efforts, took steps to reconcile their movement with the border states. In mid-September, when the French decided to send a mission to Denikin, Maklakov, who was to accompany the mission, asked Karel Kramař, a member of the Czech delegation to the peace conference, to go with him in order to persuade Denikin to adopt a more accommodating policy 'toward the Ukrainians.[141] Kramař, as we saw in chapter six, had attempted, in the early days of the peace conference, to promote an East European crusade against the Bolsheviks. At that time, and later, he had maintained good relations with the Ukrainian representatives in Paris and had even tried to work out a federal Russian constitution which would be acceptable to both the White Russians and the Ukrainians. In the role of mediator Kramař did visit Denikin in October and November 1919, but the White Russian leaders won him over and Kramař returned convinced that the Ukraine should be an integral part of Russia.[142]

This effort by Kramař was soon supplemented by that of Boris Savinkov. On the fringe of the White Russian leadership in Paris and a close friend of Churchill, Savinkov began at this time to advocate creation of a chain of independent states from Estonia to the Causasus, which could then be forged into an anti-Bolshevik alliance. Churchill naturally supported this idea, but Curzon was hesitant, commenting that it was worth considering but was not yet ripe for decision.[143] Moreover, the White

[139] *Ibid.*, 261–63. For the Polish offer, see p. 344 above.
[140] British Foreign Office, *Documents,* III, 591–92.
[141] Kramař, 16, 39, 45, 49.
[142] See an account of Kramař's views after his return in Polk Diary, November 29.
[143] Reported in a telegram from American Ambassador Davis to Washington, December 3, 1919, *U.S. Foreign Relations, 1920,* III, 484.

Russian generals, despite their dire military position, could still not bring themselves to admit the necessity of securing assistance from the non-Russian peoples by recognizing the latter's aspirations. However, the White Russian diplomats in Paris were at last becoming more accommodating. In a series of telegrams throughout November, Maklakov and Sazonov warned Denikin and Kolchak that the Allies were increasingly attracted to the idea of an anti-Bolshevik cordon of border states and that the White Russian movement, to preserve its position, should make some dramatic gesture toward the non-Russian peoples in order to forestall Allied action.[144] As rumors grew that there would soon be a conference of some sort on Russian affairs, the Russian Political Conference became increasingly alarmed that the White Russians would be forced to sit down, under pressure from the Allies, with the representatives of the border states. On December 1 Sazonov recommended to the leaders in Siberia and South Russia that a new statement of White Russian nationality policy should be issued at once, and that direct negotiations with the border states should be entered into as soon as possible. Kolchak, already nearing his end, wired his approval of this course of action on December 10, but Denikin in a reply of December 16 raised numerous objections, concluding finally that talks with the national minorities could be conducted only on the basis of the latter's autonomy and therefore as a domestic discussion and not as an intergovernmental conference among equals.[145]

But even if the White Russians had at this point made a radical departure from their rigid position, it probably would have been too late. During November Lloyd George, in part to placate his Parliamentary critics and the "activists" in the War and Foreign offices, had talked vaguely about a conference on Russia; the nature of the conference was left obscure, probably deliberately. At the end of the month Lloyd George announced that instead of a special conference, the forthcoming meeting of Allied premiers in London, called to discuss outstanding issues before the peace conference, would also consider a revised policy toward Russia. This was not exactly what Churchill and Curzon, the proponents of an anti-Bolshevik conference and alliance, had had in mind, but they were forced to settle for it. On the morning of December 11 Clemenceau and Lloyd George held a private meeting on Russian affairs, of which no record is available, but the discussion of Russia was continued in the conference that afternoon and during the next two days, with the foreign ministers of the European allies present at all the

[144] See telegrams for November in Maklakov Papers, II, Packet III, Files 1, 4, 10.
[145] Above telegrams in *ibid.*, Files 1, 4.

sessions and American and Japanese representatives attending some of them.[146]

In the sessions of December 11 and 12 Clemenceau and Lloyd George presented one point of view, Curzon another. Although they compromised, the policy finally agreed to was closer to the position of the Entente premiers. Lloyd George cleverly let the French leader do most of the talking in support of the policy on which they had agreed between themselves before the official meetings began. "The Tiger" argued that Allied intervention had failed completely and that it was pointless to give further assistance to the anti-Bolshevik forces in Russia. Instead the Allies should erect "as it were, a barbed wire entanglement round Russia in order to prevent her from creating trouble outside, and in order to stop Germany from entering into relations with Russia, whether of a political or military character." In Clemenceau's view, Poland was the key to the creation of this cordon, and the Allies should assist Poland "in order to dam up the Russian flood and to provide a check to Germany." The Allies should then, Clemenceau insisted, withdraw from Russia, watch the situation carefully, and await developments. At the same time Clemenceau objected to setting up separate states in Russia since the Russian people would consider this dismemberment of their country. The Italian and American representatives assented vaguely to the Frenchman's general views, while Lloyd George agreed completely, except that he opposed aid to Poland if this were to be used to support a Polish attack on the Bolsheviks. Clemenceau said that this was not his intention at all.

Curzon, who had finally replaced Balfour as foreign secretary on October 24, then raised his objections. First, he argued that it would be dangerous for the Allies to disinterest themselves entirely from the border areas. These states were struggling for freedom and national independence, and the Allies should continue their moral support and counsel, if not material assistance as well. He urged that consideration be given to the establishment of a conference or federation of all anti-Bolshevik states and organizations. Second, Curzon warned that it would be unwise to act too precisely and too precipitately in withdrawing from Russia: the British were already committed to assisting Denikin until the end of March, while the complete abandonment of the anti-Bolshevik forces in Siberia would lead to the overrunning of the territory by either the Red Army or by a reinforced Japanese army. Lloyd George at once rejected the idea of an anti-Bolshevik federation, reporting that he and Clemenceau had agreed that such a coalition would be

[146] British Foreign Office, *Documents,* III, 736, 764–65, 773; *Peace Conference,* IX, 847–58. Churchill met with Clemenceau privately on December 12, but to no avail.

too expensive to support. Prompted by Balfour's specific question as to what was to become of the Baltic states, Clemenceau declared that the Allies obviously could not disinterest themselves entirely from such areas but that the form and amount of the assistance to be given in each case would have to be decided on its merits by the individual Allied governments. Lloyd George maintained that the Baltic peoples seemed to be doing quite well on their own; the Allies need be concerned only if the Bolsheviks attacked in that area again.

On December 13 Lloyd George proposed that the conference adopt the following policy guidelines:

(1) The Allies would give no further aid to the anti-Bolshevik forces in Russia beyond that already promised, but the anti-Bolshevik elements could buy war material in the Allied countries and the latter could decide individually whether to leave their missions in Russia. Thus, the policy was "to leave Bolshevist Russia, as it were, within a ring fence."

After the Japanese representative had warned of the dangers of abandoning Siberia and had suggested small Japanese reinforcements to "hold the line" there, the European statesmen—at a later meeting not attended by the Japanese or Americans—decided that this was really a matter to be settled between the United States and Japan, although Curzon said he could see no great objection to the Japanese remaining in Siberia. As a result, Lloyd George's formulation was modified to include no further aid beyond that already promised, "or, in the case of Siberia, to be decided upon between the Governments of the United States of America and Japan."

(2) The Allies considered that a strong Poland was in their interests; the form and extent of assistance to her would be considered further. At the request of the Italian representative, supported by Lloyd George, this was modified to specify that the assistance to Poland would be "for the defense of her territories."

(3) The Allies rejected the calling of a conference of anti-Bolshevik states and organizations. This was later modified, apparently at the suggestion of Curzon, to read: "the Allies agreed that no useful purpose would be served by attempting to summon any general conference of the representatives of the anti-Bolshevik states at the present time."

On the proposal of Curzon a fourth guideline was added:

(4) The Allies would give the non-Russian border peoples such assistance as might be found desirable in each case. At the suggestion of Balfour it was specified finally that this assistance should be to enable them to defend their liberties.

[369]

A revised resolution covering these four points was formally approved on December 13, with the Japanese and American representatives reserving their position until they could consult their governments. It was then agreed that each government could announce the new policy publicly as it saw fit.

Thus Allied intervention in Russia, haphazard in origin, disparate in purpose, half-hearted in execution, was officially over. The hopes of Churchill and Curzon for a continuation of the anti-Bolshevik struggle through formation of an anti-Bolshevik alliance were dashed, but they did win the concession that aid to the border states might be provided individually when the need arose. Clemenceau, advocate of the idea of a *cordon sanitaire* around Soviet Russia for over a year, had carried the day, with the assistance of Lloyd George, who was interested in putting an end to the burdens and mistakes of intervention in Russia and who wanted to open the way to relations with the Soviet state. The plan for a defensive cordon, while less than Lloyd George's critics desired, was at least a gesture in their direction and could be advanced as proof that he was resolutely opposed to Bolshevik aggression. The British prime minister must have been well satisfied.

Within three weeks, however, the new policy was put to its first test by events in the Caucasus, an area of special British concern. As we saw in chapter nine, the situation there was threatening and confused at the beginning of the summer of 1919. The British generals were anxious to withdraw, but the Italians, who were to replace the British, had lost heart, while the Americans, a possible alternative if they should accept a mandate for the area, were a doubtful quantity until the question of Senate approval of the Versailles Treaty itself was settled. Despite a Cabinet decision of July 2 confirming the planned British withdrawal, Curzon continued to urge the necessity of holding this barrier against Bolshevik encroachments eastward; in late July he sent a special political mission to the Caucasus charged with keeping in close touch with the Transcaucasian governments, with preventing clashes between Denikin and the Caucasian forces by enforcing a line of separation between them laid down earlier by the British, and with advancing as far as possible British trade interests in the area.[147]

In August the Allied high commissioner in Armenia, Haskell, telegraphed Paris that starvation, massacres, and chaos would follow the British withdrawal. On August 11 and August 25 the Council of Heads of Delegations discussed the situation but since no power was willing to

[147] Callwell, *Wilson Diaries,* II, 208; British Foreign Office, *Documents,* III, 451–52.

send troops to replace the British, no solution could be found.[148] Much concerned, particularly at the possible fate of the Armenians, Polk in Paris, supported by the State Department in Washington, recommended to President Wilson that Congress be asked for special authorization to permit sending ten thousand American troops to the area. Wilson, however, doubted that Congress would consent to this; admitting at the same time that the situation was desperate, he pleaded with the British not to withdraw and approved the dispatch of a military mission under General Harbord to study the situation.[149] There was little else he could do, he confessed glumly.

At the end of August Clemenceau, anxious to extend French influence in the Near East and to curtail that of the British, offered to send twelve thousand French troops to Turkish Asia Minor. Although the peace conference approved this proposal on September 15, it was clear that the troops were intended for Cilicia and Syria and would have little impact on the situation in the Caucasus.[150] In mid-November the Council of Heads of Delegations approved Haskell's request that his authority be extended to encompass Georgia and Azerbaidjan, as well as Armenia, but this had no effect on the military situation.[151]

In the meantime, Curzon, assisted by Lord Milner, had managed to avoid carrying out the Cabinet's decision to withdraw British forces from the area. In response to urgent pleas during the fall from Oliver Wardrop, the British representative in the Caucasus, that the Caucasian states be recognized, Curzon expressed sympathy but pointed out that the lack of cooperation among the three states and their firm opposition to Denikin, whom the British were supporting, made recognition impossible for the moment.[152] Disturbed at rumors of the possible recognition of the Caucasian states, the White Russians protested strongly to London and Paris, Denikin wiring: "The Trans-Caucasus is an inalienable part of the Russian nation. . . . Such a decision by the conference [recognition] would be an act of enmity and noncooperation, which

---

[148] *Peace Conference,* VII, 647–49, 839–40. A request from London to Washington that the United States finance the British troops if they were not withdrawn was rejected by Lansing on the grounds that no funds were available and an appeal to Congress would be inopportune. *Ibid.,* II, 832–34.

[149] Memorandum on the Caucasus from the Division of Near Eastern Affairs, August 1, 1919, Lansing Correspondence, Vol. 45; Letter from Wilson to Cleveland Dodge, August 14, 1919, Wilson Papers, Series II, Box 161. See also a plea for public pressure on Congress in a letter from Lansing to John W. Gerard, September 30, 1919, Lansing Correspondence, Vol. 47.

[150] *Peace Conference,* VIII, 5, 205–08. Callwell, *Wilson Diaries,* II, 211.

[151] *Peace Conference,* VIII, 167–68, 179–80.

[152] British Foreign Office, *Documents,* III, 560, 577–78, 647, 676–68.

could not have juridical significance since it would never be accepted by Russia." [153]

After the defeat of Denikin, however, and with the United States now clearly out of the picture, Curzon, alarmed by the growth of Soviet activity and interest in the Caucasus, began to consider more favorably the question of recognizing the Caucasian states. A Foreign Office memorandum of December 24 suggested that since no power was able to assume responsibility for the Caucasus, the best course might be to support the independence of Georgia and Azerbaidjan, leaving Armenia to settlement at the time of the Turkish treaty.[154] Curzon may finally have been won over to recognition by a report of December 27 from Wardrop in Tiflis that Soviet agents and propaganda were at work in Persia, a country which had long been a special concern of the British foreign secretary.[155] In any case, in a meeting of the peace conference on January 10, 1920, with the Allied premiers in attendance, Lloyd George warned that the Caucasus was about to be caught in a Bolshevik-Turkish vise, and recommended that the military advisers at Versailles be asked to study the question of assisting the states there.[156] After the foreign ministers had withdrawn from this meeting to discuss certain issues among themselves, Curzon at once proposed that the Allies not only consider military aid to the Caucasian governments but also take the political step of granting *de facto* recognition to Georgia and Azerbaidjan, with the future of Armenia to be decided at the time of the Turkish settlement. The French and Italian representatives readily agreed, while those from the United States and Japan said they would have to consult their governments.[157]

These decisions met with little favor back in London. In a meeting there two days later, January 12, representatives of the War and Foreign offices supported the position of General Wilson, who argued that it was senseless to attempt to defend India by holding such a forward line as that in the Caucasus. He insisted on immediate evacuation of British troops remaining in Batum, while calling the action of the conference in Paris "foolish." [158] To attempt to reconcile this divergence of opinion

[153] Telegram to Sazonov, November 7, 1919, Maklakov Papers, II, Packet II, File 11; see also telegram of December 6, *ibid.*, protesting the illegality of any commercial concessions granted by the Caucasian "governments."

[154] British Foreign Office, *Documents*, III, 700–01 n. 1.

[155] *Ibid.*, 741–42.

[156] *Peace Conference*, IX, 837–38.

[157] *Ibid.*, 958–59.

[158] British Foreign Office, *Documents*, III, 753–55; Callwell, *Wilson Diaries*, II, 221–22.

within the British government Churchill and General Wilson went to Paris on January 15.

No agreement was reached within the British delegation, however. As a result, each British representative argued a different case in the Supreme Council meeting of January 19, 1920, which was largely devoted to the Caucasus and which was attended by the foreign ministers and, for part of the session, by the generals and by the representatives of Georgia and Azerbaidjan.[159] Lloyd George supported withdrawal of troops from the Caucasus but wanted to send arms and supplies to the Caucasian states for self-defense. Curzon urged both retention of the British forces and assistance to the Caucasian governments. Churchill favored withdrawal but, backed by Foch, recommended the formation and supplying of an anti-Bolshevik alliance stretching from Finland to the Caucasus. General Wilson pleaded for withdrawal but opposed both arming the Caucasian peoples and the idea of an anti-Bolshevik coalition. The report of the military advisers, requested by the Council on January 10, when the Caucasian situation had first been discussed, stated that at least two divisions would be needed to hold the Caucasus as a buffer between the Bolsheviks and Islam while local defense forces were being organized.

Since no one was prepared to supply these troops, Lloyd George urged that the best the Allies could do would be to send arms, materiel, and food. To Clemenceau's pointed objection that such help would probably fall ultimately into the hands of the Bolsheviks, as had British aid to Denikin, Lloyd George retorted that the amount involved was too small to matter. On questioning, the representatives of Georgia and Azerbaidjan bitterly criticized Denikin—"for Lloyd George's benefit and to Winston's anger," according to General Wilson—and declared that they were capable of defending themselves if they were given aid. The Council finally approved the granting of assistance. Curzon then suggested that Armenia be included, and it was agreed to extend both assistance and *de facto* recognition to Russian Armenia as well, with the proviso that her final boundaries would eventually be determined by the peace conference. Premier Nitti of Italy declared that he could not support the Council's action because his parliament had voted against any form of intervention in Russia, but he finally agreed to furnish some supplies unofficially if the British and French dispatched them. The American representative reserved the position of the United States. Washington was informed the following day but disapproved on the

[159] *Peace Conference,* IX, 890–904; Callwell, *Wilson Diaries,* II, 224–25; Riddell, 162–63.

ground that the decision of the conference violated the territorial integrity of Russia.

The Caucasian states did receive some assistance, and Lord Curzon, with remarkable tenacity, and to General Wilson's disgust, managed to keep a few British troops, supplemented by volunteer French and Italian detachments, in Batum until early July 1920, well over a year after they were due to be withdrawn.[160] But the Azerbaidjan state collapsed in the spring of 1920 under Bolshevik pressure, and the Red Army overwhelmed the Armenian republic at the end of the year and the Georgians in March 1921.

During the meeting on January 19 Marshal Foch's plea for establishment of an anti-Bolshevik alliance was sharply questioned by Lloyd George, who demanded to know if it were a strictly defensive measure and, if so, when the marshal thought the Bolsheviks were going to attack. It was clear that the British prime minister feared a renewal of Foch's plans of the preceding winter and spring for the mounting of an anti-Bolshevik crusade against the Soviet state. Although Foch's arguments received little support from anyone, and although Churchill wired Denikin on February 3 that the idea of a grand anti-Bolshevik combination had been rejected by the Allies as too expensive, the European Allies announced on February 24, a month after the official termination of the peace conference on January 21, the following summary of their Russian policy:

. . . the Allied Governments . . . cannot accept the responsibility of advising the border states to continue a war which may be injurious to their own interests.

Still less would they advise them to adopt a policy of aggression towards Russia. If, however, Soviet Russia attacks them inside their legitimate frontiers, the Allies will give them every possible support.

The Allies cannot enter into diplomatic relations with the Soviet Government, in view of their past experiences, until they have arrived at the conviction that Bolshevist horrors have come to an end and that the Government of Moscow is ready to conform its methods and diplomatic conduct to those of all civilized Governments.

Commerce between Russia and the rest of Europe which is so essential for the improvement of the economic conditions, not only in Russia, but in the rest of the world, will be encouraged to the utmost degree possible without relaxation of the attitude described above.[161]

---

[160] Callwell, *Wilson Diaries,* II, 228, 234, 240, 243; Fischer, I, 217–19.
[161] Quoted in full in Coates, *Anglo-Soviet Relations,* 21; see also Churchill, *Aftermath,* 271.

Thus, after over a year of indecision and vacillation, the leaders of the peace conference, confronted by the failure of intervention, decided that they would sponsor no more attacks on Soviet Russia but would instead encircle her with a cordon of small states whom the Allies would guarantee against Bolshevik aggression (but only where feasible, as the case of Georgia showed). Although determined not to recognize the Soviet government, the statesmen were prepared to encourage commerce with Soviet Russia. In the eyes of Lloyd George and Clemenceau, the authors of this compromise policy, the solution to the Russian question was containment and trade—containment to prevent any spread of the Bolshevik scourge, and trade to "civilize" the Red terrorists. The Bolshevik state had not been destroyed but it had been confined, at least for the moment, to Russia proper. But even this acknowledgment of the existing stalemate of power was not unanimously supported, either among the victorious Allied coalition of the war or within the English and French governments, whose leaders advocated the new policy. The United States refused to recognize the border states, and was slow to renew commercial intercourse with the Bolsheviks. Italy was less than enthusiastic about violating the territorial integrity of Russia and establishing a defensive wall of border states and believed it could restore trade on its own. Japan had no intention of relinquishing its hold on Siberia and the Maritime Provinces. And almost at once Foch, Churchill, and the most active anti-Bolsheviks in Paris and London placed their hopes on Poland. With the successes of Baron Wrangel and the eruption into open warfare of the Polish-Soviet conflict that had been smoldering since 1918–1919, the new policy of the peace conference was itself placed in abeyance, and a final bitter chapter in the history of intervention was written.

CHAPTER ELEVEN

Russia, Bolshevism, and the Peace Settlement

The Allies and Russia

▆▆▆ THIS HAS been a story of confusion, frustration, and failure.
▆▆▆ Such was the outcome of Allied efforts to solve the Russian
▆▆▆ problem in spite of the fact that the peacemakers at Paris
shared three broad and fundamental objectives respecting Russia. First,
they all wanted to draw Russia into the peace settlement being worked
out for Europe. Everyone recognized that to leave Russia out of the negotiations and out of the treaties meant an incomplete peace and the risk
of future trouble in Eastern Europe. Yet chaos ruled in Russia, and it
was difficult for the Allied leaders to see how Russia might be engaged
in the task of peacemaking. No anti-Bolshevik group seemed sufficiently
stable or representative. Few Western statesmen were prepared to deal
with the Bolsheviks; in any case the latter scornfully rejected in advance
any participation in an "imperialist" peace. Nevertheless, a small group
at Paris, hoping the Bolshevik regime would become more moderate,
was prepared to compromise with and partially sanction Soviet Russia
in an effort to secure its acquiescence in the new order and its co-
existence with the Western system. But the majority of statesmen distrusted the Bolsheviks and feared the revolutionary drive of Bolshevism.
In their view it was better to exclude Russia from the peace settlement
and to await a favorable turn of events there than to make "a contract
with crime." In any case, as George Kennan has suggested, Russia was
probably already lost to the purposes of the West by 1919, having been
driven to a hostile and bitter extremism by the misguided Allied attempt
to keep her in the war well beyond the limit of her endurance.[1]

An important reason for wishing to draw Russia into the peace settlement—and a second major purpose of the peacemakers—was to prevent a Russo-German alliance. As we saw in the first chapter, fears that
the Germans might dominate and organize the vast population and resources of Russia dated back to before the war and had been much in-

[1] Kennan, *Russia and the West*, 149–50.

tensified by the Treaty of Brest-Litovsk. Even after the defeat of Germany this anxiety continued to play a prominent role in Allied calculations. To prevent a Russo-German coalition was a major objective of the provisions respecting Russia in the Treaty of Versailles and of the French policy of erecting a large and powerful Polish buffer between Russia and Germany. As Clemenceau phrased it on June 2, 1919, in support of Polish claims, "if Germany were to colonize Russia, the war would be lost and not won." [2]

At the same time Lloyd George was concerned that too harsh terms would drive Germany into the arms of Russia, as he argued in his Memorandum of Fontainebleau. Many shared this concern. Woodrow Wilson referred to the menace of a Russo-German alliance on several occasions, as did Lansing and House, while General Smuts declared in June that "Germany should become a member of the League of Nations as soon as the Treaty was signed, it being essential to carry her with us and to remove the possibility of another combination through Germany and Russia joining hands in misfortune." [3] Even John Maynard Keynes used this argument in his famous *Economic Consequences of the Peace*.[4] In passing, it is interesting to note that fear of a Russo-German coalition so colored the thinking of the Allied statesmen that on only one occasion —during discussion of possible Russian support to Yugoslav revisionism if Italy's full claims in the Adriatic were granted—did they consider the danger of Russia coming to dominate and lead all of Slavic Europe, Wilson commenting prophetically that although it would take a generation of education and indoctrination before Russia could play such a role in Eastern Europe, "it would be necessary to watch the development of the Russian people very carefully." [5]

Most of the Western anxiety about Russia and Germany was not over what eventually transpired, a combination of Russian left and German right, but over a link between Russian Bolshevism and German Bolshevism or between Russian reaction and German reaction. Thus the peacemakers believed it essential that the Russian revolution be "civilized" in some fashion, that neither Bolshevism nor reaction be permitted to emerge triumphant from the Russian struggle for power. This,

---

[2] *Peace Conference*, VI, 143. See also Clemenceau's interview with Associated Press correspondent Melville Stone in mid-February, copy in Wilson Papers, Series VIIIA, Box 19.

[3] Quoted in Lloyd George, I, 693; for Wilson's views, see Council of Four discussions on May 7 and June 3, *Peace Conference*, V, 498, and VI, 158, and his use of the Russo-German bogey as an argument for ratification of the Versailles Treaty during a speech in Idaho on September 12, 1919, Baker and Dodd, *Wilson Public Papers*, II, 141; for the views of House and Lansing, see as examples House Diary, February 11, and Lansing Confidential Memorandum of February 20.

[4] Pp. 271–76.

[5] *Peace Conference*, VI, 212–14.

then, was their third common goal, and the attempt to realize it became the chief focus of their efforts at Paris to settle the Russian problem. If the Allied statesmen could end the fighting in Russia in such a way as to produce a moderate and at least partly representative Russian government, then Russia could be drawn into the European peace settlement and the dangers of a Russo-German combination would be minimized. In short, the peacemakers believed, probably correctly, that the key to all their hopes respecting Russia and the peace settlement lay in a resolution of the civil war favorable to their interests and in the return to more "normal" (i.e., Western) conditions in that troubled country.

But how was this to be achieved? Of the courses theoretically open to the peacemakers, one extreme of all-out intervention in Russia to overthrow the Soviet government was favored by some, such as Foch and Churchill. The other of a negotiated accommodation with the Bolsheviks to include an armistice in Russia and a *modus vivendi* between the Soviet and Western governments was supported by a liberal faction, headed by Wilson and Lloyd George. Proponents of each policy vigorously opposed the adoption of the other extreme. But paradoxically, even if the Western leaders could have agreed on one alternative or the other, the opposition of differing segments of British and American public opinion would have made it impossible to pursue *either* of these courses of action.

In his memoirs Lloyd George declared that the Allied powers would have intervened in Russia with their own armies to destroy the Soviet state if they had been able to do so.[6] Whether the advocates of intervention could have overcome his own opposition at the time, and particularly that of Woodrow Wilson, to such a policy is a moot point. Wilson's objections on principle were very strong, despite his dislike of the Bolsheviks. Lloyd George also opposed such action on principle, though this opinion was reinforced by his recognition of the practical and political difficulties of intervention. In any case, all-out intervention proved to be impossible.[7] The European Allies had no money to finance such a venture. Much of popular opinion in the West opposed intervention. The public as a whole was war-weary and dispirited and had no desire to support further foreign adventures. In America objections to interven-

[6] Lloyd George, I, 319.

[7] For general statements of the inability of the West to intervene further in Russia in 1919, see Foreign Office memorandum, "Allied Policy in Russia," by O. C. Harvey, July 28, 1919, British Foreign Office, *Documents*, III, 460; memorandum of February 24, 1919, by Samuel Eliot Morison of the Russian section of the American delegation, House Papers, Drawer 31, File 210; letter from House to Norman Hapgood, January 6, 1919, House Papers; testimony of Bullitt in *Bullitt Mission*, 18, 33; British Parliament, *1920*, Cmd. 818, pp. 5, 7; and Churchill's grudging admission of this fact in *Aftermath*, 286.

tion came from both liberals and isolationists, as well as from voters and elected officials of those states that had supplied the bulk of the American recruits stationed in North Russia and Siberia. In England both liberal and labor circles opposed intervention, and even in France few citizens were interested in paying for or manning an anti-Bolshevik crusade. Moreover, none of the Western powers had reliable troops to send to Russia, as the Odessa fiasco and the ragged performance of Allied soldiers in North Russia demonstrated.

When early in the conference, on January 16, 1919, Lloyd George demonstrated to his colleagues in Paris the impossibility of all-out intervention by asking them point-blank who would finance and supply the troops for such a venture, the interventionists turned to various substitutes. Churchill proposed an Allied military council and the use of volunteers, but was defeated by the opposition of anti-interventionists in the British and American delegations and by public apathy. Foch several times suggested a French-directed crusade of East European armies against Bolshevism, but was frustrated by the opposition of Lloyd George and Wilson and by the realization on the part of all the heads of government, including Clemenceau, that this scheme was impractical and too costly. In all the pleas of the interventionists little or nothing was said about how Russia would be ruled, should intervention succeed and White Russian rule prove to be unpopular.

One attempt, the Bullitt mission, was made to work out a settlement directly with the Soviet leadership. The proposals Bullitt brought back from Moscow provided a reasonable basis on which to negotiate such a settlement. The Bolshevik rulers, hard pressed militarily and economically, were prepared to accept an armistice, to give up—at least temporarily—substantial blocs of Russian territory, and to promise to restrict their revolutionary activity and propaganda. To make the armistice work, close supervision by an armistice commission would have been needed, and other aspects of the treaty proposed to Bullitt might have been even harder to enforce. Nevertheless, such an agreement, carefully worked out, might have ended the civil war and intervention and temporarily stabilized the situation in Russia and Eastern Europe. White Russian recalcitrance could have been overcome by Allied pressure and threats to withdraw nonmilitary, as well as military, aid. But the policy of accommodation was pursued *sub rosa* by a few members of the American and British delegations; it was never seriously considered by the top leaders at Paris or by the conference as a whole. Wilson was distrustful of the Bolsheviks and was preoccupied with the German treaty. Lloyd George, though favoring the plan, feared English conservative opinion too much to endorse it openly and to press for its adoption.

Even if Wilson and Lloyd George had advocated the Bullitt project before the conference, it is most unlikely that the French would have agreed to it under any circumstances.

So the other extreme of Allied policy toward Russia foundered. There remained, however, courses of action on which the peacemakers could agree formally and which might have been implemented under certain conditions. Impelled by their principles, encouraged by certain segments of public opinion, and attracted by Soviet offers of negotiation and compromise, Lloyd George and Wilson proposed mediation in the civil war and undertook to bring the Russian parties together to make peace. Because of technical defects in the Prinkipo plan and the failure of its sponsors to follow it up, and because of opposition to the proposal on the part of the French and of Churchill, this project met an abortive end. The Hoover-Nansen plan to give relief to Russia fared no better. The Big Four were never enthusiastic about it, considering it impractical and fearing that it might lead to direct negotiations with the Bolsheviks, as Chicherin indeed suggested in his reply to the proposal. Clemenceau consented to the plan reluctantly, and the French Foreign Office opposed it at all times. Thus when Kolchak's successes seemed to spell the downfall of the Soviet regime, the conference leaders were glad to drop the relief program.

What remained, then, was the only course that all the Allied leaders could agree on and that they were capable of carrying out: a vague and rather half-hearted anti-Bolshevism, comprising the blockading and isolation of Soviet Russia and indirect intervention through support of anti-Bolshevik Russian forces and of non-Russian minority groups struggling for independence. This policy was symbolized by the decision in May to extend Kolchak partial recognition and by the adoption in December of Clemenceau's favorite strategy of the *cordon sanitaire*. But in the long run this proved to be no more successful than the peacemakers' earlier efforts. The Russian anti-Bolsheviks were too weak and disorganized to prevail, and the Allies were powerless to prevent Bolshevik absorption of the Caucasus. As Churchill and Curzon pointed out numerous times, there was too little coordination and insufficient resources for the task of overthrowing the Bolsheviks by proxy. The basic and probably irreconcilable conflict of interests between the anti-Russian national minorities and the White Russians hampered the whole effort. Individual Allied leaders and governments had different views as to how the border areas should be treated.[8] And there were no troops to be sent to the Baltic, no

---

[8] This fact rebuts the arguments of some Soviet historians that the West tried to dismember Russia in 1919; certainly the United States and Italy did not, and an important strand of French policy favored a great undivided Russia. Those British

forces to occupy the Caucasus, no money to pay the Finns or the Poles to wage war on Soviet Russia. In short, no grand anti-Bolshevik design could be traced.

For the Allies to endeavor to resolve the Russian struggle for power on their own terms was probably an impossible task anyway, but the conditions which circumscribed their efforts and the way they went about it ensured their failure. The Western powers had little control over Russian affairs. In Germany, in Poland, even in the Balkans and the Near East, the conference leaders, although often unable completely to bend local forces and pressures to their will, had enough military, political, and economic power to influence events. In Russia their writ did not run. Without a major expenditure of effort they could not decisively shape the course of Russian developments, and as we saw earlier their electorates would not support such an effort. Some indirect weapons were at their command—they could blockade the Bolsheviks (or, conversely, promise them food and economic assistance); they could supply (or cut off) aid to the anti-Bolsheviks—but these were insufficient to control the situation. As a result, the Western statesmen could propose, but not dispose, regarding Russia.

Even more significant, however, was the fact that at no time were the Allied leaders in real agreement as to what should be done respecting Russia, except perhaps in the decision to assist Kolchak—and even in this case, Wilson had misgivings while Clemenceau wished to go further. Thus no common policy or action was possible. The French wished either to restore a Great Russia or to draw a weakened Russia into an East European alliance system; in any case they were determined to destroy Bolshevism. Lloyd George was willing to live with the Bolsheviks and perhaps trade with them; at the same time he felt honor-bound not to abandon the anti-Bolsheviks, and he believed the latter should be given enough material help to enable them to see if they represented the will of the Russian people. Concurrently, Churchill advocated an all-out effort to eradicate the Bolsheviks, and the British Foreign Office encouraged the separatist aspirations of the Baltic and Caucasian peoples. Wilson was anxious to give the Russians a chance to determine their own fate, but he disliked the antidemocratic Bolsheviks and he wished to keep the Japanese in check.

Secondary reasons for the inability of the conference to resolve the Russian question should be noted as well. In the first place the Russian problem was by no means a major preoccupation of the peacemakers.

diplomats who favored independence for the Baltic and Caucasian peoples were motivated as much by anti-Bolshevism and concern for the Empire as by a desire to break up and weaken Russia.

Their attention was fixed on the settlement with the Central Powers and on the establishment of the League of Nations. They all acknowledged the importance of the Russian question, but they believed that its resolution was less pressing than that of the German problem. None of the Western leaders was able to devote careful, considered, and consistent study to the Russian problem. The Big Four turned to it when they could, but they could not give it the day-to-day attention it required.

Another factor was the rapidly changing situation in Russia and the lack of information in Paris on Russian developments. The Allied representatives in Russia were stationed with the anti-Bolshevik forces and were partial to their cause. With the exception of Bullitt's brief visit, the conference received no direct reports from Soviet Russia. On the other hand, this factor should not be given too much weight; the intelligence sections of the British and American delegations were quite well informed and were turning out fairly accurate and well-balanced analyses, which the delegation leaders usually saw and sometimes used.[9] Moreover, while there undoubtedly existed in Paris a good deal of wishful thinking and some reasoned expectation that the Bolsheviks could not last, most of the conference discussion reflected the Allied leaders' recognition that the Bolsheviks were not about to disappear overnight and were a force to be reckoned with.

In all this, as was suggested in the second chapter, Woodrow Wilson played the key role, and he remains the chief puzzle. He, and he alone, drawing on American power and utilizing his great popularity with the peoples of Europe, might have been able to bind the Allies to a policy of negotiating with the Bolsheviks, to convince Western public opinion of the worth of such a course, and to carry it to a conclusion. But he did not. At the time of Prinkipo it seemed that he might do so. Other issues distracted him, however, and the Soviet reply irritated and repelled him. When he returned to Paris from Washington, Wilson could not seem to make up his mind what to do about Russia. He still opposed intervention on moral and practical grounds, and he spoke wistfully about withdrawing from Russia and letting the Russians settle their own affairs. Yet he showed no enthusiasm for Bullitt's proposals, which might have provided a reasonable basis for ending the Russian war and evacuating Allied troops. He was undoubtedly preoccupied, as he told House. But he was also unsure. His principles and intuition dictated that he pull out

[9] See, for example, the reports described in n. 62 of ch. four and the memorandum by Samuel Eliot Morison cited in n. 7 above. Kennan, while also emphasizing disagreements among the Allies and restraints imposed by public opinion as reasons for the peacemakers' failure, gives undue weight, in my opinion, to the handicaps of "summit" diplomacy and of biased information, discussed here in the preceding two paragraphs. Kennan, *Russia and the West,* 147–48.

of Russia, but he hesitated to leave the Russians to a Bolshevik and undemocratic fate, and he did not want to give the Japanese free rein in Siberia and the Russian Far East. Moreover, evacuating Russia and reaching an accommodation with the Bolsheviks would have meant another battle with his French allies. Thus Wilson stayed in Russia, rationalizing his decision through the effort to bind Kolchak to a democratic program.

The source of Wilson's frustration over Russia is clear. What he desired was a peaceful Russia ruled by a representative government that could express the will of the Russian people and lead them into his League of Nations. Litvinov's appeals raised Wilson's hopes that the Bolshevik leaders might after all be reasonable men with whom such a liberal solution of the Russian dilemma could be worked out. But after the Soviet reply to the Prinkipo proposal Wilson began to doubt that the Bolsheviks, "those consummate sneaks," as he called them, were prepared to negotiate in good faith. Yet he could not sanction intervention to destroy them. There was nothing he could do except wait and hope. He could not recognize the Bolsheviks because, as Christopher Lasch has pointed out, Wilson, like all American liberals, could not accept the viability of the undemocratic Bolshevik revolution without denying his rooted faith in worldwide progress. Under the precepts of liberalism Bolshevism—logically—could not last. Over a year after his departure from Paris Wilson's attitude toward Russia was unchanged from the view he had held in June 1919; writing Lloyd George on November 3, 1920, Wilson declared: "I cannot but feel that Bolshevism would have burned out long ago if let alone, and that no practicable and permanent settlement involving Russian territory and rights can be arrived at until the great Russian people can express themselves through a recognized government of their own choice." [10]

For the Russian Bolsheviks themselves the outcome of the Paris deliberations was a hard but not fatal blow. Their urgent appeals for peace and for a much-needed respite had largely gone unheeded, and indirect Allied intervention had continued throughout 1919. On the other hand, the Allies had not launched the crushing attack that Lenin had feared; time had been gained in which, the Soviet leaders believed, the world revolution would rapidly develop. And to some extent their diplomacy had been successful; their peaceful posture and professions had made it more difficult for the interventionists to persuade Western public opinion that an all-out effort against the Bolsheviks was justified and had contributed to the basic disunity over Russia among the Western powers. Finally, their proposals for peace had helped pave the way for Lloyd

[10] Quoted in Walworth, II, 405–06.

George's effort at the close of the conference to open trade with Soviet Russia.

Moreover, while the Soviet rulers publicly sought peace, they also continued revolutionary propaganda and activity. As we have seen, their dual objectives—to end intervention and to promote revolution—were pursued simultaneously. Sometimes their policies complemented each other, as when revolutionary agitation and propaganda undermined the morale of Allied soldiers in Russia and provoked protests against intervention from labor and liberal circles in the West. Sometimes they contradicted each other, as when the Soviet drive for revolution and the inflammatory appeals of the Bolsheviks spurred Allied efforts to defeat Bolshevism and caused Western leaders to doubt the sincerity of the peace proposals made by the Soviet government.

The Allies and Bolshevism

The majority of Western statesmen had little understanding of the nature of the Bolshevik Revolution in Russia or of the import of its doctrine for the postwar world. They tended to use the expressions "revolution," "Bolshevism," and "anarchy" loosely and often interchangeably. The Russian Bolsheviks were believed to be fanatical and power-hungry. Their social and economic doctrines were considered impractical, and their professed internationalism chimerical. They had at first been regarded with contempt and hatred because they had taken Russia out of the war, thereby increasing the burdens and sacrifices of the Allies. Later they had been detested for their terroristic and dictatorial practices. Soviet repudiation of Russia's debts, nationalization of foreign property, and publication of the secret treaties had angered many in the West and convinced others that the Bolsheviks were untrustworthy and immoral. There existed vague apprehension concerning the Bolsheviks' attacks on Western concepts and institutions, but most observers believed that such wild-eyed extremism could subsist only in a situation of chaos, despair, and political madness. The difficulty was that just such conditions seemed likely to exist, and indeed began to appear, after the war, especially in Eastern and Central Europe. Thus during the peace conference almost all the Allied leaders were alarmed at the possible spread of Bolshevism into Europe and at the revolutionary propaganda and agitation of the Russian Bolsheviks to this end, though they still doubted whether Bolshevism would have much attraction for the peoples of Europe under normal conditions.

Among the chief statesmen at Paris only Woodrow Wilson, and to some extent Lloyd George and House, perceived that Bolshevism was not just a means to power for a small group of Russian radicals or an act of political desperation, but partly, as Wilson phrased it, "a protest against the way in which the world has worked." In an article published four years later but reflecting his views in 1919, Wilson wrote:

> There must be some real ground for the universal unrest and perturbation. It is not to be found in superficial politics or in mere economic blunders. It probably lies deep at the sources of the spirit life of our time. . . .
>
> What gave rise to the Russian Revolution? The answer can only be that it was the product of a whole social system. . . . It was due to the systematic denial to the great body of Russians of the rights and privileges which all normal men desire. . . .[11]

Wilson went on to argue that since the capitalist system had its imperfections, its revolutionary opponents had some justification. "Our aim should be to remove the abuses which give them cause," he added, concluding that the road away from revolution lay through democracy and a broad Christian justice.

Consequently, the president was convinced that a prompt and just peace, which would reform the world and establish a better order, was the best and most direct antidote to Bolshevism.[12] When it became clear to him in the spring of 1919 that to obtain any peace at all he would have to permit incorporation into the treaty of some provisions that he considered not entirely fair, Wilson convinced himself that the League of Nations could right any such injustices and serve as the chief bulwark against revolutionary Bolshevism. This was a main theme of Wilson's speeches in September 1919 during his vain and tragic appeal to the American people to save the treaty and the League. In the first address of his Western trip, on September 4 in Columbus, Ohio, the president declared that the essence of the treaty was

> that it rectifies the age-long wrongs which characterized the history of Europe. . . . Revolutions do not spring up overnight. Revolutions come from the long suppression of the human spirit. . . . One of the chief efforts of those who made this treaty was to remove that anger

[11] In an article, "The Road Away from Revolution," published in *The Atlantic Monthly,* August 1923, cited in Baker and Dodd, *Wilson Public Papers,* II, 536–37.

[12] See his remarks at the peace conference on January 24, *Peace Conference,* III, 709, 712; his speech at the Metropolitan Opera House in New York on March 4, 1919, Baker and Dodd, *Wilson Public Papers,* I, 447; and Baker, *World Settlement,* II, 64–65. For the views of a French socialist and an American radical that if Wilson did not secure a just peace, the peoples of the world would turn to Bolshevism, see Memorandum of Conversation with M. Cachin, March 27, 1919, Wilson Papers, Series VIIIA, Box 29, and Steffens, *Letters,* I, 465–66.

from the heart of great peoples. . . . The makers of the treaty knew that if these wrongs were not removed, there could be no peace in the world.

And in Minneapolis on September 9:

> There is unrest all over the world. . . . There is not now a country in the world where the great mass of mankind is not aware of its rights and determined to have them at any cost, and the present universal unrest in the world, which renders return to normal conditions impossible so long as it continues, will not stop until men are assured by some arrangement they can believe in that their rights will be protected and that they can go about the normal production of the necessities of life and begin to enjoy the extraordinary pleasures and privileges of life without the constant shadow of some cloud of terror over them, some threat of injustice, some tyranny of control. . . .
>
> The people will not stand for a restoration of the old system of balance of power which led them to catastrophe and bloodshed. They will not let it happen again and if their governments cannot work out something better, they will destroy their governments.[13]

Although Wilson seldom referred specifically to the League in this context, it is clear that he hoped the treaty *with* the League would be ratified as a guarantee of that reordered system which he felt could alone defeat Bolshevism. It may be argued, of course, that Wilson, in depicting the treaty and the League as the only sure defense against Bolshevism, was merely attempting to use the recent wave of anti-Bolshevik feeling in the country to win support in his fight for ratification of the treaty. Reading all the speeches, however, leaves the impression that this theme was not simply political tactics but a deeply held conviction of the president. He believed fervently, as he had when he sailed for Europe ten months earlier, that a just peace and a better order were essential to turn back the challenge of Bolshevism.

As we saw in chapter six, Lloyd George argued along the same lines in his Memorandum of Fontainebleau. The treaty, he said,

> must be a settlement . . . which will constitute an alternative to Bolshevism, because it will commend itself to all reasonable opinion as a fair settlement of the European problem.
>
> It is not enough, however, to draw up a just and far-sighted peace with Germany. If we are to offer Europe an alternative to Bolshevism, we must make the League of Nations into something which will be

---

[13] Speeches in Baker and Dodd, *Wilson Public Papers,* I, 597, and II, 67–69.

both a safeguard to those nations who are prepared for fair dealing with their neighbors, and a menace to those who would trespass on the rights of their neighbors, whether they are imperialist empires or imperialist Bolsheviks.

In reply Clemenceau maintained that too lenient a peace would only lead to Bolshevism in the victors' camp.[14] To some extent Lloyd George may have been using the Bolshevist argument as a way of trying to secure amelioration of terms which he believed would ruin Germany and ensure French hegemony on the Continent, but it seems probable that he also sincerely felt, with Wilson, that a just peace and an effective League held the best promise for turning back the Bolshevik danger.

Yet the treaty itself was largely political and territorial and contained little designed to rectify the social and economic grievances which nurtured Bolshevism. Wilson, as we saw in chapter two, was little interested in the latter aspects of the peacemaking. He supported inclusion in the Covenant of the League of a provision calling for fair hours and humane conditions of labor, as well as the establishment of an international labor organization, but even a conservative such as David Hunter Miller commented to Colonel House: "The pious hope regarding hours and conditions of labor would be a cruel disillusionment to the masses who have supported and are supporting President Wilson. . . ." [15] Few of the other senior statesmen expressed any more interest than Wilson in social and economic reform. For example, when one of the architects of the future International Labor Organization, Barnes, presented proposals for the new body to the Council of Foreign Ministers on April 1, he described their reaction to Lloyd George as follows:

> But what struck me yesterday was the attitude of the Foreign Secretaries. Except for Mr. Balfour no one appeared to regard Labour settlement as of any importance. One of the Secretaries said that, in his judgment, it was not Labour but Territory which was agitating the minds of peoples. . . .
>
> And, if it gets abroad that the peace plenipotentiaries are only taking a languid interest in labour adjustment, then Labour will be very wroth and will have reason to be so. . . .[16]

At the same time, as we saw in chapter seven, some at the peace conference, particularly liberals in the American and British delegations, but Lansing and Hoover as well, insisted that relief, economic assist-

[14] See pp. 196–99 of ch. six.
[15] Miller, *Drafting of the Covenant*, I, 47. See also Canadian Prime Minister Borden's similar comment, *ibid.*, I, 361.
[16] Lloyd George, I, 655. For the meeting in question, see *Peace Conference*, IV, 537–43.

ance, and restoration of production and trade were the most effective methods to deal with Bolshevism. Anti-Bolshevism, in addition to humanitarian motives, inspired the vast relief effort in Central and Eastern Europe, in the Near East, and in the Caucasus that the West mounted after the war. After a bitter fight these measures were also extended to Germany and the Baltic in the spring of 1919. The Hoover-Nansen plan was another expression of this impulse, as were continuing discussions in the American delegation and in Washington of a major program of economic assistance to Russia. Because of the rapidly changing situation in Russia, the political difficulties of dealing with the Bolsheviks, and the opposition of the French, these hopes and projects respecting aid for Russia all came to naught for the moment, but the fundamental idea behind them—that food and economic aid would either eliminate the grievances from which Bolshevism drew its support, or would moderate and "civilize" Bolshevism itself—was eventually sanctioned early in 1920, when Lloyd George succeeded in getting the conference to lift the blockade and to encourage the resumption of trade with Russia.

Nevertheless, it is clear that for most of the peacemakers neither trade and aid nor social and economic reform was the answer to Bolshevism. Instead they hoped to counter it with traditional techniques of power and diplomacy. When direct action against the Russian Bolsheviks proved to be costly, impracticable, and objectionable to some of the Allied leaders and to much of Western public opinion, they succeeded in persuading the conference to blockade and isolate Soviet Russia and to support various anti-Bolshevik forces in and around Russia in the hope that the Soviet expression of Bolshevik power might be brought down by proxy. The opponents of Bolshevism used similar tactics against Soviet Hungary, but with greater success. After it had become clear that Russian Bolshevism would survive, they obtained conference assent to a *cordon sanitaire* around Soviet Russia. This was to be a defensive barrier, ringing the Bolsheviks in to prevent their expansion into Europe and Asia and interdicting any link between them and Germany. The Allies were to assist the economic and political development of the states bordering on Russia and were to provide military aid if the Bolsheviks should attack them. The Soviet-Polish war, the emergence of Baron Wrangel as a new "White" hope, and Soviet conquest of the Caucasus all undercut some of the assumptions and much of the effectiveness of this policy of containment, but in a modified form it remained an important aspect of Western policy toward Russia up to the Second World War and beyond. It was on the dual and somewhat contradictory notes of trade and of the *cordon sanitaire* that the peace conference ended its deliberations about the related problems of Russia and Bolshevism.

Bolshevism and the Peacemaking

A number of observers and participants of the conference, such as Nicolson, Churchill, and Baker, have published their impressions that the peacemakers in Paris worked under great pressure, believing that they must make peace quickly if they were to stave off anarchy in Europe, and these judgments have been referred to or cited earlier in this study. We need only note here, from unpublished sources, that this sense of urgency was real and significant and that it spurred the Allied leaders to their task. As early as January 22, for example—and several times thereafter—Lansing expressed his anxiety:

> We ought to make peace without delay; if we do not we may have no German government with which to make peace. . . . As it is we must go stumbling along in the present unsatisfactory way, delaying and delaying while the flames of Bolshevism eat their way into Central Europe and threaten the destruction of social order.[17]

House was also much alarmed, fearing that peace might come too late to save Europe from Bolshevism:

> From the look of things the crisis will soon be here. I hear rumblings of discontent every day. The people want peace. Bolshevism is gaining ground everywhere. Hungary has just succumbed. We are sitting on an open powder magazine and some day a spark may ignite it. . . .
>
> It is not that we are taking too much time for normal conditions, but since the world is crumbling about us, it is necessary to act with a celerity commensurate with the dangers that confront us.[18]

This problem even became a political issue to bedevil Wilson, Tumulty wiring him from Washington on March 25:

> There is great danger to you in the present situation. I can see signs that our enemies here and abroad would try to make it appear that you are responsible for delay in peace settlement and that delay has increased momentum of Bolshevism and anarchy in Hungary and the Balkans.[19]

[17] Confidential Memorandum, "Review of the Present Condition of the Peace Conference," January 22, 1919, and see Desk Diary notations for February 4, April 4, and June 5, Lansing Papers.

[18] Diary, March 22 and 24, House Papers. See also the entry for February 19 and his remarks to a correspondent on March 10, cited in Hammond, 260.

[19] Wilson Papers, Series VIIIA, Box 28.

It is fruitless to attempt to estimate the effect on the peace settlement of the pressure, of the sense of haste that this feeling of being engaged in a race with anarchy produced. One can only say that calmer, less hurried deliberations might have produced a somewhat less harsh, a more considered treaty, though this is far from certain. It is clear, however, that the belief that Bolshevism was just around the corner was an important factor in Wilson's decision not to break up the conference and go home but to remain at the council table no matter how much he felt some of his principles were being violated. Liberal critics at the time, such as William Allen White, and later historians, notably Richard Hofstadter, have argued that when the Fourteen Points began to be infringed, Wilson should have withdrawn from the conference and appealed to European public opinion over the heads of governments, or should have used the threat of a separate peace and of suspending that American financial and economic assistance which was essential to the recovery of the Allied nations, to compel compliance with his principles.[20] But as Nicolson and Baker have pointed out, the president—and many others at Paris—believed that such action would further delay peace, might upset the Allied governments, and could lead to chaos and Bolshevism.[21] The important point is not whether Wilson's withdrawal from the conference to stand on his principles would have actually had those results, but what he was convinced at the time the outcome would be. As is unfortunately the case so often, the president himself left no record of his thoughts on this question, but there is indirect evidence to show he believed that he could not risk bringing all Europe down in anarchy and that a quick if not completely just peace was essential to the stability of the world. On May 19 Colonel House, undoubtedly reflecting Wilson's views, told Bullitt that "if the President had pulled out of the conference, it would have meant revolution in every country in Europe and that the President was not ready to take this responsibility." [22] Lloyd George commented to Lord Riddell on April 23 that "I think he [Wilson] has a genuine love of liberty and . . . he has got to keep afloat in order to give effect to his principles." And on June 3 Wilson himself spoke to a meeting of the American delegation, convened to consider whether the treaty should be revised in the light of the German observations on it: "What is necessary is to get out of this atmosphere

[20] White, 430–35; Richard Hofstadter. The American Political Tradition and the Men Who Made It (New York, 1948), 272–80.

[21] Nicolson, 41–42; Baker, World Settlement, II, 62–65. Nicolson also points out, probably correctly, that the Allies would never have acceded to a peace dictated by Wilson.

[22] Memorandum of Conversation with Colonel House, May 19, 1919 [on the occasion of Bullitt's resignation in disgust over the German terms], Bullitt Papers. Steffens also reported a similar statement by House. Autobiography, 787.

of war, get out of the present exaggerated feelings and exaggerated appearances, and I believe that if we can once get out of them into the calmer airs, it would be easier to come to satisfactory solutions." [23] It seems apparent, therefore, that fear of Bolshevism helped lead Wilson to accept certain compromises in the treaty, believing that once peace was made and the League established, defects in the treaty and the problem of Bolshevism in the world could both be set to rights.

Earlier in this conclusion the prominence in the minds of the peacemakers of fear of a Russo-German combination was discussed. A corollary was their concern that Germany might turn Bolshevist, with or without help from the Russians. As we saw in the first chapter, this had worried Allied and German leaders in the fall of 1918 and had been one factor leading to fairly prompt agreement on the Armistice. As the peace conference convened, and despite suppression of the Spartacist movement in Germany, alarming reports of the danger of Bolshevism there continued to flood into Paris. Sometimes these accounts spoke of local German Bolshevism, sometimes of a combined Russo-German Bolshevism. The tenor of many of them was that if the peace terms were too harsh, this would discredit democratic government in Germany and drive the country to revolution and anarchy.

For the peacemakers this was a most unpleasant prospect. If it happened, they would be forced to occupy Germany; there was not only the cost and commitment involved, but did they have enough reliable troops for the task? An alternative suggested by some to force Germany to accept the treaty was continuation and tightening of the blockade, but others pointed out that this would only encourage despair, anarchy, and Bolshevism. It looked to the men at Paris as if their efforts might be all in vain and the world would be plunged back into war and disorder.

The Germans, as they had been at the time of the Armistice, were quick to use the Bolshevist argument in an effort to obtain better terms for themselves. Beginning with Walter Rathenau's open letter to the Allies on the eve of the conference, many German politicians, public figures, and intellectuals warned that a vindictive peace would force Germany to embrace Bolshevism and would open up the whole of Europe to the Red hordes from the East.[24] The Germans also used the Bolshevik threat to justify their actions in the Baltic and in Poland and to protest against being too completely disarmed.

[23] Riddell, 57; Baker, *World Settlement*, II, 114.

[24] Rathenau letter cited in Carr, *German-Soviet Relations*, 9. For examples of the sort of warnings which reached Wilson, see clipping of an article by Otto Hoetzch dated January 15, report of Erzberger's speech to the League of Nations Society on March 16, and Foch's report of negotiations with the Germans at Spa on April 3–4. Wilson Papers, Series VIIIA, Boxes 14, 30, 32.

These alarums and entreaties were undoubtedly partly genuine but also partly exaggerated in order to bring pressure on the peacemakers, and it is probably correct to say, as E. H. Carr does, that German Bolshevism's "strength and influence were never anything like as great as was pretended by those . . . who used German communism as a bogey." [25] But what counted was not the actual threat but rather what the Allied leaders believed it to be. And there is no doubt about their anxiety. The leaders of the American delegation repeatedly expressed their concern, and even the governor of North Carolina, T. W. Bickett, noted, in wiring the president about the desirability of shipping cotton to Germany: "I want Germany to pay every dollar she can be made to pay but it would be a fearful thing for Bolshevism to get control of Germany." [26]

The British were also worried. On March 19 General Smuts wrote Lloyd George:

> The peace terms as they are developing not only avowedly deprive Germany of the physical force required to resist external attack (which is more likely to come from Bolshevism than from any other quarter), but they deprive Germany of every atom of self-respect and reduce her morale to a point at which she may be incapable of resisting the other and perhaps more dangerous weapon of Bolshevism, namely propaganda.[27]

The South African statesman concluded that it was imperative to give the Germans sufficient force and self-respect to enable them to resist Bolshevism. Smuts' letter may have helped inspire the Memorandum of Fontainebleau a few days later. Clemenceau's sharp rebuttal that a peace that did not satisfy French needs would lead to Bolshevism not in Germany but in France was complemented during the course of the peace talks by other, though sometimes contradictory French arguments concerning the danger of Bolshevism in Germany. Such semiofficial papers as *Le Temps* maintained on the one hand that the threatening reports from Germany should be discounted as German propaganda designed to win easier terms, and on the other that the danger of Bolshe-

[25] Carr, *German-Soviet Relations*, 8.
[26] Telegram of March 11, Wilson Papers, Series VIIIA, Box 23. See also a wire from Tumulty, March 30, *ibid.,* Box 30; passages in the House Diary cited in the preceding section of this conclusion; Lansing Confidential Memorandum of February 20, "Probable Effect of an Extravagant Indemnity on the Germans," and Desk Diary for March 5 and 21, Lansing Papers; and letter from Hoover to Wilson, April 21, Wilson Papers, Series VIIIA, Box 39.
[27] Cited in Millin, II, 196–97.

vism in Germany meant that the treaty should contain even stronger guarantees against the resurgence of Germany.[28]

After the draft treaty had been completed and presented to the Germans, a new wave of anxiety swept through conference circles in Paris: would the Germans sign, or would they go Bolshevist? Lloyd George's last-minute efforts, supported by the British Cabinet and the British delegation, to obtain some amelioration of the terms were prompted in part by his fears that the Germans would not sign, or that the German government would collapse, leaving the door open to Bolshevism. Even Foch was alarmed at the prospect of a German refusal and the consequences this would entail.[29] Paradoxically, the danger of Bolshevism was one of the chief arguments used by Erzberger and Noske in persuading the German government to sign.[30] Partly as a reaction to the treaty, Nazism, not Bolshevism, later made its appearance in Germany, but the fear of Bolshevism in Germany had played its role in the complicated struggle over the peace to be imposed on Germany. It probably affected the actual terms very little, but it may have strengthened Anglo-American resistance to some of the more extreme French demands, and it undoubtedly hastened completion of the treaty.

The other states represented at Paris, both victors and vanquished, resorted to the "argument to Bolshevism" so frequently and shamelessly that like the little boy's cry of "Wolf!" it soon ceased to have much effect. "Either we get what we deserve, or we will go Bolshevik." Almost everyone used it, from the Habsburgs pleading for restoration of the dynasty through the Slovaks and Sudeten Germans protesting their incorporation into the new Czechoslovak state to the Metropolitan Bishop of Spalato arguing for Yugoslav territorial claims.[31] Those nations which used the Bolshevik argument most often, and perhaps with most justification, were Italy, Poland, and Rumania, the first raising the specter of a domestic Bolshevism, the last two primarily stressing the danger to them from Russian or Hungarian Bolshevism.

Orlando's threats that failure to satisfy Italy's claims would cause the downfall of moderate government in Italy and lead to a nationalist-Bolshevik revolution were undoubtedly sincere, but he apparently made little impression on President Wilson, though this argument did win over

---

[28] Noble, 182.

[29] Tardieu, 120, 142; *Peace Conference,* v, 899; Lansing Desk Diary, June 5.

[30] Luckau, 105–06, 111.

[31] For these, among other instances in the evidence, see respectively Baker, *World Settlement,* III, 246–48; Bliss Papers, Box 257, File 911; Memorandum from Brigadier General Thomson, April 12, *ibid.,* Box 172; and Wilson Papers, Series VIIIA, Box 29.

House and, later, Polk.[32] The Rumanians used the danger of Bolshevism to justify their demands for food, clothing, economic assistance, and arms, as well as their claims to Bessarabia and Transylvania.[33] The Poles in turn used the Bolshevik menace to support their pleas for recognition, for relief, arms, and economic assistance, and for the return of General Haller's army from France, as well as their claims to Eastern Galicia and to parts of German, Lithuanian, and Russian territory.[34] That the Allies took the threat to Poland seriously is indicated by the instructions given the Inter-Allied Commission to Poland, formed by the Council of Ten on January 22. Point three of the Commission's charge read: "to study the measures necessary to furnish to the Polish government the means to maintain order in the interior, to preserve itself against all aggression from outside, and to stop at its frontier the anarchic action of Bolshevism." [35] It was then explained that this meant the Commission was to evaluate "the immediate dangers Poland runs of Bolshevik penetration by outside military action, by troubles leading to internal disintegration, and by intensive propaganda of Bolshevik publications and agents," and to recommend what measures should be taken "to shelter Poland from this destructive action, both in its own interest and in the interest of Europe itself." The Council of Ten concluded its instructions to the Commission: "We must try to permit the new state to form itself freely . . . while escaping a new servitude worse than the preceding and we must try to build at the same time a barrier for civilized states against the criminal and dissolving action of Bolshevism."

Western concern over the menace of Bolshevism to Poland, and to Rumania as well, is clear. What is harder to evaluate is the extent to which this concern affected the peacemakers' decisions respecting these states. It is probably fair to say that for the many others who attempted to use the Bolshevik bogey to frighten the statesmen at Paris it was largely a vain effort. It appears that the Poles and Rumanians had some success, however. After detailed study Professor Low has asserted that anti-Bolshevik views of the Allies apparently had little influence, even following the Bela Kun revolution in Hungary, on final determination of

[32] Mantoux, I, 303–04; Nicolson, 165, 167; House Diary, April 19; and Polk Diary, October 26.

[33] See, for example, Brătianu before the Council of Four on June 5, *Peace Conference*, VI, 204; his appeal through the Allied ministers in Bucharest, January 11, Wilson Papers, Series VIIIA, Box 9; a copy of his letter to Clemenceau of February 8, *ibid.*, Box 19; and his appearance before the Commission on Rumanian and Yugoslav Affairs on February 22, *Recueil*, Part IV, C (4), p. 54.

[34] See, as examples, *Peace Conference*, II, 412, 421, 425; letter from Paderewski to House, January 12, 1919, in Seymour, IV, 262–64; and Dmowski before the Council of Ten on January 29, *Peace Conference*, III, 776.

[35] *Recueil*, Part IV, C (2), pp. 669–70.

the frontiers of Hungary.[36] This is probably true in the sense that the arguments of those who contended that the victors and the new states on which they hoped to rely could not be denied the just fruits of victory or the territory necessary for their viability without opening the door to Bolshevism were pretty well canceled out by the contentions of those who favored moderation toward the vanquished as a means of preventing them from turning to Bolshevism. Nevertheless, as Professor Spector has pointed out, Brătianu's clever harping on the Bolshevik theme, combined with the absence of Russia from the conference, undoubtedly helped strengthen France's determination to support Rumanian claims to Bessarabia and to Transylvania and may have won some supporters for Rumanian aspirations among others at Paris.[37] Certainly, at the very least, Rumania's requests for economic and military support were more favorably considered because of the Bolshevik menace.

Poland is both a clearer and a more complicated case. There seems little doubt that support for Poland from both the French and the Americans was encouraged by consideration of the necessity to erect a strong anti-Bolshevik bastion between Soviet Russia and Germany. As we saw in chapter six, the Big Four's decision to endorse the Polish occupation of Eastern Galicia and the use of Haller's army there may well have been motivated in large part by anti-Bolshevism.[38] At the same time the Poles' self-professed role as the defenders of Europe against Bolshevism seems not to have convinced the Allies of the justice and practicality of Polish claims to parts of Lithuanian, Byelorussian, and Ukrainain territory. The vain hope that a reconstituted democratic Russia might yet appear and the desire to strengthen the independence of the Baltic states against both German influence and Bolshevik domination operated to deny the Poles their maximum claims to the east and northeast.

The fear of Bolshevism may thus have had less effect on the peacemaking than is sometimes thought. It certainly prodded the statesmen at Paris to finish their task as quickly as possible. It apparently operated to prevent Woodrow Wilson from withdrawing from the conference in protest against violations in the treaty of his principles. It may have helped those who argued for not too harsh a peace, and it may have convinced some Germans that there was no alternative but to sign. It probably won additional material support for the Rumanians and Poles and assisted them in achieving certain territorial aspirations. But it would be difficult to prove that Bolshevism affected the general structure of the Versailles settlement in major ways.

[36] Low, 39.
[37] Spector, 237.
[38] See also the views of H. J. Paton, expert in the British delegation, in Temperley, VI, 246.

The Outcome

What then was the significance of the questions of Russia and Bolshevism for the Paris Peace Conference? First, it seems clear that the inability of the Allies to end the civil war and intervention in Russia and to reach an accommodation with the Bolsheviks embittered their relations with Soviet Russia and increased the mutual hostility and suspicion which had erupted following the Bolshevik Revolution, and especially the Treaty of Brest-Litovsk, and which was later so adversely to affect Soviet-Western relations. It is interesting, even if fruitless, to speculate on what might have occurred if Wilson and Lloyd George had pushed the Prinkipo plan to fruition or had endorsed and pursued the proposals Bullitt brought back from Russia. To be sure, it would be presumptuous to suppose that the subsequent course of Soviet development would have been much altered. Nevertheless, the student of this era cannot but wonder how the removal of the popular justification for many Soviet policies and practices—foreign attack—would have affected the Bolshevik dictatorship. Would it not have made it more difficult for the Bolshevik leaders to secure the support, or at least acquiescence, of some peasants, workers, intellectuals, and minority groups, and of all those who rallied to the Soviet regime from patriotic motives? Moreover, if the West had not only reached a negotiated settlement of intervention and civil war but had also given Russia food relief and economic aid, and had reestablished channels of political and ideological influence in Russia, how might this have affected the ability of the Soviet leadership to retain power and to suppress opposition?

In all probability the answer to these hypothetical questions is that the evolution of Soviet rule in Russia would have been little changed. Yet those closest to the situation, the leaders of the Menshevik and right Socialist Revolutionary parties in Soviet Russia in 1919, firmly believed that intervention was helping to consolidate Soviet rule and that it facilitated Bolshevik control of all aspects of life in Soviet Russia. The fate of opposition groups within and outside the Bolshevik Party in 1921 and 1922 might suggest that this was a misguided belief, but two years earlier, with large blocs of Russian territory still outside Soviet control and with the regime not yet well entrenched, the situation was markedly different. At the very least it is fair to say that a moderate attitude on the part of the powers at Paris certainly could not have made matters worse, in terms of the interests of the West and of the Russian people themselves, than did the policy ultimately adopted. But the divergence of views on Russia among the Western nations and leaders and the influence of conservative opinion in the Allied countries prevented a settlement with the Bolsheviks in 1919, and a chance, however slim, to narrow the widening gulf between the West and Soviet Russia was lost.

Emphasizing the revolutionary aspect of Soviet policy, some, such as Churchill, have argued that the conference decision to aid Russian and non-Russian anti-Bolsheviks indirectly served Western interests by containing probable Bolshevik expansion into Europe. If the Soviet leaders had not been fighting for their lives against Kolchak, Denikin, Yudenich, Wrangel, and the non-Russian border peoples, it is maintained, they might have been able to extend the Soviet system to the Baltic countries, to come to the aid of Soviet Hungary, and perhaps even to Bolshevize Poland and Germany. This seems unlikely: the Russian Bolsheviks had enough problems at home to keep them more than busy. Moreover, if they had attempted to drive westward, the Allies would have then intervened actively to stop them, and the line demarcating Bolshevism from Europe would probably have remained at about the place where it was finally delimited in 1921. Thus, although it is true that a stalemate was achieved, it is difficult to say that this was a gain, or that a more conciliatory policy would have had worse results.

Finally, it is clear that a peace settlement made, as Ray Stannard Baker phrased it, "in the teeth of one of the great powers of Europe and in complete disregard of another" was unlikely to be very successful.[39] The absence of Russia from the peace talks was certainly a disruptive influence on the future course of European history, not so much because of any specific territorial or other adjudications made without her, but because her potential power and role in Europe could not safely be ignored. In the absence of Russia the French pinned their hopes, vainly as it turned out, on Poland and on a cordon of East European states acting as buffers between Germany and Soviet Russia. But this was chimerical at best. Once Russia had regained her strength, even under a Bolshevist regime, and Germany had become inflamed by a virulent revisionist nationalism, France's East European cordon stood little chance and was engulfed in the German-Sovict Nonaggression Pact of 1939 and the Second World War.

Yet what else could the peacemakers have done? The choices open to them were limited, given the temper of the times, the nature of Bolshevism, and their own limited understanding of the great forces for change that were at work in the world. The men at Paris lacked both the power and public support to enforce their will on Russia. Unable to agree on

[39] Unpublished draft chapter, "Russia at the Paris Peace Conference," Baker Papers, Firestone Library, Princeton University.

the ideal course to be pursued and shackled by conflicting views within their electorates, they finally settled on a compromise policy that turned out to be both ineffective and injurious.

Yet if one considers the peacemakers' responses to the challenge of Bolshevism inept and haphazard, it is well to acknowledge at the same time what a striking similarity they bear to those we are familiar with today. The advocates of preventive war would find comprehensible and sympathetic the position of Foch in 1919. The proponents of containment would find familiar and recognizable the views of Clemenceau and others who favored in 1919 building "areas of strength" into a *cordon sanitaire* around the Bolsheviks. Those who a few years ago urged the "roll-back" of Communist aggression would have seen eye to eye with Churchill and others in 1919 who were convinced that Bolshevism could be turned back and eventually defeated by those bearing the banner of nationalist states and anti-Bolshevism. And, of course, those who today believe that Soviet Communism can be moderated by trade, contact, and cultural exchange would have been strong partners of Lloyd George, Bullitt, and others who in 1919 believed that accommodation and intercourse were the answer to Bolshevism's expansionism and revolutionary zeal. It is perhaps surprising how early these basic Western responses to Russian Bolshevism emerged. The essential doctrine of Bolshevism has changed relatively little, and today we are left to puzzle, just as the men at Paris did forty-five years ago, over the dangers and complexities of this challenge and over the most effective means to counter it.

Appendices

1. *Memoranda Addressed to the President of the Peace Conference by the Russian Political Conference* [1]

March 9, 1919	—The Nationality Question, 3 pp.
March 22, 1919	—Bessarabia, 6 pp. (with attached ethnographic map and a table of statistics based on the census of 1897)
April 9, 1919	—Terms Affecting Russia in the Preliminaries of Peace with Germany [2]
April 15, 1919	—Declaration of the Aims and Principles of the National Movement, 2 pp.
April 19, 1919	—Poland, 4 pp.
May 2, 1919	—The Revision of Russo-Chinese Treaties, 2 pp.
May 4, 1919	—The Nansen Plan [3]
May 8, 1919	—Finland, 2 pp. (with a four-page annex)
May 10, 1919	—The Treaty with Austria and Hungary: Eastern Galicia, Bukovina, Carpatho-Russia, and Reparations, 4 pp.
	Annex 1: Eastern Galicia and Bukovina (tables and map)
	Annex 2: Ugro-Russia (tables and map)
May 22, 1919	—Observations on the Treaty Presented to Germany, 6 pp.
May 24, 1919	—The Baltic Provinces, 3 pp.
June 23, 1919	—The Aaland Islands, 2 pp. [4]
June 24, 1919	—Observations on the Treaty Presented to Austria, 5 pp.

[1] Available unless otherwise noted at the Hoover Institution, Stanford, California, under the heading: Paris Peace Conference, 1919, Delegation Propaganda (Authenticated): Russia (Anti-Bolshevik), Documents Presented to the Peace Conference—Memoranda.

[2] Not available in the Hoover Institution but referred to in the memoranda of May 10 and May 22.

[3] Available in *1919, Russia,* 109.

[4] Available in *Recueil,* Part IV, C(7), 122–23.

July 5, 1919 —The Treaty with Turkey: the Straits and Constantinople, Armenia, Holy Places, Mt. Athos, Capitulations, Financial and Economic Claims, 14 pp.

(Annex of 7 statistical tables on Russia's exports)

July 18, 1919 —Spitzbergen, 7 pp.

July 24, 1919 —Bessarabia, 4 pp.

July 29, 1919 —The Blockade of Soviet Russia, 4 pp.

September 3, 1919 —Russia's Share in the Division of the Enemy Merchant Fleet, 1 p.

September 20, 1919—Implementation of the Allied Promise in the June 12 Reply to Kolchak and a Request for the Recognition of Kolchak [5]

September 21, 1919—Aid to Yudenich; Interdiction of Estonian Peace with the Bolsheviks, 2 pp.

October 9, 1919 —Dangers of German Technicians Aiding the Soviets, 1 p.

November 3, 1919 —Requesting Utilization of the Russian Gold Delivered to the Allies by Germany as Subsidy for a Finnish Advance on Petrograd [6]

November 26, 1919—Delivery of War Materiel Captured by Germany [7]

2. Articles Respecting Russia in the Treaty of Versailles

Article 87, Paragraph 3

The boundaries of Poland not laid down in the present Treaty will be subsequently determined by the Principal Allied and Associated Powers.

Article 116

Germany acknowledges and agrees to respect as permanent and inalienable the independence of all the territories which were part of the former Russian Empire on August 1, 1914.

In accordance with the provisions of Article 259 of Part IX (Financial Clauses) and Article 292 of Part X (Economic Clauses) Germany accepts definitely the abrogation of the Brest-Litovsk Treaties and of all other treaties, conventions, and agreements entered into by her with the Maximalist Government of Russia.

The Allied and Associated Powers formally reserve the rights of Russia

---

[5] Available in *1919, Russia,* 431–32.

[6] Available in British Foreign Office, *Documents,* III, 629.

[7] Acknowledgment of this memorandum by the secretariat of the peace conference found in Maklakov Papers, Part II, Packet III, File 6, though not the memorandum itself.

to obtain from Germany restitution and reparation based on the principles of the present Treaty.

Article 117

Germany undertakes to recognize the full force of all treaties or agreements which may be entered into by the Allied and Associated Powers with States now existing or coming into existence in future in the whole or part of the former Empire of Russia as it existed on August 1, 1914, and to recognize the frontiers of any such States as determined therein.

Article 259, Paragraph 6

Without prejudice to Article 292 of Part x (Economic Clauses) of the present Treaty, Germany confirms the renunciation provided for in Article xv of the Armistice of November 11, 1918, of any benefit disclosed by the Treaties of Bucharest and of Brest-Litovsk and by the treaties supplementary thereto.

Germany undertakes to transfer, either to Roumania or to the Principal Allied and Associated Powers as the case may be, all monetary instruments, specie, securities, and negotiable instruments, or goods, which she has received under the aforesaid Treaties.

Article 292

Germany recognizes that all treaties, conventions or arrangements which she concluded with Russia, or with any State or Government of which the territory previously formed a part of Russia, or with Roumania, before August 1, 1914, or after that date until the coming into force of the present Treaty, are and remain abrogated.

Article 293

Should an Allied or Associated Power, Russia, or a State or Government of which the territory formerly constituted a part of Russia, have been forced since August 1, 1914, by reason of military occupation or by any other means or for any other cause, to grant or to allow to be granted by the act of any public authority, concessions, privileges and favours of any kind to Germany or to a German national, such concessions, privileges and favours are *ipso facto* annulled by the present Treaty.

No claims or indemnities which may result from this annulment shall be charged against the Allied or Associated Powers or the Powers, States, Governments or public authorities which are released from their engagements by the present Article.

Article 433

As a guarantee for the execution of the provisions of the present Treaty, by which Germany accepts definitely the abrogation of the Brest-Litovsk Treaty, and of all treaties, conventions and agreements entered into by her with the Maximalist Government in Russia, and in order to ensure the restoration of peace and good government in the Baltic Provinces and Lithuania, all German troops at present in the said territories shall return to within the frontiers of Germany as soon as the Governments of the Principal Allied and Associated Powers shall think the moment suitable, having regard to the internal situation of these territories. These troops shall abstain from all requisitions and seizures and from any other coercive measures, with a view to obtaining supplies intended for Germany, and shall in no way interfere with such measures for national defence as may be adopted by the Provisional Governments of Esthonia, Latvia, and Lithuania.

No other German troops shall, pending the evacuation or after the evacuation is complete, be admitted to the said territories.

Acknowledgments

THIS STUDY could not have been undertaken or completed without the assistance provided on two occasions by the fellowship program of the Social Science Research Council. In 1952–1953 the author was the recipient of an Area Research Training Fellowship, and in the summer of 1959 he was awarded a Dissertation Completion Fellowship, both under the auspices of the Council. The author is deeply grateful for these opportunities.

He is also indebted to a number of organizations and individuals, whose mere listing here is grossly insufficient recognition for the important ways, both professionally and personally, in which they encouraged and assisted the author in the conduct of this study. At Columbia University, where an earlier version of the first eight chapters of the book was presented as a doctoral dissertation in 1960, special thanks are due the university for its award in 1952–1953 of a William Bayard Cutting Traveling Fellowship (without stipend), to Professors Philip E. Mosely and Henry L. Roberts, sponsors of the author's doctoral work, to Professors René Albrecht-Carrié, Shephard B. Clough, Alexander Dallin, and Geroid T. Robinson for consultation and advice, to Messrs. Simeon Bolan and Lev Magerovsky for bibliographic and archival assistance, and to the late Professor William L. Westermann, who gave freely of his knowledge and experience at the peace conference, and who permitted the author to consult his personal diary for that period.

At the Hoover Institution, Stanford, California, the author received special help from Professors Harold H. Fisher and C. Easton Rothwell, from Messrs. Philip McLean and Witold Sworakowski, and from Mrs. Eudin, Mrs. Perry, and Mrs. Cole. Miss Katherine Brand of the Division of Manuscripts of the Library of Congress provided invaluable guidance on the use of the Wilson Papers and on the manuscript collections available for this period in general. At the Sterling Library of Yale University, Dr. Charles Seymour and Mr. Fuller, Mrs. Powers, and Miss Smith greatly facilitated the author's use of the House Papers and of other collections in that library. Mr. Alexander Clark of the Firestone Library of Princeton University was particularly helpful in the author's consultation of the papers of Ray Stannard Baker. Dr. E. Taylor Parks of the Historical Division of the Department of State provided useful guidance and assistance on numerous occasions. The staffs of the Helsinki University Library, of the Library of the Finnish Parliament, and of the Fundamental Library of Social Sciences of the U.S.S.R. Academy of Sciences were all helpful and courteous in the final stages of preparing this study.

The author owes a special debt of gratitude to Mrs. Woodrow Wilson for permission to use her husband's papers in the Library of Congress, to Dr. Charles Seymour for permission to use the papers of Colonel House and Sir William Wiseman and for personal interviews, and to former Ambassador William C. Bullitt for a lengthy interview and for permission to use his personal papers at the Yale Library. For interviews and consultations, the author is indebted to the late Boris Bakhmetev, the late Professor Michael Karpovich, and Walter W. Pettit. Cyril E. Black, Edward H. Buehrig, Fritz T. Epstein, George F. Kennan, Dagmar Horna Perman, and John Snell, with all of whom the author discussed the study on various occasions, provided valuable encouragement and stimulation.

NOTE ON SOURCES

THIS STUDY was originally planned shortly after the State Department had finished publication, in 1947, of thirteen volumes of documents relating to the Paris Peace Conference of 1919. Although completion of the book was delayed for a variety of reasons, these documents proved, as expected, to be a major source for the study. They were supplemented by the official *Recueil* of the conference printed in a limited number of copies (one set is available at the Hoover Institution), by the two volumes of notes of meetings of the Council of Four published by Paul Mantoux, the Council's interpreter, and by the privately printed diary and papers of David Hunter Miller, a legal expert with the American delegation at Paris (available at the Law Library of Columbia University).

At the inception of the study it was hoped that access could be gained to the papers of Boris A. Bakhmetev, ambassador of the Russian Provisional Government of 1917 to the United States and an important member of the Russian Political Conference. Unfortunately, in the course of negotiations for permission to use these papers, Professor Bakhmetev died, and it was not possible to examine this collection prior to completion of the study. On the other hand, full use was made of the documents and papers of V. A. Maklakov, ambassador of the Provisional Government to France and the leading figure in the Russian Political Conference. This extremely valuable collection of telegrams, reports, and letters relating to the White Russian movement in 1918–1921, which undoubtedly duplicates many of the materials in the Bakhmetev papers, is at the Hoover Institution. Also located there are other documents on the same subject; of particular revelance to this study were the papers of S. P. Mel'gunov and General Yudenich, the diary of P. V. Vologodsky, prime minister of Kolchak's government in 1919, and memoranda, leaflets, and pamphlets relating to the peace settlement issued by the Russian Political Conference and by the unofficial delegations in Paris which represented many of the national minorities of the former Tsarist empire. Also important for the analysis of relations among the White Russian governments, their representatives in Paris, and the Allied governments were the published memoirs of Generals

Denikin and Lukomsky and of Paul N. Miliukov, as well as their private papers held at the Archive of Russian and East European History and Culture at Columbia University.

When the Red Army captured Omsk and Irkutsk in late 1919, the Soviet government seized the files of the Ministry of Foreign Affairs of the Kolchak government. Louis Fischer used these valuable materials in the 1920's during the preparation of his excellent two-volume study, *The Soviets in World Affairs*. They were also drawn on to some extent by I. Subbotovsky, a Siberian historian, in *Soiuzniki, Russkiye reaktsionery i interventsiia* (*The Allies, Russian Reactionaries, and Intervention*), published in 1926. Selections of the same documents have been printed in *Krasnyi Arkhiv* and other Soviet journals. The complete collection remains, nevertheless, a significant source for any history dealing with the period of foreign intervention in Russia. Unfortunately, the author's request in April 1959 to use these materials was never granted.

In the analysis of Soviet foreign policy in 1918 and 1919, the most valuable sources were Lenin's collected works, the excellent compilation of translated Soviet documents relating to foreign affairs edited by Jane Degras, and the first two volumes of an official Soviet series of documents on foreign policy which began to appear in 1957.

In dealing with the period of the Armistice of November 1918, the minutes of the Supreme War Council sessions at which the Armistice terms were drafted were particularly helpful. A complete set of these minutes is in the Bliss Papers at the Library of Congress. When the major research for this study was undertaken, the bulk of the official documents of the German government captured at the close of World War II were not available to individual scholars.

In addition to the State Department series of published documents on the peace conference and on American-Russian relations in 1918 and 1919, the most important sources for the analysis of United States policy toward Russia in this period were the papers of various American leaders, notably those of Woodrow Wilson, Robert Lansing, and General Tasker H. Bliss at the Library of Congress; of Colonel House, Frank Polk, Gordon Auchincloss, and William C. Bullitt at the Sterling Library, Yale University; of Ray Stannard Baker at the Library of Congress and the Firestone Library, Princeton University; and of Vance McCormick at the Hoover Institution (principally McCormick's diary). The private papers of Herbert Hoover are at present not open to general use, although specific inquiries may be directed to the curators of the papers. Of supplementary importance were the files of the Department of State and of the American Commission to Negotiate Peace in the National Archives.

As indicated, the documentation on the American side is voluminous and fairly inclusive. Together with the important materials in the Maklakov papers, it provided most of the original sources for this study. By contrast, primary materials respecting British and French policy toward Russia at the time of the peace conference are limited. This presented problems at various places in the study, but especially in chapter six. The series of official documents dealing with the interwar period published by the British Foreign Office begins in June 1919; the third volume of the first series, in the preparation of which the private papers of Balfour and Curzon were consulted, was particularly useful for this study. The published memoirs of David Lloyd George, Winston Churchill, General Sir Henry Wilson, and Sir Robert Borden, the Canadian prime minister, were all most helpful, as were the private papers of Sir William Wiseman, a confidential British representative, who acted as liaison with Colonel House (papers available in the House collection at Yale). The private papers of Lloyd George, an important source, especially for events in the latter half of 1919, were in the possession of Lord Beaverbrook. With the latter's death these may soon become available for general scholarly use.

The documentation respecting French policy is even scantier. Memoirs of French leaders are few and not very revealing. Until the archives of the Quai d'Orsay and of the French Ministry of War are opened to scholars, several aspects of French policy toward Russia and Eastern Europe in 1919 cannot be definitively analyzed.

Bibliography

Bibliographies

Nina Almond and H. H. Fisher, *Special Collections in the Hoover Library on War, Revolution, and Peace* (Stanford, 1940).

Nina Almond and R. H. Lutz, *An Introduction to a Bibliography of the Paris Peace Conference* (Stanford, 1935).

Samuel Flagg Bemis and G. G. Griffin, *Guide to the Diplomatic History of the United States, 1775–1921* (Washington, 1935).

Bibliothèque et musée de la guerre, *Catalogue méthodique du fonds russe de la bibliothèque* ed., A. Dumesnil (Paris, 1932).

Robert C. Binkley, "Ten Years of Peace Conference History," *Journal of Modern History,* I (1929), 607–29.

Paul Birdsall, "The Second Decade of Peace Conference History," *Journal of Modern History,* XI (1939), 362–78.

Jane Degras, comp., *Calendar of Documents on Soviet Foreign Policy, 1917–1941* (London, 1948).

Foreign Affairs Bibliography, 1919–32; 1932–42; 1942–52 (3 vols.; New York, 1933, 1945, 1954).

Philip Grierson, *Books on Soviet Russia, 1917–42* (London, 1943).

Hoover War Library, *A Catalogue of Paris Peace Conference Delegation Propaganda in the Hoover War Library* (Stanford, 1926).

Klaus Mehnert, ed., *Die Sowjet-Union, 1917–33* (Berlin, 1933).

Russkii zagranichnyi istoricheskii arkhiv (Prague), *Bibliografiia russkoi revoliutsii i grazhdanskoi voiny, 1917–21* (*Bibliography of the Russian Revolution and Civil War, 1917–21*) ed., Ia. Slavik (Prague, 1938).

Laura Shearer Turnbull, ed., *Woodrow Wilson: A Selected Bibliography* (Princeton, 1948).

U.S. Library of Congress, Division of Bibliography, *A Selected List of References on the Diplomatic and Trade Relations of the United States with the USSR, 1919–35* (Washington, 1935).

United States Department of State, Historical Division, "Survey of Published Records and Documents of the Paris Peace Conference, 1919," unpublished guide compiled in 1938.

Vladimir Victoroff-Toporoff, *Rossica et Sovietica* (St. Cloud, 1931).

Unpublished Papers

Gordon Auchincloss, E. M. House Collection, Sterling Library, Yale University

Newton D. Baker, Library of Congress

Ray Stannard Baker, Library of Congress and Firestone Library, Princeton University

General Tasker H. Bliss, Library of Congress

William H. Buckler, E. M. House Collection, Sterling Library, Yale University

Arthur Bullard, Firestone Library, Princeton University

William C. Bullitt, Sterling Library, Yale University

General A. I. Denikin, Archive of Russian and East European History and Culture, Columbia University

Leland Harrison, Library of Congress

George D. Herron, Hoover Institution

E. M. House, Sterling Library, Yale University

General Pierre Janin, Hoover Institution

Robert L. Lansing, Library of Congress

I. G. Loris-Melikov, Archive of Russian and East European History and Culture, Columbia University

V. A. Maklakov, Hoover Institution

Vance C. McCormick, Hoover Institution

S. P. Mel'gunov, Hoover Institution

Frank Polk, E. M. House Collection, Sterling Library, Yale University

General P. A. Tomilov, Archive of Russian and East European History and Culture, Columbia University

Henry White, Library of Congress

Sir William Wiseman, E. M. House Collection, Sterling Library, Yale University

General Nicholas N. Yudenich, Hoover Institution

Records of the American Commission to Negotiate Peace, National Archives

Records of the United States Department of State, National Archives

Interviews

William C. Bullitt, Washington, D.C., February 25, 1953.

Professor Michael Karpovich, New York, N.Y., May 9, 1949.

Walter W. Pettit, Ridgefield, Conn., May 10, 1953.

Dr. Charles Seymour, New Haven, Conn., January 22, 1953.

Unpublished Documents and Manuscripts

Ray Stannard Baker, "Russia at the Paris Peace Conference," uncompleted draft chapter originally intended for inclusion in *Woodrow Wilson and the World Settlement,* Firestone Library, Princeton University.

J. S. Beddie and P. M. Burnett, "The Organization of the Paris Peace Conference of 1919 and of the American Commission to Negotiate Peace" (1943), files of the Historical Division, U.S. Department of State.

Charles A. Beling, "The Question of Allied Recognition of the Kolchak Government," master's essay, Columbia University, 1949.

P. M. Burnett, "Organizational Aspects of the Paris Peace Conference, 1919," files of the Historical Division, U.S. Department of State.

David T. Cattell, "Soviet Russia and the Hungarian Revolution of 1919," master's essay, Columbia University, 1949.

Irving G. Cheslaw, "An Intellectual Biography of Lincoln Steffens," doctoral dissertation, Columbia University, 1952.

[409]

Ann C. Gerhart, "The United States and the Problem of Russia at the Paris Peace Conference," honors thesis, Bryn Mawr College, 1956 (microfilm, Library of Congress).

Rudolf Holsti, "Herbert Hoover and the Coming Into Being of the Finnish Republic" (1925), draft manuscript, Hoover Institution.

Allen McConnell, "The French Search for an Eastern Counterweight to Germany, November, 1918–April, 1919," master's essay, Columbia University, 1950.

J. L. McEvitt, "Wilson's Russian Policy, 1917–21," master's essay, Columbia University, 1948.

Letter of V. A. Maklakov to H. H. Fisher, March 31, 1934, Hoover Institution.

S. E. Mezes, "The Inquiry Papers of S. E. Mezes" ed. Ingram Bander, microfilm copy of typescript collection, American Documentation Institute, Special Collections, Columbia University Library.

Letter of General E. Miller to N. V. Chaikovsky, April 1, 1919, Hoover Institution.

J. Q. Reber, "American Opinion on the Status of Lithuania," files of the Historical Division, U.S. Department of State.

B. M. Sapin, "The Origins of American Intervention in the Russian Revolution," master's essay, Columbia University, 1947.

Diary of P. V. Vologodsky, translated excerpts from the original, Hoover Institution.

Documents

Ray Stannard Baker and William E. Dodd, eds., *The Public Papers of Woodrow Wilson* (8 vols.; New York, 1925–1927).

S. L. Bane and R. H. Lutz, eds., *The Blockade of Germany after the Armistice, 1918–19* (Stanford, 1942).

The Bullitt Mission to Russia: Testimony of William C. Bullitt Before the Committee on Foreign Relations, United States Senate (New York, 1919).

James Bunyan, *Intervention, Civil War, and Communism in Russia, April–December, 1918* (Baltimore, 1936).

C. K. Cumming and Walter W. Pettit, eds., *Russian-American Relations, March 1917–March 1920* (New York, 1920).

Jane Degras, ed., *The Communist International, 1919–1943:* Vol. I, *1919–1922* (London, 1956).

———, ed., *Soviet Documents on Foreign Policy* (3 vols.; London, 1951–1953).

Hamilton Foley, ed., *Woodrow Wilson's Case for the League of Nations* (Princeton, 1923).

France. Comité d'Études, *Travaux* (2 vols.; Paris, 1919).

Great Britain. Foreign Office, *Documents on British Foreign Policy, 1919–39*, Series One (3 vols.; London, 1948–1949).

Great Britain. Foreign Office, Historical Section, *Peace Handbooks*, Volumes VIII, IX, XII (London, 1920).

Great Britain. Parliament, House of Commons, *Accounts and Papers, 1919*, Vol. 1, Cmd. 307 and 395; Vol. 22, Cmd. 8.

Great Britain. Parliament, House of Commons, *Accounts and Papers, 1920*, Vol. 2, Cmd. 772 and Cmd. 818.

Great Britain. Parliament, House of Commons, *Accounts and Papers, 1921,* Vol. 25, Cmd. 1240.

Great Britain. Parliament, House of Commons, *Debates, 1919.*

Iu. V. Kliuchnikov and A. Sabanin, eds., *Mezhdunarodnaia politika noveishego vremeni v dogovorakh, notakh, i deklaratsiiakh* (*International politics of recent times in treaties, notes, and declarations*) (3 vols.; Moscow, 1925–1926).

Herbert Kraus and Gustav Rodiger, comps., *Urkunden zum Friedensvertrage von Versailles vom 28 Juni 1919* (2 vols.; Berlin, 1920).

Paul Mantoux, *Les délibérations du Conseil des quatre* (2 vols.; Paris, 1955).

David Hunter Miller, *My Diary at the Conference of Paris* (21 vols.; privately printed, New York, 1924–1928).

Recueil des actes de la conférence (8 parts; Paris, 1922–1934).

République Française. Chambre des Députés, *Débats, 1918* (Paris, 1918).

———. Chambre des Députés, *Débats, 1919* (Paris, 1919).

RSFSR, Narodnyi komissariat po inostrannym delam, *Godovoi otchet (1919–20) k VIII s'ezdu sovetov* (*Annual Report, 1919–1920, of the People's Commissariat of Foreign Affairs to the Eighth Congress of Soviets*) (Moscow, 1921).

U.S. Department of State, *Memorandum on the Bolshevist or Communist Party in Russia and its Relations to the Third or Communist International and to the Russian Soviets* (Washington, 1920).

———, Papers Relating to the Foreign Relations of the United States: *The Lansing Papers, 1914–1920* (2 vols.; Washington, 1939–1940).

1914, Supplement (Washington, 1928).

1917, Supplement 2, Vol. I (Washington, 1932).

1918, Russia (3 vols.; Washington, 1931–1932).

1918, Supplement I, Vol. I (Washington, 1933).

1919, Russia (Washington, 1937).

Paris Peace Conference (13 vols.; Washington, 1942–1947).

———, *Russian Series* (pamphlets), No. 3, 1919.

———, *The Treaty of Versailles and After: Annotations of the Text of the Treaty* (Washington, 1947).

U.S. Senate, 1919 (66th Congress, 1st session), Senate Document 106, *Treaty of Peace with Germany: Hearings before the Committee on Foreign Relations* (Washington, 1920).

———, (66th Congress, 2nd session), Senate Document 172, *Memorandum on Certain Aspects of the Bolshevist Movement in Russia* (Washington, 1920).

U.S.S.R., Ministerstvo inostrannykh del, *Dokumenty vneshnei politki SSSR* (*Documents on the Foreign Policy of the USSR*) (Moscow, 1957–   ), Vols. I and II.

"Vneshniaia politika kontrrevoliutsionnykh 'pravitel'stv' v nachale 1919 g." ("The Foreign Policy of the Counterrevolutionary 'Governments' in the Beginning of 1919"), *Krasnyi Arkhiv* (*Red Archives*), XVII (1929).

Memoirs, Autobiographies

Vernon Bartlett, *Behind the Scenes at the Peace Conference* (London, 1919).

R. H. Beadon, *Some Memories of the Peace Conference* (London, 1933).

[411]

Stephen Bonsal, *Suitors and Suppliants: The Little Nations at Versailles* (New York, 1946).

Henry Borden, ed., *Robert Laird Borden: His Memoirs* (2 vols.; Toronto, 1938).

Major-General Sir C. E. Callwell, *Field Marshal Sir Henry Wilson: His Life and Diaries* (2 vols.; London, 1928).

Winston S. Churchill, *The Aftermath, 1918–28* (Vol. IV of *The World Crisis*) (New York, 1929).

———, *The Hinge of Fate* (Boston, 1950).

Georges Clemenceau, *Grandeur and Misery of Victory* (New York, 1930).

Bainbridge Colby, *The Close of Woodrow Wilson's Administration and the Final Years* (New York, 1930).

A. I. Denikin, *Ocherki russkoi smuty* (*Sketches of the Russian Turmoil*) (5 vols.; Paris, 1921?–1926?).

E. J. Dillon, *The Inside Story of the Peace Conference* (New York, 1920).

M. Erzberger, *Erlebnisse Im Weltkrieg* (Berlin, 1920).

H. H. Fisher and Elena Varneck, eds., *The Testimony of Kolchak and Other Siberian Materials* (Stanford, 1935).

Ferdinand Foch, *The Memoirs of Marshal Foch,* tr., Col. T. Bentley Mott (Garden City, 1931).

David R. Francis, *Russia from the American Embassy* (New York, 1921).

William S. Graves, *America's Siberian Adventure, 1918–20* (New York, 1931).

Joseph C. Grew, *Turbulent Era: A Diplomatic Record of Forty Years, 1904–45* (2 vols.; Boston, 1952).

George K. Guins, *Sibir', Soiuzniki i Kolchak* (*Siberia, the Allies, and Kolchak*) (Peking, 1921).

Lord Maurice Hankey, *The Supreme Control at the Paris Peace Conference* (London, 1963).

Harry Hansen, *The Adventures of the Fourteen Points* (New York, 1919).

H. Wilson Harris, *The Peace in the Making* (London, n.d.).

Herbert Hoover, *My Memoirs* (3 vols.; New York, 1951–1952).

———, *The Ordeal of Woodrow Wilson* (New York, 1958).

David F. Houston, *Eight Years With Wilson's Cabinet* (2 vols.; Garden City, 1926).

Frederic C. Howe, *The Confessions of a Reformer* (New York, 1925).

Sisley Huddleston, *Peace-Making at Paris* (London, 1919).

General Pierre Janin, *Ma Mission en Sibérie, 1918–20* (Paris, 1933).

Michael Karolyi, *Memoirs* (London, 1956).

G. Kirdetsov, *U vorot Petrograda, 1919–20* (*At the Gates of Petrograd, 1919–1920*) (Berlin, 1921).

Vladimir Nikolaevich Kokovtsov, *Out of My Past* (Stanford, 1935).

Karel Kramař, *Kramářuv Soud Nad Benešem* (Prague, 1938).

Robert Lansing, *The Peace Negotiations: A Personal Narrative* (Boston, 1921).

———, *War Memoirs* (Indianapolis, 1935).

David Lloyd George, *The Truth About the Peace Treaties* (2 vols.; London, 1938).

———, *War Memoirs* (6 vols.; London, 1933–1936).

Erich Von Ludendorff, *Ludendorff's Own Story* (2 vols.; New York and London, 1919).

Peyton C. March, *The Nation at War* (Garden City, 1932).

Arnold D. Margolin, *From a Political Diary: Russia, the Ukraine, and America, 1905–45* (New York, 1946).

T. G. Masaryk, *The Making of a State* (New York, 1927).

General Jean J. Mordacq, *Le Ministère Clemenceau: journal d'un témoin* (3 vols.; Paris, 1930–1931).

Constantin Nabokov, *The Ordeal of a Diplomat* (London, 1921).

Fridtjof Nansen, *Russia and Peace* (London, 1923).

Harold Nicolson, *Peacemaking 1919* (Boston and New York, 1933).

Gen. A. Niessel, *L'évacuation des pays baltiques par les Allemands* (Paris, 1935).

Joseph Noulens, *Mon Ambassade en Russie Soviétique, 1917–19* (2 vols.; Paris, 1933).

Harry Pollitt, *Serving My Time, An Apprenticeship to Politics* (London, 1940).

Arthur Ransome, *Russia in 1919* (New York, 1919).

Raymond Recouly, *Le Mémorial de Foch* (Paris, 1929).

Lord Riddell, *An Intimate Diary of the Peace Conference and After, 1918–23* (London, 1933).

Charles Seymour, ed., *The Intimate Papers of Colonel House* (4 vols.; Boston and New York, 1926–1928).

James T. Shotwell, *At the Paris Peace Conference* (New York, 1927).

Henry Wickham Steed, *Through Thirty Years, 1892–1922: A Personal Narrative* (2 vols.; Garden City, 1924).

Lincoln Steffens, *Autobiography* (2 vols.; New York, 1931).

Oscar S. Straus, *Under Four Administrations: From Cleveland to Taft* (Boston, 1922).

André Tardieu, *The Truth About the Treaty* (Indianapolis, 1921).

Charles T. Thompson, *The Peace Conference Day by Day* (New York, 1920).

Leon Trotsky, *My Life: An Attempt at an Autobiography* (New York, 1930).

Joseph P. Tumulty, *Woodrow Wilson As I Know Him* (Garden City, 1921).

Oswald Garrison Villard, *Fighting Years: Memoirs of a Liberal Editor* (New York, 1939).

Colonel John Ward, *With the "Die-Hards" in Siberia* (London, 1920).

William Allen White, *Autobiography* (New York, 1946).

Jean Xydias, *L'intervention française dans le sud de la Russie, mémoires d'un témoin* (Paris, 1927).

Collected Works and Speeches

Vladimir Il'ich Lenin, *Collected Works,* Vols. XVIII, XX, XXI, XXIII, (New York, 1927–1945).

———, *Leninskii sbornik* (*Lenin collection*) (35 vols.; Moscow, 1924–1945).

———, *Rech' na pervom vserossiiskom s'ezde trudovykh Kazakov* (*Speech at the First All-Russian Congress of Kazakh Workers*) (Moscow, 1920).

Vladimir Il'ich Lenin, *Selected Works,* Vols. VIII, X (New York, n.d.).
———, *Sochineniia (Collected Works)* (30 vols.; Moscow, 1928–1937).
David Lloyd George, *Is It Peace?* (London, n.d.).
I. I. Mints and A. I. Gukovskii, eds., *Lenin ob interventsii (Lenin on Intervention)* (Moscow, 1931).
Leon Trotsky, *Sochineniia (Collected Works)*, Vols. II, III, IX, XII, XV, XX, XXI (Moscow, 1925–1927).
Ella Winter and Granville Hicks, eds., *The Letters of Lincoln Steffens* (2 vols.; New York, 1938).
Grigorii Evseevich Zinoviev, *Sochineniia (Collected Works)*, Vols. I, III, IV, V, VII, VIII, XV, XVI (Moscow, 1924–1926).

Secondary Works

Leonid Andreev, *SOS,* Russian Liberation Committee pamphlet No. 6 (London, 1919).
Thomas A. Bailey, *Wilson and the Peacemakers* (2 vols.; New York, 1947).
Ray Stannard Baker, *Woodrow Wilson: Life and Letters* (8 vols.; Garden City, 1927–1939).
———, *Woodrow Wilson and the World Settlement* (3 vols.; Garden City, 1922).
———, *What Wilson Did at Paris* (New York, 1919).
H. C. F. Bell, *Woodrow Wilson and the People* (Garden City, 1945).
A. V. Berezkin, *SSHA—aktivnyi organizator i uchastnik voennoi interventsii protiv Sovetskoi Rossii, 1918–20 gg. (USA—Active Organizer and Participant in Armed Intervention against Soviet Russia, 1918–20)* (Moscow, 1949).
Paul Birdsall, *Versailles Twenty Years After* (New York, 1941).
C. E. Black, ed., *Rewriting Russian History* (New York, 1956).
Boris L. Brasol, *The World at the Cross Roads* (Boston, 1921).
Mitchell Pirie Briggs, *George D. Herron and the European Settlement* (Stanford, 1932).
Edward H. Buehrig, ed., *Wilson's Foreign Policy in Perspective* (Bloomington, 1957).
E. H. Carr, *The Bolshevik Revolution, 1917–1923* (3 vols.; New York, 1951–1953).
———, *German-Soviet Relations between the Two World Wars, 1919–39.* (Baltimore, 1951).
William H. Chamberlin, *The Russian Revolution* (2 vols.: New York, 1935).
G. Chicherin, *Two Years of Soviet Foreign Policy* (New York, 1920).
Winston S. Churchill, *Great Contemporaries* (London, 1937).
W. P. and Zelda K. Coates, *A History of Anglo-Soviet Relations* (London, 1943).
———, *Armed Intervention in Russia, 1918–22* (London, 1935).
Francis Deak, *Hungary at the Paris Peace Conference* (New York, 1942).
Alfred L. P. Dennis, *The Foreign Policies of Soviet Russia* (New York, 1924).
William Diamond, *The Economic Thought of Woodrow Wilson* (Baltimore, 1943).
Blanche E. C. Dugdale, *Arthur James Balfour* (2 vols.; London, 1936).

Klaus Epstein, *Matthias Erzberger and the Dilemma of German Democracy* (Princeton, 1959).

Louis Fischer, *The Soviets in World Affairs* (2 vols.; 2nd printing, Princeton, 1951).

H. H. Fisher, *The Famine in Soviet Russia, 1919–1923* (New York, 1927).

Peter Fleming, *The Fate of Admiral Kolchak* (New York, 1963).

Louis L. Gerson, *Woodrow Wilson and the Rebirth of Poland, 1914–20* (New Haven, 1953).

Samuel Gompers and William English Walling, *Out of Their Own Mouths* (New York, 1921).

Malbone W. Graham, *New Governments of Eastern Europe* (New York, 1927).

———, *The Diplomatic Recognition of the Border States* (3 parts; Berkeley, 1935, 1939, 1941).

Whitney A. Griswold, *The Far Eastern Policy of the United States* (New York, 1938).

A. I. Gukovskii, *Frantsuzskaia interventsiia na iuge Rossi 1918–19* (*French Intervention in the South of Russia, 1918–19*) (Moscow, 1925).

J. L. Hammond, *C. P. Scott of the Manchester Guardian* (New York, n.d.).

C. H. Haskins and R. H. Lord, *Some Problems of the Peace Conference* (Cambridge, 1920).

George D. Herron, *The Defeat in the Victory* (London, 1921).

Richard Hofstadter, *The American Political Tradition and the Men Who Made It* (New York, 1948).

Andreas Hohlfeld, *Versailles und die russische Frage* (Hamburg, 1940).

E. M. House and Charles Seymour, eds., *What Really Happened at Paris* (New York, 1921).

William C. Huntington, *The Homesick Million, Russia-out-of-Russia* (Boston, 1938).

Gerald W. Johnson, *Woodrow Wilson* (New York, 1944).

Firuz Kazemzadeh, *The Struggle for Transcaucasia, 1917–21* (New York and London, 1951).

George F. Kennan, *Russia and the West under Lenin and Stalin* (Boston, 1961).

———, *The Decision to Intervene* (Princeton, 1958).

James Kerney, *The Political Education of Woodrow Wilson* (New York and London, 1926).

John Maynard Keynes, *The Economic Consequences of the Peace* (London, 1920).

Henry S. King, *Russia during the War* (London, 1919).

Titus Komarnicki, *Rebirth of the Polish Republic* (London, 1957).

A. G. Shliapnikov, R. A. Muklevich, and B. I. Dolivo-Dobrovolsky, eds., *Kto Dolzhnik?* (*Who Is the Debtor?*) (Moscow, 1926).

Christopher Lasch, *The American Liberals and the Russian Revolution* (New York, 1962).

Earl Latham, ed., *The Philosophy and Policies of Woodrow Wilson* (Chicago, 1958).

Arthur S. Link, *Wilson the Diplomatist: A Look at His Major Foreign Policies* (Baltimore, 1957).

———, *Wilson: The Road to the White House* (Princeton, 1947).

Alfred D. Low, *The Soviet Hungarian Republic and the Paris Peace Conference* (Transactions of the American Philosophical Society, New Series, Vol. LIII, Part 10; Philadelphia, 1963).

Alma Luckau, *The German Delegation at the Paris Peace Conference* (New York, 1941).

Ian Malcom, *Vacant Thrones: A Volume of Political Portraits* (London, 1931).

F. S. Marston, *The Peace Conference of 1919: Organization and Procedure* (London, 1944).

S. P. Mel'gunov, *N. V. Chaikovskii v gody grazhdanskoi voiny* (*N. V. Chaikovsky in the Years of the Civil War*) (Paris, 1929).

P. N. Miliukov, *Bolshevism: An International Danger, Its Doctrine and Practice through War and Revolution* (London, 1920).

————, *La politique extérieure des Soviets* (Paris, 1936).

————, *Russia and England*, Russian Liberation Committee Pamphlet No. 13 (London, 1920).

————, *Russia Today and Tomorrow* (New York, 1922).

David Hunter Miller, *The Drafting of the Covenant* (2 vols.; New York, 1928).

Sarah Gertrude Millin, *General Smuts* (2 vols.; Boston, 1936).

I. I. Mints, *Angliiskaia interventsiia i severnaia kontrrevoliutsiia* (*English Intervention and the Northern Counterrevolution*) (Moscow, 1931).

General Jean J. Mordacq, *Pouvait-on signer l'armistice à Berlin?* (Paris, 1930).

James William Morley, *The Japanese Thrust into Siberia, 1918* (New York, 1957).

Allan Nevins, *Henry White: Thirty Years of American Diplomacy* (New York, 1930).

Harold Nicolson, *Curzon: The Last Phase, 1919–25* (London, 1934).

George Bernard Noble, *Policies and Opinions at Paris, 1919* (New York, 1935).

Harley Notter, *The Origins of the Foreign Policy of Woodrow Wilson* (Baltimore, 1937).

Frank Owen, *Tempestuous Journey: Lloyd George, His Life and Times* (London, 1954).

Frederick Palmer, *Bliss, Peacemaker* (New York, 1934).

————, *Newton D. Baker: America at War* (New York, 1931).

M. N. Pokrovsky, *Vneshniaia politika Rossii v XX veke* (*The Foreign Policy of Russia in the Twentieth Century*) (Moscow, 1926).

V. P. Potemkin, ed., *Istoriia diplomatii* (*A History of Diplomacy*) (3 vols.; Moscow-Leningrad, 1941–1945).

Karl Radek, *Vneshniaia politika Sovetskoi Rossii* (*The Foreign Policy of Soviet Russia*) (Moscow, 1923).

Arthur J. Ransome, *Russia in 1919* (New York, 1919).

John S. Reshetar, Jr., *The Ukrainian Revolution, 1917–1920* (Princeton, 1952).

Ronaldshay, Earl of (Lawrence, J. L. D.), *The Life of Lord Curzon* (3 vols.; London, 1928).

Edward A. Ross, *The Russian Soviet Republic* (New York, 1923).

Harry R. Rudin, *Armistice, 1918* (New Haven, 1944).

The Russian Almanac, N. Peacock, ed. (London, 1919).

Frederick L. Schuman, *American Policy toward Russia since 1917* (New York, 1928).

Hugh Seton Watson, *From Lenin to Khruschchev: The History of World Communism* (New York, 1960).

Boris E. Shtein, *Burzhuaznye fal'sifikatory istorii, 1919–39* (*Bourgeois Falsifiers of History, 1919–39*) (Moscow, 1951).

———, *"Russkii vopros" na parizhskoi mirnoi konferentsii, 1919–20* (*"The Russian Problem" at the Paris Peace Conference, 1919–20*) (Moscow, 1949).

George Stewart, *The White Armies of Russia* (New York, 1933).

Leonid I. Strakhovsky, *Intervention at Archangel* (Princeton, 1944).

———, *The Origins of American Intervention in North Russia, 1918* (Princeton, 1937).

I. Subbotovsky, *Soiuzniki, russkiye reaktsonery, i interventsiia* (*The Allies, Russian Reactionaries, and Intervention*) (Leningrad, 1926).

Timothy A. Taracouzio, *War and Peace in Soviet Diplomacy* (New York, 1940).

H. W. V. Temperley, ed., *A History of the Peace Conference of Paris* (6 vols.; London, 1920–1924).

Gabriel Terrail (pseud. Mermeix), *Le combat des Trois* (Paris, 1922).

Seth P. Tillman, *Anglo-American Relations at the Paris Peace Conference of 1919* (Princeton, 1961).

Pauline Tompkins, *American-Russian Relations in the Far East* (New York, 1949).

Leon Trotsky, *The Bolsheviki and World Peace,* introd. by Lincoln Steffens, (New York, 1918).

M. I. Trush, *Vneshnepoliticheskaia deiatel'nost' V. I. Lenina: 1917–20, den' za dnyom* (*The Foreign Political Activity of V. I. Lenin: 1917–20, Day by Day*) (Moscow, 1963).

Betty Miller Unterberger, *America's Siberian Expedition, 1918–20* (Durham, 1956).

Arthur Walworth, *Woodrow Wilson* (2 vols.; New York, 1958).

Piotr S. Wandycz, *France and Her Eastern Allies, 1919–25* (Minneapolis, 1962).

John A. White, *The Siberian Intervention* (Princeton, 1950).

William Allen White, *Woodrow Wilson: The Man, His Times, and His Task* (Boston and New York, 1924).

Arthur Willert, *The Road to Safety: A Study in Anglo-American Relations* (London, 1952).

William A. Williams, *American-Russian Relations, 1781–1947* (New York, 1952).

Edward F. Willis, *Herbert Hoover and the Russian Prisoners of World War I* (Stanford, 1951).

F. C. Zitelmann, *Russland im Friedensvertrag von Versailles: Kommentar Nebst einschlagen Noten* (Berlin, 1920).

BIBLIOGRAPHY

Journals and Newspapers

American Slavic and East European Review
Bulletin of the American Relief Administration
L'Humanité
Istoriia SSSR
Izvestia
Krasnyi Arkhiv
London *Times*
Manchester Guardian
Mezhdunarodnaia zhizn'
The Nation
New York Times
Obshchee Delo (Paris)
Pravda
Vestnik NKID
Voprosy istorii
Weekly Bulletin of the Bureau of Information on Soviet Russia

Index

Aaland Islands, 6n, 7, 399
Ackerman, Carl, 279n
Alby, General, 137, 182
Alexander I, Tsar of Russia, 320
Alexander, Prince Regent of Yugoslavia, 179
Alexeev, General, 269
Allied and American soldiers in Russia, poor morale of, 12–13
Allied policy: on use of Germany against Bolshevism, 25–32; alternative open to Allies, 38–39; on Bolshevism, 50–51; consideration of recognition of an anti-Bolshevik government, 277–78, 282–83; note to Kolchak of May 26, 298–303; anti-Bolshevism after June 1919, 322–25; toward Baltic states, 333–43, 367–70; toward Poland, 343–46, 367–70; role of British in formulating in late 1919, 347–48; cordon around Soviet Russia, 363–75; toward Caucasus, 370–75; summary of toward Russia, 376–81; evaluation of, 381–84; summary of toward Bolshevism, 384–88; fear of Bolshevism in Germany, 391–93; fear of Bolshevism in Poland, 394–95
Allied war aims, 17
American-Japanese relations: conflict in Siberia, 283–87, 294–95, 369
American policy, 46–49, 375; public opposition to intervention, 96; proposal to support Kolchak, 97; relief to Germany, 222–30; relief to Russia, 230–33, 238, 247–67; question of recognizing Kolchak, 278–79, 282–83, 287–96; conflict over U.S. role in Siberia, 283–87, 294–95; note to Kolchak of May 26, 298–303; possible mandate for Armenia, 316–18; toward Baltic states, 335–43; support of territorial integrity of Russia, 341–42; on trade with Soviet Russia, 360–63. *See also* Wilson, Woodrow

anarchy, race with, 19–20, 389–90
Anglo-French agreement on "spheres" in Russia, 54–55
Anglo-Soviet negotiations on prisoners of war, 355–56
Anglo-Soviet trade agreement, 1921, 362
anti-Bolshevik alliance, proposals for, 365–67
anti-Bolshevik army, plans to form in Eastern Europe, 197
anti-Bolshevik crusade, plans for, 104
anti-Bolshevik Russians: pro-German sentiments, 27; fear of Bolshevism, 62; appeals to the Allies for aid, 63; various "governments" in Russia, 64–65; efforts to form a unified all-Russian government, 64–66, 268–77; efforts to secure recognition of Kolchak, 65–66, 280–82, 290–96; attitude toward non-Russian minorities, 126, 330–33, 366–67; reaction to Hoover-Nansen plan, 261–62; reaction to note of May 26 to Kolchak, 303–04; views on Versailles Treaty, 312–14; attitude toward Finland, 331–33; relations with Poland, 344n. *See also* Russian Political Conference
Armenia, 7, 400; proposal for American mandate, 316–18. *See also* Caucasus
Armistice of November 11, 1918, 391; effect of fear of Bolshevism on, 20–23; German reasons for seeking, 21–22; German arguments concerning Bolshevism in negotiations for, 22–23; Foch's views on Bolshevism and, 23; provisions affecting Russia, 23–24; Article XII, 24–32, 310–11, 334 *evacuation of German troops in East*, 29–32; views of Foch, 29–31; views of Germans, 29–30; views of anti-Bolshevik Russians, 31; faults in provision for, 31

STUDIES OF THE RUSSIAN INSTITUTE

PUBLISHED BY COLUMBIA UNIVERSITY PRESS

THAD PAUL ALTON, *Polish Postwar Economy*

JOHN A. ARMSTRONG, *Ukranian Nationalism*

ABRAM BERGSON, *Soviet National Income and Product in 1937*

EDWARD J. BROWN, *The Proletarian Episode in Russian Literature, 1928–1932*

HARVEY L. DYCK, *Weimar Germany and Soviet Russia, 1926–1933: A Study in Diplomatic Instability*

RALPH TALCOTT FISHER, JR., *Pattern for Soviet Youth: A Study of the Congresses of the Komsomol, 1918–1954*

MAURICE FRIEDBERG, *Russian Classics in Soviet Jackets*

ELLIOT R. GOODMAN, *The Soviet Design for a World State*

DAVID GRANICK, *Management of the Industrial Firm in the USSR: A Study in Soviet Economic Planning*

THOMAS TAYLOR HAMMOND, *Lenin on Trade Unions and Revolution, 1893–1917*

JOHN N. HAZARD, *Settling Disputes in Soviet Society: The Formative Years of Legal Institutions*

DAVID JORAVSKY, *Soviet Marxism and Natural Science, 1917–1932*

DAVID MARSHALL LANG, *The Last Years of the Georgian Monarchy, 1658–1832*

GEORGE S. N. LUCKYJ, *Literary Politics in the Soviet Ukraine, 1917–1934*

HERBERT MARCUSE, *Soviet Marxism: A Critical Analysis*

KERMIT E. MCKENZIE, *Comintern and World Revolution, 1928–1943: The Shaping of Doctrine*

CHARLES B. MCLANE, *Soviet Policy and the Chinese Communists, 1931–1946*

JAMES WILLIAM MORLEY, *The Japanese Thrust into Siberia, 1918*

ALEXANDER G. PARK, *Bolshevism in Turkestan, 1917–1927*

MICHAEL BORO PETROVICH, *The Emergence of Russian Panslavism, 1856–1870*

OLIVER H. RADKEY, *The Agrarian Foes of Bolshevism: Promise and Default of the Russian Socialist Revolutionaries, February to October, 1917*

OLIVER H. RADKEY, *The Sickle Under the Hammer: The Russian Socialist Revolutionaries in the Early Months of Soviet Rule*

ALFRED J. RIEBER, *Stalin and the French Communist Party, 1941–1947*

ALFRED ERICH SENN, *The Emergence of Modern Lithuania*

ERNEST J. SIMMONS, editor, *Through the Glass of Soviet Literature: Views of Russian Society*

THEODORE K. VON LAUE, *Sergei Witte and the Industrialization of Russia*

ALLEN S. WHITING, *Soviet Policies in China, 1917–1924*

PUBLISHED BY TEACHERS COLLEGE PRESS

HAROLD J. NOAH, *Financing Soviet Schools*

PUBLISHED BY PRINCETON UNIVERSITY PRESS

PAUL AVRICH, *The Russian Anarchists*

JOHN M. THOMPSON, *Russia, Bolshevism, and the Versailles Peace*